THE SHORTEST LEAP

The Rational Underpinnings of Faith in Jesus

A. L. VAN DEN HERIK

WESTBOW
PRESS®
A DIVISION OF THOMAS NELSON
& ZONDERVAN

Copyright © 2020 A. L. van den Herik.

All rights reserved. No part of this book may be used or reproduced by any means, graphic, electronic, or mechanical, including photocopying, recording, taping or by any information storage retrieval system without the written permission of the author except in the case of brief quotations embodied in critical articles and reviews.

This book is a work of non-fiction. Unless otherwise noted, the author and the publisher make no explicit guarantees as to the accuracy of the information contained in this book and in some cases, names of people and places have been altered to protect their privacy.

WestBow Press books may be ordered through booksellers or by contacting:

WestBow Press
A Division of Thomas Nelson & Zondervan
1663 Liberty Drive
Bloomington, IN 47403
www.westbowpress.com
1 (866) 928-1240

Because of the dynamic nature of the Internet, any web addresses or links contained in this book may have changed since publication and may no longer be valid. The views expressed in this work are solely those of the author and do not necessarily reflect the views of the publisher, and the publisher hereby disclaims any responsibility for them.

Any people depicted in stock imagery provided by Getty Images are models, and such images are being used for illustrative purposes only. Certain stock imagery © Getty Images.

THE HOLY BIBLE, NEW INTERNATIONAL VERSION®, NIV® Copyright © 1973, 1978, 1984, 2011 by Biblica, Inc.® Used by permission. All rights reserved worldwide.

ISBN: 978-1-9736-8980-5 (sc)
ISBN: 978-1-9736-8981-2 (hc)
ISBN: 978-1-9736-8979-9 (e)

Library of Congress Control Number: 2020906963

Printed in the United States of America.

WestBow Press rev. date: 05/12/2020

CONTENTS

Acknowledgements xii
Dedication xiii
Introduction xv
    Every Person Takes a Leap of Faith xvi
    Finding the Shortest Leap xix
    Questions for Comprehension and Discussion xxi

PART 1: THE SCIENTIFIC EVIDENCE

Chapter 1: Out to the Stars 1
    The Big Bang 3
    The Fine-Tuning of the Universe 7
    Positioned for Universe Exploration 12
    The Changing Flow of Time 12
    Questions for Comprehension and Discussion 18

Chapter 2: Into the Cell 23
    Where We Are in the Discussion 25
    The Complexity of Life 26
    The Language of DNA 31
    Specified Complexity 35
    Questions for Comprehension and Discussion 38

Chapter 3: Back in Time 43
    Stasis and Sudden Appearance 44
    The "Sociocultural Big Bang" 49
    One Ancestral Couple Made in God's Image? 53
    Questions for Comprehension and Discussion 57

Chapter 4: Science and God 63
    1. God Exists 64
    2. God is the Creator 64
    3. God Is Distinct from Creation 66

    4. God Is Infinite and Omnipresent.. 66
    5. God Is Omnipotent, Omniscient, Logical, and Wise 69
    6. God Is Supernatural 72
    7. God Is Personal... 73
    Questions for Comprehension and Discussion 76

Chapter 5: Please Believe Me! 83
    Truthful or Delusional? 85
    Tests of Historical Reliability 86
    Eyewitness Claims 88
    Other Eyewitness Statements in Acts and Luke.............................. 92
    Eyewitness Statements Elsewhere in the New Testament.............. 94
    Questions for Comprehension and Discussion 99

Chapter 6: Eyewitness Details 105
    Inclusion of Irrelevant Details... 105
    Inclusion of Embarrassing Details 110
    Inclusion of Confusing Details 113
    Questions for Comprehension and Discussion 117

Chapter 7: Not a Myth 123
    1. Osiris, Isis, and Horus 124
    2. Dionysus 126
    3. Adonis 130
    4. Attis 132
    5. Mithras 133
    Questions for Comprehension and Discussion 142

Chapter 8: Eyewitness Testimony 147
    Not Your Typical Miracle Stories 147
    Contradictions or Different Eyewitness Perspectives?................. 156
    Questions for Comprehension and Discussion 163

Chapter 9: More Eyewitness Evidence 167
    The Early Dates of the New Testament Documents 168
    Fictional Material Inserted Early? 176
    Questions for Comprehension and Discussion 183

Chapter 10: Secular Confirmation 189
    Confirmation by Non-Christian Sources 190
    1. Tacitus 191
    2. Suetonius 192

- 3. Thallus 193
- 4. Phlegon 194
- 5. Pliny the Younger 195
- 6. Trajan, and 196
- 7. Hadrian 196
- 8. Lucian of Samosata 196
- 9. Celsus 197
- 10. The Talmud 198
- 11. Josephus 199
- 12. Mara Bar-Serapion 200
- Questions for Comprehension and Discussion 202

Chapter 11: Archaeological Consistency 207
- Archaeological Support for the Old Testament 211
- Evidence for the Exodus Arrival 218
- Evidence for the Exodus Population Increase 223
- Evidence for the Exodus Enslavement 224
- Evidence for the Exodus Judgment and Exodus 228
- Evidence for the Exodus Conquest 232
- Archaeological Support for the New Testament 234
- Questions for Comprehension and Discussion 240

Chapter 12: The Chain of Testimony 249
- Proximity of Manuscripts to the Originals 249
- Multiplicity of Manuscripts and the Counting of Variants 251
- Many Early "Christianities"? 257
- Comparing Composition Dates 260
- Questions for Comprehension and Discussion 268

Chapter 13: Not Gnosticism 275
- God and Creation 276
- Was Jesus Human or Divine? 279
- What Does Redemption Entail? 282
- What Is Jesus' Purpose? 284
- Questions for Comprehension and Discussion 286

Chapter 14: The Anti-Supernatural Opinions 291
- Did Jesus Really Say It? 293
- Atheistic Assumptions 294
- Jesus, The Wandering Pagan Philosopher? 296
- The Non-Apocalyptic Jesus 298
- Throwing Out the Baby with the Bathwater? 301

    Not Pithy Enough? 303
    Questions for Comprehension and Discussion 306

Chapter 15: Trusting the Selection 311
    What Belongs in the Bookchest? 313
    Four Gospels and Four Only... 316
    Early Recognition of Other New Testament Books........................ 320
    Constantine, the Council of Nicaea, and the Deity of Jesus 322
    Questions for Comprehension and Discussion 324

Chapter 16: He Is Risen! 329
    The Internal Evidence.. 331
    The Five "Minimal Facts"... 338
    Questions for Comprehension and Discussion 343

Chapter 17: He Is Risen Indeed!... 351
    1. Legendary Development... 353
    2. Resurrection Was Intended as a Symbol 355
    3. Resurrection Copied from Other Religions 356
    4. The Disciples Stole the Body.. 357
    5. Someone Else Stole the Body... 358
    6. They Went to the Wrong Tomb... 359
    7. Jesus Didn't Really Die.. 359
    8. Psychological Phenomena Explain the Appearances................. 361
    Additional Evidence for the Resurrection 366
    Questions for Comprehension and Discussion 368

PART 2: THE BIBLICAL EVIDENCE

Chapter 18: Claims of Divinity 373
    Is God One, or Three?.. 376
    New Testament Statements That Jesus Is God................................ 377
    Jesus Demonstrated His Divinity 379
    Questions for Comprehension and Discussion 389

Chapter 19: Divinity on Display.. 395
    The HANDS of Jesus... 397
    The "H" – Jesus Shares the Honors Due to God 398
    The "A" – Jesus Shares the Attributes of God................................ 399
    The "N" – Jesus Shares the Names of God..................................... 400
    The "D" – Jesus Shares the Deeds that God Does 402

    The "S" – Jesus Shares the Seat of God's Throne.................................403
    Questions for Comprehension and Discussion 407

Chapter 20: Jesus' Coming Foretold.. 413
    Prophecies Relating to Jesus' Lineage 415
    Prophecies Relating to Jesus' Birth... 418
    Prophecies of Jesus' Triumphal Entry.. 422
    Questions for Comprehension and Discussion 424

Chapter 21: Crucifixion and Resurrection Foretold 429
    Prophecies Relating to Jesus' Suffering 430
    Prophecies Relating to Jesus' Crucifixion 440
    Prophecies Relating to the Resurrection 446
    Questions for Comprehension and Discussion 449

Chapter 22: The Victory to Come 455
    Prophecies of Jesus' Second Coming 456
    The First Prophecies About Jesus..463
    Questions for Comprehension and Discussion 467

Chapter 23: Old Testament Objects.. 473
    Noah's Ark... 476
    The Stairway to Heaven...477
    Manna in the Wilderness..479
    Symbolism of the Tabernacle and Temple... 481
    1. The Structure of the Tabernacle...483
    2. The Furniture of the Tabernacle 484
    Questions for Comprehension and Discussion 489

Chapter 24: Old Testament Fathers 493
    Adam and Eve 493
    Abel 497
    Abram/Abraham..499
    Jacob..506
    Joseph..508
    Questions for Comprehension and Discussion 510

Chapter 25: Old Testament Leaders.. 515
    Moses... 515
    David..522
    Questions for Comprehension and Discussion 531

Chapter 26: Old Testament Outsiders 535
    Tamar 537
    Rahab 539
    Ruth 543
    Mephibosheth 547
    Naaman 551
    Questions for Comprehension and Discussion 557

Chapter 27: Spring and Summer Feasts 561
    The Hebrew Calendar 562
    The Passover (Pesach) 564
    The Feast of Unleavened Bread (Hag HaMatzot) and the
        Feast of Firstfruits (Reishit) 569
    The Feast of Weeks (Shavuot) 571
    Questions for Comprehension and Discussion 574

Chapter 28: Fall and Winter Feasts 577
    The Feast of Trumpets (Rosh Hashanah, the Jewish New Year) 577
    Day of Atonement (Yom Kippur) 581
    The Feast of Tabernacles (Sukkot) 586
    The Feast of Dedication (Hanukkah) and Purim 588
    The Sabbath 590
    Questions for Comprehension and Discussion 594

PART 3: THE EXPLANATORY EVIDENCE

Chapter 29: Human Nature and Purpose 599
    The "Castle" of Evidence 605
    What an Amazing Yet Terrible World 606
    A Purpose-Driven Life 612
    Questions for Comprehension and Discussion 619

Chapter 30: Morality and Other Aspects of Real Life 623
    Is There Such a Thing as Right and Wrong? 624
    The Existence of Love 632
    The Reality of Beauty 635
    The Supernatural All Around Us 639
    Questions for Comprehension and Discussion 645

Chapter 31: Unique Among Philosophies 651
    The Unique Trajectory of the Gospel 653

    Why Human Nature Instinctively Dislikes Grace 657
    Eternal Rest for Our Souls 660
    Can I Live Any Way I Want? 661
    Questions for Comprehension and Discussion 666

Chapter 32: Power to Truly Transform 671
    The Drive Shaft of the Human Heart 671
    Instinctual Self-Justifiers 675
    How the Gospel Transforms Our Relationships 683
    Questions for Comprehension and Discussion 692

Chapter 33: Receiving the Free Gift 697
    The Great Barriers to Belief 698
    Two Ways to Avoid God 701
    Which Is True Freedom, Freedom in Christ or Freedom
        from Christ? 703
    The Object of Faith Is What's Important, Not the Strength
        of the Faith 706
    The Dartboard of Evidence 709
    The Promises and the Prayer 713
    Questions for Comprehension and Discussion 717

ACKNOWLEDGEMENTS

Special thanks to Bob and Amy Beasley, Dennis and Jane Johnson, Rhonda Telfer, Ted and Linda Hamilton, Brad and Honey Burke, Ross and Holly Colt, Brian and Kathleen Melonakos, Janice Baldwin Desterhaft, Charles and Janet Morris, Peter and Rebecca Jones, Harvey and Lynn Katzen, Kevin and Kathy Daane, John and Jessie Robertus, Mark van den Herik, Beth DeBona, Brooke and Chuck Anderson, Jim and Sukey Ridgway, Ramzi AbuJambra, and Tom and Tambra Murphy.

DEDICATION

For Willem and Hannah, who give me a
wee glimpse into God's infinite love for us.

People almost invariably arrive at their beliefs not on the basis of proof, but on the basis of what they find attractive.

—Blaise Pascal, 17th century French mathematician, physicist, and religious philosopher[1]

The unexamined life is not worth living.
—Socrates, 5th century BC Greek philosopher[2]

INTRODUCTION

The Unavoidable Leap

You stare in disbelief at the two doctors who are debating your diagnosis. The first emphatically insists that you have a life-threatening disease. The second calmly claims that there is no need to worry, offering this reassuring news: "You're going to be just fine. You simply need more rest." Whom do you believe? It should be quite obvious that you wouldn't believe the second doctor just because you want her diagnosis to be true. Instead, you would ask each expert for specific evidence to support his opinion. With the ultimate goal of achieving the best prognosis, you would most likely also seek expertise from other specialists to obtain the most accurate diagnosis and set up the ideal treatment plan.

If the desire for evidence is so strong in matters of physical health at the doctor's office, why then do so many of us fail to review the evidence when faced with questions of potentially greater consequence, questions that could determine our eternal fate beyond the grave rather than our health for mere decades? These weighty questions include: Do my beliefs and actions now affect my eternal destiny? Will I experience an unseen spiritual reality after I die? What will happen to me personally at that frightening moment when I take my last breath?

Our answers to these and other questions about life and death, whether or not we have purposefully thought them through, comprise our *worldview*. We may have imbibed our worldview from our culture, our family, our school or university, our friends, the media, or our house of worship. But why do we believe what we do? Is our worldview based on rational thinking? Or have we simply not considered evidence for the other options? Or worse, do we believe what we do simply because we want it to be true, perhaps so we can live life any way we want? If that's the case, we are like the patient choosing to believe the doctor who says we're fine while ignoring the evidence from the specialist who claims we're terminally ill.

Every Person Takes a Leap of Faith

For most of my life I disregarded the supernatural. I figured that it was acceptable to seek truth in the natural world through scientific investigation, but no one could claim to have found the "absolute truth" about God, right and wrong, and spiritual matters in general. Therefore (so my thinking went), anyone claiming to have "The One Truth" was exclusive and narrow-minded. In my opinion, no one had any basis to claim that there is absolute truth with regards to religion.

Furthermore, I used to think, if no one can claim to have the one truth about God, then all religious and spiritual claims are equally valid. The truly important thing—the mark of a good person—is to be open-minded and to respect the validity of every path to God. This open-minded worldview appealed to me because it seemed to alleviate—and perhaps even eliminate—the explosive conflicts that plague the world as a result of religious extremism. If we could just respect each other's beliefs as different but equally true, we could achieve world peace. I proudly displayed a "Coexist" bumper sticker on my car.

What I didn't realize until later in life was that my open-minded worldview, though well-intentioned, had a huge logical flaw. To believe that there is no absolute truth—that is, that there is no single correct opinion about the unobservable supernatural world—is itself a claim of absolute truth. I was actually violating my own rule. I was essentially saying: "The absolute truth is that there is no absolute truth," thus making my worldview self-contradictory. I was using what I thought was the correct worldview to look down on others who disagreed with me, insisting that they must agree with me for there to be world peace. I was therefore doing exactly what I criticized religious extremists for doing. But I was worse: I didn't admit that I was doing it. I was being the worst kind of extremist: a hypocritical one.

Moreover, my thinking was faulty because I thought I based all of my reasoning and opinions on fact. I therefore insisted that I had no faith. But no one can know for sure that there is no absolute truth. Therefore, the belief that there is no absolute truth also requires a leap of faith. When I believed that there was no absolute truth, I unknowingly had even more faith than someone who holds a strong religious conviction. How so? My opinion that there was no absolute truth required me to hold a worldview that violates the Law of Non-Contradiction. Let me explain. In order for me to believe there is no absolute truth—that is, that all beliefs are equally valid—I had to believe that two contradictory statements, such as "Jesus is God" and "Jesus is not God," are both equally valid and true. But according to simple logic, either one statement is correct and the other is incorrect, or both are incorrect.

As it turns out, much to the surprise of my earlier atheistic, presumably logical self, the truth of a supernatural worldview is not a matter of personal taste, such that you can say "That may be true for you, but not for me." If it is true that Jesus really did create the universe, as the Bible teaches,[3] how can it also be true that Jesus was just a good moral teacher? Similarly, if Jesus really *did* rise from the dead in a transformed physical body, as Christians believe, how could he have also *not* risen from the dead? These are all truth claims that may or may not be really true, not something you like or dislike, like a flavor of ice cream.

With western society's emphasis on democracy, human equality, and religious freedom, it's easy to understand why I so badly wanted to believe that all paths lead to God. (I would also include the atheistic path, in which case "God" could be a personal goal, such as making the world a better place, saving the environment, or the pursuit of another source of happiness, fulfillment, and significance.) This open-minded worldview also suited my conflict-averse nature, since life is so much easier if we don't have to talk about sensitive subjects like what happens to us when we die. For me, it was so much more peaceful and relaxing to reassure myself with thoughts like, "To each his own! We all end up in the same place anyway!"

As I thought more about these issues, I realized that I was confusing two ideas: religious freedom and religious equality. I believed that the idea that all religions are equally true was essential for there to be religious freedom. I would think to myself, how dare those Christians insist that the only way I can go to heaven is to believe in their God? It surely sounded to me like religious intolerance that severely impinged upon religious freedom. But I eventually realized that, again, there were logical flaws in my seemingly logical thinking.

Here's the very important distinction I came to understand over many years of much deliberation and research: it is possible to *both* believe that there is one absolute truth about God and *at the same time* believe in religious tolerance and freedom. In fact, Jesus calls his followers to love their neighbors "as themselves," whether or not those neighbors believe in the Christian God. However, that does not mean that Jesus calls his followers to believe that their neighbors' views of God are as true as their own, nor does it mean that Christians should refrain from lovingly sharing their faith with others. (In fact, if you truly believe what the Bible teaches—that no one can earn eternal life but can only receive it as free gift from God through faith in Jesus—it would be *unloving* for you *not* to share this with others. It would be as if you knew about a towering waterfall a few hundred feet downriver, but you don't want to warn the kayakers heading in that direction because you'd hate to interrupt their fun.)

Here's how religious truth claims become dangerous, and even deadly: The believer rejects religious tolerance and resorts to threats and violence to force all others to believe "the truth." This type of intolerance is completely at odds with the teachings of Jesus. In fact, in the parable of the Good Samaritan, one of his most famous moral lessons, Jesus provides an example of a Samaritan man who sacrificially cares for a wounded and helpless Jewish stranger. In those days, Samaritans and Jews disagreed on many theological topics and were notorious enemies. Jesus tells this parable as an example of a true neighbor, someone who loves and cares for another person, *even* when that person's spiritual beliefs are markedly different.

In addition to believing that "all paths lead to God," I also used to hold this other belief: God, if he exists, is a "God of love," and he doesn't care how you live as long as you're a "good person." But what proof did I have that God is loving? I certainly didn't deduce that from looking at the state of the world. Moreover, exactly *how good* did I have to be to get into heaven (or achieve nirvana, or perfect harmony with nature, and so forth)? My belief in a God of love who lets good people into heaven, while a wonderful idea, was also based on a leap of faith at least as large as that required by any other belief system.

I also came to realize that even an atheistic worldview requires faith. I could say, "I'll believe in God if I have 100% certain proof that he (or she) exists," or even, "There is no need to disprove something that isn't proven in the first place." But in making these statements I was actually making another truth claim: God, if he existed, would make himself known to me in an undeniably certain way. What evidence did I have that God would give irrefutable proof for his existence? And on top of this leap of faith, I would still have to take another leap of faith to trust that when I died, I would simply cease to exist. There is no way to prove this. It must be accepted on faith.

Finding the Shortest Leap

In summary, what I have come to discover is this: whatever our belief system regarding life after death and spiritual matters in general, they all require us to take a leap of faith. Perhaps you are like me when I made this realization—I was tempted to just throw up my hands and say, "No one can know anything! Why even bother to evaluate truth claims? Why not just choose what works best for me?" Fortunately, I have discovered that you don't have to conclude that spiritual truth is unknowable. As with scientific inquiry, you can use your reason to determine which worldview is closest to the truth based on the evidence that supports it or refutes it.

Even though God, if he exists, is unobservable, it is still possible to investigate whether he exists and what he is like by observing his *effects*. This is exactly how we study other unobservable phenomena. For example, we can't see the molecules of gas that constitute a gentle breeze, but we can measure their effects on objects that we *can* see. Similarly, we can't see the forces of gravity or magnetism, but we can see the effects that these forces have on visible materials.

Another example of unobservable phenomena are events that have already occurred. For this reason, historians, archaeologists, investigative journalists, attorneys, and forensic scientists also use rational induction as they seek to determine the truth about what happened in the past. They cannot rewind time and observe the original events, but they can study the effects of those events—eyewitness memories in recorded interviews and accounts, footprints and fingerprints, DNA evidence found at the scene, notes, letters and other documentary evidence, traces of dust, pollen, or other chemicals, and so forth—to reconstruct the past based on the weight of the evidence.

Consider a detective or crime scene investigator, fictional examples of which range from Sherlock Holmes in nineteenth-century London to Gil Grissom in the TV series "C.S.I." These detectives are the ultimate, dispassionate rationalists. They would never allow the investigative team to accuse someone of a crime without a thorough, rational investigation. They can't claim a person is guilty just because they have a "strong feeling" he or she did it, or because they grew up being taught that certain people commit certain crimes. Similarly, they can't let a suspect go free because they wish him or her to be innocent.

With regards to spiritual claims, most people (including my younger self) base their decisions largely on emotions, rather than on rational evidence. They choose to disregard the claims of Christianity for many reasons: it seems too good to be true, or they don't like the way Christians have acted throughout history, or because they believe they're good enough to get into heaven, or because they want to live life without the "shackles" they believe Christianity will place on them.

But while emotions are an important element of one's personal decision-making process, one should not rely upon them wholly for crucial decisions, especially those with potentially eternal consequences, like where we go, if anywhere, when we die. Moreover, one should judge Christianity for its teachings, rather than for the incorrect implementation of its teachings by error-prone humans over the course of history. As St. Augustine put it so succinctly: "Never judge a philosophy by its abuse."

I like to think of the core tenets of Christianity (salvation by faith alone) as a beautiful treasure that has unfortunately been covered by barnacles over the centuries as a result of human pride and selfishness. Instead of recoiling at the ugly barnacles, it is better to first remove them to view the treasure beneath. At that point, you have a better vantage point and can determine a more accurate estimate of the value of the treasure.

My goal in this book is to help you evaluate the Christian faith with the same techniques used to investigate scientific phenomena and historical events. First and foremost, I wrote this book for those who know little about Christianity and are willing to learn more. At best, they aren't sure why Christians believe what they do, or at worst, they are completely offended by the claims of Christianity (as I used to be). Secondly, this book is for Christians who want to learn how to share their faith with others, as well as for Christians who want to believe in

Jesus more wholeheartedly. The ultimate goal of this book is to present evidence that demonstrates the truth of Christianity.

While only God can "open your eyes" to his truth,[4] one way he does this is through rational evidence that breaks down roadblocks impeding your belief in Jesus. Please recognize that, whatever your current beliefs about the existence of God and the purpose of life, they are based on a leap of faith. It is my sincere hope and prayer that you will take the leap of faith to Jesus, which I sincerely believe requires the *shortest leap*.

QUESTIONS FOR COMPREHENSION AND DISCUSSION

1. What is a worldview? What types of questions does a worldview address? Can you describe your own worldview? Where did you get your worldview?
2. Do you identify with one or more of these common beliefs? Why? On what evidence do you base these beliefs?
   a) All religions are basically the same.
   b) All paths lead to God. Traditional Christianity is too closed-minded.
   c) You just have to be a good person to get into heaven.
   d) I will believe in God if he does [fill in the blank] for me, or if he gives me [fill in the blank].
   e) God is love, so he loves everyone no matter what.
   f) My spiritual beliefs work for me, so I don't feel the need to investigate others.
   g) God is impossible to prove, so there is no need to figure out if he exists.
   h) I don't believe in God because I believe only the natural world exists.
3. Why is the claim, "There is no absolute truth," a logical contradiction?
4. What is the difference between the belief in religious freedom and the belief that all religions are equally true?
5. How are all worldviews, including the atheistic worldview, based on leaps of faith?

6. What other truth claim is someone making when he or she states: "I will believe in God if he can be proven with 100% certainty"?
7. How can we go about investigating the truth of an unseen God? How is it similar to the work of scientists, historians, and crime scene investigators?
8. What are some common ways people reject Christianity for emotional reasons? How is it similar to judging the value of a treasure covered with barnacles?
9. What did St. Augustine mean when he encouraged people not to "judge a philosophy by its abuse"?
10. What are your feelings as you embark on this overview of the rational evidence for Christianity? Do you truly want to see this evidence, or are you—in a little way—hoping you can refute it?

INTRODUCTION ENDNOTES

[1] Blaise Pascal, *De l'Art de persuader* ["On the Art of Persuasion"], written 1658; published posthumously.
[2] Plato, *Apology*, 38a5-6.
[3] The Bible teaches that Jesus created the universe in John 1:3, 1 Corinthians 8:6, Colossians 1:16, and Hebrews 1:2.
[4] In John 6:44, Jesus says, "No one can come to me unless the Father who sent me draws them, and I will raise them up at the last day."

PART I
The Scientific Evidence

This most beautiful system of the sun, planets and comets, could only proceed from the counsel and dominion of an intelligent and powerful Being.

> – Isaac Newton, 17th/18th century English mathematician, physicist, astronomer, theologian, and author [1]

Astronomy leads us to a unique event, a universe which was created out of nothing and delicately balanced to provide exactly the conditions required to support life. In the absence of an absurdly improbable accident, the observations of modern science seem to suggest an underlying, one might say, supernatural plan.

> – Arno Penzias, Nobel Laureate in physics and co-discoverer of the radiation afterglow from the Big Bang [2]

Out to the Stars

Before we make any rational arguments concerning the truth of Christianity, we should first address the fundamental question of whether God exists. If there is sufficient evidence to argue that God cannot exist, that he is simply a figment of our imagination and what some atheists have called the most dangerous ideological invention of mankind, then the claim that Jesus is God also loses validity.

While some may claim that God's existence is supernatural and therefore not provable, there are actually very compelling, rational reasons to believe that God does exist. In fact, these reasons are so compelling that I can confidently state that the belief that there is no God requires a bigger leap of faith than the belief that a supernatural Being created the universe and everything in it.

Evidence from recent secular science, ranging from physics and biology to paleontology and anthropology, clearly points to a Creator, as we will explore in the first part of this book. In fact, while it may seem at first blush that discoveries about the natural world in the last few centuries have resulted in a conflict between science and religion, the two disciplines—science on the one hand and religion and philosophy on the other—are actually quite consistent. The apparent contradiction arose whenever new scientific discoveries replaced theistic explanations of the universe, and people started to view God as the "God of the gaps." That is, God was only needed to explain the gaps in our understanding of the universe, and if we didn't know how something happened, it must have been "by the hand of God."

Over time, those gaps in scientific knowledge were filled, and people started thinking that "God's hand" wasn't really necessary to explain how the world worked. And with Darwin's theory of evolution, which appeared to explain how organisms have developed on their own through chance mutations over billions of years, God no longer seemed necessary at all. In fact, many evolutionary scientists claim that the theory of evolution has made belief in God the equivalent of belief in the tooth fairy and Santa Claus, such that no completely rational adult would be a theist.[3]

Thus, the apparent conflict between science and religion results from thinking of God as the way to fill in the gaps in our knowledge of the universe. But the conflict vanishes if we instead view him as the engineer behind the intricate complexity that our scientific knowledge has revealed. While it is important that we don't immediately rush to a theistic explanation of events in our universe when natural explanations aren't obvious, the existing evidence from secular science is pointing convincingly towards the existence of a "divine engineer," a Being outside our time and space who designed the universe, brought it into existence, created life, and guided the development of all living things.

While there is a plethora of evidence that fills many books, for our purposes we will focus on seven main lines of scientific evidence that point to a Creator:

1. the Big Bang
2. the fine-tuning of the universe
3. the variable flow of time demonstrated by Einstein's law of relativity
4. the irreducible complexity of living systems
5. the specified complexity, or coded nature, of DNA
6. the characteristics of stasis and sudden appearance in the fossil record
7. the Sociocultural Big Bang.

This chapter will cover the first three lines of scientific evidence for God, which are obtained from studying astronomy and physics. The next chapter will discuss the fourth and fifth lines of scientific evidence, which come from recent discoveries in biochemistry and molecular biology. Chapter 3 will focus on the sixth and seventh lines of scientific evidence, which are from the fossil and anthropological records, as well as from phylogenetics (the genetics of ancestral relationships).

Finally, in Chapter 4, we will discuss how these seven lines of scientific evidence are consistent with the biblical description of God and the biblical worldview.

THE BIG BANG

In the 1920s, the Belgian astronomer Georges Lemaître was the first to theorize that the universe was expanding. Soon thereafter the American astronomer Edwin Hubble confirmed this theory when he noticed that all observable galaxies were moving away from earth, and those galaxies that are farther away from earth were moving away faster than closer galaxies (a fact now known as "Hubble's Law"). His logical conclusion was that the universe has been expanding at an ever-increasing rate since an initial moment in time when it was a singular extremely dense point of matter. After this initial "explosion" from the singularity, the universe has expanded and cooled, permitting the formation of elements (hydrogen, helium, and lithium at first). Gravity caused these elements to coalesce, with the resulting formation of stars, galaxies, planets, moons, and everything else that comprises our universe. Astrophysicists have conclusively demonstrated that this initial explosion took place 13.77 billion years ago. And it is quite true that this discovery has itself been explosive in its impact on philosophical worldviews, especially those that hold to the claim that the universe is infinite.

Prior to the recent scientific consensus that the universe had a beginning, most people assumed that it had always existed, and an infinite universe has no need for a creator. But scientists now agree that our universe is *finite*. Demonstrating the current position by astronomers on the finite nature of our universe, an article on the National Aeronautics and Space Administration website states: "Because the universe has a finite age (~13.77 billion years) we can only see a finite distance out into space: ~13.77 billion light years."[4] As the NASA article points out, the evidence for the Big Bang demands that the universe is finite.

It is a philosophically important fact that the universe is finite for the simple reason that a finite universe requires a creator. Why is that? The principles of logic require that all effects must have an associated cause. If something has begun to exist, something else must have created it. There can be no exception. In fact, to deny this Law of Cause and Effect

CHAPTER 1: OUT TO THE STARS

would be to deny the very premise of all of science, which is essentially the study of causes and their effects. So, if everything that is finite has a cause, what caused the universe? What initiated the singularity that expanded at the moment of the Big Bang? There must be something that exists outside the dimensions of time and space that could bring about those dimensions of time and space that we call the universe.[5]

Not only must there exist "something" outside of the dimensions of time and space, this "something" cannot be finite itself—it must be infinite, eternal, and without a beginning—and thus has no need for a creator. That is, there must be something infinite that caused the finite universe.

Materialist scientists, who deny the existence of anything beyond the physical world, are aware of the implications of a finite universe. To defend their materialist worldview, they have advanced many theories to explain how a creator need not be involved in the creation of our known universe.

After it became increasingly evident that the universe had a beginning, one early theory that emerged was the Big Bounce theory, or the Oscillatory Universe theory, which claimed that the universe has been in existence eternally (and thus doesn't need a creator) but has been "bouncing" between its tiny size and its fully expanded size for an infinite amount of time. We are currently only seeing it in the latest expansion phase of its latest bounce. However, this theory violates the Second Law of Thermodynamics (an infinite bouncing universe would have stopped bouncing by now, just as a ball stops bouncing eventually). And the Big Bounce theory was replaced by others as astrophysicists discovered more and more about the universe and its expansion since the Big Bang.

The Multiverse, or Multiple Universe theory, is another popular way that materialist scientists have tried to get around the religious implications of a universe with a beginning. This theory claims that, while our universe may *not* be eternal, it is one of many parallel universes in a "multiverse" that *is* eternal. Because it is eternal, the multiverse has no need for a creator.

The idea of a multiverse is not new, of course. You may recognize it from some science fiction books you've read, and even in a classic Christian children's book, *The Lion, the Witch and the Wardrobe* and a more recent favorite, the Harry Potter series. In various twists of the idea, many terms have been used: "alternate dimensions, universes, realities or timelines," "quantum universes or realities," "parallel dimensions, worlds, or realities," "interpenetrating dimensions," or "dimensional planes."[6] In fact, this is how many people envision the heaven and hell of the Bible, not real places in our existing universe, but nearby us somehow, perhaps in a different dimension. So, the idea of multiple universes feels quite plausible.

But does the multiverse really disprove God? Stephen Hawking, the initial author of this theory, said it does: "So long as the universe had a beginning, we could suppose it had a creator. But if the universe is really completely self-contained, having no boundary or edge, it would have neither beginning nor end: it would simply be. What place, then, for a creator?"[7] And one astrophysicist from UC Berkeley, Mike Wall, stated:

> The Big Bang could've occurred as a result of just the laws of physics being there. With the laws of physics, you can get universes.... The question, then, is, "Why are there laws of physics?" And you could say, "Well, that required a divine creator, who created these laws of physics and the spark that led from the laws of physics to these universes, maybe more than one." The "divine spark" was whatever produced the laws of physics. And I don't know what produced that divine spark. So let's just leave it at the laws of physics.[8]

So, we are left with the question of what created the laws of physics. Wall summarized the problem in this way: "But that answer just continues to kick the can down the road, because you still need to explain where the divine creator came from. The process leads to a never-ending chain that always leaves you short of the ultimate answer."[9] But Wall's reasoning is faulty: since an infinite Creator has no beginning, and therefore has no creator, there is no need to explain the origins of the divine creator.

After studying the multiverse theory, physicist Paul Davies made this comment: "Such a belief must rest on faith rather than observation."[10] In fact, even if the multiverse were true, it still does not disprove God. Multiverse or no multiverse, what we choose to believe must rely on faith (and other supporting evidence, such as you find in the remainder of this book).

CHAPTER 1: OUT TO THE STARS

Antony Flew, the English religious philosopher who ultimately decided to renounce atheism, explained it this way in his book, *There Is a God: How the World's Most Notorious Atheist Changed His Mind*:

> I did not find the multiverse alternative very helpful. The postulation of multiple universes, I maintained, is a truly desperate alternative. If the existence of one universe requires an explanation, multiple universes require a much bigger explanation: the problem increased by the factor of whatever the total number of universes is. It seems a little like the case of a schoolboy whose teacher doesn't believe his dog ate his homework, so he replaces the first version with the story that a pack of dogs—too many to count—ate his homework.[11]

So, what does it mean that a belief requires faith? Is faith limited to religious people? As we mentioned in the Introduction, everyone has faith, especially when it comes to the big questions about the meaning of life and what happens after we die. One has faith that a certain truth claim—let's call it XYZ—is true even when there isn't sufficient proof that XYZ is true. XYZ can be as simple as, "When I get into this elevator, I have faith that its cable will not snap while I am in transit to the 30th floor." Probability dictates that this will not happen, but you still do not have 100% proof that the elevator cable won't break on this next trip to the 30th floor. And XYZ can be as mysterious as what will happen after you die. We cannot prove with 100% accuracy what will happen after you die, but we can look at evidence to arrive at the most plausible description of what will happen at the unfortunate time of your death.

But back to our discussion of the universe's origin. As we have seen, it takes just as much faith (if not more) to believe in the infinite multiverse as it does to believe in a single finite universe that was created by a Supreme Engineer (or a series of parallel universes created by the laws of physics that were created by a Supreme Engineer). So why is it that scientists accuse proponents of "intelligent design" of being biased by their faith? Isn't it also the case that atheists have faith in "infinite laws of physics"? And perhaps this faith then clouds their own analysis of the evidence?

Religious philosophers Norman Geisler and Frank Turek summarize it this way:

> When those scientists let their personal preferences or unproven philosophical assumptions dictate their interpretation of the evidence, they do exactly what they accuse religious people of doing—they let their ideology dictate their conclusions. When that's the case, their conclusions should be questioned, because they may be nothing more than philosophical presuppositions passed off as scientific fact.[12]

Let me clarify that it is perfectly acceptable—in fact, desirable—that scientists seek to explain the creation of the universe in a way that doesn't necessitate a God. In fact, if we always threw up our hands and said, "God did it!" for everything we didn't understand in nature, we would revert to "a God of the gaps" and would still believe that the sun revolved around the earth. Nonetheless, the current evidence in favor of a single creation event approximately 14 billion years ago now far outweighs the evidence in favor of an infinite universe.

THE FINE-TUNING OF THE UNIVERSE

The evidence increasingly points to a universe that suddenly appeared 14 billion years ago. (Or, if you accept the multiverse, the evidence at least points to the creation of the laws of physics, which in turn are responsible for "universe creation.") We have already discussed the logical premise that something finite cannot come into existence without a cause. Put more succinctly, something cannot come from nothing (or, *ex nihilo*, as a philosopher would say in Latin). But for the moment let's take the leap of faith that the universe either "just appeared out of nowhere" or has existed infinitely.

Another problem arises: how to explain the "fine-tuning" of the many physical constants that comprise the laws of physics and the universe. Unless these physical constants are "just right," the universe couldn't exist at all, much less provide the necessary prerequisites for life

CHAPTER 1: OUT TO THE STARS

to exist. How can we account for this if there is no Creator who knew how to set the constants in our laws of physics "just so"?

Astrophysicist Hugh Ross has listed dozens of characteristics of the universe that must be set with extreme precision, such that a minuscule change in any of them would disrupt the balance of the universe enough to prevent it from existing at all. For example, Ross states:

> Unless the number of electrons is equivalent to the number of protons to an accuracy of one part in 10^{37} [one followed by 37 zeros] or better, electromagnetic forces in the universe would have so overcome gravitational forces that galaxies, stars, and planets never would have formed.[13]

Such a tiny probability is difficult to imagine. Ross uses the following analogy to clarify how finely tuned this one variable must be: Suppose we cover an area of land equivalent to one million North American continents with dimes up to the height of the moon (239,000 miles). We then mix in one dime that has been painted red and ask a blindfolded friend to pick out one dime. The chance that your friend would select the red dime is one in 10^{37}, the same probability that the "just right" ratio of protons to electrons in atoms happened by chance alone (that is, without any guidance by "someone turning the knobs" to make it that way).

And this ratio is just one of the many parameters describing the universe that must be balanced on a razor's edge. Here are just a few more: If molecules are to form, the strength of the electromagnetic force holding two atoms together must be within a very narrow range of values. If the electromagnetic force were a tiny bit stronger, atoms would not share their electrons with other atoms, keeping molecules from forming. If it were a tiny bit weaker, atoms would not hold onto electrons at all, also preventing molecular bonding. Moreover, if electrons were slightly bigger relative to protons, or vice versa, the same bonding would be impossible.[14] These are just two additional parameters out of dozens that physicists have discovered so far that point to a universe that is so finely tuned that it couldn't have happened by chance.

Given such fine-tuning, it is miraculous that the universe exists at all. What is even more miraculous is that life exists. There are dozens of additional characteristics that must be just right in order for living organisms to survive within the universe.[15] For one, the earth is in just the right type of galaxy. The Milky Way is a spiral galaxy, which permits stars to have more stable orbits than other types of galaxies. Moreover, the earth is perfectly situated within our galaxy: far enough from the center to avoid the dangerous radiation emitted by our galaxy's central "supermassive black hole" and the super-hot comets that orbit it. And yet the earth is not too far from the center of the galaxy. If it were any further from the center of the Milky Way, the earth would not have sufficient heavy elements to create life (elements like carbon, nitrogen, and oxygen, which are heavier than the simplest elements, hydrogen, helium, and lithium).

The earth is also at just the right distance from the sun, and its near-circular orbit around the sun is just right to stabilize temperature fluctuations throughout the year. The earth takes just the right amount of time to go around the sun and is surrounded by just the right number of planets for life to thrive. The moon is just the right size to stabilize the tilt of the earth so that temperature changes from summer to winter are not excessive. The earth itself is just the right size—any smaller and it would be unable to hold on to the atmosphere or create a magnetic field strong enough to protect us from cosmic rays; any larger, and its gravity would be so strong there would be only minor differences in altitude, causing water to cover its surface.[16] The list of such fine-tuned parameters exceeds one hundred, and it grows with each passing year as scientists make new discoveries about our universe.

As mentioned above, one way that materialists have tried to downplay the overwhelming evidence in favor of a Creator is to suggest that there have been an infinite number of universes. Therefore, the chances of getting it just right, while extremely small, are attainable. Given an infinite number of tries, eventually the right universe will happen.

The problem for those who want to disprove God is that it is scientifically impossible to prove this theory. We cannot know any universe outside our own. Again, it takes just as much faith to believe the multiverse theory as to admit the possibility that an extra-dimensional, divine Being created the universe with the right parameters the first time around. Moreover, if it is the same laws of physics that govern all of the universes within the multiverse, how do these laws "alter themselves" with each universe until they finally get it just right? Do the constants change within the laws of physics after each "universe launch failure" until they finally produce the one, finely tuned universe that doesn't collapse on itself?

CHAPTER 1: OUT TO THE STARS

Edward Harrison, the Emeritus Distinguished Professor of Physics and Astronomy at the University of Massachusetts summarizes it well: "The fine tuning of the universe provides *prima facie* evidence of deistic design. Take your choice: blind chance that requires multitudes of universes or design that requires only one."[17]

According to the calculations of astrophysicist Hugh Ross, the probability that all known constants necessary for life would be "just right" is one in 10^{138} (that's 1 with 138 zeros after it)![18] To clarify this probability, if you roll a six-sided die, the chance of rolling a two is one in six, so on average, for every six rolls, you'll roll a two. Thus, it would take 1,000,000...000,000 attempts (the three dots representing 126 additional zeros) at creating a universe by chance before eventually getting it just right.

Oxford mathematical physicist Roger Penrose calculated the odds that the constants of the universe were just right as one followed by quadrillions more zeros than there are elementary particles in the universe.[19] To put these numbers into perspective, there are "only" 10^{80} atoms in the entire universe. We can thus confidently assert that there is essentially zero chance that any planet, including the earth, would be just right for life without the interference of an engineer.

In response to the "fine-tuning argument," materialists point out that there are many other observable phenomena that also have a very low probability. Thus, just because the universe seems "just right" for man's existence does not prove God. One example they give is the lottery—the chances of winning are very low, but that doesn't mean there won't be a winner. The problem with this analogy is that lotteries are designed to have a winner. If someone doesn't win, the pot gets bigger until a winner is eventually drawn.

Another example they might give is seeing the license plate "5ARD894" followed by the license plate "3PKJ986" followed by the license plate "4THR284." Materialists would say that no one would ever exclaim, "Wow, can you believe it? What are the chances that I'd see these three license plates in a row!?" Thus, we shouldn't be surprised when we see a universe that is "finely tuned" to exist and support life.

Let's take a short look at this issue now, though we will explore it at more length in the next chapter when we discuss the concept of "specified complexity." In short, calculating the odds for everyday events after they happen is a completely different situation than assigning probabilities to the more than 100 finely tuned parameters of the universe. To illustrate this, I'll use an impressive poem I found on the Internet, in which each stanza contains all 100 letters in a Scrabble set. Here's the first stanza:

> Through sentient, gauzy flame
> I view life's dread, quixotic, partial joke.
> We're vapour-born,
> by logic and emotion seen as dead.[20]

What are the chances this stanza could have come together accidentally by throwing the 100 Scrabble tiles up in the air? There are "100!" (pronounced "one hundred factorial") ways of arranging the 100 tiles in a Scrabble game, or 100x99x98x97 and so on down to x3x2x1. That's $9x10^{157}$ ways (9 with 157 zeros after it). Thus, the chance that the tiles fall in line with the words of this poem is one in $9x10^{157}$, which is exactly the same probability that they will fall in a completely nonsensical way, like this:

> htouxghsetieartgarzyfaemteiviwliep
> sdrgyeaduioticpariaelujomkeweevaro
> bronbloincnantudeqoionlsenasdfedu

But what would you think if you walked into a room and saw the "sentient, gauzy flame" poem in Scrabble tiles on the table? Would you think someone must have dumped the Scrabble tiles on the table, and the poem happened by accident? Of course not. We can recognize design when we see it, even though the probability that they happened by chance is the same for both the poem and the nonsensical letters.

Amazingly, against enormous odds, the universe does exist. There are only two rational conclusions we can draw. Either we can assume that there have been an infinite number of attempts at universe generation and our universe was the one that "got lucky," or we can assume that there is a Being outside the universe who designed it and caused it. The Big Bang demonstrates that our universe had a beginning, which necessitates a Beginner. And the fine-tuning of our universe suggests that there was an Engineer who designed it. Unless there had been an infinite number of "universe creation attempts," our universe could not have happened by chance.

CHAPTER 1: OUT TO THE STARS

POSITIONED FOR UNIVERSE EXPLORATION

When we see how the universe is perfectly fine-tuned for mankind's existence, it appears that a Creator—let's call him the Supreme Engineer—created the earth with our comfort in mind. Not only that, it also appears that he wants humans to investigate the universe he created, possibly so that we can find him at its source.

Physicist Guillermo Gonzalez explains: "Not only do we inhabit a location in the Milky Way that's fortuitously optimal for life, but our location also happens to provide us with the best overall platform for making a diverse range of [astronomical and cosmological] discoveries."[21]

If the earth were in any number of other locations, we couldn't observe the many aspects of the universe that we have been able to discover, such as the cosmic background radiation, which provided initial proof of the Big Bang. Also, we are in just the right section of the Milky Way to allow us to see other galaxies. In almost all other positions, the view outside the galaxy would be obstructed.[22] Moreover, our atmosphere is just thick enough to protect us from cosmic rays and to permit us to breathe, but not so thick as to obstruct our view of stars.[23] The moon is also the precise size and distance from the Earth to allow us to view full solar eclipses, which have provided tremendous opportunities for scientists to study the stars that otherwise would not be available.[24]

The list of the conditions that allow optimal study of the universe from planet Earth is lengthy, and it continues to increase as astronomers discover more about the universe. If you envision all the possible positions of our planet as seats in a huge indoor stadium, with a tiny window at one end through which the universe can be studied, the earth is in the front row seat right next to the tiny window.

THE CHANGING FLOW OF TIME

There is one question that rational people often have in response to someone who claims that the Bible is true: You don't really believe that God created the universe in six days, do you?

Many believers in the biblical account of creation claim that each "day" of creation isn't meant as a literal twenty-four-hour period, but instead represents much longer "epochs" of time. Moreover, the earth hadn't even settled into its revolution around the sun on the first "day" of creation—in fact, the sun and the earth hadn't even been created yet—so the term cannot literally mean the length of time it takes for the earth to rotate on its axis while on its orbit around the sun.

But the days of Genesis need not be dismissed as merely epochs, even though this explanation is a fine one and satisfies many believers. In fact, time itself is variable, depending on where you are in the universe. In 1915, Albert Einstein published the theory of relativity, which radically changed our understanding of time. Time is not absolute, but the flow of time that you experience is dependent on the velocity at which you are traveling and the force of gravity that is acting on you. In fact, at the speed of light, time ceases to flow altogether.

We can't imagine the concept of time standing still, and at first it may seem just as implausible as the Genesis creation story, but scientists now regard Einstein's discovery as a law, the *law of relativity*, and no longer just a theory. Time *does* stop when an object travels at the speed of light, and time *does* slow down as the force of gravity increases. So, the first proper response to the question above is, "Whose six days are we talking about?"

The best explanation of the six days of creation, I believe, is provided in the book, *The Science of God*, by Gerald L. Schroeder, an MIT physicist who is also a faithful Jew.[25] Although it will not do justice to Schroeder's explanation, allow me to attempt a quick summary of how the universe could very well have been created in six twenty-four-hour days.

To illustrate the strange concept of the variability of the speed at which time passes, Schroeder provides a useful example. He asks us to imagine a planet that is so much larger than Earth that its time is slowed by a factor of 350,000 relative to Earth's time. In the same amount of time that it takes for our heart to beat once on Earth, our hearts would beat 350,000 times on the much heavier planet. Events that take one year on Earth would take 350,000 years on the planet with the much larger force of gravity.

According to Schroeder, if we can figure out the speed of the universe's clock at the point when it came into being, we can then understand time from the point of view of the Creator, since the Earth—and therefore "Earth time"—didn't exist at the moment of creation.

But how do we determine the speed of time at the start of the universe? To get to that answer, Schroeder first explains how we can determine the rate at which time flows on the sun. Just as in the example of the much larger planet above, time flows more slowly on the sun than on Earth because the sun's mass is much larger than the Earth's. This slowing of time is directly evident in the stretching of light as it leaves the sun and arrives at the surface of the Earth. By the way, this is similar to the Doppler Effect, which we experience, for example, when a fire truck passes us with its sirens blaring. The wavelength of the sound emitted from the siren changes depending on whether the truck is approaching us or going away from us.

The stretching of the wavelength of light from the sun has been measured at 2.12 parts per million, which can be translated into a corresponding shortening of time on the sun: for every million seconds that pass on Earth, time is slowed by 2.12 seconds on the sun. This works out to be about 67 seconds per year (here's the math: 365.25 days per year, times 24 hours per day, times 60 minutes per hour, times 60 seconds per minute, divided by 1,000,000, times 2.12). This 67-second annual delay in the speed of time on the sun is exactly what Einstein's law of relativity would predict and *exactly* what scientists observe using their finely tuned instruments.

Schroeder uses the same process to estimate the speed of time at the birth of the universe. Scientists can measure the wavelength of the radiation that was emitted by the Big Bang, called the cosmic background radiation (or CBR), just as they can measure the wavelength of the light that travels to us from the sun. We don't have to make any guesses about what the universe was like 14 billion years ago. This cosmic background radiation is exactly the same as it was very soon after the Big Bang.

We only have to measure the frequency of the CBR on Earth today to know how fast time passed at the moment the universe was created. As Schroeder puts it: "Any one of a dozen physics textbooks all bring the same number. The general relationship between time near the beginning and time today is a million million."[26] That is, independently verified, secular measurements of the CBR demonstrate a wavelength that was a million million (10^{12}) times shorter at the birth of the universe.

What does this indicate about the flow of time at the birth of the universe? It means that for each minute at the start of the universe, a million million minutes would pass in "Earth time." Similarly, for every six days that passed at the beginning of the universe, six million million days would pass on Earth today. To convert six million million days to years, you divide by 365.25, the number of days in a year. The result is 16 billion years. While this may not be exactly the 13.77 billion years that astronomers have recently stated is the age of the universe, 16 billion years should strike you as an amazing guess for a book that was written thousands of years ago!

To summarize, depending on whether you're looking from "Earth perspective" or from the perspective of the universe at the moment of the Big Bang, the universe is either 16 billion years old or 6 days old. A useful analogy is our measurement of weight, which varies depending on the force of gravity acting on the object being weighed. A man who weighs 200 pounds on Earth will weigh 33 pounds on the moon, 75 pounds on Mars, and 473 pounds on Jupiter. These varying weights are all equally true. And just as the man's weight varies depending on the force of gravity acting upon the man when you weigh him, the rate at which time flows varies depending on the force of gravity acting on the person whose time perspective you are using.

Could it just be a coincidence? Perhaps. But Schroeder goes on to give us much more confidence in the Genesis creation story by comparing what happened in the course of each day according to the Bible to what scientists have discovered about the history of the universe. Schroeder puts it this way:

> The Bible goes out on a limb and tells you what happened on each of those days. Now you can take cosmology, paleontology, archaeology, and look at the history of the world, and see whether or not they match up day-by-day. And I'll give you a hint. They match up close enough to send chills up your spine.[27]

Without going into the mathematical details here, suffice it to say that with each doubling of the size of the universe, time (from the perspective of the Creator) changed by a factor of two. Therefore, "day one" lasted approximately 8 billion Earth years, "day two" lasted approximately 4 billion years, "day three" lasted approximately 2 billion years, "day four" lasted approximately 1 billion years, "day 5" lasted approximately 500 million years, and "day 6" lasted approximately 250 million years. Each of the six days, therefore, started approximately 16 billion, 8 billion, 4 billion, 2 billion, 1 billion, and 500 million years ago respectively. And we are now in the "seventh day" (and every day afterward) when God rested and did not create anything.

So, how does this live up to what scientists have discovered about the development of the universe, our planet, and life?

On the first day (approximately 16 billion to 8 billion years ago), Genesis states that "God created the heavens and the earth,"[28] and light was separated from darkness. Scientific evidence has shown that the creation of the universe started with the Big Bang, and that light came into being as electrons bonded to atomic nuclei.[29] By the way, this is also the point at which the cosmic background radiation mentioned above was emitted.

According to Genesis, on the first day "the earth was formless and empty, darkness was over the surface of the deep, and the Spirit of God was hovering over the *waters*." That seems like a strange detail. Was there really water soon after the Big Bang? Cosmologists have estimated that the smallest elements (hydrogen, helium, and lithium) were probably formed about two hundred seconds after the Big Bang, while oxygen was formed when two or more lighter elements collided and fused. Once oxygen was created, there was enough hydrogen around to create water (H_2O) immediately. In fact, water is the most stable molecule that can be formed from oxygen and hydrogen, and it was therefore created in large quantities very soon after the Big Bang.[30]

On the second day of the Genesis creation account (approximately 8 to 4 billion years ago): "God said, 'Let there be an expanse between the waters to separate water from water. So, God made the expanse and separated the water under the expanse from the water above it. And it was so. God called the expanse 'sky.'"

According to scientific evidence, between 8 billion years ago and 4 billion years ago many of the stars of the Milky Way were formed. One of these stars, our own sun, is approximately 4.5 billion years old.[31] With the help of a special satellite called the SWAS (Submillimeter Wave Astronomy Satellite), scientists have recently discovered that water is a primary by-product of star formation, lending credibility to the Genesis account of water being separated from water on the second day.

The principal investigator of SWAS, an astronomer from the

Harvard-Smithsonian Center for Astrophysics, describes the discovery of water in other parts of the universe: "Most of the water we've seen is forming at incredible rates in these star-forming regions." When a star is being born, it produces water so efficiently that just one cloud becoming a star could fill the Earth's oceans with water once every twenty-four minutes! The water that is produced by the collapsing cloud in turn produces photons of energy that propagate further formation of the star.[32]

Therefore, it is quite possible that verses 2, 6, and 8 of Genesis 1 refer to the water that was formed as an initial by-product of the Big Bang, mentioned above, and the birth of the stars in the Milky Way, including our sun.

On day three (approximately 4 billion to 2 billion years ago), the Bible states that the oceans and dry land appear, as well as the first life. Scientific evidence has shown that the Earth cooled, and liquid water formed on it approximately 4 billion years ago.[33] Also, the first life appeared on Earth between several hundred million to a billion years after the earth was formed,[34] that is, about 3 billion years ago.

On the fourth day (approximately 2 billion to 1 billion years ago), God said, "Let there be light in the expanse of the sky to separate the day from the night."[35] Even though the sun, moon, and stars had already existed since day two, they wouldn't be able to separate the day from the night from Earth's perspective (since "day" and "night" are Earth-relative terms) if the earth's atmosphere weren't clear. This verse could thus be referring to the point in Earth's history when the sun, moon, and stars became visible as the atmosphere became transparent. In fact, according to scientific evidence, at this time in "cosmic perspective" the earth's atmosphere became transparent as photosynthesis from plants and certain bacteria released more and more oxygen into the air.[36]

On day five, the Bible says the first animal life appears. The cosmic equivalent of the fifth day, from 1 billion to 500 million years ago, corresponds with the earliest fossils of multi-cellular organisms and the "Cambrian explosion" of animal fossils, which we will discuss in Chapter 3.

Finally, during the course of the sixth day of the Genesis creation account, land mammals and humans were created, corresponding very well with the fossil record and the "cultural explosion" we see in the

CHAPTER 1: OUT TO THE STARS

archaeological record (also discussed in Chapter 3). You may not feel chills going up your spine, but hopefully you have a new respect for the Bible and a better understanding of why many people believe it is the Creator's inspired revelation of himself to mankind.

So, perhaps you aren't convinced by the similarity of the Genesis timeline of creation to what scientists have discovered happened in Earth's history, nor by the eerily accurate prediction of the age of the universe using the law of relativity and the CBR wavelength to convert six days into 16 billion years. But even if the Big Bang and fine-tuning of the universe were the only evidence we had to go on, let's just call it a tie between the theistic and atheistic explanations for the origin of our universe. However, as you will see in the next chapters, when we carry our investigation into other scientific disciplines, such as molecular and cellular biology, we find even more rational evidence that the universe is not just a fortuitous product of unguided chance.

QUESTIONS FOR COMPREHENSION AND DISCUSSION

1. Why has an apparent conflict between science and belief in God arisen in the last few centuries? How does it help resolve the conflict to view God as the "Supreme Engineer" instead of a "God of the gaps"?
2. If the universe has a beginning, what are the philosophical implications regarding the origin of this universe?
3. What are some theories that scientists have proposed to explain that a finite universe need not require a divine creator?
4. What are some issues with the multiverse theory? Can it be proven?
5. Why is it not necessary to discover what created a divine Creator?
6. What does it mean to say the universe had to be "finely tuned" in order to exist and to enable life to exist? What are some examples of those finely tuned parameters?
7. What are the conclusions we can draw from this precise tuning? Could it have happened by blind chance? Why or why not?
8. What about the position of the Earth enables discoveries about the universe?

9. How does the speed at which time flows change depending on the force of gravity? Why are six days from the Creator's perspective the same as 16 billion years from a modern-day Earth perspective?
10. How do the days of Genesis in the Bible match up with the scientific evidence for the origin of the universe, the sun, the earth, single-celled organisms and plants, a transparent atmosphere, more complex life forms, and modern humans?

CHAPTER 1 ENDNOTES

[1] Isaac Newton, "General Scholium," in *The Principia: Mathematical Principles of Natural Philosophy*, 1687.

[2] Quoted in Walter Bradley, "The 'Just-so' Universe: The Fine-Tuning of Constants and Conditions in the Cosmos," in William Dembski and James Kushiner, eds., *Signs of Intelligence* (Grand Rapids, MI: Baker, 2001), 168.

[3] For example, in an interview with the British paper, *The Guardian*, evolutionary biologist Richard Dawkins stated: "Santa Claus again could be a very valuable lesson because the child will learn that there are some things you are told that are not true. Now isn't that a valuable lesson? Unfortunately, it doesn't seem to have had the desired effect in some cases, because after children learn that there is no Santa Claus, mysteriously they go on believing that there is a God." *The Guardian*, June 5, 2014. Available online at https://www.theguardian.com/books/2014/jun/05/richard-dawkins-fairytales-not-harmful.

[4] See "Foundations of Big Bang Cosmology," NASA Website, https://map.gsfc.nasa.gov/universe/bb_concepts.html.

[5] Interestingly, one discovery of physicists who study string theory is that at least ten dimensions—the four that we observe in the universe (length, height, width, and time) plus at least six more—were created at the moment of the Big Bang. See Hugh Ross, *Beyond the Cosmos* (Colorado Springs, CO: NavPress, 1999), 27-46.

[6] For more examples of the idea of a multiverse in science fiction, see Elizabeth Howell, *Science & Astronomy*, May 10, 2018, https://www.space.com/32728-parallel-universes.html.

[7] Stephen Hawking, *A Brief History of Time* (New York: Bantam, 1990), 140-141.

[8] Mike Wall, "The Big Bang Didn't Need God to Start Universe, Researchers Say," Space.com, June 24, 2014. https://www.space.com/16281-big-bang-god-intervention-science.html.

CHAPTER 1: OUT TO THE STARS

9. Ibid.
10. Paul Davies, *God and the New Physics* (New York: Simon & Schuster, 1983), 174.
11. Antony Flew, *There Is A God: How the World's Most Notorious Atheist Changed His Mind* (New York: HarperCollins, 2007), 124.
12. Normal L. Geisler and Frank Turek, *I Don't Have Enough Faith to Be an Atheist* (Wheaton, IL: Crossway Books, 2004), 128.
13. Hugh Ross, *The Creator and the Cosmos*, 3rd ed. (Colorado Springs, CO: NavPress, 2001), 150.
14. Ibid, 146-148.
15. Ibid, 154-157.
16. Guillermo Gonzalez and Jay W. Richards, *The Privileged Planet: How Our Place in the Cosmos Is Designed for Discovery* (Washington, DC: Regnery Publishing, 2004), 6-7, 55-60, 127-36.
17. Edward Harrison, *Masks of the Universe* (New York: Macmillan-Collier Books, 1985), 252.
18. Hugh Ross, "Why I Believe in Divine Creation," Norman Geisler and Paul Hoffman, eds., *Why I Am a Christian: Leading Thinkers Explain Why They Believe* (Grand Rapids, MI: Baker, 2001), 138-141.
19. Roger Penrose, *The Emperor's New Mind* (New York: Oxford University Press, 1989), 344.
20. This poem is attributed to Mike Keith, 2000, http://www.cadaeic.net/scrpoem.htm.
21. As quoted in Lee Strobel, *The Case for a Creator* (Grand Rapids, MI: Zondervan, 2004), 187.
22. Gonzalez and Richards, *The Privileged Planet*, 146-151.
23. Hans Blumenberg, *The Genesis of Copernican Revolution*, translated by Robert M. Wallace (Cambridge: MIT Press, 1987), 3.
24. Gonzalez and Richards, *The Privileged Planet*, 1-19.
25. Gerald L. Schroeder, *The Science of God* (New York: Simon and Schuster, 1997), 41-71.
26. From "The Age of the Universe" on Gerald Schroeder's website, http://www.geraldschroeder.com/AgeUniverse.aspx.
27. Schroeder, "The Age of the Universe."
28. Genesis 1:1.
29. Schroeder, *The Science of God*, 66.
30. William Speed Weed, "What's Water Got to Do with It?", *Astronomy*, August 2001.
31. A. Bonanno, H. Schlattl, and L. Patern, "The age of the Sun and the relativistic corrections in the EOS," *Astronomy and Astrophysics* 390, 1992, 1115–1118.

32. Ibid.
33. G.B. Dalrymple, *The Age of the Earth* (California: Stanford University Press, 1991).
34. Kevin A. Maher & David J. Stephenson (1988), "Impact frustration of the origin of life," *Nature* 331 (6157): 612–614.
35. Genesis 1:14.
36. C. Allegre and S. Schneider, "The Evolution of the Earth," *Scientific American*, October 1994.

The complexity of the simplest known type of cell is so great that it is impossible to accept that such an object could have been thrown together suddenly by some kind of vastly improbable event. Such an occurrence would be indistinguishable from a miracle.

—Michael Denton, PhD, biochemist[1]

An honest man, armed with all the knowledge available to us now, could only state that in some sense, the origin of life appears at the moment to be almost a miracle, so many are the conditions which would have had to have been satisfied to get it going.

—Francis Crick, recipient of the Nobel Prize for his discovery of DNA[2]

Into the Cell

As we have just seen, the weight of the evidence suggests that our universe has existed for a finite period of time. In addition, the conditions for the universe to exist at all—much less to support life—are precisely as they must be. Moreover, the implications of the law of relativity and discoveries about the history of our universe are remarkably consistent with the Genesis creation account. All of these findings are consistent with a "Divine Engineer," who invented the laws of physics and brought the universe into existence in a way that enabled life to flourish.

In addition, scientists have discovered that the chances that life spontaneously arose out of non-living chemicals, a process termed *abiogenesis*, are infinitesimally small. Even after decades of research in modern laboratories, scientists are still perplexed about how life originated on Earth. A foremost origin-of-life researcher summarized the situation: "At present all discussions on principle theories and experiments in the field either end in stalemate or in a confession of ignorance."[3] Many scientists have found that conditions on the early earth approximately 4.5 billion years ago were not nearly as suitable for the formation of life from non-living chemicals as they had originally thought. Moreover, the first simplest life forms appeared "only" a billion years at most after the earth came into existence. Though a billion years may sound like a long time, it is not even close to long enough for even the simplest, single-celled organisms to develop by chance alone.

As a result, many origin-of-life scientists have postulated that life must have originated elsewhere in the universe and then traveled to

Earth, a theory called *panspermia*.[4] One of the authors of this theory (who later distanced himself from it) was Leslie Orgel. Orgel admitted that getting non-life to assemble itself into life without a chemist to prod things along would require multiple, spontaneous steps:

> There is no agreement on the extent to which metabolism could develop independently of genetic material. In my opinion, there is no basis in known chemistry for the belief that long sequences of reactions can organize spontaneously—and every reason to believe that they cannot. The problem of achieving sufficient specificity, whether in aqueous solution or on the surface of a mineral, is so severe that the chance of closing a cycle of reactions as complex as the reverse citric acid cycle, for example, is negligible.[5]

Biologists J. T. Trevors and D. L. Abel published an article in the journal, *Cell Biology International*, in which they conclude the following regarding the improbability of genetic material appearing on its own, even given billions of years:

> The argument has been repeatedly made that given sufficient time, a genetic instruction set and language system could have arisen. But extended time does not provide an explanatory mechanism for spontaneously generated genetic instruction. No amount of time proposed thus far can explain this type of conceptual communication system.[6]

And according to another scientist who is an expert on the evidence for abiogenesis: "No one has been able to demonstrate a process by which life has developed out of non-life."[7] Despite this lack of evidence, materialists continue to assert that there are ways that natural selection can generate life out of non-life; we just have to keep looking for the mechanism. While it is understandable that scientists continue to seek an explanation for how non-living chemicals can give rise to life, their efforts reflect a leap of faith, not in God, but in the assumed power of unguided evolution.

WHERE WE ARE IN THE DISCUSSION

As we have seen, it takes quite a lot of faith to believe the following three statements:

1. Our universe, with its perfect laws of physics and perfect conditions for life, either came from nothing, or it is just one universe in an eternal multiverse that we cannot prove.
2. Living, self-replicating genetic material spontaneously arose out of non-living chemicals.
3. Because there wasn't enough time for them to arise on the Earth, the earliest life forms survived a journey here from another part of the universe.

But even if we make these implausible assumptions, the chances are infinitesimal that the simplest life in a "primordial soup" evolved *through blind chance alone* into human beings and the millions of other species on this planet.

Let's back up and explain a few things. According to the theory of evolution by natural selection, an environment with scarce resources favors more "fit" organisms over less "fit" organisms. It thereby ensures that only the fittest organisms survive to pass on their beneficial traits to their offspring. Over millions of years of helpful mutations, organisms gradually became more complex. The end result is the variety of life we see in the world today.

For example, the eye would have originated when a mutation caused some cells to detect light, an ability that gave the organism a better chance of surviving and having more offspring than others without the mutation. Over millions of years, other beneficial mutations eventually caused the complete eye to form, first in simpler organisms and eventually in the more complex mammals and human beings. (By the way, even Darwin realized that explaining the development of an organ as complex as the human eye through a series of helpful chance mutations would be a huge challenge. Long after he published his theory of natural selection, he admitted to a friend, "The eye to this day gives me a cold shudder."[8])

As a biology major at Stanford University, I learned how evolution could be applied to explain the origin of all living organisms, including human beings. In my favorite class, Human Behavioral Biology, I learned how evolution even explains why humans behave the way we do, since the origin of many of our emotions and behaviors can be traced back to our primate ancestors. Blind natural selection even seemed to offer a good explanation for the origin of altruism, since helping our relatives would ensure that their genes, which were similar to ours, would be passed on to the next generation.[9]

My introductory anthropology class, Anthropology 101, explained how the discovery of many fossils of primitive human "ancestors" conclusively demonstrated the transition from apes to early "hominids" and eventually to the modern *Homo sapiens*. I was convinced that Darwin had hit the nail on the head. God didn't seem necessary if you conceded that everything that exists, even our emotions and morals, could have developed gradually through a series of chance mutations and natural selection over hundreds of millions of years.

But what I hadn't been taught was this: though Darwinism appears to work quite well at explaining most biological systems on a larger scale, when you examine life at the level of the individual molecule, you begin to see enormous difficulties. It is no longer quite so simple to explain how chance mutations alone are responsible for the increasing complexity of life.

The Complexity of Life

In his book *Darwin's Black Box*, biochemist Michael Behe impressively articulates the failure of unguided evolution to explain the origin of complex biochemical processes. He provides numerous examples in minute detail, including the development of the cilium (the hair-like projections on cells used for motion or brushing), the coagulation of blood, the intracellular transport system, the immune system, and the synthesis of molecules that are crucial to life. Each of these processes requires the precise interrelationship of multiple components and steps, such that a disturbance in any one component or step would be detrimental to the organism.

Behe explains how gradual, chance mutations cannot account for the formation of such systems because they are composed of multiple, interdependent parts. In such a system, each part is absolutely necessary, and each part must precisely interact with all other parts in order for the entire system to function. He uses the mousetrap as a simple analogy for such a system.

For the mousetrap to work, it must have five precisely interworking parts: a base, a hammer, a spring, a catch, and a holding bar. Moreover, each part must be in just the right place and be just the right size and shape for the mousetrap to catch a mouse. The interdependence of these multiple parts makes the mousetrap what Behe calls *irreducibly complex*.

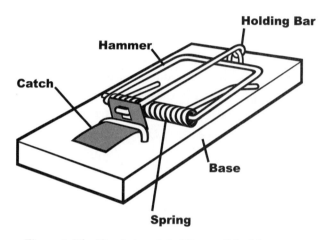

Figure 1: The Five Interrelated Parts of the Mousetrap

The question is: could a system like the mousetrap have evolved from a precursor without someone putting it together? (We'll call this precursor the "mousetrap ancestor," and we'll assume that this mousetrap ancestor is like a biological organism and can mutate gradually and pass on traits to its offspring, which are also mousetrap ancestors up to the point when they become the mousetrap.)

Even though they wouldn't be working together for a long time, the future base, hammer, spring, catch, and holding bar must each arise independently for reasons that would benefit the mousetrap ancestor in its lifetime. That is, the five separate parts would each have to mutate—on their own—to give the mousetrap ancestor a better chance at survival than other competing contraptions. The mousetrap ancestor would therefore pass on all five future parts to its offspring, even though they haven't begun working together as a mousetrap yet. And the five parts

CHAPTER 2: INTO THE CELL

would then have to start working together at the exact same time. If you had only four out of the five parts, it wouldn't function. And even if you had all five parts, if one wasn't perfect (for example, the hammer was too short to be held by the holding bar, permitting the mouse to escape), you still wouldn't have a functioning mouse trap.

There is a major problem preventing the mousetrap ancestors from gradually evolving into a functioning mousetrap: evolution doesn't work by first setting a long-term goal and then taking multiple, coinciding short-term steps to reach that goal (though this may be the way a creator would work). Each of the independent parts must mutate in ways that benefit the organism *in its lifetime*, long before they start working together in the future as an interdependent system.

Behe describes how a wide array of biochemical processes—even those in the simplest single-celled organisms—consist of multiple interdependent components. And these "molecular machines" are vastly more complex than the mousetrap. If the five-part mousetrap is irreducibly complex, these biochemical processes are orders of magnitudes more so. For example, this is how Behe describes the complexity of the long, hair-like flagellum that a single-celled bacterium uses for self-propulsion:

> Just picture an outboard motor on a boat and you get a pretty good picture of how the flagellum functions; only the flagellum is far more incredible. The flagellum's propeller is long and whip-like, made out of a protein called *flagellum*. This is attached to a drive shaft by a hook protein, which acts as a universal joint, allowing the propeller and drive shaft to rotate freely. Several types of protein act as bushing material (like a washer/donut) to allow the drive shaft to penetrate the bacterial wall (like the side of a boat) and attach to a rotary motor.... Not only that but the propeller can stop spinning within a quarter turn and instantly start spinning the other direction at 10,000 rpms.[10]

In this example, the interdependent components include the propeller, the hook, the drive shaft, the bushing material, and the motor, each of which are composed of numerous unique and interdependent proteins. To identify which proteins are essential to the functioning of the flagellum, scientists can disable the genes that code for each of the many proteins in the five components of the flagellum. In this way, the bacterium can only make certain parts of the flagellar "motor." When any *single one* of the genes that produce the many required proteins is disabled, the flagellum doesn't work.[11] Why does this matter? It demonstrates that *all* of its component parts are necessary for the flagellum to function. Each protein in each component plays a role that is essential for the flagellum to function, just as each of the five parts of the mousetrap were essential. The flagellum is therefore like the mousetrap described above, but far more complex because it has many more necessary interdependent components.

A biologist from Brandeis University compared the bacterial flagellum to other molecular motors in the cell and stated: "More so than other motors, the flagellum resembles a machine designed by a human."[12] There has been no satisfactory biochemical explanation for how the complex proteins that comprise the flagellum could have evolved by blind chance to create the marvel of engineering that propels the single-celled *E. coli*. In fact, instead of finding a means by which the flagellum could arise through chance alone, additional research has revealed even more complexity, identifying a sort of "clutch" that disables the forces that run the flagellum's motor.[13]

Some scientists have tried to demonstrate that the flagellum could have evolved from another molecular structure, the type three secretion system, or TTSS, which some pathogenic bacteria use to inject toxins into their victim's cells. These scientists claim that the TTSS was probably "co-opted by Darwinian evolution" to create the flagellum. However, other scientists have pointed out that the flagellar motor contains dozens of proteins that are not found in the TTSS, nor in any other living system, raising the question, "From whence, then, were these proteins co-opted?"[14]

Despite the decades of research in biochemistry since the structures of proteins were first discovered, there has not been a single successful Darwinian explanation for the origin of the many complex biochemical systems in organisms, of which the flagellum is but one. Behe writes:

> Molecular evolution is not based on scientific authority. There is no publication in the scientific literature—in prestigious journals, specialty journals, or books— that describes how molecular evolution of any real,

complex, biochemical system either did occur or even might have occurred. There are assertions that evolution occurred, but absolutely none are supported by pertinent experiments or calculations.[15]

When scientists aren't sure how unguided mutations created a complex system, they simply assert that evolution *must have* been responsible. Materialist scientists may accuse proponents of "intelligent design" of falling back on a "God of the gaps" explanation for complex molecular machinery. But they themselves resort to "evolution of the gaps" to explain the development of highly complex molecular machinery. Intelligent design supporters may say, "God did it," but materialists would say, "Evolution did it." *Both* statements rely on faith.

There have been numerous attempts in the scientific literature to demonstrate how complex systems could have originated through successive, chance mutations, but most of these systems are far simpler than the mousetrap example, which itself is far simpler than the molecular machinery of even the simplest single-celled organisms.

Interestingly, the complexity that scientists have discovered at the biochemical level of living organisms has inspired human engineers who want to improve man-made machinery. An institute associated with Harvard University claims to be "inspired by Nature." Known as the Wyss Institute for Biologically Inspired Engineering, they use "biological design principles to develop new engineering innovations that will transform medicine and create a more sustainable world."[16] While many may claim that "Nature" is the engineer responsible for these remarkable feats of molecular engineering, it is far more likely that a Supreme Engineer designed the biological machinery that inspires man-made machinery, and far less likely that ingenious machinery self-assembled over billions of years.

To summarize, while Darwinism appears to explain the origin of higher-level systems, such as how a fin became a leg, or how a moth may change color in response to its environment, it fails miserably at explaining the basic building blocks of life. And this is not a situation in which we just need to do more research. The "irreducibly complex" nature of these biochemical systems screams out for a Supreme Engineer, since the chance that they developed gradually on their own is extremely remote.[17] In order for these molecular machines to have developed solely through chance mutations, trillions of trillions of years would have been necessary, definitely far more than the 13.77 billion years since the Big Bang.

THE LANGUAGE OF DNA

Additional evidence that the development of organisms was guided by a Supreme Engineer rather than by blind chance alone can be found in the basic blueprint of all life: *deoxyribonucleic acid*, or DNA. An organism's DNA is the code used to build every protein in the organism. These proteins, in turn, completely determine all of the structures and functions within that organism.

DNA is composed of a string of molecules called *nucleotides*. There are four different nucleotides: adenosine, cytosine, guanine, and uracil (or abbreviated, A, C, G, and U).[18] Just as we can use the 26 letters of our own alphabet to construct a huge variety of words, particular sequences of these four nucleotides in DNA can code for a huge variety of proteins that are the building blocks of life. To give you an idea, a single-celled yeast microorganism contains *42 million* proteins.[19]

Let's break it down a bit further. While DNA is composed of four different types of nucleotides, proteins are composed of twenty different types of amino acids. These twenty amino acids combine in different ways to form billions of unique proteins. The order of amino acids in a protein is determined by the order of nucleotides in the string of DNA that codes for that protein. This string of DNA that codes for a protein is called a protein-encoding *gene*. A sequence of three nucleotides, called a *codon*, specifies which amino acid goes next in a protein.

For example, the three nucleotides that code for the amino acid Tryptophan are UGG (uracil, followed by guanine, followed by another guanine). The codon for the amino acid Methionine is AUG (adenosine, followed by uracil, followed by guanine). And there are two possible codons for the amino acid Histidine: CAC (cytosine, then adenosine, then cytosine again) and CAU (cytosine, adenosine, then uracil).[20] Thus, the DNA instructions for a protein with just three amino acids in this order, Tryptophan, then Methionine, then Histidine, would be either UGGAUGCAC or UGGAUGCAU (notice how the last three are the two alternative codons for Histidine). This DNA code, consisting of 9 nucleotides, or *base pairs*, would form a protein with just three amino acids, but most proteins have far more than three amino acids.

To give you an idea of how long proteins are: the average protein in your body has 375 amino acids. (Interestingly, the average protein in a common fruit fly has 378 amino acids, only three more than the average human protein. Obviously, the length of the average protein doesn't always translate into greater complexity in the organism!)[21]

A specific series of DNA codons therefore can be translated into a specific series of amino acids. And a protein is like a necklace of amino acids, based on the sequence of nucleotides in the gene that codes for that protein. Without getting too complex, just know that there is another type of genetic material called RNA (the transfer RNA and messenger RNA in the diagram below). The messenger RNA (*mRNA*) delivers the instructions to build a certain protein from the DNA. It brings the instructions from the DNA that is stored in the cell nucleus to a cell structure called a *ribosome* (where proteins are built). The transfer RNA (*tRNA*) recognizes and "picks up" specific amino acids and joins them to the correct corresponding codon on the mRNA. Thus, the protein chain is assembled in a specific order that depends on the order of nucleotides in the DNA.

Confused?! Don't worry! If this doesn't make sense to you, the important point is that the nucleotides in the DNA translate into the proteins that make our body work, just as the letters of our alphabet translate into words that make up your favorite novel. The nucleotides of DNA have to be in a *specific order* or else the proteins just won't work.

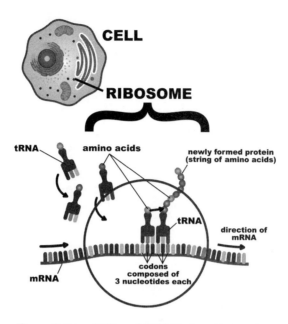

Figure 2: How DNA and RNA Codons Determine
the Order of Amino Acids in Proteins

The beauty of amino acids is that when they are in the correct order in a protein they will cause the protein to fold up into an intricate, three-dimensional shape. This precise folding happens because the different amino acids have positive or negative charges that magnetically repel and attract each other. Depending on the magnetic interactions between the amino acids in the protein chain, the protein will "crumple up" into a precise shape that is essential for it to function effectively in an organism.

In fact, some genetic diseases are caused by mutations in the DNA that affect the shape of the protein, making it less effective or even ineffective. For example, the genetic disease, sickle cell anemia, results when a single nucleotide, an adenosine, is replaced by a uracil, causing one codon to change from GAG to GUG. The result is that the amino acid, Valine, replaces the correct amino acid, Glutamic Acid, at position 6 in the protein that is responsible for carrying oxygen in the body (a protein called *hemoglobin*). As a result, the protein doesn't fold correctly, and those with this defective gene have blood that cannot carry oxygen as effectively.[22]

There are approximately 23,000 protein-encoding genes in the

CHAPTER 2: INTO THE CELL

human body, each of which contains a specific order of nucleotides (either adenine, cytosine, guanine, or uracil), and these genes code for 23,000 unique proteins.[23] Amazingly, these 23,000 proteins are responsible for every structure, function, and action of your body. Thus, by specifying the order of the amino acids in the protein molecules in your body, your DNA contains the basic blueprint for your body and all of the processes that allow you to survive and reproduce. The same goes for all other organisms, ranging from the single-celled bacterium, *Mycoplasma genitalium*, which has 580,070 base pairs (nucleotides) and 470 genes, the fewest genes of any organism,[24] to the near-microscopic crustacean, *Daphnia pulex*, which has 31,000 genes, the most of any organism.[25] As with the protein count, more genes does not mean higher intelligence!

Darwinian natural selection occurs at the most basic level, the level of the DNA code, when there is a change, or *mutation*, in the sequence of nucleotides (similar to what happens with sickle cell anemia). When a mutation occurs, nucleotides may be deleted, added, or interchanged. For example, the series UAGACA may become UAGAA if the cytosine is somehow deleted, or it may become UAGCACA if another cytosine is somehow inserted in the middle, or it may become UAAGCA if the middle guanine and adenine somehow exchange places. The end effect is a change in the amino acid sequence, and thus the three-dimensional structure, of the resulting protein molecule.

While the vast majority of mutations are harmful to an organism (as in sickle cell anemia), natural selection requires that some of these "accidental" changes end up benefiting the organism, which then passes the better trait onto its offspring.

The important questions we must ask at this point are these: Has this intricate molecular code of nucleotides really developed "by accident"? Do beneficial mutations—ones that cause enormous leaps in the complexity and capability of an organism—really happen completely by chance? Mathematician and evolutionist Amir Aczel poses another question: "Having surveyed the discovery of the structure of DNA... and having seen how DNA stores and manipulates tremendous amounts of information (3 billion separate bits for a human being) and uses the information to control life, we are left with one big question: What created DNA?"[26]

Even the devoted Darwinist Richard Dawkins, currently an "emeritus fellow" at Oxford University, admits that the DNA found in a tiny amoeba contains more information than 1,000 complete sets, thirty volumes each, of the *Encyclopaedia Britannica*.[27] Moreover, this information is not random combinations of nucleotides A, C, G, and U. The nucleotides are in a *specific order* that cannot be accounted for by chemical affinities between them, just as letters don't fall automatically into order in an encyclopedia. And this specific order of nucleotides is the code guiding every process necessary for all organisms to live.

Stephen Meyer, who earned his Ph.D. from Cambridge in the field of origin-of-life science, explains the infinitesimal probability of a certain sequence of DNA "getting it right" when constructing a protein that is useful to an organism:

> First, you need the right bonds between the amino acids. Second, amino acids come in right-handed and left-handed versions, and you've got to get only left-handed ones. Third, the amino acids must link up in a specified sequence, like letters in a sentence. Run the odds of these things falling into place on their own and you find that the probabilities of forming a rather short functional protein at random would be one chance in a hundred thousand trillion trillion trillion trillion trillion trillion trillion trillion trillion trillion. That's a ten with 125 zeros after it![28]

If it's so improbable for even one short functional protein to come together by blind chance, how likely is it that the millions of proteins in living organisms "self-assembled" through unguided evolution? Even trillions of years would be insufficient!

SPECIFIED COMPLEXITY

On top of these extremely low probabilities, there is even more evidence that DNA points to an extremely intelligent "Supreme Engineer." Mathematician William Dembski, a professor at Baylor University, has developed an "explanatory filter" to determine whether a certain occurrence has happened by pure chance or by design.

He uses three steps to make this determination. He first asks whether the occurrence is *necessary* or *contingent*. If you throw a set of Scrabble tiles up in the air, and some land face up and some face down, he calls that "necessary" because the natural laws governing the physical objects involved are sufficient to explain the occurrence. But if they all land face up, Dembski calls that occurrence "contingent." If the occurrence is necessary, you can conclude that it happened by chance. But if the occurrence is contingent, you then proceed to the second step, which is to ask whether the occurrence is *simple* or *complex*. If the order of the Scrabble tiles was random, with no meaningful words formed, you can conclude that the occurrence is "simple" and therefore a product of chance. But if the Scrabble tiles fall in a sequence with a few letters lined up in a way that has some meaning (for example, the words "HI" and "BYE" appear among the many tiles), the occurrence is "complex," and you can proceed to the third and final step.

This last step determines whether the occurrence is *ad hoc* or *specific*. (We alluded to this step in the previous chapter with the stanza of the poem containing one of each of the 100 letters from a Scrabble game.) For now, let's consider 20 Scrabble tiles. The chance that twenty randomly scattered Scrabble tiles spell out "LNWHIEHEDAONLREERBYE" is approximately one in 10^{28}, but it would be considered "ad hoc" because there was no meaning to the series of letters (except for a few words, like "HI" and "BYE," which can be attributed to chance). But what if the tiles spelled "BILLANDHONEYWEREHERE"? Even though the probability is still one in 10^{28}, that occurrence would be considered "specific" and conclusively a sign of design. In this case, the designer was probably either Bill or Honey.

In the same manner, you can determine whether events in nature occurred by chance or by design. For example, if you came across the faces of American presidents on Mount Rushmore, you could use the same process to determine that it was a product of design rather than solely the result of wind and water erosion. Similarly, if you happened upon a sentence written in the sand at the beach, you would assume it was the product of a writer, not the effects of the tide going out. These are both examples of occurrences that are contingent, complex, and specific, or to use Dembski's term, occurrences that display *specified complexity*.[29]

Because DNA consists of a complex code of information, it also displays specified complexity. Dembski explains:

> The fundamental claim of intelligent design is straightforward and easily intelligible: namely, there are natural systems that cannot be adequately explained in terms of undirected natural forces and that exhibit features which in any other circumstance we would attribute to intelligence.[30]

Noted atheist Antony Flew renounced his atheism after hearing arguments in favor of intelligent design. When he first announced his change of mind, he gave the following statement to the media: "It now seems to me that the findings of more than fifty years of DNA research have provided materials for a new and enormously powerful argument [for] design."[31] His statement caused a huge outcry among scientists who claimed that Flew was disregarding the latest findings of abiogenesis (as mentioned above, the study of how life originated from non-life). Flew responds to these critics in this way:

> The latest work I have seen shows that the present physicists' view of the age of the universe gives too little time for these theories of abiogenesis to get the job done.... The philosophical question that has not been answered in origin-of-life studies is this: How can a universe of mindless matter produce beings with intrinsic ends, self-replication capabilities, and 'coded chemistry'?[32]

Flew raises a very good question, one that materialists have yet to answer in a credible way.

Stephen Meyer explains the implication of coded chemistry when he states, "Whenever you find a sequential arrangement that's complex and corresponds to an independent pattern or functional requirement, this kind of information is always a product of intelligence. Books, computer codes, and DNA all have these two properties."[33] Geneticist Francis Collins, formerly the director of the National Human Genome Research Institute and the current director of the National Institutes of Health, even entitled one of his books, *The Language of God*, to reflect his opinion that the complex code we see in the DNA of every living organism is more than just an accident.[34]

To summarize, the molecular machines in even the simplest, single-celled organisms, along with the coded nature of DNA, give us strong evidence that life cannot be explained merely as the product of unguided natural forces. If we add the evidence of design from biochemistry and molecular biology to the evidence of design from astronomy and physics, the case for God's existence is enormously more convincing than is the case for materialism and atheism. Those who hold on to a belief in the multiverse, abiogenesis, panspermia, and unguided evolution do so not because these are the most rational deductions based on the evidence, but because they are unwilling to allow for any supernatural explanation, no matter how well it fits the evidence.

QUESTIONS FOR COMPREHENSION AND DISCUSSION

1. What is *abiogenesis*? Why have some scientists proposed that life began in a different part of the universe (*panspermia*) and not on Earth?
2. How would you explain the theory of evolution by natural selection? Why does it seem to explain the origins of all life forms so well?
3. What is *irreducible complexity*? Can you explain how a mousetrap displays this characteristic?
4. What problems arise with the theory of evolution by unguided natural selection when you consider biochemical processes that have multiple, interdependent parts?
5. Why is the bacterial flagellum so similar to a machine that is designed by humans? How is it irreducibly complex?
6. Why would it be so difficult—and therefore very unlikely—for an irreducibly complex system to arise from unguided evolution?
7. Try to explain how the order of nucleotides (A, C, G, and U) translates into the order of amino acids in a protein. How are these four nucleotides like the letters of the alphabet?
8. What is the meaning of the terms in the three tests for determining whether something is an accident or designed: *necessary, contingent, simple, complex, ad hoc,* and *specific*?

9. Can you define "specified complexity"? What are some examples of specified complexity in the world?
10. How is DNA like a computer program, a book, or other types of information? What does this reveal about its origin?

CHAPTER 2 ENDNOTES

[1] Michael Denton, *Evolution: A Theory in Crisis* (Bethesda, MD: Adler & Adler, 1985), 264.
[2] Francis Crick, *Life Itself* (New York: Simon and Schuster, 1981), 88.
[3] Klaus Dose, "The Origin of Life: More Questions Than Answers," *Interdisciplinary Science Review* 13 (1998).
[4] F. H. Crick & L. E. Orgel (1973), "Directed Panspermia," *Icarus* 19: 341-348.
[5] Leslie Orgel, "The origin of life – a review of facts and speculations," *Trends in Biochemical Sciences*, 23 (Dec 1998): 491-495 (pp. 494-495).
[6] J. T. Trevors and D. L. Abel, "Chance and Necessity Do Not Explain the Origin of Life," *Cell Biology International* 28 (2004), 729-739.
[7] Ian Hutchison, author of *Can a Scientist Believe in God? An MIT Professor Answers Questions on God and Science* (Downers Grove, IL: InterVarsity Press, 2018). Quote from an interview with Ian Hutchison on the White Horse Inn podcast, October 27, 2018.
[8] Charles Darwin (1860) in letter to Asa Gray, F. Darwin, ed., *The Life and Letters of Charles Darwin*, vol. 2 (London: John Murray, 1888), 273.
[9] I discovered later, however, that evolution cannot account for universal human rights nor for a moral code that is beyond the variation of human opinion by which good and evil can be evaluated. We'll go into more detail on this topic in Chapter 30.
[10] Michael Behe, *Darwin's Black Box* (New York: Free Press, 2003), 22.
[11] Robert M. Macnab, "Flagella," 70-83 in Frederick C. Neidhardt, et al. (editors), *Escherichia coli* and *Salmonella typhimurium*: Cellular and Molecular Biology (Washington, DC: American Society for Microbiology, 1987), Volume 1. Howard C. Berg, "The Rotary Motor of Bacterial Flagella" *Annual Review of Biochemistry* 72 (2003), 19-54. Available online at https://www.ncbi.nlm.nih.gov/pubmed/12500982.
[12] David J. DeRosier, "The Turn of the Screw: The Bacterial Flagellar Motor," *Cell* 93 (1998), 17-20.
[13] Kris M. Blair, Linda Turner, Jared T. Winkelman, Howard C. Berg, and Daniel B. Kearns, "A Molecular Clutch Disables Flagella in the Bacillus subtilis Biofilm", *Science*, http://science.sciencemag.org/content/320/5883/1636.

CHAPTER 2: INTO THE CELL

14   Scott A. Minnich and Stephen C. Meyer, "Genetic Analysis of Coordinate Flagellar and Type III Regulatory Circuits," 295-304 in M. W. Collins and C. A. Brebbia (editors), *Proceedings of the Second International Conference on Design & Nature* (Rhodes, Greece: WIT Press, 2004). See also Liu, Renyi and ochman, Howard, "Stepwise formation of the bacterial flagellar system," US National Library of Medicine, National Institutes of Health, https://www.ncbi.nlm.nih.gov/pmc/articles/PMC1852327.

15   Behe, *Darwin's Black Box*, 185.

16   From the home page of the Wyss Institute for Biologically Inspired Engineering website: https://wyss.harvard.edu.

17   Some people may still criticize the arguments of irreducible complexity as a "God of the gaps" approach to proving the existence of a Creator. But in his recent book *The Cell's Design*, molecular biologist Fazale Rana makes the case that the complexity of the cell points to a Creator, not because we don't understand how the complexity could arise through blind natural causes, but because the cell's complexity reveals patterns that are indicative of design. For example, Rana makes the following statement to introduce his case for an intelligent designer: "Rather than use a negative approach that relies on gaps in understanding, the subsequent chapters make use of pattern recognition to identify the God of the Bible's involvement in bringing life into being. Such a method makes it possible to build a positive case for biochemical intelligent design. This approach inherently depends on what science currently knows about life's chemistry and how the organization of biochemical systems relates to the characteristics of humanly designed systems—not on what science doesn't know." (Fazale Rana, *The Cell's Design: How Chemistry Reveals the Creator's Artistry* [Grand Rapids, MI: Baker Books, 2008], 33.)

18   Note: I list Uracil here, but it is actually the nucleotide Thymine that appears in the DNA. Uracil appears in Thymine's place in the RNA, which is derived from DNA for the purpose of creating a protein.

19   "A cell holds 42 million protein molecules, scientists reveal," *Science Daily*, University of Toronto, January 17, 2018, https://www.sciencedaily.com/releases/2018/01/180117131202.htm.

20   Below are the 20 amino acids, along with their symbols and codons: (1) Alanine (Ala, or A): GCA, GCC, GCG, GCU; (2) Cysteine (Cys or C): UGC, UGU; (3) Aspartic acid (Asp or D): GAC, GAU; (4) Glutamic acid (Glu or E): GAA, GAG; (5) Phenylalanine (Phe or F): UUC, UUU; (6) Glycine (Gly or G): GGA, GGC, GGG, GGU; (7) Histidine (His or H): CAC, CAU; (8) Isoleucine (Ile or I): AUA, AUC, AUU; (9) Lycine (Lyc or K): AAA, AAG; (10) Leucine (Leu or L): UUA, UUG, CUA, CUC, CUG, CUU; (11) Methionine (Met or M): AUG; (12) Asparagine (Asn or N): AAC, AAU;

(13) Proline: (Pro or P): CCA, CCC, CCG, CCU; (14) Glutamine: Gln or Q: CAA, CAG; (15) Arginine (Arg or R): AGA, AGG, CGA, CGC, CGG, CGU; (16) Serine (Ser or S): AGC, AGU, UCA, UCC, UCG, UCU; (17) Threonine (Thr or T): ACA, ACC, ACG, ACU; (18) Valine (Val or V): GUA, GUC, GUG, GUU; (19) Tryptophan (Trp or W): UGG; (20) Tyrosine (Tyr or Y): UAC, UAU.

21 Ron Milo and Rob Phillips, *Cell Biology by the Numbers*, "How Big Is the 'Average' Protein?', available online at http://book.bionumbers.org/how-big-is-the-average-protein/.

22 Suzanne Clancy (2008). "Genetic mutation". *Nature Education*. 1 (1): 187. Available online at https://www.nature.com/scitable/topicpage/genetic-mutation-441.

23 Elena A. Ponomarenko, Ekaterina V. Poverennaya, Ekaterina V. Ilgisonis, Mikhail A. Pyatnitskiy, Arthur T. Kopylov, Victor G. Zgoda, Andrey V. Lisitsa, and Alexander I. Archakov, "The Size of the Human Proteome," *International Journal of Analytical Chemistry*, 2016: 7436849, available online at https://www.ncbi.nlm.nih.gov/pmc/articles/PMC4889822/.

24 J. Craig Venter et al., "The Minimal Gene Complement of *Mycoplasma genitalium*," *Science*, 20 Oct 1995: Vol. 270, Issue 5235, pp. 397-404, https://science.sciencemag.org/content/270/5235/397.

25 "The Most Genes in an Animal? Tiny Crustacean Holds the Record," National Science Foundation website, February 3, 2011, https://www.nsf.gov/news/news_summ.jsp?cntn_id=118530.

26 Amir D. Aczel, *Probability 1* (New York: Harvest, 1998), 88.

27 Richard Dawkins, *The Blind Watchmaker* (New York: Norton, 1987), 17-18, 116.

28 Behe, *Darwin's Black Box*, 185.

29 William Dembski, *The Design Revolution* (Madison, WI: InterVarsity Press, 2004), 87-93.

30 William Dembski, No Free Lunch: Why Specified Complexity Cannot Be Purchased Without Design (New York: W. W. Norton, 1986), 47-49.

31 Quoted in Gary Habermas, "My Pilgrimage from Atheism to Theism": Interview with Antony Flew, *Philosophia Christi*, (Winter, 2005).

32 Flew quoted in Habermas, "My Pilgrimage from Atheism to Theism," 124.

33 Quoted in Lee Strobel, *The Case for a Creator* (Grand Rapids, MI: Zondervan, 2004), 237.

34 See Francis Collins, *The Language of God* (New York: Free Press, 2006).

Why, if species have descended from other species by insensibly fine gradations, do we not everywhere see innumerable transitional forms? Why is not all nature in confusion instead of the species being, as we see them, well-defined?

—Charles Darwin, 19th century biologist[1]

For millennia upon millennia, we had been churning out the same forms of stone utensils, for example. But about 40,000 years ago, a perceptible shift in our handiwork took place. Throughout the Old World, tool kits leapt in sophistication with the appearance of Upper Paleolithic-style implements.... It is an extraordinary catalogue of achievements that seem to have come about virtually from nowhere— though obviously they did have a source. The question is: What was it?

—Christopher Stringer, paleoanthropologist[2]

3

Back in Time

Let's take the leap of faith that the coded information (DNA) of complex life forms assembled itself through chance mutations over millions of years. Even though mutations in this DNA code are predominantly harmful to the organism, let's assume that a sufficient number—billions or more—of these chance mutations were beneficial and conferred survival benefits to their host. Such gradual, beneficial mutations would create small changes in the amino acid sequence of proteins, which would then result in small, gradual changes in the fossil record. But there's a problem: the fossil evidence for gradual changes just isn't there.

Even Darwin recognized that his theory of natural selection depended on evidence for such gradual modifications over time. In *On the Origin of Species*, he writes: "If it could be demonstrated that any complex organ existed which could not possibly have been formed by numerous, successive, slight modifications, my theory would absolutely break down."[3]

Let's back up a bit. We have already seen how the theory of gradual, unguided evolution *does* break down when we try to explain the development of complex biochemical systems, such as the bacterial flagellum. These irreducibly complex systems abound in organisms, even in the simplest single-celled amoeba or bacterium. Scientists have yet to explain how these complex systems evolved gradually over time, and it is extremely unlikely that they appeared within 14 billion years without the guidance of an outside power, some sort of "Supreme Engineer." If there have been an infinite number of universes before one finally appeared with just the right conditions for life, then there would have to be another infinite number of "attempts" for irreducibly complex systems to arise in the simplest organisms.

But let's take the leap of faith, as well-meaning scientists do, that DNA and irreducibly complex systems did develop through mindless, unguided chance. Remember, we're also assuming that (1) the universe either was created out of nothing or is a part of an infinite multiverse, (2) it just happened to have the extremely precise features necessary to maintain its own existence and sustain life, and (3) the first life arose from lifeless chemicals against enormous odds. As we'll see, even with these additional assumptions, Darwin's theory of evolution—that is, evolution by *unguided*, chance mutations—also loses credibility upon examination of the fossil and anthropological records.

STASIS AND SUDDEN APPEARANCE

When Darwin first published his theory, he claimed that "the number of intermediate and transitional links, between all living and extinct species, must have been inconceivably great."[4] That is, he expected to see evidence of gradual changes between various species in the fossil record. For example, if a fish became a land mammal, fossil hunters around the globe should have amassed innumerable samples that showed a step-by-step transition from the fish to the mammal.

When his *On the Origin of Species* came out in 1859, the fossil record didn't reveal evidence of transitional forms, but Darwin expected additional fossils would eventually be unearthed that would demonstrate a gradual change from one species to another. Unfortunately for the paleontologists and geologists who have been eager to find these transitional forms, the fossil record has not provided overwhelming support for such gradualism. In the century and a half of digging since the publication of *On the Origin of Species*, two predominant characteristics of the fossil record have become increasingly apparent: *stasis* and *sudden appearance*. The late paleontologist and evolutionist Stephen Jay Gould of Harvard University explains these two characteristics:

> The history of most fossil species includes two features particularly inconsistent with gradualism: 1). Stasis. Most species exhibit no directional change during their

tenure on Earth. They appear in the fossil record looking much the same as when they disappear; morphological change is usually limited and directionless. 2). Sudden Appearance. In any local area, a species does not arise gradually by the steady transformation of its ancestors; it appears all at once and "fully formed."[5]

In an attempt to account for stasis and sudden appearance, Gould went on to propose the theory of *punctuated equilibrium*, which we will discuss later in this chapter.

For now, let's consider one of the most significant challenges to Darwinian evolution, the "Cambrian explosion," also called the "Big Bang of animal evolution."[6] Prior to the Cambrian Period, there is no evidence of animal species in the fossil record. But during a geologically brief period of time starting about 540 million years ago, organisms from almost every animal phylum appear "all at once" in the fossil record.

One of the biggest discoveries of these early animal fossils was made in the Burgess Shale of western Canada, which paleontologists have determined is approximately 505 million years old.[7] Not only do the fossils from the Burgess Shale include more than thirty different animal body types, there is no sign of any predecessors for these animals. Organs such as fully functional, highly complex eyes appear suddenly in the Cambrian Period in five different phyla, without a trace of a common ancestor.

Charles D. Walcott, the former director of the Smithsonian Institute, was the first to discover the Burgess Shale fossils. By 1909, he had collected and removed approximately 60,000 fossils from the Burgess Shale, storing them rather surreptitiously (perhaps realizing the implications of what he had found) in drawers at the Smithsonian Institute. In 1989 the drawers were finally reopened.

In response to the rediscovery of the fossils, *Time* magazine did a cover story called "Evolution's Big Bang," raising the question, "Has the mechanism of evolution altered?" One of the article's subheadings declared, "For billions of years, simple creatures like plankton, bacteria, and algae ruled the Earth. Then, suddenly, life got very complicated."[8] Another thing that became more complicated was defending Darwin's theory, as he himself anticipated when he wrote, "If numerous species, belonging to the same... families, have really started life at once, that fact would be fatal to the theory of evolution through natural selection."[9]

CHAPTER 3: BACK IN TIME

Many paleontologists speculated that the Burgess Shale did not preserve the missing predecessors, and they assumed that fossil excavations at other sites would eventually uncover them. But additional excavations in Canada, China, Greenland, Namibia, and Siberia have confirmed the Burgess Shale evidence: complex animal species from many phyla suddenly appeared in the Cambrian Period with no obvious predecessors.[10]

Moreover, paleontologists have found fossils of microscopic bacteria in rocks that are billions of years *older* than the Cambrian Period, so any smaller Cambrian fossils of precursors should also have been preserved. And many of the Cambrian fossils themselves were soft-bodied, so the softness of their bodies can't be the reason intermediate forms weren't showing up.[11] Cambridge University paleontologist Simon Conway Morris describes the soft body parts of some of the Cambrian fossils in this way: "These remarkable fossils reveal not only their outlines but sometimes even internal organs such as the intestines or muscles."[12] According to William Schopf, a paleobiologist at UCLA, "The long-held notion that Precambrian organisms must have been too small or too delicate to have been preserved in geological materials... [is] now recognized as incorrect."[13]

So, if the millions of fossil discoveries in the last few decades show little evidence of transitional forms, do we just need to do more digging? Paleontologist Whitey Hagadorn of Amherst describes his own reaction to the lack of transitional fossils: "Paleontologists have the best eyes in the world. If we can't find the fossils, sometimes you have to think they just weren't there."[14]

One proponent of guided evolution explains that even the latest research into the sudden appearance of complex organisms in the Burgess Shale fails to explain how even a relatively "small" number of entirely new organisms appeared without any precursors:

> They can call it small, but the morphospace [collection of organisms] includes at least 20, and up to 30, new body plans, each distinctive, bearing complex systems like muscles, nerves, digestive systems, sensory systems, locomotion, and reproductive systems with no precursors in the Precambrian. They all appear suddenly. Where are the "intermediate taxa"? They are

nowhere in the rock record, 158 years after Darwin had hoped they would be found.[15]

Scientists are understandably dismayed at the scarcity of fossil evidence demonstrating gradual transformations from one species to another. There has been a great deal of debate about whether species do indeed evolve gradually, or whether there is such a thing as "saltatory evolution," or evolution by "jumps."

Recognizing the absence of gradual transformation in the fossil record, Stephen Jay Gould and Niles Eldredge proposed the theory of *punctuated equilibrium*. They contend that evolution progresses rapidly when a small group splits off from a larger group. When the members of this smaller group face new environmental conditions, such as different food sources, predators, or weather conditions, their features change rapidly, and they soon look very different from the members of the original population. However, researchers at the University of Oregon found that such an isolation-and-adaptation process actually leads to extinction, not evolution.[16] Other studies by scientists at Washington University in St. Louis corroborated these findings: when a small subpopulation splits off from a larger group, the result is not a new species, but an extinct subpopulation.[17]

Evolutionists have also attempted to explain the sudden appearance of complex animal species in the Cambrian Period by demonstrating that mutations to certain parts of an organism's genetic code may lead to a quick jump in the organism's complexity. For example, scientists have proposed that rapid change in an organism may result from mutations to its *homeobox* genes (also called *homeotic* or *Hox* genes). These genes are the part of the DNA that controls the development of an organism from fertilized egg to adult. Simple organisms such as jellyfish only have three homeobox genes, while insects have eight, and other primitive precursors of vertebrates have ten. Some scientists have therefore hypothesized that mutations in these genes may enable big evolutionary jumps in complexity.

However, they have yet to conclusively explain how additional genetic material can spontaneously arise out of nowhere, much less how the original homeobox gene appeared. What's more, in the vast majority of these genes, mutations have devastating effects on the organism, if it survives at all, and the organism does not become more advanced,

CHAPTER 3: BACK IN TIME

but rather has a drastic deformity, such as a leg growing out of its head. Here is how one scientist describes changes to the appearance—what he refers to as the *phenotype*—of *Drosophila* fruit flies caused by mutations in these homeotic genes:

> Control genes like homeotic genes may be the targets of mutations that would conceivably change phenotypes, but one must remember that, the more central one makes changes in a complex system, the more severe the peripheral consequences become.... Homeotic changes induced in *Drosophila* genes have led only to monstrosities, and most experimenters do not expect to see a bee arise from their *Drosophila* constructs.[18]

With scientists in a quandary about how exactly evolution happened without leaving a trace of intermediate forms, it seems reasonable to consider this: The mutations to DNA that caused the huge evolutionary jumps in the Cambrian explosion may not have been accidental after all.

But let's assume that at some time in the future the intermediate forms for all organisms will have been found in the fossil record. *Even this* would not disprove God's existence. Christian philosopher Alvin Plantinga makes this point in his review of *The God Delusion* by atheist Richard Dawkins: "After all, couldn't it be that God has directed and overseen the process of evolution?"[19] While God may very well have created each species individually from scratch, he also may have used genetic variation and natural selection to create the amazing diversity and complexity of life on our planet. Even evolutionist Francis Collins, the former director of the National Human Genome Research Institute, is very comfortable admitting that he is both a steadfast believer in evolution *and* a steadfast believer in God.[20]

Christian pastor Dr. Timothy Keller clarifies this position in his book, *The Reason for God*:

> Christians may believe in evolution as a process without believing in 'philosophical naturalism'— the view that everything has a natural cause and that organic life is solely the product of random forces guided by no one.... When evolution is turned into an All-encompassing

Theory explaining absolutely everything we believe, feel, and do as the product of natural selection, then we are not in the arena of science, but of philosophy.[21]

In other words, the belief that *unguided* evolution is responsible for the world we see is grounded on philosophical assumptions, not scientific evidence. Moreover, the belief in a supernatural Being who created and guided the evolution of all living things does not conflict with Christianity, as many believe, but it is actually quite consistent with the Christian faith and an all-powerful Creator.[22]

THE "SOCIOCULTURAL BIG BANG"

For nearly 2.5 million years, the tools used by hominids (the term evolutionists use for the ancestors of the modern human) never improved beyond the most basic stone technology. But an interesting change occurred between 40,000 and 150,000 years ago. In a relatively short time from an evolutionary perspective, human technology made a huge leap, and humans began to use complex tools such as rope, bone spears, fishhooks, harpoons, and even ivory needles for sewing clothes.

In this same brief time period, anthropologists have also unearthed the first occurrence of an array of cultural items such as musical instruments, jewelry, sculptures, and painting. There is also evidence of long-distance trade in beads and stones, and discoveries include objects created from diverse materials that sometimes came from hundreds of miles away. Moreover, the first burial practices that strongly suggest a belief in the afterlife, such as the inclusion of special items and ornaments with the body, have been found in excavations of early human sites dating to the same period.[23]

Even with hundreds of new archaeological excavations in recent decades, there has been little evidence of a gradual improvement of technology over hundreds of thousands of years, as scientists who hold to unguided evolution would expect. Instead, scientists have discovered a "quantum change" in human behavior, which has been termed a "creative explosion," the "sociocultural Big Bang," the "Big Bang of human consciousness," the "great leap forward," the "dawn of human culture," and the "human revolution."[24]

CHAPTER 3: BACK IN TIME

Due to recent advances in genomics, which we will discuss in more detail later in this chapter, scientists have been able to identify how long ago the first ancestors of modern humans lived. Using mitochondrial DNA for females and Y chromosome DNA for males, researchers have narrowed down the date for "Mitochondrial DNA Eve" and "Y Chromosome Adam" to approximately 150,000 years ago.[25] Scientists have also found that those ancestors started to migrate out of Africa around 72,000 years ago.[26] Researchers in linguistics have independently confirmed the "out-of-Africa model," which argues that all humans on Earth are descended from common ancestors in Africa, who then migrated into the Middle East and from there around the entire globe.[27]

Based on this genetic and anthropological evidence, the advanced technologies and cultural practices arose approximately 50,000 to 90,000 years after the appearance of the first *Homo sapiens sapiens* (modern humans). And one anthropologist, John Shea, has argued that the first anatomically modern humans were *already* capable of these advanced technologies and practices even 150,000 years ago. Based on his study of stone tools in Omo Kibish in Ethiopia, along with his survey of the finds in other sites throughout Africa, Shea claims that the earliest modern humans had the same cognitive ability as humans do today, but at that time their lifestyle did not require sophisticated tools (which is why you don't find them in excavations of the earliest *Homo sapiens sapiens*). Thus, the advance in technology and culture that is observed 40,000 to 100,000 years ago was not due to increased cognitive ability but instead was the result of humans using the cognitive ability they already had to adapt to new cultural situations as they spread throughout the globe.[28]

One amazing difference between the first ancestors of modern humans and the hominids that immediately preceded them is their brain capacity. Prior to the appearance of modern humans, the brain capacity of hominids was much smaller, and as a result, these hominids were incapable of the type of conceptualizing required for more advanced technology and the flourishing of culture. According to Ian Tattersall, the evolutionist curator of the American Museum of Natural History, "Something extraordinary, if totally fortuitous, happened with the birth of our species."[29] John Maynard Smith, Professor Emeritus of Biology at the University of Sussex further elaborates: "Something very puzzling happened.... The fossil evidence is patchy, but it seems that hominids suddenly developed brains that, in terms of size, were much like ours."[30]

Evolutionist Ernst Mayr writes: "What is perhaps most astonishing is the fact that the human brain seems not to have changed one single bit since the first appearance of *Homo sapiens*."[31]

Coinciding with this big jump in our ancestors' brain size was their ability to speak to one another. Language is a complex process that necessitated the concurrent development of the structures of the tongue, larynx, vocal cords, and brain. Evolutionist Steve Olson summarizes the issue this way:

> Of course, language could not have come from nowhere. To speak, early humans needed particular vocal and neural mechanisms. But here a notorious problem arises. Any adaptations produced by evolution are useful only in the present, not in some vaguely defined future.[32]

In other words, evolution doesn't happen by first determining a long-run beneficial goal (in this case, language) and then making successive short-run changes to achieve that goal. As we mentioned in our discussion of irreducible complexity in the last chapter, evolutionary change happens only when mutations confer benefits to the *current* generation. To achieve a long-term goal such as language, multiple, interdependent parts—tongue, larynx, vocal cords, and brain—must each mutate separately in ways that confer survival-enhancing benefits to the organism during its lifetime, even though they wouldn't necessarily be working together to produce language for thousands of generations. The process of acquiring language is not a simple matter at all, and the chances that it arose so quickly are extremely tiny, unless, of course, the process was guided.

The power of the human brain is difficult to fathom. To better grasp the enormity of its computing power, imagine an Olympic size swimming pool, which holds a volume of 2,500 cubic meters of water (50 meters long times 25 meters wide times 2 meters deep). This is the equivalent of 88,000 cubic feet (35.3 cubic feet per cubic meter), or 505 million teaspoons of water. According to one researcher, there are at least *86 billion neurons* in the human brain.[33] If the human brain were enlarged to fit perfectly inside the Olympic pool, and you used a teaspoon to scoop out a tiny portion of the big brain, there would be 170 neurons in that teaspoon. To put this in perspective, a teaspoon of salt contains approximately 88 grains of salt, so each neuron in our Olympic pool full of neurons would be about half the size of a grain of salt. Now consider that each of these neurons is connected with more than a thousand other neurons to make about *125 trillion* connections (synapses). By the way, this is the number of connections in our cerebral cortex alone, which would comprise about 40% of the full Olympic pool.[34] And these connections between neurons are not random, but they are each made in a very precise way to ensure proper brain function.

Stephen Hawking emphasizes the computing power of the human brain when he writes, "In comparison with most computers which have one central processing unit, the brain has millions of processing units... all working at the same time."[35] Evolutionist Carl Sagan wrote that the information content of the human brain "would fill some twenty million volumes, as many as in the world's largest libraries."[36] One writer, describing the findings of Stephen Smith, a scientist at the Stanford School of Medicine, put it this way:

> Observed in this manner, the brain's overall complexity is almost beyond belief, said Smith. "One synapse, by itself, is more like a microprocessor–with both memory-storage and information-processing elements–than a mere on/off switch. In fact, one synapse may contain on the order of 1,000 molecular-scale switches. A single human brain has more switches than all the computers and routers and Internet connections on Earth."[37]

And according to anthropologists, this is the same brain that suddenly appeared in the fossil record.

It's worth mentioning one other interesting aspect of research on the human brain. Some neuroscientists have concluded from their experiments that the mind and the brain are distinct from each other. That is, the neurons and neurotransmitters that compose the brain cannot alone account for consciousness, which gives humans the ability to have subjective thoughts, to experience hope, to be aware of ourselves, and to talk to ourselves in our mind about what we are experiencing and feeling.

Dr. Wilder Penfield, who is considered the father of modern neurosurgery, has conducted thousands of experiments to determine whether the material brain alone determines consciousness. In response to evidence that consciousness is a separate entity from the brain, he writes, "What a thrill it is, then, to discover that the scientist, too, can legitimately believe in the existence of the spirit."[38] Neurophysiologist and Nobel laureate John Eccles agreed after he looked at the evidence for a non-material part of the mind: "I am constrained to believe that there is what we might call a supernatural origin of my unique self-conscious mind or my unique selfhood or soul."[39]

A few questions stand out at this point. Could it really just have been a "fortuitous mutation," as some anthropologists propose, that converted the smaller hominid brain into the complex *Homo sapiens sapiens* brain that is capable of such higher-level thinking, culture, and consciousness? Or, like the "Cambrian explosion" of the earliest mammals 500 million years ago, and like the Big Bang 14 billion years ago, are the cultural explosion, leap in brain capability, and the existence of consciousness best explained as the work of a Creator?

ONE ANCESTRAL COUPLE MADE IN GOD'S IMAGE?

In the first chapter, we discussed the remarkable consistency of the Genesis creation story with the scientific evidence for the origin of the universe, the solar system, our planet, and plant and animal life. One event that we didn't consider was the creation of the first two humans, Adam and Eve. Could it be that these biblical characters really existed?

Based on numerous studies in anthropology and human phylogenetics (the study of human genetic code to reveal ancestral connections), there is indeed recent scientific evidence to support the claim that all humans descended from one man and one woman. Dr. Fazale Rana and Dr. Hugh Ross explain:

> An ensemble of genetic markers collectively indicates that humanity originated recently from a single location (apparently East Africa, close to where theologians believe the Garden of Eden was located) and from a small population. Those markers include mitochondrial DNA (mtDNA) variants, and Y-chromosomal variants. Both

types of DNA trace back to single ancestral sequences that some anthropologists take as corresponding to a single female ("mitochondrial Eve") and male ("Y-chromosomal Adam") individual.[40]

Using the most recent and most accurate estimate for the mutation rate of mitochondrial DNA, a type of DNA that is passed from mother to child, secular scientists have determined that "mitochondrial Eve" lived between 137,000 and 177,000 years ago.[41] And recent phylogenetic studies in which researchers have examined larger sections of the Y chromosome, including rare Y chromosome variants, have provided more confident estimates that "Y-chromosomal Adam" lived between 101,000 and 208,000 years ago.[42]

Thus, these ancient parents of the human race most likely lived in the overlap of these time ranges, 137,000 to 177,000 years ago, and the fossil record and archaeology confirm these dates. Scientists estimate that humans migrated out of Africa into Europe, Asia, and the Americas in the last 50,000 to 80,000 years.[43] Importantly, these studies disprove the theory that human evolution occurred separately in different areas, which would mean that humans today descend from different sets of unrelated ancestors. Thus, it is now widely agreed that all humans come from a single man and a single woman. You may not believe that this one couple—the ancestors of all humans today—are the Adam and Eve described in the Bible. But you should at least recognize that the Genesis story is consistent with the latest scientific research.

Let's return to the anthropological and archaeological evidence that we started to discuss earlier in the chapter. This evidence reveals a sudden leap in human technology approximately 100,000 years ago, soon after the first appearance of modern humans in the fossil record. For millions of years, toolmaking had never progressed beyond the most basic stone implements, and the brain size of early hominids remained relatively stable. All of a sudden, in evolutionary terms, early humans began to make rope, bone spears, fishhooks, harpoons, and ivory needles, and they concurrently began to express their creativity, as evidenced by the appearance in the anthropological record of musical instruments, jewelry, sculptures, and painting. In addition, evidence of trade between geographically separate communities also appeared, as well as the first evidence of a belief in the afterlife, such as ritualistic burial practices.

Moreover, as we've covered, the earliest modern humans had a brain size much larger than the earlier hominids, and this brain size hasn't changed in the tens of thousands of years leading up to the present day. And as we've most recently discussed, there is solid genetic evidence—in addition to linguistic evidence mentioned briefly earlier—that all modern humans originated from a single ancestral couple approximately 150,000 years ago.

To sum it all up, the earliest appearance of modern humans coincides with evidence for distinctly human traits that earlier hominids did not display. These traits include:

1. superior cognitive ability,
2. symbolic thinking,
3. a creative imagination,
4. craftsmanship,
5. inventiveness and adaptability,
6. artistic and musical expression, and
7. ritualistic and religious beliefs.[44]

Why is it that these traits appeared suddenly, rather than gradually over hundreds of thousands of years as Darwinian evolutionists would expect? Was it really just a "fortuitous mutation" that caused the brain to make the quantum leap in complexity that enabled human culture?

While the Darwinian explanation of gradual evolution by natural selection falls short of explaining the "dawn of human culture," the biblical explanation fits the evidence quite well. The Bible claims that humans were created in the image of God. Interestingly, the seven characteristics of early *Homo sapiens* listed above are among the attributes that Jewish and Christian theologians have used to describe what it means for humans to be made in God's image. In the first chapter of Genesis, God says, "Let us make man in our image, in our likeness. So God created man in his own image, in the image of God he created him; male and female he created them."[45]

But what does it mean to be created in the image of God? Christian theologian Wayne Grudem provides the following definition: "The fact that man is made in the image of God means that man is like God and represents God."[46] He points out that the Hebrew word for "image" (*tselem*) and the Hebrew word for "likeness" (*demût*) both describe something that is similar but not identical to the thing it represents, just as the image of Thomas Jefferson on an American nickel is not the real Thomas Jefferson. This is an important distinction: The Bible teaches that humans are God's image-bearers, but they themselves are not divine. In other words, humans are *like* God, but they are not gods.

One way that theologians classify God's attributes is to distinguish between the attributes that are *incommunicable*, the ones that God does not "communicate to," or share, with humans, and those attributes that are *communicable*, the ones that God does "communicate to" us. God's incommunicable attributes—understandably—include his *omnipresence* (that he is in all places at once), *omnipotence* (that he is all-powerful), *omniscience* (that he is all-knowing), *eternality* (that he is infinite), and so forth.

Examples of God's communicable attributes include love, mercy, knowledge, and justice. God is perfect in his love, mercy, knowledge, and justice, but humans are *able* to love others, display mercy, attain knowledge, and seek justice, though in a much more limited sense. The Bible also describes God's communicable attributes in these ways: God is spiritual, wise, truthful, good, holy, righteous, powerful, perfect, blessed, beautiful, and glorious. He also promotes peace, displays wrath against evil, and is jealous of other gods that his people worship instead of him. While humans can demonstrate each of these qualities in shadows, only God is the perfect expression of all of these characteristics at once (that is, he doesn't display some attributes sometimes and other attributes at other times).

Materialists try to explain the uniquely human pursuit of love, beauty, wisdom, justice, and goodness in terms of strictly evolutionary forces. But could the biblical description of humans being made in the image of God provide a better explanation for the "sudden" dawn of human culture approximately 100,000 years ago?[47]

Having seen scientific evidence supporting the existence of God, in the next chapter we'll focus on the *type* of God that best fits this scientific evidence. As we'll see, the God described in the Bible is incredibly consistent with the latest discoveries of secular science.

QUESTIONS FOR COMPREHENSION AND DISCUSSION

1. What future discoveries did Darwin expect fossil hunters would find that would prove his theories? Instead, what has been found?
2. What is the Cambrian Explosion? Why does this present a conundrum for the theory of unguided evolution?
3. Even if we discovered all of the intermediate forms in the fossil record, would this disprove the existence of God? Why or why not?
4. What have anthropologists discovered about the types of tools first used by humans who lived between 40,000 and 150,000 years ago?
5. What does the fossil record indicate about the development of the modern human brain?
6. Why would it be very difficult for human language and communication to have evolved through chance?
7. What are some ways to visualize the complexity of the human brain? How have some scientists described the computing power and storage capacity of the human brain?
8. How does the scientific evidence support the existence of a single ancestral couple from whom all humans descended? What is the time range during which this ancestral couple lived, and when did their ancestors migrate out of Africa?
9. How is the anthropological evidence for early human culture and religious beliefs consistent with the claim that humans were created in the image of God?
10. What are some communicable attributes of God that humans, as opposed to animals, share, albeit imperfectly? How does this lend credibility to the Bible's description of God and humans?

CHAPTER 3 ENDNOTES

[1] Charles Darwin, *On the Origin of Species by Means of Natural Selection, or the Preservation of Favoured Races in the Struggle for Life* (1859), Chapter 6.

[2] Christopher Stringer and Robin McKie, *African Exodus: The Origins of Modern Humanity* (New York: Henry Holt, 1996), 195-196.

CHAPTER 3: BACK IN TIME

3   Darwin, *On the Origin of Species*, 154.
4   Ibid.
5   Stephen Jay Gould, "Evolution's Erratic Pace," *Natural History*, vol. 86, May 1977.
6   James W. Valentine, Stanley M. Awramik, Philip W. Signor, and Peter M. Sadler, "The Biological Explosion at the Precambrian-Cambrian Boundary," *Evolutionary Biology* 25 (1991): 279-356. Jeffrey S. Levinton, "The Big Bang of Animal Evolution," *Scientific American* 267, (November 1992), 84-91. J. Madeleine Nash, "When Life Exploded," *Time Magazine*, December 4, 1995.
7   Derek Briggs, Douglas Erwin and Frederick Coller, *Fossils of the Burgess Shale* (Washington: Smithsonian Institute Press, 1995).
8   "Evolution's Big Bang," *Time Magazine*, December 4, 1995.
9   Darwin, *On the Origin of Species*, 344.
10   For a list of Cambrian fossil sites, I recommend this site: https://www.sciencenews.org/article/iconic-fossils-some-worlds-top-cambrian-sites.
11   J. William Schopf and Bonnie M. Packer, "Early Archean (3.3 Billion to 3.5 Billion-Year-Old) Microfossils from Warrawoona Group, Australis," *Science* 237 (1987):70-73.
12   Simon Conway Morris, *The Crucible of Creation* (Oxford: Oxford University Press, 1998), 2.
13   J. William Schopf, "The Early Evolution of Life: Solution to Darwin's Dilemma," *Trends in Ecology and Evolution* 9 (1994): 375-77.
14   Quoted in Thomas Hayden, "A Theory Evolves," *U.S. News and World Report*, July 29, 2002, 2.
15   "In Cambridge Explosion Debate, ID Wins by Default," *Evolution News*, Discovery CSC, December 6, 2018. Available online at https://evolutionnews.org/2018/12/in-cambrian-explosion-debate-id-wins-by-default/.
16   Kevin Higgins and Michael Lynch, "Metapopulation extinction caused by mutation accumulation," *Proceedings of the National Academy of Sciences of the United States of America*, http://www.pnas.org/cgi/content/abstract/98/5/2928, February 20, 2001.
17   Alan R. Templeton, Robert J. Robertson, Jennifer Brisson, and Jared Strasburg, "Disrupting evolutionary processes: The effect of habitat fragmentation on collared lizards in the Missouri Ozarks," *Proceedings of the National Academy of Sciences of the United States of America*, May 8, 2001, http://www.pnas.org/cgi/ content/abstract/98/10/5426.
18   C. Schwabe, Mini-Review, "Theoretical limitations of molecular phylogenetics and the evolution of relaxins." *Comp. Biochem. Physiol.* 1994, 107B: 167-177.

19 Alvin Plantinga, "The Dawkins Confusion: Naturalism *ad absurdium*," *Christianity Today*, March/April, 2007.
20 See Francis Collins, *The Language of God* (New York: Free Press, 2006).
21 Timothy Keller, *The Reason for God* (New York: Penguin Group, 2008), 87.
22 I encourage Christians to think about the way God works in the process of sanctification. At the moment of conversion, when a person professes Jesus Christ as their Savior, they are immediately *justified*, but the process whereby they become more holy, *sanctification*, is a gradual, step-by-step process that lasts for the rest of their lifetime. Yes, God could certainly make a person perfectly sanctified immediately if he so chooses (and he does at the moment of a believer's death!), but he chooses not to do so in this life. Similarly, there may be reasons he chose to create organisms gradually over time through slow genetic changes.
23 Christopher Stringer and Robin McKie, *African Exodus: The Origin of Modern Humanity* (New York: Henry Holt, 1996), 195-196.
24 Richard G. Klein and Blake Edgar, *The Dawn of Human Culture: A Bold New Theory on What Sparked the "Big Bang" of Human Consciousness* (New York: Wiley, 2002), 261.
25 G. David Poznik et al., "Sequencing Y-Chromosomes Resolves Discrepancy in Time to Common Ancestor of Males versus Females," *Science* 341 (2013): 562-65.
26 Adrien Rieux et al., "Improved Calibration of the Human Mitochondrial Clock Using Ancient Genomes," *Molecular Biology and Evolution* 31 (2014): 2780-92.
27 Quentin D. Atkinson, "Phonemic Diversity Supports a Serial Founder Effect Model of Language Expansion from Africa," *Science* 15 April 2014: Vol. 332, Issue 6027, 346-349. Available online at http://science.sciencemag.org/content/332/6027/346.
28 John Shea, "*Homo sapiens* Is as *Homo sapiens* Was," *Current Anthropology* 52 (2011):1-11; Michael Balter, "Archaeologist Hammers Away at 'Modern' Behavior," *Science* 339 (2013):642-43.
29 Ian Tattersall, *The Fossil Trail: How We Know What We Think We Know About Human Evolution* (Oxford: Oxford University Press, 1996), 246.
30 John Maynard Smith, "The Importance of Gossip," article in Rita Carter, *Mapping the Mind* (London: Phoenix Books, 2002), 257.
31 Ernst Mayr, *What Evolution Is* (New York: Basic Books, 2001), 253.
32 Steve Olson, *Mapping Human History: Genes, Race, and Our Common Origins* (New York: Houghton Mifflin Co., 2002), 87.
33 Herculano-Houzel S., "The human brain in numbers: a linearly scaled-up primate brain," *Frontiers in Human Neuroscience*. 2009 Nov 9; 3:31. doi:

10.3389/neuro.09.031.2009. eCollection 2009. Available online at https://www.ncbi.nlm.nih.gov/pubmed/19915731.

34 Micheva KD, Busse B, Weiler NC, O'Rourke N, Smith SJ. "Single-synapse analysis of a diverse synapse population: proteomic imaging methods and markers." *Neuron*. 2010 Nov 18; 68(4):639-53. doi: 10.1016/j.neuron.2010.09.024. Available online at https://www.ncbi.nlm.nih.gov/pubmed/21092855.

35 Stephen Hawking, *The Universe in a Nutshell* (London: Bantam, 2001), 169.

36 Carl Sagan, *Cosmos* (New York: Random House, 1980), 278.

37 "Stunning details of how brain connections are made," *Science Daily*, November 17, 2010. Available online at https://www.sciencedaily.com/releases/2010/11/101117121803.htm. (This article describes the study referenced in note 33 above.)

38 Wilder Penfield, *The Mystery of the Mind* (Princeton: Princeton University Press, 1975), 85.

39 Karl R. Popper and John C. Eccles, *The Self and the Brain* (New York: Springer-Verlag, 1997), 559-60.

40 Fazale Rana and Hugh Ross, *Who Was Adam?* (Covina, CA: Reasons to Believe, 2015), Location 4282.

41 Qiaomei Fu et al., "A Revised Timescale for Human Evolution Based on Ancient Mitohondrial Genomes," *Current Biology* 23 (2013): 553-59, and Adrien Rieux et al., "Improved Calibration of the Human Mitochondrial Clock Using Ancient Genomes," *Molecular Biology and Evolution* 31 (2014): 2780-92.

42 Fulvio Cruciani et al., "A Revised Root for the Human Y Chromosomal Phylogeetic Tree: The Origin of Patrilineal Diversity in Africa," *American Journal of Human Genetics* 88 (2011): 814-18; Wei Wei et al., "A Calibrated Human Y-Chromosomal Phylogeny Based on Resequencing," *Genome Research* 23 (2013): 388-95; Rebecca L. Cann, "Y Weigh In Again on Modern Humans," *Science* 341 (2013); 465-67; G. David Poznik et al., "Sequencing Y Chromosomes Resolves Discrepancy in Time to Common Ancestor of Males and Females," *Science* 341 (2013): 562-65; Paolo Francalacci et al., "Low-Pass DNA Sequencing of 1200 Sardinians Reconstructs European Y-Chromosome Phylogeny," *Science* 341 (2013): 565-69.

43 Rana and Ross, *Who Was Adam?*, Location 5975.

44 Ibid, 91-92.

45 See Genesis 1:26-27. Even though the Bible teaches that there is only one God, the use of the plural words "our" and "us" in this verse and others imply that God himself is composed of multiple persons. This is consistent with the Christian doctrine of the Trinity, that a single God exists eternally as three persons, Father, Son and Holy Spirit, each of which is fully God.

Interestingly, one of the Hebrew names for God that appears in the first verse of Genesis and throughout the Old Testament is "Elohim," the *plural* form of the word "Eloah." The use of the term *Elohim* has therefore been used as another support for the doctrine of the Trinity.

[46] Wayne Grudem, *Systematic Theology: An Introduction to Biblical Doctrine* (Grand Rapids, MI: Zondervan, 1994), 442.

[47] Tim Keller writes: "We may, therefore, be secular materialists who believe truth and justice, good and evil, are complete illusions. But in the presence of art or even great natural beauty, our hearts tell us another story." (Keller, *The Reason for God*, 134.)

The first swallow from the cup of the natural sciences makes atheists, but at the bottom of the cup God is waiting.

> Werner Heisenberg,
> Nobel laureate in physics, 1932[1]

For since the creation of the world God's invisible qualities— his eternal power and divine nature— have been clearly seen, being understood from what has been made, so that men are without excuse.

> The Apostle Paul, Letter to the Romans[2]

4

Science and God

Before drawing conclusions about what type of God is consistent with science, let's quickly review the relevant science that we have discussed thus far:

1. The universe began with a huge explosion approximately 13.77 billion years ago.
2. More than one hundred conditions must be just right for the universe to exist and to sustain life.
3. The flow of time has changed since the universe came into existence, such that 13.77 billion years from the current earth time perspective is roughly equivalent to six days from the perspective at the universe's beginning.
4. The biochemical systems and molecular machinery of even the simplest single-celled organisms are irreducibly complex, and the chances that they self-assembled—even given 13.77 billion years—are infinitesimally small.
5. DNA, the basic blueprint within every living organism, displays "specified complexity," in that it is coded information that resembles computer programs, books, and other information that has a designer.
6. Despite more than 150 years of serious effort by paleontologists to confirm Darwin's evolutionary theory, the fossil record contains no convincing proof of gradual transformations between the major phyla of organisms. In fact, around 500 million years ago, the fossil evidence shows that the first animal organisms suddenly appeared in very rapid progression during the "Cambrian Explosion."

CHAPTER 4: SCIENCE AND GOD

7. Human culture and the greatly enlarged *Homo sapiens* brain appeared suddenly in the fossil and anthropological records, not gradually over hundreds of thousands of years as evolutionists would expect.

Based on this scientific evidence, what can we conclude about God? We'll divide our discussion into the following seven conclusions: (1) God exists, (2) God is the creator, (3) God is distinct from creation, (4) God is infinite and omnipresent, (5) God is omnipotent, omniscient, logical, and wise, (6) God is supernatural, and (7) God is personal. Let's get started.

1. God Exists

To begin with, believing that a Creator exists is more rational than concluding that there is no Creator. To hold an atheistic position, you have to take the following leaps of faith:

1. Our universe is just one of an infinite number of universes in an eternal multiverse, a theory that cannot be empirically proven and which still does not address the origin of the laws of physics.
2. Life arose out of non-life against enormous odds, and since the conditions on the early earth were not suitable, the first life may have had to travel to Earth from another part of the universe.
3. Huge jumps in the complexity of even the simplest living systems, not to mention the human brain, resulted from a fortuitous sequence of extremely improbable mutations that left no evidence of gradual evolution in the fossil record.

These three assumptions are either impossible to prove or infinitesimally improbable.

2. God is the Creator

Secondly, the evidence points to a Creator who was responsible for initiating the Big Bang and for precisely tuning the one hundred plus parameters to enable the universe to exist and to sustain life. Moreover, the evidence from complex biochemical machinery, the coded nature of DNA, and the complexity of the human brain in general—and language in particular—suggests that the Creator is a powerful engineer with extraordinary creative skills.

The Bible clearly states that God created the universe out of nothing. Its first words are: "In the beginning God created the heavens and the earth."[3] The apostle John wrote: "Through him all things were made; without him nothing was made that has been made."[4] Moreover, the most common description of the universe in the Bible is that it has been "stretched out," which is quite consistent with the evidence of an expanding universe.[5] For example, the Creator states, "It is I who made the earth and created mankind upon it. My own hands stretched out the heavens; I marshaled their starry hosts."[6]

Not only does the Bible consistently state that the universe is finite, it also describes the universe as constantly wearing out, a description that is consistent with the Second Law of Thermodynamics, a law of physics that maintains that the disorder, or *entropy*, of the universe is always increasing.

On the other hand, belief systems such as those of eastern pantheistic religions and the Greek philosopher Aristotle, have claimed that the universe is eternal. They describe it as an eternal cycle of change, similar to the change of seasons from year to year. Because an eternal universe cannot be wearing out, it contradicts the Second Law of Thermodynamics. For example, consider radioactive isotopes, which are constantly undergoing radioactive decay. If the universe were eternal, all of the radioactive isotopes would have decayed by now, which they have not. Therefore, both the Big Bang and the Second Law of Thermodynamics conflict with religions that claim the universe has been in existence eternally.

The universe's unidirectional march towards greater disorder was not obvious to Aristotle and to proponents of pantheistic philosophies, but it is clearly stated in the Bible. For example, one biblical psalmist writes: "In the beginning you laid the foundations of the earth, and the heavens are the work of your hands. They will perish, but you remain; they will all wear out like a garment. Like clothing you will change them and they will be discarded."[7] Similarly, the apostle Paul notes that the universe is "in bondage to decay,"[8] a remark that is consistent with the evidence for a finite universe that is growing more and more disordered.

3. God Is Distinct from Creation

Third, it is more rational to conclude that the Creator is not the same as the universe but is instead *outside* the universe and therefore *distinct* from it. We have already seen the solid evidence that the universe has a finite age of 13.77 billion years. Because anything finite must have a beginning, and because something cannot create itself, the finite universe must have been caused by something that existed before it. And because physicists agree that the dimensions of time and space came into existence at the Big Bang, this eternal Creator must have existed *before* time and space and is therefore *outside* time and space.

The Bible's teaching about God is consistent with the scientific evidence for a Creator who is distinct from creation. One analogy that the Bible uses to describe God's relationship to his creation is the way the potter relates to his clay. One Hebrew prophet describes it this way:

> Woe to those who quarrel with their Maker, those who are nothing but potsherds among the potsherds on the ground. Does the clay say to the potter, "What are you making?" Does your work say, "The potter has no hands"?[9]

Similarly, one New Testament author likens God to the "architect and builder" of a great city.[10] Just as clay does not mold itself and a building neither designs nor builds itself, the finite, physical universe could not create itself. Clay pots and buildings must have a creator. Just as the potter and the architect are not the same as the clay and the building, but are distinct from their creation, the Creator of the physical universe is not the same as the physical universe, but distinct from it.

Scientific evidence for a finite universe is consistent with the biblical description of God, but it is inconsistent with pantheistic worldviews, which claim that the universe has existed eternally and that God either is the universe or is otherwise not distinct from the universe.

4. God Is Infinite and Omnipresent

The fourth conclusion about God that we can make from the scientific evidence is that he must be infinite and therefore not require a creator himself. We can further deduce that *monotheism*, the belief in one God, is more consistent with the scientific evidence than *polytheism*, the belief in multiple gods. Why is this logical? An infinite God lacks nothing. If there is more than one god, they must each be distinguishable from the others. For one god to be distinguishable from another, it must lack something that the other has. Because they lack something, they are not infinite, but finite. As a result of their finiteness, each of the gods would need a single infinite, beginning-less Creator, and we're back to needing the single God of monotheism.

The Bible clearly describes God as the eternal Creator, who existed before the physical universe and time itself. In what is probably one of the earliest psalms recorded, the author addresses the Creator when he writes, "Before the mountains were born, or you brought forth the earth and the world, from everlasting to everlasting, you are God."[11] A couple of verses later, he further explains God's relationship to our dimension of time: "For a thousand years in your sight are like a day that has just gone by, or like a watch in the night."[12] In other words, the biblical God sees all points of history in the universe—whether they happened 13.77 billion years ago or yesterday or a billion years from now—"equally vividly."[13] Christian theologian Wayne Grudem describes the biblical God's relation to time in this way: "Thus God somehow stands above time and is able to see it all as present in his consciousness."[14]

This timelessness is reflected in the way God describes himself to the Old Testament character Moses from the burning bush. Moses asked God for his name so that he could tell his people who had sent him. In response, God tells Moses: "This is what you are to say to the Israelites: 'I AM has sent me to you.'"[15] The name "I AM" suggests that we cannot place God at any point along the axis of our dimension of time. While everything within our universe has a constantly changing position on the axis of time, God can't be measured in the same way. He simply *is*.

An infinite, eternal God is also necessarily *omnipresent*, or present everywhere. The description of the biblical God is thoroughly consistent with this logical deduction. The Bible consistently portrays God as both distinct from our dimensions of space and time, yet simultaneously present at all points in our space. This view, called *henotheistic*, differs from the *pantheistic* view that God *is* the creation, which, as mentioned earlier, would only be possible if the creation were also eternal. The Bible, instead, teaches that God is present *throughout* creation, but he is *distinct* from it. He is not confined to the space of our universe, but he is present everywhere at the same time. A useful but imperfect analogy is a sponge soaked with water: the water is present throughout the sponge but is distinct from the sponge.[16]

In approximately 1,000 BC, the most famous king of Israel, David, wrote this: "But will God really dwell on earth? The heavens, even the highest heaven, cannot contain [him]. How much less this temple I have built!"[17] In one of his psalms, David also speaks to God about his omnipresence:

> Where can I go from your Spirit?
> Where can I flee from your presence?
> If I go up to the heavens, you are there;
> if I make my bed in the depths, you are there.
> If I rise on the wings of the dawn,
> if I settle on the far side of the sea,
> even there your hand will guide me,
> your right hand will hold me fast.[18]

Because the biblical God existed before the creation of the dimensions that arose at the moment of the Big Bang, he is extra-dimensional and operates both within and outside all of these dimensions.

Once we grasp the idea of God's extra-dimensionality—as strange as it is—we are in a better position to understand many concepts that previously seemed mysterious at best or completely impossible at worst. For example, the Christian doctrine of the Trinity—that there is only one God who consists of three separate persons, Father, Son, and Holy Spirit, each of whom is fully God—appears to many critics as intellectual nonsense, even though there is nothing inherently illogical to the claim that one God can exist in three *persons* (that is, it is *not* three gods in one God). The Trinity may appear less odd if you realize that God exists outside the dimensions of this universe.

To help us understand how the extra-dimensionality of God could explain a concept like the Trinity, physicist Hugh Ross poses the following analogy. Imagine a being that is confined to a two-dimensional world (such as a flat piece of paper, or the flat surface of water in a glass). If a three-dimensional person sticks a finger through the two-dimensional world, it would appear to the two-dimensional being as a circle, since the two-dimensional being would only see the cross-section of the finger that transects his world. If the three-dimensional being now sticks three fingers through the two-dimensional world, the two-dimensional observers would view the single being as three disconnected circles. A single three-dimensional being could therefore appear as three completely separate "objects" within the two-dimensional world.

Another strange concept is the idea that God is extremely close to each of us, yet he remains completely invisible to us. To help understand this concept, imagine another two-dimensional piece of paper that is a nanometer (a billionth of a meter, or a millionth of a millimeter) from the two-dimensional world we were just discussing. Because it doesn't intersect the two-dimensional world, this piece of paper would be invisible in that world, yet it is still only a billionth of a meter from every single point within that two-dimensional world. Similarly, an extra-dimensional God could be close to us at all times yet not be visible to us.

These analogies, though far from perfect, give us an idea of the relationship between an extra-dimensional God and the four observable dimensions of our universe. In *Beyond the Cosmos*, Hugh Ross also demonstrates how the extra-dimensionality of God can elucidate other seemingly impossible biblical claims, including the concept that God can be both completely in control of all events and yet also completely honor free will, how the extra-dimensional God could become a human being in Jesus of Nazareth (the *incarnation*), and more.[19]

5. God Is Omnipotent, Omniscient, Logical, and Wise

A fifth conclusion that we can draw from the scientific evidence about the nature of God is that he is *omnipotent*, or all-powerful, a description of God that characterizes the Bible from start to finish. The Bible describes God as omnipotent in many ways, including these two very clear statements: "With God, all things are possible" and "Nothing is impossible with God."[20]

It may seem like common sense that only an extremely powerful God could create the universe in all of its fine-tuned complexity, but some belief systems hold to a God or gods of limited power. Not only does the Bible consistently describe God as eternal, such that he did not need to be created, but it also claims that he does not need *anything*. The apostle Paul proclaimed this attribute of the biblical God to the people of Athens:

> The God who made the world and everything in it, being Lord of heaven and earth, does not live in shrines made by man, nor is he served by human hands, as though he needed anything, since he himself gives to all men life and breath and everything.[21]

The God of the Bible himself expresses this concept with the question: "Who has given to me, that I should repay him? Whatever is under the whole heaven is mine."[22]

It logically follows from the Creator's omnipotence that he is also *omniscient*, or all-knowing. That is, if God can do anything, one of the things he has the power to do is to know all things. The Bible describes God as omniscient, as well as *logical* and *wise*. Not only does God know all things, he invented the laws of logic, and he operates in accordance with those laws. And the wisdom of the biblical God supersedes both his omniscience and logic, in the sense that God's decisions will always bring the best results and achieve those results via the best possible means.[23]

The Bible does not describe the Creator as merely an impersonal force that is all-knowing. The Bible instead describes God as a person or a mind, with thoughts that are far superior to the thoughts of our own finite minds. For example, the God of the Bible makes this statement:

> "For my thoughts are not your thoughts, neither are your ways my ways," declares the LORD. "As the heavens are higher than the earth, so are my ways higher than your ways and my thoughts than your thoughts."[24]

The Bible describes God's wisdom as infinitely greater than ours, and God is the source of any finite wisdom that humans may claim to have. The biblical God even speaks to the humans he created—something an impersonal force doesn't do. And in the following example, he is quick to correct a mere human who dared to question his wisdom:

> "Who is this that darkens my counsel with words without knowledge? Brace yourself like a man; I will question you, and you shall answer me. Where were you when I laid the earth's foundation? Tell me, if you understand.... Who endowed the heart with wisdom or gave understanding to the mind? Who has the wisdom to count the clouds?"[25]

The omniscience, logic, and wisdom of the Creator can be seen throughout the natural world. The fine-tuning of the many parameters of physical laws, the specified and irreducible complexity of even the simplest organisms, the incredible computing power of the human brain, and the logic and "beauty" of the laws of physics and mathematics are consistent with a logical Creator, which is exactly how the Bible describes God.

You can summarize these attributes of the biblical God by claiming that he is the *perfect mind*. Just as a computer program is created by the mind of a programmer, and a book is created by the mind of a writer, the complexity of information contained within the simplest single-celled amoeba—1,000 sets of encyclopedias, 30 volumes each—also requires a highly intelligent mind. Dr. Stephen Meyer remarks, "Information is the hallmark of mind. And purely from the evidence of genetics and biology, we can infer the existence of a mind that's far greater than our own—a conscious, purposeful, rational, intelligent designer who's amazingly creative. There's no getting around it."[26]

The logic and order of creation cry out for a logical and extremely wise Creator. But this logic and order also contradict the belief that God would appear to different people in different, contradictory ways. If the Creator was so careful to imbue the universe with such logic and order, whether it is seen in the laws of physics, the principles of mathematics, or the complexity of living organisms, why would he appear to some people as multiple gods and to others as a single infinite God? Why would he claim to be one with his creation to some people and then claim that he is above and distinct from his creation to others? Thus, the teachings of the Bible are consistent with the logical argument that an omniscient, logical, and wise Creator would not reveal himself in logically contradictory ways.

6. God Is Supernatural

Sixth, the scientific evidence is consistent with the belief that there is a reality beyond the physical universe. Thus, the claim that nothing exists beyond the physical world, a belief called either *materialism* or *naturalism*, is most likely false. Since the Creator would have already existed eternally even before the physical universe, the nature of this Creator is most likely not physical, but supernatural or spiritual. Logically, if this spiritual Being created the universe and all that is in it, it is highly likely that other supernatural or spiritual beings also exist.

Moreover, if the Creator has already performed the greatest work of all by creating the universe and the precise laws of physics that govern it, we can deduce that it is also possible for the Creator to act upon his creation as he chooses.[27] In other words, once you make the rational deduction that an all-powerful God exists, it follows logically that his power would also enable him to intervene in the universe in ways that nothing or no one else could.

God may have chosen not to intervene after he first created the universe, as the religious philosophy of *deism* maintains, but he certainly is powerful enough to tinker with the physical laws he himself created. Christian pastor Dr. Timothy Keller explains it this way:

> If there is a Creator God, there is nothing illogical about the possibility of miracles. After all, if he created everything out of nothing, it would hardly be a problem for him to rearrange parts of it as and when he wishes. To be sure that miracles cannot occur you would have to be sure beyond a doubt that God didn't exist, and that is an article of faith.[28]

In fact, many scientists maintain a strictly materialistic worldview because they do not want to admit the possibility of miracles. Evolutionary biologist Richard Lewontin puts it this way: "To appeal to an omnipotent deity is to allow that at any moment the regularities of nature may be ruptured, that miracles may happen."[29] At that point, he would claim, the scientist cannot depend solely on the laws of cause and effect to explain phenomena. However, there are many scientists who believe in a supernatural Creator yet feel quite comfortable seeking strictly materialistic explanations for natural phenomena. A belief in God should not keep a scientist from honest intellectual investigation of the natural world.

To summarize, the scientific evidence of a finite physical universe does not rule out a realm that is beyond the natural world, and it does not rule out miracles. Instead, it is very logical that the supernatural realm exists, since it existed before the birth of the physical universe. And miracles are philosophically plausible, given an all-powerful Creator.

7. God Is Personal

A seventh conclusion that we can draw from the scientific evidence is that the Creator is most likely personal, as opposed to an impersonal force. The fine-tuning of the universe for life, the irreducible complexity of even the simplest, single-celled organisms, not to mention the human brain, and the specified complexity of DNA all point to a Creator with a creative and logical mind. Moreover, the placement of the Earth at the edge of the Milky Way galaxy, the transparency of our atmosphere, the moon's precise size and distance from the earth such that it completely covers the sun during a solar eclipse, and many other "just so" phenomena point to a Creator who wants humans to make discoveries about the universe he created.

So why would the Creator want to design the universe in such a way that humans would both thrive in it and be able to study it? The Bible gives us a reasonable answer: He wants to have a personal relationship with us. While the biblical God is independent and self-sufficient, and therefore did not *need* to create us, the Bible teaches that he is a personal God of love who created us to share the universe with him for all eternity. As a personal God, the biblical God interacts with his creation as a person would interact with another person.

Many people today think of God as an impersonal force that permeates the universe. Many eastern philosophies maintain that the universe itself is god. Islam maintains that God is too transcendent to condescend to a personal relationship with humans.[30] The scientific evidence is not only more compatible with a God who is distinct from the universe, but it is also more consistent with a God who created the universe for a purpose, one in which humans play a key role.

CHAPTER 4: SCIENCE AND GOD

Examples of God's desire to have a personal relationship with humans abound in the Bible. Throughout both the Old and New Testaments, the Creator of the universe refers to himself as the "bridegroom" of his people, who are described as "his bride."[31] One of the Old Testament prophets even makes this outrageous claim: "For your Maker is your husband—the LORD Almighty is his name—the Holy One of Israel is your Redeemer; he is called the God of all the earth."[32] And near the end of the Bible the apostle John describes his vision of what will happen when the history of the current world comes to an end:

> Then I saw a new heaven and a new earth, for the first heaven and the first earth had passed away.... I saw the Holy City, the new Jerusalem, coming down out of heaven from God, prepared as a bride beautifully dressed for her husband. And I heard a loud voice from the throne saying, "Now the dwelling of God is with men, and he will live with them. They will be his people, and God himself will be with them and be their God. He will wipe every tear from their eyes. There will be no more death or mourning or crying or pain, for the old order of things has passed away."[33]

Christian scholars almost universally interpret the "New Jerusalem" as God's people, whom he created so that they would live with him for eternity.

The Bible also describes the Creator of the universe as a parent. God even states that his relationship to his people is equivalent to the intimate connection between a mother and her newborn: "Can a mother forget the baby at her breast and have no compassion on the child she has borne? Though she may forget, I will not forget you!"[34]

Speaking to his own disciples, whom he describes as "evil" relative to the perfectly loving God, Jesus emphasizes the care and love that God has for his people:

> "Which of you, if his son asks for bread, will give him a stone? Or if he asks for a fish, will give him a snake? If you, then, though you are evil, know how to give good gifts to your children, how much more will your Father in heaven give good gifts to those who ask him!"[35]

In fact, even though the Old Testament rarely refers to God as "Father," Jesus uses the term "Father" throughout the New Testament to describe our relationship to God. Jesus even instructs us to begin our prayers, "Our Father in heaven."[36]

While the perfect conditions for life on Earth may not prove that God is personal, the Bible's depiction of God explains why the earth is such a wonderful environment for us. That the earth, unsullied, makes an ideal home for humans is obvious to anyone who has marveled at a sunset, the vast array of plant and animal life, the majesty of the snow-capped mountains and tropical beaches, and the incredible variety of delicious vegetables, fruit, herbs, and spices that grow from the soil. While atheists may argue that they can still appreciate the beauty of the universe, this beauty is much more consistent with the idea that there is a Creator who created the world with humans in mind than it is with an accidental universe that has no particular purpose.

People may have reasons to hold atheistic, pantheistic, polytheistic, and naturalistic worldviews, but it isn't because these belief systems are the most consistent with the scientific evidence. To clarify, these belief systems are not *entirely* untrue, just because their description of God is inconsistent with the scientific evidence. They still contain many beautiful and useful teachings, from which mankind can learn and benefit. But the explanation of God that is the most consistent with the evidence summarized in the last three chapters is a single, infinite, spiritual Creator who is distinct from the physical universe and powerful enough to fiddle with or suspend the laws of physics he created. Moreover, the evidence suggests that the Creator desires a personal relationship with the humans he created, such that they can more easily study the universe and find him at its source. The only world religions that describe God in this way are Judaism and Christianity, and to a lesser extent, Islam.[37]

Of course, you are free to believe in any type of God that you would like, but the goal of this book is to demonstrate that the God of the Bible, specifically the God as revealed in Jesus Christ, is the most consistent with the evidence. In fact, for a book that was written thousands of years before the discovery of scientific evidence for a finite, finely tuned universe, the Bible provides a description of the Creator that is remarkably compatible with this evidence.

In summary, the description of the Creator of the universe provided

CHAPTER 4: SCIENCE AND GOD

in the Bible fits extremely well with the scientific evidence: The biblical God created the universe out of nothing at a specific point in time in the past. Unlike the universe, the Creator is described in the Bible as infinite, and therefore doesn't himself need a creator. He exists outside the universe he created and is therefore distinct from it, yet he is constantly present at all points within the universe. He is timeless, since he exists outside our dimension of time. The biblical God is omnipotent, omniscient, logical, and wise, as we would expect from the Being that initiated the Big Bang, set the laws of physics in motion, and orchestrated the development of plants, animals, and humans. And the Bible's claim that God created us to discover and enjoy a relationship with him is consistent with our sense that the universe has purpose, beauty, and significance. At this point, it is my hope that you would consider the God of the Bible worthy of further investigation.

QUESTIONS FOR COMPREHENSION AND DISCUSSION

1. Can you list the seven primary lines of scientific evidence for God that were presented in the last three chapters?
2. Can you list the three main leaps of faith that materialists must make to defend their belief that there is no Creator?
3. This chapter summarizes seven conclusions that we can draw from the evidence regarding the nature of God. What are these seven conclusions, and how is the biblical God consistent with them?
4. Why must God be infinite? Why can there only be one infinite Being?
5. How are pantheistic religions inconsistent with the concept of an infinite Creator who is distinct from his creation?
6. If God existed before the creation of the physical realm, in what other realm could he be? If God is in this other realm, could there also be other creatures there?
7. Why are miracles possible, given an all-powerful Creator who exists outside the physical realm?
8. How would you define these three terms: omniscient, logical, and wise? How does the scientific evidence regarding the origin

of the universe and the complexity of life require that there be a Creator who is omniscient, logical, and wise?
9. How does a personal God differ from an impersonal force? In what ways does the Bible describe God as a personal God?
10. What aspects of the world give us a hint that God loves humans? (For now, think of the aspects of the world that are beautiful, as we will address the problem of evil in a later chapter.)

CHAPTER 4 ENDNOTES

[1] As quoted by Gerald Schroeder in the Foreword to Timothy P. Mahoney and Steven Law, *Patterns of Evidence: Exodus, A Filmmaker's Journey* (St. Louis Park, MN: Thinking Man Media, 2015), Location 60.
[2] Romans 1:20.
[3] Genesis 1:1.
[4] John 1:3. Other passages that describe God as creating the universe out of nothing include Psalm 33:6, 9; Isaiah 45:18; Acts 14:15, 17:24-25; Hebrews 11:3; Colossians 1:16; and Revelation 4:11 and 10:6.
[5] Hugh Ross, *The Creator and the Cosmos*, 3rd ed. (Colorado Springs, CO: NavPress, 2001), 24.
[6] Isaiah 45:12. A few of the biblical references to a Creator who stretched out the universe are Job 9:8; Psalm 104:2; Isaiah 40:22, 42:5, 44:24, 45:12, 48:13, and 51:13; Jeremiah 10:12, 51:15; and Zechariah 12:1.
[7] Psalm 102:25-26.
[8] Romans 8:21.
[9] Isaiah 45:9.
[10] Hebrews 11:10.
[11] Psalm 90:2.
[12] Psalm 90:4.
[13] Wayne Grudem, *Systematic Theology: An Introduction to Biblical Doctrine* (Grand Rapids, MI: Zondervan, 1994), 170.
[14] Ibid, 171.
[15] Exodus 3:14.
[16] Grudem, *Systematic Theology*, 175.
[17] 1 Kings 8:27.
[18] Psalm 139:7-10. A few other Bible passages that describe God's omnipresence include Isaiah 66:1-2; Jeremiah 23:23-24; Acts 17:28; and Colossians 1:17.
[19] Hugh Ross, *Beyond the Cosmos* (Covina, CA: RTB Press, 2017). Ross devotes a chapter to explaining each Christian doctrine that can be better understood in light of the extra-dimensionality of God.

CHAPTER 4: SCIENCE AND GOD

20 Matthew 19:26b and Luke 1:37. For just a few other examples of biblical descriptions of an omnipotent God, see Mark 10:27, Luke 18:27, and Ephesians 3:20.
21 Acts 17:24-25.
22 Job 41:11.
23 Grudem, *Systematic Theology*, 193.
24 Isaiah 55:8-9.
25 Job 38:14, 36-37a.
26 As quoted in Lee Strobel, *The Case for a Creator* (Grand Rapids, MI: Zondervan, 2004), 244.
27 Note: Research in quantum physics has revealed possible mechanisms whereby a supernatural power could influence the physical universe at a subatomic level. Moreover, a phenomenon called quantum tunneling could explain how a particle—and possibly entire objects or people—could move through barriers such as walls, without altering the structure of the barrier. For more information about the revelations of quantum physics, see Michio Kaku and Jennifer Thompson, *Beyond Einstein: The Cosmic Quest for the Theory of the Universe* (New York: Anchor Books, 1995). For more recent research on quantum tunneling, see D. Shafir, H. Soifer, B. D. Bruner, M. Dagan, Y. Mairesse, S. Patchkovskii, M. Y. Ivanov, O. Smirnova, N. Dudovich, "Resolving the time when an electron exits a tunnelling barrier." *Nature*. 2012 May 16; 485(7398):343-6. DOI: 10.1038/nature11025. Available online at https://www.ncbi.nlm.nih.gov/pubmed/22596157.
28 Timothy Keller, *The Reason for God* (New York: Penguin Group, 2008), 86.
29 Richard Lewontin, "Billions and Billions of Demons," *The New York Review of Books*, January 9, 1997, 150.
30 Tim Keller writes: "Later on, after I became a minister, I was a speaker and panelist for several years in a monthly discussion program in Philadelphia between a Christian church and a mosque. Each month a speaker from the church and a speaker from the mosque would give a Biblical and Qu'ranic perspective on a topic. When we covered the topic of God's love, it was striking how different our conceptions were. I was told repeatedly by Muslim speakers that God was indeed loving in the sense of being merciful and kind to us. But when Christians spoke of the Lord as our spouse, of knowing God intimately and personally, and of having powerful effusions of his love poured into our hearts by the Holy Spirit, our Muslim friends balked. They told us that it was disrespectful, in their view, to speak of anyone knowing God personally." (Timothy Keller, *The Reason for God* [New York: Penguin Group, 2008], 82.)
31 Among the passages that describe God in this way are Psalm 19:5; Isaiah 49:18, 54:5, 61:10, 62:5; Jeremiah 2:2, 32; Ezekiel 16:8-14; Matthew 9:15,

25:1-13; Mark 2:19-20; Luke 5:34-35; John 3:29; and Revelation 19:7, 21:2,9, 22:17.

[32] Isaiah 54:5.
[33] Revelation 22:1-4.
[34] Isaiah 49:15.
[35] Matthew 7:9-11.
[36] Matthew 6:9.
[37] As mentioned in footnote 30, Islam places less emphasis on the personal nature of God. For example, Muslims would never consider God to be their father.

PART II
The Historical Evidence

We did not follow cleverly invented stories when we told you about the power and coming of our Lord Jesus Christ, but we were eyewitnesses of his majesty.

        Peter, one of Jesus' original disciples[1]

Extraordinary claims require extraordinary evidence.

        Carl Sagan, atheist and astronomer[2]

Please Believe Me!

The Bible was written over a period of 1,400 years by more than forty authors from a wide variety of backgrounds ranging from kings to herdsmen. Some wrote in times of war, and others wrote in times of peace. With literary styles spanning poetry, romance, and song to allegory, satire, and parables to historical narrative, prophecy, and biography, the Bible deals with many controversial subjects that cut to the core of questions about the meaning of life.

Yet despite this diversity of writers, styles, historical periods, and topics, the Bible's message about the relationship between God and humans is consistent throughout: God created men and women to live eternally with him, but they rebelled against him. As a result, we could no longer live peaceably with a perfectly pure God. Evil, suffering, and death all resulted when humans made the choice to live independently of their Creator. God then disclosed his plan to rescue his people from sin and death, a plan that was foretold in the Old Testament and implemented in the New, culminating in the establishment of an eternal Kingdom of perfect peace and flourishing that is still future to us. To summarize this consistent storyline from the beginning to the end of the Bible, Norman Geisler and William Nix put it, "The 'Paradise Lost' of Genesis becomes the 'Paradise Regained' of Revelation."[3]

So, why should we believe this story? There are many religious writings that have very different claims about the nature of God and his relationship to us. Why believe exclusively in this one? Moreover, why not pick and choose the parts of the Bible that we want to believe and chuck the rest? And let's not forget that many people come to different conclusions about what the Bible says about the relationship between God and man. What then are we to believe?

Following the overview in the last four chapters of the consistency of the biblical God with science, you have a better understanding of why many people consider the Bible to be God's revelation of himself and his plan for the world. The compatibility of the biblical description of God with recent, secular scientific discoveries about our universe is strong evidence that the Bible is divinely inspired. How else could men writing thousands of years ago make so many statements that are harmonious with modern science? But there's even more evidence that the Bible has a divine origin—that is, that it was written down by humans who were "inspired" to write what God told them to write.

Having seen this scientific support for the Bible, we now turn to an analysis of its historical reliability to answer questions such as these: Does the Bible pass the same tests that historians use to determine the truthfulness of other historical documents? Can we determine whether the Bible is trustworthy in its claims about God, or must we conclude that it is just a collection of man-made myths?

If, after close scrutiny, we find sufficient reason to believe the Bible is just a series of fictional stories, then we can discard it or base our worldview on the selected parts that appeal to us. Of course, we cannot use tests of historical truthfulness to prove that the Bible is true in its entirety. But if we can demonstrate that the Bible is a historically reliable collection of truthful narratives—especially when it comes to its claims regarding Jesus' deity, miracles, and resurrection—then we have a greater basis for trusting that the claims it makes about God and our relationship to him are also true.

Christian theologians use the term *general revelation* to describe the means by which God reveals himself to all humanity through nature. Through general revelation, God demonstrates his omnipotence, eternity, omniscience, wisdom, creativity, and other attributes. Even before modern science, God demonstrated his existence through nature loudly and clearly.

Ironically, as new scientific discoveries have been made, humans began to deny that nature points to God—they have further "suppressed the truth," as the apostle Paul calls it.[4] Yet the evidence from science for God's existence has never been stronger. In fact, scientific discoveries (or the lack thereof) continue to provide more and more evidence for a "Supreme Engineer" who is the source of all things.

Psalm 19 starts with a description of God's general revelation to all humans throughout the world:

> The heavens declare the glory of God;
> the skies proclaim the work of his hands.
> Day after day they pour forth speech;
> night after night they display knowledge.
> There is no speech or language
> where their voice is not heard.
> Their voice goes out into all the earth,
> their words to the ends of the world.[5]

But the "non-verbal communication" of nature does not provide more explanatory details about God. This additional information about God, what Christian theologians call *special revelation*, was given to us at various times throughout human history: through the Old Testament prophets, through Jesus, and through the New Testament apostles.[6] It is to this special revelation that the rest of this book is devoted.

TRUTHFUL OR DELUSIONAL?

One of my favorite movies is *Terminator 2: Judgment Day*, which came out in 1991 soon after I graduated from Stanford. The first scene takes place in an insane asylum, where a woman named Sarah Connor has been locked up following her claims that a super-computer is using human-like robots called Terminators to take over the planet. Despite her desperate attempts to convince them that she is not crazy but in fact has just endured a true experience facing one such Terminator (played by Arnold Schwarzenegger in the first Terminator movie), the psychiatrists don't believe her. Facing no other alternative, she escapes from the asylum in order to defend the world from certain additional attacks by Terminators.

I don't blame the psychiatrists. Their opinion of her mental instability is completely understandable. Her claims were outrageous and exactly what you'd expect from someone who had gone insane. When I put myself in Sarah Connor's place, it brings to mind the frustration and urgency that the first disciples must have felt if the New Testament stories were really true. As they pleaded with people and tried to convince them they were telling the truth, they instead were often rejected as insane.

As we will cover in more detail later, the people of the ancient world—whether they were Jews, Greeks, Romans, or otherwise—did not believe in the bodily resurrection of a dead person any more than modern scientific people do. For example, when the apostle Paul was imprisoned for the claims he had been making about Jesus' resurrection, he was brought out of his jail cell to be interviewed by the Jewish King Agrippa and the Roman Governor Festus. Festus interrupted Paul's defense and shouted at him: "You are out of your mind, Paul! Your great learning is driving you insane."[7]

But were the first Christians out of their minds? Are the stories of the miracles and resurrection of Jesus trustworthy, or can we discard them as delusional claims that are merely symbolic at best, or purposeful lies at worst? Did they want to believe so badly that Jesus was resurrected that they convinced themselves it was true? Did they have a hallucination of what looked like the risen Jesus? Or did they report what actually happened?

Incredibly, the historical record leaves us many clues that actually support their amazing claims.

TESTS OF HISTORICAL RELIABILITY

Let's begin our historical evaluation of the biblical claims with a definition of the techniques historians use to reconstruct the past, collectively called *historiography*: "the narrative evaluation of history based on a critical examination, evaluation, and selection of material from primary and secondary sources and subject to scholarly criteria."[8] In other words, a historiographer examines, analyzes, and evaluates various historical source documents (letters, government records, books, and so forth) in an attempt to determine the truth, or *historicity*, of past events.

After scrutinizing the various sources available and taking bias and other influences into account, the historiographer aims to construct a picture of what happened that is as realistic as possible. While no ancient historical event can be confirmed with 100% accuracy, historiography—just like scientific research—can get us as close as possible.

Using the techniques of historiography, we can try to answer questions such as "Did Jesus really exist?" and "Are the stories about him in the New Testament true, mythological, or a combination of both?"

As a fan of both science and history, I find it especially interesting that Christianity is not only consistent with modern science, but the Christian faith is also unique among world religions in that it can be evaluated using methods of historiography. Because it is based on historical events, the most important of which is the resurrection of Jesus, these events can be either confirmed or refuted through documentary, archaeological, and other historical evidence.

While some Christians may believe it is unnecessary to determine whether the events of Jesus' life really happened, the truth claims of Christianity really *do* depend on the truthfulness of these events. In other words, we can and should ask questions like these: Did God really enter space and time on the planet Earth as a human named Jesus? Did this Jesus really live in ancient Palestine? Did he really die on a Roman cross? Did he really rise again from the dead three days later? Did he really appear to hundreds of people in a transformed physical body? If we can't demonstrate that he really did these things, especially that he rose from the dead, then the apostle Paul is right: Christians are "of all people most to be pitied."[9]

It is thus very important to defend and demonstrate the historicity of these events. Prominent biblical historian F. F. Bruce explains it this way:

> For the Christian gospel is not primarily a code of ethics or a metaphysical system; it is first and foremost good news, and as such it was proclaimed by its earliest preachers…. And this good news is intimately bound up with the historical order, for it tells how for the world's redemption God entered into history…. This historical 'one-for-all-ness' of Christianity, which distinguishes it from those religious and philosophical systems which are not specially related to any particular time, makes the reliability of the writing which purport to record this revelation a question of first-rate importance.[10]

If Jesus never existed, the Christian faith may still provide a useful ethical code to guide our lives, but its essential doctrine— the redemption of humanity through Jesus' perfectly lived life and his death on the cross—loses all credibility.

Amazingly, historiographical analysis can give us confidence that the core doctrines of Christianity are firmly based on solid historical evidence.

To begin the analysis of this historical evidence, let's first go over the primary tests that historiographers use to determine whether the claims of any historical document are trustworthy. Historiographers use three primary tests to determine the truth of past events described in historical documents:

1. The *internal evidence test* asks whether the writer of the document claims to be telling the truth and whether the document itself contains other evidence of trustworthiness.
2. The *external evidence test* asks whether the document can be confirmed by outside evidence, such as archaeology or other reliable historical documents, especially those with an opposing bias.
3. The *bibliographical test* asks how many early copies of the document exist and how closely they correspond to the originals.[11]

We will spend this chapter and the next four chapters evaluating the internal evidence that supports the truth of the New Testament stories. In Chapters 10 and 11, we will examine the external evidence for the Gospel accounts' historicity, first from secular historical documents and then from archaeology. Finally, we'll take a look at how the New Testament fares on the bibliographical test in Chapter 12. Let's start where the authors of the New Testament started when they wrote down details of the events of Jesus' life: with the eyewitness evidence.

Eyewitness Claims

To determine how well a document fares on the internal evidence test of historicity, historiographers first ask whether the author of the document claims to be telling the truth. Of course, he or she could be lying, or the document could have been altered posthumously, but if the author claims to be truthful, it is highly unlikely that the book is an intentional work of fiction or mythology. As we will see, the New Testament writers go out of their way to emphasize that they are telling the truth. Moreover, they stress that they are providing eyewitness testimony to support their claims that the miracles and resurrection of Jesus really happened.

Not only do they claim that Jesus physically rose from the dead, but they also claim that he is the Messiah, the leader that the Jewish people had been expecting for thousands of years to usher in a new kingdom of peace on Earth. They even claim that Jesus is the creator of the universe and the judge of all mankind, positions that the Jews only ever attributed to God. They knew full well that people would doubt them, even vilify and punish them. No one in that society expected someone to rise from the dead—not even the eventual Messiah,[12] nor did the Jews believe that God could become a man or that the Messiah would come without immediately establishing peace on earth. What is even more incredible is that these early Christians[13]—most of them devout Jews—made these outrageous claims fully aware that they would suffer or even be put to death as a result.

So, let's take a look at some of the New Testament passages in which the first Christians claim to be eyewitnesses of Jesus' miracles and resurrection. Many of these claims are found in the Acts of the Apostles, the book that describes the earliest years of the Christian church.

Early church historians claim that the author of Acts traveled with the apostle Paul and had opportunities to interview eyewitnesses of Jesus. The Muratorian Canon, written by an early church historian in circa AD 170, tells us that a man named Luke authored both the Gospel of Luke and the Book of Acts, and that Luke was Paul's physician.[14] This is consistent with one of Paul's letters when he sends greetings to the Colossian church from "our dear friend Luke, the doctor."[15] Luke was also Paul's traveling companion, which is implied in Colossians and confirmed by the writings of Irenaeus, a bishop and church historian around AD 180.[16]

Irenaeus also talks about the extensive discussions he had with Polycarp, whom the original disciple John had ordained as bishop of Smyrna (modern-day İzmir, Turkey). In a letter to Florinus, a fellow Christian in Rome whom he was accusing of heresy, Irenaeus wrote:

CHAPTER 5: PLEASE BELIEVE ME!

> These opinions, Florinus, to say no more, are not of sound judgment; these opinions are not in harmony with the Church... these opinions the elders before us, who also were disciples of the apostles, did not hand down to you. For when I was still a boy I saw you in lower Asia in the company of Polycarp, faring brilliantly in the imperial court and trying to secure his favour. For I distinctly recall the events of that time better than those of recent years (for what we learn in childhood keeps pace with the growing mind and becomes part of it), so that I can tell the very place where the blessed Polycarp used to sit as he discoursed, his goings out and his comings in, the character of his life, his bodily appearance, the discourses he would address to the multitude, how he would tell of his conversations with John and with the others who had seen the Lord, how he would relate their words from memory; and what the things were which he had heard from them concerning the Lord, his mighty works and his teaching, Polycarp, as having received them from the eyewitnesses [*autopton*] of the Logos, would declare altogether in accordance with the scriptures.[17]

Thus, there is evidence that Irenaeus had access to reliable information about Jesus and the authors of the Gospels. In fact, it is likely that the authors of the four Gospels and the Book of Acts obtained their information directly from these eyewitnesses—that is, *through oral history*—and not through *oral tradition*, which is not as trustworthy because it involves intermediaries between the eyewitnesses and the authors of the Gospels.

The author of the Book of Acts and the Gospel of Luke, whether or not it was Paul's companion and doctor, Luke, clearly asserts that Jesus appeared in physical form to many eyewitnesses over an extended period of time after his crucifixion. Note how the Book of Acts begins:

> In my former book, Theophilus, I wrote about all that Jesus began to do and to teach until the day he was taken up to heaven, after giving instructions through

THE SHORTEST LEAP

> the Holy Spirit to the apostles he had chosen. After his suffering, he showed himself to these men and gave many convincing proofs that he was alive. He appeared to them over a period of forty days and spoke about the kingdom of God.[18]

Because the author calls it his "former book," the Gospel of Luke was written even earlier than Acts, probably within twenty to thirty years of Jesus' death, when eyewitnesses were still alive who could support or refute his testimony.

But even if we assume that Luke's Gospel was written much later than Jesus' death, its author makes it very clear that he depended on eyewitness testimony for its subject matter. As a case in point, the author goes out of the way to insist that he is not writing a legend. In fact, the beginning of Luke sounds like the typical preamble of an ancient historical document, not at all what you would see at the start of a legend:[19]

> Many have undertaken to draw up an account of the things that have been fulfilled among us, just as they were handed down to us by those who from the first were eyewitnesses and servants of the word. Therefore, since I myself have carefully investigated everything from the beginning, it seemed good also to me to write an orderly account for you, most excellent Theophilus, so that you may know the certainty of the things you have been taught.[20]

Luke is going out of his way to convince his audience that his account is based on substantiated evidence from actual eyewitnesses and that he has fastidiously researched and confirmed everything. Note also that in the Gospel of Luke and the Book of Acts, the author is specifically addressing a man named Theophilus, whose title "most excellent" suggests that he was a powerful and educated Roman authority figure,[21] who—like "most excellent Festus" above—would not have been easily convinced of the truth of miracles and other supernatural experiences.[22]

CHAPTER 5: PLEASE BELIEVE ME!

OTHER EYEWITNESS STATEMENTS IN ACTS AND LUKE

In the very beginning of Acts, it is obvious that eyewitnesses were of utmost importance to the early Christian faith. When the eleven remaining disciples were deciding who should replace Judas Iscariot, the disciple who had betrayed Jesus and subsequently committed suicide, they wanted to be sure to choose someone who had also witnessed Jesus' ministry and resurrection. The author of Acts emphasizes that Peter clearly understood the importance of selecting a fellow eyewitness, which is evident when Peter makes the following statements:

> Therefore it is necessary to choose one of the men who have been with us the whole time the Lord Jesus went in and out among us, beginning from John's baptism to the time when Jesus was taken up from us. For one of these must become a witness with us of his resurrection.[23]

The disciples knew that it was crucial to their credibility that their circle included only eyewitnesses.

When Peter addressed a crowd in Jerusalem, he stated, "God has raised this Jesus to life, and we are all *witnesses* of the fact."[24] Peter wasn't just claiming to be an eyewitness; he was claiming to be one of multiple eyewitnesses present at that moment. Another way of interpreting his statement is: "You saw this yourselves, or if you didn't, you can just ask those guys over there to confirm what I'm saying is true."

Similarly, when Peter addressed another crowd in Jerusalem, he stated: "You killed the author of life, but God raised him from the dead. We are *witnesses* of this."[25] Peter not only emphasized that he and others present were witnesses of Jesus' resurrection, but he also demonstrated his understanding of Jesus as the divine Creator when he called him "the author of life."

When the Jewish high priests commanded Peter and the other disciples "not to speak or teach in the name of Jesus," Peter and John replied, "Judge for yourselves whether it is right in God's sight to obey you rather than God. For we cannot help speaking about *what we have seen and heard*."[26]

They weren't just inventing their belief in Jesus' resurrection because they wanted it to be true—it certainly wasn't helping them avoid criticism, imprisonment, and suffering. They claimed they were simply reporting what they had seen and heard. Unless they were telling the truth, why would Peter and John continue to make these claims if it could easily lead to prison time and their execution?

Again, when the Jewish leaders commanded them to stop preaching about Jesus or else face punishment, Peter and the other apostles replied: "The God of our fathers raised Jesus from the dead.... We are witnesses of these things."[27] Moreover, Peter made the following statement:

> "We are witnesses of everything he did in the country of the Jews and in Jerusalem. They killed him by hanging him on a tree [a term for crucifixion], but God raised him from the dead on the third day and caused him to be seen. He was not seen by all the people, but by witnesses whom God had already chosen—by us who ate and drank with him after he rose from the dead. He commanded us to preach to the people and to testify that he is the one whom God appointed as judge of the living and the dead. All the prophets testify about him that everyone who believes in him receives forgiveness of sins through his name."[28]

Despite the enormous risks, Peter proclaimed that Jesus was the judge that God had appointed, a role that the Jewish leaders knew only God could fill. What's more, Peter stated that the Jewish Scriptures (the "prophets") pointed to Jesus as the one who would forgive sins, also a power the Jews believed was reserved only for God.

Peter claimed that he and others present had witnessed Jesus' actions, including his resurrection. He even claimed they ate and drank with him after he had risen. A non-physical being has no need to eat and drink, so Peter's statement reveals that Jesus *had a body*—he was alive physically, not just spiritually or symbolically.

Not only did they claim to have been eyewitnesses, the earliest apostles also claimed that the miracles of Jesus were public knowledge. For example, in response to Festus' claim that he had gone insane, mentioned above, Paul said:

CHAPTER 5: PLEASE BELIEVE ME!

> "I am not insane, most excellent Festus. What I am saying is true and reasonable. The king is familiar with these things, and I can speak freely to him. I am convinced that none of this has escaped his notice, because it was not done in a corner."[29]

Paul emphasized that the miracles and resurrection of Jesus were "not done in a corner" because there had been many witnesses: if Paul were making it up, there were many people who could refute him, and if he weren't making it up, there were many people who could confirm the truth of his statements.

Moreover, since there had already been widespread reports of Jesus' miracles, which Paul was certain the Roman and Jewish leaders had also heard, he could confidently claim that "none of this has escaped [their] notice." Note also that Paul didn't believe in Jesus because "it worked for him"—he was in chains and facing his possible execution for political dissidence!

In fact, in response to King Agrippa's teasing question, "Do you think that in such a short time you can persuade me to become a Christian?", Paul made this statement reminding us of his imprisonment for the cause of Christ: "Short time or long—I pray to God that not only you but all who are listening to me today may become what I am, except for these chains."[30] Paul believed not because he wanted it to be true, but because he knew it to be true. He himself experienced the risen Jesus and talked with others who had similar eyewitness experiences.

EYEWITNESS STATEMENTS ELSEWHERE IN THE NEW TESTAMENT

In addition to the Book of Acts and Luke's Gospel, other eyewitness claims can be found in Paul's letters to the first Christian churches, which scholars agree are the earliest documents of the New Testament. Paul was executed in Rome in the mid-60's,[31] but he had begun preaching and writing letters to the first Christians a few decades before his death and only a short time after Jesus' death.

Paul includes one of the earliest statements of Christian beliefs, called a *creed*, in the first letter he wrote to the new church in Corinth,

THE SHORTEST LEAP

which most scholars believe was written between 53 and 57.[32] However, the creed that Paul quotes ("passes on") was originally written much earlier. Paul introduces the creed with these words: "For what I received [*paralambanō*] I passed on [*paradidōmi*] to you as of first importance": These were Greek technical terms that indicated that material was being passed along by oral tradition from the eyewitnesses. The original audience would have easily recognized that Paul was passing on important oral tradition that had been faithfully memorized and carefully controlled to prevent distortion.[33]

He then continues with the creed, which many scholars believe most likely originated within a few years of Jesus' death:

> that Christ died for our sins according to the Scriptures, that he was buried, that he was raised on the third day according to the Scriptures, and that he appeared to Peter, and then to the Twelve.

Paul then appends the following to the creed that had been "passed down" to him:

> After that, he appeared to more than five hundred of the brothers at the same time, most of whom are still living, though some have fallen asleep [a common ancient metaphor for dying]. Then he appeared to James, then to all the apostles, and last of all he appeared to me also.[34]

Paul is essentially saying, "We're not making this up. More than five hundred of us saw him!"

Craig Blomberg, one of the foremost experts on the biographies of Jesus, explains how early this creed was in circulation among the Christian church:

> If the crucifixion was as early as A.D. 30, Paul's conversion was about 32.... His first meeting with the apostles in Jerusalem would have been about A.D. 35. At some point along there, Paul was given this creed, which had already been formulated and was being used in the early church.[35]

The early date of this creed, along with the claims it makes, give solid evidence that soon after Jesus' death—within as little as a few years—Christians were proclaiming the truth of his resurrection. In other words, the belief that Jesus physically rose from the dead wasn't legendary material that developed over time as church leaders embellished earlier documents to suit their purposes.

An additional example of eyewitness claims comes from the author of the First Epistle of John. The majority of scholars believe this document was written between AD 75 and 100 by the same author as the Gospel of John, who was most likely Jesus' original disciple John.[36] But whether or not he was the original disciple John, the author of First John makes it quite clear at the very beginning of the document that he was an eyewitness of Jesus:

> That which was from the beginning, which we have heard, which we have seen with our eyes, which we have looked at and our hands have touched—this we proclaim concerning the Word of life. The life appeared; we have seen it and testify to it, and we proclaim to you the eternal life, which was with the Father and has appeared to us. We proclaim to you what we have seen and heard, so that you also may have fellowship with us.[37]

Even though the author is more theological in his explanation—for example in his use of "the Word of life" to mean Jesus—this does not read like a work of fiction. Notice how many times he emphasizes objective observations, with the words "appeared," "seen," "touched," and "heard." What reason would the author possibly have to invent such stories? The only things John stood to gain by his writings were criticism, ostracism, suffering, and death.

The Gospel of John also contains claims of truthfulness. Consider for example the following statement, written by the author about himself:

> The man who saw it has given testimony, and his testimony is true. He knows that he tells the truth, and he testifies so that you also may believe.[38]

If the author of the Gospel of John really did witness what he is describing—if Jesus really did die on the cross and rise again on the third day—he certainly would have understandable and unselfish reasons to try to convince you that his testimony is true. You can sense his urging the reader to believe him and not just assume it's too good to be true.

Interestingly, the author of John doesn't give a name to one of the disciples, whom he calls "the disciple whom Jesus loved"[39] or "another disciple."[40] The second to last verse of John clarifies that this "other disciple" is the one who wrote the Gospel:

> Peter turned and saw that the disciple whom Jesus loved was following them. (This was the one who had leaned back against Jesus at the supper and had said, "Lord, who is going to betray you?")... This is the disciple who testifies to these things and who wrote them down. We know that his testimony is true.[41]

F. F. Bruce, one of the most prominent biblical scholars of the twentieth century, uses the following logic to identify this unnamed disciple as Jesus' disciple John: Because this "beloved disciple" was present at the Last Supper,[42] and because the "Synoptic Gospels" (Matthew, Mark, and Luke[43]) indicate that only the twelve disciples were at the Last Supper, we can conclude that the beloved disciple was one of the twelve. Moreover, this disciple was most likely one of the three disciples who had the closest relationship with Jesus: that is, Peter, James, or John. Peter is clearly distinguished from the unnamed disciple three times,[44] and James was martyred by AD 44, long before the Gospel of John was composed. Therefore, the beloved disciple is most likely John.[45]

Another reason we can trust that the Gospel of John was written by the disciple John is that it records many of Jesus' private conversations that aren't mentioned in the other Synoptic Gospels. (In fact, the author of John probably knew of these earlier Gospels, which explains why he sought to supplement their stories rather than simply retell the same ones.[46])

The private conversations that are unique to John's Gospel include Jesus' dialog with Nicodemus in John 3, his talk with the Samaritan woman at the well in John 4, the healing of the blind man in John 9, the teaching about the Good Shepherd in John 10, the occasion when Jesus washed his disciples' feet in John 13, the discussion of the way to the Father in John 14, the teaching of the vine and the branches in John

15, the explanation of the work of the Holy Spirit in John 16, and Jesus' prayers in John 17. Since these conversations aren't recorded in the other Synoptic Gospels, it is likely that the Gospel of John indeed provides eyewitness testimony from the disciple John, who had been one of the few people present at these events.[47]

Moreover, as the only disciple to live to old age, John would have been alive to write down his testimony at the end of the first century, the date that scholars give this Gospel. To further support the authorship of the Gospel of John by the disciple John, Irenaeus (the late-second-century bishop who had been instructed by Polycarp, who had in turn been instructed by John) makes this claim: "John—the Lord's own follower, the one who leaned against his chest—composed the Gospel while living in Ephesus, in Asia."[48]

In addition to Irenaeus, many other second-century writers attribute the authorship of the Gospel of John to Jesus' original disciple John, including Clement of Alexandria (c. 150-c. 211), Theophilus of Antioch (mid-second century), Tertullian of Carthage (c. 160-c. 220), and the Gnostic Heracleon of Italy (second half of the second century).[49]

The New Testament therefore clearly passes the internal evidence test of historicity because the authors make numerous claims to convince their readers that they were being truthful reporters of eyewitness testimony. The New Testament actually passes the internal evidence test far better than other historical documents, since the claims of its authors put them in grave danger of being killed. In fact, it is a well-supported historical fact that ten of the eleven original disciples of Jesus (the original twelve minus Judas Iscariot, the one who betrayed Jesus) were martyred, and there is no evidence that any of them ever recanted their belief in Jesus' resurrection. While it is relatively common for people to die for a tightly held belief, no one would die for something they know is a lie.

So, the authors claim to be telling the truth, and they're willing to die for something they insist they had seen with their own eyes. But are these claims of truth really true? Are there other ways to determine whether these stories are really based on truthful eyewitness reportage? Do we have evidence that substantiates the New Testament authors' claims?

Indeed, we do.

Questions for Comprehension and Discussion

1. How is the Bible consistent in its message, despite the variety of historical periods, authors, literary styles, and topics? Can you summarize the main storyline of the Bible?
2. What is *general revelation*, and how does it differ from *specific revelation*? What types of information about God do each convey?
3. How is Christianity unique among world religions in that the truth of its claims depends on historical events? Why does it matter so much to the validity of Christianity that Jesus really existed, that he died on the cross, and that he rose again?
4. What are the three tests of historicity that historiographers use to determine whether a historical document is truthful and accurately describes events that actually happened?
5. Why is it so important that the authors of the New Testament documents claim to have been eyewitnesses of the events they record?
6. Why does it matter that the author of the Books of Luke and the Acts of the Apostles really was Luke, the doctor who accompanied Paul on his travels, including his journey to Rome?
7. Who was Theophilus, and why did the author of Luke and Acts sound desperate to make him believe that what he was writing wasn't made up?
8. Can you name at least five instances in Luke, John, Acts, and 1 John where the author claims to have been an eyewitness of Jesus or to have interviewed eyewitnesses?
9. What is a creed, and why do scholars believe that 1 Corinthians 15 contains one of the earliest Christian creeds? Why does it matter that it was written so soon after Jesus' death?
10. How many of Jesus' original disciples (except Judas Iscariot) were killed because they refused to recant? What is the difference between dying for a strongly held belief and dying for something that you have seen with your own eyes?

CHAPTER 5 ENDNOTES

1. 2 Peter 1:16.
2. Carl Sagan (writer/host), "Encyclopaedia Galactica," *Cosmos: A Personal Voyage*. PBS Episode 12. 01:24 minutes in. December 14, 1980.
3. Norman L. Geisler and William E. Nix, *A General Introduction to the Bible* (Chicago: Moody Press, 1986), 28.
4. See Romans 1:18.
5. Psalm 19:1-4.
6. Wayne Grudem, *Systematic Theology: An Introduction to Biblical Doctrine* (Grand Rapids, MI: Zondervan, 1994), 123.
7. Acts 26:24.
8. *The American Heritage Dictionary of the English Language, Fourth Edition*. Retrieved from Dictionary.com: https://www.dictionary.com/browse/historiography.
9. 1 Corinthians 15:19. See also 1 Corinthians 15:6-18 and 29-32.
10. F. F. Bruce, *The New Testament Documents: Are They Reliable?* (Grand Rapids, MI: Eerdmans, 1981), 2.
11. From C. Sanders, *Introduction to Research in English Literary History* (New York: Macmillan Co., 1952) as referenced in Josh McDowell, *The New Evidence That Demands a Verdict* (Nashville, TN: Thomas Nelson Publishers, 1999), 33.
12. According to N. T. Wright, "No Second-Temple Jewish texts speak of the Messiah being raised from the dead. Nobody would have thought of saying, 'I believe that so-and-so really was the Messiah, therefore he must have been raised from the dead." (N. T. Wright, *The Resurrection of the Son of God* [Minneapolis, MN: Fortress Press, 2003], 25.)
13. The very first followers of Jesus weren't called "Christians," but instead were referred to as believers in or followers of Christ Jesus (or "Messiah"). At first, their movement or sect was called "the Way" (see Acts 9:2, 19:9, 23, 24:14, 22), which is probably a reference to Isaiah 40:3 ("Prepare the way of the Lord."). The followers of Jesus were first called "Christians" or "Messianists" in Antioch, Syria, as noted in Acts 11:26.
14. See Lee M. McDonald, *The Formation of the Christian Biblical Canon: Revised and Expanded Edition* (Peabody, MA: Hendrickson, 1995), 209-210.
15. Colossians 4:14.
16. See Irenaeus, *Against Heresies* 3.1.1 and 3.11.8-9, in Alexander Roberts and James Donaldson, eds., *The Ante-Nicene Fathers*, reprint ed. (Grand Rapids, MI: Eerdmans, 1978-1980). Available online at http://www.newadvent.org/fathers/0103301.htm and http://www.newadvent.org/fathers/0103311.htm. For a defense of Irenaeus' claims, see Richard Bauckham, *Jesus and the*

17 *Eyewitnesses: The Gospels as Eyewitness Testimony* (Grand Rapids, MI: Eerdmans, 2006).

17 Quoted by Eusebius, *Church History*, 5.20.4-7. Translation from R.M. Grant, *Second Century Christianity: A Collection of Fragments* (London: SPCK, 1946), 115-16. Cited in Bauckham, *Jesus and the Eyewitnesses*, 456.) For more information on the relationship between Irenaeus, Polycarp, and the original disciples of Jesus, see Bauckham, *Jesus and the Eyewitnesses*, Chapter 17 "Polycrates and Irenaeus on John".

18 Acts 1:1-3.

19 Richard Bauckham notes that research by scholar Loveday Alexander demonstrates that the beginning of Luke's Gospel more closely resembles the prefaces of technical or professional documents, with which Luke, a doctor, would have been quite familiar. However, scholars still consider the preface to the Gospel of Luke a strong indication that Luke intended that both his Gospel and the Acts of the Apostles should be considered historical documents, in that the preface still contains terminology and concepts typical of Greek historiography. For a more detailed discussion of Luke's preface, see Bauckham, *Jesus and the Eyewitnesses*, 116-124.

20 Luke 1:1-4.

21 According to chapter 28 of the Acts of the Apostles, Luke accompanied Paul by ship to Rome, where Luke may have composed both Acts and the Gospel of Luke. According to prominent Biblical scholar F. F. Bruce, "Luke's arrival with Paul in Rome suggests itself a fitting occasion for Luke's taking in hand to draw up his orderly and reliable account of Christian beginnings. If the official and cultured classes of Rome knew anything of Christianity before, they probably dismissed it as a disreputable eastern cult; but the presence in the city of a Roman citizen [Paul], who had appealed to Caesar for a fair hearing in a case which involved the whole question of the character and aims of Christianity, made it necessary for some members of these classes to examine Christianity seriously. The 'most excellent Theophilus,' to whom Luke dedicated his twofold history, was possibly one of those who were charged with investigating the situation, and such a work as Luke's, even in a preliminary draft, would have been an invaluable document in the case." (Bruce, *The New Testament Documents*, 41.)

22 Kenneth L. Barker and John R. Kohlenberger III, *NIV Bible Commentary, Volume 2: The New Testament* (Grand Rapids, MI: Zondervan, 1994), 211.

23 Acts 1:21-22.

24 Acts 2:32.

25 Acts 3:15.

CHAPTER 5: PLEASE BELIEVE ME!

26. Acts 4:18-20.
27. Acts 5:30, 32.
28. Acts 10:39-43.
29. Acts 26:25-26.
30. Acts 26:28-29.
31. This is based on the writings of Eusebius of Caesarea in the fourth century. Eusebius claimed that Paul was beheaded under the Roman Emperor Nero, who reigned from 54 to 68. Paul's martyrdom under Nero is confirmed by the following other sources: Lactantius, *Of the Manner in Which the Persecutors Died* II (third century); John Chrysostom, *Concerning Lowliness of Mind* 4 (fourth century); Sulpicius Severus, *Chronica* II.28–29 (late third century to early fourth century).
32. "The First Epistle to the Corinthians," *The International Standard Bible Encyclopedia*, ed. James Orr, 1915.
33. Timothy Paul Jones, *Misquoting Truth: A Guide to the Fallacies of Bart Ehrman's Misquoting Jesus* (Downers Grove, IL: InterVarsity Press, 2007), 91.
34. 1 Corinthians 15:3-8.
35. In an interview with Craig Blomberg, Lee Strobel, *The Case for Christ* (Grand Rapids, MI: Zondervan, 1998), 35.
36. The early church father Irenaeus quotes from First John at length and attributes its authorship to John, the original disciple of Jesus. (See Irenaeus, *Against Heresies*, 3.16.5, 8, available online at http://www.newadvent.org/fathers/0103316.htm.) The Muratorian Canon (c. AD 170) also attributes the authorship of both First John and the Gospel of John to the original disciple John. For a more comprehensive defense of the authorship of John's Gospel and First John, see Leon Morris, *The Gospel According to St. John, New International Commentary* (Grand Rapids, MI: Eerdmans, 1971), 8-30.
37. 1 John 1:1-4.
38. John 19:35.
39. John 13:23, 19:26-27, 20:2, 21:7, 20.
40. John 18:15.
41. John 21:20, 24.
42. See John 13:23.
43. Because they can be arranged synoptically and therefore can easily be studied together, the Gospels of Matthew, Mark, and Luke were first called the "Synoptic Gospels" by the textual scholar J. J. Griesbach in 1774 (from Bruce, *The New Testament Documents*, 27f).
44. John 13:24, 20:2, and 21:20.
45. Bruce, *The New Testament Documents*, 45.

[46] Ibid, 53.
[47] Normal L. Geisler and Frank Turek, *I Don't Have Enough Faith to Be an Atheist* (Wheaton, IL: Crossway Books, 2004), 263.
[48] Eusebius, *Church History*, 5.8.
[49] Bruce, *The New Testament Documents*, 48.

Testimony should be treated as reliable until proven otherwise. First, trust the word of others, then doubt if there are good reasons for doing so.

—Richard Bauckham, New Testament scholar, Cambridge University[1]

Rather than love, than money, than fame, give me truth.

— Henry David Thoreau, *Walden*[2]

6

Eyewitness Details

We now turn to additional internal evidence that attests to the reliability and historicity of the New Testament. Not only are there numerous claims by the authors of the New Testament documents that they were writing down what actually happened—what they saw with their own eyes—but there are many other clues within the documents as to their historical reliability. In this chapter, we will examine three characteristics of the biblical record that are typical of eyewitness accounts and atypical of concocted stories: (1) they mention details that are irrelevant to the story, (2) they include embarrassing details that the writers would never have included if the stories were concocted, and (3) they contain details that would confuse or even turn away potential converts.

INCLUSION OF IRRELEVANT DETAILS

Modern readers are accustomed to fictional narratives that use detailed description to embellish a story in order to make it more realistic. But this technique is a very recent literary invention. Ancient fiction writers only included details that were necessary to further the plot. C. S. Lewis, who taught literature and mythology at Oxford University, explains how these secondary details demonstrate that the Gospels contain eyewitness testimony:

> I have been reading poems, romances, vision literature, legends, and myths all my life. I know what they are like. And I know none of them is like this. There are

CHAPTER 6: EYEWITNESS DETAILS

only two possible views of these gospel texts. Either this is reportage pretty close to the facts.... Or else, some unknown writer... without known predecessors or any successors suddenly anticipated the whole technique of modern novelistic, realistic narrative. The reader who doesn't see this has simply not learned how to read.[3]

In other words, because the Gospels contain many details that aren't essential to the story, it is very likely that someone actually noticed the details while observing the event. An ancient fiction writer wouldn't think to include such details. It makes much more sense that an eyewitness must have remembered them while recounting the story.

It is human nature for you to remember small details of momentous events that had a deep emotional impact on you. These types of memories are sometimes called "flashbulb" memories. For example, many people have clear memories of exactly where they were and what they were doing when they first heard that John F. Kennedy had been shot or that terrorists had flown planes into the World Trade Center towers. Unfortunately, the majority of these commonly held historical flashbulb memories are related to tragic events that characterize the fallen world.

According to psychological research, our memories are most detailed and accurate when the remembered event falls into one or more of these categories:

1. The remembered event was unique or unusual.
2. The remembered event had important consequences for our lives.
3. The remembered event had an emotional impact on us.
4. After experiencing the event, we repeatedly told others about it or "rehearsed" it in our own minds.

Moreover, our recollections of these types of events generally have several characteristics:

1. They contain vivid imagery.
2. They contain irrelevant detail.
3. They can be told either from our own point of view or from the perspective of another outside observer of the event.

4. The exact date or timing of the event is often not remembered.
5. They are extremely accurate when reporting the general "gist" of the event, even if some of the exact details are not accurate.⁴

Interestingly, not only were the events in the Gospels unique, consequential, and emotionally charged, but those who experienced them repeatedly told others about them soon after they occurred. Moreover, while the Gospel stories may not contain the vivid imagery we would expect in the best modern, novelistic fiction, they contain many irrelevant details and are told from a diverse array of perspectives, features that are atypical of mythological accounts.

Let's look at a few examples of small details in the Gospel record that carry no thematic, doctrinal, or historic significance. Mark records the miracle of Jesus calming the Sea of Galilee and prefaces it with this description: "Jesus was in the stern, sleeping on a cushion."⁵ Does the cushion have any significance? It makes no difference to the story—in fact, it seems redundant—and so this detail was most likely included because the eyewitness remembered it when recounting the experience.

In John's Gospel, we read that Peter tried to defend Jesus when soldiers came to arrest him and take him to be crucified. John writes: "Then Simon Peter, who had a sword, drew it and struck the high priest's servant, cutting off his right ear. (The servant's name was Malchus.)"⁶ A short while later, we read about Peter's denial of Jesus, and John writes, "One of the high priest's servants, a relative of the man whose ear Peter had cut off, challenged him, 'Didn't I see you with him in the garden?'"⁷ One can imagine an ancient writer mentioning the name of an important official, perhaps to bolster his document's credibility. But what is gained by naming a mere servant? And why include the relationship between this servant and an unnamed man who occurs later in the story? The best explanation is the least dramatic: John happened to know the man's name and knew that he was related to another servant also in the account.

In fact, the frequent mention of named individuals alongside unnamed individuals throughout the Gospels is strong evidence that they record eyewitness testimony. This is the case made by Richard Bauckham, who earned his Ph.D. from Cambridge University and is one of the foremost scholars on the reliability of the Gospels. In his recent book, *Jesus and the Eyewitnesses*, Bauckham publishes the results of a detailed study of the dozens of names in the New Testament that belong neither to

CHAPTER 6: EYEWITNESS DETAILS

important historical figures nor to Jesus' disciples, noting that the names in the New Testament not only accurately reflect first-century Jewish and Greek names, but they also occur in the same relative frequency in the New Testament as in the Palestinian world at the time.[8] In Bauckham's opinion, the numerous named individuals in the Gospels are significant because "they indicate the eyewitness sources of the individual stories in which they occur."[9] In other words, certain people are named because they were the original eyewitnesses of the story being recounted, and their names served as a way to document the source of the story.

Another example of an irrelevant detail comes from the description of Jesus' burial. Describing the events after Jesus' crucifixion, John writes: "Later, Joseph of Arimathea asked Pilate for the body of Jesus. He was accompanied by Nicodemus, the man who earlier had visited Jesus at night. Nicodemus brought a mixture of myrrh and aloes, about seventy-five pounds."[10] In this case, the names are expected, since they are of important or wealthy men (though they were also the likely eyewitness sources of this information). But another detail—the number of pounds of spices—would not have been included if this were a work of fiction.

After Jesus' resurrection, John records that Peter and several other disciples were out on the fishing boat when the risen Jesus appeared to them on the shore. He states that Peter "wrapped his outer garment around him (for he had taken it off) and jumped into the water."[11] It would make more sense to read that Peter removed his outer garment before swimming to shore. The only logical reason to mention this unexpected detail was that Peter actually did, odd as it seems, put his outer garment back on before jumping in the water.

A few sentences later, John writes, "So Simon Peter climbed back into the boat and dragged the net ashore. It was full of large fish, 153, but even with so many the net was not torn."[12] Biblical scholars over the years have tried to figure out the spiritual significance of 153, but to no avail. If there is no special meaning to the number 153, why even mention it? The most logical reason is also the most mundane: it was simply a tally taken by career fishermen, as remembered by one of them (possibly Peter himself).

Notice that most of the examples of unimportant details above are from the Gospel of John, which skeptics believe is less trustworthy in its description of Jesus. It was written later than the Synoptic Gospels (Matthew, Mark, and Luke) and contains many more claims that Jesus is God. Its later date has caused skeptics to claim that the deity of Jesus must have been an invention of later church leaders, who thought this doctrine would be a good way to attract converts and increase the power of the Christian church.

The first problem with this theory is that there is solid evidence that the Gospel of John was completed by the end of the first century, while some eyewitnesses of Jesus were still alive and able to dispute its claims. It generally requires centuries for legendary material about ancient historical figures to develop—a few decades would not allow sufficient time for a legend to evolve.[13] A second problem is that the Synoptic Gospels and the even earlier letters of the apostle Paul also make it very clear that the first Christians worshiped Jesus as God, even within a few years of his crucifixion.

Though there are many other irrelevant details throughout the gospels, one other detail is especially interesting for our purposes. After Mary Magdalene delivered the astounding news that Jesus was alive again, Peter and John ran to the tomb. This is how John describes it:

> So Peter and the other disciple [John] started for the tomb. Both were running, but the other disciple outran Peter and reached the tomb first. He bent over and looked [*blepō*] in at the strips of linen lying there but did not go in. Then Simon Peter came along behind him and went straight into the tomb. He saw [*theōreō*] the strips of linen lying there, as well as the cloth that had been wrapped around Jesus' head. The cloth was still lying in its place, separate from the linen. Finally the other disciple, who had reached the tomb first, also went inside. He saw [*horaō*] and believed.[14]

In this account, John mentions the strips of linen that had been wrapped around Jesus' body, along with the cloth that had been wrapped around Jesus' head. The mention that the cloth was "still lying in its place, separate from the linen" implies that they were not lying in a pile on the floor, as you would expect if someone had removed the linen strips and cloth from the body. And when Peter and John enter and see the scene, what they saw was sufficient to cause them to believe Jesus was alive. It could very well have been the position of the linen strips and the cloth that convinced Peter and John. For one thing, if someone had stolen the body, which is the most probable reason Jesus was no longer in the tomb, why would the thief have unwrapped the body?

A second reason the linen strips may have caused John and Peter to believe Jesus had risen from the dead is the way the linen strips and cloth were laying in place. It may have looked like the body had risen right through them, causing them to fall into place as if the body had just disappeared within them. (This is similar to how the Gospels describe Jesus' body later in John 20, when John implies that Jesus walked through the walls: "Though the doors were locked, Jesus came and stood among them."[15])

Another interesting point is that John uses the Greek verb, *theōreō*, for the English word "saw" to describe what Peter did when "he *saw* the linen cloths." This word is not one of the two words that were usually used to describe seeing, *horaō* or *blepō*, but instead describes a type of seeing that involves investigation or questioning, typical of what a detective would do when looking at crime scene evidence. (Appropriately, this Greek word *theōreō* is the source of the English word "to theorize.")

Another irrelevant detail is how John emphasizes that he beat Peter in the foot race and arrived at the tomb first. This strikes me as the type of detail a competitive young man would want to include!

Ancient works of fiction would not include the incidental and irrelevant details that are found throughout all four Gospels. Ancient writers would not invent a story and purposefully include these types of side notes to make it seem real. The fact that these details are there gives us much greater reason to trust that these stories are not invented but are instead truthful accounts of what actually happened.

INCLUSION OF EMBARRASSING DETAILS

A second reason we can trust that the documents of the New Testament were neither concocted to begin with nor altered over the years by church leaders is that they include many details that would reflect poorly on the early Christians. Historiographers call this the *criterion of embarrassment*, which is one of the primary criteria by which you can determine the authenticity of a historical claim. According to this criterion, a document is more likely to be true if the author makes embarrassing, humiliating, or counterproductive statements about himself or another person or event with which he is aligned. You can trust these embarrassing statements are truthful, for why would the author invent them, if they could only harm the cause he was promoting?

When you apply this principle to the Gospels, they sound like eyewitness testimony recorded by authors who placed a high value on telling the truth, even when the truth would seem unhelpful to their cause. There are numerous examples of how the criterion of embarrassment reveals the reliability of the Gospels. First of all, whether or not he was the Son of God, we would expect Jesus to have the good sense to select a more dedicated and astute group of men as his first representatives. Yet each of the four Gospels repeatedly portrays Jesus' disciples as self-absorbed, foolish, and undependable.

These men, including Peter, James, and John, would hold the first leadership roles in the church, and the Christian church honored them as its first heroes. But the behavior of the first disciples in the Gospels actually reflects poorly on all other Christian leaders. Why, then, didn't the authors of the Gospels make the disciples look more impressive? Or why didn't early church leaders simply alter the original accounts to depict the disciples as worthy of greater respect? The most plausible answers are: (1) the authors wanted to tell the truth no matter how unflattering, and (2) it was not so easy to alter the original documents.

Let's take a look at just a few examples of embarrassing information about the first Christian leaders. All four gospels tell the story of how Peter, whom you may call the most eager and dedicated disciple, denied knowing Jesus three times after Jesus had been arrested and Peter's own life was potentially on the line. In fact, Mark states that Peter "began to call down curses" or "began to curse and swear."[16] The English translation goes easy on Peter. The literal translation from the ancient Greek is that Peter was "anathematizing" [*anathematizō*]. Commentators note that Peter wasn't cursing, but was actually calling down the anathema, or curse of God, on his own head if what he told them—that he didn't know Jesus—wasn't true.[17] Some commentators even believe that Peter was actually calling down curses on Jesus.[18] This is a terrible thing for the most dedicated disciple to do, and one would expect the early church leaders to remove or edit it to portray their leader in a better light. But Peter's denials of Jesus remain in all four Gospels to this day.[19]

Jesus also strongly rebuked Peter at another point, saying, "Get behind me, Satan! You are a stumbling block [*skandalon*] to me; you do not have in mind the things of God, but the things of men."[20] The Greek word *skandalon* is where we get the English word, "scandal," though the original meaning was "stumbling block," "hindrance," or "offense." Jesus rebuked Peter because he didn't want Jesus to have to suffer and die and was determined to convince Jesus that this shouldn't be the plan. Why would the early church leaders make Peter out to be so dense that he thought he could improve on God's plan of salvation?

Jesus repeatedly referred to his disciples as "you of little faith."[21] They fell asleep on him at his moment of greatest need in the Garden of Gethsemane, just before he was arrested and executed. Jesus' "soul was overwhelmed with sorrow to the point of death,"[22] but Peter, James, and John could not stay awake. When Jesus roused them, he asked the question we would be asking too: "Couldn't you men keep watch with me for one hour?"[23] These men are clearly not depicted as impressive models of commitment and dependability that you would expect in builders of a popular religious movement.

Even worse, all of Jesus' disciples abandoned him once he was taken to be crucified. Peter denied him, as mentioned above, and nine others were nowhere to be found. Only one disciple, John, seems to have been present while Jesus was on the cross.[24]

What's more, while the male disciples were still in hiding, it was women followers who were the first to visit his tomb following the Sabbath rest, as recorded in all four Gospels. Women held such a low rank in that society that the courts of law did not accept the testimony of a woman.[25] Yet the documents state that the women were the first to witness the empty tomb. And when they ran to tell the men that Jesus had risen from the dead, the male disciples didn't believe them. You can imagine them saying, "Silly, irrational women! Just because you want him to come back to life doesn't make it happen!"

Luke describes the eleven remaining disciples' initial reaction to the women's report in this way:

> When they came back from the tomb, they told all these things to the Eleven and to all the others. It was Mary Magdalene, Joanna, Mary the mother of James, and the others with them who told this to the apostles. *But they did not believe the women, because their words seemed to them like nonsense.*[26]

They doubted the resurrection, even though Jesus had repeatedly told them he would die and rise again.[27] The disciple Thomas, who has gone down in history as the "doubting Thomas," responded to the news of the risen Jesus by claiming, "Unless I see the nail marks in his hands and put my finger where the nails were, and put my hand into his side, I will not believe it."[28] (By the way, Thomas soon did get his request for solid evidence, causing him to believe and call Jesus, "My Lord and my God!"[29])

Matthew states that some of the original followers of Jesus, perhaps including the eleven primary disciples, *still doubted* even after seeing the risen Jesus:

> Then the eleven disciples went to Galilee, to the mountain where Jesus had told them to go. When they saw him, they worshiped him; but *some doubted*.[30]

If you were an early church leader intent on making yourself and this new religion look good, why record the embarrassing details about the earliest disciples? Wouldn't it make more sense to portray the founders as brave men of the utmost integrity? If you were going to fabricate a resurrection, why would you claim women were the first witnesses when it would only make your story less credible? If you wanted to convince others that Jesus really did rise from the dead, why would you mention that some of his original followers doubted?

All of these details are more consistent with honesty than with concoction. They constitute solid evidence against the claim that the early church leaders either invented these stories or altered them over time. If they had invented or changed these stories, there were many ways they could have done a better job of furthering their cause!

INCLUSION OF CONFUSING DETAILS

We find further evidence that the Gospel stories are truthful and unaltered by the "powers that be" in the many verses throughout the Gospels that would turn off or unnecessarily confuse potential converts. For example, Jesus made several statements that diminished the case that he was God. When Jesus visited his hometown of Nazareth during his ministry, he was unable to do miracles because the people there

CHAPTER 6: EYEWITNESS DETAILS

doubted him. After all, they had seen him grow up as the son of a carpenter—how could he be the Son of God? Mark states:

> Jesus said to them, "Only in his hometown, among his relatives and in his own house is a prophet without honor." *He could not do any miracles there*, except lay his hands on a few sick people and heal them. And he was amazed at their lack of faith.[31]

Why would this account portray Jesus as so powerless, if the early church leaders were so eager to portray Jesus as God? As you may deduce from the passage, commentators note that Jesus' miracles were always in response to faith, so his apparent inability to do miracles in his hometown was not because he did not have the power, but because the people did not have faith.[32] But why leave it in, if it only caused doubt about whether Jesus was all-powerful?

Moreover, when Jesus taught his disciples about his second coming, he admitted that even he, the "Son of God," didn't know when it would happen, saying: "No one knows about that day or hour, not even the angels in heaven, nor the Son, but only the Father."[33] If Jesus was supposed to be divine, why bother mentioning that he wasn't quite omniscient? The scholars' explanation is that the New Testament teaching regarding the incarnation—God taking on human flesh—involved some limits on Jesus' omniscience. Jesus willingly and temporarily set aside some of his knowledge as a part of becoming human and experiencing the same suffering that we humans experience.[34] But, again, why even create a question in anyone's minds about Jesus' omniscience if you were making this up?

What's more, many Christians would eventually face death with more bravery than Jesus appeared to face it. In the Garden of Gethsemane, Jesus prayed that he didn't have to go through with the plan for him to die.[35] Why bother mentioning that Jesus wanted to get out of the ultimate reason he came to earth, to die for his people's sins? Scholars now note that when he prayed in the Garden of Gethsemane, Jesus was not merely facing death; he was about to bear the infinite punishment for the sins of all humanity who trust in him.[36][37] Yes, there is an explanation for Jesus' apparent lack of courage, but someone who was intent on making Jesus out to be God could have easily left out this part.

And when Jesus was hanging on the cross, the Gospel accounts show him crying out in confused desperation, "My God, my God, why have you forsaken me?"[38] Commentators today tell us that at the time of Jesus, there were no chapter and verse numbers in Scripture, but instead it was common to use the first line to reference a section of Scripture. Thus, Jesus quoted the first line of Psalm 22 while he was dying on the cross because he was living out what Psalm 22 foreshadowed, the forsaking of the Son by the Father in order to accomplish the forgiveness of sins.[39] However, if you wanted to make people believe Jesus was God, why make him sound like he doesn't understand what is going on? Why leave these strange comments in if they may potentially cause doubt, controversy, or confusion?

In addition, many of the descriptions of Jesus throughout the Gospels wouldn't have sounded very appealing to potential converts. Mark records that Jesus' mother and brothers thought he was "out of his mind."[40] Matthew records that some people called Jesus "a glutton and a drunkard."[41] Also, Luke describes an event in which a prostitute wiped Jesus' feet with her hair, which could potentially cause people to believe Jesus was allowing her to make a sexual advance.[42] If the early church leaders held so much sway over what the Gospels recorded, why not alter these statements—or just remove them—in order to attract more believers?

We've provided examples so far from the Synoptic Gospels. But the later Gospel of John also contains many statements that could hurt rather than help the new Christian movement. In his historical analysis of John's Gospel, New Testament scholar Craig Blomberg lists details that seem unhelpful at best, and misleading or contradictory at worst, demonstrating that they are most likely historically accurate:[43]

1. Jesus hardly sounded like the infallible God when he said, "By myself I can do nothing; I judge only as I hear, and my judgment is just, for I seek not to please myself but him who sent me. If I testify about myself, my testimony is not valid."[44] Why would church leaders make up statements that could call one of their central doctrines, the divinity of Jesus, into question?
2. Consider how unappealing this statement must have sounded to the original audience: "Jesus said to them, 'I tell you the truth, unless you eat the flesh of the Son of Man and drink his blood, you have no life in you.'"[45]
3. A statement that follows soon thereafter reveals one of the consequences of what Jesus said about his body and blood:

"From this time many of his disciples turned back and no longer followed him."[46] Why mention this if you were inventing these accounts? Why leave it in there if you were a later church leader and it was easy to edit it out (which, by the way, as we will see later, it wasn't)?

4. John states that there were two predominant opinions about Jesus: "Some said, 'He is a good man.' Others replied, 'No, he deceives the people.'"[47] A few verses later, the crowd called Jesus "demon-possessed."[48] Even the kinder description, "good man," isn't quite the picture of divinity that John gives Jesus in other parts of his Gospel, so why include it?

5. When Jesus washes his disciples' feet in John 13, the earliest hearers would have been appalled that a Jewish rabbi like Jesus would lower himself to perform such a menial task, which even Jewish slaves didn't have to do. If John's Gospel were concocted to portray Jesus as God, it's unlikely that this story would have made the cut.

Another compelling reason to trust that the Gospels accurately record Jesus' words is that Jesus was never heard making statements that would have settled key controversies of the early Christian church. If church leaders could so easily alter these documents to suit their purposes, they would likely have put clear dictates in his mouth, such as, "All men should be circumcised," or "Never eat meat that has been sacrificed to pagan idols."[49] Instead, it was left to the disciples to argue and to clarify where the church should stand on these issues.

It is notable that Paul carefully distinguished his own statements from those of Jesus. For example, when Paul was teaching on marriage and divorce, he specifically stated, "I, not the Lord" to clarify that these were his own teachings and that he was not quoting Jesus.[50] This is evidence that the earliest Christians were careful to preserve the teachings of Jesus as distinct from their own.

Based on the occurrence of many irrelevant, embarrassing, and counterproductive details in the Gospel stories about Jesus, we can be more confident that the authors of these documents were recording events truthfully, not concocting them. It is also unlikely that later church leaders altered the documents, if they could have, because they would have changed quite a bit to make their religion more popular.

These details demonstrate that the authors placed a high value on telling the truth, as remembered by eyewitnesses, even when the truth was inconvenient.

Questions for Comprehension and Discussion

1. What are three types of details in the Gospel accounts (covered in this chapter) that support the authors' claims that they are truthfully recording eyewitness testimony about Jesus?
2. According to psychological research, in what circumstances are our memories the most detailed? What are common characteristics of eyewitness accounts of these events, and how are the accounts about Jesus similar?
3. What are examples of unnecessary details that are included in the Gospels? Why do these unnecessary details demonstrate that these stories are eyewitness accounts?
4. What detail did Peter and John notice in the empty tomb that made them believe that Jesus had risen from the dead? Why was this detail so convincing?
5. Why is the Gospel of John considered more likely than the other Synoptic Gospels to be a legend about Jesus? How can you rebut the argument that John's account is legendary?
6. Why does Richard Bauckham believe the inclusion of named individuals (who aren't in positions of power) throughout the Gospels is a sign that they are eyewitness accounts?
7. What is the criterion of embarrassment?
8. What are some examples of embarrassing information in the Gospel accounts that would have been excluded if someone biased in favor of Christianity were inventing them?
9. How do confusing or counterproductive statements in the Gospel accounts support the claim that they were neither concocted nor altered by later church leaders?
10. What are some examples of confusing statements that Christians who wanted to make up a story to win converts would not have included?

CHAPTER 6 ENDNOTES

1. Richard Bauckham, *Jesus and the Eyewitnesses: The Gospels as Eyewitness Testimony* (Grand Rapids, MI: Eerdmans, 2006).
2. Henry David Thoreau, *Walden*, 249. Available online at http://www.literaturepage.com/read/walden-249.html.
3. C. S. Lewis, *Christian Reflections*, Walter Hooper, ed. (Grand Rapids, MI: Eerdmans, 1967), 154-155.
4. Richard Bauckham summarizes these characteristics in *Jesus and the Eyewitnesses*, 330-335. Bauckham cites the following psychology publications as sources for this information: W. F. Brewer, "What Is Recollective Memory?" in D. C. Rubin, ed. *Remembering Our Past: Studies in Autobiographical Memory* (Cambridge: Cambridge University Press, 1996), 19-66; W. F. Brewer, "What is Autobiographical Memory?" in D. C. Rubin, ed., *Autobiographical Memory* (Cambridge: Cambridge University Press, 1986), 25-49; S. A. Christianson and M. A. Safer, "Emotional Events and Emotions in Autobiographical Memories," in Rubin, ed., *Remembering Our Past*, 238; D. Reisberg and F. Heuer, "Memory for Emotional Events," in D. Reisberg and P. Hertel, eds., *Memory and Emotion* (Oxford: Oxford University Press, 2004), 35; B.A. Misztal, *Theories of Social Remembering* (Philadelphia: Open University, 2003), 80-81; M. A. Conway and D. A. Bekerian, "Characteristics of Vivid Memories," in M. M. Gruneberg, P. E. Morris, and R. N. Sykes, eds., *Practical Aspects of Memory*, vol. 1: *Memory in Everyday Life* (Chichester: Wiley, 1988), 519-524; C. R. Barclay, "Truth and Accuracy in Autobiographical Memory," in Gruneberg, Morris, and Sykes, eds., Memory in Everyday Life, 289-93; A. Baddeley, *Human Memory: Theory and Practice* (revised edition; Hove: Psychology, 1997), 218-221.
5. Mark 4:38.
6. John 18:10.
7. John 18:26.
8. See Bauckham, *Jesus and the Eyewitnesses*, Chapters 3 and 4.
9. Ibid., 84.
10. John 19:38-39.
11. John 21:7b.
12. John 21:11.
13. For example, King Arthur is alleged to be a sixth-century British leader, who valiantly fought to defend Britain against Saxon invaders. Historians debate whether King Arthur really was a historical figure or simply a product of folklore and legendary development, especially during the Middle Ages. The earliest historical references to King Arthur date to the ninth and tenth centuries, but the reliability of these sources is debated.

Even if these sources are accurate, they occur *three hundred years after* King Arthur was supposed to have lived, sufficient time for legendary material about him to be inserted. By contrast, the Gospel accounts were written within a few decades of Jesus' life.

14   John 20:6-8.
15   John 20:26.
16   Mark 14:71.
17   D. Guthrie, J. A. Motyer, A. M. Stibbs, and D. J. Wiseman, eds., *The New Bible Commentary: Revised* (London: InterVarsity Press, 1970), 883.
18   R. T. France, *The Gospel of Mark* in the New International Greek Testament Commentary (Grand Rapids, MI: Eerdmans, 2002), 622; R. E. Brown, *The Death of the Messiah*, vol. 2 (New York: Doubleday, 1994), 604-5, as referenced by Bauckham, *Jesus and the Eyewitnesses*, 170.
19   Richard Bauckham makes the case that one of the many reasons we can trust that Peter was the eyewitness source for Mark's Gospel is *because* of this admission of failure. Bauckham writes: "Only by failing as a disciple could Peter come to understand the necessity for the Messiah to take the way of the cross.... In this sense it is not difficult to imagine Peter telling this story of his own failure, perhaps with a corresponding account of his restoration (cf. John 21:1519)." (Bauckham, *Jesus and the Eyewitnesses*, 179.)
20   Matthew 16:23.
21   See Matthew 8:26, 14:31, and 16:8, and Luke 12:28.
22   Matthew 26:38 and Mark 14:34.
23   Matthew 26:40 and similarly, Mark 14: 37b.
24   See John 19:26-27.
25   In *Antiquities* 4.8.15, the Jewish historian Josephus writes, "But let not the testimony of women be admitted, on account of the levity and boldness of their sex, nor let servants be admitted to give testimony on account of the ignobility of their soul; since it is probable that they may not speak the truth, either out of hope of gain, or fear of punishment." Also, in Rosh Hashanah 1.8, the Jewish Talmud records, "Any evidence which a woman [gives] is not valid (to offer), also they are not valid to offer. This is equivalent to saying that one who is Rabbinically accounted a robber is qualified to give the same evidence for a woman." In Sotah 19a, the Talmud states, "Sooner let the words of the Law be burnt than delivered to a woman." And in Kiddushin 82b, the Talmud states, "The world cannot exist without males and without females—happy is he whose children are males, and woe to him whose children are females."
26   Luke 24:9-11.
27   See Matthew 26:32; Mark 9.31, 10.34, 14:28; Luke 18:33, 24:46.
28   John 21:25.

CHAPTER 6: EYEWITNESS DETAILS

29. John 21:28.
30. Matthew 28:16-17.
31. Mark 6:4-6.
32. See Kenneth L. Barker and John R. Kohlenberger III, *NIV Bible Commentary, Volume 2: The New Testament* (Grand Rapids, MI: Zondervan, 1994), 158.
33. Matthew 24:36.
34. For Biblical teaching on the limitations of the incarnation, see Philippians 2:6-8, John 4:34, 5:30, 6:38, and 15:15.
35. See Mark 14:36 and Matthew 26:39.
36. Jesus anticipated the time when he "drink the cup the Father has given to him." The "cup" to which Jesus refers (in Matthew 20:22-23, Mark 10:38-39, and John 18:11) is a common Old Testament symbol for God's just punishment for sin (for example, see Psalm 75:7-8, Isaiah 51:19, 22, and Jeremiah 25:15-16). Because he wasn't simply anticipating pain and death but knew he would soon have to drink this cup, it is understandable why Jesus was experiencing intense stress and why he had the genuine human desire to find another way to accomplish the task.
37. Timothy Keller writes: "On the cross [Jesus] went beyond even the worst human suffering and experienced cosmic rejection and pain that exceeds ours as infinitely as his knowledge and power exceeds ours." Timothy Keller, *The Reason for God* (New York: Penguin Group, 2008), 30.
38. Matthew 27:46 and Mark 15:34.
39. I encourage you to read Psalm 22 to see that Jesus cried out, "My God, my God, why have you forsaken me?" not because he was questioning what was happening to him, but instead because he was *explaining to us what was happening*. Jesus was pointing out to us what he was doing for those who trust in him, allowing God the Father to forsake him so that those who trust in Jesus won't ever be forsaken. We will discuss this psalm in greater detail in Chapter 21.
40. Mark 3:21, 31.
41. Matthew 11:19.
42. See Luke 7:36-39.
43. Craig Blomberg, *The Historical Reliability of John's Gospel* (Downers Grove, IL: InterVarsity Press, 2001).
44. John 5:30-32.
45. John 6:53.
46. John 6:66.
47. John 7:12.
48. John 7:20.

[49] For example, see Acts 15 for the discussion at the first church council meeting in Jerusalem about whether men should be circumcised in order to be saved, and whether or not to eat food that had been sacrificed to idols.
[50] 1 Corinthians 7:12.

When you read the accounts of Mary's unsuspected pregnancy, what is particularly notable... is an underlying tone of realism that runs through the narratives. These seem to be real people, living in real times and places. In contrast the birth stories in Greco-Roman literature have a decidedly legendary flavor to them.

James Tabor, Chair of the Religious
Studies Department, UNC-Charlotte[1]

In the New Testament, the thing really happens. The Dying God really appears—as a historical Person, living in a definite place and time.... The old myth of the Dying God... comes down from the heaven of legend and imagination to the earth of history. It happens—at a particular date, in a particular place, followed by definable historical consequences. We must not be nervous about "parallels" [in other religions].... They ought to be there—it would be a stumbling block if they weren't.

C. S. Lewis, Christian apologist,
novelist, and professor[2]

Not a Myth

Before we proceed with our analysis of how the internal evidence supports the truthfulness of the Gospel accounts of Jesus' life and teachings, it is helpful to provide an overview of the nature of the mythologies of ancient Egypt, Greece, Rome, and Asia Minor. These myths were recorded and embellished in the centuries before and after the life of Jesus, and they therefore offer a point of comparison by which we can evaluate the relative truthfulness of the biblical accounts.

There is another useful reason to take a look at these myths: to evaluate the credence of claims that the beliefs of Christianity grew out of these earlier stories. Some skeptics claim that Jesus is simply a myth, much like other mythological characters such as Zeus, Osiris, and Mithras, and Christians have all been duped into believing that Jesus actually existed. They assert that Jesus was not a real man, let alone God in human form. One example comes from the award-winning book *The Jesus Mysteries*, in which Timothy Freke and Peter Gandy pose the following question:

> Why should we consider the stories of Osiris, Dionysus, Adonis, Attis, Mithras, and other Pagan Mystery saviors as fables, yet come across essentially the same story told in a Jewish context and believe it to be the biography of a carpenter from Bethlehem?[3]

As we aim to demonstrate, the nature of the biblical accounts of Jesus and his early followers are extremely different than the myths of ancient Egypt, Greece, Rome, Phrygia, and Persia. First of all, the

New Testament accounts are more detailed and historically accurate. Moreover, they are also not nearly as bizarre and vulgar as the other myths, which lends them further credibility. In addition, the accounts of Jesus are sufficiently different from other ancient myths that it is illogical to conclude that the myths influenced Christian beliefs. In fact, the "Christ-myth" argument often falls apart because many of the myths with similarities to Christianity were recorded *after* the New Testament documents.

For our overview of ancient mythology, we will focus on the myths that skeptics claim most influenced Christianity: the Egyptian myths about Osiris, Isis, and Horus, the Greek myths (and their Roman counterparts) about Dionysus and Adonis, the Phrygian—and eventually Greek and Roman—myths about Attis, and the Roman "cult of Mithras."

1. Osiris, Isis, and Horus:

Osiris was the ancient Egyptian god of life, death, and fertility. According to the most popular story about Osiris—and there are a few accounts that differ in their primary details—his brother, Set, murders him and drops his coffin into the Nile River. Isis, who is both Osiris' wife and sister, subsequently revives him long enough for him to impregnate her. Unfortunately, Set kills Osiris again, chops him into fourteen pieces, and scatters his parts throughout the world. His faithful wife and sister, Isis, sets out to gather Osiris' fourteen pieces, but only finds thirteen. She puts him (partially) back together in order to give him a proper burial. Osiris then becomes the god of the underworld, never to return to this world.

Their son Horus, who is famous for his falcon head and his "Eye of Horus," was born after Osiris' first "resurrection." Horus thus came to represent new beginnings, and the Osiris-Horus combination became the life-death-rebirth deity, which was associated with the annual harvest. Some people have claimed that the Christian rite of baptism was influenced by the sinking of Osiris' coffin in the Nile, and the Christian belief in Jesus' resurrection was influenced by the story of Osiris' death followed by Horus' birth.

Around 100 AD, the Greek biographer Plutarch, who had become a citizen of Rome, recorded much of what we know about the religious rites of the worshipers of Osiris, Isis, and Horus in his work, *On the Worship of Isis and Osiris*. Here is one sample of Plutarch's record, describing the fourteenth piece of Osiris that Isis was unable to locate:

> Of the parts of Osiris's body the only one which Isis did not find was the male member, for the reason that this had been at once tossed into the river, and the lepidotus, the sea-bream, and the pike had fed upon it; and it is from these very fishes the Egyptians are most scrupulous in abstaining. But Isis made a replica of the member to take its place, and consecrated the phallus, in honour of which the Egyptians even at the present day celebrate a festival.[4]

To help you make a comparison between these stories and Jesus' physical resurrection, it's helpful to know that, according to Plutarch, worshipers of Osiris sought to be buried in the same ground where the body of Osiris was located, indicating that they never believed his physical body had risen again.[5] This is consistent with the ancient Egyptians' belief that a person's personality, composed of the *Ba* and the *Ka*—that is, not their physical body—was what lived on in the after-life. The body remained to rot in the grave, which clearly differs from the bodily resurrection of Jesus.[6]

Ancient historian N. T. Wright clarifies the difference between Jesus' resurrection and the dying and rising fertility gods in the following way:

> From very early times, in Egypt and elsewhere, some of the major religions centred their symbols, stories and praxis on the cycles of nature, and on the gods and goddesses who were believed to enact, or to have enacted, these cycles themselves.... Did any worshiper in these cults, from Egypt to Norway, at any time in antiquity, think that actual human beings, having died, actually came back to life? Of course not. These multifarious and sophisticated cults enacted the god's death and resurrection as a metaphor, whose concrete referent was the cycle of seed-time and harvest, of human reproduction and fertility.... Nobody actually expected

the mummies to get up, walk about and resume normal living; nobody in that world would have wanted such a thing, either.[7]

The Egyptians may have believed in a resurrection of Osiris, but only insofar as it symbolized the cycle of the seasons and the changing productivity of their fields.

2. Dionysus:

Also known as Bacchus, Dionysus was the Greek god of the vine, the grape harvest, winemaking and wine, fertility, ritual madness, religious ecstasy, and theater. Depending on the version of the myth, he was either the son of Zeus, the king of the gods, and the princess Semelê, or the son of Zeus and Persephone, the goddess of death. According to the first version, Zeus disguises himself as a human and impregnates Semelê. When Zeus' wife, Hera, finds out about the pregnancy, she slyly suggests to Semelê that she ask Zeus to reveal himself fully to her (knowing it would kill Semelê, since mere mortals cannot look at an undisguised god and live). Zeus finally agrees to Semelê's request, and she is then reduced to ashes because she could not endure the splendor of his godly radiance. However, Zeus is able to rescue their baby from her womb and sews him into his thigh. Dionysus is born a few months later upon his release from Zeus' thigh.

In Greek and Roman art, Dionysus is generally depicted as arriving by a chariot pulled by tigers or lions with a procession of *maenads* and *satyrs*. The maenads, whose name is literally translated "the raving ones," were females who had nursed Dionysus from his youth and whom Dionysus would put into a state of "ecstatic frenzy" as they danced and drank. The satyrs are described as naked men with the tail and ears of a horse, snub noses, mane-like hair, and a permanent erection. They were notoriously ribald lovers of wine, music, dancing, and pursuing women, often attempting to rape women and nymphs. They are also sometimes depicted while they are masturbating or engaging in bestiality. Over time, the satyrs became more goat-like and evolved into fauns, men with the legs and horns of goats.

One interesting story about Dionysus is found in "Homeric Hymn 7 to Dionysus," a Greek epic written between the 7th and 4th centuries BC.

Because Dionysus was so handsome, some Aegean pirates believed he was a prince and kidnapped him (when he was disguised as a mortal), hoping to earn a ransom or to sell him into slavery. After setting sail with their prisoner, the pirates discovered they could not bind him with even the strongest ropes. Dionysus caused a vine to grow, blossom, and bear fruit, winding itself around the sails and mast. The story proceeds as follows:

> But the god [Dionysus] changed into a dreadful lion there on the ship, in the bows, and roared loudly: amidships also he showed his wonders and created a shaggy bear which stood up ravening, while on the forepeak was the lion glaring fiercely with scowling brows. And so the sailors fled into the stern and crowded bemused about the right-minded helmsman, until suddenly the lion sprang upon the master and seized him; and when the sailors saw it they leapt out overboard one and all into the bright sea, escaping from a miserable fate, and were changed into dolphins.[8]

Thus, Dionysus was able to break even the strongest rope that bound him, to change himself into a lion, to conjure up a bear, and to turn men into dolphins.

Some people have claimed that this myth influenced Judaism, even though the accounts in the Bible that describe humans as not being able to survive after looking at God were written in advance of the Dionysus myths. The strength of Dionysus may also have influenced the story of Samson in the biblical book of Judges, but this book is believed to date to approximately 1000 BC, so it also probably pre-dates the *Homeric Hymn 7 to Dionysus*.

Skeptics also theorize that the birth of Dionysus (from Zeus' thigh) contributed to the idea of the virgin birth of Jesus. Christ-myth theorists also claim that Jesus' conversion of water to wine was influenced by Dionysus, who encouraged the consumption of wine. But it is especially unlikely that the first Christians invented or copied the water-to-wine miracle, since on the whole they did not consume alcohol.[9]

Copycat theorists also claim that Dionysus' birthday was December 25, which was why Christians chose that day for Jesus' birthday. The

CHAPTER 7: NOT A MYTH

problem with this theory is that Jesus' earliest followers didn't know his birthday and initially selected January 6 as the date to celebrate his birth. (In fact, the Armenian Apostolic Church still celebrates Christmas on January 6.) The official date of Jesus' birth was changed to December 25 in AD 336, the year before the death of Constantine, the first Christian Roman emperor. Prior to becoming a Christian, Constantine had worshiped the god Sol Invictus, and the temple of Sol Invictus had been dedicated on December 25. Therefore, many historians believe Constantine may have changed the date on which Christians celebrate Jesus' birth so that it would coincide with the pagan holiday on December 25. Instead of banishing pagan celebrations on that day, it was most likely easier to just transition the celebration of Jesus' birth to the existing pagan holiday. So, the fact that Dionysus and Jesus share the same birthday in no way implies that Jesus was a myth modeled on Dionysus.

Let's look at one other way that skeptics see a consistency between Dionysus and Jesus: Both were under investigation by rulers of their day for making claims to deity. Jesus appeared before Pontius Pilate for questioning, while the Theban king Pentheus investigated Dionysus. But even though both did stand trial before powerful political figures, the outcome of each trial differed dramatically. After Jesus' trial, Pontius Pilate remained unhurt, while Jesus was sentenced to death. On the other hand, after investigating Dionysus, King Pentheus was torn limb from limb by mad women, including his mother, Agave, and his aunts, Ino and Autonoë. Because Dionysus had put the women into a crazed state of mind, Agave only realized who her son Pentheus was once she had returned to Thebes with his head on a stick.

The British mythographer Thomas Bulfinch translated and retold this myth in the nineteenth century, basing his story on Ovid's *Metamorphoses*, which had been first published in 8 AD. This is how Bulfinch described the scene that ensued after King Pentheus insisted on going to investigate the worshipers of Bacchus on the mountain of Cithaeron:

> [Pentheus] penetrated through the wood and reached an open space where the chief scene of the orgies met his eyes. At the same moment the women saw him; and first among them his own mother, Agave, blinded by the

> god [Dionysus], cried out, "See there the wild boar, strike the wild boar!" The whole band rushed upon him, and while he now talks less arrogantly, now excuses himself, and now confesses his crime and implores pardon, they press upon him and wound him. In vain he cries to his aunts to protect him from his mother. Autonoë seized one arm, Ino the other, and between them he was torn to pieces, while his mother shouted, "Victory! Victory! We have done it; the glory is ours!"[10]

Note that even here Bulfinch went to great pains to "tone down" the myths he retold so that they would be more suitable for the sensibilities of his audience in the Victorian era.

For the sake of comparison, it is helpful to read the earliest recorded version of the myth, as recorded by the ancient Greek playwright Euripides in the fifth century BC. In the play, *Bacchae*, Pentheus has already been killed and his servant, having returned to the palace, explains how everything went down:

> His mother first, a priestess for the nonce, began the bloody deed and fell upon him; whereon he tore the snood [ribbon] from off his hair, that hapless Agave might recognize and spare him, crying as he touched her cheek, "O mother! it is I, thy own son Pentheus, the child thou didst bear in Echion's halls; have pity on me, mother dear! oh! do not for any sin of mine slay thy own son." But she, the while, with foaming mouth and wildly rolling eyes, bereft of reason as she was, heeded him not; for the god possessed her. And she caught his left hand in her grip, and planting her foot upon her victim's trunk she tore the shoulder from its socket, not of her own strength, but the god made it an easy task to her hands; and Ino set to work upon the other side, rending the flesh with Autonoe and all the eager host of Bacchanals; and one united cry arose, the victim's groans while yet he breathed, and their triumphant shouts. One would make an arm her prey, another a foot with the sandal on it; and his ribs were stripped of flesh

by their rending nails; and each one with blood-dabbled hands was tossing Pentheus' limbs about. Scattered lies his corpse, part beneath the rugged rocks, and part amid the deep dark woods, no easy task to find; but his poor head hath his mother made her own, and fixing it upon the point of a thyrsus, as it had been a mountain lion's, she bears it through the midst of Cithaeron, having left her sisters with the Maenads at their rites.[11]

The reader should have no problem finding the stark differences between Dionysus' effects on his worshipers in this story and Jesus' effects on his worshipers in the stories of the New Testament.

3. ADONIS:

Similar to Osiris-Horus, Adonis is sometimes considered a life-death-rebirth deity, though nowhere in any existing ancient Greek written record is Adonis described as having risen from the dead.[12] While there are multiple accounts of his birth, the most popular version recounts that the goddess Aphrodite encourages a woman named Myrrha to commit incest with her father, Cinyras, the king of Cyprus. (In alternate versions, his name is Theias, and he is the king of Smyrna, or Syria.) After her incestuous act, Myrrha becomes pregnant. When her father discovers that she had deceived him into sleeping with her, he pursues her in a rage. Aphrodite then turns Myrrha into a myrrh tree, Cinyras shoots the tree with an arrow, and Adonis is born from the tree. Some skeptics have suggested that this story influenced the idea of Jesus' virgin birth.

Though there is a brief reference to Adonis in a poem by Sappho that was composed in the sixth century BC, the earliest record that describes the myth of Adonis comes from the Roman poet Publius Ovidius Naso, known simply as Ovid, who lived from 43 BC to AD 17 or 18. To give you a flavor of the narrative, following is the section that describes the love affair between Myrrha and her father and her subsequent transformation into a myrrh tree:

> She left the room impregnated by her father, bearing impious seed in her fatal womb, carrying the guilt she

had conceived. The next night the crime was repeated: nor did it finish there. Eventually, Cinyras, eager to discover his lover after so many couplings, fetching a light, saw his daughter and his guilt, and speechless from grief, he snatched his bright sword out of the sheath it hung in. Myrrha ran, escaping death, by the gift of darkness and secret night.... Tired of living, and scared of dying, not knowing what to pray for, she composed these words of entreaty: "O, if there are any gods who hear my prayer, I do not plead against my well-deserved punishment, but lest, by being, I offend the living, or, by dying, offend the dead, banish me from both realms, and change me, and deny me life and death!" Some god listened to her prayer: certainly, the last request found its path to the heavens. While she was still speaking, the soil covered her shins; roots, breaking from her toes, spread sideways, supporting a tall trunk; her bones strengthened, and in the midst of the remaining marrow, the blood became sap; her arms became long branches; her fingers, twigs; her skin, solid bark. And now the growing tree had drawn together over her ponderous belly, buried her breasts, and was beginning to encase her neck: she could not bear the wait, and she sank down against the wood, to meet it, and plunged her face into the bark.[13]

This is most definitely an interesting and artfully conveyed miracle, quoted primarily to give you a flavor of the ancient myths with which we are comparing the New Testament. But back to Adonis, who is born from the tree his mother became. Because he is so beautiful, Aphrodite, the goddess of love, and Persephone, the goddess of death, argue over who would spend time with him. The dispute is finally settled when they agree that Adonis will spend four months of the year with Aphrodite, four months of the year with Persephone, and four months of the year with the goddess of his choice (he chooses Aphrodite). After Adonis is killed by a wild boar, Aphrodite sprinkles nectar on his body, which causes each drop of Adonis' blood to become a red anemone flower. While there are some variations of the myth that claim Adonis was resurrected from the dead, these didn't appear until the second half of the second century, at least fifty years after the Gospel accounts of Jesus' life had been written.[14]

4. ATTIS:

Attis is another ancient god whom skeptics claim also rose from the dead. One version of the story goes like this: Near the Phrygian city of Pessinos was a mountain called Mount Agdistis. The locals believed that the mountain would become a *daemon*, a supernatural being that was part human. In human form, Agdistis originally had both male and female body parts, but the Olympian gods, fearing him, cut off his male organ and threw it away. His phallus subsequently grew into an almond tree. In her new disfigured state, Agdistis became known as Cybele or Magna Mater ("Great Mother").

Meanwhile, the daughter of the river Sangarios, by the name of Nana, became pregnant when she picked an almond from the tree and put it in her bosom. She gave birth to a son, Attis, whom she then abandoned. Attis was instead reared by a billy goat. Because he was so beautiful, Attis' mother Cybele (formerly the hermaphroditic Agdistis) fell in love with him. Eventually, Cybele caused Attis to go mad and cut off his own genitals. His father-in-law followed suit. In fact, all newly initiated priests of Cybele would perform self-castration in a bloody festival on March 24, known as *Dies Sanguinis*, or "Day of Blood." The worship of Cybele and Attis moved from Phrygia to Greece, and from Greece to Rome, with the Roman senate officially naming Cybele the state goddess in 204 BC.[15] But the senate also pronounced that Roman citizens were not allowed to castrate themselves, so all of the priests of Cybele, known as *Galli*, were either slaves or from Asia Minor.[16]

The earliest written record of this story of Agdistis, Cybele, and Attis is from the second century AD, when it appears in a work by the Greek traveler Pausanias, called *Description of Greece*. After relating one version of the story of Attis, Pausanias continues:

> But the current view about Attis is different, the local legend about him being this. Zeus, it is said, let fall in his sleep seed upon the ground, which in course of time sent

up a demon, with two sexual organs, male and female. They call the demon Agdistis. But the gods, fearing Agdistis, cut off the male organ. There grew up from it an almond-tree with its fruit ripe, and a daughter of the river Sangarius, they say, took of the fruit and laid it in her bosom, when it at once disappeared, but she was with child. A boy was born, and exposed, but was tended by a he-goat. As he grew up his beauty was more than human, and Agdistis fell in love with him. When he had grown up, Attis was sent by his relatives to Pessinus, that he might wed the king's daughter. The marriage-song was being sung, when Agdistis appeared, and Attis went mad and cut off his genitals, as also did he who was giving him his daughter in marriage. But Agdistis repented of what he had done to Attis, and persuaded Zeus to grant that the body of Attis should neither rot at all nor decay.[17]

Though there is a reference to Zeus agreeing not to allow Attis' body to decay, there is no mention of his resurrection in this account (which was recorded after Jesus had already lived anyway). A story about Attis appeared in the third century at the earliest claiming that he was reborn as an evergreen pine tree, but of course, it was too late to have influenced Christianity.[18]

5. MITHRAS:

Finally, let's take a look at the Persian god Mithras, which a few people claim is the god that Christianity most copied as it developed its beliefs. The primary book that pushes this theory is called *The Christ Conspiracy: The Greatest Story Ever Sold*. In it, the late Dorothy Mayne Murdock, also known by her pen name, Acharya S, claims that Mithras was born of a virgin in a cave on December 25, where shepherds subsequently visited him. She also claims he was considered a "great traveling teacher," he had twelve disciples, his followers were promised immortality, he performed miracles, he "sacrificed himself for world peace" as the "great bull of the Sun," and he was buried in a tomb and rose again after three

CHAPTER 7: NOT A MYTH

days. According to Murdock, his followers celebrated his resurrection every year and called him the Good Shepherd, the Way, the Truth, and the Light, the Logos, Redeemer, Savior, Messiah, Creator of the World, God of Gods, the Mediator, Mighty Ruler, King of Gods, Lord of Heaven and Earth, and Sun of Righteousness.

Moreover, Murdock asserts that hundreds of years before Jesus, the followers of Mithras observed Sunday as the "Lord's Day," and their main festival was Easter. In addition, Mithras had a special Eucharist meal at which he claimed, "He who shall not eat of my body nor drink of my blood so that he may be one with me and I with him, shall not be saved."[19]

Let's take a brief look at the misleading, distorted, and unfounded arguments that are used to support the "copycat" theories in books like *The Jesus Mysteries* and *The Christ Conspiracy*. First, let me provide a little background on Mithraism, a Roman mystery religion that coexisted with the earliest Christian believers during the first through fourth centuries AD. Its followers were primarily male soldiers and merchants, and it involved secret rituals and initiation rites that took place in a cave-like structure called a *mithraeum*.

There is very little written documentation of the beliefs of Mithraism, and it has long been a dead religion. Therefore, we know very little about Mithras except what can be gleaned from artistic inscriptions and other iconography. While there was an ancient god called Mithras in Persia around 1400 BC, there is little evidence that the Roman god had anything in common with this older god other than his name.[20]

The earliest Roman Mithraic inscription dates to AD 101, the earliest *mithraea* are dated to the early second century AD, and most of the evidence of Roman Mithraism is found in the second, third, and fourth centuries AD. This suggests that if any religion is copying another, it's Mithraism copying Christianity.[21] As prominent scholar Ronald Nash claimed, "The flowering of Mithraism occurred after the close of the New Testament canon, too late for it to have influenced the development of first-century Christianity."[22] And after looking at the evidence of early Mithraism, archaeologist and historian Richard Gordon concluded, "It is therefore reasonable to argue that Western Mithraism did not exist until the mid-second century, at least in a developed sense."[23]

Not only does she claim that Mithraism existed centuries before Jesus, which it did not, Murdock's list of similarities between Christianity and Mithraism is far from accurate. In the *Proceedings of the First*

International Congress of Mithraic Studies, scholars of Mithraism rejected the "Christian copycat" theories that had been initially proposed by Franz Cumont, the only academic to have extensively studied Mithraism up until the middle of the twentieth century. This group of prominent academic scholars claimed: "The only domain in which we can ascertain in detail the extent to which Christianity imitated Mithraism is that of art."[24] And the artistic copying occurred during the third and fourth centuries, at the earliest. Moreover, it was common in that period for different religious groups to seek to outdo one another in the artistic renderings of their beliefs. Christians may have copied elements of Mithraic art, but that was the extent of their copying.

Contrary to the claims of copycat theorists, Mithras was not born of a virgin but emerged fully-grown from a rock, perhaps creating a cave in the process. Though the idea that Jesus was born in a cave is mentioned in the *Letter of Barnabas*, an early Christian writing that scholars believe was composed between AD 70 and 130, the New Testament never makes this claim.

As mentioned earlier, December 25 had become a common holiday for a variety of religious groups in the Roman Empire, especially after AD 336 when Constantine made it the official day for Christians to celebrate the birth of Jesus.

From Mithraic art, we know that there were indeed shepherds at the birth of Mithras, but all of this art postdates the first century. Since scholars universally agree that the New Testament Gospels about Jesus' life (at least Matthew, Mark, and Luke) were written in the first century, this Mithraic art couldn't have influenced the Gospel writers. (Interestingly, Mithras was supposedly born before the creation of humans, so the fact that shepherds visited him at his birth makes the story even less credible!)

Mithras may very well have been a great traveling teacher, but again, there is no evidence for this belief. Like the gods of other Roman myths, he may have assumed human form and imparted some wisdom about life.

The claim that Mithras had twelve disciples apparently comes from a stone carving of Mithras slaying a bull, which is framed by two vertical rows of six human figures each. Not only was this carving completed after the four Gospels of the New Testament were already written, but many Mithraic scholars believe that the twelve figures correspond to the signs of the zodiac. This is the most logical explanation because there is other evidence that Mithraic rituals incorporated star constellations and signs of the zodiac.[25]

Copycat theorists rely on two main pieces of evidence for the claim that Mithras promised his followers immortality. One is an inscription found in a *mithraeum*: "And us, too, you saved by the spilling of eternal blood."[26] Of course, one of the main reasons people take up any set of beliefs is to achieve immortality, but even this inscription doesn't seem to suggest that the "eternal blood" causes "salvation" in the same sense that Christians believed Jesus' atonement did. Moreover, it's a moot point, since this Mithraic inscription has been dated to no earlier than AD 200, much later than the Christian belief that faith in Jesus leads to eternal life.

Some copycat theorists claim that another practice of Mithraism, a rite called the *taurobolium*, inspired the Christian belief in eternal salvation "through the blood of Jesus." In this rite, the worshipers slaughtered a bull on top of a grate, causing its blood to spill down into a pit below the grate where the Mithraic initiate had been placed. One inscription in a *taurobolium* reads, "*in aeternum renatus*," or "reborn for eternity," which parallels the Christian belief in eternal life through the "blood of the Lamb."

The main problem with this theory, other than the fact that the Christian belief in Jesus' atonement is utterly different from this gruesome ritual, is that the inscription has been dated to AD 375, long after the New Testament documents had been written. According to Swiss scholar Günter Wagner, "The idea of rebirth through the instrumentality of the *taurobolium* only emerges in isolated instances towards the end of the fourth century AD."[27] Again, this looks more like Mithraism borrowed and twisted a few Christian beliefs, rather than the other way around.

As for the claim that Jesus' miracles were a copy of Mithras, which ancient Roman god didn't perform miracles? As we will see in the next chapter, the miracles of Jesus differed greatly from the miracles of mythology. Moreover, there is no evidence that Mithras performed any miracles like calming a storm, walking on water, or turning water into wine.

Despite the "copycat" theorists' claims, Mithras never sacrificed himself, although he did kill a bull. Some have charged that Mithras and the bull were one and the same, so he really did sacrifice himself.

In response to this far-fetched theory, one Mithraic scholar notes that "neither the temples nor the inscriptions give any definite evidence to support this view and only future finds can confirm it."[28] There is also no evidence that Mithras ever died. In his book *Image and Value in the Greco-Roman World*, historian Richard Gordon claims there was "no death of Mithras."[29] If there was no death of Mithras, there can be no resurrection of Mithras.

There is also no evidence that Mithras was ever called the Good Shepherd, the Way, the Truth, and the Light, Redeemer, Savior, Messiah, Creator of the World, God of Gods, Mighty Ruler, King of Gods, Lord of Heaven and Earth, and Sun of Righteousness. Since there are very few written records of Mithraism, copycat theorists somehow derived these names from non-verbal Mithraic art, and they read specifically Christian terms into the iconographic evidence with no proof that these terms were ever used of Mithras.

There is some evidence that Mithras was considered a mediator, but only between the good and bad gods. Christianity, on the other hand, considers Jesus the mediator between God the Father and human beings, and even the earliest Christians denied polytheism, often to the point of death.

In one Mithraic initiation rite, there is a reference to a "Logos," but this term, which means "word" or "logic," was in common use in philosophy at the time. Dating back to 300 BC, the Stoic philosophers of Greece used the term *logos* to describe the reason or logic that pervades the universe. The term was often used in the Greco-Roman world to identify Nature or God. It is in this latter sense that John uses "Logos" as a term for Jesus in the first chapter of his Gospel: "In the beginning was the Word [Logos], and the Word was with God, and the Word was God.... The Word became flesh and made his dwelling among us."[30] Just because Mithraism used the term "Logos" in some of its inscriptions only proves that the religion had been exposed to Greek philosophy, and based on the pattern we've seen, followers of Mithras were likely to steal this term from Christians and apply it to their central god as well.

While it is true that Roman Mithraism did observe Sunday as their sacred day, this post-dates the Christian observance, so if anyone copied anyone, again, it was Mithraism copying Christianity. Mithraism did have a festival at the spring equinox, but this was just one of four equally important festivals that corresponded with each of the four seasons. So, their spring festival wasn't their main holiday, as Easter is for Christians. Moreover, there is no parallel with the Christian celebration of Jesus' resurrection on Easter, since there is no evidence that Mithras was resurrected.

It is true that Mithraism did have a common "sacramental" meal similar to the Christian celebration of Eucharist, but this meal was typical of many pagan religions. Manfred Clauss, professor of ancient history at Free University of Berlin, explains:

> The ritual meal was probably simply a component of regular common meals. Such meals have always been an essential part of religious assembly; eating and drinking together creates community and renders visible the fact that those who take part are members of one and the same group.[31]

Moreover, the earliest evidence for the saying, "He who shall not eat of my body... shall not be saved" comes in the Middle Ages, and even then it isn't attributed to Mithras. The attempts by Freke and Gandy and Murdock to connect this saying to the Roman Mithraic common meal are considered by scholars to be extremely dubious.[32]

Edwin Yamauchi, who is considered one of the foremost experts on ancient history, summarized the primary differences between Mithraism and Christianity in the following way:

> Christianity is quite distinct in that it rose from a Jewish background, which is monotheistic, and it centers around a historical figure who was put to death in a barbaric manner, which is attested in non-Christian sources. Jesus' followers were eyewitnesses in the first generation.... Christianity flourished and expanded in spite of persecution from Roman authorities. It was a new message of love and God's intervention in the world, and it incorporated all people, including slaves and women, the educated and noneducated—unlike Mithraism, which was confined primarily to soldiers.... And it wasn't comfortable, as were the polytheistic

pagan religions, in being eclectic or syncretistic—that is, enfolding beliefs and practices from other religions. That's why, in fact, Christianity was persecuted.[33]

The enormous differences between Christianity and the myths of the ancient world have caused serious scholars of ancient history to confidently dismiss the "copycat theories" as hogwash. Unfortunately, these theories have been re-marketed to a generally gullible mass market that is unaware of the scholarly research that long ago debunked the claim that Jesus is just one myth among many similar ones.

Dr. Michael Grant of Cambridge summarizes the opinion of leading scholars on such theories:

> To sum up, modern critical methods fail to support the Christ-myth theory. It has again and again been answered and annihilated by first rank scholars. In recent years no serious scholar has ventured to postulate the non-historicity of Jesus.[34]

F. F. Bruce, one of the most respected biblical scholars of the last century, concurs:

> Some writers may toy with the fancy of a 'Christ-myth', but they do not do so on the ground of historical evidence. The historicity of Christ is as axiomatic for an unbiased historian as the historicity of Julius Caesar. It is not historians who propagate the 'Christ-myth' theories.[35]

Those who brush off Christianity as "just another myth" demonstrate their ignorance of history and the clear distinction between the Gospels and the literary genre of mythology.

Another tendency of skeptics is to reduce all ancient myths, and Christianity along with them, down to symbolic stories that are helpful in conveying moral lessons to guide our lives and to improve society. While the teachings of Jesus do contain parables to illustrate moral truths, Christianity is far more than simply a set of moral principles.

CHAPTER 7: NOT A MYTH

It is essentially "good news" about historical events—the life, death, resurrection, and ascension of a man named Jesus. And if these events are not historically true, there is really no use in following this man, except in what we can glean from his teachings that makes us enjoy life as long as we're alive. In the absence of historical evidence for Jesus, selfishness should continue to rule the day. As the apostle Paul wrote, if Jesus didn't rise again, "let us eat and drink, for tomorrow we die."[36]

Moreover, many people have tried to excuse the distasteful elements in the ancient myths, like the ones we've discussed in this chapter, by insisting that they were merely employing symbolism to teach moral lessons. But unfortunately, this often was not the case. For example, when Thomas Bulfinch retold the story of how the Titan Saturn eats his own children, he relates it as an allegory and claims that the Greek translation of Saturn, *Chronos*, means "time," so the story symbolized how time "brings to an end all things which have had a beginning, [and] may be said to devour its own offspring."[37] In the introduction to a recent edition of Bulfinch's *Mythology*, which consists of three works that were originally published in the mid-nineteenth century, Dr. Stephanie Lynn Burdin writes:

> In such an analysis Bulfinch may be doubly faulted. It is clear that Bulfinch did not read Greek; if he did, he would have known that the Greek equivalent of Saturn is actually *Kronos*, not *Chronos*, and the name Kronos bears no relation to time. Furthermore, the ancient Greeks and Romans who told this tale, presented originally in Hesiod's *Theogony*, believed it literally: Kronos ate his children. Eventually, his wife Rhea gave him an emetic which caused him to vomit them up again, a detail that probably also came under the rubric of "distasteful."[38]

Thus, in his effort to make the ancient myths suitable for the Victorian Age, Bulfinch tried to make them symbolic, or simply cut out the portions that couldn't be viewed as allegory. Often, the myths actually weren't intended to be allegorical, and there was no polite excuse for their unsavory aspects.

One final point is worth mentioning, as it helps to reframe the connection between the New Testament stories and the myths of other cultures. Many theologians have proposed—and the Bible supports—the idea that humans have an instinctual understanding of good and evil, an inborn desire to live beyond the grave, an innate sense that they must do something to earn God's (or the gods') approval or appease him, her, or them by some sort of sacrifice, and a fundamental desire to feel worth, purpose, and significance. There also is evidence for a common human experience—one that crosses historical periods, geographical regions, racial differences, and socioeconomic levels—that absolute good and evil exist, that justice and injustice are real, and that even the best experiences in life can never satisfy our deepest longings, try as we may. In fact, the common threads within myths, legends, epics, fairy tales, and lore of all cultures may reflect these universal human desires for immortality, the defeat of evil, the approval of one's Creator, and the reign of a good king. You could describe it as an instinctual yearning of all humans across history, a "collective consciousness" of sorts. As the Israelite King Solomon claimed approximately 3,000 years ago, God "has set eternity in the human heart."[39]

While he was an atheist, the professor of literature and mythology C. S. Lewis lamented to his friend J. R. R. Tolkien, the author of the *Lord of the Rings* trilogy, that it was too bad that none of the myths about the eventual vanquishing of evil were true. Tolkien begged to differ, and it was through his conversations with Tolkien that Lewis came to a confident faith in Jesus. Lewis went on to become one of the world's greatest defenders of Christianity. In a famous lecture called "On Fairy Stories," Tolkien stated that readers of myths can get a "fleeting glimpse of Joy, Joy beyond the walls of the world."[40] (Most likely, he was referring to myths other than the ones we covered in this chapter!)

These glimpses, according to both Tolkien and Lewis, are simply reflections of the "one True Myth": the coming, dying, and rising of Christ, who will defeat evil, renew and restore the world, and give immortality to all who have faith in him. Dr. Timothy Keller put it very succinctly in this way: "Jesus is not one more story pointing to these underlying realities. Jesus is the underlying reality to which all the stories point."[41]

CHAPTER 7: NOT A MYTH

QUESTIONS FOR COMPREHENSION AND DISCUSSION

1. Describe the Egyptian myth of Osiris, Isis, and Horus. In what ways do skeptics claim these stories influenced Christianity?
2. Describe the Greek myth of Dionysus (equivalent to the Roman myths of Bacchus) and the effect that this god had on his followers. What miracles did Dionysus perform? In what ways do skeptics claim Dionysus influenced Christianity?
3. Describe the Greek myth of Adonis. In what way did Adonis supposedly influence Christian beliefs, according to skeptics?
4. Describe the Phrygian myth of Attis and Cybele (worship of whom eventually moved to Greece and Rome). What did the priests of this pagan religion practice, and how did the Roman senate limit this practice? How did this myth influence Christianity, according to skeptics?
5. What are some reasons people claim the stories of Jesus were based on Mithraism?
6. What time period was the cult of Mithras active, according to archaeological evidence?
7. What are the ways that Christianity differs from Mithraism, according to ancient historian Edwin Yamauchi?
8. How do you counter the argument that Christianity was influenced by Osiris, Isis, and Horus, Dionysus, Adonis, Attis and Mithras?
9. Why do people love stories of redemption, sacrificial love, good defeating evil, and other aspects of the Gospel stories of Jesus?
10. What do you think Timothy Keller meant when he stated, "Jesus is not one more story pointing to these underlying realities. Jesus is the underlying reality to which all the stories point"?

CHAPTER 7 ENDNOTES

[1] James D. Tabor, *The Jesus Dynasty: The Hidden History of Jesus, His Royal Family, and the Birth of Christianity* (NY: Simon & Schuster, 2006), 60.

[2] C. S. Lewis, *God in the Dock: Essays on Theology and Ethics* (Grand Rapids, MI: William B. Eerdmans Publishing Company, 1970), 58.

3. Timothy Freke and Peter Grandy, *The Jesus Mysteries* (New York: Three Rivers, 1999), 9.
4. Plutarch, *On the Worship of Isis and Osiris*, in *Moralia* 18. Available online at http://penelope.uchicago.edu/Thayer/E/Roman/Texts/Plutarch/Moralia/Isis_and_Osiris*/A.html.
5. Bruce M. Metzger, "Methodology in the Study of Mystery Religions and Early Christianity," in Metzger, *Historical and Literary Studies*, 21.
6. In an interview with Edwin Yamauchi, Lee Strobel, *The Case for the Real Jesus* (Grand Rapids, MI: Zondervan, 2007), 177.
7. N. T. Wright, *The Resurrection of the Son of God* (Minneapolis, MN: Fortress Press, 2003), 80-81.
8. "Homeric Hymn 7 to Dionysus" (trans. Evelyn-White) (Greek epic c. 7th to 4th BC), available online at https://www.theoi.com/Olympios/DionysosWrath.html#Tyrrhenian.
9. Craig Blomberg, *The Historical Reliability of John's Gospel* (Downers Grove, IL: InterVarsity Press, 2001), 86.
10. Thomas Bulfinch, *Bulfinch's Mythology* (San Diego, CA: Canterbury Classics, 2014). This book comprised three volumes written by Bulfinch, *The Age of Fable* (1855), *The Age of Chivalry* (1858), and *Legends of Charlemagne* (1863).
11. Euripides, *The Bacchantes*, available online at https://sourcebooks.fordham.edu/ancient/euripides-bacchant.txt.
12. Paul Rhodes Eddy and Gregory A. Boyd, *The Jesus Legend: A Case for the Historical Reliability of the Synoptic Jesus Tradition* (Grand Rapids, MI: Baker Academic, 2007), 143.
13. Ovid, *Metamorphoses*, X, 431-502. Available online at http://ovid.lib.virginia.edu/trans/Metamorph10.htm#484521424.
14. Günter Wagner, *Pauline Baptism and the Pagan Mysteries* (Edinburgh: Oliver and Boyd, 1967), 197-201.
15. Luther H. Martin, *Hellenistic Religions: An Introduction* (Oxford: Oxford University Press, 1987), 83.
16. Maarten J. Vermaseren, *Cybele and Attis: The Myth and the Cult*, trans. A. M. H. Lemmers (London: Thames and Hudson, 1977), 96.
17. Pausanias, *Description of Greece*, 7.17.10-12. Available online at https://www.theoi.com/Text/Pausanias7B.html.
18. Wagner, *Pauline Baptism and the Pagan Mysteries*, 213, 219, 221, 223-224, 229, 251, 265.
19. Acharya S, *The Christ Conspiracy: The Greatest Story Ever Sold* (Adventures Unlimited Press, 1999), 118-120.
20. *Mithraic Studies: Proceedings of the First International Congress of Mithraic Studies* (Manchester U. Press, 1975), xiii.

CHAPTER 7: NOT A MYTH

21. From an interview with Dr. Edwin Yamauchi in Strobel, *The Case for the Real Jesus*, 169.
22. Ronald Nash, *The Gospel and the Greeks* (Phillipsburg, NJ: P&R, 2003), 137.
23. As quoted in Edwin Yamauchi, *Persia and the Bible* (Grand Rapids, MI: Baker, 1996), 510.
24. *Mithraic Studies*, 508n.
25. David Ulansey, "The Cosmic Mysteries of Mithras," http://www.well.com/~davidu/mithras.html, which is an online adaptation of David Ulansey, "Solving the Mithraic Mysteries," *Biblical Archeology Review*, vol. 20, #5, September/October 1994, 40-53. Also see David Ulansey, *The Origins of the Mithraic Mysteries* (Oxford: Oxford University Press, 1991).
26. Michael Spiedel, *Mithras-Orion, Greek Hero and Roman Army God* (Leiden: J.J. Brill, 1980), 45.
27. Wagner, *Pauline Baptism and the Pagan Mysteries*, 266.
28. M. J. Vermaseren, *Mithras the Secret God* (New York: Barnes and Noble, 1963), 103.
29. Richard Gordon, *Image and Value in the Greco-Roman World* (Aldershot: Variorum, 1996), 96.
30. John 1:1,14.
31. Manfred Clauss (trans. Richard Gordon), *The Roman Cult of Mithras* (New York: Routledge, 2000), 7.
32. Vermaseren, *Mithras the Secret God*, 103.
33. Quoted in Strobel, *The Case for the Real Jesus*, 184.
34. Michael Grant, *Jesus* (London: Rigel, 2004), 200.
35. F. F. Bruce, *The New Testament Documents: Are They Reliable?* (Downers Grove, Illinois: InterVarsity Press, 1973), 123.
36. A quote by the apostle Paul in 1 Corinthians 15:32.
37. As quoted by Stephanie Lynn Budin, PhD, in the Introduction to Thomas Bulfinch, *Bulfinch's Mythology*, xiv.
38. Ibid.
39. Ecclesiastes 3:11.
40. From J. R. R. Tolkien, "On Fairy Stories," in *The Monsters and the Critics and Other Essays* (San Francisco: HarperCollins, 1997).
41. From Timothy Keller's sermon, "Jesus' Meal with Zacchaeus," December 5, 2005. Available online at https://gospelinlife.com/downloads/jesus-meal-with-zaccheus-5436.

Miracles are a retelling in small letters of the very same story which is written across the whole world in letters too large for some of us to see.

— C. S. Lewis, Christian apologist, novelist, and professor[1]

One eyewitness weighs more than ten hearsays. Seeing is believing, all the world over.

— Titus Maccius Plautus, Roman dramatist (254-184 BC)[2]

Eyewitness Testimony

Having examined the nature of the ancient myths that preceded and coincided with early Christianity, we now return to our discussion of the internal evidence—that is, evidence from the New Testament documents themselves—that demonstrates the historicity of the events they describe.

As we saw in Chapter 5, the authors of the New Testament documents go out of their way to emphasize that they are writing what they themselves have witnessed. Sure, the authors could have been lying, but we at least know that the documents were not intentional works of fiction or meant to be read as myths. Moreover, in Chapter 6, we discussed how the inclusion of embarrassing, confusing, and counter-productive details gives us greater confidence that the New Testament documents record actual events, rather than legends or myths. It appears that the writers placed great value on the truth, even if it wasn't helpful to their cause.

Let's now take a look at the nature of the Gospels' miracle stories and the conflicting secondary details of the Gospel accounts, both of which unexpectedly support the claim that the New Testament records what actually happened.

NOT YOUR TYPICAL MIRACLE STORIES

Ironically, the miracles of Jesus themselves provide strong evidence for the truthfulness of the Gospel stories. Reading the Gospel miracle accounts side by side with accounts of miracles in other works of ancient

CHAPTER 8: EYEWITNESS TESTIMONY

literature, enormous differences pop out. The miracles of the New Testament don't resemble the ones you'd typically find in myths, legends, and other literary works of the ancient world.

In the myths of ancient Egypt, Greece, and Rome, the miracles were very dramatic and extremely far-fetched, even as far as miracles go. The Greek god of the sky and rain, Zeus (or "Jupiter" in Roman mythology), rode his winged horse, Pegasus, and threw lightning bolts at his foes. One of Zeus' most impressive miracles was to change the direction of the sun's course in the sky. This miracle was part of a series of events leading up to what became known as "The Atrean Curse." Here is the *Cliffs Notes'* summary that describes these events and the origin of the Atrean curse:

> Of his many sons Pelops [the grandson of Zeus] loved the bastard Chrysippus the most, which made Hippodamia [Pelops' wife] fear that her own children would lose the throne. When Chrysippus was murdered by Hippodamia two of her sons were implicated, so [they, her sons] Atreus and Thyestes fled to Mycenae. Atreus acquired a golden fleece there, which would have established his right to rule. But Thyestes made love to Atreus' wife, Aerope, and obtained the fleece from her. Having been made king, Thyestes agreed that if the sun should move backward in its course Atreus could take over the throne. Zeus sent the sun backward across the sky, and Atreus acquired the kingdom of Mycenae. He had two sons by Aerope, Agamemnon and Menelaus [the Greek leaders famous for their involvement in the Trojan War]. When Atreus learned that Thyestes had cuckolded him he invited Thyestes to a banquet and served his brother Thyestes' own sons, who had been butchered and boiled. Nauseated, Thyestes laid a curse [the Atrean curse] on Atreus and his sons.[3]

This story resembles the ancient myths we discussed in the last chapter and provides additional confirmation that this type of drama—and the miracles therein—are typical of ancient literature, whether it is Greek, Roman, Egyptian, Persian, or otherwise.

In stark contrast, Jesus' miracles are described in simple, everyday language, with minimal embellishment and extravagance. As one example of many, consider this story from Mark's Gospel:

> They came to Bethsaida, and some people brought a blind man and begged Jesus to touch him. He took the blind man by the hand and led him outside the village. When he had spit on the man's eyes and put his hands on him, Jesus asked, "Do you see anything?"
>
> He looked up and said, "I see people; they look like trees walking around."
>
> Once more Jesus put his hands on the man's eyes. Then his eyes were opened, his sight was restored, and he saw everything clearly. Jesus sent him home, saying, "Don't go into the village."[4]

Unlike the extravagant style used to present the power of gods in other works of ancient literature, Jesus doesn't appear all that dramatic. If the early church leaders were inventing this, why would they have made Jesus appear to have failed at first?[5] And notice how Jesus took the blind man by the hand and led him outside the village, where they could avoid the numerous gawkers. You'd think that Jesus would want to spread the news of the healing far and wide. Jesus even instructed the blind man not to return to the village, indicating that the healing was done for the man's sake, not as a way to impress the crowds. Why such an insistence on secrecy, if you wanted to attract others to follow your new religion?

Another interesting question is why Jesus had to touch the blind man's eyes to heal him, since he had been powerful enough to calm a storm merely by uttering a few words.[6] After further study, it seems that Jesus knew exactly what this man needed, and he sensitively sought to communicate with him through his primary senses of hearing and touch. By taking his hand and touching his eyelids, Jesus lovingly communicated to the man what he was doing.

As opposed to the sensational quality of ancient mythological miracles, this story has an air of everyday life, making it in many ways

CHAPTER 8: EYEWITNESS TESTIMONY

more believable, despite the supernatural elements. And this is how all of Jesus' miracle stories read: matter of fact, simple, unembellished narratives that you might hear from anyone describing an event they had witnessed, almost as if they're stating, "I know it sounds crazy, but this is what happened."

To emphasize this unembellished nature of the miracle stories of Jesus, let's take a look at the account of Jesus' resurrection in the *Gospel of Peter*, which is one of the Gnostic texts discovered in Nag Hammadi, Egypt in 1945. Most scholars agree that this document was written more than 100 years after Jesus died.[7] One of the clues of its late writing is the embellished, extravagant style used to describe Jesus' resurrection, a style that characterizes legends. The *Gospel of Peter* records that, following his death and burial, two men descended from the sky, the stone rolled itself back from the entrance to the tomb, and the following ensued:

> Now when these soldiers saw that, they woke up the centurion and the elders (for they also were keeping watch). While they were yet telling them the things which they had seen, they saw three men come out of the tomb, two of them sustaining the other one, and a cross following after them. The heads of the two they saw had heads that reached up to heaven, but the head of him that was led by them went beyond heaven. And they heard a voice out of the heavens saying, "Have you preached unto them that sleep?" The answer that was heard from the cross was, "Yes!"[8]

Compared to this account of a talking cross and heads extending into heaven, the resurrection accounts in the canonical gospels of Matthew, Mark, Luke, and John[9] are plain, understated, and seemingly commonplace. To illustrate, let's take a look at the resurrection stories in the Gospel of John, which scholars agree are the latest accounts of Jesus' life found in the New Testament. (It is thus the one that you would expect to have the greatest legendary development, if any.) John describes the first appearance of Jesus after his resurrection in this way:

> Now Mary stood outside the tomb crying. As she wept, she bent over to look into the tomb and saw two angels

in white, seated where Jesus' body had been, one at the head and the other at the foot.

They asked her, "Woman, why are you crying?"

"They have taken my Lord away," she said, "and I don't know where they have put him." At this, she turned around and saw Jesus standing there, but she did not realize that it was Jesus.

He asked her, "Woman, why are you crying? Who is it you are looking for?"

Thinking he was the gardener, she said, "Sir, if you have carried him away, tell me where you have put him, and I will get him."

Jesus said to her, "Mary."

She turned toward him and cried out in Aramaic, "Rabboni!" (which means "Teacher").

Jesus said, "Do not hold on to me, for I have not yet ascended to the Father. Go instead to my brothers and tell them, 'I am ascending to my Father and your Father, to my God and your God.'"

Mary Magdalene went to the disciples with the news: "I have seen the Lord!" And she told them that he had said these things to her.[10]

Compared to the first witnesses of the resurrection in the *Gospel of* Peter, who were male soldiers and Jewish "elders," John records that a woman was the first to see the empty tomb and the risen Jesus. Moreover, Mary was in tears at the time, which makes her an even less credible witness. And even though she was looking at two angels dressed in white, she unexpectedly and confusingly still assumed that Jesus' body must have been stolen. Then she turned around and didn't recognize

CHAPTER 8: EYEWITNESS TESTIMONY

Jesus, mistaking him for a gardener, but then recognized his voice. Why would anyone concoct a story like this, if you wanted to convince people that it is true? Why wouldn't you make the first witness more credible? Why wouldn't Mary suspect something else was going on when she saw two angels in Jesus' tomb? Why wouldn't Mary recognize Jesus with joy and exhilaration, rather than mistake him for a gardener? The details in this story are strange, but strange in a different way compared to the strange details of the account of the "heads that reached up to heaven" in the Gnostic *Gospel of Peter*.

Now let's look at how the Gospel of Luke describes the risen Jesus when he first appeared to his disciples:

> While they were still talking about this, Jesus himself stood among them and said to them, "Peace be with you."
>
> They were startled and frightened, thinking they saw a ghost. He said to them, "Why are you troubled, and why do doubts rise in your minds? Look at my hands and my feet. It is I myself! Touch me and see; a ghost does not have flesh and bones, as you see I have."
>
> When he had said this, he showed them his hands and feet. And while they still did not believe it because of joy and amazement, he asked them, "Do you have anything here to eat?" They gave him a piece of broiled fish, and he took it and ate it in their presence.[11]

Standing in front of them for the first time after his disfiguring death, Jesus simply asked for something to eat. No profound comments. No fanfare. And the disciples appear incredulous, not what you would expect if unscientific, ancient people found it so easy to believe in a bodily resurrection. And, as we discussed in Chapter 6, no ancient fictional account would have used such understatement and ordinariness to convey realism. The most logical explanation for this commonplace, mundane account of Jesus' first appearance after his death is, strange as it was, it happened this way.

In addition to the everyday nature of their miracle narratives, the Gospel accounts emphasize that Jesus never performed miracles to put on a dramatic show of his power, as was typical of the miracle accounts in ancient literature. Rather than attempting to impress and electrify the crowds and draw attention to himself, Jesus' primary purpose in performing miracles was simple: to help people. He often even told the person he had just healed not to tell anyone else about it.[12] Jesus also consistently refused when people asked him for a dramatic display of his power.[13]

Rather than using miracles to increase his popularity, Jesus used them to help people and thereby teach them about his overarching goal: the restoration of the world to the way it had originally been created before evil entered it. His miracles thus involved forgiving sin, feeding the hungry, healing the sick, vanquishing evil, and conquering death.

To illustrate this pattern, let's consider a series of five miracles that are recorded in chapters 8 and 9 of Matthew's Gospel. These miracles follow a specific order that demonstrates Jesus' power over progressively more powerful enemies. Jesus first demonstrates his power over sickness when he healed Peter's mother-in-law.[14] He again demonstrates his power over nature when he calms the storm on the Sea of Galilee. And next, when he restores two demon-possessed men, Jesus demonstrates his power over the spiritual world. Fourth, he demonstrates his power over sin when he forgives (and heals) the paralyzed man. And fifth, he displays his power over death itself when he brings the daughter of a synagogue leader back to life. This progression also demonstrates Jesus' ultimate plan to eventually rid the world of the same enemies: sickness, natural disaster, evil spirits, sin, and death itself.[15]

If the stories of Jesus' ministry were invented by people who wanted to impress others with Jesus' power in order to attract more converts, you could imagine that they may record that Jesus could fly through the air, blow the tops off mountains, cause objects to spontaneously combust, or uproot trees for all to see. But the Gospels never show Jesus using his power in this way, though the New Testament proclaims him in many other ways to be quite capable of doing so. Instead, Jesus' miracles always helped others in a way that taught them the fundamental lesson that he was the Messiah, the one who would usher in the Kingdom of God as the Scriptures foretold, culminating in the defeat of hunger, disease, evil, and death.[16]

CHAPTER 8: EYEWITNESS TESTIMONY

To demonstrate the primary educational purpose of Jesus' miracles, biblical scholar F. F. Bruce makes this point:

> The miracles of the fourth Gospel are always called 'signs', and elsewhere in the New Testament the word for 'miracle' or 'wonder' is regularly linked with the word for 'sign'. 'Signs and wonders' is a frequent phrase, as if to teach us that the miracles are not related merely for their capacity of begetting wonder in the hearers and readers, but also because of what they signified. [Jesus] did not esteem very highly the kind of belief that arose simply from witnessing miracles. His desire was that men should realize what these things signified. They were signs of the messianic age, such as had been foretold by the prophets of old.... They are 'mighty works,' signifying that the power of God has entered into human life; they are 'the powers of the age to come' (Heb. 6:5), signifying that the age to come has in Christ invaded this present age.[17]

Likewise, pastor Timothy Keller underscores that the ultimate goal of Jesus' miracles was to point to how he would renew the world:

> We modern people think of miracles as the suspension of the natural order, but Jesus meant them to be the restoration of the natural order. The Bible tells us that God did not originally make the world to have disease, hunger, and death in it. Jesus has come to redeem where it went wrong and heal the world where it is broken. His miracles are not just proofs that he has power but also wonderful foretastes of what he is going to do with that power. Jesus' miracles are not just a challenge to our minds, but a promise to our hearts, that the world we all want is coming.[18]

In short, Jesus didn't do miracles to gain converts; he did miracles to teach us about his identity and his purpose.

F. F. Bruce notes that Jesus' miracles are not just more believable than the typical miracles of ancient literature, but they are exactly what we'd expect from a man who is consistently portrayed as divine:

> In literature there are many different kinds of miracle-stories; but the Gospels do not ask us to believe that Jesus made the sun travel from west to east one day, or anything like that; they do not even attribute to Him such monstrosities as we find in the apocryphal [Gnostic] Gospels of the second century.... As we have seen, not even in the earliest Gospel strata can we find a non-supernatural Jesus, and we need not be surprised if supernatural works are attributed to Him. If we reject from the start the idea of a supernatural Jesus, then we shall reject His miracles, too; if, on the other hand, we accept the Gospel picture of Him, the miracles will cease to be an insuperable stumbling block.[19]

Therefore, his miracles are consistent with who Jesus claimed to be (stay tuned for more on this topic in Chapter 18). In other words, the earliest records of Jesus' teachings confirm that he claimed to be much more than an average human being, and thus, his miracles are to be expected and are signs that confirm his self-proclaimed identity.

One final quote on this topic serves to summarize the difference between Jesus' miracles and those in other works of ancient literature. C. S. Lewis made the distinction this way:

> When we open such books as Grimm's *Fairy Tales* or Ovid's *Metamorphoses* or the Italian epics, we find ourselves in a world of miracles so diverse that they can hardly be classified.... If such things really happened they would, I suppose, show that Nature was being invaded. But they would show that she was being invaded by an alien power. The fitness of Christian miracles, and their difference from these mythological miracles, lies in the fact that they show invasion by a Power which is not alien. They are what might be expected to happen when she is invaded not simply by a god, but by the God of Nature: by a Power which is outside her jurisdiction not

as a foreigner but as a sovereign. They proclaim that He who has come is not merely a king, but the king, her King and ours.[20]

As we continue to examine the historical evidence for Jesus' deity in the chapters to come, especially the evidence for his bodily resurrection, the historicity of Jesus' miracles will gain even more solid footing. If Jesus really is the creator of the universe, and he really did come in human form to draw humans into a personal relationship with him as their creator, these miracles are not just plausible, they are to be expected.

CONTRADICTIONS OR DIFFERENT EYEWITNESS PERSPECTIVES?

One of the reasons that some people dismiss the Gospels as untrustworthy, especially the accounts of miracles, is that the same stories vary from one Gospel to another. But, ironically, much as the nature of miracles is evidence for the truthfulness of the Gospel accounts, the discrepancy in the secondary details actually *lends support* to their being eyewitness accounts rather than fiction. If the Gospels were based on eyewitness accounts of Jesus' life and ministry, we would *expect* variations in the secondary details. In fact, if the accounts were exactly alike, it would seem that the writers had colluded with one another, or had simply copied from one another, making it much more likely that their accounts were invented.

A similar principle operates in a court of law. When two eyewitnesses report the exact same details of their experience in a particular situation, it should tip off the lawyers and jury that they had prepared their statements together in order to cover up what actually happened. But if they provide a consistent account of the event but have varying secondary details due to their different vantage points, their accounts would be more trustworthy. Because each individual remembers different details, and because they observed the scene from different places and heard or saw different things, you'd expect two eyewitnesses to tell the story slightly differently, but to be consistent in the primary details. This is exactly what you see in the Gospels.

Simon Greenleaf, a prominent Harvard law professor, compared the accounts of each of the four Gospel authors, concluding:

> There is enough of a discrepancy to show that there could have been no previous concert among them; and at the same time such substantial agreement to show that they all were independent narrators of the same great transaction.[21]

Many generations of law students have used Greenleaf's textbook, *Treatise on the Law of Evidence*, to determine what constitutes legal evidence. Initially a skeptic of Christianity, Greenleaf eventually claimed that the origin of his Christian faith was his legal analysis of the Gospel accounts of Jesus' life. He concluded that the dissimilarity in the secondary details of the accounts was strong evidence that each Gospel presents eyewitness testimony. However, though they were dissimilar in their secondary details, the accounts were so similar in their primary details that he considered the main events of Jesus' life to be historically trustworthy.

Let's look at just a few examples of apparent "contradictions" that do not detract from the reliability of the primary accounts. One common difference between the Gospels is their chronology of events. For example, Luke places the imprisonment of John the Baptist nearer the beginning of his Gospel,[22] grouping it with his description of John the Baptist's ministry. Mark, however, puts it in the middle of Jesus' ministry to the people of Galilee.[23] Is this a contradiction that weakens the trustworthiness of the accounts?

One of the reasons Luke and Mark organized their narratives differently was in order to more effectively convey their main points. As a result, the secondary details in their accounts appear to contradict each other. Craig Blomberg, widely considered an expert on the reliability of the New Testament, explains how authors often chose to arrange their stories by theme rather than in chronological order:

> But at least as long ago as Saint Augustine, it has been recognized that the gospels did not set out to supply a detailed itinerary of Jesus' ministry with every event in its proper chronological sequence, but frequently

arrange passages in topical or thematic order instead.... If one applies the principle of assuming a chronological connection between two portions of the Synoptics only when the text explicitly presents one, then the apparent contradictions of sequence vanish. This is especially true when one realizes that the Greek words sometimes translated as 'now' or 'then' in English (e.g. *kai* or *de*) often need only mean 'and,' without implying that one event happened after the one previously narrated.[24]

Therefore, differences in the chronology of events in the Gospels shouldn't cause us to doubt the authenticity of the events themselves.

It is interesting to note that the later Gospel of John provides the most accurate chronology of events in the ministry of Jesus, another reason to believe it was written by the original disciple John or another close eyewitness.[25] In the opinion of F. F. Bruce, most experts trust the Gospel of John's chronology of Jesus' ministry and use it to understand the order of events in the Synoptic Gospels. He explains:

> John's record, by its recurring mention of periodic festivals, provides a helpful chronological framework for the Synoptic narrative, which is lacking in chronological indications for the period between Jesus' baptism and His last visit to Jerusalem.... Indeed, several scholars who decline to accept as historical John's portrait of Christ are quite willing to accept the chronological framework.[26]

The early church father Papias was a young man when several of Jesus' earliest disciples were still alive. He claims to have talked with these earliest followers, most likely including John,[27] one of the original twelve disciples. Perhaps as a way to emphasize the superior chronology of John's Gospel without undermining the importance of Mark's, Papias wrote the following regarding the arrangement of Mark's Gospel. Note the people whom Papias calls "elders" had been *eyewitnesses* of Jesus' ministry. He wrote:

> I won't hesitate to arrange alongside my interpretations whatever things I learned and remembered well from the elders, confirming the truth on their behalf.... The

> elder said this: Mark, who became Peter's interpreter, wrote accurately as much as he remembered—*though not in ordered form*— of the Lord's sayings and doings. For [Mark] neither heard the Lord nor followed after him, but later (as I said) he followed after Peter, who was giving his teachings in short anecdotes and thus did not bring forth an ordered arrangement of the Lord's sayings; so, Mark did not miss the point when he wrote in this way, as he remembered. For he had one purpose—to omit nothing of what he had heard and to present no false testimony in these things.[28]

Thus, the early church father Papias, who in his youth had met the apostle John, claims that Mark recorded the stories that Peter told him, though not necessarily in the order in which they occurred. Thus, this difference in chronology should not be a reason to discount the truthfulness of his accounts.

Early church historian Richard Bauckham summarizes this point as follows:

> Mark's Gospel, then, in Papias's view was really an incomplete historical work: Mark had accomplished the first stage of the historian's task, that of recording the eyewitness source, but was not able to complete the work by putting the material in order.... These evaluations of Mark and Matthew make excellent sense once we realize that Papias valued above all the Gospel of John, which was directly written by an eyewitness and offered a much more precise chronological sequence of events. It was by comparison with John that Papias had to see the Gospels of Mark and Matthew as lacking order, but, not wishing to dismiss these Gospels, Papias set out to explain why they lacked order but were nevertheless of great value because of their closeness to eyewitness testimony.[29]

Thus, chronological differences between the Gospels don't necessarily imply that the stories are untrue, only that some of the original authors were more inclined to put the stories into an accurate chronological framework, while others preferred to organize the stories thematically.

In addition to chronological differences, the Gospels also differ in the phrasing of quotations, something that especially bothers modern historians who want to pinpoint the actual words that Jesus said. But because there were no symbols for quotation marks in Greek and Hebrew, quotations in Scripture should be understood as paraphrases of what was actually said.

One example of quotes that are paraphrases rather than exact word-for-word transcriptions is when a loud voice spoke at the baptism of Jesus. Mark and Luke record, "You are my beloved son with whom I am well pleased,"[30] while Matthew records, "This is my beloved son with whom I am well pleased."[31] Does this difference invalidate the historical record? Not when you realize that ancient historians were more concerned with recording the main meaning of the statement than the actual words used. Matthew may very well have thought it was better to emphasize that God spoke not just directly to Jesus, but for the benefit of both Jesus and the crowd witnessing the baptism.

In addition to variations in chronology and paraphrasing, the four Gospels differ with respect to the stories they recount. Why some stories are in all four Gospels and some only in one or two? John gives us a clue to the answer with the words he uses to conclude his Gospel:

> Jesus did many other things as well. If every one of them were written down, I suppose that even the whole world would not have room for the books that would be written.[32]

Obviously, there were many other events in Jesus' life that the Gospel writers could have included in their account, but instead of including everything, they chose to include the events that conveyed the primary truths about Jesus that they wanted their audience to understand. This is especially true because they had to fit their accounts within the length of the typical scroll, since the book-like *codex* hadn't been invented yet.

The authors may have chosen to tell a certain story in detail (such as the revivification of Jairus' daughter in Mark[33]) or to give a short summary of what happened (such as the quick overview of the same event in Matthew[34]). In fact, Matthew's accounts generally use fewer words than the corresponding accounts in Mark.

Because Jesus' resurrection is so central to Christianity, the most commonly cited "contradictions" in the Gospel accounts are those related to the initial discovery of Jesus' empty tomb.[35] In Matthew, there is one angel, and the women who visited Jesus' tomb were "Mary Magdalene and the other Mary." Mark agrees that there was one angel—"a young man dressed in a white robe"—but he claims that the women were "Mary Magdalene, Mary the mother of James, and Salome." Luke says the women included "Mary Magdalene, Joanna, Mary the mother of James, and the others with them," and he claims that there were "two men in clothes that gleamed like lightning." Finally, John records that Mary Magdalene went to the tomb, and there were "two angels in white." So, which women really went to the tomb, and how many angels were there anyway? Are these details contradictory, or do they resemble eyewitness accounts heard in a courtroom, when different people notice and recall different details?

First, you'll note that none of the Gospels say that *only the women they mention* went to the tomb. In fact, Luke even says, "and the others with them." The main aim of the writers was not to provide exhaustive detail, but to record that the tomb was empty and that women were the first to discover it.

Also, Matthew and Mark never say there was *only* one angel. They may simply be mentioning only the angel who was speaking, and the other one may have been in the background. (John actually describes that one was sitting where Jesus' head had been, and the other was "at the foot.")

Moreover, each Gospel may record a different aspect of the women's experience, just as different witnesses in a courtroom would report different perspectives of the same event. The important point is that the various accounts match up in the primary details: women went to Jesus' tomb early in the morning after the Sabbath, they saw the stone had been rolled away, and an angel told them Jesus had risen.[36]

Thus, when the secondary details differ in the stories of Jesus' life, death, and resurrection, it is not a sign of fabrication, but instead indicates that these are eyewitness accounts of historical events.[37] N. T. Wright emphasizes that the differences in the four canonical resurrection accounts actually support their historicity, explaining it this way:

> In the ancient world, someone who was intending to tell people what actually happened did not feel obligated (any

CHAPTER 8: EYEWITNESS TESTIMONY

more than a good journalist, or indeed a real practicing historian, would today) to mention every single feature of every single incident. Peter went to the tomb; "some of our number" went to the tomb. If I say, "the bishop went to the party", and if somebody else says "the bishop and his two daughters went to the party", we have not contradicted one another.[38]

Wright goes on to summarize the historical value of the four slightly varying resurrection accounts in this way:

When Luke fits all the resurrection appearances into a single day in chapter 24 [of his Gospel], and spreads them over forty days in Acts 1, we should not suppose that we have caught him out in some terrible historical oversight. By the same token, it would be wrong to highlight the small-scale discrepancies between the four canonical narratives as though they constituted evidence that nothing at all actually happened. If anything, the argument should work the other way. If nothing happened, and if someone, years later, invented a story of women discovering an empty tomb, we should expect, not four slightly different stories, but one story.[39]

When we discuss the historical evidence for the resurrection in Chapters 16 and 17, we will cover additional reasons to trust that the resurrection accounts are truthful.

So far, the New Testament receives top marks on the internal evidence test. The authors' numerous claims that they are basing their accounts on eyewitness testimony shift the burden of proof to the historian who claims that they are liars or that their original testimony was altered at a later date. We have also seen evidence from the New Testament documents themselves that provides further support for the authors' claims to be telling the truth: the inclusion of unimportant, embarrassing, and confusing details, miracle stories that are more mundane and believable than the miracles typical of ancient literature, and differences in secondary details that indicate different eyewitness perspectives of the same event. But that's not all. Let's explore more internal evidence in the next chapter, which gives us even more reason to trust the truthfulness of the Gospel accounts of Jesus' life, death, and resurrection.

QUESTIONS FOR COMPREHENSION AND DISCUSSION

1. By way of review, can you summarize the main lines of *internal evidence* covered in Chapters 5 and 6 that demonstrate the historicity of the New Testament accounts?
2. Why is it unlikely that the leaders of the early Christian church changed the Gospel stories? How might they be different if they were able to change them?
3. What is the Atrean Curse, and can you describe events that led up to it?
4. How do the accounts of miracles in the New Testament differ from Zeus' miracle that changed the direction of the sun and the miracles described in the last chapters?
5. What was Jesus' primary purpose when he performed miracles? What did he aim to teach through his miracles?
6. How does the account of Jesus' resurrection in the Gnostic document, the *Gospel of Peter*, differ from the New Testament accounts of this event? How are the events describing the discovery of the empty tomb in the New Testament more believable?
7. If two authors write accounts that are consistent in the primary details but differ in the secondary details, how does this strengthen the case that they are each telling the truth?
8. How can you explain differences in the chronology of the events in the various Gospel stories?
9. What did the early church leader Papias say about the order of events in Mark's Gospel? From whom did Papias get his information?
10. What are the differences between the four different accounts of the discovery of the empty tomb? How do these differences demonstrate varied perspectives of the event, rather than that the stories were invented?

CHAPTER 8 ENDNOTES

[1] C. S. Lewis, *Miracles*, in *The Complete C. S. Lewis* (San Francisco: HarperCollins San Francisco, 2002).

CHAPTER 8: EYEWITNESS TESTIMONY

2   Tacitus Maccius Plautus, *Truculentus*, Act II, sc. 6, line 8.

3   "Summary and Analysis: Greek Mythology, The Tragic Dynasties—Mycenae: The House of Atreus," Cliffs Notes Website, https://www.cliffsnotes.com/literature/m/mythology/summary-and-analysis-greek-mythology/the-tragic-dynasties-8212-mycenae-the-house-of-atreus.

4   Mark 8:22-26.

5   Some commentators interpret this two-step healing as Jesus' demonstration that spiritual healing happens in stages. For example, refer to Timothy Keller's sermon titled "Do You See Anything?" from June 18, 2006, available online at http://sermons.redeemer.com.

6   See the story in Matthew 8, Mark 4, and Luke 8.

7   Mark D. Roberts, *Can We Trust the Gospels?* (Wheaton, IL: Crossway, 2007), 60. See also Lee Strobel, *The Case for the Real Jesus* (Grand Rapids, MI: Zondervan, 2007), 44-46 and Craig A. Evans, *Fabricating Jesus* (Downers Grove, IL: InterVarsity Press, 2006), 78-85.

8   *The Gospel of Peter* 10:1-5. See Ron Cameron, *The Other Gospels* (Philadelphia, PA: Westminster, 1982), 80-81.

9   For example, compare the *Gospel of Peter* account to Matthew 28:2-7, Mark 16:4-8, Luke 24:2-8, and John 20:1-12.

10   John 20:11-18.

11   Luke 24:36-43.

12   See Matthew 8:4, Mark 7:36 and 9:9, and Luke 5:14.

13   See Matthew 4:6-7, 12:39, and 16:4, Mark 15:29-30, and Luke 4:9-12, 11:29, and 23:37-39.

14   See Matthew 8:14-9:26. As explained in Lawrence O. Richards, *Bible Teacher's Commentary* (Colorado Springs, CO: Cook Communications Ministries, 2002), 553.

15   See Matthew 4:6-7, 12:39, 16:4, Mark 15:29-30, Luke 4:9-12, 11:29, 23:37-39.

16   For a discussion of the historicity of Jesus' miracles, see Craig A. Evans, *Fabricating Jesus* (Downers Grove, IL: IVP Books, 2006), Chapter 7.

17   F. F. Bruce, *The New Testament Documents: Are They Reliable?* (Downers Grove, Illinois: InterVarsity Press, 1973), 69.

18   Timothy Keller, *The Reason for God* (New York: Penguin Group, 2008), 95-96.

19   Bruce, *The New Testament Documents*, 61.

20   C. S. Lewis, *Miracles*, 419.

21   Simon Greenleaf, *The Testimony of the Evangelists* (Grand Rapids, MI: Baker, 1984), vii.

22   Luke 3:1-20.

23   Mark 6:14-29.

24. Craig Blomberg, *The Historical Reliability of the Gospels* (Downers Grove, IL: InterVarsity Press, 1987), 127-128.
25. Richard Bauckham, *Jesus and the Eyewitnesses: The Gospels as Eyewitness Testimony* (Grand Rapids, MI: Eerdmans, 2006), 227.
26. Bruce, *The New Testament Documents*, 54.
27. For evidence that Papias did know John and other earlier followers who had been eyewitnesses of Jesus' ministry, see Monte A. Shanks, *Papias and the New Testament* (Portland, OR: Wipf and Stock Publishers, 2013).
28. Papias as quoted in Eusebius, *Church History*, 3.39.15. Emphasis mine. Available online at http://www.newadvent.org/fathers/250103.htm.
29. Bauckham, *Jesus and the Eyewitnesses*, 228. For a complete defense of the reliability of Papias' accounts, see Chapter 2 ("Papias on the Eyewitnesses"), Chapter 9 ("Papias on Mark and Matthew"), and Chapter 16 ("Papias on John").
30. Mark 1:11, Luke 3:22.
31. Matthew 3:17.
32. John 21:25.
33. Mark 5:21-43.
34. Matthew 9:18-26.
35. See the accounts of the discovery of the empty tomb in Matthew 28:1-8, Mark 16:1-8, Luke 24:1-11, and John 20:1-18.
36. For a helpful examination of a wide range of the most commonly cited gospel variations, see Blomberg, *The Historical Reliability of the Gospels*, Chapters 4 and 5.
37. For a helpful examination of a wide range of the most commonly cited gospel variations, see Craig Blomberg, *The Historical Reliability of the Gospels*, Chapters 4 and 5.
38. N. T. Wright, *The Resurrection of the Son of God* (Minneapolis, MN: Fortress Press, 2003), 648.
39. Ibid, 649.

The Gospels were written within living memory of the events they recount. Mark's Gospel was written well within the lifetime of many of the eyewitnesses, while the other three canonical Gospels were written in the period when living eyewitnesses were becoming scarce, exactly at the point in time when their testimony would perish with them were it not put in writing.

—Richard Bauckham, theologian and historian[1]

If skeptics are looking for an early version of Jesus that is less divine, less miraculous and less supernatural, they aren't going to find it in the writings of the first generation that followed the apostles. Instead, they're going to find the very same Jesus that you and I know from the writings of the New Testament.

—J. Warner Wallace, author of *Cold-Case Christianity*[2]

More Eyewitness Evidence

Many skeptics claim that leaders of the early Christian church altered the original documents of the New Testament to suit their theological and political agenda. Thus, the original documents may be somewhat accurate, they'd say, but Jesus' miracles and resurrection and his claims to be God must have been inserted later. They argue either that the New Testament we read today bears little resemblance to the original documents because of this alteration over time, or that the original documents themselves were fabricated in order to further the agenda of the first Christians and thus do not accurately represent the real Jesus.

We have already covered many of the weaknesses of these claims, so before we proceed to additional evidence against them, let's summarize a few reasons we can trust that the New Testament tells us the truth about Jesus:

1. The authors of the Gospels of Luke and John, the Book of Acts, the Pauline epistles, and at least the First Epistle of John claim to be eyewitnesses of the events of Jesus' life or insist that their accounts are based on eyewitness testimony. While these claims could have been invented, at least we know that the documents weren't intentionally meant to be symbolic, mythological, or legendary.
2. The Gospels contain numerous incidental details that do not characterize ancient works of fiction or mythology.
3. The Gospels include potentially embarrassing and counterproductive information that later church leaders would have removed if they were concocting or able to edit the documents.

CHAPTER 9: MORE EYEWITNESS EVIDENCE

4. Ancient myths and mystery religions differ greatly from early Christianity, and the chronology of evidence demonstrates that Christianity influenced these pagan religions and not the other way around.
5. The accounts of miracles in the Gospels are unembellished and "matter of fact," which is not typical of miracle stories in legends and myths.
6. The differences in the secondary details of the various stories in each of the Gospels are a sign of eyewitness reportage.

In this chapter, we will summarize even more evidence to disprove the allegations that the early church invented or altered the first accounts of Jesus' life. In order to demonstrate that they were written within the lifetime of eyewitnesses, we will first discuss the dates that the majority of scholars give the New Testament documents. Secondly, we'll present additional evidence to counter the claim that the authors of these documents fabricated their stories in the years between the events described and the time when the Gospels were written.

THE EARLY DATES OF THE NEW TESTAMENT DOCUMENTS

As we saw in Chapter 5, the Gospels' authors claim to be eyewitnesses or, in Luke's case, to have interviewed eyewitnesses of the events they describe. It is thus extremely important to pinpoint when the Gospels were written in order to determine whether the authors are telling the truth. If the Gospels were written early enough, when they began to circulate, true eyewitnesses could have spoken out to support or refute what the documents claimed. If the documents contained falsehoods, eyewitness disputes would have put a serious damper on the growth of the Christian movement. The enemies of Christianity, of which there were many, would have been eager to publicize it far and wide if anyone who had been present during Jesus' ministry could refute the accounts about him that were being circulated.[3]

It would be especially easy for eyewitnesses to point out inaccuracies or exaggerations in the stories if the documents were first circulated in the very place Jesus lived, as opposed to a distant location where no one would know whether the stories were false. Conversely, if the documents were true reports, you'd expect eyewitnesses to confirm their claims and for this new movement to spread rapidly from its place of origin.

Historians have indeed confirmed that many of the New Testament documents were written within the lifetime of eyewitnesses, and as one would expect, the Christian movement started in Jerusalem, the region where the events of Jesus' life took place and where eyewitnesses would still be living. Further, the rapid spread of the Christian faith throughout the Roman Empire—despite lethal persecution—suggests that the Gospel authors were indeed telling the truth about Jesus.

From a survey of New Testament scholarly opinion, ranging from liberal to conservative, we attain the following plausible date ranges for the completion of the four canonical Gospels:

Matthew: AD 65-85
Mark: AD 60-75
Luke: AD 65-95
John: AD 75-100[4]

Jesus' crucifixion was most likely between 30 and 33 AD.[5] Thus, the majority of New Testament scholars believe that all of the Gospels that we read in the New Testament today were written within twenty-seven to seventy years of Jesus' death. Moreover, as we will discuss in more detail later, it is likely that the Gospels were based in part on sources that were written down even earlier. Thus, we have more reason to trust the authors' claims that they either saw the events of Jesus' life, death, and resurrection, or that they were basing their accounts on interviews with first-hand eyewitnesses of Jesus' life, death, and resurrection.

According to many respected New Testament scholars, it is highly likely that the Synoptic Gospels (Matthew, Mark, and Luke) were written even earlier than the date ranges given above. They point to numerous historical events that occurred between AD 60 and 70 that aren't included in the Book of Acts, a document dedicated to recording the history of the early Christian church.

Acts ends suddenly when Paul is under house arrest in Rome. It thus never records Paul's martyrdom, which happened around AD 68.[6] Acts also fails to mention the death of Jesus' brother James in AD 62,[7] the outbreak of the Jewish War in AD 66, and the destruction of Jerusalem in AD 70.

CHAPTER 9: MORE EYEWITNESS EVIDENCE

The destruction of Jerusalem by the Romans in AD 70 is among the most important events of the early years of Christianity, for it completely altered the political and religious landscape of the Mediterranean world. If Luke was writing Acts after AD 70, it is very hard to believe that he would omit this catastrophic event, especially since he had recorded Jesus' prediction that it would happen:

> "When you see Jerusalem being surrounded by armies, you will know that its desolation is near. Then let those who are in Judea flee to the mountains, let those in the city get out, and let those in the country not enter the city. For this is the time of punishment in fulfillment of all that has been written. How dreadful it will be in those days for pregnant women and nursing mothers! There will be great distress in the land and wrath against this people. They will fall by the sword and will be taken as prisoners to all the nations. Jerusalem will be trampled on by the Gentiles until the times of the Gentiles are fulfilled."[8]

Why wouldn't Luke want to record the fulfillment of an event that Jesus had so accurately predicted?

Acts includes events in the life of Paul and James, who were prominent leaders of the early church, and it includes the martyrdom of Stephen. However, it doesn't include the martyrdoms of James and Paul, which Luke surely would have included as an encouragement to other Christians facing persecution and death. The conclusion is quite logical: Luke wrote Acts before James died in AD 62. Including this one reason, the classical historian Colin Hemer provides a total of seventeen reasons why Acts was most likely written prior to AD 62.[9]

Many scholars believe that one of Luke's sources was Mark's Gospel, and they have concluded that Mark could have been composed as early as twenty years after Jesus' death.[10] Many scholars also recognize that Mark's Gospel contains even earlier material, as the respected New Testament scholar William Lane Craig explains:

> We can tell from the language, grammar, and style that Mark got his empty tomb story—actually his whole passion narrative—from an earlier source. In fact, there

is evidence it was written before AD 37, which is much too early for legend to have seriously corrupted it.[11]

Not only is there evidence that Mark wrote his Gospel in the 50's and that he incorporated even earlier eyewitness material about Jesus' death and resurrection, there is strong evidence that Mark was a companion of the apostle Peter. This was attested to by the early church father Papias, who was the leader of the church in Hierapolis (modern-day Pamukkale, Turkey) and whom we mentioned in the last chapter. Papias had known the daughters of the original apostle Philip,[12] and it is likely that he had spoken with many early Christians who had known Jesus, possibly including the original disciple John.[13]

As we covered in the last chapter, Papias recalled one of the earliest followers of Jesus saying, "Mark, who became Peter's interpreter, wrote accurately as much as he remembered—though not in ordered form—of the Lord's sayings and doings."[14] So, according to an early church leader who had contact with eyewitnesses of Jesus, Mark was careful to base his account about Jesus on the teachings of Peter, one of the eleven original disciples who willingly died for his beliefs.

Papias' claims about the authorship of Mark's Gospel are independently confirmed by another early church leader, Irenaeus, who lived at the other end of the Roman Empire in the province of Gaul (modern-day France). Irenaeus had been a student of Polycarp, who in turn had been a student of the original disciple John.[15] Writing in the early second century, Irenaeus had this to say concerning the authorship of the four Gospels:

> Matthew composed his Gospel among the Hebrews in their language, while Peter and Paul were preaching the Gospel in Rome and building up the church there. After their deaths, Mark—Peter's follower and interpreter—handed down to us Peter's proclamation in written form. Luke, the companion of Paul, wrote in a book the Gospel proclaimed by Paul. Finally, John—the Lord's own follower, the one who leaned against his chest—composed the Gospel while living in Ephesus, in Asia.[16]

Thus, Irenaeus claims that all four Gospels were written either by eyewitnesses or based on eyewitness accounts.

CHAPTER 9: MORE EYEWITNESS EVIDENCE

Based on these independent testimonies from disparate parts of the Mediterranean world, we have good reason to believe that all four of the Gospels were either written by original eyewitnesses or—in Mark and Luke's case—by men who interviewed eyewitnesses.

We can also glean even earlier information about Jesus and early Christian belief from the letters of the apostle Paul. The majority of New Testament scholars agree that Paul definitely wrote these seven biblical books: Romans, First Corinthians, Second Corinthians, Galatians, Philippians, First Thessalonians, and Philemon. The earliest Christian writers quoted from these seven, they were included in every official early collection of Christian documents, and they are consistent in terms of themes, style, vocabulary, and emphases. Moreover, there is consensus among scholars that at least these seven letters were written in the 50's while Paul was traveling throughout the Mediterranean.[17]

Many scholars believe that some, if not all, of the six other Pauline Epistles were also written by Paul. In fact, in addition to the Epistles mentioned above, the early church father Clement (writing in AD 95) quoted from the Pauline Epistles to the Ephesians, First Timothy, and Titus. The early church father Ignatius (writing circa AD 107) also quoted from the Pauline Epistles to the Colossians and Second Timothy. And the early church father Polycarp (writing in AD 110) also quoted from the Pauline Epistle of Second Thessalonians.

We can therefore be confident that all of the Pauline Epistles were written in the first century or, at the very latest, the first decade of the second century. However, to be conservative for our purposes, we'll confine our analysis to the seven letters that are widely acknowledged as written by Paul in the 50's.

These letters contain numerous early Christian *creeds*, or statements of faith, which had begun to circulate among the early churches a few years after Jesus' death.[18] One creed, which we mentioned in Chapter 5, bears repeating. It makes these claims:

> For what I received I passed on to you as of first importance: that Christ died for our sins according to the Scriptures, that he was buried, that he was raised on the third day according to the Scriptures, and that he appeared to Cephas, and then to the Twelve. After that, he appeared to more than five hundred of the brothers

and sisters at the same time, most of whom are still living, though some have fallen asleep [i.e., died]. Then he appeared to James, then to all the apostles, and last of all he appeared to me also.[19]

This creed confirms that the earliest followers of Jesus believed he rose from the dead and that Jesus appeared to several groups of people after his resurrection, including one group of more than five hundred individuals.

Prominent New Testament scholar Craig Blomberg notes the importance of this creed:

> Almost no one doubts that Paul wrote this letter or that he was telling the truth when he 'delivered' to the Corinthians the list of witnesses of the resurrection in verse 3-7 as one which he had 'received' from Christians who preceded him. The Greek words for 'deliver' (*paradidomi*) and 'receive' (*paralambanō*) in this context are often used as fairly technical terms for the transmission of tradition. Almost certainly such information would have been related to Paul by the disciples in Damascus (*c.* AD 33) or in Jerusalem during his first visit there after becoming a Christian (*c.* AD 35). Regardless of one's attitude towards the gospels' testimony, therefore, it is extremely difficult to deny that here at least is accurate information.[20]

Another early creed is recorded in Paul's letter to the first group of believers in Philippi (in modern-day Greece between Thessaloniki and Istanbul, Turkey). Because of its poetic style, early Christians likely would sing it as a hymn.[21] Paul uses this creed to emphasize how believers should look to Jesus as the ultimate example of humility because, even though he was God, Jesus became a man and humbled himself in service to us. The creed describes Jesus in this way:

> Who, being in very nature God,
> did not consider equality with God something to be used to his own advantage;

> rather, he made himself nothing
> by taking the very nature of a servant,
> being made in human likeness.
> And being found in appearance as a man,
> he humbled himself
> by becoming obedient to death—
> even death on a cross!
> Therefore God exalted him to the highest place
> and gave him the name that is above every name,
> that at the name of Jesus every knee should bow,
> in heaven and on earth and under the earth
> and every tongue acknowledge that Jesus Christ is Lord,
> to the glory of God the Father.[22]

The ending of this creed, specifically the part claiming that every knee will bow and every tongue will acknowledge Jesus as Lord, clearly connects Jesus to the God of the Jewish Scriptures. The prophet Isaiah, writing some seven hundred years before Paul, records this proclamation:

> "Turn to me and be saved, all you ends of the earth; for I am God, and there is no other. By myself I have sworn, my mouth has uttered in all integrity a word that will not be revoked: Before me every knee will bow; by me every tongue will swear."[23]

The first Christians (many of them Jews) may not have understood how a statement about God from the Old Testament could be applied to a man, but here we find one of the first clear statements that the earliest Christians believed Jesus deserved the same honor as the God of the Old Testament.[24]

Moreover, when it describes Jesus as "Lord," this creed uses *kyrios*, the word used for God in the Greek translation of the Hebrew Old Testament, called the *Septuagint*. The Jewish community of the first century was very familiar with the Greek Old Testament, and the New Testament writers regularly quoted from it. (In fact, most of our Bibles today use "Lord" instead of "*Yahweh*" or "*Jehovah*" in the Old Testament because the Greek Old Testament used *kyrios* instead of these usual Hebrew names for God.)

Prominent biblical scholar James Montgomery Boice emphasizes the importance of using this word to reference Jesus:

> The disciples of Christ knew that the word [*kyrios*] was repeatedly used to translate this great name for God [*Yahweh* or *Jehovah*]. Yet, knowing this, they did not hesitate to transfer the title to Jesus, thereby indicating that in their view Jesus is Jehovah.[25]

The creed also applies to Jesus the name "Christ," or "*Christos*," the *Septuagint's* translation of "Messiah," the anointed ruler chosen by God to institute peace on earth. Therefore, the Philippians 2 creed is clearly claiming that Jesus is both God and the Jewish Messiah. In fact, "Jesus Christ is Lord" ("*Xristos Iesous Kyrios*") was the earliest Christian confession of faith, and many Christians were executed for saying Jesus was Lord, and not Caesar.[26] Paul refers to this simple but important early creed, or statement of faith, in several other places.[27]

Let's discuss one more book of the New Testament that provides additional insight into early Christian beliefs, the First Epistle of John. As mentioned in Chapter 5, the First Epistle of John begins with the claim that the author saw, heard, and touched Jesus after he had risen. Here, and in other sections, First John makes it clear that Jesus appeared in the flesh after his resurrection, not in a spiritual form, as some people were starting to claim.[28] Again, this provides evidence that Christians were claiming they had seen him *physically* alive after his death on the cross.

Two different types of objections can be made at this point: First, skeptics may claim that the early Christians concocted the stories about Jesus—especially his miracles, claims of deity, and resurrection—in the period of time between his death and when the Gospels were recorded a few decades later. Second, skeptics may claim that legendary material was inserted over the centuries after the Gospels were first written down, perhaps by zealous church leaders or scribes who wanted to put words in Jesus' mouth or exaggerate his actions and claims.

While we have already addressed these objections in part, let's take another look to more fully understand why both of these scenarios are very unlikely. We'll respond to the first skeptical claim now, and Chapter 12 will address the second claim.

CHAPTER 9: MORE EYEWITNESS EVIDENCE

FICTIONAL MATERIAL INSERTED EARLY?

Scholarly consensus is that the Gospel of Mark was written between AD 60 and 75, within twenty-seven to forty-five years of Jesus' death. Moreover, many aspects of Jesus' life were recorded in the Pauline Epistles, the earliest of which were written within twenty to twenty-five years of Jesus' death.

These gaps may seem huge to us, but they are actually very small for ancient documents. Unlike people today, who have access to books and can easily write things down, the majority of people in Jesus' day were unable to read and write. Therefore, many people were able to memorize lengthy stories and accurately pass them along orally.[29] In fact, the earliest followers of Jesus probably did not see a need to write their recollections down immediately, since they were accustomed to an oral recitation of Scripture. Moreover, eyewitnesses were still around to ensure that the oral testimony was accurate. It was only when the eyewitnesses started to die that the accounts were finally written down in the forms we read today in the New Testament.

New Testament scholar William Lane Craig explains that oral transmission was dependable in that culture:

> In an oral culture like that of first century Palestine the ability to memorize and retain large tracts of oral tradition was a highly prized and highly developed skill. From the earliest age children in the home, elementary school, and the synagogue were taught to memorize faithfully sacred tradition. The disciples would have exercised similar care with the teachings of Jesus.[30]

If anything, they would allow only small changes in less important, secondary details in the retelling of the story. One study of ancient literature of the Middle East found that in any given retelling of sacred tradition, the *secondary* details would vary by ten to forty percent, but the *primary* points were *always unaltered*. Perhaps not coincidentally, the variations among the Synoptic Gospels (Matthew, Mark, and Luke) constitute approximately ten to forty percent of the text, but these variations are only in the secondary details, as we saw in Chapter 8.[31]

This oral tradition was definitely not like the our game of "telephone," in which one person whispers a statement to another person, who whispers it to the next person, and so on down a long line of people, such that by the time it reaches the last person, the statement has changed dramatically, and everyone has a good laugh when they compare the first and last versions. In cultures dependent on oral tradition, the stories were told repeatedly, and the listeners—especially the original eyewitnesses—could always correct the storyteller if there was any error. If you were to alter the game of telephone to make it analogous to the passing on of oral tradition, each person would have to say the statement out loud so that everyone could hear it each time and have an opportunity to correct the speaker if he or she made a mistake.

In his well-researched and highly lauded book, *Jesus and the Eyewitnesses*, Richard Bauckham lays out the plentiful evidence that the Gospels were based directly on eyewitness testimony. He also demonstrates that the eyewitnesses played a crucial role in preserving the accounts of Jesus' life exactly as they were passed along within the earliest Christian communities. As a result of the direct influence of these eyewitnesses, Bauckham clarifies that the Gospels are more accurately described as *oral history*, as opposed to *oral tradition*. Oral history depended directly on the testimony of eyewitnesses and was passed along during their lifetimes and in their presence. Oral tradition, on the other hand, is a more general category of oral transmission and doesn't require that the eyewitnesses were still alive. If something was passed down "by oral tradition," the general implication is that the stories were probably handed down orally when the eyewitnesses were no longer around to ensure their accuracy.

Of particular note, the authors of the Gospels often provide names for some individuals in an account, but not for others who play an equally important role in the same story. Bauckham asserts that the named individuals in the Gospels were most likely the eyewitnesses who had provided their testimony of the events that are recorded. Bauckham summarizes the issue by posing these questions:

> Why should one of two disciples on the road to Emmaus be named (Cleopas) and the other not? While most beneficiaries of Jesus' healings and resuscitation miracles are anonymous, Jairus (whose daughter is raised) is named in Mark and Luke, Bartimaeus in Mark,

CHAPTER 9: MORE EYEWITNESS EVIDENCE

Lazarus in John. Since people who encounter Jesus on one occasion are usually not named, why should the Pharisee who entertains Jesus to dinner in Luke 7 be named (Simon, 7:40)? Why should Simon of Cyrene be named? There are also cases where a person who is anonymous in one Gospel is named in another. For example, John alone identifies the woman who anoints Jesus as Mary of Bethany, the name of the man who cut off the ear of the high priest's slave as Peter, and the slave as Malchus.[32]

Bauckham also notes that, in general, the Gospel writers did not provide names to the individuals in their accounts (for example, the Samaritan woman, the paralyzed man, and the man born blind). In fact, in all four of the Gospels, individual benefiting from a healing, exorcism, or resuscitation are only named three times (Jairus, Bartimaeus, and Lazarus).[33] Thus, individuals who *do* have a name stand out—most likely because, as Bauckham states, they "were eyewitnesses who not only originated the traditions to which their names are attached but also continued to tell these stories as authoritative guarantors of their traditions."[34]

Bauckham lists more than forty named individuals in the four Gospels (that is, besides Jesus, individuals from the Old Testament, public persons, the twelve disciples, and the names in the two genealogies of Jesus).[35] He notes that the presence of these named individuals has "never been satisfactorily explained."[36] And Bauckham emphasizes that the practice of assigning a fictional name to characters in stories was very uncommon before the fourth century.[37] Furthermore, personal names are generally the most difficult parts of stories to remember and the first to be dropped as stories are told over time. Therefore, in the few cases when these personal names are remembered, there must be a good reason for it. The best reason, Bauckham claims, is that the names represent the eyewitness sources of the stories.[38] He concludes that "all these people joined the early Christian movement and were well known at least in the circles in which these traditions were first transmitted."[39]

One interesting aspect of Bauckham's proposal that named individuals were the eyewitnesses is that it clarifies the divergence in the names of the women who first visited Jesus' empty tomb, as we discussed in Chapter 8. The variation in the women's names from Gospel to Gospel could actually be evidence that the named women were the ones who provided eyewitness testimony to each of the Gospel writers. Bauckham emphasizes the significance of the different lists of women as follows:

> The divergences among the lists have often been taken as grounds for not taking them seriously as naming eyewitnesses of the events. In fact, the opposite is the case: these divergences, properly understood, demonstrate the scrupulous *care* with which the Gospels present the women eyewitnesses.... In this way my proposal that the Evangelists were careful to name precisely the women who were well known to them as witnesses to these crucial events in the origins of the Christian movement explains the variations among their lists of women as no other proposal has succeeded in doing.[40]

Not only did the Gospel writers only mention the women whom they trusted had actually witnessed the empty tomb and the risen Jesus, but, Bauckham claims, the differences in the narratives of the empty tomb and resurrection also reflect the unique perspective of the eyewitnesses each writer interviewed. Each woman had a different vantage point, which led her to recall different aspects of the same event, which in turn led to the differences in the secondary details of each Gospel account.

Bauckham lays out similar evidence that other named individuals—such as Simon of Cyrene, Jairus, Bartimaeus, Zacchaeus, Cleopas, and Lazarus—were also key providers of eyewitness testimony to the Gospel writers. He points out that the stories involving named individuals are "among the most vividly told." The following stories are especially vivid: the raising of Jairus' daughter, the healing of Bartimaeus, the story of Zacchaeus, and the story of Cleopas and his companion.[41] As we discussed in Chapter 6, this vivid detail (from "flashbulb" memories) is exactly what we would expect from a story that had originally been told by an emotionally involved eyewitness.[42]

Bauckham also proposes that the divergence in names provided in each Gospel is a reflection of how well-known a given person was in a Christian community. For example, Bauckham hypothesizes that Mark

CHAPTER 9: MORE EYEWITNESS EVIDENCE

names Bartimaeus because he was known to the people who would read Mark's account. But by the time of Matthew and Luke, Bartimaeus was "no longer a figure of wide repute,"[43] one explanation why he is simply described as one of the blind beggars that Jesus heals by the side of the road. Such examples of divergences in the use of personal names give credence to the claim that the Gospels were based on the testimony of certain specific individuals who had seen, heard, touched, and received healing from Jesus.

The most important eyewitnesses and guarantors of the oral history about Jesus were, of course, the eleven original disciples of Jesus, along with the twelfth disciple, Matthias, who the others selected to replace Judas Iscariot. As mentioned in Chapter 5, Peter specifically emphasizes the importance of selecting a fellow eyewitness of Jesus who had been with them "the whole time the Lord Jesus went in and out among us," and he also insists that "one of these [fellow eyewitnesses] must become a witness with us of his resurrection."[44] Two men were proposed to fill Judas Iscariot's vacancy, which suggests that more than just the twelve disciples qualified as having been with Jesus "the whole time."[45] Based on this and other passages, Bauckham notes that there was special emphasis on the testimony of those who had known Jesus from the beginning of his ministry:

> Evidently in the Christian movement a special importance attached to the testimony of disciples who had been eyewitnesses of the whole ministry of Jesus, from its beginning when John was baptizing to Jesus' resurrection appearances. This was a necessary qualification for membership of the Twelve, but there were also other disciples who fulfilled the qualification and whose witness would have been especially valuable for that reason.[46]

Therefore, while the numerous named individuals throughout the Gospels played an important role as providers of eyewitness testimonies to their own stories, the disciples who had been with Jesus throughout his ministry were the most important guarantors of the tradition. Luke calls these individuals the *"autoptai"* in the preface to his Gospel, stating that he has written an "orderly account" of the events of Jesus' life as they were "handed down" to him from "those who from the first were eyewitnesses [*autoptai*]."[47]

By using the term *autoptai*, Luke asserts that he is following the best practices of ancient historiography, since most ancient historians believed first-hand eyewitness interviews were the most accurate way to determine the truth of past events.[48] Not only did the Twelve play a crucial role in starting the oral history of Jesus' life, but they continued to play a role as prominent teachers in the early Christian movement, ensuring that this oral history did not become distorted.[49]

There is further internal evidence within the Gospel of Mark indicating that it is based on Peter's eyewitness testimony. First, Mark uses a unique "plural-to-singular narrative device" that is not found in Matthew and Luke. There are twenty-one passages in Mark in which a plural verb appears without a subject and is immediately followed by a singular verb or pronoun referring to Jesus alone. This narrative device, which was originally described by C. H. Turner in 1925,[50] indicates that Mark is writing his Gospel from the perspective of an eyewitness of the original events. In one example of a "plural-to-singular narrative device," Turner also describes an awkward construction that Mark uses at the beginning of his Gospel, when he describes how Jesus healed Simon's mother. We read, "As soon as *they* left the synagogue, *they* went with James and John to the home of Simon and Andrew."[51] Turner notes that substituting "they" in this verse with "we" makes this statement less awkward: "As soon as *we* left the synagogue, *we* went with James and John to *our* house." The "we" therefore refers to Simon (whose name Jesus changed to Peter) and his brother Andrew. It is as if the author were directly transcribing a story that Peter or Andrew was telling, simply substituting "they" whenever Peter or Andrew said "we."[52]

The Gospel of Mark uses a second narrative device, what Bauckham terms the "*inclusio* of eyewitness testimony," to indicate that Peter was the eyewitness source for Mark's stories. Peter is both the first and the last disciple mentioned by Mark.[53] As Bauckham notes, "The two references form an *inclusio* around the whole story, suggesting that Peter is the witness whose testimony includes the whole."[54] This literary device is also found in the Gospels of John and Luke, as well as in other ancient historical documents.[55]

Let's take a quick look at how the "*inclusio* of eyewitness testimony"

CHAPTER 9: MORE EYEWITNESS EVIDENCE

is also possibly used to indicate the author of John's Gospel. The first disciples mentioned in John are two unnamed individuals who had followed John the Baptist.[56] In John 1:40, the identity of one of these unnamed individuals is revealed as Andrew, who then proceeds to look for his brother, Simon Peter, to tell him they have found the Messiah (Jesus). This eliminates Peter as the second unnamed individual, who remains anonymous.

As mentioned in Chapter 5, the disciple who claims to have written the Gospel of John never tells us who he is, referring to himself only as "the disciple whom Jesus loved" or "another disciple." John's Gospel ends with this anonymous individual's claim that he is the "disciple who testifies to these things and who wrote them down."[57] Again, we see the "*inclusio* of eyewitness testimony" with the first and last disciple mentioned in the Gospel of John most likely the actual author who relied on his own experience as an eyewitness for much of the Gospel. Interestingly, biblical scholar Derek Tovey notes that "at every point where the beloved disciple appears… the narrative includes items of close detail which suggest 'on the spot,' eyewitness report."[58]

Some final notes on memorization and historical authenticity: Over eighty percent of Jesus' sayings were originally recorded in poetic form.[59] When the sayings of Jesus are translated into Aramaic, the language Jesus spoke, they display regular poetic rhythm and rhyme. Biblical scholar F. F. Bruce states: "A discourse that follows a recognizable pattern is more easily memorized, and if Jesus wished His teachings to be memorized His use of poetry is easily explained."[60] Also, there are numerous compact sections of text that succinctly summarize teachings in a way that could easily be memorized. Biblical scholar Gary Habermas has identified forty brief sections of the New Testament that also fit the description of a creed, such as the creeds in First Corinthians 15:3-8 and Philippians 2:6-11. These numerous creeds provide further strong evidence that the beliefs of the earliest followers of Jesus—that is, those beliefs formulated soon after the crucifixion—are accurately preserved in the New Testament.[61]

In sum, scholars who claim that the four Gospels were fabricated and thus present a false picture of the teachings of Jesus are ignoring an abundance of historical evidence demonstrating that the accounts are based on eyewitness testimony. You might say these skeptics are taking a huge leap of faith. The most reasonable approach to these documents uses responsible historiographical methods. In doing so, the "shortest leap" is this: we can regard the New Testament accounts as historical.

Questions for Comprehension and Discussion

1. For the sake of review, what are six main lines of evidence that have been covered in previous chapters that provide support for the trustworthiness of the accounts of Jesus' life?
2. Why is it important that the documents describing Jesus' life and the early church were (a) written within the lifetime of possible eyewitnesses and (b) started to circulate in the same places where the events had occurred?
3. Why do many scholars believe that the Book of Acts was written before AD 62? Why is it likely that Luke was written before Acts, and that Mark was written before Luke?
4. What is the likely range of dates assigned to the seven Pauline epistles that scholars agree were written by Paul? What are examples of even earlier material that is included in the Pauline epistles?
5. What is especially significant about the description of Jesus in the creed or hymn that Paul includes in Philippians 2:9-11?
6. Why is it significant that the Jewish authors of the accounts of Jesus' life call him *kyrios*?
7. What is the distinction between oral history and oral tradition? Why is it more appropriate to classify the Gospel accounts of Jesus' life as oral history?
8. Why does Richard Bauckham claim that some individuals in the Gospel accounts are named, while others are not? What are some examples of this, and how does it explain the different names of the women in the resurrection accounts?
9. What are two narrative devices that are used in Mark and John to indicate that the stories are based on eyewitness testimony?
10. How are more than eighty percent of Jesus' sayings written, and how does this affect the reliability of oral transmission?

CHAPTER 9: MORE EYEWITNESS EVIDENCE

CHAPTER 9 ENDNOTES

1. Richard Bauckham, *Jesus and the Eyewitnesses: The Gospels as Eyewitness Testimony* (Grand Rapids, MI: Eerdmans, 2006), 7.
2. J. Warner Wallace, "Can We Construct the Entire New Testament from the Writings of the Church Fathers?" June 13, 2016. https://coldcasechristianity.com/2016/can-we-construct-the-entire-new-testament-from-the-writings-of-the-church-fathers.
3. F. F. Bruce, *The New Testament Documents: Are They Reliable?* (Grand Rapids, MI: Eerdmans, 1981), 43.
4. Mark D. Roberts, *Can We Trust the Gospels?* (Wheaton, IL: Crossway, 2007), 58.
5. Paul Barnett, *Jesus and the Rise of Early Christianity: A History of New Testament Times* (Downers Grove, IL: InterVarsity Press, 1999), 19.
6. Basing his history on previous church historians, Eusebius of Caesarea, writing in the fourth century, claimed that Paul was beheaded under the Roman Emperor Nero, who reigned from 54 to 68. Paul's martyrdom under Nero is confirmed by the following other sources: Lactantius, *Of the Manner in Which the Persecutors Died* II (3rd century); John Chrysostom, *Concerning Lowliness of Mind* 4 (4th century); Sulpicius Severus, *Chronica* II.28–29 (late 3rd century to early 4th century).
7. The Jewish historian Josephus records the stoning of James in AD 62 (during the interregnum of the rules of Festus and Albinus) in *Antiquities* 20:9, from *The Works of Josephus*, transl. by William Whiston (Philadelphia: David McKay, n.d.).
8. Luke 21:20-24.
9. Hemer, *The Book of Acts in the Setting of Hellenistic History*, 376-382. These reasons are also summarized in Norman L. Geisler, *Baker Encyclopedia of Christian Apologetics* (Grand Rapids, MI: Baker, 1999), 5-6.
10. Normal L. Geisler and Frank Turek, *I Don't Have Enough Faith to Be an Atheist* (Wheaton, IL: Crossway Books, 2004), 241.
11. Quoted in Lee Strobel, *The Case for Christ* (Grand Rapids, MI: Zondervan, 1998), 220.
12. The daughters of Philip are mentioned in Acts 21:8-9. From Bruce, *The New Testament Documents*, 40. Bruce cites Eusebius, *Church History*. iii.31, 39.
13. Bauckham, *Jesus and the Eyewitnesses*, 13,18-19. For a scholarly summary of the eyewitness evidence from the writings of Papias, as well as a defense of the Papias source documents, see chapters 2, 9, and 16.
14. Quoted in Eusebius, *Church History*, 3.39.15. The translation is from Philip Schaff and Henry Wace, eds., *A Select Library of Nicene and Post-Nicene Fathers*, 2nd series (Grand Rapids, MI: Eerdmans, 1952-1957).

15 See Bauckham, *Jesus and the Eyewitnesses*, 18f and Chapter 17. Irenaeus wrote that Polycarp "would tell of his conversation with John and with others who had seen the Lord, how he would relate their words from memory; and what the things were which he had heard from them concerning the Lord, his mighty works and his teaching" (quoted in Eusebius, *Church History*, 5.20.6; translation from R. M. Grant, *Second-Century Christianity* [London: SPCK, 1946], 116.)

16 Quoted in Eusebius, *Church History*, 3.39.15. The translation is from Philip Schaff and Henry Wace, eds., *A Select Library of Nicene and Post-Nicene Fathers*, 2nd series (Grand Rapids, MI: Eerdmans, 1952-1957).

17 I. Howard Marshall, ed., *New Testament Interpretation: Essays on Principles and Methods*, Grand Rapids, MI: William B. Eerdmans Publishing Co., 1977. According to F. F. Bruce, ten of the Pauline epistles were written between AD 48 and 60. From Bruce, *New Testament Documents*, 75.

18 As quoted by Craig Blomberg in Strobel, *The Case for Christ*, 35.

19 First Corinthians 15:3-8.

20 Craig Blomberg, *The Historical Reliability of the Gospels* (Downers Grove, IL: InterVarsity Press, 1987), 108.

21 Kenneth L. Barker and John R. Kohlenberger III, *NIV Bible Commentary, Volume 2: The New Testament* (Grand Rapids, MI: Zondervan Publishing House, 1994), 796. See also Robert M. Bowman and J. Ed Komoszewski, *Putting Jesus in His Place: The Case for the Deity of Christ* (Grand Rapids, MI: Kregel, 2007), 57-58.

22 Philippians 2:9-11.

23 Isaiah 45:22-23.

24 D. Guthrie, J.A. Motyer, A.M. Stibbs, and D.J. Wiseman, eds., *The New Bible Commentary: Revised* (London: InterVarsity Press, 1970), 1132.

25 James Montgomery Boice, *An Expositional Commentary of Romans: Volume 3* (Grand Rapids, MI: Baker Books, 1993), 1191.

26 Ibid.

27 Paul includes the creed "Jesus Christ is Lord" ("*Xristos Iesous Kyrios*") in 1 Corinthians 12:3, 2 Corinthians 4:5, and Romans 10:9.

28 See 1 John 4:2.

29 The fact that ancient people could remember long stories far better than modern people is demonstrated in Plato's *Phaedrus* 274c-275a, when Socrates warns against replacing oral traditions with written documents because people will stop using their memories. This indeed has been a repercussion of our modern dependence on written documents! But whether or not their memories were better in ancient times, their education emphasized memorization much more than ours does today. For more information on the importance of the skill of memorization in

CHAPTER 9: MORE EYEWITNESS EVIDENCE

the ancient world, see Richard Bauckham, *Jesus and the Eyewitnesses*, 280-287.

30 William Lane Craig, "The Evidence for Jesus." Posted online at http://www.leaderu.com/offices/billcraig/docs/rediscover2.html.
31 In an interview with Craig Blomberg in Strobel, *The Case for Christ*, 41.
32 Bauckham, *Jesus and the Eyewitnesses*, 40.
33 Ibid, 53.
34 Ibid, 39.
35 Ibid, Table 5, 65-66.
36 Ibid, 45.
37 Ibid, 44.
38 Ibid, 55.
39 Ibid, 45.
40 Ibid, 49-51. Emphasis his.
41 See Mark 5:22-24a, 35-43, 10:46-52, Luke 19:1-10, and Luke 24:13-35 respectively.
42 Bauckham, *Jesus and the Eyewitnesses*, 46-47.
43 Ibid, 54.
44 Acts 1:21-22.
45 Bauckham, *Jesus and the Eyewitnesses*, 115.
46 Ibid, 116.
47 Luke 1:2.
48 For a discussion of the ancient historiographic preference for eyewitness testimony, as well as his discussion of Luke's preface, see Bauckham, *Jesus and the Eyewitnesses*, 21-30, 116-124.
49 Bauckham, *Jesus and the Eyewitnesses*, 30.
50 C. H. Turner, "Marcan Usage: Notes Critical and Exegetical, on the Second Gospel V. The Movements of Jesus and His Disciples and the Crowd," *Journal of Theological Studies* 26 (1925) 225-40. Turner's article is reprinted, along with the rest of his eleven "Notes on Marcan Usage," in J. K. Elliott, *The Language and Style of the Gospel of Mark* (Leiden, The Netherlands: E. J. Brill, 1993).
51 Mark 1:29.
52 For a more detailed explanation of this Marcan narrative pattern, see Bauckham, *Jesus and the Eyewitnesses*, 156-164.
53 See Mark 1:16 and 16:7.
54 Bauckham, *Jesus and the Eyewitnesses*, 125.
55 For a more detailed discussion of the "*inclusio* of eyewitness testimony" in the Gospels and other works of ancient literature, see Ibid, 124-147.
56 See John 1:35.

57 John calls himself "the disciple whom Jesus loved" in John 13:23, 19:26, 20:2, 21:7, and 21:20, and he calls himself "another disciple" in John 18:15. The final reference is in John 21:24.
58 D. Tovey, Narrative Art and Act in the Fourth Gospel (*Journal for the Study of the New Testament Supplement Series* 151; Sheffield: Sheffield Academic, 1997), 124, as quoted in Bauckham, *Jesus and the Eyewitnesses*, 398.
59 In an interview with Craig Blomberg in Strobel, *The Case for Christ*, 43.
60 Bruce, *The New Testament Documents*, 36. Bruce cites C. F. Burney, *The Poetry of Our Lord* (1925).
61 Gary Habermas, *The Historical Jesus* (Joplin, MO: College Press, 1996), Chapter 7.

Ancient extrabiblical sources do present a surprisingly large amount of detail concerning both the life of Jesus and the nature of early Christianity.... We should realize that it is quite extraordinary that we could provide a broad outline of most of the major facts of Jesus' life from 'secular' history alone.

—Gary Habermas, apologetics
and philosophy professor[1]

I have yet to see a piece of writing, political or non-political, that does not have a slant. All writing slants the way a writer leans, and no man is born perpendicular, although many men are born upright.

—E. B. White, author[2]

10

Secular Confirmation

During a 2010 broadcast of CNN's *Larry King Live*, millions of viewers heard an extraordinarily confident claim about human history. Larry King's guest was Ellen Johnson, the president of American Atheists. Their topic was life after death, and King suddenly threw out this question:

> KING: We got to take a break. Ellen, what do you believe about Jesus Christ?
> JOHNSON: Well, I'm here to give the reality point of view, I guess. Because the reality is there is not one shred of secular evidence there ever was a Jesus Christ. Jesus Christ and Christianity is a modern religion. And Jesus Christ is a compilation from other gods: Horus, Mithra, who had the same origins, the same death as the mythological Jesus Christ.
> KING: So you don't believe there was a Jesus Christ.
> JOHNSON: There was not. It is not what I believe. There is no secular evidence that JC, Jesus Christ, ever existed.[3]

Following these statements, a commercial aired, and there was no later opportunity to provide any evidence to the contrary. Viewers were left with the impression that one of the foundational claims upon which Western civilization has been built is as unsubstantial as a forgotten fairytale. Was Jesus really just a mythological figure, like Zeus, Apollo, or Hercules? And even if Jesus really did exist, could the New Testament authors have written about him with a bias, making him out to be the person they wanted him to be?

CHAPTER 10: SECULAR CONFIRMATION

Our first clarification is this: Just because the authors of the New Testament wanted people to believe in Jesus, we can't automatically assume their accounts are false. It is just as logical (and actually more logical, considering they were willing to die for their statements) that the authors of the New Testament wanted people to believe in Jesus because Jesus really did rise from the dead. Christian apologist Norman Geisler explains that bias doesn't necessarily lead to historical inaccuracy:

> The objection that the writings are partisan involves a significant but false implication that witnesses cannot be reliable if they were close to the one about whom they gave testimony. This is clearly false. Survivors of the Jewish holocaust were close to the events they have described to the world. That very fact puts them in the best position to know what happened.... The New Testament writers should not be disqualified because they were close to the events they relate.[4]

So, we can't discard the eyewitness testimony described in the last four chapters simply because it's biased. Let's instead look at historical viewpoints concerning Jesus from sources that were not Christian, and even anti-Christian. In this chapter, we will continue our historiographical analysis of these early descriptions of Jesus' life, death, resurrection, and teachings to further assess their truthfulness. Having evaluated the documents using the internal evidence test of historicity, let's now determine whether the accounts of Jesus' life pass the *external* evidence test. In so doing, we ask whether there are other outside historical sources that tell us about a man named Jesus in the early first century. If we can confirm the details of the stories about Jesus using other historical documents as well as using archaeological evidence, we can be much more confident that the New Testament accounts are truthful.

CONFIRMATION BY NON-CHRISTIAN SOURCES

Ellen Johnson's dismissal of the New Testament record as mythmaking stands on her claim that there is "not one shred of secular evidence" that Jesus existed. As it turns out, there are many non-Christian sources that mention Jesus within one hundred fifty years of his life, so many that what begins to "shred" is the argument that this public figure never existed. We turn now to these outside sources, some of which display a clear anti-Christian bias. Ironically, their attacks on this young religion now serve to confirm its claims, even to the twenty-first century skeptic.

1. TACITUS:

The Roman historian Cornelius Tacitus lived during the reigns of more than six Roman emperors, from circa AD 55 to 120. His most important works, the *Annals* and the *Histories*, record the history of ancient Rome from the death of Augustus in AD 14 to the death of Domitian in AD 96. The *Annals*, written around 115, contain his most important reference to Jesus and early Christians.

We can learn much about Jesus and early Christianity from Tacitus' claim that the emperor Nero blamed the Christians for setting a fire that destroyed much of Rome in July of 64:

> Consequently, to get rid of the report, Nero fastened the guilt and inflicted the most exquisite tortures on a class hated for their abominations, called Christians by the populace. Christus, from whom the name had its origin, suffered the extreme penalty during the reign of Tiberius at the hands of one of our procurators, Pontius Pilate, and a most mischievous superstition, thus checked for the moment, again broke out not only in Judaea, the first source of the evil, but even in Rome, where all things hideous and shameful from every part of the world find their centre and become popular.[5]

Note these historical claims:

1. Christians were named for their founder, Christus (the Latin form of the title, "Christ," "Messiah," or "King").
2. This Christus was put to death by the local Roman leader (procurator) Pontius Pilate during the reign of Tiberius (AD

14-37). (As F. F. Bruce states: "It may surely be accounted one of the ironies of history that the only mention Pilate receives from a Roman historian is in connection with the part he played in the execution of Jesus!"[6])

3. We also learn that the Christians' "superstition" was ended for a short time, but it broke out again after the death of their founder. This could be a reference to the Christian beliefs that Jesus had risen from the dead and was the Son of God, since his followers lost hope after his crucifixion, but then started worshiping him as God again and claiming that he had physically risen from the dead. While the "superstition" arose initially in Judea, where the teaching of Christus originated, his followers soon brought it to Rome (at the latest by AD 64, the year of the fire).

4. Finally, the emperor Nero put the blame for the great fire on the Christians who lived in Rome.[7]

2. SUETONIUS:

The Roman historian Suetonius, short for Gaius Suetonius Tranquillus, lived from approximately AD 69 to 130. He served as the chief secretary of the emperor Hadrian, who reigned from AD 117 to 138. Writing around the same time as Tacitus in the early part of the second century, Suetonius makes a reference to Jesus when he is writing about the emperor Claudius, who reigned from AD 41 to 54:

> Because the Jews at Rome caused continuous disturbances at the instigation of Chrestus, he expelled them from the city.[8]

The translator notes that "Chrestus" is an alternate Latin spelling of "Christus," or "Christ." Suetonius is referring to the riots that broke out in a Jewish community in Rome in AD 49 and that led Claudius to order all Jews to leave Rome. Lending further credibility to the Book of Acts, Luke actually mentions this event when he notes that Paul met a man and his wife who had come from Italy:

There [Paul] met a Jew named Aquila, a native of Pontus, who had recently come from Italy with his wife Priscilla, because Claudius had ordered all the Jews to leave Rome.[9]

In his record of the emperor Nero, Suetonius makes another reference to the early Christians that corroborates Tacitus' reference above, claiming that Nero blamed the great fire of Rome on the Christians, "a sect professing a new and mischievous religious belief."[10]

3. Thallus

In approximately AD 52, a historian named Thallus wrote a history of the Eastern Mediterranean world from the Trojan War up to his own day.[11] Although this work has been lost, it has in part lived on because many other early historians quote from it.[12] One quote is found in the works of Sextus Julius Africanus, a Christian who wrote around AD 221. Africanus references a part of Thallus' history in a discussion of the darkness that coincided with Jesus' death. He writes:

> Thallus, in the third book of his histories, explains away this darkness as an eclipse of the sun—unreasonably, as it seems to me (unreasonably, of course, because a solar eclipse could not take place at the time of the full moon, and it was at the season of the Paschal full moon that Christ died).[13]

While it is not 100% certain that Thallus was referring to the mid-day darkness that coincided with the death of Jesus on the eve of the Jewish Passover, the fact that Africanus is countering Thallus' naturalistic explanation suggests that Thallus was indeed commenting on this event. Africanus was arguing that the Passover, when Jesus was killed, was always at the time of a full moon. The moon is full because the sun is on the other side of the Earth from the moon, thus shining directly on the moon and fully lighting it. Thus, at the time of a full moon at Passover, the Earth is between the sun and the moon (sun – Earth – moon). But if the darkness was caused by a solar eclipse, the moon would be blocking the sun from the Earth's perspective. The moon would thus be between the Earth and the sun (Earth – moon – sun).

Africanus' counterargument that a solar eclipse cannot be the explanation for the darkness at the time of Jesus' crucifixion therefore implicitly acknowledges that Thallus was referring to the darkness he had heard occurred on the day Jesus died. Why would Africanus even bring up Thallus' argument if Thallus had been talking about a solar eclipse that was completely unrelated to Jesus? This reference could very well confirm that non-Christians as early as AD 52 were looking for naturalistic explanations for the darkness described by Matthew, Mark, and Luke.[14]

4. Phlegon:

Phlegon was another early Roman historian whose work has been partially preserved in the works of other historians. In the same debate about the darkness at Jesus' death, Julius Africanus quotes from Phlegon's work, *Chronicles*. Africanus claims that Phlegon wrote: "During the time of Tiberius Caesar an eclipse of the sun occurred during the full moon."[15]

Like Thallus, Phlegon may have been trying to use a natural explanation to silence early Christian claims that the darkness at Jesus' death had a miraculous source. It was likely for this reason that Africanus quotes his statement about the eclipse during the reign of Tiberius Caesar. Again, since it is impossible for a solar eclipse to take place during the full moon, Phlegon implicitly—perhaps unknowingly—acknowledges that something completely extraordinary happened to darken the sun during the reign of Tiberius.

Because of Luke's careful record keeping (as he puts it, "having investigated everything carefully from the beginning to write an orderly account"[16]), we have specific references for the reign of Tiberius to demonstrate that it coincided with the death of Christ. We know that Tiberius reigned from 14 to 37 AD.[17] Luke claims that John the Baptist began his ministry "in the fifteenth year of the reign of Tiberius Caesar."[18] Jesus was crucified approximately three years after John the Baptist began his ministry, in the eighteenth year of Tiberius' reign. Thus, Luke's Gospel confirms that Jesus did in fact die under the reign of Tiberius (approximately AD 32), which is when the disputed darkness occurred.

In addition to Africanus, early church fathers Origen Adamantius (also known simply as Origen) and John Philoponus (also known as John the Grammarian or John of Alexandria) referred directly to this quote from Phlegon in the third and sixth centuries respectively, providing further evidence that Phlegon actually wrote it, even though the original has been lost.[19]

5. PLINY THE YOUNGER:

In the early second century, a man named Pliny the Younger was the Roman *legate*, or military ruler, of Bithynia-Pontus (in what is now north-central Turkey). He wrote a letter to the Roman emperor Trajan to ask for advice in dealing with Christians who were refusing to worship Trajan and the other Roman gods. This letter, dated to AD 112, reveals many characteristics of early Christian beliefs. One section reads:

> They were in the habit of meeting on a certain fixed day before it was light, when they sang in alternate verses a hymn to Christ, as to a god, and bound themselves by a solemn oath, not to do any wicked deeds.[20]

Note that Pliny does not say that they sang "to their god Christ." Instead, he implies that it is remarkable that they sang to an actual person "as to a god."

Other than the very important confirmation that the earliest believers worshiped Jesus as God, this letter from Pliny, as well as the response from the emperor Trajan (discussed below), provides historians with a wealth of information about the early Christian believers. For example, they refused to worship the Roman gods or the emperor, even when Pliny threatened to torture and execute them. Pliny even admits that he could discern who had falsely been accused of being a Christian because he "made them curse Christ, which a genuine Christian cannot be induced to do."[21]

6. Trajan, and

7. Hadrian:

The emperors Trajan and Hadrian both wrote letters that attest to the early Christian refusal to worship any other gods besides Jesus. In Trajan's response to the letter from Pliny the Younger mentioned above (dated AD 112), he confirms that Christians must be punished when they refuse to worship the Roman gods or the emperor, although he does provide restraints on this punishment, including the restriction that Christians aren't to be sought out for punishment.

Moreover, he states: "When the party denies himself to be a Christian and shall give proof that he is not (that is, by adoring our Gods) he shall be pardoned on the ground of repentance."[22]

A letter from the emperor Hadrian to another Roman political leader also recommends restrictions on the punishment of Christians, though he does state that Christians should be punished for their belief in a god other than the Roman gods and the emperor.[23] These letters from two Roman emperors thus demonstrate that the Christians worshiped Jesus as God from an early date, and that they were willing to suffer punishment for worshiping Jesus instead of the Roman gods or the Roman emperor.

8. Lucian of Samosata:

The Greek satirist Lucian of Samosata, who wrote during the first half of the second century, was fond of criticizing Christians as "misguided creatures." His sarcastic commentary includes the following:

> The Christians, you know, worship a man to this day—the distinguished personage who introduced their novel rites, and was crucified on that account.... You see, these misguided creatures start with the general conviction that they are immortal for all time, which explains the contempt of death and voluntary self-devotion which are so common among them; and then it was impressed on them by their original lawgiver that they are all brothers,

from the moment that they are converted, and deny the gods of Greece, and worship the crucified sage, and live after his laws. All this they take quite on faith, with the result that they despise all worldly goods alike, regarding them merely as common property.[24]

It is clear from this outsider's criticism that Christians were worshiping a historical man who had been crucified because of his teachings. The term *sage*, though used sarcastically here, is usually applied to Greek philosophers and wise men, which suggests that Lucian was poking fun at the Christians' belief that their crucified leader was a wise man. Moreover, no other followers of an executed Jewish religious leader had ever continued to worship their leader, simply because, once dead, they knew that the leader no longer had any power.[25] And yet now these Christians continued to worship a man who had been executed by crucifixion.

9. CELSUS:

Another Greek writer in the second century, Celsus, criticized Christians because he felt they threatened the stability of the social structures of the day. Although his works have been lost, they are preserved in *Against Celsus*, a work by the early church father Origen that was devoted to answering Celsus' criticisms of Christianity. Origen writes that Celsus accused Jesus of inventing his birth from a virgin. He also quotes many of Celsus' derogatory comments about Jesus, including the following:

> [Jesus was] born in a certain Jewish village, of a poor woman of the country, who gained her subsistence by spinning, and who was turned out of doors by her husband, a carpenter by trade, because she was convicted of adultery; that after being driven away by her husband, and wandering about for a time, she disgracefully gave birth to Jesus, an illegitimate child, who having hired himself out as a servant in Egypt on account of his poverty, and having there acquired some miraculous powers, on which the Egyptians greatly pride

themselves, returned to his own country, highly elated on account of them, and by means of these proclaimed himself a God.[26]

While Celsus' opinions definitely differ from those of the New Testament writers, his statements serve to support the fact that Jesus did exist, that he "proclaimed himself a God," and that he had "miraculous powers."

Although his description of Jesus' life is quite skewed (after all, he wrote these statements in an effort to combat the spread of Christianity), even these twisted facts confirm that Jesus was a historical person and that his early followers worshiped him as God.

10. The Talmud:

The Jewish Talmud is a written record of the oral tradition of the Jewish people. It is composed of the *Mishnah*, the Jewish code of religious jurisprudence, and the *Gemaras*, the commentary on the Mishnah. Because the Talmud was limited to the Jewish law and commentaries on the law, we actually should not expect to learn anything about Jesus from it. As biblical scholar F. F. Bruce notes:

> As the Mishnah was a law-code, and the Talmud's commentaries on this code, there is little occasion in these writings for references to Christianity, and what references there are are hostile. But, such as they are, these references do at least show that there was not the slightest doubt of the historical character of Jesus.[27]

For example, the earliest portion of the Talmud, which was recorded between AD 70 and 200, contains this reference:

> On the Eve of the Passover Yeshu [Hebrew for "Jesus"] was hanged. For forty days before the execution took place, a herald went forth and cried, "He is going forth to be stoned because he has practiced sorcery and enticed Israel to apostasy. Any one who can say anything in his

favour, let him come forward and plead on his behalf."
But since nothing was brought forward in his favour he
was hanged on the eve of the Passover![28]

The New Testament also uses the Greek term for "hanged," *kremamenos*, to describe the crucifixion of Jesus.[29] Not only do we learn from this passage that Jesus was an actual person who was crucified, but we also learn that the crucifixion took place on the eve of the Passover, which confirms the New Testament accounts. We also learn that Jesus "practiced sorcery," a probable reference to his miracles, and that he "enticed Israel to apostasy," a possible reference to Jesus' blasphemous statements and his criticism of the ritual-focused Jewish leaders. In a work that certainly did not wish to promote the Christian religion, there is no suggestion that Jesus was a product of people's imagination.

11. JOSEPHUS:

Flavius Josephus was a Jewish historian who wrote during the reign of the Roman emperor Vespasian following the destruction of Jerusalem in AD 70. Josephus makes two references to Jesus in his *Antiquities* (written circa AD 90-95). In the first reference, Josephus describes how the Jewish council sentenced "James, the brother of Jesus, who was called Christ" to death by stoning.[30] Josephus explains that the Jewish council took advantage of a period when there was no Roman ruler overseeing events in Judea, since the Roman ruler Festus had just died and his successor, Albinus, was still *en route* to Judea to take over the leadership. From this information, we know that the date was AD 62. This reference to Jesus tells us a few useful facts: First, Jesus existed. Second, he had a brother named James, who was stoned to death in AD 62 because of his beliefs. Third, Jesus' followers called him "Christ," the Greek translation of the term "Messiah."

Referring to the time of Pontius Pilate's rule, Josephus also writes:

> At this time there was a wise man who was called Jesus.
> His conduct was good and he was known to be virtuous.
> And many people from among the Jews and the other
> nations became his disciples. Pilate condemned him

to be crucified and to die. But those who had become his disciples did not abandon his discipleship. They reported that he had appeared to them three days after his crucifixion, and that he was alive; accordingly he was perhaps the Messiah, concerning whom the prophets have recounted wonders.[31]

This reference clearly recognizes that his followers claimed to have seen Jesus alive after he was crucified. Even though this source has been disputed because it gives such great corroboration of the Gospel accounts and because there is another version that does appear to have been altered by Christians, New Testament scholar Gary Habermas describes its credibility in this way:

> There is nothing really sensational in such a list of facts from a Jewish historian. Jesus' ethical conduct, his following, and his crucifixion by the command of Pilate are what we would expect a historian to mention. Even the account of the disciples reporting Jesus' resurrection appearances (if it is allowed) has an especially authentic ring to it. Josephus, like many historians today, would simply be repeating the claims, which were probably fairly well known in the first century Palestine.[32]

Another reason to trust Josephus' report regarding the beliefs of the early Christians is that it provides a very good explanation for the rapid growth of the Christian church in the face of severe persecution. We'll have more to say on this topic in chapters 16 and 17 when we discuss the historical evidence for the resurrection.

12. MARA BAR-SERAPION:

A Syrian philosopher named Mara Bar-Serapion wrote to his son in AD 73. In this letter, he compared the "wise King" of the Jews—most likely a reference to Jesus—to Socrates and Pythagoras, since they were all executed by their own people, whom were subsequently "avenged" by God. In the case of the Jews, he says they were "ruined and driven from their land" and "live in complete dispersion," which is a reference to the events of AD 70, when the Romans destroyed Jerusalem.[33]

From these twelve non-Christian sources, all written within 150 years of Jesus' life, historians can glean the following information about Jesus and his first followers:

1. Jesus was a real man who lived during the reign of the Roman emperor Tiberius Caesar.
2. He lived a wise and virtuous life.
3. He had miraculous powers.[34]
4. He had a brother named James.
5. His followers called him the Messiah ("Christus").
6. He was crucified in Palestine when Pontius Pilate was the local Roman ruler.
7. He was crucified on the eve of the Jewish Passover.
8. His death may have coincided with darkness.
9. His disciples believed he rose from the dead.
10. His disciples were willing to die for their beliefs.
11. Christianity spread rapidly from Palestine at least as far as Rome.
12. His disciples denied the Roman gods, lived moral lives, and worshiped Jesus as God.

According to both biblical and secular historical documents, Jesus lived during the reign of the Roman emperor Tiberius Caesar. No one has ever suggested that Tiberius Caesar did not exist, and yet he is only mentioned in nine non-Christian sources in the same 150-year period during which these *twelve* sources provided information about Jesus. Moreover, if you include Christian sources, Jesus is mentioned forty-three times versus Tiberius' ten![35] [36] Since ancient historians readily admit that Tiberius was a real man, we can be extremely confident that Jesus was also.

If someone announced on national television that Tiberius Caesar never actually existed, many viewers would hurriedly fact-check this claim during the commercial break. Such ignorance of history could hardly go unchallenged, and many people would swiftly call attention to the ten ancient documents that mention Tiberius Caesar. But forty-three historical documents mention Jesus of Nazareth. Why then should Jesus be so quickly dismissed as a mere myth?

CHAPTER 10: SECULAR CONFIRMATION

QUESTIONS FOR COMPREHENSION AND DISCUSSION

1. What is the external evidence test of historicity? How does it compare to the internal evidence test discussed in chapters 5 through 9?
2. Why is it so important that Jesus is mentioned in other sources besides documents written by early Christians? Why are secular sources—especially those with an anti-Christian bias—helpful in proving that Jesus was a real person?
3. What are the four main conclusions about Jesus that we learn from Roman historian Tacitus?
4. What do we know from Roman historian Suetonius that confirms an event mentioned in Acts 18?
5. Describe the debate that was taking place in the ancient world, to which Roman historians Thallus and Phlegon contributed their thoughts. Why is it logical to conclude that they were talking about an event that happened at the death of Jesus?
6. What can we conclude from Pliny the Younger and the Roman emperors Trajan and Hadrian regarding what the early Christians believed about Jesus?
7. What can we glean about Jesus from the reference to "Yeshua" in the Talmud? Why is it surprising that the Talmud even mentions Jesus?
8. Why is there a debate regarding the authenticity of Josephus' second reference to Jesus? Why is it plausible for a Jewish historian to describe Jesus in this way, according to New Testament scholar Gary Habermas?
9. What can we glean about Jesus from the Syrian, Mara Bar-Serapion?
10. What are the twelve main points that we learn about Jesus from just these twelve non-Christian sources, all written within one hundred fifty years of his death? How do the number of non-Christian and Christian sources mentioning Jesus compare to the number that mention Tiberius Caesar in the same 150 years?

CHAPTER 10 ENDNOTES

1. Gary R. Habermas, *The Historical Jesus: Ancient Evidence for the Life of Christ* (Joplin, MO: College Press Publishing Company, 1996), 224.
2. E.B. White, "Bedfellows", *Essays of E.B. White* (HarperCollins Publisher, 2014).
3. *Larry King Live*, CNN, April 14, 2005. Available online at http://transcripts.cnn.com/TRANSCRIPTS/0504/24/lkl.01.html.
4. Norman L. Geisler, *Baker Encyclopedia of Christian Apologetics* (Grand Rapids, MI: Baker, 1999), 381.
5. Tacitus, *Annals* 15.44. Available online at https://en.wikisource.org/wiki/The_Annals_(Tacitus)/Book_15#44.
6. F. F. Bruce, *The New Testament Documents: Are They Reliable?* (Downers Grove, Illinois: InterVarsity Press, 1973), 121.
7. Habermas, *The Historical Jesus*, 189.
8. Suetonius, *Claudius*, 25. Available in Latin online at http://www.thelatinlibrary.com/suetonius/suet.claudius.html#25.
9. Acts 18:2.
10. Suetonius, *Nero Claudius Caesar, XVI*. Available online at https://www.gutenberg.org/files/6400/6400-h/6400-h.htm#link2H_4_0007.
11. F. F. Bruce, *Jesus and Christian Origins Outside the New Testament* (Grand Rapids, MI: Eerdmans, 1974), 29-30.
12. Other historians that mention the histories of Thallus are Eusebius (*Chronicle*, I. K125.2), Tertullian (*Apologeticum* 19), Theophilus (*Ad Autolycum* 3.29), Lactantius (*Divine Inst.* I.23), Minucius Felix 21, Justin (*Cohortatio* 9), Syncellus, and John Malalas VI.
13. Julius Africanus, *Chronography*, 18.1. Available online at http://www.newadvent.org/fathers/0614.htm.
14. See Matthew 27:45, Mark 15:33, and Luke 23:44.
15. Julius Africanus, *Chronography*, 18.1.
16. Luke 1:3.
17. C. A. Robinson Jr., (Holt, Rinehart and Winston: 1964). "Introduction". *Selections from Greek and Roman historians*, pp. xxix.
18. Luke 3:1.
19. Origen, *Contra Celsum*, 2. 14, 33, 59 and Philopon, *De. Opif. Mund.* II 21, as referenced by Josh McDowell and Bill Wilson, *He Walked Among Us: Evidence for the Historical Jesus*. (San Bernardino, CA: Here's Life Publishers, 1988), 36. *Contra Celsum* is available online at http://www.newadvent.org/fathers/04162.htm.
20. Pliny the Younger, *Letters*, X:96. Available online at http://www.attalus.org/old/pliny10b.html#96.

CHAPTER 10: SECULAR CONFIRMATION

21 Ibid.
22 Trajan, *Letters*, X:97. Available online at http://faculty.georgetown.edu/jod/texts/pliny.html.
23 Eusebius, *Church History*, IV:9. Available online at http://www.newadvent.org/fathers/250104.htm.
24 Lucian, *The Death of Peregrine*, 11-13, in *The Works of Lucian of Samosata*, transl. by H.W. Fowler and F.G. Fowler, 4 vols. (Oxford: Clarendon, 1949), vol. 4. Available online at http://www.tertullian.org/rpearse/lucian/peregrinus.htm.
25 Describing the other first-century messianic movements whose leader had been executed, early Christian historian N. T. Wright makes the point this way: "In not one single case do we hear the slightest mention of the disappointed followers claiming that their hero had been raised from the dead. They knew better. Resurrection was not a private event. Jewish revolutionaries whose leader had been executed by the authorities, and who managed to escape arrest themselves had two options: give up the revolution, or find another leader. Claiming that the original leader was alive again was simply not an option. Unless, of course, he was." (N. T. Wright, *Who Was Jesus?* [Grand Rapids, MI: Eerdmans, 1993], 63.)
26 Origen, *Contra Celsum*, published in *The Ante-Nicene Fathers* (Edinburgh: T&T Clark Publishers, 1867-1872), Vol. 4, Book 1, Chapter 28.
27 Bruce, *The New Testament Documents*, 103.
28 *The Babylonian Talmud*, transl. by I. Epstein (London: Soncino, 1935), vol. III, *Sanhedrin* 43a, 281.
29 For example, see Galatians 3:13.
30 *Antiquities* 20:9 from *The Works of Josephus*, transl. by William Whiston (Philadelphia: David McKay, n.d.).
31 This is the less disputed Arabic version of Josephus' quote, presumably of *Antiquities* 18.63. From Agapios' Kitab al-'Unwan ("Book of the Title," 10th c.). See also James H. Charlesworth, *Jesus Within Judaism* (London: SPCK, 1989).
32 Habermas, *The Historical Jesus*, 195-196.
33 This source most likely confirms the crucifixion of Jesus and corroborates the Gospels' claim that Jesus was called "the king of the Jews" (for example, in Matthew 2:2, 27:11, 29, and 37; Mark 15:2, 9, 12, 18, and 26; Luke 23:3, and 37-38; and John 18:33, 39, 19:12, 14. See Bruce, *The New Testament Documents*, 117.
34 F. F. Bruce writes this concerning the external historical evidence for Jesus' miracles: "If we do proceed to ask what the independent non-Christian evidence for the Gospel miracles is, we shall find that early non-Christian writers who do refer to Jesus at any length do not dispute

that He performed miracles. Josephus, as we shall see, calls Him a wonder-worker; later Jewish references in the rabbinical writings, as we shall also see, attribute miracles to sorcery, but do not deny them, just as some in the days of His flesh attributed His powers to demon-possession. Sorcery is also the explanation given by Celsus, the philosophic critic of Christianity in the second century. The early apostles referred to His miracles as facts which their audiences were as well acquainted with as they themselves were; similarly, the early apologists refer to them as events beyond dispute by the opponents of Christianity." (Bruce, The *New Testament Documents*, 67-68.)

[35] The nine non-Christian sources that mention Tiberius are Tacitus, Suetonius, Velleius Paterculus, Plutarch, Pliny the Elder, Strabo, Seneca, Valerius Maximus, and Josephus. The one Christian source that mentions Tiberius is the Gospel of Luke (Luke 3:1). From Gary Habermas and Michael Licona, *The Case for the Resurrection of Jesus* (Grand Rapids, MI: Kregel, 2004), 128.

[36] Normal L. Geisler and Frank Turek, *I Don't Have Enough Faith to Be an Atheist* (Wheaton, IL: Crossway Books, 2004), 222.

Archaeological work has unquestionably strengthened confidence in the reliability of the Scriptural record. More than one archaeologist has found his respect for the Bible increased by the experience of excavation in Palestine.

—Millar Burrows, archaeologist and former director of the American School of Oriental Research in Jerusalem[1]

Archaeology holds all the keys to understanding who we are and where we come from.

—Sarah Parcak, remote-sensing archaeologist and 2016 winner of $1 million TED prize[2]

11

Archaeological Consistency

The myths of ancient Egypt, Greece, and the Near East, as we saw in Chapter 7, may mention real geographical names, such as Mount Olympus, the Nile, and the River Sangarios. And they may also mention historical rulers who were well-known in their day, such as kings, emperors, and pharaohs. However, you wouldn't expect myths and legends to paint a comprehensive picture of a particular place at a particular time in history with details such as minor political titles, architectural landmarks, means of travel, cultural practices, trade routes, and geographical features.

For that level of detail, you wouldn't look to myths, but instead to works that are more worthy to be classified as *historiography*. To find information about the first few centuries BC, you might consult Greek historians like Herodotus or Thucydides, or Roman historians like Sallust or Quintus Fabius Pictor. If you want to go back further in time in the Mediterranean region, you may be surprised to learn that—of all literary options—the most historiographical are the books of the Bible. The *Encyclopædia Britannica* explains it this way:

> The Hebrew Bible (Old Testament) was as fundamental to Western historiography as the dynastic histories were to Chinese historiography. Although the Bible is many things, it is substantially a work of history. Seventeen of its 39 books are historical, and the 5 major and 12 minor prophets also offer moral interpretations of historical events.[3]

CHAPTER 11: ARCHAEOLOGICAL CONSISTENCY

So, the Bible contains at least some accurate historical information to shed light on the events that took place millennia ago.

But can we really trust that the Bible—a book filled with many anti-scientific miracles—records these events accurately? Isn't it possible that the writers of the Old Testament simply invented many of the historical details they record as a way to explain their origins, boost the significance of their cultural heritage, grant themselves the impressive status of "God's people," establish moral statutes to guide their lives, and instigate comforting traditions that create a cohesive culture? Settling on this explanation is especially understandable, since relatively little historical evidence remains after almost four millennia.

Before proceeding in this discussion, it is useful to remind ourselves of a topic we briefly discussed in chapter 6: literary realism is a recent invention. It has only been in the last few centuries that writers have started to add descriptive details in order to make a fictional story sound historical. In *The Rise of the Novel,* the Stanford English professor and literary historian Ian Watt demonstrated that the modern novel arose in the 1700s due to economic and social trends, along with new ways of thinking inspired by the Scientific Revolution. Watt wrote that modern realism "begins from the position that truth can be discovered by the individual through the senses," and thus realism in literature "has its origins in Descartes and Locke and received its first full formulation by Thomas Reid in the middle of the eighteenth century."[4] Therefore, the detail we find in ancient literature—especially if it isn't necessary to further the story—is generally attributed not to fabrication but instead to eyewitness testimony, testimony that was recorded by the eyewitnesses themselves or by those who had interviewed the eyewitnesses.

Nearly every page of the Bible contains this type of eyewitness detail. Moreover, much of the biblical detail is the type of information—confirmed by archaeology—that someone would only know if he or she were living during that historical period in that geographic area. Such details provide extraordinary evidence that the biblical histories are trustworthy. For example, suppose you read a book that includes a description of your hometown. You are surprised that it includes numerous details just as you remember them many years ago, details that a present-day visitor would not see. You would logically assume that the author had actually visited your hometown in the same period when you lived there, or at least interviewed someone who had.

Similarly, if the writers of the Bible accurately present the geography, cultural practices, and political leaders of the area they are describing, you have strong reason to trust that they were there to record this information. This is especially true of ancient histories. Unlike today, when we can just visit the library or watch a video documentary to learn details about other historical periods, there were no easily accessible records in the ancient world for this information.

As we will see in part, time and again, archaeology has confirmed the historicity of events in both the Old and New Testaments. William F. Albright, one of the greatest archaeologists of all time, describes how well archaeology confirms the truthfulness of many biblical events:

> The excessive skepticism shown toward the Bible by important historical schools of the eighteenth and nineteenth centuries, certain phases of which still appear periodically, has been progressively discredited. Discovery after discovery has established the accuracy of innumerable details and has brought increased recognition to the value of the Bible as a source of history.[5]

Although parts of the Bible are best described as allegorical or visionary,[6] the writers of the majority of the Bible make it clear that they are recording actual history (as we saw in Chapter 5), and the events they describe have been repeatedly confirmed by archaeological discoveries and other reliable historical documents.

You may see the importance of confirming the truthfulness of what the New Testament writers claim Jesus said and did. But does the historicity of the *Old* Testament matter to our discussion of whether Jesus of Nazareth lived, died, and rose again? Though it is by no means an exhaustive reply to this question, here is one plausible answer: if we can trust that the Hebrew Scriptures—the Old Testament—accurately present real events in the history of the nation of Israel, our classification of the Bible moves towards history and away from mythology. And as our classification becomes more historical and less mythological, we have more reason to trust what the Bible tells us on other matters.

Of course, by repeatedly confirming the truthfulness of events in Israel's history, we cannot logically prove that *every* event in the Bible

CHAPTER 11: ARCHAEOLOGICAL CONSISTENCY

happened exactly as it is described. But as additional archaeological evidence confirms the historicity of the Old Testament, we can have greater trust in what the Bible tells us about the nature of God and his message to us. In other words, the more we can trust the truth of the Bible's events, the more faith we have that the message it delivers to us is truly from God. One Old Testament scholar explains it this way:

> Israel's neighbors expressed their beliefs through fantastic, elaborate, "out-of-this-world" myths. In contrast, Old Testament narratives about Israel describe real events in real time involving real people and a real God. The reality of Israel's faith rested on the reality of Israel's history.[7]

Christians trust that God has acted in history in order to reveal himself to us, first to the Israelite people in the ancient Near East and later, with the birth of Jesus, to the rest of the world. The earliest Christians—and on many occasions Jesus himself—proclaimed that he had come to *fulfill* the Hebrew Scriptures.[8] Thus, it is important to demonstrate that the events through which God communicated his purpose are actual historical events, events that often pointed forward to Jesus' coming.

As another biblical scholar writes, the reality of the Bible's message is correlated with the connection between its stories and a real historical and geographical setting:

> Archeology is one of the disciplines that shed light on the historical nature of the Scriptures; it reveals the setting and background in which the story of the Bible occurs. Moreover, archeology demonstrates the earthiness of the Bible; in other words, it helps to bear witness to the Bible's rootedness in time and space.[9]

If the stories are rooted in time and space, we have much more reason to trust that God actually is communicating to us through them, since only an all-powerful God could steer the events of history and use them to impact humans in frequently miraculous ways. Let's dive into the fascinating study of ancient Near East archaeology and the consistency of the archeological evidence with the biblical accounts.

Archaeological Support for the Old Testament

Though the archaeological evidence for the historical events of the Old Testament fills many books, we will focus on a mere handful of the archaeological finds that have bolstered the case that the Old Testament accurately describes ancient history. We will then focus on the historicity of one of the earliest periods of biblical history, the time of the "Exodus," asking whether the events leading up to and following this mass departure of the Israelites from Egypt really occurred nearly four millennia ago. If we can demonstrate that some of the earliest events of the Bible are historically credible, it is likely that the later historical accounts, for which we have more evidence, are also credible.

One of the most popular artifacts in the British Museum is the Rosetta Stone. Discovered by French soldiers in el-Rashid (Rosetta), Egypt in 1799, this stone is a much smaller part of what was originally a huge slab called a *stela*. The inscription, written in 197 BC, is not exciting in itself, as it simply communicates that the Egyptian priests supported the rule of the current king, Ptolemy V. The importance of the Rosetta Stone lies in the fact that the same message was inscribed in three scripts, one on top of the other:

1. *ancient Greek*, which had become the language used for administrative purposes in Egypt after Alexander the Great conquered the area in 332 BC,
2. *hieroglyphics*, the script that the Egyptian priests had been using for centuries for this type of royal decree, and
3. *Demotic*, an Egyptian script that was newer and more commonly used than hieroglyphics.

Knowing ancient Greek, scholars were able to use the Rosetta Stone to decipher hieroglyphics, thereby removing much of the mystery that had enshrouded ancient Egyptian history.

The understanding of hieroglyphics has shed light on many biblical events, and it has also confirmed many of the details of ancient Egyptian administration mentioned in Genesis, the first book of the Bible. For example, the Bible tells the story of a man named Joseph, one of the twelve great-grandsons of the patriarch Abraham and one of the heads of the

CHAPTER 11: ARCHAEOLOGICAL CONSISTENCY

twelve tribes of Israel. Because Joseph was the favored son and had been boasting of his superiority, his brothers sold him to a passing caravan of slave traders traveling towards Egypt. While he was a slave in Egypt, Joseph rose to power within the household of one of pharaoh's officers, Potiphar, who is called a "captain of the guard." Potiphar promotes Joseph to a position called "over the house" or "overseer." Having deciphered hieroglyphics, scholars have confirmed that these titles, though transliterated into Hebrew in the Bible, were actual official titles in ancient Egypt, though not necessarily titles that the average Israelite would know.[10] We will return to the topic of Joseph and his brothers shortly.

Additional historical credibility for the Old Testament comes from another stone tablet, this time with an inscription in the language of Moab (in present-day Jordan, on the other side of the Dead Sea from Israel). Called the "Moabite Stone" (or *Mesha Stele*), this stela dates to the ninth century BC and describes the victory of the Moabite King Mesha over the Israelites in a war that historians believe happened in 850 BC. The Bible records the same battle skirmishes between the Israelites and the Moabites—but from the Israeli perspective—in Second Kings chapter 3. Understandably, on the Moabite Stone King Mesha emphasizes his victory over Israel, while in the biblical record the Israelites emphasize their successful counterattacks against the Moabites.

Another reason that scholars claim the Moabite Stone is so important is that it contains the first reference outside of the Bible to the Israelite God, "Yahweh" or "Jehovah," recorded as "JHWH" in Moabite script. In the inscription, the king boasts that he defeated the Israelites, took the objects they used in their worship of Jehovah, and offered them to the Moabite national deity, Chemosh:

> And Chemosh said to me, Go take Nebo against Israel, and I went in the night and I fought against it from the break of day till noon, and I took it: and I killed in all seven thousand men, but I did not kill the women and maidens, for I devoted them to Ashtar-Chemosh; and I took from it the vessels of *Jehovah*, and offered them before Chemosh.[11]

Interestingly, Nebo is the area of Jordan where the Israelite leader Moses died just before the people entered Canaan after the Exodus.

Also of interest: the Bible describes Chemosh with the Hebrew word, שִׁקּוּץ [šiq-quṣ], which is translated "vile," "disgusting," "abomination," and "detestable,"[12] an understandable description given that, according to the Bible and confirmed by archeology, the Moabite king offered his son to Chemosh as a human sacrifice.[13]

In 1993, archaeologists uncovered another inscribed fragment of stone, this time in northern Israel. Called the "Tel Dan" inscription, it describes the victory of a king of Aram (in present-day Syria) over the kings of two neighboring nations to the south: "the king of Israel" and the "king of the House of David." Here is the English translation of one part of the Aramaic inscription, with brackets around the missing parts that scholarly research has filled in:

> [I killed Jeho]ram son [of Ahab] king of Israel, and [I] killed [Ahaz]iahu son of [Jehoram kin]g of the House of David, and I set [their towns into ruins and turned] their land into [desolation].[14]

Like the Moabite Stone, this find has been dated to the ninth century BC. It provides the first archaeological evidence for the biblical King David, whom scholars believe lived in approximately 1010-970 BC. The stela most likely corresponds to the defeat of Jehoram of Israel and Ahaziah of Judah by Hazael of Damascus.[15] As a result of this archaeological find, we can be more confident that King David was an actual historical figure.[16]

Many skeptics have claimed that the Old Testament was written as late as 400 to 200 BC, such that legends had developed over the centuries since the original events occurred (if they occurred at all). However, the discovery of two tiny silver scrolls in 1979 has provided evidence that the Old Testament is even older than previously thought. The older the records, the closer they are to the time of the events they describe, and the greater their potential accuracy. The scrolls, which have been dated to the late seventh century BC, were found in a box within a burial cave in Ketef Hinnom, just southwest of Jerusalem.[17] It took three years to carefully unroll the delicate scrolls, and it was eventually determined that they contained the Hebrew priestly benediction from Numbers 6:24-26.[18] [19] Also of note, these scrolls contain the earliest known *Hebrew* inscription of the holiest word for

CHAPTER 11: ARCHAEOLOGICAL CONSISTENCY

God, YHWH.[20] (It is inscribed in an ancient version of Hebrew called *paleo-Hebrew*.[21])

But most biblical scholars would agree that the most important archaeological find of the twentieth century is the "Dead Sea Scrolls." Though they date to several hundred years *after* the Ketef Hinnom silver scrolls, the Dead Sea Scrolls make up for it in number. Consisting of more than a thousand biblical manuscripts written on parchment, papyrus, and even bronze, they provide excellent evidence that the Old Testament we read today is remarkably similar to the Old Testament as it circulated two millennia ago. Prior to the discovery of the Dead Sea Scrolls in 1946, the oldest complete copy of the Old Testament dated to the late tenth century. By contrast, the approximately two hundred copies of biblical books in the Dead Sea Scrolls have been dated to between the third century BC and the first century AD.[22]

With regard to the similarity of the Dead Sea Scrolls to the modern Old Testament, biblical scholar Gleason Archer states:

> Even though the two copies of Isaiah discovered in Qumran Cave 1 near the Dead Sea in 1947 were a thousand years earlier than the oldest dated manuscript previously known (AD 980), they proved to be word-for-word identical with our standard Hebrew Bible in more than 95 percent of the text. The 5 percent variation consisted chiefly of obvious slips of the pen and variations in spelling.[23]

The similarity of the Dead Sea scrolls to the modern Hebrew Bible was both greatly unexpected and highly consequential. It demonstrated that the ancient scribes who had the high honor of creating copies of the Scriptures were extremely careful to ensure that no errors, omissions, or insertions were made.

In fact, following the Israelites' return from exile in Babylon at the end of the sixth century BC, the scribes were careful to follow certain rules to maintain the fidelity of copies. First of all, the scribe had to have another manuscript from which to make the copy. (That is, he was not permitted to make a copy of Scriptures from memory, though he probably could!) As he was copying a word, the scribe had to state the word out loud. Every thirty days a review of the copy was done, and if one error was found on a sheet, it invalidated that sheet. And if there were three errors on a sheet, the entire manuscript was declared invalid.

Moreover, the paragraphs, words, and letters had to be counted, and if the middle paragraph, word, or letter from the copy did not correspond exactly to the middle paragraph, word, and letter in the original, the copy was invalid. (By the way, the sheets that had been invalidated could not be destroyed, since they contained God's Word, so they were stored in a special "hiding place," or *genizah*, within the synagogue or cemetery.) And to demonstrate just how seriously the Israelites considered the copyist's task, before he could write the holy name "YHWH," he had to wipe his pen and wash his entire body in the ceremonial bath, called the *mikvah*.[24] Considering these rules, it is understandable that the modern Hebrew Bible so closely matches the biblical manuscripts in the Dead Sea Scrolls.

This extreme care demonstrates the importance that the Israelites placed on accuracy when transmitting the stories from their ancestors. It also demonstrates how unlikely it was that the details of the biblical stories would change over the years. We can therefore be confident that the scribes did not add new details in order to make the stories more interesting or to make them sound more historical (not that this was a practice in those days anyway). The historical details are *in* the documents because—simply put—the documents are *historical*.

In fact, secular archaeologists have depended in large part on the historical details from the Bible to guide them in their search for evidence of the ancient Israelites. One important example of a detail that archaeologists and historians have depended upon in their reconstruction of ancient chronologies is found in the first chapter of the second book of the Bible, Exodus. At that time, Joseph had invited his father Jacob and his eleven brothers and their extended family to come from Canaan to live in Egypt, where he had become second-in-command to Pharaoh. But several generations later, the new pharaoh began to fear that the Israelites living in his territory had grown too numerous, and he therefore ordered that they be enslaved. The story goes like this:

> Then a new king, to whom Joseph meant nothing, came to power in Egypt. "Look," he said to his people, "the Israelites have become far too numerous for us. Come, we must deal shrewdly with them or they will become

CHAPTER 11: ARCHAEOLOGICAL CONSISTENCY

even more numerous and, if war breaks out, will join our enemies, fight against us and leave the country."

> So they put slave masters over them to oppress them with forced labor, and they built *Pithom and Rameses* as store cities for Pharaoh. But the more they were oppressed, the more they multiplied and spread; so the Egyptians came to dread the Israelites and worked them ruthlessly. They made their lives bitter with harsh labor in brick and mortar and with all kinds of work in the fields; in all their harsh labor the Egyptians worked them ruthlessly.[25]

First off, the criterion of embarrassment is one reason historians believe this story is historical. Why would the Israelites invent a story that their ancestors were slaves? The founder and editor of *Biblical Archaeology Review* compared this story to other origin stories:

> We do have a lot of legends, or myths if you wish, about foundations and creations of people, but this is the only one that traces [a people's] origins back to slaves, not to princes and kings, but to slaves. This gives it a ring of truth, and I'm not ready to throw this out.[26]

A second interesting detail about this story is its claim that the Israelites built two cities, Pithom and Rameses. These Egyptian cities were in fact built in the thirteenth century BC during the reign of Ramesses II, known as "Ramesses the Great." Though there is debate over which archaeological site corresponds to Pithom, historians agree that the ancient city of Rameses is located in the Nile River delta quite near the area where the Bible says the ancient Israelites settled, a region known as the "Land of Goshen."[27]

Using this biblical detail as a starting point, assuming the biblical story is true, historians believe that the Israelites' escape from Egypt— an event known as the "Exodus"– most likely happened during or soon after the reign of Ramesses the Great in the 1200s BC. And because they conclude that the biblical Exodus must have happened in the 1200s BC (if at all), archaeologists have appropriately been looking for evidence for a mass exodus of slaves from Egypt in the archaeological strata of that period, i.e., the 1200s BC.[28] But a problem has emerged: they haven't found any evidence of a mass exodus of slaves in the 1200s BC. As a result, many archaeologists have concluded that the Exodus didn't really happen; it's simply a mythical account that the Israelites concocted to explain their origins.

However, one Egyptologist by the name of David Rohl has noted multiple lines of evidence in the archaeological record that support the biblical story of the Israelites' Exodus from Egypt. This extensive evidence is not found in the 1200s BC, but instead in the period several hundred years *before* the reign of Ramesses the Great. After being interviewed by filmmaker Timothy Mahoney for the documentary film, *Patterns of Evidence: Exodus*, Rohl decided to lay out the evidence in his own book, entitled *Exodus: Myth or History?*

In his interview for the documentary, Rohl explains how archaeologists have dismissed the Exodus as fictional because they have been looking in the wrong historical period:

> The issues that I and others have identified lie in how we have dated the ancient world, not in the biblical text. And the historical credibility of the Bible is what has suffered as a result. And the joke, if you like, is that I have no biblical axe to grind here because I am an agnostic. I don't need these stories to be true. But the reality is, although archaeologists have been looking in all the right places for the biblical stories, they have been looking in the entirely wrong time.[29]

In other words, archaeologists have looked for evidence for the truth of the biblical stories, and when they didn't find any evidence, they blamed the Bible for being inaccurate. But instead, Rohl argues, what should receive the blame was the archaeologists' assumption regarding the time period of the Exodus. It is ironic that archeologists' dismissal of the Exodus as fictional stems from the original assumption that a biblical detail (the slaves built the city of Ramesses) was historical, which caused archaeologists to limit their search for evidence of the Exodus to the 1200s BC.

For our purposes here, I will provide a high-level summary of the

CHAPTER 11: ARCHAEOLOGICAL CONSISTENCY

main lines of evidence for the historicity of the Exodus that David Rohl and other archaeologists have described. To organize the evidence, we'll follow the same six stages of the biblical story that Mahoney used to organize the archaeological evidence in the film:

1. The arrival of the Israelites in Egypt,
2. The increase in the population of the Israelites,
3. The enslavement of the Israelites,
4. The judgment of Egypt after the pharaoh refused to free the Israelites,
5. The Exodus of the Israelites from Egypt, and
6. The conquest of the land of Canaan.[30]

Let's begin our overview of the evidence with the Israelites' arrival in Egypt.

EVIDENCE FOR THE EXODUS: ARRIVAL

As mentioned earlier, Joseph ascended as a slave to the position of "overseer" for a man named Potiphar, the Pharaoh's "captain of the guard." But after he refused the advances of Potiphar's wife, Joseph was falsely accused of a crime and sent to prison. Many years later, Joseph gained a reputation for accurately interpreting dreams and eventually had the opportunity to interpret two distressing dreams that the Pharaoh hadn't been able to understand. Pharaoh was so impressed not only with Joseph's interpretation of his dreams, but also with his recommendations for addressing the issues that the dreams predicted. In response to Joseph's display of intelligence, foresight, and leadership acumen, Pharaoh released him from prison and gave him the second most powerful office in Egypt, most likely the position known as the *vizier*. It was in this position that Joseph implemented his recommendations to prepare the Egyptians for the coming famine, which had been the subject of Pharaoh's dreams.

Through his planning, Joseph saved the Egyptian people from what would have been sure starvation. In their search for grain during the famine, Joseph's brothers eventually came from Canaan to Egypt, and in their ensuing reunion, Joseph eventually reconciled with them and forgave them for selling him into slavery. And because grain was plentiful in Egypt at that time, but not in Canaan, and because he longed for his family to live near him, Joseph arranged for his father Jacob and their extended family to travel from Canaan and settle in the Land of Goshen in the Nile River delta, the same area where the store city of Ramesses was built.

As mentioned before, there hasn't been evidence that the Israelites lived in this area in the 1200s BC. However, a recent excavation *under* the town of Ramesses has yielded significant evidence that the Israelites did live here, but *centuries before the 1200s*. This older city, called Avaris, was occupied from the 1700s to the 1500s BC. At the time the story of Joseph was written down, the name of the town had been changed from Avaris to Ramesses, thus explaining the source of the confusion about the time period. Rohl explains why the Bible says the Israelites built "Ramesses," not "Avaris":

> This particular mention of the city of Ramesses—the building of Ramesses—is what we call an anachronism. It's been something that's been added into the text later by an editor. So what the editor is basically saying is, 'This is the place where the Israelites built the store city, and we know it today as Ramesses.'[31]

There is a plethora of evidence that Avaris was settled by non-Egyptians, specifically those from a Syrian origin. Dating back to the earliest layer of settlement in Avaris are houses that were built in a style typical at that time in Syria, known as the "Mittselsaalhaus" or "middle-room-house." This house, which consisted of a large central room or court surrounded by smaller rooms, was clearly distinct from the typical Egyptian homes of the same era.[32] Even though the Israelites who settled in Egypt had come from Canaan (modern-day Israel and Palestine), their patriarch, Abraham, had originally come from the Syrian city of Harran, and this middle-room-house, was, according to Rohl, "exactly the same style of house you'd expect [Abraham's grandson] Jacob to build for himself in Egypt."[33] Rohl writes:

> The Book of Genesis mentions a number of occasions when the Patriarchs or their sons return to the Harran

CHAPTER 11: ARCHAEOLOGICAL CONSISTENCY

region in north Syria to search out brides from the greater family or tribe. So the cultural connection between Harran and the Jacob clan remained strong. It would not therefore be surprising to find the clan chief, Jacob, building his new Egyptian home in the traditional style of his Syrian ancestors.[34][35]

It is worth reiterating that in the Bible story, Joseph implemented the projects that prepared the Egyptians to survive a seven-year famine, and as a result of his acumen, Joseph saved many lives. There is evidence that Joseph may have been the historical vizier who recommended broadening a tributary of the Nile and setting up a reservoir to collect water in years when excess rain fell in the highlands at the source of the Nile. These measures served to prevent the larger than usual floods that would cause severe famines (since too much flooding prevented the planting of crops). For millennia, this canal has been called "Bahr Youseff" ("Joseph's Canal" in English), and it has been diverting excess water from the Nile headwaters since the time of Pharaoh Amenemhat III, whose rule coincided with the early development of Avaris.[36] Could it be that this canal was one of the ways Joseph helped the nation he served?

Returning to the excavations at Avaris, archaeologists have also found an Egyptian-style palace that had been built on top of the remains of one of the oldest middle-room-houses. Rohl describes it in this way:

> The palace had courtyards, colonnades, audience chambers. There was even a robing room. It obviously belonged to some high official of state who was very, very important to that state. Because when somebody gets a palace like this given to them, it means they've been honored for what they've done for the state.[37]

In addition to a colonnade with twelve columns, the palace grounds held twelve memorial chapels that were built over twelve graves. It may be a coincidence, but there were also twelve tribes of Israel, each of which was descended from the twelve sons of Jacob (Joseph and his eleven brothers), whom the Bible claims originally settled in this area. Even more intriguing, one of the memorial chapels was in the shape of a pyramid. This surprised the archaeologists because at this time pyramid tombs were built only for pharaohs and their queens. Commenting on its original occupant, Rohl stated that the tomb "marked the man out as someone very special."[38]

Inside this pyramid tomb was a colossal statue of a seated man. Twice life size, this man was sculpted with red hair in a meticulously combed "mushroom-style," pale yellow skin, a throw stick (similar to a large boomerang) across his shoulder, and remnants of paint showing stripes of color on his shoulder. At the time the statue was made, Egyptians used this same hairstyle and skin color to depict foreigners from the north (whom they called "Asiatics"). Moreover, the term for "Asiatic" in hieroglyphics uses a throw stick, and this character often denoted "foreigner."[39] The stripes of color are reminiscent of the ornate, multi-colored robe that Joseph received from his father Jacob just before his brothers sold him into slavery,[40] and this robe had probably become Joseph's insignia. Rohl claims that there are no other statues similar to this one "in the whole of Egyptian history."[41] He concludes: "There is no doubt therefore that the statue represents a high official of the Egyptian state who was of Asiatic origin."[42]

Moreover, the leading art historian and curator of the Metropolitan Museum in New York, Dorothea Arnold, examined the statue and compared it to statues of pharaoh Amenemhat III, concluding that it had been carved in the workshops of Hawara by the same sculptors who had created that pharaoh's statues. This suggested that "the owner of the statue had close connections with the court of Amenemhat III,"[43] who is the pharaoh Rohl had believed as early as 1995 had appointed Joseph as vizier to prepare Egypt for the coming famine.

Another fascinating feature of the pyramid tomb was that archaeologists found no bones within it, which is consistent with the Bible's story: Joseph asked that his bones be carried to the land that God had promised his family in Canaan once his descendants settled there.[44] Egyptologist Charles Aling comments on the significance of this statue: "Either it is Joseph, or it's somebody who had a career remarkably the same as Joseph did."[45]

In addition to the palace with twelve columns and twelve tombs, the middle-room-house under this palace, the waterway of Joseph, and the statue and missing bones in the pyramid tomb, we'll mention one other piece of evidence for the historicity of the biblical account concerning

CHAPTER 11: ARCHAEOLOGICAL CONSISTENCY

the arrival of Joseph's family in Egypt. Rohl notes that in the same period that Avaris was first being settled, there is evidence that all of the wealth in Egypt became consolidated in the hands of the Pharaoh, causing a significant decline in the power of the local governors, called *nomarchs*. Archaeologists and historians have noted this transfer of wealth but have never successfully explained it. One possible explanation, in Rohl's opinion, is the plan that the Bible says Joseph implemented to prepare for the famine. One particular verse mentions what happened: "So Joseph bought all the land in Egypt for Pharaoh. The Egyptians, one and all, sold their fields, because the famine was too severe for them. The land became Pharaoh's."[46] Rohl explains:

> If you examine Joseph's famine policy, you'll see he was very astute. He didn't simply give the grain away, as some kind of giant welfare program. He sold the grain, and so the people had to buy [it]. So over those seven years all the wealth of Egypt came into Joseph, which meant that it came to Pharaoh.... If you read the Egyptian history books, there is no explanation for it.... Instead of the nomarchs having all this power and authority and wealth, it's all concentrated with the pharaoh.... Well, we have the answer in the Bible, and it's Joseph's famine policy.[47]

It is also interesting to note that, coinciding with the transfer of power from the nomarchs to the Pharaoh, historians have evidence that a new agency was set up in Egypt, called the "Department of the People's Giving" (*kha en djed remetj*). Rohl believes this agency "was set up to organize the gathering of crops by a conscription workforce and for the store of grain in government silos."[48] Here is the biblical account, which fits this historical detail quite remarkably:

> Joseph collected all the food produced in those seven years of abundance in Egypt and stored it in the cities. In each city he put the food grown in the fields surrounding it. Joseph stored up huge quantities of grain, like the sand of the sea; it was so much that he stopped keeping records because it was beyond measure....When the famine had

spread over the whole country, Joseph opened all the storehouses and sold grain to the Egyptians, for the famine was severe throughout Egypt. And all the world came to Egypt to buy grain from Joseph, because the famine was severe everywhere.[49]

EVIDENCE FOR THE EXODUS: POPULATION INCREASE

According to the biblical story, a Pharaoh who didn't know Joseph eventually came to power, and he decided to enslave the Israelites in order to keep them from becoming overly numerous and powerful. Yet despite their harsh lives, the Israelites continued to grow in number. So, our question now becomes: Is there evidence for this population expansion in the archaeological record? Again, David Rohl insists that there is.

Based on the recent excavations of Avaris, the city was approximately 250 hectares, or just under a square mile, which is very large by ancient standards. This is how Rohl describes the growth of the ancient city, as determined by the archaeological excavation and the dates assigned to different layers:

> At first there is a virgin land with no population at all. And suddenly there is a small group of Semitic people settled there.... There's probably a dozen or 15 houses – let's say about 70 or 100 people all told. And over a period of maybe three or four generations it becomes a very large city, one of the largest cities in the ancient world.[50]

Moreover, there is evidence of Semitic settlements throughout the region in this same period. Old Testament scholar James Hoffmeier explains:

> We do know that there was a large Semitic speaking population, which probably came from Syria, Canaan, sometime in the early part of the second millennium BC. Their remains have been found at a number of sites. We

have tombs that are clearly those of foreigners, Semites; we can tell this by the pottery, by the kind of weapons. These are not Egyptian-type axes and daggers.[51]

And Professor John Bimson further explains the evidence for the multiplication of the Israelites in Egypt:

> If we go back to the 18th and 19th centuries BC, you've got a good many settlements, 20 or more, which would fit the land of Goshen where the Bible says the Israelites were settled. Many of these settlements have not been fully excavated yet.[52]

Thus, there is evidence of a significant expansion of the Semitic settlers in Egypt in the period following the first settlements in Avaris.

EVIDENCE FOR THE EXODUS: ENSLAVEMENT

We now turn to the question of whether there is any evidence that the Semitic peoples who had settled in Avaris and other locations throughout Egypt went from apparently free and prosperous to enslaved and impoverished. Let's first ask if there is evidence of Semitic slaves in Egypt in this period, the type of slave that Joseph had become when his brothers first sold him to the Ishmaelite caravan, as recounted in the Bible. We'll also ask whether there is evidence that the Israelites were forced into slavery several generations later when the new Pharaoh didn't know Joseph.

One helpful clue comes from the tomb of an 18th Dynasty Egyptian official named Rekhmire (dated to approximately the 1300s to 1500s BC). In Zone 4 of his tomb, wall paintings depict slaves of Semitic and Nubian origin engaged in building and agricultural work, which is what the Bible claims the Israelites did when they were slaves in Egypt.[53] The hieroglyphics adjacent to the paintings describe the scene. Here is the English translation: "The captives [slaves] that His Majesty has bought back to work in the temple of Amun… making bricks to rebuild nine workshops of Amun in Karnak."[54]

THE SHORTEST LEAP

Figure 3: A wall painting from Zone 4 of the Rekhmire Tomb in Thebes, Egypt, depicting enslaved Semites and Nubians, fifteenth century BC.

Historians note that there was a large slave trade that brought many slaves to Egypt from Canaan (modern-day Israel, Palestine, Jordan, and Lebanon), Syria, Hatti (modern-day Turkey), and Mesopotamia (modern-day Iraq, southeastern Turkey, eastern Syria, and western Iran). In fact, the Egyptian word translated "Asiatics" was originally used to describe the origin of these people groups, but due to the large number of Asiatic slaves in Egypt, the term became synonymous with "slaves."[55]

Thus, we have evidence of a slave trade in Egypt that brought slaves like Joseph from the north. Further, the details of the biblical story describing how Joseph was sold into slavery in Egypt have historical plausibility. At the beginning of the Joseph story, before he was sold into slavery, Joseph and his brothers lived in Hebron. According to the biblical story, Jacob asked Joseph to bring food to his brothers, who were pasturing their flock of sheep in nearby Shechem. When Joseph didn't find his brothers in Shechem, he encountered a man who had overheard the brothers' plans to go to Dothan. After his brothers saw Joseph approaching them in Dothan, they vengefully threw him into an empty cistern with initial plans to kill him. But upon seeing a caravan of slave traders passing by, they instead decided to sell Joseph into slavery.

Not only have archaeologists identified the location of each of these

CHAPTER 11: ARCHAEOLOGICAL CONSISTENCY

ancient cities (Hebron, Shechem, and Dothan), but they also note that Dothan was near "a major highway of antiquity,"[56] a route that slave traders took on their way to sell their slaves in Egypt. It therefore makes sense that a caravan of traders happened upon Joseph and his brothers while they were in the region of Dothan. Moreover, cisterns and other types of pits, like garbage dumps, grain storage bins, and latrines, were a common feature of the land in those days, and they were often as big as ten feet wide by sixteen feet deep.[57]

An additional detail in the biblical story is that Joseph's brothers sold him for "twenty shekels of silver,"[58] which, according to laws 116, 214, and 252 of the Code of Hammurabi, was the common price of a male slave between the ages of 5 and 20 in the first half of the second millennium BC.[59] It is important to note that the price of a slave increased to thirty shekels by the mid- to early second millennium BC and to fifty shekels by the first millennium. Egyptologist James Hoffmeier explains the pertinence of the Bible's mentioning the twenty-shekel price: "That's the kind of detail in the story that is not only authentic, but hardly one that a later writer a thousand years later could have dreamt up and gotten right, knowing the economic considerations of the day."[60]

Dated to the late 1700s BC, a document known as the "Brooklyn Papyrus" provides additional evidence that a large population of Semitic people was enslaved in Egypt in the period of time after the first settlement in Avaris. The entire papyrus measures seven feet in length (though it is no longer intact), but one section in particular is relevant to our discussion. The Brooklyn Museum's website describes it in this way:

> The most important text recounts the efforts of a Thirteenth Dynasty Theban noblewoman named Senebtisi to establish legal ownership of ninety-five household servants, whose names indicate that forty-five were of Asiatic origin. The presence of so many foreigners in a single household suggests that the Asiatic population was increasing rapidly in Thirteenth Dynasty Egypt.[61]

Rohl comments further on the relevance of the list of servant names in this document:

> When we look at these names, 70 percent of them are Semitic names. And some of these names actually occur in the Bible: Menahem; Issachar and Asher, the names of two of the tribes of Israel; Shiphrah, one of the Hebrew midwives in the Exodus.[62]

This papyrus, therefore, confirms that there were Hebrew slaves in Egypt after the original settlement at Avaris, and that the names of slaves are also shared by Israelites mentioned in the Genesis and Exodus.

So, there is clearly archaeological evidence that Semitic peoples were used as slaves in Egypt, and that the population of Semitic slaves was increasing after the settlement of Avaris. But is there evidence to support the biblical story that the Israelites who had settled in Goshen were prosperous before they became enslaved? As before, the excavations at Avaris shed light on this question.

Based on the excavation of the Egyptian-style palace, there is evidence that the original settlers of Avaris were prosperous, but they didn't resemble the prosperous native Egyptians. For one thing, the bodies found in the tombs (except for the pyramidal tomb that didn't contain bones) were buried on their sides with their knees bent, which was typical of Canaanite, not Egyptian, burials. Moreover, the style of pottery, weapons, and other artifacts in the graves indicate that most of the settlers of Avaris (including the palace) were of Semitic origin. In the words of the archaeologist in charge of excavating Avaris, the distribution of housing in the earliest period of settlement was "egalitarian" and, "the archaeological and anthropological evidence indicates that the settlers were not Egyptians but people from nearby Canaan, albeit highly Egyptianised."[63] Thus, in the earliest strata of the archaeological excavation at Avaris, the evidence shows that the residents were Semites, but they were not enslaved. And far from it—they were instead quite prosperous, living in substantial homes and even in one palace.

But the evidence changes when you examine the later burials in Avaris, where the bodies show evidence of malnourishment and growth retardation. Moreover, in these later strata, the average age at death decreases markedly from former levels: the average lifespan of those who lived past childhood was 29.7 years for females and 34.4 years for males.[64] Also, fifty percent of these later burials were infants or children, a rate that is much higher than the 25% typical of a civil society in that ancient period. Further, the adult burials consisted predominantly of females, a sign that most of the infants who died had been males.[65] The signs of malnutrition, the earlier age at death, the increase in the infant mortality rate, and the predominance of females in the adult burials are all consistent with the biblical story. Not only does the Bible claim that the Israelites became enslaved, but also that their youngest males were killed in an effort to weaken their population: "Then Pharaoh gave this order to all his people: 'Every Hebrew boy that is born you must throw into the Nile, but let every girl live.'"[66]

EVIDENCE FOR THE EXODUS: JUDGMENT AND EXODUS

Despite Pharaoh's orders, one Hebrew boy was saved, and this boy, named Moses, grew up to become the man God used to save the Israelites from slavery and to lead them to the promised land. According to the Book of Exodus, God told Moses to deliver this message to Pharaoh: "This is what the LORD, the God of the Hebrews, says: 'Let my people go, so that they may worship me.'"[67] Each time Pharaoh refused to release the Israelites, God sent a plague. A total of ten plagues tormented the Egyptians until Pharaoh ultimately relented and permitted them to leave. First, the Nile turned to blood, killing the fish and depriving the Egyptians of drinking water. Then God sent a plague of frogs, followed by a plague of gnats, and then a plague of flies. The fifth plague caused the death of all of Egypt's livestock. Sixth, God caused all of the Egyptians to break out in boils, and the seventh plague brought a hailstorm, which killed all of the crops and stripped all of the trees bare. The plague of locusts, eighth, devoured all of the remaining crops and fruit, and ninth, the plague of darkness plunged Egypt into pitch black for three days.

The final and most devastating plague, the death of the firstborn, caused Pharaoh to finally give in. He granted permission to Moses to lead the Israelites out of Egypt (though he changed his mind after they began to depart). Interestingly, each of the plagues corresponds to one or more Egyptian deities, which was clearly intended as a symbol of Jehovah's superiority to and power over all of the Egyptian gods. The biblical story also claims that Moses instructed the people, as they were leaving, to ask the Egyptians for their silver, gold, and clothing, and that

God caused the Egyptians to give them what they asked for, and "so they plundered the Egyptians."[68]

Though this story seems far-fetched and definitely sounds like a legend, there is evidence that Egypt did experience this devastation in the middle of the second millennium BC. The first line of evidence comes from a papyrus that dates to approximately 1250 BC.[69] Entitled "Admonitions of an Egyptian Sage," but known more commonly as the "Ipuwer Papyrus," this document contains a description of events that sound eerily similar to what occurred during the ten plagues. Scholars debate whether this papyrus actually describes the events of the Bible, but consider these excerpts:

> The river is blood! As you drink of it you lose your humanity and thirst for water....

> Gone is the grain of abundance! Food supplies are running short. The nobles hunger and suffer. Upper Egypt has become a wasteland. Grain is lacking on every side. The storehouse is bare. Women say, "Oh, that we had something to eat!...

> What can we do about it? All is ruin!...

> Those who had shelter are now in the dark of the storm. The whole of the delta cannot be seen....

> There is fire in their hearts! If only he [Pharaoh] had perceived their [the Israelites'?] nature in the first generation! Then he would have smitten the evil – stretched out his arm against it. He would have destroyed their seed and their heritage....

> Behold, plague sweeps the land; blood is everywhere with no shortage of the dead. Children are dashed against the walls. The funeral shroud calls out to you before you come near. Woe is me for the grief of this time. He who buries his brother in the ground is everywhere.... Wailing is throughout the land mingled with lamentations....

CHAPTER 11: ARCHAEOLOGICAL CONSISTENCY

> The slave takes what he finds. What belongs to the palace has been stripped. Gold, lapis lazuli, silver and turquoise are strung on the necks of female slaves. See how the poor of the land have become rich whilst the man of property is a pauper.[70]

Rohl summarizes the conclusions that we can draw from the similarity of the Ipuwer Papyrus and the biblical account of the ten plagues:

> It seems, then, that Ipuwer was an eyewitness to a calamitous era in Egyptian history when, towards the end of the 13th Dynasty, foreigners had brought the great civilization of Egypt to its knees.[71]

Corresponding with this same period of history, excavations at Avaris reveal numerous "death pits," into which multiple bodies were tossed without the usual ceremonial burial rites. The archaeologist in charge of the excavation, Manfred Bietak, describes the death pits in this way:

> Over the course of this period [the Middle Bronze Age, 1500-1250 BC], the settlement expanded considerably but suffered a crisis near its end. Tombs found in excavation areas F/I and A/II, areas which are more than 500m apart from each other, were obviously emergency graves. Some of them are merely pits into which bodies were thrown. Most were without offerings. We think the evidence suggests that an epidemic swept through the town. It may have been the bubonic plague, perhaps the disease referred to as "Asiatic disease" in the medical papyri of the early 18th Dynasty. It is possible that the plague acquired this name as it raged within this Asiatic community in the Delta. However, this is speculation as there is, as yet, no scientific evidence for such a plague.[72]

Though Bietak links the death pits to a plague of some sort, another possible explanation is the biblical account of the death of the first-born in Egypt (at least those who lived in households that hadn't protected themselves with the "blood of the lamb" on the door post as God had instructed).

Another interesting quote provides further evidence of a judgment similar to the Exodus story. The Egyptian historian Manetho, who lived in the third century BC, wrote these comments about the period when the Tutimaos was Pharaoh (the 1500s to 1600s BC):

> In his reign, for what cause I know not, God smote us [the Egyptians]. And, unexpectedly, from the regions of the east, invaders of an obscure race marched in confidence of victory against our land. By main force they easily seized it without striking a blow; and, having overpowered the rulers of the land, they then burned our cities ruthlessly, razed to the ground the temple of the gods, and treated all the natives with a cruel hostility, massacring some and leading into slavery the wives and children of others.[73]

Rohl explains the relevance of this comment by Manetho:

> There are two separate events here: first God smites the Egyptians, then... a second blow occurs. With Egypt already on its knees, foreigners invade across Sinai and easily seize Egypt without meeting any significant resistance... due to the face that Egypt had already been smitten by God.[74]

The biblical explanation, though its inclusion of miracles makes it difficult to believe, is that the Egyptian army had been drowned in the sea as they pursued the Israelites, and thus Egypt was no longer able to defend itself.[75]

Excavations at Avaris indicate that soon after the death pits appeared, the Asiatic portion of the city was abandoned. And the date of this abandonment corresponded to the reign of Dudimose, the same pharaoh mentioned in Manetho above, but spelled "Tutimaos." Bietak, the archeologist at Avaris, notes that the area had been "substantially settled during the 13th Dynasty," but "was afterwards partly abandoned, perhaps as a result of an epidemic."[76] Were the death pits and the abandonment of the Asiatic portion of Avaris a result of an epidemic, or could this be evidence of the Exodus of the Israelites from Egypt? In conjunction with the evidence from the Ipuwer Papyrus and Manetho, the biblical story of the Exodus provides a plausible explanation.

EVIDENCE FOR THE EXODUS: CONQUEST

Lastly, let's briefly examine the main archaeological evidence supporting the historicity of the Israelites' conquest of the land that the Bible says God had promised to their forefather, Abraham. According to the story in the Books of Exodus and Joshua, after they left Egypt, the Israelites wandered for forty years in the desert. They then crossed the Jordan River into Canaan and conquered the land city-state by city-state. Again, David Rohl explains that evidence for the conquest of Israel exists, but archaeologists haven't found it because they have been looking for it in the Late Bronze Age, which is too late:

> Moving back to the Middle Bronze Age (several centuries earlier),... we do indeed find a series of city destructions that closely parallels the Conquest narratives.... What was actually needed [in archaeological scholarship] was a rejection of the baseless nineteenth-century assumption that the Pharaoh of the Exodus was Ramesses II. That catastrophic error and the equally damaging misidentification of Shoshenk I with the biblical Shishak are the two guilty parties here... not the biblical narrative, which really comes to life as a historical work once its stories are relocated to the Middle Bronze Age.[77]

One of the reasons that archaeologists have debated whether the Israelites had conquered the city of Jericho, the first one they encounter after crossing the Jordan, is that Jericho already was in ruins in the Late Bronze Age. The question thus becomes, why was it in ruins? Perhaps an earlier invading force had left it that way, and that earlier invading force had been the Israelites.

In the 1950s, Dame Kathleen Kenyon excavated the ruin mound of Jericho and discovered a city from the Middle Bronze Age whose exterior walls had collapsed. There was also evidence that it had been burned to the ground. This is precisely what the Bible describes happened to Jericho: the exterior walls collapsed, and the city was burned. Kenyon describes the collapsed walls and fire as follows:

> The destruction was complete. Walls and floors were blackened or reddened by fire, and every room was filled with fallen bricks, timbers, and household utensils; in most rooms the fallen debris was heavily burnt, but the collapse of the walls of the eastern rooms seems to have taken place before they were affected by fire.[78]

Another interesting detail of the Jericho excavation that the archaeologists discovered was that an abundant supply of grain had been left in the city upon its destruction. Multiple storage jars were filled with grain and, though they were charred, the grain remained inside of them. These full storage jars confirm two details of the biblical story: first, the siege happened soon after harvest, which is exactly when the Bible claims the siege of Jericho happened,[79] and second, the city of Jericho fell rather quickly, since if it had been a long siege, more of the grain would have been eaten. The evidence for a brief siege is also consistent with the biblical story.[80]

In addition, excavations of Jericho by Ernst Sellin and Carl Watzinger between 1907 and 1909 revealed a part of the outer mudbrick wall that hadn't been destroyed and to which homes were attached. These homes were "definitely on the seedy side of town," and consisted of "shops on the ground floors and living quarters above, suggesting that this was the town market district."[81] The homes that were built right into the outer walls looked out on the mountains and would have afforded "an easy escape from the city."[82] This archaeological find is incredibly consistent with the story in Joshua 2 about the prostitute Rahab, who helped the Israelite spies escape: "she let them down by a rope through the window, for the house she lived in was part of the city wall."[83] It is also interesting that these structures remained intact, which would have been necessary if Rahab and her family were to survive the destruction of the walls before the spies came to rescue her and the fire burned the city.

Rohl describes the evidence from Jericho:

> Only the Middle Bronze Age city fits the story of Joshua's Conquest. This fact alone is surely sufficient evidence to demonstrate when the Exodus and Conquest really took place... yet scholars continue to ignore the unambiguous archaeological picture in their preference for a mythical Bible with no Joshua and no Conquest at the end of the Late Bronze Age – all on the basis of one isolated anachronistic mention of the city of Ramesses in the Book of Exodus.[84]

While there is much more evidence that demonstrates the historicity of Old Testament events, let's now turn our attention to the New Testament. Like the older Scriptures, the New Testament is filled with historical detail that archaeological excavations have confirmed time and again.

ARCHAEOLOGICAL SUPPORT FOR THE NEW TESTAMENT

The Acts of the Apostles provides our first example of the historical accuracy of the New Testament. Colin Hemer, a noted Roman historian, has identified eighty-four facts in Acts that have been confirmed by archaeological and historical research.[85] For example, the author of Acts gives the correct names of ports used in the first-century Roman world, correct slang for Athenian words used at the time, accurate descriptions of shrines in ancient Athens, correct titles and names of the chief magistrates and other political rulers at the time, and proper terms in use in the first century for geographical features, political and judiciary processes, and much more.

These are all details that later writers, even in the second century, would not have known. In other words, Luke, the author of Acts, not only lived and traveled widely in the first-century Mediterranean world, but he was also a first-class, first-century historian. Biblical scholar and archaeologist Merrill Unger explains:

> The Acts of the Apostles is now generally agreed in scholarly circles to be the work of Luke, to belong to

the first century and to involve the labors of a careful historian who was substantially accurate in his use of sources.[86]

Sir William Ramsay, who is regarded as one of the world's foremost archaeologists, described Luke's accuracy: "Luke is a historian of the first rank; not merely are his statements of fact trustworthy... this author should be placed along with the very greatest of historians."[87]

In addition, biblical scholar F. F. Bruce points out that Luke's detailed accuracy "extends also to the more general sphere of local color and atmosphere." Luke describes first-century cities in a way that accurately reflects what historians know about these cities from other sources:

1. Jerusalem, with, in Bruce's words, "its excitable and intolerant crowds";
2. Syrian Antioch, "where men of different creeds and nationalities rub shoulders and get their rough corners worn away, so that we are not surprised to find the first Gentile church established there";
3. Philippi, "a Roman colony with its self-important magistrates and its citizens so very proud of being Romans";
4. Athens, "with its endless disputations in the marketplace and its unquenchable thirst for the latest news"; and
5. Ephesus, "with its temple of Artemis, one of the seven wonders of the world, and so many of its citizens depending for their living on the cult of the great goddess."[88]

In short, Luke's descriptions of the cities of the first-century Roman Empire provide a wealth of trustworthy historical information that has been confirmed by many other historical sources.

Bruce also notes that the Book of Acts contains three "we-sections," called such because Luke switches his narrative from the third person ("they") to the first-person plural ("we"). This indicates that Luke himself was present when the events occurred.[89] In Bruce's opinion, the most interesting "we-section" is the last one, which contains a description of Paul's sea voyage and shipwreck. Many historians have studied this account in order to understand ancient seamanship. In fact, in his mid-nineteenth century book, *The Voyage and Shipwreck of St. Paul*, the

CHAPTER 11: ARCHAEOLOGICAL CONSISTENCY

yachtsman James Smith of Jordanhill describes the uncanny accuracy of Luke's account, which enabled him to retrace the route of the voyage and pinpoint the exact location on the coast of Malta where the shipwreck occurred.[90]

The same remarkable detail also characterizes what Luke calls his "former book,"[91] the Gospel of Luke, which describes the life of Jesus. In the first three chapters of his Gospel, Luke names eleven historically confirmed political and religious leaders.[92] As an example of Luke's attention to detail, consider this excerpt:

> In the fifteenth year of the reign of Tiberius Caesar— when Pontius Pilate was governor of Judea, Herod tetrarch of Galilee, his brother Philip tetrarch of Iturea and Traconitis, and Lysanias tetrarch of Abilene— during the high priesthood of Annas and Caiaphas, the word of God came to John son of Zechariah in the desert. He went into all the country around the Jordan, preaching a baptism of repentance for the forgiveness of sins.[93]

F. F. Bruce explains how Luke is going out on a limb by recording all of these historical details:

> A writer who thus relates his story to the wider context of world history is courting trouble if he is not careful; he affords his critical readers so many opportunities for testing his accuracy. Luke takes this risk, and stands the test admirably.[94]

On top of this plentiful evidence of Luke's attention to detail, historians have investigated and confirmed the accuracy of Luke's references to thirty-two countries, fifty-four cities, and nine islands. Moreover, Luke mentions ninety-five people by name in Acts, sixty-two of whom are not mentioned anywhere else in the New Testament, indicating that he understood the importance of historical detail and naming his eyewitness sources.[95]

If Luke was so careful concerning the historical and geographic details in his accounts of Jesus' life and the early Christian church, we must ask whether he would distort the truth in describing the actions, claims, and miracles of Jesus. Perhaps Luke would have reason to do so, but at least we can't discard his account of Jesus' life because he was sloppy with the historical details. F. F. Bruce makes the point this way:

> Now, all of these evidences of accuracy are not accidental. A man whose accuracy can be demonstrated in matters where we are able to test it is likely to be accurate even where the means for testing him are not available. Accuracy is a habit of mind, and we know from happy (or unhappy) experience that some people are habitually accurate just as others can be depended upon to be inaccurate. Luke's record entitles him to be regarded as a writer of habitual accuracy.[96]

It is hard to believe that an accurate historian like Luke would then insert inaccurate details about the ministry and teachings of Jesus. We may question Luke's motives to stray from the truth in theological matters, but we certainly can't do so because he hasn't already proven to be habitually accurate.

Since Luke appears to be telling the truth, at least with regard to the historical details, Mark and Matthew also appear to tell the truth, since the primary details of their story of Jesus' life are very similar to Luke's. Moreover, much like Luke, the author of John was extremely accurate in his description of historical details.

Biblical scholar Craig Blomberg did a complete study of the Gospel of John and found numerous details that have been confirmed by archaeology and other historical documents.[97] For example, John writes that "there is in Jerusalem... a pool, which in Aramaic is called Bethesda and which is surrounded by five covered colonnades."[98] Archaeologists have discovered a pool in Jerusalem that accurately fits John's description of the five colonnades. What's even more interesting is that this pool was covered in rubble in AD 70, when the Romans destroyed Jerusalem, yet John uses the present tense to describe the pool's location: "there *is* in Jerusalem." This is strong evidence that the author of John had either seen the pool himself or had heard about it from someone who saw it before its destruction. We cannot prove that Jesus really healed the invalid man by

CHAPTER 11: ARCHAEOLOGICAL CONSISTENCY

the side of this pool, but this archaeological confirmation at least lends substantial support to the claim that John was either written before AD 70 or was written by someone who had lived in Jerusalem before AD 70.

Let me give just a few other examples of how archaeology has confirmed the accuracy of the Gospel of John. In 2004, archaeologists uncovered another pool in Jerusalem that has been confirmed as the "Pool of Siloam," where Jesus healed the blind man.[99] Coins dating to the years around the life of Jesus were found in the plaster of the pool, giving little doubt that this is the same pool described in John's Gospel.[100]

Upon hearing that his friend Lazarus was sick, Jesus traveled from Jerusalem to the town where Lazarus lived, Bethany. We read, "Now Bethany was fifteen stadia from Jerusalem."[101] Fifteen stadia convert to a little less than two miles, which is the actual distance between Jerusalem and Bethany. If the author were inventing the story, it is unlikely that he would include this type of detail, which is not essential to the story.

After Jesus walked these fifteen stadia, he discovered that Lazarus had died. John then records these details:

> Jesus, once more deeply moved, came to the tomb. It was a cave with a stone laid across the entrance. "Take away the stone," he said.
>
> "But, Lord," said Martha, the sister of the dead man, "by this time there is a bad odor, for he has been there four days."
>
> Then Jesus said, "Did I not tell you that if you believe, you will see the glory of God?"... When he had said this, Jesus called in a loud voice, "Lazarus, come out!" The dead man came out, his hands and feet wrapped with strips of linen, and a cloth around his face. Jesus said to them, "Take off the grave clothes and let him go."[102]

In the first century, Jews did in fact wrap the deceased in strips of linen before burial. However, after the first century, this burial practice was no longer common. This detail been confirmed as consistent with historical practice, and it demonstrates that the Gospel of John must have been written in the first century. If it had been written any later, it is highly unlikely that this detail would have been included.

Of the many details about Jesus that John's Gospel records, one detail of Jesus' death has been confirmed not by archaeology but by modern medicine. As Jesus was hanging on the cross, one of the Roman soldiers pierced his side with his spear, causing a "sudden flow of blood and water."[103] According to modern medical knowledge, one of the effects of crucifixion is the accumulation of fluid around the heart and lungs, respectively known as *pericardial effusion* and *pleural effusion*. The soldier's spear most likely punctured Jesus' right lung and heart, causing the watery substance that had built up in his heart and lung to flow out before the blood.[104]

This type of detail—regarding the mixture of water and blood—is consistent with eyewitness testimony. If someone were inventing the story, why would he include the detail about the water when only blood would be expected? This is just one of the many more eyewitness-like details of Jesus' final hours found in the Gospel of John, suggesting that John really was written either by an eyewitness or by someone who interviewed an eyewitness.

The Book of Acts and the Gospel stories—including those in the later Gospel of John—perform phenomenally well when submitted to the scrutiny of archaeologists. These accounts contain numerous historical details, and these details have been confirmed time and again by the archaeological record. In all, the books of the New Testament mention at least thirty historical figures that have been confirmed by archaeology or by non-Christian historical sources.

Moreover, as we saw in the last chapter, many early non-Christian— even anti-Christian— historical sources have confirmed the main details of Jesus' life and the beliefs of early Christians as summarized throughout the New Testament. Any claim that the Gospels are works of fiction is simply not substantiated by the external evidence. Furthermore, it is also inconsistent with the historical evidence to claim that the beliefs in the deity and resurrection of Jesus were later inventions of the Christian church. Non-Christian sources confirm that Christians were worshiping Jesus as God and proclaiming his resurrection from a very early date.

While the Old and New Testaments both receive an excellent score on the external evidence test of historicity, that doesn't necessarily mean

CHAPTER 11: ARCHAEOLOGICAL CONSISTENCY

that they are true in their entirety. However, because the archaeological record confirms them so well, the claims of the New Testament writers, especially those who professed to base their account on eyewitness testimony, merit further investigation.

QUESTIONS FOR COMPREHENSION AND DISCUSSION

1. Before even reading this chapter, what evidence do we have from previous chapters that Jesus was an actual historical figure, not a myth?
2. How does archaeological evidence help to determine whether a document is mythological or describes true history?
3. Why is it important to confirm the historicity of the Old Testament, in addition to the New Testament (except for the parts that are allegorical or visionary)?
4. Describe the following discoveries and how they have confirmed details of the Old Testament: the Rosetta Stone, the Moabite Stone (or Mesha Stele), the Tel Dan inscription, the Ketef Hinnom scrolls, and the Dead Sea Scrolls.
5. Describe the rules that the scribes were required to follow when they copied the Hebrew Scriptures, as set out in the *Mishneh Torah*.
6. Why have many archeologists thought that the biblical Exodus must have happened in the 1200s BC? Why have these archaeologists concluded that the story of the Exodus is a myth?
7. What is some of the evidence that David Rohl has summarized to support the historicity of the biblical stories of:
   a) the arrival of the Israelites in Egypt
   b) the increase in their population
   c) their enslavement
   d) the judgment of pharaoh, followed by the Israelites' departure from Egypt, and
   e) their conquest of the land of Canaan (Jericho in particular)?
8. What is the evidence that Luke has an excellent attention to detail with regards to the historical details in the Gospel of Luke and the Book of Acts? How does this detail provide more reason

to trust the truthfulness of these books, as well as the Gospels of Matthew and Mark?
9. What are some examples of archaeological confirmation of details in the Gospel of John?
10. What is the significance of the detail that both blood and water emerged from Jesus' body after a spear pierced his side?

CHAPTER 11 ENDNOTES

[1] Millar Burrows, *What Mean These Stones?* (New York: Meridian, 1957), 1.

[2] Quoted in Jessica Laber, "The Future of Archeology Is Not Digging Something Up," *Fast Company*, November 23, 2015. Available online at https://www.fastcompany.com/3053674/the-future-of-archaeology-is-not-digging-anything-up.

[3] "Ancient historiography: The first histories," *Encyclopædia Britannica*, https://www.britannica.com/topic/historiography/Ancient-historiography.

[4] Ian Watt. *The Rise of the Novel: Studies in Defoe, Richardson and Fielding* (Berkeley: University of California Press, 1957), 12.

[5] William F. Albright, *The Archeology of Palestine* (Baltimore, MD: Penguin, 1949), 127-28.

[6] One example of visionary literature in the Bible is the last book, the Revelation to John, in which the author uses symbols to represent future realities.

[7] David Murray, "5 Reasons to Study Old Testament History," Ligonier Ministries blog, June 27, 2012. Available at https://www.ligonier.org/blog/5-reasons-study-old-testament-history.

[8] See John 1:45, 5:39-40, 46, 10:25-26, Matthew 5:17, Luke 24:27, 44, Acts 3:18-25, 8:32-35, 10:43, 17:2, 3, 28:23, Romans 3:21.

[9] John D. Currid and David W. Chapman, eds., *The ESV Archeology Study Bible* (Wheaton, IL: Crossway, 2017), vii.

[10] Ibid, 67, 69, 71. These titles occur in Genesis 39:1 and 4.

[11] James King, *Moab's Patriarchal Stone: being an account of the Moabite stone, its story and teaching.* (London: Bickers and Son, 1858), 56, lines 14-18a. Available online at https://archive.org/details/moabspatriarcha01fundgoog/page/72.

[12] 2 Kings 23:13.

[13] See 2 Kings 3:27. Child sacrifice by the Moabites and other Canaanites is also attested to by the Greek author Kleitarchos in the 4th century BC (Scholia on Plato's *Republic* 337a).

CHAPTER 11: ARCHAEOLOGICAL CONSISTENCY

14. Avraham Biran and Joseph Naveh, "The Tel-Dan Inscription: A New Fragment," *Israel Exploration Journal*, Vol. 45, No. 1 (1995), pp. 1-18, available online at https://www.jstor.org/stable/27926361.
15. See the story of these kings in 2 Kings 8-11. Specifically, 2 Kings 10:32-33 states: "In those days the Lord began to reduce the size of Israel. Hazael overpowered the Israelites throughout their territory east of the Jordan in all the land of Gilead (the region of Gad, Reuben and Manasseh), from Aroer by the Arnon Gorge through Gilead to Bashan." Note that the Bible claims that Jehu killed Ahaziah and Jehoram, while the Tel-Dan stela claims that Hazael killed them. To resolve this discrepancy, scholars have noted that they were wounded by Hazael (who may have been boasting and thus exaggerating) and then killed by Jehu.
16. "The Tel Dan Inscription: The First Historical Evidence of King David from the Bible," *The Biblical Archeology Society*, May 2, 2019. Available at https://www.biblicalarchaeology.org/daily/biblical-artifacts/the-tel-dan-inscription-the-first-historical-evidence-of-the-king-david-bible-story.
17. John Nobel Wilford, "Solving a Riddle Written in Silver," *The New York Times*, September 28, 2004. Available at https://www.nytimes.com/2004/09/28/science/solving-a-riddle-written-in-silver.html.
18. Gabriel Barkay, "News from the Field: The Divine Name Found in Jerusalem," *Biblical Archaeology Review* 9:2, March/April 1983, https://www.baslibrary.org/biblical-archaeology-review/9/2/8.
19. The priestly blessing from Numbers 6:24-26 is "The Lord bless you and keep you; the Lord make his face shine on you and be gracious to you; the Lord turn his face toward you and give you peace.'"
20. YHWH would have been pronounced "Yahweh" or "Jehovah." But for fear of misusing it and breaking the third commandment, the Israelites did not say this holy name out loud. They often used the word "Adonai" in place of YHWH, and the English Old Testament uses the all-caps word "Lord" to translate this sacred name.
21. For a very interesting comparison of paleo-Hebrew to the letters used in this book, I recommend this link: https://en.wikipedia.org/wiki/Phoenician_alphabet#Table_of_letters.
22. From the Israel Museum of Jerusalem website: The Digital Dead Sea Scrolls, "Nature and Significance," http://dss.collections.imj.org.il/significance.
23. Gleason Archer, *A Survey of Old Testament Introduction* (Chicago, IL: Moody Press, 1964), 19.
24. The rules come from Maimonides, *Mishneh Torah*, "Tefillen, Mezuzah and Sefer Torah," English translation available at https://www.chabad.org/library/article_cdo/aid/925369/jewish/Tefillin-Mezuzah-and-Sefer-Torah.htm.

25   Exodus 1:11. All emphases in Bible passages are mine.
26   From an interview with Hershel Shanks in Timothy Mahoney and Steven Law, *Patterns of Evidence: Exodus, A Filmmaker's Journey* (St. Louis Park, MN: Thinking Man Media, 2015), Location 456.
27   "Goshen" occurs in Genesis 45:10, 46:28, 29, 34, 47:1, 4, 6, 27, 50:8, Exodus 8:22, 26, Joshua 10:41, 11:16, 15:51. For a more extensive description of the location of Goshen, see John Van Seters, "The Geography of the Exodus," in Neil Ash Silberman, ed., *The Land That I Will Show You: Essays in History and Archaeology of the Ancient Near East in Honor of J. Maxwell Miller* (Sheffield Academic Press, 1997), 267-269.
28   Scholars have also justified this timeline through another line of evidence from an inscription carved relief on a gateway in the ruins of the Temple of Amun-Re in Thebes, Egypt. In 1828, one of the first scholars who was able to translate hieroglyphics interpreted the name of the pharaoh in the inscription as "Shishak," which scholars assume is the same pharaoh mentioned in 2 Chronicles 12:9: "When Shishak king of Egypt attacked Jerusalem, he carried off the treasures of the temple of the Lord and the treasures of the royal palace. He took everything, including the gold shields Solomon had made." David Rohl explains that the inscription does not refer to Shoshenk, and instead it more likely refers to Ramesses the Great, whose nickname was "Sysa" or "Shysha." This misapplication of the inscription, in addition to the assumption that the Israelites built the city of Ramesses, have led to an inaccurate date for the Exodus. For more detail of Rohls' case, see Chapter Four: "Shishak," in Rohl, *Exodus: Myth or History.*
29   David Rohl, as quoted in Mahoney and Law, *Patterns of Evidence*, Locations 1659-1660.
30   The corresponding stories in the Bible are: (1) Arrival: Genesis 45:16-47:12, (2) Population increase: Genesis 47:13- 50:26, (3) Enslavement: Exodus 1:1-22, 5:1-21, (4) Judgment: Exodus 7:14-11:10, 12:29-30, (5) Exodus: Exodus 12:31-42, 13:17-22, 14:1-31, 15:19, (6) Conquest: Joshua 1:1-24:33.
31   Mahoney and Law, *Patterns of Evidence: Exodus*, Locations 1715-1716.
32   This is how the Austrian archaeologist in charge of the excavation at Avaris, Manfred Bietak, describes the architecture of the oldest structures they discovered: "The houses of this settlement reveal that the settlers were not Egyptians but people from the Levant [modern-day Israel, Palestine, Lebanon, Syria, and Jordan]. According to [archaeologist] Eigner, the layout of the houses resembles closely both the 'Mittelsaalhaus' and the 'Breitraumhaus'—ancient architectural types which occur in northern Syria in the second half of the fourth millennium BC." From David Rohl,

CHAPTER 11: ARCHAEOLOGICAL CONSISTENCY

Avaris: The Capital of the Hyksos, Recent Excavations at Tell el-Dab'a (London: The British Museum Press, 1996), 10.

33   David Rohl, as quoted in Mahoney and Law, *Patterns of Evidence: Exodus*, Location 1773.
34   Rohl, *Exodus: Myth or History*, 107.
35   Jacob's grandfather Abraham had come from Harran (Genesis 11:31-32, 12:4-5), the wife of Jacob's father Isaac had come from Harran (Genesis 24:2-4, 29), and Isaac had sent his servant to Harran to find a wife for his son Jacob (Genesis 27:43, 29:19-20). Jacob also lived in Harran for 20 years and had 11 sons and a daughter while he lived there (Genesis 31:38-41).
36   For an overview of Joseph's Canal, see Mahoney and Law, *Patterns of Evidence: Exodus*, Locations 1937-1958, and Rohl, *Exodus: Myth or History?*, 99-102.
37   David Rohl, as quoted in Mahoney and Law, *Patterns of Evidence*, Location 1790.
38   Rohl, *Exodus: Myth or History?*, 110.
39   Charles E. Nichols, *Egyptian Hieroglyphic to English Dictionary*, 304, and E. A. Wallis Budge, *An Egyptian Hieroglyphic Dictionary*, Vol. 1 (London: John Murray, 1920), cxxxvii.
40   See the story in Genesis 37, with references to the "ornate" or "multi-colored" robe in verses 3, 23, and 32.
41   David Rohl, as quoted in Mahoney and Law, *Patterns of Evidence*, Location 1833.
42   Rohl, *Exodus: Myth or History?*, 115.
43   Ibid, 114.
44   See Genesis 50:24-25.
45   Charles Aling, as quoted in Mahoney and Law, *Patterns of Evidence*, Location 1871.
46   Genesis 47:20.
47   Rohl, as quoted in Mahoney and Law, *Patterns of Evidence*, Locations 2015-2017, 2022, 2024, 2032.
48   Rohl, *Exodus: Myth or History?*, 98.
49   Genesis 41:48-49, 56-57.
50   Rohl, as quoted in Ibid, Locations 2228-2230.
51   James Hoffmeier, as quoted in Ibid, Location 2261.
52   John Bimson, as quoted in Mahoney and Law, *Patterns of Evidence*, Location 2361.
53   See Genesis 11:3; Exodus 1:14, 5:7-8, 14, 16, 18-19.

54 Hieroglyphic translation from Osirisnet, "The Tombs of Ancient Egypt," https://www.osirisnet.net/tombes/nobles/rekhmire100/e_rekhmire100_07.htm.
55 Currid and Chapman, *The ESV Archeology Study Bible*, 65.
56 Ibid.
57 Ibid.
58 See Genesis 37:28.
59 The Code of Hammurabi was a law code authored by Hammurabi, the king of Babylon from 1792 to 1750 BC. To see an English translation of this code, visit https://avalon.law.yale.edu/ancient/hamframe.asp. Note that "one-third of a mina" is equivalent to 20 shekels of silver.
60 James Hoffmeier, as quoted in Mahoney, *Patterns of Evidence*, Locations 1871-1885.
61 The Brooklyn Museum Website, "Portion of a Historical Text," https://www.brooklynmuseum.org/opencollection/objects/3369. For a description of the findings of the archeological analysis of the Brooklyn Papyrus, see William C. Hayes, *A Papyrus of The Late Middle Kingdom In the Brooklyn Museum (Papyrus Brooklyn 35.1446)* (Brooklyn, NY: Brooklyn Museum, 1972).
62 Rohl, as quoted in Mahoney and Law, *Patterns of Evidence*, Locations 2520-2522.
63 Bietak, *Avaris: The Capital of the Hyksos, Recent Excavations at Tell el-Dab'a*, 5.
64 Ibid, 36.
65 Rohl, *Exodus: Myth or History?*, 127.
66 Exodus 1:22.
67 Exodus 9:1, 13, 10:3.
68 The plagues are described in Exodus 7:14-11:10. A useful chart that summarizes the ten plagues and the corresponding Egyptian gods can be found at http://www.biblecharts.org/oldtestament/thetenplagues.pdf.
69 Ian Shaw. "Pharaonic Egypt", Peter Mitchell, Paul Lane, eds., *The Oxford Handbook of African Archaeology* (Oxford University Press, 2013).
70 These excerpts are taken from Rohl, *Exodus: Myth or History?*, 150-152. To view the translation of the Ipuwer Papyrus, see http://dlib.nyu.edu/awdl/sites/dl-pa.home.nyu.edu.awdl/files/admonitionsofegy00gard/admonitionsofegy00gard.pdf.
71 Rohl, *Exodus: Myth or History?*, 150.
72 Bietak, *Avaris: The Capital of the Hyksos*, 35.
73 Quoted in Rohl, *Exodus: Myth or History?*, 156. From Manetho, *Aegyptiaca.*, frag. 42, 1.75-79.2. Available online at https://ryanfb.github.io/loebolus-data/L350.pdf, page 79 (115-802).

CHAPTER 11: ARCHAEOLOGICAL CONSISTENCY

74 Rohl, *Exodus: Myth or History?*, 156-157.

75 Exodus 14:26-28: "Then the Lord said to Moses, 'Stretch out your hand over the sea so that the waters may flow back over the Egyptians and their chariots and horsemen.' Moses stretched out his hand over the sea, and at daybreak the sea went back to its place. The Egyptians were fleeing toward it, and the Lord swept them into the sea. The water flowed back and covered the chariots and horsemen—the entire army of Pharaoh that had followed the Israelites into the sea. Not one of them survived."

76 Bietak, *Avaris: The Capital of the Hyksos*, 7.

77 Rohl, *Exodus: Myth or History?*, 264, 272.

78 Joshua 6:20, 24: "When the trumpets sounded, the army shouted, and at the sound of the trumpet, when the men gave a loud shout, the wall collapsed; so everyone charged straight in, and they took the city....Then they burned the whole city and everything in it, but they put the silver and gold and the articles of bronze and iron into the treasury of the Lord's house."

79 K. Kenyon, *Digging Up Jericho* (London, 1957), 254.

80 The Israelites crossed the Jordan River at the time of the harvest, as described in Joshua 3:14-16a: "So when the people broke camp to cross the Jordan, the priests carrying the ark of the covenant went ahead of them. Now the Jordan is at flood stage all during harvest. Yet as soon as the priests who carried the ark reached the Jordan and their feet touched the water's edge, the water from upstream stopped flowing. It piled up in a heap a great distance away, at a town called Adam in the vicinity of Zarethan, while the water flowing down to the Sea of the Arabah (that is, the Dead Sea) was completely cut off. So the people crossed over opposite Jericho."

81 Rohl, *Exodus: Myth or History?*, 278.

82 Ibid, 281.

83 Joshua 2:15.

84 Rohl, *Exodus: Myth or History?*, 280.

85 Colin J. Hemer, *The Book of Acts in the Setting of Hellenistic History* (Winona Lake, IN: Eisenbrauns, 1990).

86 Merrill F. Unger, *Archaeology and the New Testament*. (Grand Rapids, MI: Zondervan Publishing House, 1956), 24.

87 W. M. Ramsay, *The Bearing of Recent Discovery on the Trustworthiness of the New Testament* (Grand Rapids, MI: Baker Book House, 1953), 222.

88 F. F. Bruce, *The New Testament Documents: Are They Reliable?* (Grand Rapids, MI: Eerdmans, 1981), 89.

89 These "we-sections" occur in Acts 16:10-17, 20:5-21:18, and 27:1-28:16.

90 James Smith, *The Voyage and Shipwreck of St. Paul* (Eugene, OR: Wipf and Stock, 2001).

91 Luke calls his Gospel his "former book" in Acts 1:1.

92. Bruce, *The New Testament Documents*, 90.
93. Luke 3:1-3.
94. Bruce, *The New Testament Documents*, 82.
95. Bruce M. Metzger, *The New Testament: Its Background, Growth, Content* (New York: Abingdon Press, 1965), 171.
96. Bruce, *The New Testament Documents*, 90-91.
97. Craig L. Blomberg, *The Historical Reliability of John's Gospel* (IVP Academic, 2011).
98. John 5:2.
99. John 9:7.
100. Hershel Shanks, "The Siloam Pool: Where Jesus Cured the Blind Man," *Biblical Archeology Review*, September/October 2005, 16-23.
101. John 11:18.
102. John 11:38-41a, 43-44.
103. John 19:34.
104. See William D. Edwards, Wesley J. Gabel, Floyd E. Hosmer, "On the Physical Death of Jesus," *Journal of the American Medical Association* 255, no. 11 (March 21, 1986): 1455-1463.

The interval then between the dates of original composition and the earliest extant evidence becomes so small as to be in fact negligible, and the last foundation for any doubt that the Scriptures have come down to us substantially as they were written has now been removed.

—Sir Frederic Kenyon, paleographer and biblical scholar[1]

To be skeptical of the resultant text of the New Testament books is to allow all of classical antiquity to slip into obscurity, for no documents of the ancient period are as well attested bibliographically as the New Testament.

—John Warwick Montgomery, lawyer and apologist[2]

12

The Chain of Testimony

Having put the biblical documents through the *internal* and *external tests of historicity* in the last seven chapters, we are now ready to put the New Testament through the *bibliographical test of historicity*. To perform this test, you first identify the earliest existing copies (or *extant manuscripts*) of the document in question in order to determine how much time has passed between the earliest copies and the originals.

A second component of the test is to count the early extant manuscripts, and the third component is to compare the extant manuscripts to one another. If there are many early manuscripts, it is much easier to identify when changes were inserted, either accidentally or intentionally, and then to most accurately determine the content of the original documents. Let's get started.

PROXIMITY OF MANUSCRIPTS TO THE ORIGINALS

The original New Testament documents were written on papyrus, a paper-like material made from the pith of the papyrus plant. Because papyrus becomes brittle and disintegrates with age, none of the originals, called *autographs*, still exist. Amazingly, however, more than one hundred papyrus copies of portions of the New Testament have survived to the 21st century, and in excess of fifty of these were created between AD 125 and 200. Thanks to its dry climate, Egypt is the source of most of these surviving early manuscripts.

CHAPTER 12: THE CHAIN OF TESTIMONY

The oldest extant manuscript is known as P_{52} (for "Papyrus 52"), or the "Rylands Library Papyrus," after the library in Manchester, England, where it is kept.[3] Copied between AD 125 and 200, this small fragment contains verses 31, 32, 33, 37, and 38 from chapter 18 of John's Gospel. The other papyri manuscripts include a significant portion of each of the four Gospels, as well as many portions of the other books of the New Testament.

From the third century on, copies of the New Testament documents were made on *parchment*, the higher quality version of which is called *vellum*. Made from animal skins, parchment lasts much longer than papyrus. The most significant parchment copy of the Bible that exists today is the *Codex Sinaiticus*, which was created between AD 330 and 350. It contains all of the New Testament, as well as portions of the Old Testament in Greek. Another important early parchment manuscript is the *Codex Vaticanus*, which contains nearly the entire Bible and was created between AD 325 and 350.[4]

In sum, much of the New Testament can be reconstructed from early papyri manuscripts, and the rest can be filled in by early parchment manuscripts. Using the widely accepted date range for the composition of the four Gospels (AD 60 to 100), the earliest manuscripts date between 25 to 290 years of the originals.

While this lapse between the earliest extant manuscripts and the originals may seem huge, it is a relative blink of the eye for an ancient document. When compared to other reliable ancient historical documents, it's the winner by a huge margin. A quick comparison of the New Testament to other trusted historical documents demonstrates its superiority:

1. The oldest extant manuscripts of the Roman historians Tacitus and Suetonius, who wrote between AD 95 and 120, are from the ninth century, 800 years after the originals.
2. The oldest extant copies of Josephus, the Jewish historian writing between AD 75 and 100, are from the eleventh century, 900 years after the originals.
3. The oldest extant manuscript of Caesar's *Gallic Wars*, written between 58 BC and AD 17, is also dated 900 years after the original.
4. The earliest extant manuscript of Thucydides' *History*, written between 460 and 400 BC, is dated circa AD 900, 1,300 years after the original.

5. The oldest extant manuscript of Herodotus' *Histories*, written between 488 and 428 BC, was also written down approximately 1,300 years later than the originals.

After the New Testament, the ancient document with the shortest span of time between the originals and the first complete copy is Homer's *Iliad*, with a 600-year span. Written in the ninth century BC, the first complete copy of the *Iliad* dates to the third century BC.[5]

The respected biblical scholar F. F. Bruce observes:

> The evidence for our New Testament writing is ever so much greater than the evidence for many writings of classical authors, the authenticity of which no one dreams of questioning.... But we do not quarrel with those who want more evidence for the New Testament than for other writings; firstly, because the universal claims which the New Testament makes upon mankind are absolute, and the character and works of its chief Figure so unparalleled, that we want to be as sure of its truth as we possibly can; and secondly, because in point of fact there *is* much more evidence for the New Testament than for other ancient writings of comparable date.[6]

Let's take a closer look at the abundant evidence that historians have at their disposal as they assess the authenticity of the New Testament documents.

Multiplicity of Manuscripts and the Counting of Variants

Not only were the earliest extant manuscripts of the Gospels recorded just 25 to 290 years after the originals, but we can be confident about the content of the original documents because we have a huge collection of manuscripts. At the latest count, there are at least 5,600 Greek manuscripts of the New Testament, both partial and complete, both papyri and parchment.[7][8]

CHAPTER 12: THE CHAIN OF TESTIMONY

In addition to the Greek, there are about 9,000 manuscripts in other languages, including Latin, Coptic (the final stage in the development of the ancient Egyptian language), Syriac (the language of ancient Syria), and ancient Arabic. Many of these manuscripts in other languages were translated in the first centuries of the Christian church. There are also more than 36,000 quotations of the earliest New Testament documents in the works of the early church fathers, who lived in the second through fourth centuries: Justin Martyr (100-165), Irenaeus (*c.* 130-*c.* 202), Clement of Alexandria (*c.* 150-211/216), Origen (*c.* 185-*c.* 254), Tertullian (160-220), Hippolytus (*c.* 170-*c.* 235), and Eusebius (*c.* 265-*c.* 339).[9] These quotations cover a large portion the New Testament.[10]

In comparison to the wealth of manuscript and quotation resources for the New Testament, there are 133 manuscripts of Josephus' works, three manuscripts of Tacitus' works (none include all his writings), and 200 manuscripts of Suetonius' works.[11] We also only have eight early manuscripts of Herodotus' *History*, eight copies of Thucydides' *History*, and ten copies of Caesar's *Gallic Wars*. Again, the next best ancient document after the New Testament is Homer's *Iliad*, with 643 copies.[12]

So why is having so many manuscripts such a good thing for understanding what was in the original documents? It starts with this key assumption: it is highly unlikely that copyists across a broad geographic area would make the exact same changes at the exact same time. Therefore, by comparing the manuscripts, scholars can deduce when changes were made and thereby work back to the contents of the original document.

Figure 4 on the next page illustrates this concept in admittedly simplistic terms. The rectangle on the far left is the original document. Each column to its right is a "generation" of copies. Let's assume that only two copies are made of a document, and two copies are made of those copies, and so on. After four "generations," there are a total of sixteen copies. Now let's assume that the original no longer exists, nor do any of the other copies for the next three generations. We only have the sixteen latest copies to compare with one another.

If a change was made at point A—let's call it "Difference A"—only two documents would be affected, so we can assume that Difference A is not in the original. If a change was made at point B, four of the sixteen documents would contain "Difference B." Again, we can assume it is not in the original. If a change is made at point C, half of the documents would contain "Difference C," making it difficult to discern whether it was in the original or not.

Now imagine that we find a copy that is earlier than the others. Let's call it Copy X. We see that the change made at point C does not appear in this earlier copy. We can therefore determine that it is more than likely that change C was not in the original.

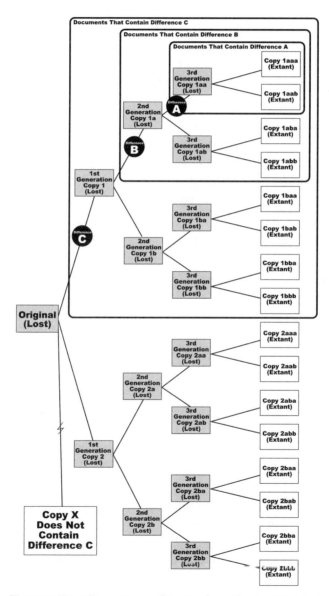

Figure 4: Four Generations of Copies from the Lost Original

CHAPTER 12: THE CHAIN OF TESTIMONY

This analogy is helpful for understanding the process that text critics use to determine the content of the original New Testament. But instead of 16 or 17 manuscripts, they have thousands. New Testament text critics also have much earlier sources, analogous to the second and third rows of our example. Therefore, any changes made in later centuries can easily be identified, and even changes made early on, especially if they are errors, are readily discovered. As a result of the comparison of thousands of manuscripts, we can be confident the New Testament we read today is remarkably similar to the original documents, even though we no longer have those original documents.

But skeptics persist. In his book, *Misquoting Jesus*, text critic Bart Ehrman has discredited the accuracy and reliability of the New Testament by making such apparently devastating claims as: "There are more variations among our manuscripts than there are words in the New Testament."[13] There are indeed many variants among the thousands of manuscripts, and Ehrman makes a big deal of the quantity of variants, which is between 200,000 and 400,000.[14] But has Ehrman demonstrated from this high number that Jesus has been misquoted all along? On the contrary, one of the world's foremost authorities on biblical text criticism, Daniel Wallace, claims that Ehrman's book, in contrast to its title, provides not even a single example of when Jesus was misquoted.[15] Moreover, he never proves that any central doctrine of Christianity was compromised because of textual variants.[16]

Another scholar with expertise in text criticism, Timothy Paul Jones, makes this statement in response to Ehrman's book:

> As I examine *Misquoting Jesus*, I find nothing that measures up to the title or to the promotional copy. What I find is a great deal of discussion about a handful of textual variants— none of which ultimately changes any essential belief that's presented in the New Testament.[17]

Not only does Ehrman exaggerate the impact of variants on the meaning of the text, but his claim that there are more variants than the number of words in the New Testament is also completely misleading.

To see why "200,000 to 400,000 variants" is not an indication that the New Testament is unreliable, it is crucial to understand that any tiny variation between manuscripts is counted as a variant, and each manuscript that contains this tiny difference is counted as one variant. Thus, if one thousand manuscripts contain the same tiny difference, it counts as one thousand variants.

For example, the name "John" appears in the New Testament at least 150 times. Some manuscripts spell the Greek version of "John" with one *n*, while other manuscripts spell it with two *n*'s. Therefore, if 100 Greek manuscripts each contain 150 occasions when the Greek word for John uses only one *n*, the total variants would be 15,000.

Another common source of variants is the "movable *nu*." The Greek letter *nu*, the equivalent of the English letter *n*, was sometimes used at the end of a word before a word beginning with a vowel, much like the English use of the indefinite article "an" instead of "a." Many manuscripts leave off this additional *nu*, resulting in thousands of variants. So, if one hundred Greek manuscripts each left off one hundred *nu*'s, that would count as ten thousand variants. According to Daniel Wallace, spelling variations as with "John" and the "movable *nu*" account for seventy to eighty percent of the textual variants.[18]

Synonyms, such as the occurrence of "the Lord" in place of "Jesus," are another common source of variants among manuscripts. The definite article is another: in Greek, it is often used in front of proper names, but sometimes it is excluded. Thus, "the Mary" would be counted as a variant of "Mary," even though the two variants are obviously referring to the same person.

This type of variant is common in manuscripts called *lectionaries*, of which there are approximately 2,200. Scribes who prepared lectionaries were dividing the Bible into sections for daily or weekly readings, over the course of a year. Because the listener would only hear a small section each day, if the reading started with a reference to Jesus as "he," the lectionary inserted the name "Jesus" to avoid ambiguity. When you multiply 2,200 lectionaries by the number of uses of "Jesus" in place of "he," you arrive at a very large number of variants.[19]

Changes in word order are another source of variants. Greek is an inflected language, so the ending of the word communicates its purpose in the sentence—subject, direct object, and so forth. That is, because the subject of a verb and the object of a verb take on different forms in Greek, if they exchange places in the sentence, it is still possible to determine which word is the subject and which is the object. For example, there are sixteen different ways to say, "Jesus loves Paul" in Greek (due to varying word order and whether or not the definite article is used with proper names), but each would be translated into English the same way.[20] But even when the meaning of a sentence is unaffected, any difference in word order would still count as a variant.

Timothy Paul Jones summarizes the significance of the variants: "In the end, more than 99 percent of the 400,000 differences fall into this category of virtually unnoticeable variants!"[21] And once you understand the nitpicky way that discrepancies are counted among the thousands of manuscripts, you can better appreciate the response Daniel Wallace has to Ehrman's claims:

> If we have 200,000 to 400,000 variants among the Greek manuscripts, I'm just shocked that there are so few!... What would the potential number be? Tens of millions! Part of the reason we have so many variants is because we have so many manuscripts. And we're glad to have so many manuscripts— it helps us immensely in getting back to the original.[22]

However, there are still differences between manuscripts that lead text critics to conclude that portions of the current New Testament most likely were not in the originals. Thus, scholars debate the alternatives for what was in the original.[23] But the outcome of any of these debates has no effect on the core doctrines of Christianity, which are the deity and resurrection of Jesus, the forgiveness of sins through his substitutionary atonement, and eternal salvation through faith in him. Mark Roberts, who earned his doctorate in New Testament studies from Harvard University, makes this point in his comments on the tiny percentage of variants that have an uncertain interpretation: "If you actually took out of the Gospels every word that was text-critically uncertain, the impact on your understanding of Jesus would be negligible."[24]

In response to Ehrman's claim that the disputed variants affect the meaning of entire books of the Bible, Timothy Paul Jones reacts this way:

> It is at this point that I must respectfully disagree with Ehrman. Here's what I find as I look at the textual evidence. In every case in which two or more options remain possible, every possible option simply reinforces

truths that are already clearly present in the writings of that particular author and in the New Testament as a whole; there is no point at which any of the possible options would require readers to rethink an essential belief about Jesus or to doubt the historical integrity of the New Testament.[25]

Benjamin Warfield, late professor of systematic theology at Princeton Theological Seminary, describes the accuracy of the New Testament text as follows:

If we compare the present state of the New Testament text with that of any other ancient writing, we must... declare it to be marvelously correct. Such has been the care with which the New Testament has been copied—a care which has doubtless grown out of true reverence for its holy words.... The New Testament [is] unrivaled among ancient writings in the purity of its text as actually transmitted and kept in use.[26]

The surprise, therefore, is not that there are so many variants, but that there are so few. Comparing the number of variants to what we would expect for an ancient document that has been copied thousands upon thousands of times over the centuries, we should be very impressed with just how well preserved the New Testament has been.

Many Early "Christianities"?

The science of text criticism has given us a remarkably accurate understanding of the content of the original documents of the New Testament, such that we can be confident that no major doctrine of the Christian faith is affected by any changes made to these documents over the centuries. However, some skeptics have raised doubts about the trustworthiness of the New Testament in another way.

These skeptics claim that there was a wide diversity of views in the first century about who Jesus was and what he taught. They theorize that the more powerful proponents of the traditional, "orthodox" view silenced

CHAPTER 12: THE CHAIN OF TESTIMONY

the views that may have provided a more accurate picture of Jesus and his teachings. Thus, they claim, the winning orthodox view has survived, while the alternative views were excluded. The Jesus we read about in the four canonical Gospels of Matthew, Mark, Luke, and John, they claim, is simply a concoction of the early orthodox church and bears very little resemblance to the true "historical Jesus." In order to find out who Jesus *really* was, they say we must read between the lines of the canonical Gospels and also look to other documents, such as the *Gospel of Thomas*, which they claim had been hidden and suppressed by "the powers that used to be."

A popular expression of this theory comes from Dan Brown's bestselling novel and the film based on it, *The Da Vinci Code*. The fictional character Sir Leigh Teabing describes the conspiracy that many modern liberal scholars also believe:

> "Fortunately for historians… some of the gospels that Constantine attempted to eradicate managed to survive. The Dead Sea Scrolls were found in the 1950s hidden in a cave near Qumran in the Judean desert. And, of course, the Coptic Scrolls in 1945 at Nag Hammadi. In addition to telling the true Grail story, these documents speak of Christ's ministry in very human terms. Of course, the Vatican, in keeping with their tradition of misinformation, tried very hard to suppress the release of these scrolls. And why wouldn't they? The scrolls highlight glaring historical discrepancies and fabrications, clearly confirming that the modern Bible was compiled and edited by men who possessed a political agenda—to promote the divinity of the man Jesus Christ and use His influence to solidify their own power base."[27]

This view makes for compelling fiction, but it is nothing new. Since the Enlightenment, scholars in religion departments of the world's foremost universities have proposed similar theories. Ironically, they claim there is bias (even misogynistic, power-thirsty bias) in the Christian church, but their views are themselves saturated in bias.

A group of liberal New Testament scholars called the Jesus Seminar has used myriad media-savvy techniques in recent decades to widely proclaim this position to an uninformed mass-market audience. In one publication they state: "With the Council of Nicaea in 325, the orthodox party solidified its hold on the Christian tradition and other wings of the Christian movement were choked off."[28] In another, they boast that they provide "for the first time anywhere all twenty of the unknown gospels from the early Christian era."[29] They especially rely on the *Gospel of Thomas*, one of the documents discovered in 1945 near the town of Nag Hammadi, Egypt.

Certainly, the Jesus of Matthew, Mark, Luke, and John is the more offensive personality. He repeatedly speaks of sin, judgment, and hell. The Gnostic Jesus is much more attractive: a traveling sage who guides his followers toward heavenly wisdom, mystical illumination, and their own inner divinity.

The Jesus Seminar has concluded that early Christianity bore no resemblance to what would become the orthodox church of later centuries, with its domineering, all-male hierarchy and emphases on liturgy and doctrine. The Nag Hammadi documents in general reveal a better Christianity, they claim, in which women held a high status and a diversity of opinions peacefully coexisted. In fact, instead of speaking of "early Christianity," they believe we should refer to "early Christianities."[30]

Based on a vote of their members, the Jesus Seminar winnowed down the four Gospels of Matthew, Mark, Luke, and John to a mere fifteen statements that Jesus really said (none of which are in the Gospel of John) and only ten acts that he actually performed. The rest of those Gospels, they claim, are simply embellishments or fabrications of the early church. Not surprisingly, none of Jesus' sayings about judgment, sin, and salvation were considered authentic, and all of his miracles were dismissed as concoctions.[31]

For modern people interested in spirituality outside the confines of organized religion, these claims that Jesus was simply a mystical teacher of wisdom—not the divine Son of God who offers atonement for sin—have been just what they wanted to hear. Assessing the mass appeal of the Nag Hammadi documents, religion professor Philip Jenkins states:

> The reasons for this development are not hard to [find], since the scholars and writers presenting the "real Jesus" and his followers were making them sound so precisely

CHAPTER 12: THE CHAIN OF TESTIMONY

compatible with strictly contemporary concerns, so relevant to modern-day debates. The marketing of alternative Christianity represents a model case study in effective rhetoric, in which a potential audience is first identified, and a message is then tailored to its particular needs and interests.[32]

N. T. Wright describes the new depiction of early Christianity as "the sort of religion that a large swathe of America yearns for: a free-for-all, do-it-yourself spirituality with a strong agenda of social protest against the powers that be and an I'm-OK-you're-OK attitude on all matters religious and ethical."[33]

While the liberal scholars accuse the original church of inventing a leader who could fortify its power base, conservative scholars accuse liberal academia of inventing a leader who appeals to a modern audience. With intelligent scholars on both sides of the debate, is it even possible to find the real Jesus? Fortunately, there are ways to sift through the data and logically determine the most accurate, historical description of Jesus.

First, since the "real Jesus" is most likely the earliest to be recorded, let's compare the dates that scholars assign to the Nag Hammadi documents with the dates for Matthew, Mark, Luke, and John, dates that even the most liberal scholars affirm. Because virtually every scholar—liberal and conservative alike—believes that the four canonical Gospels were written much closer to Jesus' life than the other noncanonical "gospels," Matthew, Mark, Luke, and John are much more likely to tell us what Jesus really said and what he really did.

Comparing Composition Dates

From a very early date—at a time when Christians were being put to death for their beliefs and the Christian church had no political power—Christian theologians ruled out certain documents because they could not be traced back to the testimony of an eyewitness. This process of determining which documents are authentic and which are not is called "canonization." The twenty-seven books of the New Testament are part of the "canon" and are therefore considered "canonical" documents. The

Nag Hammadi documents, which are not in the New Testament, are considered "noncanonical."

As discussed in Chapter 9, virtually all scholars date the four canonical Gospels of Matthew, Mark, Luke, and John to the first century. Contrary to this early dating for the canonical Gospels, the vast majority of scholars believe that the "noncanonical gospels," such as those of the Nag Hammadi Library, weren't composed until the latter half of the second century—at the earliest.[34] This is long enough after Jesus' death that no eyewitnesses would still be alive, making it easier for false material to be inserted without refutation.[35] Simply put, the later the account, the less likely it accurately portrays who Jesus really was.

Because a full analysis of the noncanonical documents is beyond the scope of this book, we will limit our discussion to the *Gospel of Thomas*, the only noncanonical "gospel" that arguably could be dated to the first century.[36]

Although parts were found at the end of the nineteenth century, the complete text of the *Gospel of Thomas* was among the documents found in Nag Hammadi. Many respected scholars believe *Thomas* was composed in the late second century, but a vocal minority argues that it belongs in the first century.

Critical New Testament scholar and Harvard Divinity School professor Helmut Koester maintains that the *Gospel of Thomas* reflects first-century views and was composed even earlier than the canonical Gospels.[37] This is also the opinion of many of the Jesus Seminar scholars, who claim that the "first edition" of *Thomas* dates to AD 50, before any of the canonical Gospels had been composed.[38] As reflected in the title of his book, *The Five Gospels*, the late Jesus Seminar founder Robert Funk even elevated the *Gospel of Thomas* to the same status as Matthew, Mark, Luke, and John.[39]

Unlike the canonical Gospels, which place Jesus' sayings within a flowing narrative of Jesus' life, *Thomas* is a list of 114 sayings (or "logia") that are attributed to Jesus and placed in no particular order. The document begins: "These are the secret words which the living Jesus spoke, and Didymus Judas Thomas wrote them down."[40] Many of the sayings are similar to those in the canonical Gospels, but a large number reflect a very different view of Jesus that is typical of a philosophy called *Gnosticism*. Rather than as a divine ruler who dies for his people's sins,

CHAPTER 12: THE CHAIN OF TESTIMONY

Jesus is portrayed in *Thomas* as the revealer of divine knowledge (or *gnosis*), through which one can attain mystical enlightenment.

The Jesus of *Thomas* offers a completely different route to eternal life than the Jesus of the canonical New Testament. This is obvious in the very first saying: "He who shall find the interpretation of the words shall not taste of death." Immortality is achieved by attaining secret knowledge, not through faith in Jesus. Consider also Saying 77, in which Jesus states: "I am the light that shines over all things. I am everywhere. From me all came forth, and to me all return. Split a piece of wood, and I am there. Lift a stone, and you will find me there." Not only does this sound like the pantheism of eastern philosophy, it is a far cry from the understanding of Jesus' divinity in the New Testament. Interestingly, it is also a far cry from the "more human" Jesus that Professor Teabing claims is revealed in the Nag Hammadi documents.

Is it credible that the *Gospel of Thomas* was written in the first century? One of the main arguments for an early composition date is its similarity to a hypothetical document, dubbed "Q."[41] The assumption is that "Q" is a list of Jesus' sayings that existed before Matthew and Luke's Gospels, and Matthew and Luke each based their Gospel on it.

There are numerous logical problems with the theory that *Thomas* and Q were composed at the same time. No ancient writers mention the existence of an independent list of sayings that Matthew and Luke used. Although many New Testament scholars do believe it may have existed, some scholars have recently proposed very logical arguments to demonstrate that Q may not have ever existed at all. Instead of Matthew and Luke being independent accounts based in part on Q, portions of Luke's Gospel may have been based directly on Matthew's Gospel. When both theories are subjected to "Occam's razor," which holds that the simplest explanation is the best, the Q theory loses the competition hands down.[42]

Scholars who base their understanding of the earliest beliefs of Christianity on Q are giving historiographical priority to a hypothetical document. It is far more rational—the shortest leap of reason—to trust actual, existing works by writers who insist they are eyewitnesses. Logically, we can conclude that the promotion of hypothetical documents over those that exist seems suspiciously biased against the traditional claims of Christianity.

With its collection of sayings, the *Gospel of Thomas* fits into a distinct genre. As New Testament scholar Craig Evans explains: "The collections genre was just as popular in Syria at the end of the second century as it was anywhere else in an earlier period."[43] Another Nag Hammadi text, the *Gospel of Philip*, is also an unordered list of Jesus' sayings, but scholars universally date it to the latter half of the third century.[44] There is also a collection called *The Sentences of Sextus* that was in use at the end of the second century, as well as a collection of sayings of the rabbis produced around the same time.[45]

Still, skeptics persevere. They argue that when sayings in *Thomas* resemble those of the Synoptic Gospels, the versions in *Thomas* appear "more primitive" or "closer to the source."[46] One study compared the order of the sayings in *Thomas* to the order of similar sayings in the Synoptic Gospels and found little correlation. This would suggest, therefore, that *Thomas* did not depend upon the canonical Gospels and therefore may have been written first.[47] Meanwhile, some scholars have pointed to the story of the "doubting Thomas" in John's Gospel[48]—when Thomas said he would have to touch Jesus before he'd believe he had physically risen—as evidence that the author of John was addressing an existing "Thomas community" that did not believe in a physical resurrection.[49]

But the credibility of these theories for a first-century *Thomas* quickly crumbles when compared to evidence on the other side. First, the different order of the sayings in *Thomas* compared to the Synoptic Gospels in no way proves that *Thomas* was written first. In fact, the Synoptic Gospels, which most likely did rely on one another to some extent, present a very different chronology for Jesus' sayings. There are other good explanations for the order of sayings in *Thomas* that demonstrate it was composed in the second century, as we will discuss below.

Second, even educated guesses regarding which sayings are earlier (or "closer to the source") are easily influenced by bias and therefore cannot definitively prove that *Thomas* was written before the canonical documents.

Third, the author of the Gospel of John likely was aware of individuals who denied the physical nature of Jesus' resurrection. Given the extraordinary nature of the claim that Jesus rose bodily from the dead, first-century people were bound to doubt it or reinterpret it as a spiritual or symbolic resurrection, just as twenty-first-century people

CHAPTER 12: THE CHAIN OF TESTIMONY

do. This in no way proves that the *Gospel of Thomas* had already been composed. Neither does it prove that this "*Thomas*-like" opinion reflects an equally authentic "early Christianity." This is especially true since the whole troubling Christian movement could have been toppled if the powerful Roman authorities had simply produced a corpse from the tomb that their armed soldiers had guarded.[50]

In fact, the New Testament book of First John, likely written by the same author as the Gospel of John, is a sermon that specifically addresses the false belief that Jesus' resurrection was only spiritual in nature.[51] Since the author repeatedly claims to have been an eyewitness of Jesus' ministry and resurrection,[52] he is responding to these skeptics precisely because their beliefs contradict the truth of events he saw with his own eyes. The deniers may have represented a subset of those who called themselves "followers of Christ" in the first century, but they weren't among the eyewitnesses. Moreover, if a more formalized "Thomas community" did exist in the first century, why don't the early church fathers make any mention of it until the late second century? In fact, the earliest surviving references to the *Gospel of Thomas* in the historical record are in the writings of Hippolytus and Origen in the first half of the third century.[53]

There are three other proofs demonstrating the *Gospel of Thomas* deserves a date in the late second century. First, it includes references to all of the canonical Gospels, the writings of Paul, and many other early Christian writings. According to Craig Evans:

> Over half of the New Testament writings are quoted, paralleled, or alluded to in *Thomas*.... [This] tells me that it's late. I'm not aware of a Christian writing prior to AD 150 [who] references this much of the New Testament. Go to the Epistles of Ignatius, the bishop of Antioch, which were written around AD 110. Nobody doubts their authenticity. They don't quote even half of the New Testament. Then along comes the *Gospel of Thomas* and it shows familiarity with fourteen or fifteen of the twenty-seven New Testament writings. And people want to date it to the middle of the first century?[54]

The author of *Thomas* clearly was writing after these other documents had widely circulated. The opposite scenario—that *Thomas* was first and thus influenced these other documents—is extremely unlikely, especially considering the Gnostic characteristics of *Thomas*.

Secondly, approximately one third of the sayings in *Thomas* reflect images, ideas, and phrasing typical of Gnostic philosophy of the mid- to late second century.[55] Saying 77, mentioned above, is just one example. Another is Saying 50:

> Jesus said, "If they say to you, 'Where did you come from?,' say to them, 'We came from the light, the place where the light came into being on its own accord and established [itself] and became manifest through their image.' If they say to you, 'Is it you?,' say, 'We are its children, we are the elect of the Living Father.' If they ask you, 'What is the sign of the father in you?,' say to them, 'It is movement and repose.'"

This saying resembles Gnostic literature of the mid-second century, which the early church father Irenaeus described in his five-volume work, *Against Heresies*, written circa AD 180.[56] Based on this similarity, the "they" in Saying 50 most likely refers to the "archons," the rulers of the material world in Gnostic mythology.[57] The statement also reflects the goal of Gnostic salvation: rest, or "repose," not the bodily resurrection of all who put their faith in the resurrected Jesus.

Thomas also uses typical second-century Gnostic symbols. Saying 7 says: "Blessed is the lion that a man will eat, and the lion will become man." In Gnostic mythology of the mid-second century, the rulers of the heavens were portrayed as lions.[58] In Saying 75, Jesus says, "Many are standing at the door, but it is the solitary who will enter the bridal chamber." The bridal chamber was a Gnostic rite that symbolized entry into a full relationship with God. Sayings 2, 3, 37, 51, 60, 84, 86, 87, 90, and many others also contain Gnostic ideas popular in the second century.

A third strong line of evidence demonstrates that Syrians in the second century wrote the *Gospel of Thomas*. The first indication of this is found in the use of the name, "Didymus Judas Thomas," for the person who wrote down the "secret words" of Jesus. The combination of "Judas" and "Thomas" is found only in the Syrian church.[59] There are

CHAPTER 12: THE CHAIN OF TESTIMONY

also many words in the Coptic version of *Thomas* (the version found at Nag Hammadi) that hint at a Syrian source. One example is the use of the Coptic word *noub* for "gold coin" in *Thomas* Saying 100. This type of coin was only used in Syria, suggesting *Thomas'* author was from Syria.[60] Moreover, *Thomas* contains many statements of belief that were very similar to the notably ascetic and mystical beliefs of the Syrian church in the second century.

Another clue pointing to the Syrian origin of *Thomas* is the order of the sayings. When the Coptic version of *Thomas* that had been found at Nag Hammadi is translated into Syriac, the 114 sayings no longer appear random. Instead, each saying ends with a Syriac "catchword" that is found in the next saying. For example, as Craig Evans explains, "Saying 2 is followed by Saying 3 because Saying 2 refers to a certain word that's then contained in Saying 3. And Saying 3 has a certain word that leads you into Saying 4. It was a memorization aid."[61] It is important to emphasize that this memorization aid only works when the sayings are in Syriac, suggesting that *Thomas* was originally written in Syriac by the later Syrian church, not in Greek, as the first-century canonical Gospels had been.[62]

But the "crippling blow"[63] to the argument that *Thomas* was written in the first century comes from its incredible similarity to a document composed circa AD 170 called the *Diatessaron* (Greek for "through four"). As the name implies, the *Diatessaron* was an attempt to blend the four canonical Gospels into a single narrative story. The author, Tatian the Assyrian, wanted to eliminate redundancy in the four Gospels of Matthew, Mark, Luke, and John and present them as a single Gospel in his native Syriac. In fact, the *Diatessaron* provided the first opportunity for Syrians to read the Gospels in their native language, and it became the main Gospel text in the Syrian church for two centuries before it was abandoned in favor of the four independent Gospels.

Commenting on an earlier study of the similarity between *Thomas* and the *Diatessaron*, ancient manuscript scholar Nicholas Perrin states:

> In comparing the *Gospel of Thomas* against our best reconstruction of textual variants in the *Diatessaron*, [Christian and Gnostic scholar] Gilles Quispel finds over 160 textual variants shared by *Thomas* and

the *Diatessaronic* tradition. These variants occur throughout the *Gospel of Thomas* and, more importantly, on examining Thomasine sayings that parallel the synoptic gospels (roughly half of the entire collection of 114 sayings) one finds that there are only a few logia [sayings] that do not bear the marks of *Diatessaronic* influence.[64]

In *Fabricating Jesus*, Craig Evans provides examples of how a saying in *Thomas* resembles the corresponding verse in the *Diatessaron* more closely than it resembles the corresponding verses in the Gospels of Matthew and Luke. He remarks: "There are many examples like this, where the form of the saying in *Thomas* agrees with either the form of the saying in Tatian's *Diatessaron* or in the later Syriac Gospels."[65]

While *Thomas* may indeed contain some of the earliest teachings of Jesus because it is based in part on the canonical documents, it was composed too late to accurately reflect, in its entirety, the historical person of Jesus of Nazareth. Historian Philip Jenkins clarifies that the Gnostic gospels represent an undependable portrait:

> Though contemporary writers use the Gnostic gospels to portray alternative models of Christianity, we see that these rival movements were much later historically than their orthodox counterparts, and were actually formulated in reaction against a preexisting orthodoxy, so they cannot claim to represent equally valid or ancient views of Jesus. The more we explore primitive Christianity, the earlier we find some of the most "catholic" and orthodox practices.[66]

Most likely, *Thomas* reflects a diversity in beliefs of later Christians, much of which can be attributed to the influence of Greco-Roman and Gnostic philosophy. To find the true, unaltered teachings of Jesus, our best bet is to stick with the far earlier canonical Gospels of Matthew, Mark, Luke, and John, of which we have thousands of early copies.

CHAPTER 12: THE CHAIN OF TESTIMONY

Questions for Comprehension and Discussion

1. What is the bibliographical test of historicity? What are the three components of this test?
2. What are some other ancient documents that historians consider trustworthy, and how do they compare to the New Testament documents in terms of elapsed time between the earliest copy and the original and the number of extant manuscripts?
3. How many manuscripts of the New Testament documents exist? What are the various types of manuscripts that are available to text critics in order to determine the content of the original documents?
4. Why do the original papyrus documents no longer exist? Is this a huge problem? Why or why not?
5. Describe the process whereby text critics compare extant manuscripts to each other in order to determine the most likely contents of the original document. What is the main assumption underlying this process?
6. What are the various causes of the vast majority of these variants, and how do they impact the meaning of the text? Do any central Christian beliefs stand or fall on these variants?
7. Describe the argument that skeptics make when they claim that the canonical Gospels' accounts of Jesus' life and teachings are simply the one opinion of Jesus that "won out" over other opinions. What do they mean by "early Christianities"?
8. Why are the beliefs of the Gnostic gospels so appealing to many people today?
9. What are the main differences between *The Gospel of Thomas* and the canonical Gospels? What are the main ways we can demonstrate that the *Gospel of Thomas* was written in Syria in the late second century?
10. If the *Gospel of Thomas* is the one Gnostic gospel that scholars have tried to demonstrate was written in the first century, and if it actually was written in the late second century, what can we then conclude about the Gnostic gospels' descriptions of Jesus' life and teachings?

CHAPTER 12 ENDNOTES

1. Sir Frederic Kenyon, *The Bible and Archeology* (New York: Harper & Brothers, 1940), 288-289.
2. John Warwick Montgomery, *History and Christianity* (Grand Rapids, MI: Bethany House Publishers, 1986), 29.
3. Bruce M. Metzger and Bart D. Ehrman, *The Text of the New Testament: Its Transmission, Corruption, and Restoration*, 4th ed. (Oxford: Oxford University Press, 2005), 53-61.
4. Josh McDowell, *The New Evidence That Demands a Verdict* (Nashville, TN: Thomas Nelson Publishers, 1999), 39-40.
5. University of Michigan Library, "Translating Homer: Translating an Oral Tradition into Writing," https://www.lib.umich.edu/online-exhibits/exhibits/show/translating-homer--from-papyri/translating.
6. F. F. Bruce, *The New Testament Documents: Are They Reliable?* (Grand Rapids, MI: Eerdmans, 1981), 10.
7. Clay Jones, "The Bibliographical Test Updated," October 21, 2013, CRI, https://www.equip.org/article/the-bibliographical-test-updated/.
8. A full list of all manuscripts of the New Testament is available at http://www.laparola.net/greco/manoscritti.php.
9. McDowell, *The New Evidence That Demands a Verdict*, 43.
10. Norman L. Geisler, *Baker Encyclopedia of Christian Apologetics* (Grand Rapids, MI: Baker, 1999), 532.
11. Mark D. Roberts, *Can We Trust the Gospels?* (Wheaton, IL: Crossway, 2007), 31.
12. McDowell, *The New Evidence That Demands a Verdict*, 38.
13. Bart D. Ehrman, *Misquoting Jesus: The Story Behind Who Changed the Bible and Why* (New York: HarperOne, 2005), 90.
14. From an interview with Daniel B. Wallace in Lee Strobel, *The Case for the Real Jesus* (Grand Rapids, MI: Zondervan, 2007), 67.
15. Strobel, *The Case for the Real Jesus*, 67.
16. As quoted in Strobel, *The Case for the Real Jesus*, 88.
17. Timothy Paul Jones, *Misquoting Truth: A Guide to the Fallacies of Bart Ehrman's* Misquoting Jesus (Downers Grove, IL: InterVarsity Press, 2007), 77.
18. As quoted in Ibid, 86.
19. Ibid.
20. As quoted in Ibid, 87.
21. Jones, *Misquoting Truth*, 44.
22. Quoted in Strobel, *The Case for the Real Jesus*, 87.

CHAPTER 12: THE CHAIN OF TESTIMONY

23   One contested passage is the end of Mark's Gospel (Mark 16:9-20). In the oldest complete manuscripts of the New Testament, the *Codex Sinaiticus* and the *Codex Vaticanus*, Mark ends after the women discover the empty tomb and an angel tells them Jesus has risen. But even without the twelve contested verses, the tomb is still empty, and the angel has pronounced Jesus risen. Though Mark doesn't mention Jesus' appearances, the angel instructs Mary to tell the disciples to expect him to meet them in Galilee.

Moreover, the other Gospels, as well as the Book of Acts and the Pauline Epistles, mention that Jesus appeared to many people after his crucifixion. Therefore, Jesus' resurrection does not stand or fall on whether the last twelve verses of Mark are in the original document. On top of this, many scholars have made the case that the original ending of Mark, which most likely did mention Jesus' appearances, may have been lost. One reason is that it was common for the endings and beginnings of scrolls to be damaged because they were on the outer edge. Another reason, scholars claim, is that there are many themes in Mark, such as the numerous predictions by Jesus that he would appear to them after his death, that indicate that the author intended to conclude with those appearances. (For example, see N.T. Wright's case in *The Resurrection of the Son of God* [Minneapolis: Fortress, 2003], 617-24.)

Another story that is missing from the original is the "let him throw the first stone" story of John 7:53-8:11. The Jewish leaders accuse a woman of adultery and sentence her to die by stoning. When they ask Jesus what they should do with her, he tells them, "If any one of you is without sin, let him be the first to throw a stone at her." They then disperse, leaving the woman alone with Jesus. The story is consistent with Jesus' ministry, especially the insinuation that even the most moral people are not free of sin, and it is reasonable to assume this event really did happen. The fact that this story doesn't appear in the earliest manuscripts of John does not invalidate Jesus' overall message. While most New Testaments still include these verses, they usually include a note to clarify that they are not in the earliest manuscripts.

While there are a number of instances when scholars debate the original text of a verse, none affect any essential doctrine of the Christian faith—that is, they don't affect Christian *orthodoxy*, or "right belief." The discrepancies may, however, affect issues of *orthopraxy*, or "right practice," which describe the correct way to live out the Christian faith. For more information, see Strobel, *The Case for the Real Jesus*, 89.

24   Roberts, *Can We Trust the Gospels?*, 34-35.
25   Jones, *Misquoting Truth*, 55.

26. Benjamin B. Warfield, *Introduction to Textual Criticism of the New Testament* (London: Hodder & Stoughton, 1907), 12-13.
27. Dan Brown, *The Da Vinci Code* (New York: Doubleday, 2003), 234.
28. Robert W. Funk, Roy W. Hoover, and the Jesus Seminar, *The Five Gospels* (New York: Macmillan, and Sonoma, CA: Polebridge Press, 1993), 35.
29. Robert J. Miller, *The Complete Gospels* rev. and expanded ed. (Sonoma, CA: Polebridge Press, 1994), cover.
30. For example, see Bart D. Ehrman's books *Lost Christianities* (New York: Oxford University Press, 2003); *Lost Scriptures: Books That Did Not Make It into the New Testament* (New York: Oxford University Press, 2003); and *The New Testament and Other Early Christian Writings*, 2nd ed. (New York: Oxford University Press, 2004).
31. See Funk et al., *The Five Gospels*.
32. Philip Jenkins, *Hidden Gospels: How the Search for Jesus Lost Its Way* (Oxford: Oxford University Press, 2001), 16.
33. N. T. Wright, "A Return to Christian Origins (Again)," *Bible Review*, December 1999, 10.
34. For a good summary of the scholarly opinions on the dating of the noncanonical documents, see Darrell L. Bock, *The Missing Gospels: Unearthing the Truth Behind Alternative Christianities* (Nashville, TN: Thomas Nelson Publishers, 2006).
35. Mark D. Roberts, *Can We Trust the Gospels?* (Wheaton, IL: Crossway, 2007), 60. Also see Chapters 3 and 4 of Craig A. Evans, *Fabricating Jesus* (Downers Grove, IL: 2006), in which Evans provides strong evidence against earlier dates for the following noncanonical texts: *The Gospel of Thomas, The Gospel of Peter, The Egerton Gospel, The Gospel of Mary*, and *The Secret Gospel of Mark*.
36. In *The Cross That Spoke* (New York: HarperCollins, 1992), John Dominic Crossan claims that another Nag Hammadi text, the *Gospel of Peter*, dates to AD 50. The vast majority of other scholars disagree. In response to the claim that the Gospel of Peter was composed earlier than the canonical gospels, Moody Smith of Duke Divinity School raised this question: "Is it thinkable that the tradition began with the legendary, the mythological, the anti-Jewish, and indeed the fantastic, and moved in the direction of the historically restrained and sober?" (Moody Smith, "The Problem of John and the Synoptics in Light of the Relation between the Apocryphal and Canonical Gospels," in Adelbert Denaux, ed., *John and the Synoptics* BETL 101 [Leuven: Peeters and Leuven University Press, 1992], 150.)
37. Helmet Koester, *Ancient Christian Gospels: Their History and Development* (Philadelphia: Trinity Press International, 1990), 84-85.
38. Miller, *The Complete Gospels*, 6.

CHAPTER 12: THE CHAIN OF TESTIMONY

39 See Funk et al., *The Five Gospels.*
40 There are many translations of the *Gospel of Thomas* available online. One place to start your search is under "Translations" in the Wikipedia article located at http://en.wikipedia.org/wiki/Gospel_of_Thomas.
41 Interestingly, two different scholars originally called this hypothetical document "Q" independently at the beginning of the 1900's. The German scholar Julius Wellhausen called it Q because it was the first initial of the German word for "source," *Quelle.* Around the same time, the Cambridge scholar J. Armitage Robinson also assigned the letter Q to the source for the similar material in Matthew and Luke. He had called the source of Mark's material "P," the first initial of Peter, whom he believed had influenced Mark's Gospel, so it was natural to use the next letter Q to name the shared source of much of Matthew and Luke's Gospel. (F. F. Bruce, *The New Testament Documents*, 34f.)
42 For one convincing argument against Q, see Mark Goodacre, *The Case Against Q* (Harrisburg, PA: Trinity Press International, 2002). See also his demonstration of how Luke was most likely based directly on Matthew in, "Ten Reasons to Question Q," http://www.markgoodacre.org/Q/ten.htm.
43 Quoted in Strobel, *The Case for the Real Jesus*, 39.
44 Evans, *Fabricating Jesus*, 76.
45 Ibid.
46 Gerd Theissen and Annette Merz, *The Historical Jesus: A Comprehensive Guide* (Minneapolis: Fortress Press, 1998), 38-39.
47 Stevan L. Davies, *Correlation Analysis*, http://users.misericordia.edu//davies/thomas/correl.htm.
48 John 20:25-29.
49 See Elaine Pagels, *Beyond Belief: The Secret Gospel of Thomas* (New York: Vintage Books, 2004).
50 We will discuss the empty tomb in much more detail in Chapter 17.
51 Kenneth L. Barker and John R. Kohlenberger III, *NIV Bible Commentary, Volume 2: The New Testament* (Grand Rapids, MI: Zondervan Publishing House, 1994), 1078-1079.
52 See John 19:35, 21:24, and 1 John 1:1.
53 Hippolytus mentioned the *Gospel of Thomas* in his *Refutation of All Heresies* 5.7.20 (c. 222-235), and Origen mentioned it in his *Homilies* on Luke 1.5.13-14 (c. 233).
54 Strobel, *The Case for the Real Jesus*, 36.
55 Jenkins, *The Hidden Gospels*, 70.
56 See Irenaeus, *Adversus Haereses* (or *Against Heresies*), available online at http://www.newadvent.org/fathers/0103.htm.
57 Jenkins, *The Hidden Gospels*, 70.

58. Ibid, 70.
59. From an interview with Craig Evans in Strobel, *The Case for the Real Jesus*, 38.
60. Nicholas Perrin, *Thomas: The Other Gospel* (Louisville, Ky.: Westminster John Knox Press, 2007), 78.
61. Evans, *Fabricating Jesus*, 74.
62. Perrin, *Thomas: The Other Gospel*, 78.
63. For more information about this argument, see Perrin, *Thomas: The Other Gospel* and Nicholas Perrin, *Thomas and Tatian: The Relationship Between the Gospel of Thomas and the Diatessaron* (Leiden: Brill, 2002).
64. Perrin, *Thomas, The Other Gospel*, 83. He references Gilles Quispel, *Tatian and the Gospel of Thomas: Studies in the history of the western Diatessaron* (Leiden: Brill, 1975), 174-190.
65. Evans, *Fabricating Jesus* (Downers Grove, IL: InterVarsity Press, 2006), 75.
66. Jenkins, *The Hidden Gospels*, 108.

Gnosticism was not a neutral variant of general Christian belief but indeed an essentially different and opposing religion that simply borrowed terminology from the New Testament Gospels and changed its meaning.

—Craig A. Evans, New Testament scholar[1]

[The Gnostics] hold that the consummation of all things will take place when all that is spiritual has been formed and perfected by Gnosis (knowledge); and by this they mean spiritual men who have attained to the perfect knowledge of God, and been initiated into these mysteries by Achamoth.

—Irenaeus, second century Christian bishop[2]

13

Not Gnosticism

In the last chapter, we demonstrated that the Gnostic documents, many of which were discovered in Nag Hammadi, Egypt in 1945, were composed in the second century at the earliest. Thus, these Gnostic documents began to circulate many decades after the biblical Gospels of Matthew, Mark, Luke, and John, not to mention the other twenty-three books of the New Testament. Not only were the Gnostic documents written and circulated much later, but their contents also reflect a very different set of beliefs than the earlier documents, the ones that comprise the New Testament we read today.

The very different belief system, combined with the later dates, serve as evidence that the original statements of Jesus were altered by these later Gnostic groups and blended with existing philosophies to create a more palatable religion for the average second-century person. Thus, there may have been "alternative Christianities" in the second and third centuries, but the only version of Christianity that can be traced back to the teachings of Jesus through eyewitness connections are the biblical books of the New Testament.

The documents that are generally classified as "Gnostic" actually reflect a wide spectrum of beliefs, so wide that scholars have long debated exactly what constitutes Gnosticism. Gnostic thinkers were syncretistic; that is, they drew their ideas from different sources, combining elements of Christianity with Greek philosophy, most notably Platonism and Neo-Platonism. There never was a "Gnostic church," and the term "Gnosticism" was first coined by English philosopher Henry More in 1669. However, there is a common theme among Gnostic texts: the quest to attain special knowledge—or *gnosis*, in Greek—that enables you to escape the material world.

CHAPTER 13: NOT GNOSTICISM

The most prominent Christian element in Gnosticism is the powerful Christ figure. As the popularity of Jesus grew and Christianity spread rapidly throughout the ancient world, Gnostic philosophers sought to incorporate a Christ figure into their own texts. For titles, they even borrowed names of the original followers of Jesus, such as Mary Magdalene, Peter, James, and Thomas, lending their documents more credibility (even among a modern audience!).

However, the Gnostics weren't quite so taken with other elements of the new Christian faith, such as the Hebrew conceptions of creation, the end of the world, and the redemption of humanity. Gnostics rejected these ideas in favor of a more pagan understanding of origins, the goal of human history, and humankind's greatest need. Let's look closely at the difference between the varied "Gnosticisms" and the Bible. Not only does this discussion respond to the skeptical claim that the New Testament is just one of many "early Christianities," it also serves to clarify the original teachings of Jesus, which were markedly different from Gnosticism.

GOD AND CREATION

While some Gnostic texts, such as the *Gospel of Thomas*, speak only of a single god creating the world, others claim that several heavenly beings were involved. The *Gospel of Thomas* actually only mentions the name "God" twice and provides very little description of him or her. This is because Gnostics generally believed that God cannot be known directly. Professor of New Testament Studies Darrell L. Bock summarizes what the *Gospel of Thomas* teaches about God in this way:

> *Thomas* says next to nothing about God as Creator other than that He creates. God is light. The goal of life is related to attaining knowledge of who we are, discovering that we are children of God, and finding the presence of the kingdom that is in us.[3]

A close look at three other Gnostic texts will suffice to help us see the difference between biblical Christianity and Gnosticism: the *Gospel of Mary Magdalene*, the *Gospel of Philip*, and the *Apocryphon of John*.

In the *Gospel of Mary Magdalene*, which most scholars date to the second century, Mary and the resurrected Jesus are engaged in an extended conversation about the afterlife. Such extended dialogs between the risen Jesus and his followers on earth were a common device of Gnostic literature, since they emphasized the revelation of secret knowledge from Jesus after he rose from the dead, rather than the historical events of his life. (As you can deduce, the Gnostic texts fare poorly on the external evidence test of historicity.)

The *Gospel of Mary Magdalene* contains a reference to an ascent of the soul (but not the body) to God, as well as two references to God as "the Good."[4] In the entire dialog between Mary and the risen Jesus, however, there is little other mention of God.

The *Gospel of Philip*, written between AD 150 and 350, contains many ideas relating to the Gnostic idea of *dualism*, the belief that the spiritual world (or the "eternal realm") is distinct from the created, material world (or "this world"). The material world is considered corrupt, evil, and incapable of fathoming the mysteries of the spiritual world, i.e. "the world above."[5] In Gnostic philosophy, the material world was actually the result of an error, as the *Gospel of Philip* states:

> The world came about through a mistake. For he who created it wanted to create it imperishable and immortal. He fell short of attaining his desire. For the world was never imperishable, nor for that matter, was he who made the world.[6]

No statement could be further from the foundation of biblical teaching: the existence of an eternal, omnipotent, infallible Being who accomplishes everything in keeping with his perfect will.[7]

The *Apocryphon of John*, which scholars date from the mid-second century to the third century, contains a more developed creation story. In this document, God consists of a Father, a Mother, and a Son. Again, creation is considered evil, the flawed work of other spiritual beings who are subordinate to God. Evil actually resulted from the female deity's failure to seek and follow God's will.[8]

In contrast to these ideas, the Judeo-Christian tradition holds that creation was the work of a single, morally perfect God, who originally created the material world to be "very good."[9] In a letter to Timothy, the

CHAPTER 13: NOT GNOSTICISM

apostle Paul states: "For everything God created is good, and nothing is to be rejected if it is received with thanksgiving."[10] Moreover, instead of being a deity's fault, the biblical view is that evil, suffering, and death resulted when humans chose to live independently from their Creator. The apostle Paul makes this clear when he summarizes the Bible's teaching on the origin of sin and death for the Christians in Rome: "Therefore... sin entered the world through one man, and death through sin, and in this way death came to all men, because all sinned."[11]

In addition, unlike the god (or more accurately, gods) of Gnosticism, who are often composed of male and female components (with the female component often bearing much of the fault in creating the evil material world), the Judeo-Christian God is genderless, and both males and females were created in the image of God.[12]

While on the topic of gender, contrary to what some liberal scholars have claimed, the New Testament's portrayal of Jesus is actually far more affirming of the dignity of women than that of the Gnostic texts. Unlike typical religious teachers of his day, Jesus included women in his ministry and showed special concern for disempowered and marginalized females, young and old. Women held the honor of being the first witnesses of the risen Jesus, and women played an important role in the early Christian church. Even secular historians note that the Christian community treated women much better than the rest of Greco-Roman society.[13] Paul makes this counter-cultural comment in his letter to the diverse group of Christians in Galatia:

> You are all sons of God through faith in Christ Jesus, for all of you who were baptized into Christ have clothed yourselves with Christ. There is neither Jew nor Greek, slave nor free, *male nor female*, for you are all one in Christ Jesus.[14]

This clear statement of the equality of men and women—*both* becoming "sons of God," who were entitled to an inheritance from the father—was completely revolutionary in the first-century world.

Along these lines, a central belief of apostolic Christianity is that *all* who put their faith in Jesus will receive eternal life, while in Gnosticism only a select few was worthy of receiving special, secret knowledge. For example, Paul claims that God is now revealing to "everyone" a formerly hidden mystery about the "unsearchable riches of Christ."[15] This revelation is announced to *all people* regardless of their ethnicity, gender, morality, socioeconomic status, intelligence, or pedigree. On the other hand, Gnostic followers formed an elite group of insiders. Biblical Christianity says that salvation is an undeserved, free gift made available to all through God's grace. Eternal life is therefore *not earned* but instead *received* by faith in Jesus: "It is by grace you have been saved... so that no one can boast."[16]

WAS JESUS HUMAN OR DIVINE?

Another crucial difference between Gnosticism and traditional Christianity is with respect to their *Christology*—that is, their opinion as to whether Jesus was divine or merely a human (or both). Even though it only makes a few statements about who Jesus is, the *Gospel of Thomas* actually displays "high Christology"—in other words, it describes Jesus as a divine figure who is sent by the Father and who is light.

The divinity of Jesus—or at least the close relationship Jesus has to God—is reflected in Saying 77: "I am the light that shines over all things. I am everywhere. From me all came forth, and to me all return. Split a piece of wood, and I am there. Lift a stone, and you will find me there." And in Saying 13, Thomas tells Jesus, "Master, my mouth is wholly incapable of saying who you are like." Because he recognizes that Jesus' role is so inexpressibly high, Jesus rewards Thomas by taking him aside and revealing secret knowledge to him that the other disciples are not worthy to hear.

Other Gnostic documents have an even higher Christology, since they purport that Jesus merely appeared human when he walked on earth. One example of this belief, called *Docetism*, can be found in the *Apocalypse of Peter*, which dates to the mid-second to third century. In this work, Peter has a series of visions, which Jesus interprets. At one point, Jesus is described as laughing above the cross as he looks down on his own crucifixion. Jesus says, "He whom you see above the cross, glad and laughing, is the living Jesus. But he into whose hands and feet they are driving the nails is his physical part, which is the substitute."[17] In this view, Jesus' body is a sort of container for his divinity, and the two are completely divisible.[18] Another second-century Docetic text, the *Second*

CHAPTER 13: NOT GNOSTICISM

Treatise of the Great Seth, also portrays Jesus as simply appearing to suffer when he is on the cross. He never actually experienced the agony a normal human would have experienced.

While not all Gnostic texts have a high Christology, neither do they portray Jesus as just a regular human being. Referring to the full range of Gnostic texts, Bock states, "None of these ancient texts presents a strictly human Christ. That option is popular in many modern-day appeals to this material as *The Da Vinci Code* exemplifies and some theologians teach. A strictly human Jesus, however, simply does not exist in any of these sources."[19]

The Christology of the New Testament documents is consistent in its portrayal of Jesus as both fully human and fully divine (as opposed to half human and half divine, or sometimes human and sometimes divine). One way that the canonical Gospels emphasize Jesus' human nature is by concerning themselves with Jesus' teaching and ministry on earth, unlike the Gnostic gospels, which emphasize Jesus' teaching from heaven after his death.

While the canonical Gospels place Jesus within a distinct and detailed historical context, the Gnostic texts are not nearly as concerned with portraying Jesus as a historical figure. In fact, because they emphasize Jesus as a divine figure and downplay his work on earth, these pseudo-gospels are much less useful in the reconstruction of the historical Jesus. As Jenkins remarks, "Characteristic of these [Gnostic] gospels, the events described occur symbolically and psychologically, in sharp contrast to the orthodox Christian concern with historical realities."[20]

Writing in the middle of the first century, the apostle Paul provides a glimpse of the early Christian understanding of Jesus' nature as both human and divine. Immediately after stating "as to his human nature [Jesus] was a descendant of David," Paul claims that Jesus "was declared to be the Son of God by his resurrection from the dead: Jesus Christ our Lord."[21] Paul calls Jesus the "image of the invisible God," by whom and for whom "all things were created" and in whom "God was pleased to have all his fullness dwell."[22]

In his letter to the church in Philippi, Paul quotes an even earlier Christian creed, which, as we've said in other chapters, was most likely sung as a hymn, and which declares that Jesus humbled himself to become a human despite being "in very nature God."[23] That is, even though he was divine, Jesus voluntarily chose to experience suffering and pain, hunger and thirst, rejection and ridicule, temptation and longing, and the other difficulties associated with being a human being. He therefore completely identifies with us in our own sufferings. As the author of Hebrews declares, Jesus is able to "sympathize with our weaknesses" because he "has been tempted in every way, just as we are."[24] In response to the heresy that Jesus was not fully human, the apostle John writes, "This is how you can recognize the spirit of God: Every spirit that acknowledges that Jesus Christ came in the flesh is from God."[25] John even calls those who claim Jesus did not come in the flesh "deceivers."[26]

No other religion makes the claim that God—the Creator of the universe!—completely identifies with us in our human condition.[27] The earliest Christians may not have clearly understood how Jesus could be both fully man and fully God, and the Christian church did not formalize its statements of belief on this topic (called "the Incarnation") until the third century, but it is clear that the earliest followers of Jesus saw him neither as solely human nor as a divine figure who only seemed human.[28]

Even the Gospel of John, which many scholars have claimed presents a more developed understanding of Jesus' divinity than the earlier Synoptic Gospels, emphasizes the humanity of Jesus. F. F. Bruce writes:

> There is, in fact, no material difference in Christology between John and the three Synoptists. He does indeed view Jesus as the pre-existent Word of God, the Eternal Father's agent in creation, revelation, and redemption; but he does not emphasize His deity at the expense of His humanity. Jesus grows tired on His journey through Samaria (Jn. 4:6); He weeps at the grave of Lazarus (Jn. 11:35), He thirsts upon the cross (19:28). Indeed, John is at pains to refute a current fancy that our Lord's humanity was only apparent and not real; that is why he insists so unambiguously that 'the Word became flesh' (Jn. 1:14) and affirms so solemnly, with the authority of an eyewitness, that there was nothing unreal about His death on the cross (19:30-35).[29]

CHAPTER 13: NOT GNOSTICISM

What Does Redemption Entail?

In addition to the role of God in creation and the question of whether Jesus is human or divine, the Gnostic thinkers and the earliest followers of Jesus also differ in their understanding of the term "redemption." That is, let's ask how each would answer this question: When we die, what lasts, the material body, the spiritual soul, or both?

Gnostics commonly believed that the material world was evil and had been created as the result of an error. Therefore, only the soul would be redeemed. The body, they believed, is a prison that must be escaped. The *Gospel of Thomas* claims that Jesus made this statement about how the soul resides in the body: "I am amazed at how great wealth has made its home in this poverty" (Saying 29). The body was considered grossly inferior compared to the value of the soul or spirit.

In fact, the *Gospel of Thomas* makes it clear that both the body and the soul are "wretched" unless they become a "living spirit" by attaining special mystical knowledge. For example, at the end of *Thomas*, when Peter wants to send Mary away because she is not worthy of becoming a living spirit, Jesus says: "I myself shall lead her in order to make her male, so that she may become a living spirit resembling you males. For every woman who will make herself male will enter the kingdom" (Saying 114). Not only is this another example of the failure of the Gnostics to live up to the feminist image modern scholars have given them, it also demonstrates the Gnostic view that redemption (or "entering the kingdom") only happens by activating one's true spirit through knowledge and by discarding the body.[30]

Another example of the Gnostic idea of redemption is found in the *Pistis Sophia*, which was written in the second century at the earliest and was primarily concerned with the question of what happens after we die. The document claims to present "eleven years of secret teaching and true knowledge that Jesus gave to his followers after his resurrection."[31] In line with its dualistic view of the evil material world and the good spiritual world, this text teaches that the soul will be saved out of the body. For example, one section declares: "God will save their souls out of all matter, and a city will be prepared in the light; and all souls which will be saved will dwell in that city, and they will inherit it" (32:36-36). According to the *Pistis Sophia*, there are two different classes of people: those who are indwelt by the power of light and possess a spirit that will be redeemed, known as the "pneumatics," and everyone else, who lacks a spirit and will not be redeemed.

Another second-century Gnostic document, the *Letter to Rheginos*, makes the case that we shouldn't expect a physical resurrection, but only a spiritual one. Moreover, this resurrection has already happened; people simply fail to recognize it. For example, consider these claims from chapter 47:

> Nothing, then, redeems us from this world. But the All which we are, we are saved. Let us think this way! Let us comprehend this way! But there are some (who) wish to understand, in the enquiry about those things they are looking into, whether he who is saved, if he *leaves his body behind*, will be saved immediately. Let no one doubt concerning this.[32]

One final example, though there are many more, comes from the *Apocryphon of James*, composed in the late second to early third centuries. Purportedly a letter from the apostle James that discloses a "secret writing" from the Savior, this document portrays the soul as a force that must choose between the good spirit or the evil body: "For it is the spirit that raises the soul, but the body that kills it." In classic Gnostic style, the *Apocryphon of James* claims that the material body is evil, and only the soul is potentially redeemed.

In contrast, the first-century Christian texts claim that all believers will be like Jesus: physically raised from the dead. That is, *both* the soul *and* the body will be redeemed. The earliest followers of Jesus risked their lives declaring that he was raised *bodily* from the dead, not just spiritually. Not only do the canonical Gospels emphasize that people could see, touch, and eat with Jesus after he rose from the dead, but Paul also makes it very clear in his early letters that, following his resurrection, Jesus had a newly restored and glorious body.[33] That is, his resurrection wasn't merely symbolic, nor did it simply entail the spiritual ascent of his soul.

Moreover, the creed Paul records in First Corinthians 15:3-8 makes it clear that Jesus' physical, bodily resurrection was a core component of the very earliest Christian beliefs. Paul even follows the creed with a declaration that if Christ was not physically raised from the dead, then his followers are "of all people most to be pitied."[34] The earliest Christians went out of their way to convince others that Jesus had appeared to them—in the flesh—following his crucifixion, giving them "many convincing proofs"[35] that he was physically alive again. And oddly, those who met the risen Jesus after his resurrection didn't recognize him at first in his newly transformed body, and his risen body, though physical, was able to walk through walls.[36] These strange aspects of the physical resurrection, which we will discuss more in Chapter 16, indicate that the redemption of the body through faith in Jesus won't simply mean believers get back the same body they had before death, but they receive a "transphysical" version of the same body, to use the term that N. T. Wright coined to describe the unique and mysterious physical body that Jesus had after his resurrection.[37]

In his letter to the Christians in Rome, Paul summarizes the implications of the physical resurrection of Jesus: "And if the Spirit of him who raised Jesus from the dead is living in you, he who raised Christ from the dead will also give life to your mortal bodies." In this life, "we groan inwardly as we wait eagerly for our adoption as sons, the redemption of our bodies."[38] The Christian hope is for a future with immortal bodies that can run, eat, and play—not an amorphous existence as disembodied spirits floating in the light, as the Gnostic documents claim.

WHAT IS JESUS' PURPOSE?

Fourth and finally, let's take a look at the difference between the Gnostic and traditional views regarding the reason Jesus came to earth. What was (and perhaps still is) his purpose? How would each answer the following questions: Why did Jesus come? What is his role? What did his death accomplish?

As mentioned earlier, the *Gospel of Thomas* claims that Jesus' main purpose was to reveal knowledge—the "secret words"—that would enable humans to achieve salvation, or eternal "repose" in a bodiless, spiritual realm. By means of the special knowledge from Jesus, one can truly "find oneself" and attain the self-knowledge necessary for an eternal life of spiritual awakening. Saying 111 emphasizes the need for self-understanding by posing the following question: "Did not Jesus say, 'Whoever finds himself is superior to the world?'"

In contrast to the free grace of biblical Christianity, only a certain elite group can achieve this knowledge-based Gnostic salvation. The *Thomas* Jesus explains in Saying 62: "It is to those worthy of my mysteries that I tell my mysteries." The *Apocryphon of James* makes similar claims, including: "So also you yourselves can receive the kingdom of heaven; unless you receive this through knowledge, you will not be able to find it" (8:23-27). Salvation, which takes you to a supposedly superior existence, must be earned.

Another text that demonstrates the Gnostic understanding of Jesus' role is the *Gospel of Truth*, composed in the mid-to-late second century by a teacher named Valentinus (or by his students).[39] The following excerpt explains how Jesus provides enlightenment, leading and guiding an elite group from the darkness into the truth:

> Through this, the gospel of the one who is searched for, which [was] revealed to those who are perfect through the mercies of the Father, the hidden mystery, Jesus, the Christ, enlightened those who were in darkness through oblivion. He enlightened them; he showed [them] the way; the way is the truth which he taught them. (18:12-21)

The *Gospel of Truth* is one of the few Gnostic texts that mention Jesus' crucifixion. It is not a payment for sin, however, but the means by which Jesus shows us the nature of existence and knowledge. After Jesus died, he became "a fruit of knowledge of the Father" (18:24-26), giving insight to believers like a book: "the living book of the living—the one written in the thought and the mind" (19:35-36). By dying on the cross, Jesus "put on that book" (20:24). Stated in a slightly different way, "he was nailed to a tree; he published the edict of the Father on the cross" (20:25-27). And his death and new life now reveal the new way of salvation: "When light had spoken through his mouth, as well as his voice which gave birth to life, he gave them thought and understanding and mercy and salvation and the powerful spirit from the infiniteness and the sweetness of the Father" (31:13-20). If this rhetoric confuses you, you are definitely not alone (and perhaps you're wondering if the Gnostics used cannabis).

The New Testament claims that Jesus himself—not special knowledge—is the means by which we are saved. That is, by dying on

CHAPTER 13: NOT GNOSTICISM

the cross and by physically rising from the dead, Jesus wasn't providing *knowledge about* salvation, he was providing *the* salvation. Though he surely is a good moral example, he is far more: he is his people's representative who acts on their behalf. As their representative, Jesus transfers his perfect moral record—the "righteousness of God"—to those who trust in him. This is what true salvation involves: the ability to stand before a perfect God, guilt-free.

Paul's teaching on true redemption stands against the elusive oddities of Gnostic writings. He writes:

> This righteousness from God comes through faith in Jesus Christ to all who believe. There is no difference, for all have sinned and fall short of the glory of God, and are justified freely by his grace through the redemption that came by Christ Jesus.[40]

Through a child-like trust in Jesus, we attain salvation; not through any effort on our part. No true Christian can claim to be "superior to the world," as Saying 111 of the *Gospel of Thomas* claims is possible. True Christianity emphasizes humility, while Gnostic philosophy emphasizes pride, since only certain people are given the special revelation needed for redemption.

But even though the traditional documents were composed far earlier than the Gnostic texts, perhaps their ideas about the way to eternal life never originated with Jesus, as some skeptics claim. Could these beliefs about sin, salvation, and physical resurrection be merely concoctions of the earliest Christians? We now turn to the claims of some liberal scholars, who insist that the "real Jesus" is nothing like the "mythical Jesus" portrayed in the first-century New Testament texts.

QUESTIONS FOR COMPREHENSION AND DISCUSSION

1. How does Gnosticism differ from the Bible with respect to its beliefs about God, creation, and the existence of evil?

2. What is meant by the term *Christology*? Does Gnosticism demonstrate "high Christology" or "low Christology"?
3. What is the *Christology* of traditional Christianity, and how does it differ from the various Gnostic beliefs about Jesus' nature?
4. What do the Gnostic gospels teach about redemption? Does one's soul or one's body survive after death, or both?
5. How do the early Christian writers present Jesus following his death and resurrection, and how does this differ from the Gnostics' presentation of Jesus?
6. Which type of redemption would you prefer? Why?
7. What did the Gnostics believe about who Jesus was and what he does for us?
8. According to the New Testament documents, why did Jesus come, and what does he do for us?
9. What did the Gnostics teach was necessary in order for humans to attain "spiritual enlightenment"?
10. What role do we play in attaining eternal life, according to the New Testament documents? How does this require humility and circumvent pride?

CHAPTER 13 ENDNOTES

[1] Craig A. Evans, *Fabricating Jesus* (Downers Grove, IL: InterVarsity Press, 2006), 66.
[2] Irenaeus of Lyon, *Against Heresies*, Book I, Chapter 6. Available online at http://www.earlychristianwritings.com/text/irenaeus-book1.html.
[3] Darrell L. Bock, *The Missing Gospels: Unearthing the Truth Behind Alternative Christianities* (Nashville, TN: Thomas Nelson Publishers, 2006), 65.
[4] Ibid, 66.
[5] Ibid, 68.
[6] *Gospel of Philip*, available online at http://gnosis.org/naghamm/gop.html.
[7] For a few examples of the biblical teaching of an all-powerful, eternal God whose will is perfect, see Deuteronomy 32:4; Numbers 23:19; Psalm 18:30, 90:2; Jeremiah 23:24; Matthew 19:26; Romans 8:28, 12:2; and 1 John 1:5.
[8] Bock, *The Missing Gospels*, 72-73.
[9] See Genesis 1:31.
[10] 1 Timothy 4:4.
[11] Romans 5:12.

CHAPTER 13: NOT GNOSTICISM

12. See Genesis 1:27.
13. For example, early Christian historian Rodney Stark notes that the early Christian church forbade the practice of leaving female infants outside to die of exposure, which was a common practice among non-Christians. The early Christians were also much more supportive of unmarried women and widows. See Rodney Stark, *The Rise of Christianity* (San Francisco: HarperSanFrancisco, 1996), Chapter 5: "The Role of Women in Christian Growth."
14. Galatians 3:26-28. All emphases in Bible passages are mine. Note that Paul uses the term "sons of God" here because the sons in that culture were the children who inherited the wealth of the fathers. He indicates that men and women are equally deserving of the same inheritance from God.
15. See Ephesians 3:8-9.
16. Ephesians 2:8-9.
17. *The Apocalypse of Peter*, in James M. Robinson, *The Coptic Gospel Library: A Complete Edition of Nag Hammadi Codices* (Leiden: Brill, 2000), 4:243.
18. Bock, *The Missing Gospels*, 107.
19. Ibid, 113.
20. Ibid, 37.
21. Romans 1:3-4.
22. See Colossians 1:15-20.
23. Philippians 2:6.
24. Hebrews 4:15.
25. 1 John 4:2.
26. See 2 John 1:7.
27. Timothy Keller makes the point as follows: "Christianity alone among the world religions claims that God became uniquely and fully human in Jesus Christ and therefore knows firsthand despair, rejection, loneliness, poverty, bereavement, torture, and imprisonment.... If we again look at the question: 'Why does God allow evil and suffering to continue?' and we look at the cross of Jesus, we still do not know what the answer is. However, we now know what the answer *isn't*. It *can't be* that he doesn't love us. It *can't be* that he is indifferent or detached from our condition. God takes our misery and suffering so seriously that he was willing to take it on himself." (Timothy Keller, *The Reason for God* [New York: Penguin Group, 2008], 30. Emphasis in original.)
28. Bock, *The Missing Gospels*, 125.
29. F. F. Bruce, *The New Testament Documents: Are They Reliable?* (Grand Rapids, MI: Eerdmans, 1981), 56-57.
30. Bock, *The Missing Gospels*, 132-133.
31. Ibid, 135.

32. James M. Robinson, ed., *The Nag Hammadi Library in English* (Leiden: E.J. Brill, 1977), 52. Available online at https://books.google.com/books?id=1bU3AAAAIAAJ&pg=PA52.
33. For example, see Philippians 3:21 and Romans 8:11.
34. See 1 Corinthians 15:12-18.
35. Acts 1:3.
36. Mary did not recognize the risen Jesus in John 20:15. His companions on the road to Emmaus did not recognize the risen Jesus in Luke 24:16. The risen Jesus enters a room with locked doors in John 20:19.
37. N. T. Wright, *The Resurrection of the Son of God* (Minneapolis: Fortress, 2003), 611.
38. Romans 8:11, 23.
39. Bock, *The Missing Gospels*, 69-70.
40. Romans 3:22-24.

But are the new views true? In fact, the iconoclastic views of early Christianity so often proposed in recent years can be challenged in many ways, so many in fact that it is amazing that these ideas have achieved the wide credence they have.

—Philip Jenkins, church historian[1]

Smart people believe weird things because they are skilled at defending beliefs they arrived at for non-smart reasons.

—Michael Shermer, founder of the Skeptics Society[2]

14

The Anti-Supernatural Opinions

In the opinion of Jesus Seminar co-founder Robert Funk, "The religious establishment has not allowed the intelligence of high scholarship to pass through pastors and priests to a hungry laity."[3] From the outset, Funk made it clear that his mission in founding the Jesus Seminar wasn't just to present the opinions of liberal Jesus scholarship, but to set people free from the confines of belief in what he believed was a mythical Jesus.

In his book, *Honest to Jesus*, Funk explains how he was hoping to free average Bible-believing Christians from their dogmatic chains: "I agonize over their slavery in contrast to my freedom. I have a residual hankering to free my fellow human beings from that bondage, which can be as abusive as any form of slavery known to humankind."[4] Relevantly, the Jesus of the traditional New Testament claims: "If you hold to my teaching, you are really my disciples. Then you will know the truth, and the truth will set you free."[5] The question then becomes, who is truly free, those who hold to the teachings of the traditional Jesus of the Gospels, or those whom Funk has sought to set free from these traditional teachings?

Before we examine the methodology employed by the Jesus Seminar in their reconstruction of the historical Jesus, let's first consider who they are. According to their website, "more than two hundred Fellows have participated in the Jesus Seminar and other Westar projects."[6] (The Westar Institute is the educational institute that sponsors the Jesus Seminar.) The Fellows "include scholars with advanced degrees

CHAPTER 14: THE ANTI-SUPERNATURAL OPINIONS

in biblical studies, religion or related fields and, by special invitation only, published authors who are recognized authorities in the field of religion."[7]

Two hundred scholars may sound like a respectable and formidable number, but it represents a tiny fraction of the total number of New Testament scholars. To put it into perspective, there are more than 8,500 members of the Society of Biblical Literature (SBL),[8] of which about half are focused on New Testament studies.[9] In addition, there are thousands of other New Testament scholars who are not members of the SBL. And to make the insignificant size of their ranks even more clear, the actual number of Jesus Seminar scholars who have met regularly to write papers and cast votes is closer to forty, not two hundred.[10]

The active Fellows of the Jesus Seminar—only forty individuals out of more than ten thousand in the field of New Testament studies—also represent only a handful of schools, far from an accurate cross-section of New Testament scholarship. As a case in point, forty of the seventy-four Fellows listed in Funk's *The Five Gospels* received their Ph.D. from only five liberal-leaning schools of theology: fourteen from the Claremont School of Theology, nine from the Vanderbilt Divinity School, eight from Harvard University, five from the University of Chicago Divinity School, and four from Union Theological Seminary in New York.[11]

Christian scholar and bishop N. T. Wright points out that there are only a few prominent scholars among those who have played a role in the Jesus Seminar's decision-making process regarding the historical Jesus. He writes:

> But one could compile a very long list of North American New Testament scholars, including several who have written importantly about Jesus, who are not among those present [in the Jesus Seminar discussions], and whose work has had no visible impact on the Seminar at all.[12]

So even before the Seminar starts its discussion of the historical Jesus, we must realize that their opinions represent a tiny subset of prominent Jesus historians. And as we will soon see, the vast majority of other scholars disagree with their assumptions.

THE SHORTEST LEAP

DID JESUS REALLY SAY IT?

In *The Five Gospels*, Robert Funk summarizes the decisions of the Jesus Seminar, providing a special "Scholars Version" translation of the four canonical Gospels, along with the *Gospel of Thomas*, which they believe deserves to be considered the "fifth gospel." In their opinion, *The Five Gospels* provides a more accurate and colloquial translation of the original Greek.[13] As the Westar website claims: "Unlike other major translations into English, the Scholars Version is being created free of ecclesiastical and religious control. The language is meant to produce in the reader an experience comparable to that of the first readers—or listeners—of the original."[14]

One example of their "improved" translation is a verse describing Jesus' healing of the leper.[15] The traditional NIV translation is "Filled with compassion, Jesus reached out his hand and touched the man. 'I am willing,' he said. 'Be clean!'" The Jesus Seminar's "Scholars" translation is: "Although Jesus was indignant, he stretched out his hand, touched him, and says to him, 'Okay—you're clean!'" Also, the Scholars translation for the traditional "Blessed are the poor in spirit" is "Congratulations to the poor in spirit!"[16]

In addition to what they claim is a more accurate translation of the original language of the four canonical Gospels, the Jesus Seminar claims that the *Gospel of Thomas* is the rightful fifth gospel based on their assumption that the first edition of Q and the first edition of the *Gospel of Thomas* are the earliest sources of Jesus' sayings.[17] As discussed in Chapter 12, it is very unlikely that the *Gospel of Thomas* was written before the second century. In his remarks on the early date that the Jesus Seminar gives *Thomas*, Wright reminds us:

> If members of the public are interested in knowing what 'scholars' think, they ought to be told fair and square that diagrams in which a hypothetical first edition of *Thomas* is placed in the 50s of the first century are thoroughly tendentious, and belong out on a limb of current scholarship.[18]

Already, we see a tremendous bias in the works of the Jesus Seminar, a bias that causes them to base their decisions on tenuous assumptions that most other New Testament scholars find extremely implausible.

Starting with a fresh "scholarly translation," *The Five Gospels* then color-coded the sayings of Jesus to reflect their authenticity: red means Jesus said it—it is authentic, pink means it is probably authentic, gray means it is probably inauthentic, and black means it is definitely inauthentic—Jesus definitely did not say it. (Funk also described the colors in the following way: red means, "That's Jesus!"; pink: "Sure sounds like Jesus"; grey: "Well, maybe"; and black: "There's been some mistake.")[19]

The colors were decided by a weighted average of the votes of Seminar Fellows. After discussing and voting on more than 1,500 sayings, the Jesus Seminar determined that *"no more than 20 percent of the sayings attributed to Jesus were uttered by him."*[20] The problem was, however, that even if the majority of voters believed a statement was red or pink, a small number of black votes could pull the saying into the grey zone.[21] One example is Jesus' statement regarding the end times, "Now learn this lesson from the fig tree: As soon as its twigs get tender and its leaves come out, you know that summer is near. Even so, when you see all these things, you know that it is near, right at the door."[22] Fifty-four Fellows voted either red or pink, while thirty-five Fellows voted black. The result was a gray compromise.

N. T. Wright summarizes one primary issue with this method:

> A voting system that produces a result like this ought to be scrapped. The average reader, seeing the passage printed as gray, will conclude that the 'scholars' think it is probably inauthentic; whereas, even with the small company of the Seminar, the majority would clearly disagree.[23]

ATHEISTIC ASSUMPTIONS

How exactly did the scholars of the Jesus Seminar determine the color of their vote? In line with their quest to objectively determine the truth about Jesus, they depended on a myriad of premises and scholarly methodologies that supposedly eliminate bias. But, ironically, their own premises and methodologies are actually founded upon clear biases.

Among the sayings of Jesus that the Seminar found authentic, a great many are found in *Q* and *Thomas*, demonstrating their biased assumptions that *Q* existed as a precursor to Matthew and Luke, and that *Thomas* was composed in the first century. Wright comments on this *Q-Thomas* bias in the voting results:

> The *Q-and-Thomas* pattern continues to predominate. The main reason why these sayings are considered 'authentic' is clearly not that each one has been tested individually against some abstract criteria, but that they have been judged to fit into the picture of Jesus *which has already been chosen*.[24]

In other words, the Jesus Seminar likes the portrait of Jesus that *Q* and *Thomas* provide, and as a result, they deem acceptable any of Jesus' statements from *Q* and *Thomas*.

So, why do they prefer the portrait of Jesus in *Q* and *Thomas*? And what was the main way the Fellows decided whether Jesus really made a certain statement or performed a certain action? The answer lies in the Jesus Seminar's philosophical methodology, which is called *methodological materialism*. Using this methodology, they base their decisions on the belief that neither God nor a supernatural realm exists. As Funk explains in his book *Honest to Jesus*, "The times call for a wholly secular account of the Christian faith."[25]

The materialistic assumptions of the Jesus Seminar are obvious in the "twenty-one theses" of the Westar Institute, a list of principles that guided the scholars as they made decisions. For example, the first thesis states:

> The God of the metaphysical age is dead. There is not a personal god out there external to human beings and the material world. We must reckon with a deep crisis in god talk and replace it with talk about whether the universe has meaning and whether human life has purpose.[26]

Based on their atheistic assumptions, therefore, it is easy to understand why the Jesus Seminar automatically dismisses as inauthentic any of Jesus' sayings and actions that depend on the supernatural, such as his miracles, prophecies, and resurrection.

A quick review of a point we touched on in Chapter 4 may be helpful at this point. As we saw in the first part of the book, the scientific evidence is overwhelmingly consistent with the existence of an infinite, non-physical Creator who is powerful enough to have caused the Big Bang. If this all-powerful Being created the laws of physics, it is entirely possible that this Being could also alter or temporarily suspend the laws of physics. And even if we may never experience miracles in our day-to-day life, this all-powerful Being may have performed miracles in the past. Thus, to deny the existence of the supernatural and the possibility of miracles is a philosophical assumption that cannot be proven or disproven using the scientific method.

In fact, to claim that miracles in the New Testament could not have happened because miracles are impossible is an excellent example of *circular reasoning*. This faulty reasoning happens when you base a logical conclusion on an unproven assumption. Let's take a look at the argument of methodological materialism:

1. Premise 1: It is impossible for anyone to do miracles.
2. Premise 2: The biblical writers claim that Jesus did miracles.
3. Conclusion: Therefore, the writers must not be telling the truth, and Jesus did not do miracles.

While the second premise is true, the first premise is unprovable, and based on the scientific evidence presented in the first part of this book, highly unlikely. The entire argument falls apart once you remove the first premise. The only reason you may keep the first premise (and therefore the conclusion) is for philosophical—not scientific—reasons.

JESUS, THE WANDERING PAGAN PHILOSOPHER?

In addition to their assumption that God doesn't exist and that miracles are impossible, the Jesus Seminar bases its conclusions on other highly debated presuppositions. For example, the Seminar assumes that Jesus was merely a wandering, "reticent sage"[27] who "does not initiate debate or offer to cast out demons, and who does not speak of himself in the first person."[28]

Based on this presupposition, the Jesus Seminar decided that Jesus did not enlist followers, rarely quoted from the Hebrew Scriptures, did not predict his own death, and did not refer to himself as the Son of God or the Messiah. For example, they claim he never would have made the famous self-referential claim, "I am the way and the truth and the life."[29] Funk and his band claim such statements are concoctions of the early church in the period between Jesus' death and when the canonical Gospels were written down.

In his book on "the historical Jesus," John Dominic Crossan makes the case that Jesus was "a peasant and Jewish Cynic" or "a hippie in the world of Augustan yuppies."[30] The conclusion that Jesus was a traveling sage is based in part on the similarity between a few of Jesus' sayings and those of ancient pagan philosophers known as "Cynics," who dressed simply, were known for unkempt personal sanitation, and encouraged others to live according to nature.[31] Moreover, Crossan claims, Jesus may have been exposed to Cynic philosophy because his hometown of Nazareth was very near Sepphoris, a large town that archaeologists in the 1980s believed was predominantly Greco-Roman, not Jewish. However, excavations in the 1990s demonstrated that Sepphoris was indeed a predominantly Jewish town during the time of Jesus' ministry, before the destruction of Jerusalem in AD 70. Therefore, in all likelihood, Jesus never even encountered a Cynic.[32]

Dr. Craig Evans calls Crossan's historical reconstruction of Jesus as a Cynic "one of the strangest proposals to come from qualified scholars in recent years."[33] Granted, some of Jesus' sayings are similar to those of the Cynics, such as his "Consider the lilies of the field" lesson about not worrying,[34] his command to love one's neighbor as oneself,[35] and his insistence that we forgive others.[36] But Evans notes that most of Jesus' teachings bear no resemblance to Cynicism and in fact are in stark opposition. For example, Jesus never taught his followers that personal happiness was the chief goal in life or to live in harmony with the natural world, which were central tenets of the Cynics (and also popular philosophies today).[37]

Summarizing the lack of proof that Jesus was exposed to Cynicism, Evans writes:

> Thus, the evidence—archaeological, literary and historical—shows that despite a Greco-Roman presence in places, Galilean Jews consciously and at times violently attempted to maintain their religious identity and

CHAPTER 14: THE ANTI-SUPERNATURAL OPINIONS

boundaries. Moreover, there is also no archaeological or literary evidence of a Cynic presence in Galilee in the early part of the first century A.D. No evidence whatsoever.[38]

In their reconstruction of Jesus, the Seminar ignores his Jewish culture completely. Their assertion that Jesus was merely a traveling sage who was not immersed in the Jewish Scriptures not only assumes that Jesus was exposed to Cynic philosophy, but also ignores a huge body of evidence about the first-century Jewish world in which this "sage" lived.

In his response to *The Five Gospels*, N. T. Wright describes the Seminar's process of revealing the historical Jesus:

> The Seminar claims, then, that a portrait of Jesus "begins to emerge" from their work at certain points (p. 340). Not so. The portrait was in their minds all along. It is, for the most part, a shallow and one-dimensional portrait, developed through anachronistic parallels (the laconic cowboy) and ignoring the actual first-century context. Its attractive and indeed sometimes compelling features, of Jesus as the subversive sage, challenging the status quo with teasing epigrams and parables, has been achieved at the huge cost of screening out a whole range of material which several of the leading Jesus-scholars around the world, in major, serious, and contemporary works of historical reconstruction, would regard as absolutely central.[39]

By divorcing Jesus from his first-century Jewish context, the historical reconstruction of Jesus is bound to be both extremely biased and extremely inaccurate. Although Funk advises his readers to "beware of finding a Jesus entirely congenial to you,"[40] that is exactly what the Jesus Seminar has done.

THE NON-APOCALYPTIC JESUS

Another major assumption of the Jesus Seminar is that Jesus was "non-apocalyptic" or "non-eschatological." In other words, they believe that all of Jesus' references to the end of the world, God's final judgment, the kingdom of God, and his second coming must have been theological fabrications of the early church. In the Seminar's opinion, Jesus would never say such things, unless he was referring to a kingdom that already exists within believers (as the *Gospel of Thomas* teaches[41]). Funk summarizes this assumption in this way:

> The expectation that Jesus will return and sit in cosmic judgment is part and parcel of the mythological worldview that is now defunct. Furthermore, it undergirds human lust for the punishment of enemies and evildoers and the corresponding hope for rewards for the pious and righteous. All apocalyptic elements *should be expunged* from the Christian agenda.[42]

It is evident that Funk's reasons for expunging the apocalyptic elements stem from his distaste for them, rather than from a logical historical argument. In fact, in the Introduction to *The Five Gospels*, Funk admits that both Jesus' mentor John the Baptist and the early Christian church had an apocalyptic message, yet he insists that Jesus did not. Early Christian historian Luke Timothy Johnson summarizes just how irrational this conclusion is: "A less sophisticated logic might naturally conclude just the opposite: If Jesus' mentor was eschatological and Jesus' followers were eschatological, it would seem logical to suppose that Jesus was eschatological!"[43]

But Funk and many of his colleagues simply choose to blot that aspect of Jesus' ministry out of the historical record. What is their explanation for doing this? For one, they assume that apocalyptic elements contained in the hypothetical document Q must not have been in an earlier edition of Q (an even more hypothetical document!). They basically assume that anything they dislike in Q was a later insertion that didn't originate with Jesus.

There is actually abundant evidence that first-century Jewish thinking was profoundly apocalyptic. The Jews were clearly looking forward to a final judgment when God would establish his kingdom of perfect justice and peace.[44] Moreover, as we already mentioned, there is very little evidence that Jesus had been influenced by—much less exposed to—Greco-Roman pagan philosophy that was more focused on "finding the Kingdom of God within oneself." But the Seminar disregards this abundant evidence, preferring to characterize Jesus as a wandering pagan philosopher instead of a Jew who had grown up steeped in the profoundly apocalyptic ideas of Jewish culture.

Echoing Evans' earlier criticisms of the Seminar's bias against the Jewish context of Jesus' ministry, N. T. Wright states:

> We do not actually know anything about wandering pagan philosophers whom Jesus might have met in the days of his youth. There is no evidence for them. But they are brought in [by Funk] of necessity; otherwise one might have to admit that Jesus' language about the Kingdom of God was thoroughly Jewish and belonged within the Jewish setting and aspirations of his day.[45]

Again, the Jesus Seminar ignores the evidence that Jesus' apocalyptic statements accurately reflected the Jewish thinking of his day, preferring instead to attribute his apocalyptic statements to insertions of the early Christian church.

In their defense, the Seminar's depiction of Jesus may not be due to bias alone. Evans provides a plausible explanation for the Jesus Seminar's distinctly non-Jewish, non-apocalyptic portrayal of Jesus:

> Whereas many of the Seminar's members have been exposed to Greek literature and Greco-Roman culture and conventions, not many of them appear to have competence in the Semitic (Jewish) world of Jesus. Few seem acquainted with the land of Israel itself. Few have done any archaeological work. Few know rabbinic literature and the Aramaic paraphrase of Scripture. As a consequence of these deficiencies, it is not surprising that the Jesus Seminar has come to so many odd and implausible conclusions.[46]

Evans cites two examples of their ignorance: Jesus' own view of "the kingdom of God" and his favorite self-referential term, "Son of Man," which has its roots in the prophetic writings of the Hebrew Scriptures. These are just two examples of the many ways Jesus expressed his Jewish background.

Throwing Out the Baby with the Bathwater?

A third assumption of the Jesus Seminar is the belief that, aside from the four gospels, most of the New Testament is irrelevant for getting at the "real Jesus." Here lies another irony: they confidently depend on a hypothetical document (Q) and one that most scholars date to the late second century (*Thomas*), but they dismiss the Acts of the Apostles, Paul's thirteen letters, and the nine other New Testament books. These, they declare, obscure rather than illuminate the truth.

Luke Timothy Johnson describes the Jesus Seminar's historical methodology as follows:

> The rest of the New Testament evidence concerning Jesus and Christian origins is casually dismissed. Paul is caricatured as "having no interest in Jesus." The narratives in Acts and the Gospels are tossed out as mythical fabrications based on faith. More than that, any sayings that are "developed" must also be dismissed from the reconstruction. What is left is a small pile of pieces. But on this basis, Jesus is declared to have "really" been one way or another. And this is announced *before* the Seminar takes up its (equally portentous) work of figuring out which deeds attributed to Jesus "really" came from him. This is not responsible, or even critical, scholarship. It is a self-indulgent charade.[47]

Even in a cursory reading of Paul's letters, the reasonable reader will see that:

1. The person of Jesus was the main subject.
2. Paul visited and interviewed original disciples.[48]
3. He delivered the same message as the eyewitness apostles.[49]
4. He took great care to pass along the earliest eyewitness testimony concerning Jesus.[50]
5. He confirms the testimony of the four canonical Gospels, which would be unexpected if the Gospel stories had been concocted at a later date.[51]

CHAPTER 14: THE ANTI-SUPERNATURAL OPINIONS

Moreover, many scholars have successfully disputed the claim that Paul (not Jesus) was the "inventor" of Christianity. Johnson remarks: "The best work done on Paul in recent years has demonstrated that Paul was not the inventor of a 'Christ cult' but was, rather, the inheritor of liturgical and creedal traditions already in place before his conversion."[52]

F. F. Bruce agrees that Paul's letters are consistent with the claims of Matthew, Mark, Luke, and John. He notes that Paul wrote his letters to Christians who were already familiar with the gospel story. Paul's primary purpose was therefore not to relate facts about Jesus' life and ministry, which he assumed his readers already knew, but to provide encouragement and guidance to the early Christian churches. Bruce notes that Paul's letters provide "sufficient material to construct an outline of the early apostolic preaching about Jesus."[53] He adds:

> Even where [Paul] does not quote the actual sayings of Jesus, he shows throughout his works how well acquainted he was with them. In particular, we ought to compare the ethical section of the Epistle to the Romans (12:1 to 15:7), where Paul summarizes the practical implications of the gospel for the lives of believers, with the Sermon on the Mount, to see how thoroughly imbued the apostle was with the teaching of his Master. Besides there and elsewhere Paul's chief argument in his ethical instruction is the example of Christ Himself. And the character of Christ as understood by Paul is in perfect agreement with His character as portrayed in the Gospels.... In short, the outline of the gospel story as we can trace it in the writings of Paul agrees with the outline which we find elsewhere in the New Testament, and in the four Gospels in particular.[54]

Thus, in their historical reconstruction of Jesus, the Jesus Seminar dismisses out of hand the early writings of Paul. This is not a sign that Paul is an undependable source of information about Jesus (he is), but instead a sign that the Seminar simply dislikes what Paul has to say about Jesus.

The Jesus Seminar also dismisses the wealth of early historical evidence that can be gleaned from the Book of Acts. Acts contains numerous early sermons that most scholars trace back to the first generation after Jesus' death.[55] Though the sermons in Acts 1-5, 10, 13, and 17 are recorded in Greek, they contain many Jewish words and traits, or semitisms, evidence of their origin in early Jewish oral tradition.[56]

Moreover, some of these early sermons, such as the one by Peter in Acts 10, are written in imperfect Greek, as if by someone who spoke Greek as a second language. Meanwhile, the Greek language of the rest of Acts was written by an educated person who could obviously speak Greek fluently. This suggests that at least some of the sermons were originally recorded in Aramaic, the language Jesus spoke, and then translated into Greek.[57] In short, the Jesus Seminar favors the *Gospel of Thomas* and the hypothetical document Q over documents that thousands of other respected scholars justifiably consider much more historical.

NOT PITHY ENOUGH?

The Jesus Seminar believes that lengthy, "less memorable" statements could not be from Jesus because he did not write down his own teachings, and because his sayings and actions were initially passed on orally. They conclude that the shorter, pithier aphorisms, such as "Turn the other cheek,"[58] are most likely to be authentic. The Seminar does approve of the lengthy parables, which, they say, would be easy to remember. (But, of course, they still disapprove of any supernatural or apocalyptic remarks contained therein.)

For example, *The Five Gospels* makes this claim about the stories Jesus tells in Mark 5: "They are not particularly memorable, are not aphorisms or parables, and would not have circulated independently during the oral period. They cannot, therefore, be traced back to Jesus."[59]

These skeptical scholars assume that Jesus' typical style was to utter paradoxical statements (such as "Love your enemies") and tales that are meant to challenge the status quo (in their view, the parable of the Good Samaritan). Therefore, if a teaching of Jesus is lengthy, not paradoxical, not ironic, or not meant to confront the religious establishment, Jesus could not have uttered it.

Furthermore, they assume that any remarks that reflect the concerns or theological agenda of the early Christian church must be a later insertion. For example, they voted black (definitely inauthentic) the claim that Peter was the "rock" on which Jesus would build his church. They also assume that the prophecy of the sheep and the goats[60] was

CHAPTER 14: THE ANTI-SUPERNATURAL OPINIONS

an insertion of the early church because it reflects a desire by Matthew to denigrate certain less worthy members of the Christian community.

In the opinion of N. T. Wright, the Jesus Seminar's Jesus is:

> ...a very peculiar human being (as one Fellow of the Seminar pointed out to me, a Jesus who always and only uttered pithy aphorisms would start to look like some of the less credible cinematic Jesuses). Such a person would in fact be quite maddening.... More importantly, as a historian I find it incredible that such a Jesus could have been a significant historical figure. It is not at all clear why people would have followed him, died for him, loved him, invented rich and powerful stories about him, and (within an almost incredibly short time, and within the context of continuing Jewish monotheism) worshiped him.[61]

In short, how did a Jesus who uttered only short, pithy, cynical statements have such a dramatic effect on the course of history?

The claim that lengthier, "less memorable" sayings could not have originated from Jesus depends on the assumption that people in an oral culture weren't able to remember longer discourses. However, not only is there strong evidence that much of the canonical Gospels is based on eyewitness testimony, but there is also strong evidence that even if they were passed on orally, lengthy teachings could be accurately preserved between Jesus' lifetime and the writing of the canonical Gospels.

We modern people depend on written records. Our attention spans, accustomed to sound bites and multiple media distractions, make retaining long oral discourse very difficult. But first-century listeners were steeped in a strong oral culture. And Jesus' stories and teachings were on the whole very memorable, characterized by vivid illustrations, engaging characters, and dramatic consequences. Again, Wright offers insight:

> Communities that live in an oral culture tend to be *storytelling* communities. They sit around on long evenings telling and listening to stories—the same stories, over and over again. Such stories, especially when they are involved with memorable happenings that have determined in some way the existence and life of the particular group

in question, acquire a fairly fixed form, down to precise phraseology (in narrative as well as recorded speech), extremely early in their life—often within a day or so of the original incident taking place.... Each village and community has its recognized storytellers, the accredited bearers of its traditions; but the whole community knows the stories by heart, and if the teller varies them even slightly they will let him know in no uncertain terms.[62]

In fact, Wright argues that stories in a narrative form, such as those in the canonical Gospels, were most likely the earliest to be recorded because they corresponded more directly to the initial stories circulating in the oral culture. On the other hand, lists of sayings, such as the *Gospel of Thomas*, were more likely to be written down later than the narrative versions. As these stories extended into the Hellenistic world, they would become detached from the original Jewish story format and gathered as lists of individual sayings, similar to other lists of wise sayings typical of the Greco-Roman world. As these lists developed, they were subject to distortion and more likely to depart from the original teachings of Jesus. Therefore, Wright argues, the story-like narratives of the Gospels are much more likely to accurately go back to Jesus than a mere list of his sayings.[63]

Finally, how logical is it that a religious teacher would make no statements regarding the concerns of his earliest followers? Would Jesus never give instructions to those he wanted to pass on his teachings, or never designate leaders to carry on for him? These assumptions seem like convenient ways for the Seminar to expunge other aspects of Jesus' teachings that they find unpalatable.

Referring to the overall picture of Jesus put forth by the Jesus Seminar, Wright makes the following summary statement:

In order to sustain their homemade view of Jesus, the authors of [*The Five Gospels*], and presumably a fair number at least of Fellows of the Jesus Seminar, have had to invent, as well, an entire picture of the early church out of not much more than thin air.... Any jigsaw puzzle can be solved if we are allowed to create new pieces for it at a whim. But we should not imagine that historical scholarship built on this principle is of any great value.[64]

Chapter 14: The Anti-Supernatural Opinions

Constructing the pieces of the jigsaw puzzle themselves, is it any surprise that the Jesus found by the Jesus Seminar looks very much like the Jesus they assumed existed in the first place?

Questions for Comprehension and Discussion

1. What did the founder of the Jesus Seminar want to do for traditional Christians? How does this ironically contrast with what the traditional Jesus says he does for his disciples?
2. What is the Jesus Seminar? How do their numbers compare to the number of scholars in the field of New Testament studies?
3. How many Fellows were involved in voting whether Jesus really said or did what the New Testament claims he said or did?
4. What does the Jesus Seminar assume about the documents Q and the *Gospel of Thomas*? Why is this assumption flawed (see Chapter 12 for help, if necessary)?
5. What does the Jesus Seminar assume about the existence of God and a supernatural world? What does the scientific evidence reveal about their assumptions concerning God and the possibility of miracles?
6. Which group of traveling philosophers does the Jesus Seminar assume that Jesus resembled in word and deed? Why is this assumption flawed?
7. What is the most logical reason that the Jesus Seminar believes Jesus would never talk about the ending of the world, God's judgment of humanity, and other "apocalyptic" themes? Does the historical evidence support the idea that Jesus was in close contact with Greco-Roman philosophy, or that he was steeped in Jewish culture? What are the implications of this evidence for determining the true teachings of Jesus?
8. Why is it more likely that a narrative story about Jesus was composed earlier than a list of his sayings, like *Thomas* and the hypothetical Q?
9. Why does the Jesus Seminar disregard the rest of the New Testament in their assessment of who Jesus really was? Why is this illogical and bound to lead to a less accurate portrayal of Jesus?

10. Why does the Jesus Seminar think Jesus would only say short, pithy saying or parables that were easy to remember? What evidence demonstrates that this assumption is flawed?

CHAPTER 14 ENDNOTES

1. Philip Jenkins, *Hidden Gospels: How the Search for Jesus Lost Its Way* (Oxford: Oxford University Press, 2001), 11.
2. Thomas E. Kida, *Don't Believe Everything You Think: The 6 Basic Mistakes We Make in Thinking* (Amherst, NY: Prometheus Books, 2006), 157.
3. Robert Funk, "The Issue of Jesus," *Forum 1/1* (Westar Institute, 1985), 8.
4. Robert Funk, *Honest to Jesus* (New York: HarperCollins, 1996), 19.
5. John 8:31b-32.
6. Westar Institute website, "Westar Fellows," https://www.westarinstitute.org/membership/westar-fellows/fellows-directory.
7. Ibid.
8. From The Society for Biblical Literature website, http://www.sbl-site.org/aboutus.aspx.
9. Luke Timothy Johnson, *The Real Jesus: The Misguided Quest for the Historical Jesus and the Truth of the Traditional Gospels* (New York: HarperCollins, 1997), 2.
10. Ibid, 2.
11. Ibid, 3.
12. N. T. Wright, "Five Gospels But No Gospel: Jesus and the Seminar," available at http://ntwrightpage.com/1999/01/01/five-gospels-but-no-gospel-jesus-and-the-the-seminary.
13. Funk et al., *The Five Gospels: The Search for the Authentic Words of Jesus* (Sonoma: Polebridge; New York: Macmillan, 1993), 43 and 138.
14. The Westar Institute website, "The Jesus Seminar," https://www.westarinstitute.org/projects/the-jesus-seminar.
15. Matthew 22:12.
16. Luke 6:20 and Matthew 5:3.
17. Funk et al., *The Five Gospels*, 18.
18. Wright, "Five Gospels But No Gospel," 5.
19. Robert Funk, ed., *The Gospel of Mark: Red Letter Edition* (Sonoma, CA: Polebridge Press, 1991), xx.
20. Funk et al., *The Five Gospels*, back of the book. Emphasis theirs.
21. Other examples are Matthew 21:28-31a (the parable of the two sons) and Matthew 21:31b (the saying, "I tell you the truth, the tax collectors and the prostitutes are entering the kingdom of God ahead of you"). According to

CHAPTER 14: THE ANTI-SUPERNATURAL OPINIONS

The Five Gospels: "Fifty-eight percent of the Fellows voted red or pink for the parable, 53 percent for the saying in v. 31b. A substantial number of gray and black votes pulled the weighted average into the gray category." (Funk, et al., *The Five Gospels*, 232.)

22. Matthew 24:32-33.
23. Wright, "Five Gospels But No Gospel," 7.
24. N.T. Wright, *Jesus and the Victory of God, Christian Origins and the Question of God*, vol. 2 (Minneapolis: Fortress, 1996), 33. Emphasis his.
25. Funk, *Honest to Jesus*, 298.
26. Robert W. Funk, "The Coming Radical Revolution," *The Fourth R* 11:4, (July/August, 1998).
27. Funk et al., *The Five Gospels*, 128.
28. Ibid, 265.
29. John 14:6.
30. John Dominic Crossan, *The Historical Jesus: The Life of a Mediterranean Jewish Peasant* (San Francisco: HarperCollins, 1991), 421.
31. Craig A. Evans, *Fabricating Jesus* (Downers Grove, IL: InterVarsity Press, 2006), 106-7, 109.
32. The evidence includes the lack of pig bones in the dump before AD 70, while after AD 70, pig bones made up about 30 percent of the animal remains. Jews did not eat pig meat, indicating that the population of Sepphoris was predominantly Jewish before AD 70. Moreover, instead of using the lighter, more portable ceramic vessels that non-Jews used, Jews used large stone vessels because they were easier to keep clean in observance of the Jewish purity rituals. Large numbers of stone vessels were found in the pre-70 AD layers of excavations in Sepphoris, again suggesting it was predominantly Jewish, not Greek. For more details on the archaeological evidence, see Evans, *Fabricating Jesus*, 113-119.
33. Ibid, 103.
34. See Matthew 6:28-33.
35. Mark 12:31.
36. See Matthew 6:12,13-15, 18:21-25, and Luke 17:3-4.
37. Evans, *Fabricating Jesus*, 109.
38. Ibid, 119.
39. Wright, "Five Gospels and No Gospel," 11.
40. Funk et al., *The Five Gospels*, 5.
41. Darrell L. Bock, *The Missing Gospels: Unearthing the Truth Behind Alternative Christianities* (Nashville, TN: Thomas Nelson Publishers, 2006), 65.
42. Robert W. Funk, "The Coming Radical Revolution." Emphasis mine.
43. Johnson, *The Real Jesus*, 25.

44 The Dead Sea Scrolls that date to the period just prior to Jesus' life, especially those called 4Q521 and 4Q246, repeatedly confirm that the Jewish world in the century before and after Jesus was extremely concerned with apocalyptic issues and the coming of the Messiah. See Evans, *Fabricating Jesus*, 40-46.

45 Wright, "Five Gospels and No Gospel," 16.

46 Evans, *Fabricating Jesus*, 12.

47 Johnson, *The Real Jesus*, 26. Emphasis his.

48 For example, see Galatians 1:18 and 2:7-9. F. F. Bruce describes Paul's time with Peter in Jerusalem as follows: "What did Peter and Paul talk about during the fortnight they spent together in Jerusalem about AD 35 (Gal. 1:18)? As Professor Dodd puts it, 'we may presume they did not spend all the time talking about the weather.' It was a golden opportunity for Paul to learn the details of the story of Jesus from one whose knowledge of that story was unsurpassed." (F. F. Bruce, *The New Testament Documents: Are They Reliable?* [Grand Rapids, MI: Eerdmans, 1981], 39. Bruce cites C.H. Dodd, *The Apostolic Teaching and Its Development* [1936], 26.)

49 For example, see 1 Corinthians 15:11.

50 For references to transmission of oral history, see 1 Corinthians 11:2, 23-25, 15:3-8, Philippians 2:6-11, Galatians 1:9, and 1 Thessalonians 2:13. For a full discussion of Pauline evidence for the formal transmission of oral history within the early Christian communities, see Richard Bauckham, *Jesus and the Eyewitnesses: The Gospels as Eyewitness Testimony* (Grand Rapids, MI: Eerdmans, 2006), 264-271.

51 Johnson, *The Real Jesus*, 122.

52 Ibid, 119.

53 F. F. Bruce, *The New Testament Documents: Are They Reliable?* (Downers Grove, IL: InterVarsity Press, 1973), 77.

54 Ibid, 78-79.

55 Gary Habermas and Michael Licona, *The Case for the Resurrection of Jesus* (Grand Rapids, MI: Kregel, 2004), 53.

56 C. H. Dodd, *The Apostolic Preaching and Its Developments* (Grand Rapids, MI: Baker, 1980), 17-31.

57 Habermas and Licona, *The Case for the Resurrection of Jesus*, 53f.

58 Matthew 5:29.

59 Funk et al., *The Five Gospels*, 62.

60 Matthew 25:31-46.

61 Wright, "Five Gospels and No Gospel," 21.

62 Ibid, 19.

63 Ibid, 21.

64 Ibid.

Growing Roman persecution, particularly by the third century, at times meant that Christians had to decide, quite literally, which books they were willing to die for.

  —Craig Blomberg, New Testament scholar[1]

If you don't stand for something, you will fall for anything.

  —Methodist church bulletin announcement

15

Trusting the Selection

Sir Leigh Teabing, the fictional historian in *The Da Vinci Code*, a bestselling novel made into a popular film, spouts his opinion about the New Testament:

> "Because Constantine upgraded Jesus' status almost four centuries *after* Jesus' death, thousands of documents already existed chronicling His life as a *mortal* man. To rewrite the history books, Constantine knew he would need a bold stroke. From this sprang the most profound moment in Christian history..., Constantine commissioned and financed a new Bible, which omitted those gospels that spoke of Christ's human traits and embellished those gospels that made Him godlike. The earlier gospels were outlawed, gathered up, and burned."[2]

Teabing goes on to explain that "Jesus' establishment as the Son of God was officially proposed and voted on by the Council of Nicaea." Cryptologist Sophie Neveu reacts with surprise: "Hold on. You're saying Jesus' divinity was the result of a vote?" Teabing replies, "A relatively close vote at that."[3]

Were the books of the New Testament really selected by a Roman emperor who thought a deified Jesus would give him more control over his subjects? And could our understanding of Jesus from the New Testament really be the outcome of a close vote of a power-thirsty religious council almost four hundred years after Jesus lived?

CHAPTER 15: TRUSTING THE SELECTION

Certainly, a work of fiction or a Hollywood film does not need to be historically accurate. But it is disturbing when documentaries on important historical events mislead the viewer by presenting disputed information as fact. One such documentary, entitled *Christianity: The First Thousand Years*, makes the claim that Constantine was the one who decisively settled the contents of the New Testament canon when he commissioned fifty Bibles for the main churches of the Roman Empire.[4] The implication was that, prior to the influence of Constantine, the churches had been reading a wide variety of texts, including the Gnostic texts, but eventually these other views were no longer acceptable. (Not surprisingly, Jesus Seminar co-founder, John Dominic Crossan, served as a historical consultant for this A&E documentary.)

Elaine Pagels, a Harvard scholar with expertise in the Gnostic gospels, makes this claim about the impact of these recently discovered Gnostic texts: "We now begin to see that what we call Christianity—and what we identify as Christian tradition—actually represents only a small selection of specific sources, chosen from among dozens of others. Who made that selection, and for what reasons?"[5] Again, the implication is that the selection of documents for inclusion in the New Testament was biased, and many deserving texts were excluded.

Bart Ehrman implies similar ideas in his book, *Misquoting Jesus*:

> We are able to pinpoint the first time that any Christian of record listed the twenty-seven books of our New Testament as *the* books of the New Testament—neither more nor fewer. Surprising as it may seem, this Christian was writing in the second half of the fourth century, nearly three hundred years after the books of the New Testament had themselves been written. The author was the powerful bishop of Alexandria named Athanasius. In the year 367 C.E., Athanasius wrote his annual pastoral letter to the Egyptian churches under his jurisdiction, and in it he included advice concerning which books should be read as Scripture in the churches. He lists our twenty-seven books, excluding all others. This is the first surviving instance of anyone affirming our set of books as the New Testament. And even Athanasius didn't settle the matter. Debates continued for decades, even centuries.[6]

Ehrman's comments, while accurate in the details, leave the reader to believe that there was no general agreement about which documents should be read in churches until a powerful bishop finally took the reins and made a unilateral decision, relegating many other worthy documents to the trash bin.

But contrary to the theories of best-selling conspiracy novels and the criticism of modern liberal scholarship, long before Constantine legalized Christianity and Athanasius wrote his letter to the Egyptian churches, there *was* consensus among the vast majority of Christian churches as to which documents accurately reflected the teachings of Jesus and which did not. Moreover, most of the books of the New Testament we read today were widely accepted by Christian churches by the mid-second century, *before* the Nag Hammadi and other excluded texts had even been written.[7]

After Emperor Constantine legalized Christianity in the early fourth century, the church did make a more deliberate attempt to officially recognize the canonical documents that had long been *unofficially* considered authoritative. But, even though the influence of Constantine and Athanasius was important, the content of that official list had already been determined to a significant extent centuries earlier.

To set the background for our discussion of the books chosen to be included in the New Testament, let's first take a look at the issues that the mid-second-century Christians were facing as it became unclear whether new documents should be read in their church services. Let's then examine the evidence for the early recognition of the four canonical Gospels. We will then briefly discuss the evidence for early recognition of the other New Testament documents. Finally, we'll look at the purpose of the Council of Nicaea and the role that this first church council played in the doctrine of Jesus' divinity and the development of the New Testament canon.

What Belongs in the Bookchest?

Drawing from Jewish tradition, the earliest followers of Jesus placed a high value on holy writings. Jewish synagogues had always safely preserved their collection of Scriptural documents in special pieces of furniture, called the *'aron* (for "chest" or "shrine").[8] Similarly, each early

Christian church maintained a chest called an *armarion* in the home where they gathered each week.[9]

The first documents were written on parchment or papyrus, which were rolled around a rod to form a *scroll*. Towards the end of the first century, a new storage method came into general use. Called a *codex* (or more than one *codices*), it consisted of a stack of folded papyri or parchment that was bound together at the edge. It was thus the ancestor of the modern book. Not only was the codex cheaper and more portable than a scroll, it could also hold much more text. Because Christians generally met in varying locations, and because Christianity was spreading rapidly, the codex soon replaced the scroll as the primary medium for copied Christian documents. The book titles were most likely written on scraps of parchment and sewn onto the side of the codices to make them easily identifiable in the *'aron*, which contained special niches to hold them.[10]

By the middle of the second century, the chests of each Christian congregation generally contained the same collection of codices. They would each have a Greek translation of the Jewish Scriptures, known as the *Septuagint*, as well as approximately twenty other documents that were connected to the original apostles, such as the four canonical Gospels and the thirteen letters of Paul.[11]

Much like the practice in modern church services, literate members of the early Christian congregations read selections from these cherished texts during each weekly meeting. In the opinion of these early believers, the codices contained the writings of Jesus' first followers, who had gone to their deaths for their faith. Therefore, each Christian community treasured and protected its *'aron*, and they treated the documents contained therein with the utmost respect.

But in the mid- to late second century, new documents began circulating among the congregations. These new codices included a gospel allegedly written by Peter (*The Gospel of Peter*), a visionary text also attributed to Peter (*The Apocalypse of Peter*), a manual for Christian living (*The Teaching of the Twelve Apostles*, also called *The Didache*), a letter from Peter to Philip (two letters from Peter had already been in the chest for many years), a letter from a church leader named Clement (the *First Epistle of Clement*), and another letter from a man named Barnabas (the *Epistle of Barnabas*). What were the Christians to make of these new documents? Should they read them alongside the texts that had already been cherished for generations? Should the church members be required to follow their teachings?

In the mid-second century, another issue arose in Rome. A pastor named Marcion declared that the *Septuagint* shouldn't be read at all, and that only certain Christian documents belonged in the bookchest. He discarded all documents except the Pauline Epistles and the Gospel of Luke. He then altered Paul's letters and Luke's Gospel to rid them of all Jewish elements, since he didn't care for the God of the Jewish Scriptures.[12] Rumors of Marcion's new list of "authoritative" books spread throughout the Christian world. Churches began to wonder: Should all documents other than Paul's letters and the Gospel of Luke be excluded from the canon? Does Marcion have a better understanding of what Jesus would have wanted than previous leaders did?

Moreover, churches started coming across other documents that claimed to be "gospels," but professed very different beliefs about God, creation, the nature of redemption, and the role of Jesus (as discussed in Chapter 13). Should these newer documents be included in the bookchest, even though they clearly conflicted with the teachings of Matthew, Mark, Luke, and John?

We can begin to understand the dilemma facing the Christians in the mid- to late second century. Seeking answers, Christians looked to their leaders for clarification regarding which documents represented the truth about their faith and practices. For generations, there had been little debate about the matter, but now that new documents were circulating, crucial decisions had to be made: Which documents were truthful representations of the life and teachings of their Lord?

These decisions were not made immediately, as you would expect at a time when communication across a wide region was so slow, but instead the debate and agreements evolved gradually over the next two centuries. Athanasius was the first to officially recognize the same twenty-seven books that we read in the New Testament today, but an informal consensus had emerged much earlier. Starting very early on, the church prioritized documents that had been circulating the longest and had the widest readership among the churches, and it was wary of new documents that lacked a strong tradition and usage. Let's take a look at the gradual process whereby the churches recognized which codices deserved an honored place in their bookchests.

CHAPTER 15: TRUSTING THE SELECTION

FOUR GOSPELS AND FOUR ONLY

By the end of the second century, church leaders recognized Matthew, Mark, Luke, and John—and only these four Gospels—as *the* dependable biographies of Jesus. These four had been in circulation since the first century, while the Gnostic documents, as we have seen, originated in the mid-second century at the earliest.

In fact, the widespread recognition of the four canonical Gospels by the end of the second century was largely a response to the emergence of heretical groups like the Gnostics and the Marcionites (the followers of Marcion). These four authentic gospels were considered "apostolic" because the church recognized that they were authored either by those who were Jesus' original apostles, as in the case of Matthew (a converted tax collector) and John (who ended his life as a prisoner for his faith), or by close associates of the original apostles, as in the case of Mark (a translator for Peter) and Luke (a physician and companion of Paul).[13] The Gnostic gospels had no such credibility, even though they often bore the names of Jesus' apostles, such as Thomas, Mary Magdalene, and Peter, or claimed to contain conversations with the risen Jesus.

Writing in AD 110 about himself decades earlier, Papias of Hierapolis notes that he depended on information that originated with the apostles and the "elders" who were eyewitnesses of Jesus:

> I shall not hesitate also to put into properly ordered form for you everything I learned carefully in the past from the elders and noted down well, for the truth of which I vouch.... [I did not] enjoy those who recall someone else's commandments, but those who remember the commandments given by the Lord to the faith and proceeding from the truth itself. And if by chance anyone who had been in attendance on the elders should come my way, I inquired about the words of the elders—[that is,] what [according to the elders] Andrew or Peter said, or Philip, or Thomas or James, or John or Matthew or any other of the Lord's disciples, and whatever Aristion and the elder John, the Lord's disciples, were saying. For I did not think that information from books would profit me as much as information from a *living and surviving voice*.[14]

Papias recognized that the only reliable information about Jesus came from those who had lived with him, walked with him, and talked with him—the original apostles and other eyewitnesses.

Apostolic origin—or lack thereof—was therefore the primary criterion by which the early Christians evaluated any information about Jesus, whether it was received orally or in written format. Richard Bauckham notes that the phrase "living and surviving voice" was used in ancient historiography to indicate the transmission of stories directly from the eyewitness, rather than through a chain of individuals across generations.[15]

Moreover, Papias' reference to "Aristion and the elder John" indicates that they were still alive at the time about which Papias is writing (probably towards the end of the first century), since he uses a form of the verb indicating progressive action, translated "were saying," for them and the past (aorist) tense, "said," for the other disciples of Jesus, such as Andrew and Peter. Papias was emphasizing that he preferred to learn the truth of what Jesus taught directly from the original disciples or those who were taught directly by these disciples.[16]

The emphasis the early Christians placed on the apostolic origin (*apostolicity*) of a text was also clearly noted by Serapion of Antioch, an early church father in the late second and early third centuries. In rejecting the *Gospel of Peter*, Serapion demonstrated his desire to distinguish between documents that had truly originated with the apostles and those that only bore the apostles' names:

> We, brothers and sisters, receive Peter and the rest of the apostles as we would receive Christ himself. But these writings that are ascribed with their names, we carefully reject, knowing that no such writings have ever been handed down to us.[17]

These early church leaders were not excluding documents because they did not fit their version of Christianity, but because they had been composed recently by those who were not associated with eyewitnesses. Christian ministers realized that a document claiming to come from Peter didn't mean it really did, especially since it had recently appeared in circulation and contained many beliefs that were completely at odds with earlier Christian documents. Therefore, apostolicity was the primary

CHAPTER 15: TRUSTING THE SELECTION

criterion used to identify the documents that legitimately reflected the teachings of Jesus. One New Testament scholar puts it succinctly: "Testimony that could be connected to eyewitnesses of the risen Lord was uniquely authoritative among early Christians."[18]

Let's now take a closer look at evidence for the widespread recognition of the four canonical Gospels by the end of the second century—over one hundred years before Constantine and Athanasius, and at a time when Christians were still being persecuted and hadn't yet been corrupted by power.

Justin Martyr, who lived from AD 100 to 160, was the first Christian *apologist*, a term that derives from *apologia*, the Greek word for "a reasoned defense." As a Christian apologist, he devoted himself to teaching and writing in defense of the Christian faith. By AD 150, Justin Martyr's Roman school was using only the four Gospels of Matthew, Mark, Luke, and John,[19] and Justin referred to these Gospels in his writings as the "memoirs of the apostles."[20]

The widespread acceptance of the four Gospels is also demonstrated by the *Diatessaron*, a harmony of Matthew, Mark, Luke, and John composed by Tatian around AD 170. As New Testament scholar Bruce Metzger states: "The *Diatessaron* supplies proof that all four Gospels were regarded as authoritative, otherwise it is unlikely that Tatian would have dared to combine them into one gospel account."[21] The debate that followed the composition of the *Diatessaron* was not about whether it excluded other worthy "gospels," but whether or not the four Gospels should be kept separate rather than blended.

Around AD 180, the church father Irenaeus eloquently insisted that the number of Gospels was only four:

> It is not possible that the Gospels can be either more or fewer in number than they are. For, since there are four zones of the world in which we live, and four principal winds, while the Church is scattered throughout all the world, and the pillar and ground of the Church is the Gospel and the spirit of life; it is fitting that she should have four pillars, breathing out immortality on every side, and vivifying men afresh.... For the cherubim, too, were four-faced, and their faces were images of the dispensation of the Son of God.[22]

His reference to the "four-faced" cherubim alludes to Revelation 4:7. Irenaeus likened each of the Gospels to the "four living creatures": the lion representing *John* with its emphasis on Jesus' royal power, the ox representing *Luke* with its emphasis on Jesus' sacrificial role, the human representing *Matthew* with its emphasis on Jesus' humanity, and the eagle representing *Mark* with its emphasis on the influence of the Holy Spirit.

In identifying the four different emphases of the four Gospels, Irenaeus was reacting to the *Diatessaron*, as well as to the emergence of new "gospels" that contradicted the long tradition in the Christian church. At this point, most of the Gnostic books hadn't even been written yet. And even the few Gnostic gospels that were in circulation at the time of Irenaeus had only been around for a few years. It is understandable, therefore, why Irenaeus doesn't consider them as authoritative as the Gospels of Matthew, Mark, Luke, and John, which had already been in circulation for approximately a century.

F. F. Bruce says this about Irenaeus: "The general impression given by his words is that the fourfold pattern of the gospel was by this time no innovation but so widely accepted that he can stress its cosmic appropriateness as though it were one of the facts of nature."[23] That is, rather than forcing his own opinion on the churches, as many liberal scholars complain that he did, Irenaeus was simply reporting what had been established for generations: the four Gospels of Matthew, Mark, Luke, and John were the only true ones.[24]

Serapion of Antioch did permit the reading of the *Gospel of Peter* in a local church around AD 200, but upon closer examination of its contents, he noted hints of Docetism (the belief that Jesus only appeared to be human) and changed his mind.[25] Around the same time, Clement of Alexandria permitted the *Gospel of the Egyptians*, but none of his successors considered it authoritative.[26] Therefore, with these minor exceptions, the Gospels of Matthew, Mark, Luke, and John were well established as canonical by the end of the second century.

Additional strong evidence for the early canonicity of our modern-day New Testament comes from a document called the Muratorian fragment, perhaps the oldest extant list of New Testament books. Written in approximately AD 170 by an unknown author, the Muratorian fragment refers to four Gospels. Although the text at the beginning of the fragment is missing, Luke and John are listed as the third and fourth

Gospels, and scholars universally agree that the missing first part of the fragment had listed Matthew and Mark as the first and second Gospels.[27]

One final quote from an early church father will serve to drive home the point regarding the early recognition of the four Gospels. In the early 200's, Origen clarified the church's opinion of the other so-called "gospels," including the *Gospel of Thomas*:

> I know a certain gospel which is called *The Gospel according to Thomas*, and a *Gospel according to Matthias*, and many others have we read—lest we should in any way be considered ignorant.... Nevertheless, among these, we have approved solely what the church has recognized, which is that only the four gospels should be accepted.[28]

It is worthwhile to note again that Origen was writing in the early third century, still at a time when Christianity was illegal, Christians were being cruelly persecuted for their beliefs, and the church had not yet been corrupted by political power.

EARLY RECOGNITION OF OTHER NEW TESTAMENT BOOKS

The Muratorian fragment of AD 170 also helps us understand whether the rest of the New Testament documents were considered worthy of a place in the armarion at the time. In addition to the four Gospels, it lists all thirteen of Paul's epistles as accepted by the churches, as well as Acts, Jude, the epistles of John,[29] and Revelation (referred to as the "Apocalypse of John").[30] Only four New Testament books are not mentioned in the Muratorian fragment: First and Second Peter, James, and Hebrews.

In its comments on two books in particular, the *Apocalypse of Peter* and the *Shepherd of Hermas*, the Muratorian fragment is particularly helpful to our understanding of how the second-century Christian churches decided which texts to read in public services. The author claims that some churches "are not willing" to read the *Apocalypse of Peter* in services, suggesting that one criterion for acceptance was how widely a document was being read among the various Christian congregations, a criterion that has been termed *catholicity*. The author also mentions that the *Shepherd of Hermas* was composed "very recently, in our own times" and "cannot be read publicly to the people in church either among the Prophets, whose number is complete, or among the Apostles, for it is after [their] time."[31]

Thus, the Muratorian fragment confirms that twenty-three of the twenty-seven books of the New Testament were recognized as authoritative by approximately AD 170. Metzger summarizes the evidence:

> It should be observed that the tone of the whole treatise is not so much that of legislation but of explanatory statement concerning a more or less established condition of things, with only a single instance of a difference of opinion among members of the Church catholic (namely, the use to be made of the *Apocalypse of Peter*). The exclusive validity of the four Gospels, with not so much as a passing reference to the apocryphal [noncanonical] gospels even by way of rejecting them, is perfectly apparent.[32]

In other words, the author of the Muratorian fragment was not presenting his personal opinion about what should or should not be accepted by the church. He was simply providing a summary of the documents that had been widely accepted already.

There is plenty of even earlier evidence from the late first century and the first half of the second century that the Christian church had already recognized much of the modern-day New Testament as authoritative. Three main church fathers—Clement of Rome, Polycarp of Smyrna, and Ignatius of Antioch—quoted from large portions of the New Testament in their writings.

Because these leaders had connections with the original apostles of Jesus, they are often called *apostolic fathers*. Clement, who was the bishop of Rome from AD 88 to 99, is reported to have known the apostle Peter.[33] Polycarp was the bishop of Smyrna in the first half of the second century and had known the apostle John, as his most famous student, Irenaeus, stated. Polycarp had also known many others who had seen and heard Jesus.[34] Ignatius (c. 35-110) was also a student of the apostle John.[35]

There is also early historical evidence that Peter appointed Ignatius to his position as bishop of Antioch.[36]

The only New Testament writings to which these apostolic fathers did not refer are Mark, Second Peter, Second and Third John, and Jude.[37] While it is surprising that they did not quote from Mark, his Gospel is widely recognized as the earliest Gospel, resembles the Gospel of Matthew, and is included among the four Gospels in many early lists. Therefore, Mark was still considered an authoritative Gospel very early, even though the three apostolic fathers do not cite it.

Clement, Polycarp, and Ignatius were also careful to distinguish between their own writings and the apostolic writings, which they considered inspired. Note that these early church fathers were already quoting from documents that they accepted as authoritative long before the Gnostic documents of the Nag Hammadi Library had even been composed.

Therefore, by the time the Roman emperor Constantine converted to Christianity and legalized its practice throughout the Empire at the beginning of the fourth century, there had been a general consensus on the authority of the same twenty-seven books, although there were still debates over a few, most notably James, Second Peter, Second and Third John, and Jude.[38]

Based on this evidence, it takes a very big leap in logic to make the claim that the canon was shaped by the political agenda of Constantine and the powerful bishops of the newly legalized Christian church. The historical record simply does not support this view. While Constantine did play an important part in the decision to close the canon and settle the remaining disputes about a few books, the canon had already been established to a large extent for more than a hundred years. Constantine simply encouraged the church to make the existing canon official.

Constantine, the Council of Nicaea, and the Deity of Jesus

Despite claims to the contrary, Jesus' deity was an early Christian doctrine, not a later invention, as we have covered in previous chapters. A quick overview may be helpful at this point. The creed in Paul's letter to the Philippians states that Jesus was "in very nature God."[39] The earliest Christian statement of faith, "Jesus Christ is Lord," uses the term *kyrios* for Jesus, the same term applied to God in the *Septuagint*, the Greek translation of the Old Testament. And the evidence from text criticism demonstrates that the four Gospels—not to mention the rest of the New Testament—haven't been altered over the centuries to make Jesus out to be God. Furthermore, early second-century non-Christian historical documents—such as Pliny the Younger's claim that Christians sing hymns "to Christ, as to a god" and Lucian of Samosata's description of Christians as "worshiping a man"—confirm that Jesus was worshiped as God by his followers.

While we can dismiss the claims that Jesus' deity was a late invention and that other noncanonical documents made Jesus to be just a man, it is true that one of the primary purposes of the Council of Nicaea in AD 325 was to officially clarify the church's position on the relationship between Jesus and God the Father. This does not mean, however, that it was an invention for the sake of political power. The need for this clarification arose when a Christian named Arius began to argue that Jesus was not God, but a special created being—higher than humans, yes, but not divine. Arius believed Jesus shared a *"similar* substance" (*homoiousios* in Greek) with God, while the church had long held that Jesus was the *"same* substance" (*homoousios*) as God.

Because the Bible clearly states that there is only one God, Arius believed Jesus could not possibly also be God, but must have been created by God. Therefore, if Arius was right, Jesus hadn't existed for all time. The church, however, had always maintained that Jesus had always existed, and therefore, that Jesus and God the Father were of the same substance. This doctrine of the Trinity, though mysterious, has been a tenet of Christianity since the beginning.

In order to bring cohesion to churches throughout the Empire, Constantine convened the Council of Nicaea in 325 (still early enough that the church hadn't been corrupted by power) to discuss the dispute and to reach a consensus among all of the bishops. Of the several hundred bishops in attendance, only two voted in favor of Arius' beliefs. The rest voted to maintain the traditionally held belief that Jesus was God, not a created being.[40] Far from being close, as our fictional Sir Leigh Teabing maintained, the vote was a landslide in favor of the full deity of Jesus.[41]

The Council of Nicaea provided the first summary of the core beliefs of Christianity. We call their statement the Nicene Creed, which is often recited by Christian congregations even today. However, neither the Council of Nicaea nor the influential bishop Athanasius *created* the

CHAPTER 15: TRUSTING THE SELECTION

New Testament canon; these leaders were recognizing the authenticity of established beliefs, in the same way that an expert recognizes a real dollar bill over a forgery.

Based on his own long career comparing the canonical and noncanonical documents, New Testament professor Craig Evans encourages his own students to decide for themselves if the early church was wise in its recognition of the canon. He writes: "When students ask me why certain Gospels were omitted from the canon of the New Testament and whether some of them ought to be included, I tell them to read these Gospels. They do, and that answers their question."[42]

When scholars dismiss the first-century New Testament documents as biased and untrustworthy and instead insist that the New Testament should have included documents that were composed much later outside of Jesus' home of Palestine, the anti-traditional bias that drives their research is exposed for all to see. Upon close scrutiny of the historical record, it turns out that the documents that give us the most accurate picture of Jesus and his teachings are the ones contained in the New Testament. We owe the early Christians a debt of gratitude for fighting the battle to make it that way.

We now turn to the most important question of all, because a negative answer renders moot all discussions up to this point: Did Jesus really rise from the dead?

QUESTIONS FOR COMPREHENSION AND DISCUSSION

1. What do skeptics accuse the emperor Constantine and the bishop Athanasius of doing that significantly altered the selection of the New Testament canon?
2. How did the early churches store the manuscripts that they received as copies from other churches? How does their respectful treatment of the scrolls and codices demonstrate the importance they placed on which books they cared for and read in their services?
3. Describe the situation in the middle of the second century, when new documents started circulating?

4. What is *apostolicity*, and how did it determine whether a document was read in a church service or not?
5. Describe the evidence that the four gospels of Matthew, Mark, Luke, and John had already been generally accepted as the official stories of Jesus' life and teachings by the end of the second century, more than one hundred years before the Council of Nicaea.
6. Of the twenty-seven books in the New Testament, how many had not yet been fully accepted by all churches by the end of the second century?
7. What is the Muratorian fragment, and what can we glean from it regarding the state of the canon in the second century?
8. What is *catholicity*, and how did it determine whether a document should be included in the official canon?
9. What was the theological issue concerning Jesus' relationship to God the Father that the Council of Nicaea was called to address? What was the result of the vote?
10. How has this chapter affected your feelings about the process that the early church leaders followed in order to hand down to us the New Testament that we have today? Can you concisely state the reasons they selected the twenty-seven books that comprise the New Testament?

CHAPTER 15 ENDNOTES

[1] Craig Blomberg, "The New Testament Canon," https://www.namb.net/apologetics-blog/the-new-testament-canon.
[2] Dan Brown, *The Da Vinci Code* (New York: Doubleday, 2003), 234.
[3] Ibid, 234.
[4] Arts & Entertainment Network, *Christianity: The First Thousand Years*, 1998.
[5] Elaine Pagels, *The Gnostic Gospels* (New York: Random House, 1999), xxxv.
[6] Bart Ehrman, *Misquoting Jesus: The Story Behind Who Changed the Bible and Why* (New York: HarperSanFrancisco, 2005), 36. Emphasis his.
[7] P. R. Ackroyd and C. F. Evans, eds., *The Cambridge History of the Bible (volume 1)* (Cambridge: Cambridge University Press, 1970), 308.
[8] H. Gregory Snyder, *Teachers and Texts in the Ancient World: Philosophers, Jews and Christians* (London: Routledge, 2000), 178.
[9] Martin Hengel, *Studies in the Gospel of Mark* (Eugene, OR: Wipf and Stock, 2003), 77-84.

CHAPTER 15: TRUSTING THE SELECTION

10   Timothy Paul Jones, *Misquoting Truth* (Downers Grove, IL: InterVarsity Press, 2007), 35.
11   Ibid, 36.
12   F. F. Bruce, *The Canon of Scripture* (Madison, WI: InterVarsity Press, 1988), 134-144.
13   Two early church fathers, Papias and Irenaeus, independently confirm this oral tradition. See Eusebius, *Church History*, 3.39.15. There is also abundant evidence in the Gospels that they were based on eyewitness testimony from the original disciples of Jesus, who played a prominent role in ensuring that the stories about Jesus were passed along intact throughout the early Christian churches before they were eventually put into writing. See Bauckham, *Jesus and the Eyewitnesses*.
14   Papias of Hierapolis, as quoted in Eusebius, *Church History* 3.39. Emphasis mine. Available online at http://www.newadvent.org/fathers/250103.htm. This translation (emphases mine) was from Richard Bauckham, *Jesus and the Eyewitnesses*, 15-16. Bauckham comments that his translation—apart from the first sentence and the translation of *parēkolouthēkōs tis* as "anyone who had been in attendance on"—was from J. B. Lightfoot, J. R. Harmer, and M. W. Holmes, *The Apostolic Fathers* (Leicester: Apollos, 1990), 314. The usual translation of *parēkolouthēkōs tis* is "anyone who had been a follower of," but Bauckham believes this translation is misleading and that the better translation of the verb *parakoloutheo* is to "go closely with, attend" rather than "come after." (See Bauckham, *Jesus and the Eyewitnesses*, 15f.)
15   Bauckham, *Jesus and the Eyewitnesses*, 21-30.
16   For a full defense of Papias, see Ibid, chapters 2, 9, and 16.
17   Tertullian of Carthage, as quoted in Eusebius, *Church History* 6.12. Available online at http://www.newadvent.org/fathers/250106.htm.
18   Jones, *Misquoting Truth*, 124.
19   Jenkins, *The Hidden Gospels*, 85.
20   Justin Martyr, *First Apology* 67.3. Available online at http://www.newadvent.org/fathers/0126.htm.
21   Bruce M. Metzger, *The Canon of the New Testament: Its Origin, Development, and Significance* (Oxford: Oxford University Press, 1987), 115.
22   Irenaeus, *Against Heresies*, 3.11.8. Available online at http://www.newadvent.org/fathers/0103311.htm.
23   Bruce, *The Canon of Scripture*, 175.
24   The possible exception was the Gospel of John, which some disliked because it contained mystical elements that they believed had Gnostic origins (Jenkins, *The Hidden Gospels*, 85.) However, according to F. F. Bruce, the Gospel of John was generally accepted in the second century by orthodox churches and heretics alike, with the exception of only one orthodox churchman, Gaius of

25. Timothy Paul Jones, *Misquoting Truth*, 127-131.
26. Jenkins, *The Hidden Gospels*, 85.
27. Metzger, *The Canon of the New Testament*, 195.
28. Origen, *Homily* on Luke 1:1.
29. The Muratorian Fragment mentions two epistles of John, which were probably First John and an epistle that was the combination of Second John and Third John (Jones, *Misquoting Truth*, 135).
30. The Muratorian fragment also includes a book called *The Wisdom of Solomon*, which the Roman Catholic Church, the Eastern Orthodox Church, the Oriental Orthodox Church, and the Assyrian Church of the East include in the Old Testament. It is considered apocryphal by Protestant churches.
31. For the text of the Muratorian Fragment, see http://www.earlychristianwritings.com/text/muratorian-metzger.html.
32. Metzger, *The Canon of the New Testament*, 200.
33. This is recorded in the biography of Clement in Liber Pontificalis. See Raymond Davis, *The Book of Pontiffs (Liber Pontificalis)*. Second Edition. (Liverpool: University of Liverpool Press, 2000).
34. See Irenaeus, *Against Heresies* 3.1.1 and 3.11.8-9, in Alexander Roberts and James Donaldson, eds., *The Ante-Nicene Fathers*, reprint ed. (Grand Rapids, MI: Eerdmans, 1978-1980). Available online at http://www.newadvent.org/fathers/0103301.htm and http://www.newadvent.org/fathers/0103311.htm. For a defense of Irenaeus' claims, see Bauckham, *Jesus and the Eyewitnesses*, 35, 295-6.
35. From *The Martyrdom of Ignatius*, available online at http://www.newadvent.org/fathers/0123.htm.
36. Theodoret, *Dialogue I—The Immutable*, I, iv, 33a. Available online at http://www.newadvent.org/fathers/27031.htm.
37. Milton Fisher, "The Canon of the New Testament," in *The Origin of the Bible*, Philip Wesley Comfort, ed. (Wheaton, IL: Tyndale House Publishers, 1992), 70.
38. Fisher, "The Canon of the New Testament," 74.
39. Philippians 2:6.
40. Schaff's *History of the Christian Church, Volume III, Nicene and Post-Nicene Christianity*, 120. The Council of Nicaea, 325. Available online at http://www.ccel.org/ccel/schaff/hcc3.iii.xii.iv.html.
41. Warren H. Carroll, *The Building of Christendom, Vol. II* (West Chester, PA: Christendom Press, 1987), 12.
42. Craig A. Evans, *Fabricating Jesus* (Downers Grove, IL: InterVarsity Press, 2006), 98-99.

Faith does not mean a leap in the dark, an irrational credulity, a believing against evidences and against reason. It means believing in the light of historical facts, consistent with the evidences, on the basis of witnesses. It would be impossible to believe in the resurrection of Jesus apart from the historical facts of His death, His burial, and the witness of his disciples.

—George E. Ladd, theologian[1]

But Christians are not merely hoping for some consolation for the life we have lost. [We] look toward the restoration of the life we wanted but never had. The resurrected Jesus was not a phantom, and neither shall we be. He received a new body, and so shall we.... You will not simply get your life back, but you will get the life you always longed for but never were able to achieve.

—Timothy Keller, pastor and author[2]

He Is Risen!

On a Sunday morning approximately two thousand years ago, an angel allegedly appeared to some women at the tomb where Jesus of Nazareth had been buried. According to Matthew, the angel gave this message to the women:

> "Do not be afraid, for I know that you are looking for Jesus, who was crucified. He is not here; he has risen, just as he said. Come and see the place where he lay. Then go quickly and tell his disciples: 'He has risen from the dead and is going ahead of you into Galilee. There you will see him.' Now I have told you."[3]

Though they differ in their secondary details, the other Gospel writers corroborate this story. And, according to Matthew, Luke, John, and the Book of Acts,[4] Jesus *did* meet the disciples in Galilee, ate with them, and allowed them to touch his scars. He had been *physically* raised from the dead, his followers steadfastly claimed, even to the point of death. They took pains to clarify that it was not merely a spiritual or symbolic resurrection.

Many people assume that this is a clever tale, spun by the creative imaginations of mortal men, the byproduct of a deep ache for something beyond this short life of toil, pain, suffering, and sorrow. The resurrection of a dead man has all the makings of a blockbuster movie, complete with special effects, a heartfelt reunion of loved ones, the victory of good over evil, and a happy ending to conclude and engulf a series of huge disappointments.

CHAPTER 16: HE IS RISEN!

But is it really just a feel-good story to help us cope with life's difficulties? Does the Easter celebration in churches worldwide only amount to beautiful symbolism? Or was the physical resurrection of Jesus an actual historical event?

If Jesus really did rise bodily from the dead, there are enormous implications. Our fear of death is eradicated; we can join the taunt of the apostle Paul and the prophet Hosea: "Where, O death, is your victory? Where, O death, is your sting?"[5] If Jesus really did appear in a newly restored body after receiving torturous lashes and suffering the excruciating disfigurement of crucifixion, there is hope that our increasingly frail, debilitated, broken, wrinkled, and withering bodies can also be restored. There is hope that we will still be able to enjoy—for all eternity—the physical pleasures of this life, sensory stimuli that a mere bodiless spirit couldn't truly appreciate.

If the resurrection is true, then all the things that Jesus claimed to be—living water, the bread of life, the way, the truth, the life, the very Son of God[6]—are credible. And his claim to be ushering in a "kingdom" of perfect peace and justice may not be a pipe dream after all.

But—if Jesus did not come back to life, the entire foundation of the Christian faith crumbles. We may still have a beautiful symbol of new life to celebrate on Easter, and we may still have a set of moral rules to guide our lives, but any hope for eternal life after death is mere wishful thinking. Moreover, any confidence that good will defeat evil and justice will be done evaporates. In fact, we may as well forget all about the moral rules and live as we please. As Paul says:

> If Christ has not been raised, your faith is futile.... If only for this life we have hope in Christ, we are to be pitied more than all men.... If the dead are not raised, "Let us eat and drink, for tomorrow we die."[7]

Let's look again at the internal evidence (the New Testament accounts themselves) and the external evidence (other historical sources) for the truth of the Gospel accounts, this time focusing on the claim that the man called Jesus Christ came back to life. Though it contradicts the metaphysical views of the materialists, we will see that Jesus' actual, physical resurrection is the only plausible explanation for the historical evidence.

THE INTERNAL EVIDENCE

In his tome, *The Resurrection of the Son of God*, N. T. Wright gives a detailed presentation of the solid historical evidence that undergirds faith in the resurrection of Jesus. In the first 583 pages (out of nearly 800), he provides a meticulous overview of the variety of beliefs in the ancient world with regard to the afterlife, demonstrating that no human being at the turn of the first century—Jewish, Greek, Roman, Egyptian, Syrian, or of any other nationality—expected that a man would come back from the grave in the middle of history in a newly restored, *physical* body.[8] And yet, within a few days, thousands of Jews and Gentiles (non-Jews) came to believe just such a thing had happened. How could this be? Wright argues that the only plausible explanation for this belief to become so widespread so quickly—the only explanation for the explosive birth of the Christian church—is that people, crazy as it sounds, *really did* see the risen Jesus and gave convincing testimony to others about their experiences.

Beyond this unexpected, overnight claim that Jesus had risen physically from the dead, Wright also presents four main surprising features that characterize the resurrection narratives, features that indicate these stories were not fabrications, but instead represented early eyewitness testimony of events that actually happened.

The first surprising feature is that there is little commentary embedded in the resurrection narratives. They are, as Wright says, "biblically unadorned."[9] Throughout the other parts of the Gospel accounts, the authors felt free to interpret the events of Jesus' life and ministry in light of Old Testament prophecies and their Jewish worldview. But this type of biblical interpretation is surprisingly not present in the resurrection stories.

Wright describes the stories prior to the resurrection in this way: "The evangelists told their stories up to this point... with a persistent build-up of scriptural quotation, allusion, reference and echo."[10] For example, Matthew often inserted phrases such as, "All this took place to fulfill what the Lord had said through the prophet...."[11] But these types of statements are curiously absent in Matthew's resurrection narratives. Not only that, they are not present in any of the other biblical resurrection narratives. We'll discuss the implications of this unexpected and strange absence shortly.

The second curious feature of the resurrection stories is their failure to comment on what Jesus' resurrection meant for his followers. The Gospel narratives never answer questions such as: Will those who believe in Jesus also be resurrected? Does Jesus' resurrection mean his followers will have eternal life? The resurrection narratives in the Gospels stand out in stark contrast to the letters of Paul, especially 1 Corinthians 15 and Romans 8, in which Paul thumbs his nose at death and expounds on the hope that believers have because they can look forward to a bodily resurrection just like Jesus'.

As Wright notes, "The significant thing to notice here is this: neither 'going to heaven when you die', 'life after death', 'eternal life', nor even 'the resurrection of all Christ's people', is so much as mentioned in the four canonical resurrection stories. If Matthew, Mark, Luke, and John wanted to tell stories whose import was 'Jesus is risen, therefore you will be too', they have done a remarkably bad job of it."[12] Since one of the main objectives of any invented story about Jesus' resurrection would have been to promote Christianity and attract believers, especially given that at the time they were being put to death for their faith, you would expect these types of "you-too-can-live-forever" statements throughout the resurrections accounts. But they aren't there.

The third surprising feature of the resurrection narratives is that they portray the risen Jesus in an unusual, completely unexpected way—a way that is inconsistent with the Jewish Scriptures. Rather than depicting him as a radiant heavenly being coming on the clouds, like the visionary "son of man" figure that the prophet Daniel saw,[13] the resurrection accounts depict the risen Jesus as a human being interacting with his fellow human beings. Rather than shining "like the brightness of the heavens," as resurrected individuals are portrayed by Daniel in the end times,[14] Jesus eats broiled fish[15] and invites people to touch him to see that he is real.[16]

Jesus' risen body has bizarre properties that no one would have expected, especially after studying what the Jewish Scriptures had to say about resurrection. Jesus could appear and disappear at will.[17] And his appearance was somehow altered; those who met him did not, at first, recognize him.[18]

Wright uses the word "transphysical" to describe the resurrected Jesus. That is, he had a physical body, but it wasn't quite like the typical human body. Because the description of the resurrected Jesus was so strange and unexpected, it is unlikely that the early church would have invented it. Wright makes the point as follows:

> If, as the consensus view has tended to say, these stories developed as the church pondered scripture and expressed and re-expressed its faith, we should have expected the resurrection stories to reflect the kind of things that the favourite 'resurrection' passages in the Old Testament had been saying. But they do not....They are not, that is, the sort of thing one would expect if the evangelists or their sources had wanted to say that Jesus had been exalted to a position of either divinity or heavenly glory.[19]

Interestingly, the Gospels' unexpected depiction of Jesus' risen body—one that is like ours, yet somehow different—fits well with Paul's understanding of things to come. In his first letter to the Corinthians, the apostle declares that someday "the dead will be raised imperishable, and we will be changed. For the perishable must clothe itself with the imperishable, and the mortal with immortality."[20] Paul didn't get this idea of a transformed embodiment—a "transphysicality"—from the Jewish Scriptures. So, where did he get it? Did he invent it out of thin air, or was he describing something that the original eyewitnesses had described to him?

The fourth surprising feature of the resurrection accounts, as we explored in Chapter 6, is that women were the first witnesses of the empty tomb. Interestingly, while Paul excludes the women from his own list of eyewitnesses in 1 Corinthians 15:3-8, all four canonical Gospels, which were written after Paul's letters, claim that women were the first to discover that Jesus' body was missing from the tomb. Why insert the detail about the women if it didn't serve your purpose, unless, of course, the women really were the first to discover the empty tomb?

Wright explains why stating that women were the first witnesses is so unusual:

> It is, frankly, impossible to imagine that they were inserted into the tradition after Paul's day.... Even if we suppose that Mark made up most of his material, and

did so some time in the late 60s at the earliest, it will not do to have him, or anyone else at that stage, making up a would-be apologetic legend about an empty tomb and *having women be the ones who find it*. The point has been repeated over and over in scholarship, but its full impact has not always been felt: women were simply not acceptable as legal witnesses. We may regret it, but this is how the Jewish world (and most others) worked.[21]

So, why would the Gospel resurrection accounts list women as the first witnesses, especially since the tradition that Paul quoted in his letter to the Corinthians excluded them? The most likely answer, according to Wright, is that the resurrection stories as recounted in the four Gospels go back to a time *before* Paul wrote in the 40s and 50s, "before anyone had time to think, 'It would be good to tell stories about Jesus rising from the dead; what will best serve our apologetic needs?'"[22]

To summarize these four curious features of the canonical resurrection narratives:

1. The stories of Jesus' resurrection are not adorned with biblical quotations or commentary.
2. They don't expound on the hope that Jesus' resurrection gives believers.
3. They don't describe the risen Jesus in a way that reflects resurrection passages in the Jewish Scriptures, but instead give him a strange, completely unexpected, "transphysical" quality.
4. They don't try to suppress the embarrassing detail that the first witnesses of the empty tomb were women.

There are only two possible historical explanations: either these stories are fabrications, or they are true. Let's weigh these two options to see which requires the "shortest leap" of faith.

The first historical explanation is that the early church invented these resurrection stories. As Wright explains, this option requires that Matthew, Luke, and John based their accounts of the risen Jesus on Paul's unprecedented description of the resurrected body—"of human bodies being neither abandoned to rot, nor yet resuscitated into the identical sort of condition they were in before, but somehow transformed, so that they are puzzlingly the same and yet different."[23]

That is, because this belief in a "transphysical resurrection body" did not derive from the expectations of the Messiah as laid out in the Jewish Scriptures, Paul must have invented it, and Matthew, Luke, and John subsequently based their resurrection accounts on Paul's invention. Then, Matthew, Luke, and John turn this "theology of transphysicality" into three completely different accounts of the risen Jesus: Matthew's account of Jesus appearing on a mountain and giving the "Great Commission" to his followers,[24] Luke's account of Jesus appearing to two men on the road to Emmaus and then to the eleven disciples,[25] and John's account of Jesus cooking breakfast on the lakeshore and speaking to Peter.[26] In Wright's words, the three accounts of the risen Jesus "show no sign of mutual influence, but... all possess this same, strange, like-and-yet-not-quite-like characteristic."[27]

Moreover, if the Gospel resurrection accounts were invented and were based on Paul's resurrection theology, how do they somehow avoid any analysis of the resurrected embodiment, but instead describe the risen Jesus in a way that most hearers would find perplexing? If you were making up a story to convince people that Jesus had risen again and had been "exalted," why even mention that some people didn't recognize him? Why would you have Mary Magdalene at first mistake the risen Jesus for a gardener?[28] Why emphasize how normal Jesus' body appeared, such that it could eat and be touched, and then immediately describe it in a way that contradicts normal experience, such as that he entered the room through a wall?[29] What's more, if these stories were written to convince people that Jesus was the fulfillment of Old Testament prophecy concerning the Messiah, why would they never allude to any Old Testament prophecy or describe the risen Jesus in a way that was consistent with Jewish expectations of what a resurrected body might look like?

All of these questions point to the implausibility of the first historical option, which Wright summarizes as follows:

> If, as a first-century Bible-reading writer, you started with Paul's theology, or indeed that of Revelation or Ignatius, and tried to turn that theology of resurrection into an artful, just-as-if-it-happened-yesterday sort

of narrative, it would be extremely difficult to avoid reference to scripture. If you try to imagine three such people doing it independently and coming up with three different stories which nevertheless all share this remarkable feature, in addition to the others we have noted, I think you will find it incredible. I certainly do.[30]

But then there is the opposing explanation: these narratives record what actually happened, as reported by the original eyewitnesses of the risen Jesus. Wright offers the following challenge:

[Suppose] Paul was providing a theoretical, theological and biblical framework for stories which were already well known—stories which, indeed, he is summarizing when he quotes an already official formula at the start of 1 Corinthians 15. Supposing the stories in Matthew, Luke and John— though almost certainly not written down until after Paul had dictated his last letter—were what they were, not because they were a late writing up, or wholesale invention, of what post-Pauline Christians thought ought to have happened, but precisely because they were not. What if they represented, with only light editing, the stories that had been told very early on, without offering theories about what sort of a thing this new, risen body might be, without attempting (except at the level of minor adjustments) to evoke wider theological themes, without adding the element of hope for one's own resurrection, and in particular without the biblical quotations or allusions that might have done for these stories what was done for so many, so recently in the same books. Supposing the reason nobody evoked Daniel 12 in the Easter stories was that everybody knew that the risen body of Jesus had not shone like a star? Supposing, wider, that the reason nobody evoked the Old Testament in the gospel accounts of the resurrection was that there was no immediately apparent point of connection between resurrection and the narratives in Jewish tradition? Supposing, in other words, that these stories have the puzzled air of someone saying, "I didn't understand it at the time, and I'm not sure I do now, but this is more or less how it was."[31]

The most plausible historical explanation is that these stories stem from accounts from those who had seen and interacted with Jesus after his resurrection. Rather than fabricating the "transphysical" nature of his resurrected body, the Gospels simply record the strange characteristics of the risen Jesus, as described by those who had seen him, touched him, eaten with him, and otherwise interacted with him. These eyewitnesses did not concern themselves with theological explanations, fulfillments of Scriptures, probable implications, or potential negative ramifications on the credibility of their stories down the road. They simply reported "how it was."

One final quote from N. T. Wright serves to drive home the point:

> The very strong historical probability is that, when Matthew, Luke and John describe the risen Jesus, they are writing down very early oral tradition, representing three different ways in which the original astonished participants told the stories. These traditions have received only minimal development, and most of that probably at the final editorial stage, for the very good reason that stories as earth-shattering as this, stories as community-forming as this, once told, are not easily modified. Too much depends on them.[32]

These accounts have the mysterious air of stories told by the bewildered and stunned individuals who had experienced the risen Jesus. Plus, it is incredibly unlikely that three separate writers would concoct different stories that were so consistent in this unexpected description of Jesus' "transphysical" body.

We now turn to the external evidence supporting the historicity of the resurrection. Once again, we will see that the most plausible explanation—the shortest leap to truth—is that Jesus really did come back to life after his crucifixion and burial.

THE FIVE "MINIMAL FACTS"

Theologians Gary Habermas and Michael Licona aim to cut to the chase of the debate by using what they call the "minimal facts approach." In their book, *The Case for the Resurrection of Jesus*, they boil down the historical data to five key facts, the truth of which is rarely disputed by experts in the field. In other words, with respect to the historical truthfulness of these five "minimal facts," there is consensus among the majority of New Testament scholars—including the most skeptical, even atheistic, critics.[33]

The first universally accepted fact is that Jesus died by crucifixion. The non-Christian sources that we covered in Chapter 10 attest to the crucifixion of Jesus: The Jewish historian Josephus records that Jesus was crucified under Pilate.[34] The Roman historian Tacitus writes that "Christus... suffered the extreme penalty [crucifixion] during the reign of Tiberius at the hands of one of our procurators, Pontius Pilate."[35] Lucian of Samosata writes that Christians "worship a man to this day—the distinguished personage who introduced their novel rites, and was crucified on that account."[36] The earliest portion of the Jewish Talmud also mentions that "on the Eve of the Passover Yeshu was hanged."[37] (By way of reminder, "Yeshu" is the Hebrew equivalent of "Jesus," and the term "hanged" was used to describe crucifixion in ancient times.) Even the most skeptical New Testament scholars agree that Jesus died by crucifixion. John Dominic Crossan of the Jesus Seminar writes, "That he was crucified is as sure as anything historical can ever be."[38] James Tabor, another scholar who is skeptical of the resurrection, admits: "I think we need have no doubt that given execution by Roman crucifixion he was truly dead."[39]

The second minimal fact is that the disciples truly believed that Jesus appeared to them after his crucifixion. This does not prove that Jesus really did appear to them, of course, and skeptical scholars postulate that the disciples must have experienced a vision of Jesus. There are two main reasons for the broad consensus among New Testament scholars that the disciples truly believed they saw Jesus: First, multiple early sources demonstrate that the disciples boldly made the claim that they saw him after his resurrection. Second, multiple early sources confirm that the disciples were transformed overnight from dejected cowards to bold martyrs. They went from denying that they even knew Jesus to steadfastly proclaiming that he was alive again, even though such a proclamation led them to imprisonment, torture, and death.

There are at least nine early, independent sources which demonstrate that the disciples themselves—not later Christian leaders—declared that Jesus had risen from the dead.[40] There are at least seven early, independent sources which demonstrate that the disciples were willing to suffer and die for their belief that Jesus had risen from the dead.[41] There are four additional early sources which confirm that the apostles Paul and James (Jesus' brother) also suffered and died for their belief that Jesus had risen from the dead.[42]

These people may have been hallucinating, but they definitely saw something convincing, and their belief was so strong that they were willing to die for it. Skeptical New Testament scholar Paula Fredriksen puts it this way:

> I know in their own terms what they saw was the raised Jesus. That's what they say and then all the historic evidence we have afterwards attest to their conviction that that's what they saw. I'm not saying that they really did see the raised Jesus. I wasn't there. I don't know what they saw. But I do know as a historian that they must have seen something.[43]

Although New Testament scholar and professed atheist Gerd Lüdemann believes the disciples saw a vision of the risen Jesus, he concurs that they definitely saw something: "It may be taken as historically certain that Peter and the disciples had experiences after Jesus' death in which Jesus appeared to them as the risen Christ."[44] Gary Habermas did a study of more than 1,400 recent scholarly publications concerning the resurrection of Jesus, and one of the study's main conclusions was that "no fact is more widely recognized than that early Christian believers had real experiences that they thought were appearances of the risen Jesus."[45] If even the scholars who deny the supernatural agree that this is a historical fact, we can be confident that the disciples really did believe and proclaim that they had seen the risen Jesus.

The third minimal fact that virtually all New Testament scholars grant is this: a man named Saul of Tarsus had an experience in which he claims the risen Jesus appeared to him, and after this experience,

CHAPTER 16: HE IS RISEN!

he went immediately from violently persecuting Christians to ardently proclaiming the truth of their message. After his conversion, Saul's name was changed to Paul, and he became one of the most influential and outspoken messengers of the Christian faith, even though he suffered greatly and was eventually killed for his beliefs. He wrote a testimony of his conversion in three different letters, those to the churches of Corinth, Galatia, and Philippi.[46] To the first, he describes what he willingly endured:

> I have worked much harder, been in prison more frequently, been flogged more severely, and been exposed to death again and again. Five times I received from the Jews the forty lashes minus one. Three times I was beaten with rods, once I was stoned, three times I was shipwrecked, I spent a night and a day in the open sea, I have been constantly on the move. I have been in danger from rivers, in danger from bandits, in danger from my own countrymen, in danger from Gentiles; in danger in the city, in danger in the country, in danger at sea; and in danger from false brothers. I have labored and toiled and have often gone without sleep; I have known hunger and thirst and have often gone without food; I have been cold and naked. Besides everything else, I face daily the pressure of my concern for all the churches.[47]

Paul left a comfortable life as a successful Pharisee for this discomfort, and why? Paul would explain that it was because Jesus appeared to him and convincingly demonstrated to him that he was God.

In the extension of his "orderly account," the Book of Acts, the detail-oriented Luke confirms Paul's story.[48] According to Luke's carefully researched account, here are the words Jesus himself used to describe Paul's purpose: "This man [Paul] is my chosen instrument to proclaim my name to the Gentiles and their kings and to the people of Israel. I will show him how much he must suffer for my name."[49] Luke describes how Paul originally persecuted Christians, was converted when he saw the risen Jesus, and subsequently proclaimed the resurrection even in the face of numerous death threats, imprisonment, and tremendous suffering.[50] Even though Acts ends when Paul is under house arrest in

Rome, we know from other early historians that he was beheaded under the emperor Nero.[51]

Why would a man who was formerly a powerful and respected Jewish religious leader lose all of his status by converting? His story—that he personally saw the risen Jesus—provides the most logical answer.

Historians in the field agree on a fourth minimal fact: the conversion of James, one of Jesus' brothers, as a result of his own experience of the risen Jesus. All four Gospels, along with Acts, 1 Corinthians, and Galatians corroborate the fact that Jesus had four younger brothers (James, Judas, Joseph, and Simon), as well as younger sisters who were unnamed.[52] The Gospels mention that Jesus' brothers did not believe that he was the Messiah, and even believed he was "out of his mind."[53] The principle of embarrassment gives us confidence that Jesus' brothers really believed that Jesus was not who he claimed to be. Why would the authors of the Gospels mention this if it weren't really true, since it could only hurt their cause? We also know from an early source that James had been a very strict and pious Jew, the least likely candidate for conversion to Christianity.[54]

Writing at the end of the first century, the Jewish historian Josephus confirms that the Jewish court sentenced James to death by stoning because of his heretical belief in Jesus,[55] and two other early historians confirm this fact.[56] Why would a devout Jew like James convert? Jews believed that God cursed anyone who was crucified; consequently, a crucified man could never be the Messiah.[57] A devout Jew like James would only be further convinced that his brother was *not* the Messiah following his crucifixion, but instead he joined the movement and remained a committed follower even though it led to his execution.

One plausible explanation: The creed that Paul included in his letter to the Corinthians lists James among the people to whom Jesus appeared after his burial. Even the skeptical scholar Reginald Fuller claims that without the creed, "we should have to invent" the appearance of Jesus to James in order to explain why a pious, skeptical Jew would become the head of the first Christian church—in Jerusalem, the beloved center of Judaism.[58]

The fifth minimal fact is the empty tomb. While New Testament scholars universally accept the previous four facts—liberal and critical, atheistic and theistic—the empty tomb doesn't enjoy the same universal acceptance. However, only 25% of New Testament scholars do not believe that Jesus' tomb was empty.[59] Though there is not universal agreement regarding the empty tomb, the 75% of scholars who do support its historicity base their reasoning on the following three lines of evidence.

First, Jesus died in Jerusalem, and the Christian church began in Jerusalem. If the body was still in the tomb, all that Jesus' enemies needed to do to extinguish the Jesus movement was produce his corpse. But no corpse was ever found. Prominent German theologian Paul Althaus emphasizes that the resurrection "could not have been maintained in Jerusalem for a single day, for a single hour, if the emptiness of the tomb had not been established as a fact for all concerned."[60]

Second, rather than produce the body, Jesus' enemies allegedly asserted that the disciples had stolen it.[61] By asserting this, they were obviously implying that the body was not in the tomb. If Jesus' body had been thrown into a mass grave or had been left for wild animals to devour, as some skeptical scholars claim, the enemies of the Jesus movement would have been all too happy to circulate this fact. Considering the uproar that Jesus had caused, you would think at least someone had seen his body being devoured or dumped. But there is no evidence that anyone had.

And third, as we have mentioned several times already because it is so surprising, the Gospels each record that women were the first to discover the empty tomb, an embarrassing admission in a society where the testimony of women wasn't even accepted in court.[62] In those days, no author would concoct a story he wanted people to believe and describe frenetic, emotional women as the ones to first discover that Jesus' body was missing from his tomb.

The evidence in favor of the empty tomb is so strong that the Oxford University church historian William Wand wrote:

> All the strictly historical evidence we have is in favor of [the empty tomb], and those scholars who reject it ought to recognize that they do so on some other ground than that of scientific history.[63]

The empty tomb is an important piece of historical evidence demonstrating that the appearances of the risen Jesus were more than mere visions or hallucinations. In fact, there is only one plausible explanation for all five minimal facts: Jesus actually rose from the dead.

In the next chapter, we'll take a look at how skeptics have attempted to explain the five minimal facts, and you'll see that none of the alternative explanations can adequately account for all five historical facts. The only historically plausible explanation—though it requires the existence of the supernatural realm—is the resurrection.

Questions for Comprehension and Discussion

1. What are the implications for humanity if Jesus really did rise again from the dead in a transformed, physical body?
2. Why are Christians to be pitied more than all others, as Paul writes, if Jesus really did not rise from the dead? What is the point of being a Christian if the resurrection didn't happen?
3. Why did N. T. Wright spend more than 500 pages describing his research into the many cultures at the turn of the first century? What did he find regarding their beliefs regarding the transformed bodily resurrection of a single dead person in the middle of history?
4. How can we account for the fact that the worldview of so many people changed so dramatically overnight once the stories of Jesus' resurrection started to circulate?
5. What are the four "surprise features" of the resurrection stories in the four Gospels, according to N. T. Wright?
6. Why are these four features more consistent with a historically accurate, eyewitness account of Jesus' resurrection, rather than with the claim that the resurrection stories were invented?
7. What are the "five minimal facts" that virtually all New Testament scholars, atheist and traditional alike, agree upon?
8. What are the secular historical sources that make scholars confident that Jesus really died by crucifixion?
9. Why can we trust what the New Testament documents say about the overnight transformation of the disciples, as well as Paul's and Jesus' brother James' conversions?
10. Describe the three lines of evidence that demonstrate that there was no body in Jesus' tomb beginning the Sunday after his burial.

CHAPTER 16 ENDNOTES

1. George Eldon Ladd, *I Believe in the Resurrection* (Grand Rapids, MI: Eerdmans, 1975).
2. Timothy Keller, *Making Sense of God: Finding God in the Modern World* (New York: Penguin Books, 2016), 171.
3. Matthew 28:5-7.
4. As discussed in Chapter 12, the earliest manuscripts of Mark's Gospel end at verse 8, after the women find the empty tomb and before the risen Jesus makes an appearance.
5. 1 Corinthians 15:55, paraphrasing Hosea 13:14.
6. See Matthew 27:43 and John 5:25, 6:35, 7:38, 11:26-27, 14:6, 19:7.
7. 1 Corinthians 15:17, 19, 32.
8. Note that the Jews did believe in a physical resurrection in the end times, but not in the middle of history. For example, the prophet Daniel describes how the "wise" will wake and "shine like stars" at the coming of the Messiah: "At that time Michael, the great prince who protects your people, will arise. There will be a time of distress such as has not happened from the beginning of nations until then. But at that time your people—everyone whose name is found written in the book—will be delivered. Multitudes who sleep in the dust of the earth will awake: some to everlasting life, others to shame and everlasting contempt. Those who are wise will shine like the brightness of the heavens, and those who lead many to righteousness, like the stars for ever and ever." (Daniel 12:1-3)
9. N. T. Wright, *The Resurrection of the Son of God* (Minneapolis: Fortress, 2003), 602.
10. Ibid, 600.
11. See, for example, Matthew 1:22, 3:15, 4:14, 5:17, 8:17, 12:17, and 21:4.
12. Wright, *The Resurrection of the Son of God*, 603.
13. See Daniel 7:13.
14. See Daniel 12:2-3.
15. See Luke 24:42-43.
16. See Luke 24:39 and John 20:27.
17. See John 20:19, 26.
18. For example, see John 20:15 with 16, 21:4 with 12, and Luke 24:15-16 with 31.
19. Wright, *The Resurrection of the Son of God*, 604-5.
20. 1 Corinthians 15:54.
21. Wright, *The Resurrection of the Son of God*, 607-8. Emphasis his.
22. Ibid, 608.
23. Ibid, 608-9.

24 Matthew 28:16-20.
25 Luke 24:13-49.
26 John 21.
27 Wright, *The Resurrection of the Son of God*, 609.
28 John 20:15.
29 See John 20:19 when Jesus appears in a room with the disciples even though the doors of the room had been locked.
30 Wright, *The Resurrection of the Son of God*, 610.
31 Ibid, 611.
32 Ibid.
33 Gary Habermas and Michael Licona, *The Case for the Resurrection of Jesus* (Grand Rapids, MI: Kregel, 2004), 43-131.
34 Josephus, *Antiquities* 18.6.4 *Josephus in Ten Volumes*, vol. 9, *Jewish Antiquities*, Loeb Classical Library, Louis H. Feldman, trans. (Cambridge, MA: Harvard University Press, 1981). Available online http://www.sacred-texts.com/jud/josephus/ant-18.htm.
35 Tacitus, *Annals* 15.44. Available in Latin at http://www.thelatinlibrary.com/tacitus/tac.ann15.shtml#44 and in English at http://classics.mit.edu/Tacitus/annals.mb.txt.
36 Lucian, *The Death of Peregrine*, 11-13, in *The Works of Lucian of Samosata*, transl. by H.W. Fowler and F.G. Fowler, 4 vols. (Oxford: Clarendon, 1949), vol. 4. Available online at http://www.sacred-texts.com/cla/luc/wl4/wl420.htm.
37 *The Babylonian Talmud*, transl. by I. Epstein (London: Soncino, 1935), vol. III, *Sanhedrin* 43a, 281.
38 John Dominic Crossan, *Jesus: A Revolutionary Biography* (San Francisco: HarperCollins, 1991), 145.
39 James Tabor, *Jesus Dynasty* (New York: Simon & Schuster, 2006), 230. Emphasis his.
40 The nine early sources that demonstrate the disciples proclaimed Jesus' resurrection are: First, the apostle Paul provided written testimony that the disciples claimed Jesus rose from the dead. Paul knew at least a few of the disciples, including Peter, James, and John, so he would have known what they proclaimed. In 1 Corinthians 15:11, Paul even states that the disciples—not just Paul himself—also proclaimed the truth of Jesus' resurrection. Second, early creeds, such as that in 1 Corinthians 15:3-8, provide testimony that the disciples proclaimed they had seen Jesus after his crucifixion. Third, sermon summaries from Acts (such as Acts 2) provide further early oral tradition demonstrating that the disciples proclaimed the resurrection of Jesus. Fourth, fifth, sixth, and seventh, the four Gospels each mention that the disciples saw Jesus after his death.

CHAPTER 16: HE IS RISEN!

Note that even if a scholar denies their divine inspiration, and even though they may contain bias, historians still consider these four documents early historical sources about Jesus. Eighth, the early church father, Clement of Rome (c. 30-100), who had been ordained as the bishop of Rome by the original disciple Peter, wrote that the disciples had "received complete certainty caused by the resurrection of our Lord Jesus Christ" (*First Clement* 42:3). Ninth, the early church father, Polycarp (c. 69-c. 155), who had been ordained by the original disciple John as bishop of Smyrna, wrote "For they did not love the present age, but him who died for our benefit and for our sake was raised by God." (*To the Philippians* 9:2) For further explanation of these sources, refer to Habermas and Licona, *The Case for the Resurrection of Jesus*, 49-62, along with the extensive accompanying endnotes.

41 The seven early sources that demonstrate that the disciples were willing to suffer and die for their belief that Jesus had risen from the dead are: First, the Book of Acts, written by Luke, attests to their willingness to suffer and die. Second, Clement of Rome (c. 30-100) writes, "The greatest and most righteous pillars have been persecuted and contended unto death." (*First Clement* 5:2) Third, Polycarp (c. 69-c. 155) writes to the church in Philippi that Paul and the rest of the apostles suffered together for their belief in Jesus' resurrection. Fourth, Ignatius, who was the bishop of Antioch in Syria at the end of the first century and beginning of the second, and who had known Polycarp and was therefore familiar with the apostles' teaching, confirmed that the disciples had touched Jesus when he appeared to them after rising from the dead, and that they were willing to die for him because they no longer feared death (*To the Smyrnaeans* 3:2). Fifth, Tertullian, an early church father at the end of the second century, recorded that Peter was crucified for his faith in Jesus and Paul was beheaded for his faith in Jesus, both during the reign of the Roman emperor Nero (AD 54-68). Sixth, the first church historian, Eusebius, records that Dionysius of Corinth wrote in approximately AD 170 that Paul and Peter had both been martyred for proclaiming the resurrection of Jesus. Seventh, Origen (c. 185-c. 254) was an early church father who wrote, "Jesus, who has both risen Himself, and led His disciples to believe in His resurrection, and so thoroughly persuaded them of its truth, that they show to all men by their sufferings how they are able to laugh at all the troubles of this life, beholding the life eternal and the resurrection clearly demonstrated to them in word and deed." (Origin, *Contra Celsum*, 2.77 in Roberts, Donaldson, and Coxe, eds. and trans., *The Ante-Nicene Fathers*). For further explanation of these sources, refer to Habermas and Licona, *The Case for the Resurrection of Jesus*, 49-62, along with the extensive accompanying endnotes.

42   The four additional sources that claim that Paul and James suffered and died for their belief in Jesus' resurrection are: First, the apostle Paul himself claims that he suffered for proclaiming the resurrection throughout his Epistles (see 1 Corinthians 15:30-32 and 2 Corinthians 11:22-29 for two examples). Second, the Jewish historian Josephus records that James, the brother of Jesus, was stoned for his faith in Jesus (*Antiquities* 20:9). Third, Hegesippus, writing around AD 165-175, records the martyrdom of James, as quoted by the church historian Eusebius. Fourth, Clement of Alexandria, writing around AD 200, also records the martyrdom of James, as quoted by Eusebius. For further explanation of these sources, refer to Habermas and Licona, *The Case for the Resurrection of Jesus*, 49-62, along with the extensive accompanying endnotes.

43   In an interview by Peter Jennings in *The Search for Jesus* (American Broadcasting Corp. [ABC], July 2000).

44   Gerd Lüdemann, *What Really Happened to Jesus? A Historical Approach to the Resurrection*, John Bowden, trans. (Louisville: Westminster John Knox, 1995), 80.

45   Habermas and Licona, *The Case for the Resurrection*, 60. The study was published in Gary R. Habermas, "Resurrection Research from 1975 to the Present: What Are Critical Scholars Saying?" *Journal for the Study of the Historical Jesus*, 3.2 (2005), pp. 135-153. Available online at http://www.garyhabermas.com/articles/J_Study_Historical_Jesus_3-2_2005/J_Study_Historical_Jesus_3-2_2005.htm.

46   See Paul's testimonies in 1 Corinthians 15:9-10, Galatians 1:12-16, 22-23, and Philippians 3:6-7.

47   2 Corinthians 11:23-28.

48   Acts 9:15b-16.

49   It is widely accepted that Luke, the doctor and Paul's traveling companion, is the author of the Acts of the Apostles and the Gospel of Luke and that Acts is a continuation of Luke's Gospel.

50   In Acts 7:58 through 8:1, Luke records that Paul (called Saul at the time) was present at the stoning of Stephen and gave his consent for his execution, the first Christian to die for his faith. In Acts 8:2-3, Saul began to persecute the church, dragging believers in Jesus from their homes and putting them in prison. In Acts 9, Luke records the story of Saul's conversion, which happened after he saw the risen Jesus on the road to Damascus. Paul's suffering for his beliefs in the risen Jesus are recounted throughout Acts: Acts 14:19 records that he was stoned to the point where his attackers thought he was dead. In Acts 16:19-24, Paul and Silas were stripped, beaten with rods, and severely flogged, then jailed with their feet fastened in stocks. In Acts 17:5, they were pursued by a mob. In Acts 21:27-36, a crowd

CHAPTER 16: HE IS RISEN!

<ol start="51">
<li value="50">tried to kill Paul, and a group of more than forty men vowed not to eat or drink until they kill Paul in Acts 23:12-35.</li>
<li>Eusebius of Caesarea, Lactantius, John Chrysostom, and Sulpicius Severus all record that Paul was beheaded during the reign of Nero.</li>
<li>The four brothers are listed by name in Matthew 13:55-56 and Mark 6:3. Jesus' siblings are also mentioned in Matthew 12:46-50; Mark 3:31-35; Luke 8:19-21; John 2:12, 7:3, 5, 10; Acts 1:13-14; 1 Corinthians 9:5; and Galatians 1:19.</li>
<li>See Mark 3:21, 31, 6:3-4, and John 7:5.</li>
<li>This comes from statements about James from the Christian chronicler, Hegesippus, writing in the second century. Even though the works of Hegesippus have been lost, Eusebius quotes Book 5 of Hegesippus' *Memoirs*, in which he describes James as a devout, law-abiding Jew. See Eusebius' *Church History* 2.23, available online at http://www.newadvent.org/fathers/250102.htm.</li>
<li>Josephus, *Antiquities* 20:9. Available online at http://www.sacred-texts.com/jud/josephus/ant-20.htm.</li>
<li>These two sources are Clement of Alexandria, who wrote about it in AD 200, and Hegesippus, who mentioned James' martyrdom in circa AD 165-175. Both sources are quoted by Eusebius in his *Church History* 2.1 and 2.23, available online at http://www.newadvent.org/fathers/250102.htm.</li>
<li>This comes from Deuteronomy 21:23b: "Anyone who is hung on a tree is under God's curse."</li>
<li>Reginald H. Fuller, *The Formation of the Resurrection Narratives* (New York: Macmillan, 1971), 37.</li>
<li>See Habermas and Licona, *The Case for the Resurrection of Jesus*, 70.</li>
<li>Paul Althaus, as cited in Wolfhart Pannenberg, *Jesus – God and Man*. Trans. by L.L. Wilkins and D.A. Priche (Philadelphia: Westminster Press, 1968), 100.</li>
<li>The claim that Jesus' disciples had stolen his body is recorded in Matthew 28:12-13. In *Trypho 108*, Justin Martyr wrote that this explanation for the empty tomb was still in circulation in the first half of the second century (available online at http://www.ccel.org/ccel/schaff/anf01.viii.iv.cviii.html). Tertullian also mentions that skeptics were using this explanation for the empty tomb in *De Spectaculis* 30, written in the late second century (available online at http://www.tertullian.org/lfc/LFC10-13_de_spectaculis.htm).</li>
<li>In *Antiquities* 4.8.15, the Jewish historian Josephus writes, "But let not the testimony of women be admitted, on account of the levity and boldness of their sex, nor let servants be admitted to give testimony on account of the ignobility of their soul; since it is probable that they may</li>
</ol>

not speak the truth, either out of hope of gain, or fear of punishment" (available online at https://www.gutenberg.org/files/2848/2848-h/2848-h.htm#link42HCH0008). Also, in *Rosh Hashannah 1.8*, the Jewish Talmud records, "Any evidence which a woman [gives] is not valid (to offer), also they are not valid to offer. This is equivalent to saying that one who is Rabbinically accounted a robber is qualified to give the same evidence for a woman." In *Sotah* 19a, the Talmud states, "Sooner let the words of the Law be burnt than delivered to a woman." And in *Kiddushin* 82b, the Talmud states, "The world cannot exist without males and without females— happy is he whose children are males, and woe to him whose children are females."

63 William Wand, *Christianity: A Historical Religion?* (Valley Forge, PA: Judson, 1972), 93-94.

Enormous forces in our culture are determined to deny Jesus was raised from the dead. And, over and over again, they use arguments which can be shown to be invalid, and they propose alternative scenarios about the rise of Christianity which can be shown to be impossible.

—N. T. Wright, bishop and early Christian historian[1]

After more than 700 hours of studying Christ's resurrection, I came to the conclusion that the resurrection of Jesus Christ is either one of the most wicked, vicious, heartless hoaxes ever foisted on the minds of human beings, or it is the most remarkable fact of history.

—Josh McDowell, Christian apologist[2]

17

He Is Risen Indeed!

As we have just seen, there are five historical facts that stand up to historiographical scrutiny:

1. Jesus was killed by crucifixion.
2. His disciples claimed to have seen him physically alive afterwards, and they were willing to die proclaiming the truth of this testimony.
3. Paul converted from being Christianity's chief persecutor to its chief missionary after claiming to have seen the risen Jesus.
4. Jesus' brother James went from a devoted Jew (one who would never imagine a human could be God or that a crucified man could be the Messiah) to a leader in the early Christian church following his brother's crucifixion.
5. No corpse was found in Jesus' tomb.[3]

These five facts can easily be accounted for if Jesus really did rise from the dead. Alternative explanations have been attempted, although even resurrection skeptics find fault with these theories.[4] In this chapter, we'll take a look at the eight main alternative theories, some of which we have already touched on. These alternative theories are:

1. The resurrection story is a legend.
2. The resurrection is merely metaphorical, and it was never intended to be understood as a historical reality.
3. The resurrection is based on myths from other religions.
4. The disciples lied or stole the body.

CHAPTER 17: HE IS RISEN INDEED!

5. Someone besides the disciples stole the body.
6. Witnesses went to the wrong tomb.
7. Jesus didn't really die.
8. The appearances of the risen Jesus can be explained by psychological phenomena, such as hallucinations, delusions, visions, or conversion disorder.

Although we will go into more detail soon, the ability of each of these theories to account for the five minimal facts is summarized in Figure 5.

Figure 5: Summary of Theories and Their Ability to Explain the Five Minimal Facts

Minimal Facts / Theories	1. Jesus died by crucifixion	2. Jesus' disciples truly believed they had seen the risen Jesus	3. After Jesus' death, Paul converted from chief persecutor to chief missionary	4. After Jesus' death, James converted from pious Jew to devoted follower of Jesus	5. Jesus' tomb was empty
Jesus rose from the dead.	✓	✓	✓	✓	✓
The resurrection is the result of legendary development.	✓				
The resurrection was intended to be nonhistorical genre.	✓				
The resurrection was copied from other religions.	✓				

352

The disciples lied or stole the body.	✓				✓
Someone else stole the body.	✓				✓
Witnesses went to the wrong tomb.	✓				
Jesus didn't die on the cross.					✓
The disciples had visions of the risen Jesus.	✓	✓			
Paul had a vision of the risen Jesus.	✓		✓		
James had a vision of the risen Jesus.	✓			✓	

1. Legendary Development

First, let's take a look at the claim that the resurrection accounts arose through legendary development within the early Christian church. As we saw in Chapter 12, textual criticism of the thousands of extant manuscripts demonstrates that the accounts of Jesus' life that we read today are essentially identical to the originals, and any minor differences have no effect on the core doctrines of Christianity, including the resurrection. Therefore, if any legendary development occurred, it was before the Gospels were written, and even then, it is highly unlikely for reasons that we've covered in many previous chapters and that we'll also touch on shortly.

There are many problems with the "legendary development" theory. For now, we will focus on the failure of this theory to explain the minimal facts. First, as we discussed above, there are numerous early sources that

CHAPTER 17: HE IS RISEN INDEED!

record that *the disciples themselves*— not later church leaders—claimed that they saw the risen Jesus, either actually or in a vision of sorts, and that *the disciples themselves* were willing to proclaim that Jesus had risen from the dead, even in the face of persecution and martyrdom. The original disciples had nothing to gain and everything to lose by proclaiming their belief that Jesus had risen from the dead.

Moreover, there is no record that anyone who claimed to have seen the risen Jesus ever recanted, even when threatened with torture or death. Christianity's many critics, including Celsus, Pliny the Younger, Tacitus, Suetonius, Lucian of Samosata, and Josephus, to name a few, would have seized the opportunity to publicize any news of recantation, if there had been any.

Historical sources report that no one recanted and only demonstrate that the very people who claimed to have seen the risen Jesus went willingly to their deaths. While someone may willingly die for something he believes in, it is unlikely that someone would willingly die for something he knows is a lie. As Habermas and Licona put it, "Liars make poor martyrs."[5]

Another insightful analysis is to compare the Gospel accounts of Jesus' resurrection to the accounts of other religions' founders who performed miracles. When we do so, we find a big difference. When an account other than the Bible describes a historical person as performing miracles, it was written much later than that religious founder's death. For example, the first miracle accounts of Mohammed, the founder of Islam, were written down 75 to 125 years after his death and are in sources that even Islamic scholars consider dubious.[6] Another example is Siddhartha Gautama, the founder of Buddhism, who lived between 563 and 483 BC and left only oral traditions of his teachings. The first written accounts of his life appear in the Pali manuscripts of the first century BC—more than 400 years after he lived. And nearly all of the accounts of Gautama's miracles appear in the later Sanskrit manuscripts, which were written in the first century AD. Therefore, given hundreds of years, it is much more likely that legend crept in.

The legendary development theory also does not explain the conversions of Paul and James. Why would an active enemy of Christianity choose to go along with a concocted story about the resurrection? And why would a formerly devout Jew like James convert to Christianity, much less be willing die as a martyr for his faith? Pious Jews like Paul and James (and most of the other initial converts) wouldn't have willingly converted without strong reason to do so, and they would have easily seen right through any legendary fabrications. Furthermore, this theory does not account for the empty tomb. The only minimal fact that the legendary development theory accounts for is Jesus' death by crucifixion, which these theorists would say launched the legend.

2. Resurrection Was Intended as a Symbol

Proponents of this theory claim that the disciples invented the resurrection as a way to honor Jesus and communicate a theological message. The resurrection of Jesus is therefore a fable much like Aesop's fables about talking animals, which communicate a moral but were never meant to be taken literally. Proponents of this theory point to Jesus' own use of parables as an example of this "nonhistorical genre."

There are many problems with this theory, not the least of which is that it accounts neither for the empty tomb nor for the conversions of Paul and James. If the resurrection wasn't intended to be taken literally, why was there discussion of the tomb being empty, and why did the Jews claim that the disciples had stolen the body? Certainly, Jewish fables already were in existence (and were later known as the Midrash), and the disciples would have understood the distinction between a metaphorical fable and something that really happened. This is especially true in Paul's case, since he himself claimed to have seen the risen Jesus. He definitely wasn't thinking Jesus' resurrection was merely symbolic.

Moreover, as mentioned in Chapter 5, the Gospel accounts of the resurrection, as well as the sermons from the Acts of the Apostles, all make it clear that the disciples saw, heard, and touched the risen Jesus. They were proclaiming Jesus' literal bodily resurrection, not a metaphorical symbol. For example, Peter makes it quite clear in his sermon at the beginning of Acts that King David died and was buried, and his "grave is here to this day," but Jesus was "not abandoned to the grave, nor did his body see decay." He even claims, "God has raised this Jesus to life, and we are all witnesses of the fact."[7] Peter emphasizes that he and others "ate and drank with Him after He arose from the dead."[8]

This is not the language of symbolism and metaphor. Peter is clearly talking about a literal, physical resurrection. Moreover, early critics of

Christianity, such as the second-century Greek philosopher Celsus, were clearly attacking the assertion that Jesus had risen physically from the dead. Celsus proposed other theories to explain Jesus' appearances, but he clearly understood that the Christians were not using symbolism. Like the previous one, this theory accounts for the death of Jesus, but for none of the other four historical facts.

3. Resurrection Copied from Other Religions

The third theory that skeptics have proposed is that early Christians were merely copying other myths about dying and rising gods. First of all, most of the parallels between pagan religions and Jesus' death and resurrection appear after the first century, suggesting that Christianity influenced those pagan religions, not the other way around. For example, the accounts of the god Adonis rising from the dead appear after AD 150, and the accounts of the god Attis being reborn as an evergreen tree first appear in the third century.[9]

Moreover, the mythological accounts of dying and rising gods that pre-date Christianity in no way resemble the resurrection of Jesus. For example, as we discussed in Chapter 7, the Egyptian god Osiris died after being cut into fourteen pieces. He was reassembled (or at least thirteen of his parts were reassembled) and became the god of the underworld. There is no mention that he appeared to others on earth again. His son, Horus, was born soon after his death, becoming a symbol of the new harvest. This mythological account most likely arose as a way to understand the annual change of seasons as a cycle of death and rebirth similar to Osiris and Horus. According to the Greek historian Plutarch, who wrote in the first century, Osiris' worshipers believed his body was still buried in the ground, and they sought to be buried nearby.[10]

Moreover, there is no evidence that any of the dying and rising gods that preceded Jesus were historical individuals. Some skeptics, however, point out that the Roman emperor Augustus, who died in AD 14, is a historical person, and he is described as having had a divine birth, a concept that Christians must have copied. But the accounts of Augustus' divine birth come from a single source, a book by Asclepiades of Mendes called *Theologumena*, copies of which no longer exist. Moreover, the sole surviving reference to Augustus' divine birth comes from the Roman historian Suetonius, who was writing 183 years after Augustus' death.[11]

This "copycat theory" is far-fetched for many reasons, not the least of which is that it explains none of the facts, other than the fact that Jesus died by crucifixion.

4. THE DISCIPLES STOLE THE BODY

This was the original theory that circulated soon after Jesus' death.[12] In *Dialogue with Trypho*, Justin Martyr also reports that skeptics in the mid-second century were still proposing this theory as the explanation for Jesus' empty tomb. Its proponents maintain that Jesus' disciples, who had been critical of the Jewish religious leaders while Jesus was alive, came to the embarrassing realization that their crucified leader wasn't who he had claimed to be. In order to cover their mistake and maintain their position at the head of a new religious movement, they stole his body and invented the story of his resurrection.

While it sounds credible at first glance, this theory has many weaknesses. It means the disciples willingly died for something they knew was a lie. There is absolutely no evidence that any of them recanted even in the face of torture and death.

Charles Colson, who served prison time for his role in the Watergate scandal of the early 1970s, draws parallels with his own experience and explains how unlikely it would be for someone to willingly die for something *they know* is a lie:

> Watergate involved a conspiracy to cover up, perpetuated by the closest aides to the President of the United States—the most powerful men in America, who were intensely loyal to their president. But one of them, John Dean, turned state's evidence, that is, testified against Nixon, as he put it, "to save his own skin"—and he did so only two weeks after informing the president about what was really going on—two weeks! The real cover-up, the lie, could only be held together for two weeks, and then everybody jumped ship in order to save themselves. Now, the fact is that all that those around the President were facing was embarrassment,

maybe prison. Nobody's life was at stake. But what about the disciples? Twelve powerless men, peasants really, were facing not just embarrassment or political disgrace, but beatings, stonings, execution. Every single one of the disciples insisted, to their dying breaths, that they had physically seen Jesus bodily raised from the dead. Don't you think that one of those apostles would have cracked before being beheaded or stoned? That one of them would have made a deal with the authorities? None did.[13]

There is a huge difference between the first disciples of Jesus and every other martyr after that. Every other Christian martyr died because they believed the disciples had told the truth. The first disciples died *claiming to have seen* Jesus alive.

Moreover, this theory doesn't explain the conversions of the skeptics Paul and James, who would have expected such a fraud. Upon hearing that Jesus' body was missing from the tomb, their first thought would have been that someone had stolen the body, not, "He must have risen! Count me in for a new religion!" The theory that Jesus' disciples stole his body just doesn't stand up as a plausible explanation for the historical data. It is no surprise that few serious scholars have maintained this opinion in the last two hundred years.[14]

5. Someone Else Stole the Body

A fifth theory proposes that someone besides the disciples stole Jesus' body; the disciples, upon finding the empty tomb, believed Jesus had risen from the dead.

But, as we've seen, an empty tomb alone is not sufficient to account for Paul's or James' conversion. Upon hearing the announcement that Jesus' tomb was empty, as we've said, they would have suspected someone had stolen the corpse, giving them little reason to become followers of a dead Jesus.

John's Gospel even reports that Mary Magdalene's first thought upon finding Jesus' tomb empty was that his body had been stolen. It was thus obvious to the average person that this was the most logical explanation. She tells Peter and John, "They have taken the Lord out of the tomb, and we don't know where they have put him!"[15] Only John believed Jesus had risen from the dead based solely on the empty tomb. John most likely believed Jesus had risen because he recalled Jesus telling him to expect it and because he saw Jesus' vacated grave clothes. He probably asked himself why someone would unwrap the body before stealing it, and the way the linen grave clothes were folded, as if Jesus had passed right through them as he got up, may have convinced him.

The biggest problem with this theory is that it also fails to explain the sightings of Jesus. It must be combined with other theories, such as the psychological theories below, to adequately explain the overnight transformation of the disciples, as well as their claims—and Paul's—that Jesus appeared to them. The only minimal facts that this theory explains are Jesus' death by crucifixion and the empty tomb.

6. They Went to the Wrong Tomb

The sixth theory is that the disciples went to the wrong tomb. Finding it empty, they concluded that Jesus must have walked out alive. This has all the weaknesses of the previous theory plus one more: if they had looked into the wrong tomb and then proclaimed a resurrection, all their opponents had to do to silence them was go to the *right* tomb and carry out Jesus' body for all to see.

There were many enemies of Christianity in the first few years after Jesus' crucifixion who would have liked to squelch the movement that was disrupting their community.[16] The sophisticated Roman society had enough infrastructure—publications, excellent roads, powerful politicians—to expose and punish undesirables. No record exists of any critic providing evidence that disproves the resurrection. Although this theory does admit that Jesus died on the cross, it only partially accounts for the empty tomb, and it leaves the other three minimal facts unexplained.

7. Jesus Didn't Really Die

This theory, often referred to as the "apparent death theory" or the "swoon theory," proposes that Jesus was still alive when they took him down from the cross and that he recuperated enough to appear to his disciples a few days later. Perhaps one of Jesus' wealthy followers paid off a Roman official to have him taken down from the cross before he died and to ensure that he received top-notch medical care.

In the best-seller, *The Jesus Papers*, speculative theorist Michael Baigent proposes a variation of this theory. Baigent claims that the Roman leaders wanted to keep Jesus alive because he advocated for the Jews to pay taxes to the Romans.[17] Therefore, in order to save the Jewish defender of Roman taxation and at the same time placate the Jewish leaders who wanted Jesus dead, they faked Jesus' death by giving him a sedative, removing him from the cross, and reviving him with medicinal herbs.[18]

There are glaring problems with every theory that claims Jesus survived his crucifixion. For one, the vast majority of scholars disagree with this position. If we trust the Gospels, the water and blood that gushed from Jesus' side when he was pierced by a spear are evidence enough that he was dead.[19] The flow of water was evidence that the sacs around the heart and lungs had been ruptured, which alone would cause death, if it hadn't yet occurred.

Three medical doctors researched the historical evidence regarding the death of Jesus and published their opinion in an issue of the *Journal of the American Medical Association*. Here is their conclusion:

> Clearly, the weight of the historical and medical evidence indicates that Jesus was dead before the wound to his side was inflicted and supports the traditional view that the spear, thrust between his right rib, probably perforated not only the right lung but also the pericardium and heart and thereby ensured his death. Accordingly, interpretations based on the assumption that Jesus did not die on the cross appear to be at odds with modern medical knowledge.[20]

Even if we assume Jesus didn't die on the cross, he could never have appeared to his disciples only a few days later in a condition that would inspire them to claim he had conquered death. The bones in his feet would have been severely crushed by the stakes that nailed him to the cross, leaving him incapable of walking. And even if he could walk, he wouldn't have presented the glorious image of divinity necessary for anyone to call him, "My Lord and my God!" as Thomas did upon first touching him.

Gary Habermas writes:

> A crucified but still living Jesus would have been in horrible physical shape: bloodied, bruised, pale, limping, unwashed, and in obvious need of medical assistance. Such a condition would have hopelessly contradicted the disciples' belief that Jesus had appeared to them in a resurrected body. True, Jesus would have been alive, but not raised! Additionally, the frequently repeated New Testament teaching that believers would someday be gloriously raised just like Jesus would be groundless. Such a sickly body would hardly be an inspiration for theology.[21]

Even scholars who deny the resurrection don't buy this "swoon" theory. One scholar called it "more miraculous even than the resurrection itself!"[22]

The Qur'an puts forth another explanation: Jesus never died, but "Allah raised him up unto Himself."[23] (Muslims have claimed that the *Gospel of Barnabas* also supports this theory, but this document turned out to be a fraud.[24]) As a historical source about Jesus, the Qur'an is far more dubious than the four Gospel accounts because it was written six hundred years later. It is a huge leap of faith to believe something written about Jesus more than half a millennium later while discarding multiple documents written within decades of Jesus' life.

Moreover, why would non-Christian writers, such as Tacitus, Josephus, Lucian of Samosata, and the Jewish Talmud, all corroborate the Gospels' account that Jesus had died by crucifixion? Were they all mistaken as well? If God really did raise Jesus up before he died—perhaps substituting a look-alike on the cross to die in his place—why would he deliberately deceive so many people? There is no evidence for this theory except for a claim in the Qur'an that post-dates Jesus' death by six hundred years.

8. Psychological Phenomena Explain the Appearances

This theory is actually a cluster of theories that can be grouped together as "psychological phenomena." According to these theories, the people who

CHAPTER 17: HE IS RISEN INDEED!

claimed to have seen the risen Jesus were experiencing hallucinations, delusions, visions, the effects of guilt or a desire for power, an illness known as "conversion disorder," a psychological mindset known as "groupthink," or some other way that neurotransmitters were playing tricks on their brains.

One Christian theologian reacts to these theories by saying, "The Christian Church is founded upon a pathological experience of certain persons in the first century of our era. It means that if there had been a good neurologist for Peter and the others to consult, there never would have been a Christian Church."[25] Could the Christian doctrine of the resurrection of Jesus be grounded only on the false perceptions of supposed eyewitnesses?

Ask any psychologist and you'll get the same answer regarding hallucinations: like dreams, hallucinations are unique to each individual. That is, two people cannot experience the same hallucination. Psychologist Gary Collins writes:

> Hallucinations are individual occurrences. By their very nature only one person can see a given hallucination at a time. They certainly aren't something which can be seen by a group of people. Neither is it possible that one person could somehow induce a hallucination in somebody else. Since a hallucination exists only in the subjective, personal sense, it is obvious that others cannot witness it.[26]

Because hallucinations can't explain the multiple appearances of Jesus to different groups of people,[27] skeptics have proposed that the appearances of Jesus are not hallucinations, but visions or illusions. Skeptics have also proposed that the early Christian claim that Jesus had risen from the dead is the result of groupthink. Because Jesus' grieving followers so desperately wanted their former leader to be alive, they convinced each other that he was.

Alternatively, skeptics say, the people who claimed to have seen the risen Jesus could have been deluded in their thinking, and their testimony was simply a result of their false perception of reality. Skeptics point to many examples of people who have willingly died for deluded beliefs, such as the followers of Jim Jones (nine hundred people who committed suicide in 1978) and members of "Heaven's Gate" (thirty-eight who committed suicide in 1997). Members of the latter group were convinced that their souls could board a spaceship hiding behind the Hale-Bopp Comet. Can the claims of the earliest Christians regarding Jesus' resurrection really be explained by deceptive groupthink? Let's investigate further.

Visions and illusions are the experience of something that isn't really there, so for our purposes, we will use the terms interchangeably. The first weakness of the vision/illusion theory is this: even though visions are common throughout the Bible, the sightings of the risen Jesus were of a totally different nature. The disciples and Paul didn't just claim to have seen Jesus, but to have touched him, to have eaten with him, and to have conversed with him.[28]

In the opening of his Acts of the Apostles, the detail-oriented historian Luke claims that Jesus appeared to many people over the course of forty days, giving them commandments and providing "many convincing proofs that he was alive."[29] It is impossible for multiple people to experience the same vision over a long period of time, much less to eat, drink, and converse with that vision. Visions, unless they are supernatural like the resurrection, are thus a lot like hallucinations.

It bears repeating that the disciples willingly faced death, believing Jesus had risen. Not only did they die defending this fact, but they were certain that their own bodies would be raised from the dead. Paul was so convinced that Jesus' physical body had been transformed into a glorious and immortal body that he teaches on numerous occasions throughout his letters that Jesus will "give life to our mortal bodies,"[30] that our mortal body will be "clothed with" the immortal,[31] that Jesus will "transform our lowly bodies so they will be like his glorious body."[32] Paul clearly understood his experience of Jesus to be an objective physical reality, not a spiritual vision.

Another weakness of the vision/illusion theory is that the disciples themselves needed convincing that this supernatural event had taken place—they were certainly using their mental faculties correctly. They were acutely aware that a mutilated corpse coming to life was outrageous. Jesus, we read, had to convince them he really was alive: "Why are you troubled, and why do doubts rise in your minds? Look at my hands and my feet. It is I myself! Touch me and see; a ghost does not have flesh and bones, as you see I have."[33]

CHAPTER 17: HE IS RISEN INDEED!

Campbell's Psychiatric Dictionary defines an illusion as "an erroneous perception, a false response to a sense-stimulation."[34] The dictionary clarifies that "in a normal individual this false belief usually brings the desire to check often another sense, or other senses may come to the rescue and satisfy him that it is merely an illusion."[35] This is precisely what the witnesses of the risen Jesus did. They couldn't believe their eyes, so they turned to other senses. Hearing and touching Jesus, they were convinced it was he.

Here is how one Christian apologist emphasizes that the sightings of Jesus in the Gospels could not just be illusions or visions:

> The very kind of evidence which modern science, even psychologists, are so insistent upon for determining the reality of any object under consideration is the kind of evidence that we have presented to us in the Gospels regarding the Resurrection of the Lord Jesus, namely, the things that are seen with the human eye, touched with the human hand, and heard by the human ear. This is what we call empirical evidence.[36]

The first witnesses knew that subsequent generations would need proof as well. That is why they wrote their testimonies, which are found in the histories and letters of the New Testament.

Moreover, only certain types of people experience visions, and the likelihood that a diverse group would all have a vision, much less the same one, is extremely remote. In order for the psychological phenomena theories to explain all of the minimal facts, there would have to be different reasons to account for the visions of each of the disciples, of Paul, and of James, the probability of which is infinitesimally low.

We can also rule out groupthink and delusion as explanations for the sightings of Jesus. Groupthink occurs in a highly cohesive group whose members are reticent to voice dissent for fear of upsetting the group's cohesion. Paul and James were not part of the group, and though James may have wanted to see his brother again, groupthink would not account for his motivation to assume his brother had risen from the dead. Similarly, groups of people share the same delusion when they share similar convictions and acquire their deluded beliefs through the influence of a very persuasive and charismatic leader who generally is *alive* at the time of their delusion.

Perhaps if the disciples were the only ones to have seen the risen Jesus, their belief in the resurrection could be explained away. But neither Paul nor James shared the disciples' same longing to see Jesus again, so neither was in the frame of mind to be influenced by the forces of groupthink or delusional persuasion.

So, what psychological reasons *could* account for Paul's conversion? Some skeptics claim that Paul was suffering from "conversion disorder," a psychosis that causes someone to experience sensory distortions. That is, the distortions originate in his or her brain, not in the external world. The person suffering from conversion disorder may lose his sight, become paralyzed, experience pain, lose his voice, have seizures or tics, and so forth, all for neurological rather than the usual biological reasons. Conversion disorders usually affect women, adolescents, men who are or have been in a battle situation, people of low socioeconomic status, or people with a low IQ.[37]

Some skeptics claim that Paul had a conversion disorder because, as Luke records, he was blinded after an appearance of Jesus, possibly as a result of the disorder.[38] However, Paul fits none of the typical profiles of those who suffer from conversion disorder. Skeptics also claim that Paul also had an auditory hallucination because he heard Jesus speaking to him. But even if Paul did have both a conversion disorder and an auditory hallucination, this explanation still doesn't account for Jesus' appearances to all of the others, nor does it account for the empty tomb.

The same weaknesses apply to all of the other theories for Paul's conversion, including his desire for power or his guilt over having persecuted a group of people whom he came to admire. While these theories may provide some level of explanation for Paul's own conversion, they have to be combined with other theories to account for the conversion of the disciples, James, and the empty tomb.

Let's take a look at an explanation of the five minimal facts that uses one combination of the various theories. Skeptics may propose that someone stole the body from the tomb, causing the disciples to believe that Jesus really rose from the dead. Due to their state of grief and disillusionment, they had visions of the risen Jesus and confidently proclaimed this experience far and wide. On hearing these claims, Paul began to feel guilty for persecuting Christians. He then suffered from a conversion disorder, causing him to lose his sight, and he had an auditory hallucination that the risen Jesus spoke to him. Meanwhile, the devout Jew James, after refusing to believe in his brother's claims, also felt guilty, was missing his brother, and began to believe the disciples' claims, which were based on groupthink. James may also have had a vision of what he claims was the risen Jesus, explaining why he is mentioned in the 1 Corinthians 15 creed and why he willingly went to his death for his belief in Jesus.

In order for this theory to work, many different events (each of which is itself very rare) must coincide, an extremely remote possibility. Let's illustrate by putting it in mathematical terms: Even if we claim that there is a 10% chance that someone stole the body (and no one ever found it, which would have crushed the new Jesus movement), a 1% chance that all of the disciples had the same vision or convinced one another Jesus was alive due to groupthink, a 1% chance that Paul had a conversion disorder, a 1% chance that Paul also had an auditory hallucination, and a 1% chance that James changed his mind and subsequently had the same vision of his resurrected brother, the probability that all five happened is the product of their probabilities, $0.1 \times 0.01 \times 0.01 \times 0.01 \times 0.01$, or one in a billion.

Historians refer to these types of combination theories as "ad hoc" because they rely too much on speculation in order to achieve a pre-determined final purpose, in this case, to disprove the resurrection. Those who insist on such combination theories do so because, at the onset, they rule out a supernatural explanation. However, the likelihood of this combination of explanations is ridiculously low.

ADDITIONAL EVIDENCE FOR THE RESURRECTION

A man rising physically from the dead is certainly extraordinary, to say the least. Skeptics may still say, "Well, it was easy for ancient folks with their primitive ideas to believe something like that." But people back then were not unsophisticated. They were just as skeptical, just as insistent on proof, as people are today. First-century people knew that the dead did not rise. They may have believed in *revivification*—that someone could bring a dead person back to life (as Elijah had done in

THE SHORTEST LEAP

the Old Testament[39])—but for a dead person to actually come back to life in a completely restored body that could walk through walls was unheard of. As we've mentioned, N. T. Wright spent hundreds of pages explaining that no one expected this type of phenomenon. He puts it this way:

Proposing that Jesus of Nazareth was raised from the dead was just as controversial nineteen hundred years ago as it is today. The discovery that dead people stay dead was not first made by the philosophers of the Enlightenment.[40]

Before and after Jesus, there were many movements whose Jewish leaders claimed to be the Messiah. However, each of these movements ended abruptly upon the execution of their leader. No one else claimed to have seen their leader gloriously alive after his death. They knew people would mock that claim. So, what motivated Jesus' followers to make the outrageous claim that he had come back to life? Such a claim amounted to an entire shift in worldview. The only logical explanation is that the resurrection of Jesus really happened.

The Jewish religion was distinct in many ways but marked especially by the belief in only one God and by the faithful observance of the Sabbath. Yet shortly after Jesus' death, thousands of Jews began professing that Jesus, a man, was God, and they started gathering to worship him on "the Lord's Day"—Sunday, the day of the resurrection. This new belief contradicted everything monotheistic Jesus had believed for *millennia*.

There is only one plausible explanation for the birth of the Christian church, with its very different views of the afterlife and its distinct symbols and rituals. That single plausible explanation is that the resurrection happened. As Wright puts it, "The proposal that Jesus was bodily raised from the dead possesses unrivalled power to explain the historical data at the heart of early Christianity."[41]

If Jesus rose from the dead, taking on a new, indestructible body, what does this say about who he is? If the resurrection happened, Jesus either was God in the flesh or had a unique relationship with God—only the creator could accomplish a bodily resurrection from the dead. We now turn to Jesus' claims to divinity, claims that are much more credible if he really did rise from the dead, as the historical evidence suggests.

CHAPTER 17: HE IS RISEN INDEED!

Questions for Comprehension and Discussion

1. Why is it unlikely that the claim that Jesus rose from the dead was the result of legendary development?
2. What is the evidence that the story of Jesus' resurrection was not just intended as a beautiful symbol of rebirth and renewal?
3. Summarize the evidence countering the claim that Jesus' resurrection stories were copied from other myths and legends. You are welcome to also incorporate evidence you remember from previous chapters.
4. Why isn't it plausible that the disciples stole Jesus' body?
5. If someone else stole Jesus' body, how does this not account for the five minimal facts?
6. Why is it unlikely that the disciples thought Jesus had risen from the dead because they went to the wrong tomb?
7. What are the problems with the theory that Jesus didn't really die, which is why he appeared to his disciples after the crucifixion?
8. Explain the various types of theories that claim psychological phenomena account for the resurrection appearances. What are the problems with these theories?
9. What is the weakness of using a combination of theories to account for the five minimal facts?
10. Which two aspects of Jewish worship changed overnight soon after Jesus' crucifixion? Why is the truth of the resurrection the best explanation for these changes and for the birth of the Christian church?

CHAPTER 17 ENDNOTES

[1] From N. T. Wright's opening statement in his dialog with John Dominic Crossan, "The Resurrection: Historical Event or Theological Explanation? A Dialogue," recorded in Robert B. Stewart, ed., *The Resurrection of Jesus: John Dominic Crossan and N. T. Wright in Dialogue* (Minneapolis, MN: Fortress Press, 2006), 18.

[2] From an interview with Josh McDowell on CBN, available at http://www1.cbn.com/700club/josh-mcdowell-proof-risen-christ.

3   This discussion of the failure of alternative theories comes primarily from Gary Habermas and Michael Licona, *The Case for the Resurrection of Jesus* (Grand Rapids, MI: Kregel, 2004).
4   As mentioned in *The Case for the Resurrection of Jesus*, Gary R. Habermas and J.P. Moreland write in *Beyond Death* (Wheaton, IL: Crossway, 1998), 125: "David Strauss delivered the historical deathblow to the swoon theory held by Karl Venturini, Heinrich Paulus, and others. On the other hand, while Strauss popularized the hallucination theory, Friedrich Schleiermacher and Paulus pointed out errors in it. The major decimation of the hallucination theory came later in the century at the hands of Theodor Keim. Liberal scholars had long before dismissed fraud theories, while legend theories, popular later in the century, were disproved by later critical research. So these scholars demolished each other's theories, thereby burying the major naturalistic attempts to account for Jesus' resurrection by the late 1800s."
5   Habermas and Licona, *The Case for the Resurrection of Jesus*, 59.
6   Ibid, 91.
7   Acts 2:29-32.
8   Acts 10:40-41.
9   Günter Wagner, *Pauline Baptism and the Pagan Mysteries* (Edinburgh: Oliver and Boyd, 1967), 197-201, 213, 219, 221, 223-224, 229, 251, 265.
10 Bruce M. Metzger, "Methodology in the Study of Mystery Religions and Early Christianity," in Metzger, *Historical and Literary Studies*, 21.
11 Ibid, 170.
12 See Matthew 28:11-15.
13 Charles Colson, "An Unholy Hoax? The Authenticity of Christ," *BreakPoint* syndicated column, March 29, 2002.
14 Habermas and Licona, *The Case for the Resurrection of Jesus*, 95.
15 John 20:2.
16 Acts 17:6 indicates that the authorities believed the followers of Jesus were "turning the world upside down" (ESV translation) or "causing trouble all over the world" (NIV translation). There is ample historical evidence supporting the fact that the first followers of Jesus were causing a problem for the local political authorities because of the growing popularity of their message.
17 Jesus said, "Give to Caesar that which is Caesar's." (Matthew 22:21, Mark 12:17, and Luke 20:25).
18 Michael Baigent, *The Jesus Papers* (San Francisco: HarperSanFrancisco, 2006).
19 As we discussed in Chapter 10, the detail about the blood and water strengthens the case that this was eyewitness testimony, since most people would have expected only the blood.

CHAPTER 17: HE IS RISEN INDEED!

20 See William D. Edwards, Wesley J. Gabel, Floyd E. Hosmer, "On the Physical Death of Jesus," *Journal of the American Medical Association* 255, no. 11 (March 21, 1986), 1463.
21 Gary Habermas, *The Risen Jesus and the Future Hope* (Oxford: Rowman and Littlefield Publishers, 2003), 16.
22 E. Le Camus, *The Life of Christ*, Vol. III (New York: The Cathedral Library Association, 1908), 486.
23 See Sura 4:157-158 of the Qur'an.
24 See Norman L. Geisler and Abdul Saleeb, *Answering Islam*, 2nd ed. (Grand Rapids, MI: Baker, 2002), appendix 3.
25 J. Gresham Machen in Ernest F. Kevan, *The Resurrection of Christ* (London: The Campbell Morgan Memorial Bible Lectureship, Westminster Chapel, Buckingham Gate, S. W. I., 14 June 1961), 10-11.
26 As quoted in Lee Strobel, *The Case for Christ* (Grand Rapids, MI: Zondervan, 1998), 238.
27 Based on the early Christian creed from 1 Corinthians 15:3-8, Jesus appeared to Peter, then to the rest of the disciples, then to a group of more than five hundred people, then to James, then to all of the apostles, and finally to Paul.
28 See Matthew 28:9-10, Luke 24:13-35, 36-49, John 20:10-18, 19-23-24, 1 John 1:1-3, and Acts 1:4-8, 10:39-43.
29 Acts 1:3.
30 Romans 8:11.
31 1 Corinthians 15:54.
32 Philippians 3:21.
33 Luke 24:28-39.
34 Robert Jean Campbell, M.D., *Psychiatric Dictionary*, 8th ed (New York: Oxford University Press, 2003), 328.
35 L.E. Hinsie and J. Shatsky. *Psychiatric Dictionary (Definitions and Illustrative Quotations for All Important Terms and Concepts Since Hippocrates) 4th Ed* (New York: Oxford University Press, 1970), 280.
36 Wilbur Smith, *Therefore Stand* (Grand Rapids, MI: Baker Book House, 1945), 400.
37 Habermas and Licona, *The Case for the Resurrection of Jesus*, 114-115.
38 See the story in Acts 9 and 22.
39 See 1 Kings 17.
40 Wright, *The Resurrection of the Son of God*, 10.
41 Ibid, 718.

PART III
The Biblical Evidence

Buddha said unequivocally that he was a mere man, not a god—almost as if he foresaw later attempts to worship him. Jesus, on the other hand, claimed... to be divine.

—Huston Smith, religious scholar[1]

Frankly, it's hard to escape the feeling that our culture has taken the question 'Who do you say that I am?' and changed it to 'Who do you want me to be?'

— Robert M. Bowman, Jr. and J. Ed Komoszewski, Christian scholars[2]

18

Claims of Divinity

A helpful analogy for our systematic analysis so far is the step-by-step ascent of a steep mountain. Each line of evidence enables sure-footed progress toward the summit. In our case, that summit symbolizes a confident affirmation that Jesus of Nazareth truly is God in human flesh, who came to live, die, and rise again to give his followers eternal life.

My unabashed goal is to lead you, dear reader, to a spectacular vista at that summit—a "viewpoint"—where out of all the possible philosophical stances on the existence or absence of a deity, believing that Jesus is God is rooted in the most rational evidence, thus requiring the "shortest leap of faith."

Believing that this man was (and still is) God still requires faith—we cannot see him after all—and many people will still dismiss the evidence for this claim for a variety of reasons. Ironically, a rejection of Jesus despite the evidence is actually quite consistent with the Bible's teachings, specifically the claim that God must first enable us to take that leap of faith, regardless of any rational proof that may be staring us in the face.[3] One of the best explanations for why so many people refuse to take the leap of faith to Jesus was insightfully provided by a non-Christian man, who explains it this way:

> Christianity, alone among world religions, was founded by God in person. God came down from heaven to earth and launched the salvific movement that came to be known as Christianity. From this premise it seems obvious that God must wish all human beings to enter this stream of saved life, so that Christianity

CHAPTER 18: CLAIMS OF DIVINITY

shall supersede all other world faiths. They may perhaps have some good in them and be able to function to some extent as a preparation for the gospel, but nevertheless Christianity alone is God's own religion.... It is therefore divinely intended for all men and women without exception. All this follows logically from the central dogma of the deity of Jesus.[4]

That is, he's saying: if Jesus really is God in human form, the Creator of all humans, then logically Christianity is the belief system that all humans are obligated to adopt.

But returning to our metaphor of a logical ascent to a vantage point of the truth: In the first part of this book, we examined the scientific evidence, demonstrating that it takes much less faith to believe in a single all-powerful, infinite Creator than to believe that the universe and all of life resulted simply from a "glorious evolutionary accident," as atheist Stephen Jay Gould has called it.[5]

In the second part, we examined the historical evidence, setting down more steppingstones in our pursuit of the truth. These logical footholds were: (1) the internal evidence (the biblical authors' claims to be telling the truth and their inclusion of many details that are consistent with eyewitness testimony), (2) the external evidence (archaeological evidence, accuracy of historical details, confirmation by outside, secular sources, and the stark differences of the accounts compared to myths and later Gnostic philosophy), and (3) the bibliographical evidence (the multiplicity of extant documents demonstrating that the New Testament documents we read today are the same as those written soon after Jesus' death, as well as the evidence that the books that comprise the New Testament canon were selected due to their apostolicity and catholicity).

As we have provided evidence, we have also cleared away the debris that could cause our trust to slip, such as skeptics' claims that Jesus is not described in outside secular historical documents, or that he is a myth based on earlier myths, or that his life is a mere legend that developed over time as his followers idealized him, or that early church leaders invented a Jesus of their choosing (and buried "true" alternate versions of him) because they sought power and wealth.

We have come a long way. At this point, the evidence gives us confidence to boldly claim the following:

1. An extra-dimensional, infinite, all-powerful, all-knowing Creator God exists, and he has provided evidence that he wants a personal relationship with humans, the pinnacle of his creation. Moreover, this God is very consistent with the single deity, *Yahweh*, of the world's monotheistic religions, and he is much less consistent with the deities of other world religions.[6]
2. Jesus really existed in history, and his life, teachings, death, and resurrection are accurately preserved in the documents of the New Testament.
3. The New Testament is a dependable document, not just for historical details, but also in its most outrageous claim: that Jesus rose from the dead in a new, "transphysical" body after dying by crucifixion.

Now, in the third part of the book, we turn to the biblical evidence that Jesus truly is the monotheistic God of the Hebrew Scriptures, *Yahweh*, and that the biblical documents written hundreds of years before Jesus' birth predicted the coming of a Savior who looks exactly like him. These Old Testament prophecies of Jesus' life, death, and resurrection are fulfilled so accurately in the New Testament that their similarity can be neither a coincidence nor a concoction.

God appeared as a poor carpenter from a podunk town in ancient Palestine? Yes, it is a huge claim. Kenneth Bowman and J. Ed Komoszewski put it this way:

> The Christian belief that Jesus Christ is God incarnate has been around so long that many people familiar with Christianity do not realize just how astonishing such a claim was and still is. Jesus was very much a real human being.... Indeed, by some measures, he was not a particularly remarkable man. He led no army, held no political office, wrote no books, had no wife and children, left no estate, and never traveled even a hundred miles from home. Yet billions of people during the past two millennia all over the world have worshiped him as their Lord and their God. How did this happen?[7]

In this chapter, we will try to answer the question of why a seemingly simple man two thousand years ago has had such a huge impact on the world. Our focus will be on the ways that Jesus gave his audience—both those to whom he spoke audibly two millennia ago and those to whom he speaks through the Bible even today—the clear message that *he is God*.

IS GOD ONE, OR THREE?

The Hebrew Scriptures—what Christians call the Old Testament—make it abundantly obvious that the Jews worshiped one God and one God only. In fact, this unequivocal belief in monotheism distinguished the ancient Jews from their neighbors, such as the Egyptians, Babylonians, and Greeks, who worshiped multiple gods (polytheism) or worshiped one particular god but acknowledged others (henotheism).

The monotheism of the Jews is succinctly stated in one of the most important verses in the Hebrew Scriptures, known as "the Shema Yisrael" (in Hebrew, שְׁמַע יִשְׂרָאֵל) and translated as "Hear, O Israel." "Shema Yisrael" are the first two words of God's instructions to the people of Israel soon after they had received the ten commandments: *"Hear, O Israel: The Lord our God, the Lord is one."*[8] In fact, when asked which of God's commandment is the greatest, Jesus immediately pointed to the Shema Yisrael, since all of the other commandments flow out of that one belief.[9] The apostle Paul—following his conversion—also confirms the belief in only one God: "We know that... 'There is no God but one.'"[10]

Furthermore, the second of the ten commandments further clarifies that the Jews were to worship *only* the one true God, *Yahweh*, though there would be many other people groups enticing them to worship other "gods."[11] Following Jesus' death and resurrection, Paul explained monotheism to the people of Athens, emphasizing that the gods represented by man-made idols are *not* the one true God who created the universe:

> "The God who made the world and everything in it is the Lord of heaven and earth and does not live in temples built by human hands. And he is not served by human hands, as if he needed anything. Rather, he himself gives everyone life and breath and everything else.... Therefore since we are God's offspring, we should

not think that the divine being is like gold or silver or stone—an image made by human design and skill."¹²

Despite many warnings by their own prophets not to worship the imaginary gods of other people groups, the story of the Israelites in the Old Testament is fraught with examples of the Jews breaking the second commandment, often with frightful consequences.¹³ The worship of Yahweh alone was, in fact, a life-or-death matter.

So how do we account for the historical fact that soon after Jesus' death, pious Jews, like Jesus' brother James and the strict, law-abiding Pharisee Saul (who became Paul), began to claim—at the risk of death—that Jesus of Nazareth was God, seemingly in addition to God the Father? The only plausible answer is that Jesus did in fact teach them that he was "one with the Father."¹⁴

They may not have understood how this was possible, but something convinced them it was true. As mentioned in the last chapter, the most plausible cause for this drastic, overnight change in belief—something that would have amounted to heresy otherwise—was the resurrection. In combination with actions and the statements that he made about himself, the resurrection demonstrated to the early eyewitnesses that Jesus was indeed God in human flesh, the physical "image of the invisible God."¹⁵

New Testament Statements That Jesus Is God

Before we turn to Jesus' own claims concerning his divinity, let's start with the statements of those who wrote the documents that comprise the New Testament, accounts that we have seen were based on extensive eyewitness testimony.

Many believe the most beautifully worded expression of Jesus' deity can be found in the words John wrote to powerfully launch his Gospel:

> In the beginning was the Word, and the Word was with God, and the Word was God. He was with God in the beginning. Through him all things were made; without him nothing was made that has been made. In him was

CHAPTER 18: CLAIMS OF DIVINITY

> life, and that life was the light of all mankind.... The Word became flesh and made his dwelling among us. We have seen his glory, the glory of the one and only Son, who came from the Father, full of grace and truth.... No one has ever seen God, but the one and only Son, who is himself God and is in closest relationship with the Father, has made him known.[16]

John is clearly stating that Jesus is God. And though he may not have understood how it could be possible, he claims that Jesus was "with God in the beginning" and simultaneously "was God." Over the centuries, Christian thinkers coined the term "Trinity" for this mysterious relationship that the Bible describes regarding the existence of three persons (Father, Son, and Holy Spirit) within a single God.[17]

An aside is helpful at this point: It had become common in Greek philosophy by the first century AD to use the term *Logos* (translated here as "Word") to describe the logic that pervades the universe. Today we may call it "ultimate reality," which some believe is found in Nature. Others may find this ultimate reality in science, specifically in the laws of physics or the principles of mathematics. It is to this ultimate reality that John equates Jesus.

John also penned the document we call First John, the one that we have noted specifically addresses the physical nature of Jesus' resurrection in order to rebut those who were saying Jesus' resurrection was merely symbolic or spiritual. In this letter, possibly even a written sermon, John concludes with a clear statement that he and his fellow eyewitnesses believed that Jesus was God:

> And we know that the Son of God has come and has given us understanding, so that we may know him who is true; and we are in him who is true, in his Son Jesus Christ. He is the true God and eternal life.[18]

Another summary of what the early Christians believed about Jesus can be found in Paul's letter to the church in Colossae, written within a decade or two of Jesus' life (and most likely containing even earlier material, possibly hymns, that had been circulating among Christians from the time of the resurrection appearances):

> The Son is the image of the invisible God, the firstborn over all creation. For in him all things were created: things in heaven and on earth, visible and invisible, whether thrones or powers or rulers or authorities; all things have been created through him and for him.... For God was pleased to have all his fullness dwell in him.[19]

Paul's readers then and now could not fully grasp how a man could have all God's "fullness" in him. But here is clear evidence that the earliest Christians believed that Jesus was equal to the Creator.[20]

An important point: other religious groups may call themselves "Christian" even though they do not hold to the core Christian belief that Jesus is God. These include the Mormon Church (also known as The Church of Jesus Christ of Latter-Day Saints), Jehovah's Witnesses, Christian Scientists, and the Unitarian Universalist Church. These groups deny this distinct doctrine even though there is overwhelming evidence that the authors of the New Testament clearly communicated that Jesus *was* (and, since he is eternal, still is) God.

JESUS DEMONSTRATED HIS DIVINITY

We've seen that the earliest Christians did believe that Jesus was equal to God. But did Jesus himself claim to be God? Or were John, Paul, and others misinterpreting his message and thus mislabeling him? As we will see, throughout the Gospels, Jesus made it very clear that he wasn't just a representative of God—though he certainly was. He made it clear that he *was God*.

Let's start with the Gospel of John, which most liberal, atheistic scholars reject for the very reason that it contains so many claims to the deity of Jesus. From there, we will proceed to Jesus' statements concerning his deity in the less disputed Synoptic Gospels.

Jesus' most famous statements of his deity are called his "I Am" statements. The most concise, telling "I Am" statement comes while Jesus is in a discussion with a group of fellow Jews right after he has said: "Very truly I tell you, whoever obeys my word will never see death." In response, they ask Jesus the same question you and I would ask: "Who

CHAPTER 18: CLAIMS OF DIVINITY

do you think you are?" Jesus then explains that their forefather Abraham was looking forward to the day when he, Jesus, would come. He then says, "Very truly I tell you, before Abraham was born, *I am*!"[21]

Two lines of reasoning demonstrate that Jesus is claiming to be God in this statement. First, by comparing his age to Abraham, and by using the present tense, "I am," instead of "I was," Jesus is stating that his existence is timeless. But there is even more to it than that. The name, "I am," is the name that Yahweh provided for himself when he spoke to Moses from the burning bush:

> Moses said to God, "Suppose I go to the Israelites and say to them, 'The God of your fathers has sent me to you,' and they ask me, 'What is his name?' Then what shall I tell them?"

God said to Moses, "*I am who I am*. This is what you are to say to the Israelites: '*I am* has sent me to you.'"[22]

Secondly, note the reaction he elicits from his Jewish hearers: "At this, they picked up stones to stone him, but Jesus hid himself, slipping away from the temple grounds."[23] The Jewish leaders clearly understood that Jesus was claiming to be Yahweh—a sin they considered deserving of capital punishment.

Here are the other "I am" statements recorded by John:

1. "I am the living bread that came down from heaven. Whoever eats this bread will live forever. This bread is my flesh, which I will give for the life of the world."
2. "I am the light of the world. Whoever follows me will never walk in darkness, but will have the light of life."
3. "I am the gate; whoever enters through me will be saved. They will come in and go out, and find pasture."
4. "I am the good shepherd. The good shepherd lays down his life for the sheep."
5. "I am the resurrection and the life. The one who believes in me will live, even though they die."
6. "I am the way and the truth and the life. No one comes to the Father except through me."[24]

THE SHORTEST LEAP

Jesus says he is the light of the world who gives people eternal life, he claims to be the one who saves people, he predicts that he will die in order to save those he shepherds, he declares that he is the source of eternal life after death, and he states that he is the truth, the source of life, and the only way to God the Father. Suffice it to say that Jesus is making claims that the average prophet or moral teacher would never have made. It was not surprising, therefore, that the Jewish leaders were accusing Jesus of making himself equal to God.

These self-designated titles would be obnoxious, even insane, coming from a mere man. To be the chief source of life and illumination? The only one who can save everybody else? Not merely a truth*ful* person but *Truth itself*?

Let's take a look at just a few of the other verses from John's Gospel demonstrating that Jesus considered himself God. In response to questions regarding his healing a man on the Sabbath, which the Pharisees claimed was not allowed, Jesus makes a few startling statements, including claims that he shares with his Father both the ability to give life and the authority to judge all people. Jesus said:

> "For just as the Father raises the dead and gives them life, even so the Son gives life to whom he is pleased to give it. Moreover, the Father judges no one, but has entrusted all judgment to the Son, that all may honor the Son just as they honor the Father. Whoever does not honor the Son does not honor the Father, who sent him. Very truly I tell you, whoever hears my word and believes him who sent me has eternal life and will not be judged but has crossed over from death to life. Very truly I tell you, a time is coming and has now come when the dead will hear the voice of the Son of God and those who hear will live. For as the Father has life in himself, so he has granted the Son also to have life in himself. And he has given him authority to judge because he is the Son of Man."[25]

By the way, the title that Jesus used for himself most often, the "Son of Man," is a reference to a divine Messianic figure in the Old Testament book of Daniel, where it is used as a title of divinity. We'll return to this title later in the chapter.

CHAPTER 18: CLAIMS OF DIVINITY

The Hebrew Scriptures clearly teach that only God is the giver of life and the ultimate judge of humans. Jesus' brother James, a pious Jew, likely had heard his brother make statements regarding his authority to judge. But rather than stating that Jesus *and* God *each* have the authority to judge, James reiterates the belief that Jews have always held: "There is only one Lawgiver and Judge, the one who is able to save and destroy. But you—who are you to judge your neighbor?"[26]

With regard to his ability to give eternal life, Jesus repeats this claim before his arrest and crucifixion, while he is praying in the Garden of Gethsemane:

> After Jesus said this, he looked toward heaven and prayed: "Father, the hour has come. Glorify your Son, that your Son may glorify you. For *you granted him authority over all people that he might give eternal life to all those you have given him.* Now this is eternal life: that they know you, the only true God, and Jesus Christ, whom you have sent. I have brought you glory on earth by finishing the work you gave me to do. And now, Father, glorify me in your presence with the glory I had with you *before the world began.*"[27]

Did Moses, or Isaiah, or David, or any other prophet, priest, or king say anything remotely like this in the Old Testament? No. They always communicated God's words of instruction to the people with, "Thus saith the Lord," or a similar introductory phrase. And the prophets in the Old Testament, and even Muhammed, who claimed to be another prophet in succession after Jesus, never claimed to have been with God before the world began.

In addition to claiming the powers to give life and to judge all people, Jesus claimed to have the authority to forgive sins, which Jews had always believed God alone could do. Listen to this one interchange between Jesus and his fellow Jews:

> Then they asked him, "Where is your father?"
>
> "You do not know me or my Father," Jesus replied. "If you knew me, you would know my Father also."...

THE SHORTEST LEAP

> Once more Jesus said to them, "I am going away, and you will look for me, and you will die in your sin. Where I go, you cannot come."
>
> This made the Jews ask, "Will he kill himself? Is that why he says, 'Where I go, you cannot come'?"
>
> But he continued, "You are from below; *I am from above*. You are of this world; *I am not of this world*. I told you that you would die in your sins; if you do not believe that *I am he*, you will indeed die in your sins."[28]

Here Jesus makes the audacious claims that he is "from above" and "not of this world," unlike other humans, and that we will die in our sins (that is face judgment and not receive eternal life in heaven, based on other New Testament teachings) if we do not believe he is God. Jewish prophets of the Old Testament never dared to make these types of claims.

Moreover, Jesus mysteriously claimed to be "one with the Father," which prompted the crowd to pick up stones to kill him:

> The Jews who were there gathered around him, saying, "How long will you keep us in suspense? If you are the Messiah, tell us plainly."
>
> Jesus answered, "I did tell you, but you do not believe. The works I do in my Father's name testify about me, but you do not believe because you are not my sheep. My sheep listen to my voice; I know them, and they follow me. I give them eternal life, and they shall never perish; no one will snatch them out of my hand. My Father, who has given them to me, is greater than all; no one can snatch them out of my Father's hand. *I and the Father are one.*"
>
> Again, his Jewish opponents picked up stones to stone him, but Jesus said to them, "I have shown you many good works from the Father. For which of these do you stone me?"

CHAPTER 18: CLAIMS OF DIVINITY

> "We are not stoning you for any good work," they replied, "but for blasphemy, because *you, a mere man, claim to be God.*" [29]

Jesus indicates that he is the Messiah, but he is much more than the kind of Messiah the Jews had been expecting.

He makes yet another claim of equality with God the Father four chapters later:

> Philip said, "Lord, show us the Father and that will be enough for us." Jesus answered: "Don't you know me, Philip, even after I have been among you such a long time? *Anyone who has seen me has seen the Father.* How can you say, 'Show us the Father'? Don't you believe that I am in the Father, and that the Father is in me? The words I say to you I do not speak on my own authority. Rather, it is the Father, living in me, who is doing his work. Believe me when I say that I am in the Father and the Father is in me; or at least believe on the evidence of the works themselves."[30]

Some skeptics interpret this verse by saying that the Father is in all people, and Jesus happened to be more "full of" the Father than the rest of us "less enlightened" folk. But the rest of the New Testament contradicts this theological position, including Jesus' own statement that he is "from above," as opposed to all other humans. And in context, when he says, "Anyone who has seen me has seen the Father," he is clearly *not* saying, "Just look at anyone who is fully enlightened, and you'll see the Father." Jesus never suggests anything remotely like that (though later Gnostic philosophy and members of the modern-day Mormon church would like to believe he did).

Let's take a look at a few statements recorded in the other, even earlier gospels which demonstrate that Jesus believed himself to be divine. First, Jesus claims repeatedly to be the Son of God. Here is one example:

> When Jesus came to the region of Caesarea Philippi, he asked his disciples, "Who do people say the Son of Man is?" They replied, "Some say John the Baptist; others say

Elijah; and still others, Jeremiah or one of the prophets." "But what about you?' he asked. 'Who do you say I am?' Simon Peter answered, "You are the Messiah, the Son of the living God." Jesus replied, "Blessed are you, Simon son of Jonah, for this was not revealed to you by flesh and blood, but by my Father in heaven."[31]

Jesus also claims to be the Son of Man, as mentioned earlier, a reference to the divine figure of Daniel. The title "Son of Man" is used for Jesus more than eighty times in the gospels. Jesus uses the term often in place of the first person "I" and frequently in association with actions that are usually attributed to God.[32]

So, what is the implication of Jesus' use of this term for himself? The only reference to the term "Son of Man" in Jewish literature up to the time of Jesus[33] are these statements from the Book of Daniel:

> In my vision at night I looked, and there before me was one like a son of man, coming with the clouds of heaven. He approached the Ancient of Days and was led into his presence. He was given authority, glory and sovereign power; all nations and peoples of every language worshiped him. His dominion is an everlasting dominion that will not pass away, and his kingdom is one that will never be destroyed.[34]

This description of a "son of man" sounds very similar to other statements in the Hebrew Scriptures about God and his establishment of an everlasting Kingdom that would be ruled by someone who is of ancient origins.[35] We'll have more to say on this topic in upcoming chapters.

Another interesting aspect of Jesus' use of the title, "Son of Man," is that Daniel describes this "one like a son of man" as coming "with the clouds of heaven." Not only does that sound familiar to ways that God is described in the Old Testament,[36] but when he is being questioned just prior to his crucifixion, Jesus also says he himself will come again in that way:

> Again the high priest asked him, 'Are you the Messiah, the Son of the Blessed One?" "I am," said Jesus. "And you

CHAPTER 18: CLAIMS OF DIVINITY

> will see the Son of Man sitting at the right hand of the Mighty One and coming on the clouds of heaven."
>
> The high priest tore his clothes. "Why do we need any more witnesses?" he asked. "You have heard the blasphemy. What do you think?" They all condemned him as worthy of death.[37]

The high priest readily recognized that Jesus was claiming to be God, causing him to immediately tear his clothes and accuse Jesus of blasphemy deserving of death.

Continuing our exploration of Jesus' self-identity in the Synoptic Gospels, we see that he also claims to forgive sins, which only God can do:

> When Jesus saw their faith, he said to the paralyzed man, "Son, your sins are forgiven."
>
> Now some teachers of the law were sitting there, thinking to themselves, "Why does this fellow talk like that? He's blaspheming! Who can forgive sins but God alone?"
>
> Immediately Jesus knew in his spirit that this was what they were thinking in their hearts, and he said to them, "Why are you thinking these things? Which is easier: to say to this paralyzed man, 'Your sins are forgiven,' or to say, 'Get up, take your mat and walk'? But I want you to know that the Son of Man has authority on earth to forgive sins."
>
> So he said to the man, "I tell you, get up, take your mat and go home." He got up, took his mat and walked out in full view of them all.[38]

In this passage, Jesus is "claiming to exercise a prerogative belonging only to God."[39] It is clear that the Jews considered that Jesus' claim to forgive sins was in direct contradiction to the Shema, their belief that there is only one God and therefore only one Being who can forgive sins.

THE SHORTEST LEAP

Another way that Jesus claims he is divine in the Synoptic Gospels is when he calls himself "David's Lord." At a point in Luke's Gospel when his fellow Jews were questioning his authority, Jesus caps the discussion with this confusing, riddle-like question:

> Then Jesus said to them, "Why is it said that the Messiah is the son of David? David himself declares in the Book of Psalms: 'The Lord said to my Lord: "Sit at my right hand until I make your enemies a footstool for your feet."' David calls him 'Lord.' How then can he be his son?"[40]

Though enigmatic, this rhetorical question may be Jesus' clearest expression of his divinity. He is referencing the beginning of Psalm 110, where King David wrote, "The Lord says to my Lord." David was describing God talking to the future Messiah, the one whom God had promised would be victorious over his enemies, who would then become his footstool.

David knew very well that the Messiah, "his Lord," would come through his own descendants. God had told him so through the prophet Samuel:

> "Now then, tell my servant David, 'This is what the Lord Almighty says... I will raise up your offspring to succeed you, your own flesh and blood, and I will establish his kingdom. He is the one who will build a house for my Name, and I will establish the throne of his kingdom forever."[41]

So what does it all mean? Jesus is claiming to be the answer to his own question: he is *both* the "Son of David"—the promised "offspring" whose throne God would establish forever—*and* David's "Lord," that is, God Himself. Jesus is essentially asking, if the future Messiah is David's son (or descendant), why would David call him "my Lord"? The answer to the enigma is that the promised Messiah will be *both* a human descendant of David *and* divine (deserving of David calling him "Lord"). In short, Jesus is communicating that he himself is the Messiah and is—in some mysterious way—*both* divine *and* human.[42]

CHAPTER 18: CLAIMS OF DIVINITY

Another interesting event in Luke's Gospel draws attention to Jesus' awareness of his own deity. Jesus sent out seventy-two disciples as his laborers for the "harvest" of believers. He said that he sent them out as "lambs in the midst of wolves," and he instructed them to tell others that the Kingdom of God is near.[43] When they returned, they excitedly reported to him, "Lord, even the demons are subject to us in your name!"[44] Jesus' reply seems off-hand and nonchalant, but it includes quite a remarkable claim: "And he said to them, 'I saw Satan fall like lightning from heaven.'"[45]

Yes, Jesus claimed that he was present at the fall of Satan. Moreover, Jesus claimed to give his disciples "authority over all power of the enemy," and he insisted they should rejoice that they have eternal life, not that they have power over demons. It is quite implausible that a mortal man would make these statements, unless he was either lying or a lunatic.

Moreover, Jesus claimed to have all authority in heaven and on earth. He made the clearest statement of this all-encompassing authority when he gave what is known as the "Great Commission" at the end of Matthew's Gospel:

> Then Jesus came to them and said, "All authority in heaven and on earth has been given to me. Therefore go and make disciples of all nations, baptizing them in the name of the Father and of the Son and of the Holy Spirit, and teaching them to obey everything I have commanded you. And surely I am with you always, to the very end of the age."[46]

Jesus believed he had serious influence, to say the least! If he were a mere man, it would seem he had narcissistic personality disorder (notwithstanding his exceptional concern for others, which is the opposite extreme in terms of symptoms).

Within this claim, Jesus also succinctly lists the three members of what the church calls the Trinity, and Jesus specified his role in the single Godhead as "God the Son," alongside God the Father and God the Holy Spirit. Moreover, Jesus said he will be with his followers as they go "to all nations" until the "very end of the age," implying that he considered himself both omnipresent and eternal.

C. S. Lewis provides a great summary for the reaction that Jesus elicited in his hearers:

> Then comes the real shock. Among these Jews there suddenly turns up a man who goes about talking as if He was God. He claims to forgive sins. He says He always existed. He says He is coming to judge the world at the end of time. Now let us get this clear. Among Pantheists, like the Indians, anyone might say that he was a part of God, or one with God.... But this man, since He was a Jew, could not mean that kind of God. God, in their language, meant the Being outside the world, who had made it and was infinitely different from anything else. And when you have grasped that, you will see that what this man said was, quite simply, the most shocking thing that has ever been uttered by human lips.[47]

Jesus made it quite clear he wasn't merely a wise teacher, another prophet, or a rabbi intent on helping his students improve their lives. He clearly communicated that he was the fulfillment of "God with us," the "ancient of days" who would one day gather all the nations under his glorious and never-ending rule.

Questions for Comprehension and Discussion

1. How is a logical journey to the truth similar to an ascent of a mountain to see a view?
2. Why is it so offensive to many people to claim that Jesus is God?
3. Based on the evidence presented in the first seventeen chapters, what are the three main conclusions we can draw?
4. Why would it have been so unlikely for Jews to believe that Jesus could be God? What is the most likely explanation for the overnight change in the worldview of formerly pious, law-abiding Jews?
5. What are a few examples from the New Testament that the earliest Christians considered Jesus to be equal to God?

6. What are a few examples of Jesus' own statements from the Book of John that indicate he considered himself God?
7. What are a few examples of Jesus' own statements from the Synoptic Gospels that indicate he considered himself God?
8. Why did Jesus use the term "Son of Man" to refer to himself? At what point in his earthly life did he indicate that he was going to come like the "son of man" referenced in the Old Testament? What did he say?
9. What did Jesus say to the paralyzed man that raised questions in the minds of the teachers of the law? How did Jesus demonstrate that he had authority to do this?
10. Explain what Jesus probably meant when he referenced Psalm 110, where King David wrote, "The Lord says to my Lord." How was Jesus expressing both his deity and humanity?

CHAPTER 18 ENDNOTES

[1] Paraphrased from Smith, Huston, *The World's Religions* (HarperCollins, 1991), 82. Quoted in Peter Kreeft and Ronald K. Tacelli, *Handbook of Christian Apologetics* (Downers Grove, IL: InterVarsity, 1994), 150.

[2] Robert M. Bowman, Jr. and J. Ed Komoszewski, *Putting Jesus in His Place: The Case for the Deity of Christ* (Grand Rapids, MI: Kregel Publications, 2007), 17.

[3] See Ephesians 2:8-9: "For it is by grace you have been saved, through faith—and this not from yourselves, it is the gift of God—not by works, so that no one can boast." Jesus claims that is necessary to "be born again of the Spirit" in order "enter the Kingdom of God" (see John 3:3-8). In the Old Testament, God speaks through Ezekiel and describes what he does in this way: "I will give them an undivided heart and put a new spirit in them; I will remove from them their heart of stone and give them a heart of flesh" (Ezekiel 11:19). Christians have described it as "seeing the light" or "having my eyes opened," but the main point is it is God's work in us, not our own logic that will empower us to take the leap of faith to believe in Jesus as God. Other verses that support this teaching that we are saved by faith alone, and not through any works include: Galatians 2:16, 21, 3:6, 10, 14, 22, 24; Romans 1:17, 3:10, 20, 24-25, 27-28, 4:1-25, 5:1-2, 9, 6:23, 9:30, 10:4, 10, 11:6; Philippians 3:9; John 1:17, 3:16, 18, 5:24, 6:28-29, 40, 47, 8:47; James 2:1-26 (especially vv10, 14, 16, 20, 24); Genesis 15:6; Acts 10:43, 13:39, 16:31, 26:18; Timothy 3:5; 1 Corinthians 5:17, Mark 16:16; Ephesians

1:13; and 2 Colossians 4:4. Some Christians wholly emphasize that we can do nothing for our own salvation, such that God has complete power over whether we are "His" or not. This doctrine of *election* is debated, but the goal is to remove any credit for salvation from believers and give all credit to God. For biblical evidence that demonstrates that God *chooses* those who have faith, that is, He alone has complete power of saving us, see John 15:16; Acts 9:15; Ephesians 1:4-5; 2 Thessalonians 2:13; John 6:28-29; and Philippians 1:29.

4   John Hick, "A Pluralist View," in *More Than One Way? Four Views on Salvation in a Pluralist World*, Dennis L. Okholm and Timothy R. Phillips, eds. (Grand Rapids, MI: Zondervan, 1995), 51-52. As quoted in Bowman and Komoszewski, *Putting Jesus in His Place*, 19.

5   Stephen Jay Gould writes, "Through no fault of our own, and by dint of no cosmic plan or conscious purpose, we have become, by the power of a glorious evolutionary accident called intelligence, the stewards of life's continuity on earth. We did not ask for this role, but we cannot abjure it. We may not be suited to such responsibility, but here we are." (Stephen Jay Gould, *The Flamingo's Smile: Reflections in Natural History* [New York: W.W. Norton & Company, 1987], 431.)

6   As a reminder, an infinite God is inconsistent with materialism (the belief that nothing exists beyond the material world), atheism (the belief that there is no God), and pantheism (the belief that there are multiple gods).

7   Hick, "A Pluralist View," 29.

8   Deuteronomy 6:4.

9   Mark 12:29. By worshiping the one true God, humans were to deny other idols in their lives and obey the God's wishes, which would result in love for one's neighbor and a desire to pursue a God-honoring life. The Lutheran Book of Concord states this succinctly: "Just this is also the meaning and true interpretation of the first and chief commandment, from which all the others must flow and proceed, so that this word: Thou shalt have no other gods before Me, in its simplest meaning states nothing else than this demand: Thou shalt fear, love, and trust in Me as thine only true God. For where there is a heart thus disposed towards God, the same has fulfilled this and all the other commandments. On the other hand, whoever fears and loves anything else in heaven and upon earth will keep neither this nor any." *Book of Concord*, "The Large Catechism: The Ten Commandments", Paragraph 324, available online at http://bookofconcord.org/lc-3-tencommandments.php#para324.

10 1 Corinthians 8:4.

11 Deuteronomy 5:7.

12 Acts 17:24-25, 29.

CHAPTER 18: CLAIMS OF DIVINITY

13   For examples of God's warnings, see Deuteronomy 8:19, 11:16, 12:2, 13:1-2, 6-8, 12-14, 16:21-22, 17:3, 20:18, 29:26, 27:19, 22; 1 Kings 9:6-9, 14:23, 35-38; Isaiah 57:6, 17:2, 22:9; and Ezekiel 6:13. For examples of the Jews worshiping other gods, see Deuteronomy 29:25-27; Judges 2:17-19; 2 Kings 16:4, 17:7-12; Jeremiah 3:6, 13, 16:11, and 17:2.

14   In John 10:30, Jesus says, "I and the Father are one."

15   Colossians 1:15.

16   John 1:1-4, 14, 18.

17   The New Testament authors didn't use the term, "trinity," but expressed the concept in various ways. Indeed, to express the authors' teaching about the Father, the Son, and the Holy Spirit, it took several centuries to fully encapsulate the Bible's statements about the triune God with the term, *Trinity*. New Testament verses which explain the concept of the Trinity include: 1 Corinthians 8:6; 2 Corinthians 1:21-22, 13:14; Ephesians 4:4-6; John 1:1, 3:16, 34-35, 5:19, 14:16, 26, 15:26; Hebrews 1:3; Isaiah 48:16; Luke 1:35, 3:22; Matthew 2:16-17, 3:16, 28:19; Mark 12:29; Romans 8:9-11; 1 Peter 1:2; Philippians 2:5-8; and 1 Timothy 2:5. Old Testament verses that support the concept of the Trinity include: Genesis 1:1 (uses a plural word, *Elohim*, for God), 1:2 ("the Spirit of God was hovering"), 1:26 (God uses the plural pronouns for himself: "Let *us* make mankind in *our* image, in *our* likeness," Genesis 3:22 (God uses the plural for himself: "the man will become like one of *us*"), Genesis 11:7 (uses the plural "let *us* go down"), Genesis 48:15-16 (when Jacob blesses his son Joseph, he mentions God three times with different names for God), Exodus 23:20-21, Psalm 2:6-7,12, Proverbs 30:4, Isaiah 6:8 (the Lord uses the plural for himself: "who will go for *us*?"), Isaiah 11:2-3, 54:5 (uses a plural word in Hebrew for "Maker" in "your Maker is your husband"), Isaiah 48:16,17 (mentions the "Spirit" as well as "your Redeemer, the Holy One of Israel," who is sent by God), Isaiah 61:1, Jeremiah 23:5-6, and others.

18   1 John 5:20-21.

19   Colossians 1:15-16, 19.

20   See G.J. Wenham, J.A. Motyer, D.A. Carson, R.T. France, eds., *New Bible Commentary, 21st Century Edition* (Leister, England: Inter-Varsity Press, 2003), 1266-1267.

21   John 8:58. All emphases in Bible passages are mine.

22   Exodus 3:13-14.

23   John 8:59.

24   These can be found respectively in John 6:51, 8:12, 10:9, 10:11, 11:25, and 14:6.

25   John 5:21-27.

26   James 4:12.

27. John 17:1-5.
28. John 8:19, 21-23.
29. John 10:24-33.
30. John 14:8-11.
31. Matthew 16:13-17, also found in Mark 8:27-30 and Luke 9:18-20.
32. For example, in Mark 2:10, Jesus claims to have the authority to forgive sin, in Mark 2:28, he claims to have authority over the Sabbath, and in Matthew 13:37, he makes a reference to being the Lord of the harvest.
33. Walter A. Elwell, ed., *The Evangelical Dictionary of the Theology* (Grand Rapids: Baker Academic), 1127.
34. Daniel 7:13-14.
35. See Psalm 145:13; Isaiah 9:6, 11:10; Ezekiel 37:26; Daniel 7:27; Micah 5:2; and many others.
36. See Deuteronomy 33:26; Psalm 18:9, 68:33; and Isaiah 19:1.
37. Mark 14:61-62, also recorded in Matthew 26:63-65.
38. Mark 2:5-12b, also in Luke 5:19-25.
39. Bowman and Komoszewski, *Putting Jesus in His Place*, 239. Emphasis theirs.
40. Luke 20:41-44.
41. 2 Samuel 7:8a,12b-13. For more detail on God's promise to David, read 2 Samuel 7:8-16.
42. For more information about this enigmatic claim to deity, I recommend Timothy Keller's sermon, "The Deity of Jesus," available at https://gospelinlife.com/downloads/the-deity-of-jesus-5298/.
43. Luke 10:1-3.
44. Luke 10:17.
45. Luke 10:18-20.
46. Matthew 28:18-20.
47. C. S. Lewis, *Mere Christianity* (San Francisco: HarperOne, 2009), 52. Originally published in 1952.

This Jesus of Nazareth, without money or arms, conquered more millions than Alexander, Caesar, Mohammed, and Napoleon; without science and learning, He shed more light on things human and divine than all philosophers and scholars combined; without the eloquence of schools, He spoke such words of life as were never spoken before or since, and produced effects which lie beyond the reach of orator or poet; without writing a single line, He set more pens in motion, and furnished themes for more sermons, orations, discussions, learned volumes, works of art, and songs of praise than the whole army of great men of ancient and modern times.

—Philip Schaff, 19th century Swiss theologian[1]

Through the pages of the Gospels Jesus emerges as a man of surpassing charm and winsomeness who bore about him, as someone has said, no strangeness at all save the strangeness of perfection.... It came to the point where they felt that as they looked at Jesus they were looking at the way God would be if he were to assume human form.

— Huston Smith, religious scholar[2]

19

Divinity on Display

The biblical passages that we read in the previous chapter are only a subset of many in which Jesus asserts that he was not just a prophet or representative of God, but God himself, in the flesh. At this point, some of you may be asking, why should we bother proving that Jesus is God? Isn't it just important to follow his teachings? Shouldn't we all just get along and move beyond the controversy?

Let's take a moment to summarize the various opinions: Mormons claim that Jesus is the eldest of God's "spirit children," just a human who fully expressed his divinity, and by emulating him, we can become more like God, too. Unitarian Universalists claim that Jesus, if a god, is just one of many gods, but not equal to one "single, true God." The Jehovah's Witnesses believe that Jesus was the first created being, and that God somehow used him to create everything else, but he is definitely not equal to God. Christian Scientists, who like many eastern philosophies claim that the physical world is an illusion, believe that Jesus was merely a man who was the first to identify the "way" to a vague spiritual reality and to somehow manifest the "truth" of God. And most Jews and Muslims believe that Jesus was just a human who claimed to have a special relationship with God the Father, as all other prophets have also claimed. With so many religions disputing the deity of Jesus, why can't each person determine who Jesus is for themselves? Why insist that Jesus is God, if it only causes heated division?

The essential reason that Christians consider this doctrine "non-negotiable" is their belief that salvation—that is, living forever in the absence of judgment, sin, sickness, and death—*depends on* Jesus being God in human form. It is therefore critical to demonstrate that Jesus really is both fully God and fully human.

CHAPTER 19: DIVINITY ON DISPLAY

Why must Jesus be both fully divine and fully human in order to provide salvation? In simple, admittedly insufficient words: Only if Jesus were fully human could he stand in place of his followers and facilitate the "Great Exchange," giving them his perfect moral record and taking on himself the penalty for their sin. And only if Jesus were fully divine could he have lived a sin-free life.[3] The Bible clearly teaches that only God is holy enough that he could never sin.[4] Moreover, only an infinite God could have endured the one-time penalty for the sins of all humanity, unlike the ineffective, merely symbolic animal sacrifices that had to be repeatedly presented in the temple by an unclean high priest (stay tuned for this in Chapter 27).[5] Thus, the only way that Jesus could fully pay the penalty for his followers' sins and give them his perfect moral record was for him to be both *fully* human and *fully* divine.[6]

Moreover, if Jesus was not really God, his followers could not confidently trust any of the promises he gave to them. Interestingly, Jesus claimed to be delivering the words that the Father had given to him, but he didn't say it in the same way that the Old Testament prophets always had. Jesus had a unique way of introducing his statements. The Jewish prophets who had come before him prefaced their proclamations with "The Lord says" (that is "God says"). Instead, Jesus always said, "Truly I tell you." A search of the Old Testament for the exact phrases, "the Lord says" or "the Sovereign Lord says" or "God says," yields 326 matches. On the other hand, Jesus used the phrase "I tell you" or "Truly I tell you" approximately 150 times in the New Testament.[7] As we transition from the time of the prophets to the time of Jesus, "the Lord says" becomes "I tell you."

One New Testament writer explains it this way:

> In the past God spoke to our ancestors through the prophets at many times and in various ways, but in these last days he has spoken to us by his Son, whom he appointed heir of all things, and through whom also he made the universe.[8]

Thus, before the physical birth of Jesus, God had used humans to deliver his messages. Having thus prepared humanity for his arrival, *he himself* came in human form to deliver the rest of his messages and to carry out the "ultimate rescue plan" that would enable his people to live with him for eternity. As God in human form, Jesus ushered in what he called the "New Covenant"[9] that makes salvation dependent only on one's faith in what he himself had done. This replaced the "Old Covenant," which based salvation on one's perfect obedience to the law and was thus something that no human could possibly attain. If this confuses you, hang in there, as we will clarify it in coming chapters.

THE HANDS OF JESUS

Professors Robert Bowman and J. Ed Komoszewski have developed a useful method to summarize their case that Jesus is divine. They proposed the acronym "HANDS" to classify the various means by which Jesus revealed himself during his time on earth. The acronym references Jesus' hands, which provided sufficient proof to the disciple Thomas that Jesus was divine. That is, after Thomas saw the nail marks in Jesus' hands, he famously exclaimed, "My Lord and my God!" Here is their explanation of the acronym:

> Just as an examination of the nail prints convinced Thomas he was beholding the hands of deity, a closer look at the Bible reveals that Jesus shares the HANDS of God:
> **Honors:** Jesus shares the *honors* due to God.
> **Attributes:** Jesus shares the *attributes* of God.
> **Names:** Jesus shares the *names* of God.
> **Deeds:** Jesus shares the *deeds* of God.
> **Seat:** Jesus shares the *seat* of God's throne.[10]

They clarify that the acronym is "not a gimmick" but a "tested and proven device for enabling people of different backgrounds to remember and explain the biblical evidence for identifying Jesus as God."[11] Though they fill their lengthy book with plentiful evidence from the New Testament, for our purposes I will briefly summarize each of the five aspects of Jesus' deity using the "HANDS of Jesus" mnemonic device.

CHAPTER 19: DIVINITY ON DISPLAY

THE "H" – JESUS SHARES THE HONORS DUE TO GOD

The authors note that the earliest Christian believers gave the same honors to Jesus that traditional Jews would only give to God. They shared the same belief in the Shema as the Jews, and they also sought to obey the second commandment to worship God alone. They worshiped Jesus *as if he were God*, prayed to him *as if he were God*, sang hymns to and about him *as if he were God*, believed in him *as if he were God*. They sought to serve, love, fear, revere, and obey his teaching *as if he were God*.

The Gospels record numerous examples of Jesus receiving worship. When sages from the far east found him as a child, "they bowed down and worshiped him."[12] As an adult, Jesus walked on the water and his disciples "worshiped him, saying, 'Truly you are the Son of God.'"[13] And when he appeared to his disciples after his resurrection, they "came to him, clasped his feet and worshiped him."[14] Similarly, after forty days in his resurrected body, Jesus was just about to give the "Great Commission" and ascend into heaven, and "when they saw him, they worshiped him."[15]

Jesus' followers also *believe in* him as if he were God. Jesus taught that "the Father loves the Son and has placed everything in his hands. Whoever *believes* in the Son has eternal life, but whoever rejects the Son will not see life, for God's wrath remains on them.'[16] And, in one of the most amazing statements that Jesus ever makes, he clarifies one reason we ought to believe in him:

> "I am the resurrection and the life. The one who *believes* in me will live, even though they die; and whoever lives by believing in me will never die."[17]

Furthermore, Jesus claims that to honor him is equivalent to honoring God the Father, and "Whoever does not *honor* the Son does not honor the Father, who sent him."[18]

Peter instructs his audience to honor Jesus as God, and he follows it with one actionable way that they could do so, by being ready to rationally and respectfully defend their faith:

> But in your hearts *revere Christ as Lord. Always be prepared* to give an answer to everyone who asks you *to give the reason for the hope that you have.* But do this with gentleness and respect.[19]

These are but a few of the many claims throughout the New Testament that Jesus' earliest followers believed he deserves the same honors that in the Old Testament had only been bestowed on Yahweh.[20]

THE "A" – JESUS SHARES THE ATTRIBUTES OF GOD

The second line of evidence that Jesus is God is that Jesus shares the same attributes as God, and he "possesses them in the same sense and to the same extent that God possesses them."[21] In short, the New Testament documents claim: (1) that Jesus is like God in the same way that a son inherits traits from a father, (2) that Jesus came from God in heaven and is returning to God in heaven (that is, he was with God before and after his time on earth), and (3) that Jesus is like God the Father in that he is also eternal, uncreated, unchanging, perfectly loving, omnipotent, omnipresent, omniscient, and incomprehensible.

There are some who like to point out instances when Jesus did not appear omniscient or omnipotent, such as when he admits he doesn't know when the ends times will come[22] or when he could not perform miracles in his hometown.[23] As we discussed in Chapter 6, there are theological explanations for these apparent contradictions to Jesus' divinity, but they are beyond the scope of this book. Suffice it to say that Jesus performed his miracles in response to the faith of the people.[24] Those who had seen Jesus grow up, the son of a carpenter, were jaded and refused to believe he was who he claimed to be. The saying, "Familiarity breeds contempt" may apply here.[25]

Moreover, Jesus was willing to humble himself and deny some of his divine powers as a part of his taking on human flesh, which is termed the *incarnation*. One of the earliest Christian hymns, which Paul quotes, explains that Jesus, though he was "in very nature God, did not consider equality with God something to be used to his own advantage; rather, he made himself nothing by taking the very nature of a servant."[26] Jesus purposefully limited his powers and knowledge for his role when he came to earth, just as he purposefully became a baby who required the care of human parents. When Jesus prayed right before he was arrested and taken away to be crucified, he gave us a hint that he had given up some of his "glory" while he was on earth: "And now, Father, glorify me in your presence with the glory I had with you before the world began."[27][28]

THE "N" – JESUS SHARES THE NAMES OF GOD

Throughout the New Testament, Jesus is given names that had *always only ever* been ascribed to God. The New Testament authors frequently call him "Savior," "Lord," and "God." They often combined the terms, calling him "our Lord and Savior," or "my Lord and my God," and so forth. Bowman and Komoszewski explain why this would be so unusual, if the writers considered Jesus a mere mortal:

> One can find a few texts here and there in the Bible that refer to some men over here as "saviors," or to a man over there as a "rock," but one cannot find texts referring to the same mere human being as god, lord, savior, shepherd, rock, first and last, and king of kings and lord of lords! The application of all these designations to the one person, Jesus Christ, often with two or more in the same immediate context, is highly significant.[29]

What's more, the New Testament documents give these names to Jesus while referencing Old Testament passages where the name had been applied to the one true God, *Yahweh* or *Jehovah*. The New Testament even teaches that Jesus' name itself has power, which is evident in the phrase, "in Jesus' name." In fact, the name "Jesus" means "Jehovah saves." And another of Jesus' names, "Immanuel," means "God with us."[30] Clearly, we are being told that Jesus is God, who saves us from death and is physically present with us, his creatures.

Following Jesus' resurrection, Peter healed a lame beggar, saying, "In the *name* of Jesus Christ of Nazareth, walk."[31] Because they were "proclaiming in Jesus the resurrection of the dead," the "priests and the captain of the temple guard and the Sadducees" detained Peter and John in jail overnight. The next day, the two men appeared before the Jewish ruling council, the Sanhedrin. It was here that Peter made an amazing claim regarding the power of Jesus' name. When the rulers, elders, and the teachers of the law asked them, "By what power or what name do you do this?" Peter replied in this bold way:

> "Rulers and elders of the people! If we are being called to account today for an act of kindness shown to a man who was lame and are being asked how he was healed, then know this, you and all the people of Israel: It is by the *name* of Jesus Christ of Nazareth, whom you crucified but whom God raised from the dead, that this man stands before you healed. Jesus is 'the stone you builders rejected, which has become the cornerstone.' Salvation is found in no one else, for there is *no other name* under heaven given to mankind by which we must be saved."[32]

Not only is Jesus the name by which Peter and John claimed they had power to heal, but Jesus is the *only name* by which people can be saved—that is, saved from sin and death to live in God's presence for all eternity.

Another very telling verse is found in Jesus' lengthy discourse to his disciples prior to his departure. Jesus said: "You did not choose me, but I chose you and appointed you so that you might go and bear fruit—fruit that will last—and so that whatever you ask *in my name* the Father will give you."[33] (Note, however, that this promise is tied with the goal of bearing fruit for God's eternal kingdom, so believers shouldn't expect to receive a billion dollars just because they ask for it in Jesus' name! This verse has been misunderstood and misused by many "health and wealth" preachers whose teach what has been called the "prosperity gospel.")

There are many other verses that specifically assign to Jesus names that had formerly only been used for Yahweh, as well as numerous verses that otherwise reference the power of the name of Jesus in order to emphasize his deity.[34]

CHAPTER 19: DIVINITY ON DISPLAY

THE "D" – JESUS SHARES THE DEEDS THAT GOD DOES

Not only does Jesus deserve the same honors as God, possess the same attributes as God, and share the same names as God, but he also performs the same deeds as God. His most impressive display on earth was his resurrection from the dead in a transphysical body. In the last chapter, we also discussed how he forgave sins, an act God alone could perform.

An outstanding deed (to say the least) that the New Testament attributes to him is creation itself. John is most clear: "All things came into being through him, and without him not one thing came into being."[35]

For those who object that Jesus is not mentioned in the Genesis creation account, it is helpful to point out that the opening verse ("In the beginning, God created the heavens and the earth") uses a plural form for the term "God"—the Hebrew word *Elohim*. Later in the first chapter, God states, "Let *us* make man in *our* image, in *our* likeness." This very well could be God's way of giving a "sneak peek" of his triune nature in the very first book of the Bible.

Moreover, the New Testament teaches that Jesus is participating in the ongoing activity of maintaining and directing the universe. Paul eloquently states that Jesus is "before all things, and in him all things hold together"[36] and it is Jesus through whom "all things came and through whom we live."[37] Also, John's use of the term *Logos* supports the idea that Jesus is the sustaining force throughout the universe, as if he is the cause of the laws of physics that hold the material world together.

Jesus also had the power to seemingly suspend the laws of physics. For example, he calmed the storm,[38] walked on water,[39] made food appear from nowhere,[40] converted water to wine,[41] and brought a dead man back to life (which, by the way, is called a "resuscitation," as opposed to a resurrection).[42]

There are many more examples of the ways he suspended the laws of nature, that is, performed miracles. The main distinction between Jesus and all other "miracle workers" in the Bible is that Jesus never called on the power of God to perform the miracle, as prophets in the Old Testament had. Men like Moses required God to intervene to perform miracles. Jesus did them by his own power.

One scholar studied the full range of Jewish literature prior to and contemporaneous with Jesus, and his conclusion was that "the Gospel portrayals of Jesus break with Jewish tradition by characterizing Jesus as a 'bearer of numinous power' (BNP) and his miracles as pointing to him as Yahweh."[43] That is, Jesus performed his miracles directly, without appeal to a higher power, prayer to a higher power, or mediation by a higher power. His disciples, however, were like the Old Testament prophets who performed miracles, "petitioners of numinous power" (PNPs), calling on the name of Jesus in order to perform healings and exorcisms. Moses, whom God used as a mediator to perform miracles, falls into a third category of miracles workers, a "mediator of numinous power" (MNP).[44]

Finally, as wondrous as creation and sustenance are, Jesus' best divine deed is the salvation he provides from sin and death. The following statement from Jesus' mouth is among the most amazing ever uttered, which is why it is so controversial: "I am the way, the truth and the life. No one comes to the Father except through me."[45] This verse is debated for good reason: how dare Jesus claim to be the only way to eternal life with God? Unless he's crazy or has been misquoted (both of which are unlikely based on his teachings in the rest of the New Testament), the only way he can confidently claim to be the only way to eternal life is if he himself is the *only one* with the power to provide eternal life.[46]

Furthermore, when he returns to earth, Jesus will "judge the living and the dead,"[47] which, as we discussed in the last chapter, is another deed that was reserved for God alone. Jesus himself stated that he has this particular role, not the Father: "Moreover, the Father judges no one, but has entrusted all judgment to the Son."[48] These are but a small sample of the many other verses that describe Jesus' power to judge humans.[49]

THE "S" – JESUS SHARES THE SEAT OF GOD'S THRONE

After his arrest, Jesus made another audacious claim: "From now on, the Son of Man will be seated at the right hand of the mighty God."[50] He was about to be tortured, and rather than pleading innocent or trying to pacify his enemies, he made a statement that roused them even more: when they asked, "Are you the Messiah, the Son of the Blessed One?" he

CHAPTER 19: DIVINITY ON DISPLAY

replied: "I am. And you will see the Son of Man sitting at the right hand of the Mighty One and coming on the clouds of heaven."[51] Claiming that he is worthy of sitting at God's right hand was over the top, and the high priest tore his clothing and accused Jesus of blasphemy for understandable reasons. That is the place of greatest honor, representing exalted rule and the right to judge.[52]

In the documents of the New Testament, Jesus made it abundantly clear what he thought of himself. Skeptics would like to disprove it, but we have shown that the accounts of his extraordinary life are trustworthy, and they unequivocally show that Jesus claimed to be equal to God. For this, he was accused of blasphemy. He repeatedly received death threats for this crime. The people who believed his self-testimony worshiped him—and they, too, faced death for it.

In his classic work *Mere Christianity*, C. S. Lewis memorably writes:

> I am trying here to prevent anyone saying the really foolish thing that people often say about Him: I'm ready to accept Jesus as a great moral teacher, but I don't accept his claim to be God. That is the one thing we must not say. A man who was merely a man and said the sort of things Jesus said would not be a great moral teacher. He would either be a lunatic — on the level with the man who says he is a poached egg — or else he would be the Devil of Hell. You must make your choice. Either this man was, and is, the Son of God, or else a madman or something worse. You can shut him up for a fool, you can spit at him and kill him as a demon or you can fall at his feet and call him Lord and God, but let us not come with any patronizing nonsense about his being a great human teacher. He has not left that open to us. He did not intend to.[53]

There is another way that Jesus demonstrated his divinity while on earth: his unmatched character and history-shaping, awe-inspiring life. The author H. G. Wells said, "I am a historian, I am not a believer, but I must confess as a historian that the penniless preacher from Nazareth is irrevocably the very center of history. Jesus Christ is easily the most dominant figure in all history."[54] Yale University historian Kenneth Stott

THE SHORTEST LEAP

Latourette makes a similar claim regarding Jesus: "As the centuries pass by, the evidence is accumulating that measured by its effect on history, Jesus is the most influential life ever lived on this planet."[55]

After being exiled to the island of Saint Helena, Napoleon Bonaparte wrote an argument for the divinity of Jesus, which was printed as a tract by a publisher in Paris. A professor from the theological seminary at Montauban, France, submitted a translation of this tract to the *New York Observer* on April 16, 1842. He also included an English translation of a conversation between Napoleon and his friend, the Count de Montholon, that took place on Saint Helena in the years before Napoleon's death. The former emperor purportedly said, "I know men, and I tell you that Jesus is not a man!" He then stated:

> The religion of Christ is a mystery which subsists by its own force, and proceeds from a mind which is not a human mind. We find in it a marked individuality, which originated a train of words and maxims unknown before – Jesus borrowed nothing from our knowledge. He exhibited in himself the perfect example of his precepts. Jesus is not a philosopher; for his proofs are miracles, and from the first his disciples adored him. In fact, learning and philosophy are of no use for salvation; and Jesus came into the world to reveal the mysteries of heaven and the laws of the Spirit.... Alexander, Caesar, Charlemagne, and I have founded empires. But on what did we rest the creation of our genius? Upon *force*. Jesus Christ founded His empire upon *love*; and at this hour millions of men would die for Him.... I die before my time, and my body will be given back to the earth to become food for worms. Such is the fate which so soon awaits him who has been called the great Napoleon. What an abyss between my great misery and the eternal Kingdom of Christ, which is proclaimed, loved, and adored, and which is extending over the whole earth! Call you this dying; is it not living rather? The death of Christ is the death of a God![56]

I found it interesting that the same publication mentioned that Napoleon had read the French professor's "Essay on the Divine Authority of the New Testament," which "eye-witnesses attest that he read with interest and satisfaction." The professor also stated that "similar witnesses attest that [Napoleon] read much of the Bible, and spoke of it with profound respect; and, further, that there was a religious revival among the inhabitants of St. Helena, which extended to the soldiers, who prayed much for the conversion and salvation of the noble prisoner."[57]

Of Jesus' character, Timothy Keller writes:

> In [Jesus] we see qualities and virtues we would ordinarily consider incompatible in the same person. We would never think they could be combined but, because they are, they are strikingly beautiful. Jesus combines high majesty with the greatest humility, he joins the strongest commitment to justice with astonishing mercy and grace, and he reveals a transcendent self-sufficiency and yet entire trust in and reliance upon his heavenly Father. We are surprised to see tenderness without any weakness, boldness without harshness, humility without any uncertainty, indeed accompanied by a towering confidence. Readers can discover for themselves his unbending convictions but complete approachability, his insistence on truth but always bathed in love, his power without insensitivity, integrity without rigidity, passion without prejudice.[58]

When one reads the Gospel narratives, it is hard to conclude that such a man is an invention. Jesus comes across without artifice, and he never appears to do or say anything out of selfish ambition. Indeed, Jesus is so different from all man-made, mythological accounts of a divine being in human form, that it is hard to imagine that early church leaders—even those with creative imaginations and extensive education in morality—could have created such a believable and admirable character.

Timothy Keller recounts a conversation between a pastor and a man who said he'd believe in God if someone would simply give him a watertight argument. The pastor replied, "What if God hasn't given us a 'watertight argument,' but rather a watertight person?"[59] Is it possible that the Creator decided to answer our longing for perfect proof of his existence by coming himself as the perfect human being?

QUESTIONS FOR COMPREHENSION AND DISCUSSION

1. Explain the acronym that Bowman and Komoszewski developed as a way to remember how the New Testament portrays Jesus as God: HANDS.
2. What are some of the honors that early Christians gave to Jesus that the Old Testament claims should be given to God alone? What are some examples of times that Jesus or his followers claim that Jesus deserves these honors?
3. What are some of the attributes that Jesus shares with God? What are some examples of when Jesus demonstrated these divine attributes?
4. How did Jesus purposefully humble himself through the incarnation? Why might it have appeared that he did not possess the full attributes of God while he was in human flesh?
5. Provide a few names normally reserved for God in the Old Testament that are then given to Jesus in the New Testament?
6. What are some examples of what the disciples were able to do "in Jesus' name"?
7. What are some examples of Jesus' deeds that the Jewish people had expected only God could do?
8. What does it mean that Jesus shares the same "seat" as God?
9. How do Jesus' character and actions demonstrate his divinity? Why is it so unlikely that Jesus is merely an invention of mankind?
10. What was it about Jesus that caused Napoleon, a man who had experienced the height of human power, to so admire him?

CHAPTER 19 ENDNOTES

[1] Philip Schaff, *The Person of Christ*, American Tract Society, 1913. As quoted in Peter Kreeft, "Why I Believe Jesus Is the Son of God," in Norman

CHAPTER 19: DIVINITY ON DISPLAY

L. Geisler and Paul K. Hoffman, eds., *Why I Am a Christian: Leading Thinkers Explain Why They Believe* (Grand Rapids, MI: Baker Books, 2001), 220-221.

2   Huston Smith, *The Religions of Man* (New York: Harper & Row, 1958), 310.

3   Note that we will get into more detail on the need for an innocent sacrifice in Chapter 27 when we discuss the symbols of the Old Testament that point to Jesus, in particular, the "Passover lamb."

4   For example, see Psalm 14:1, 3, 53:1, 3, Isaiah 64:6, Romans 3:12, and Hebrews 4:15. Compare to Number 23:19.

5   The need for an infinite God—and only an infinite God—to take on the sins of humans in order to give them eternal life is not clarified in only one verse. But I recommend the following verses as a starting point for further research: Ezekiel 18:4, Galatians 2:21, Romans 6:23, 8:3-4, 2 Corinthians 5:21, 1 Peter 2:24, Galatians 3:13, Hebrews 8:1-2, 9:11-14.

6   Stephen L. Wellum, "The Deity of Christ in the Synoptic Gospels" in Christopher W. Morgan and Robert A. Peterson, eds. *The Deity of Christ* (Wheaton, IL: Crossway, 2011), 61-90.

7   These searches were done in the NIV translation.

8   Hebrews 1:1-2.

9   See Luke 22:20 and 1 Corinthians 11:25 for Jesus' statement. See also Jeremiah 31:31 for the prophecy of this new covenant. And for other explanations of the New Covenant, see 2 Corinthians 3:6-7 and Hebrews 8:1-8, 9:15, 12:24.

10   Robert M. Bowman and J. Ed Komoszewski, *Putting Jesus in His Place: The Case for the Deity of Christ* (Grand Rapids, MI: Kregel Publications, 2007), 23.

11   Ibid.

12   Matthew 2:11.

13   Matthew 14:33.

14   Matthew 28:9.

15   Matthew 28:17.

16   John 3:34-35.

17   John 11:25-26.

18   John 5:23b.

19   1 Peter 3:15-16.

20   A few of the other verses that demonstrate that Jesus received the honors due to God from his earliest followers include: Matthew 20:31; John 6:35, 7:37-39, 10:37, 14:4, 21, 15:10; Acts 1:24-25, 3:16, 7:59-60, 10:43, 16:31, 20:21, 22:19, 24:24, 26:18; Philippians 2:6-11; 1 Corinthians 1:2; 2 Corinthians 5:10-11, 12:8-9; Galatians 3:26; Ephesians 5:18-21, 6:7-8,

21. Colossians 3:22-25; 2 Peter 3:18; 1 John 3:23, 5:1, 10, 13; Revelation 1:17, 4:11, 5:12-14, 22:20-21.
22. It is important to note that, though the Son shares the same *attributes* as the Father and the Holy Spirit, theologians do make the distinction regarding how the persons of the Trinity differ from one another using the term *property*. For example, "being the Son of the Father is a property that applies to the Son, not to the Father (or the Holy Spirit)." (Bowman and Komoszewski, *Putting Jesus in His Place*, 75.)
23. Matthew 24:36.
24. Mark 6:5.
25. For example, see Matthew 8:13, 9:2, 22, 29, 14:31, 16:8, 21:21; Mark 2:5, 5:28-29, 34, 36, 10:52, 11:22-23; Luke 5:20, 7:9, 50, 8:48, 17:6, 19, 18:42.
26. G.J. Wenham, J.A. Motyer, D.A. Carson, R.T. France, eds., *New Bible Commentary* (Leicester, England: InterVarsity Press, 2003), 961.
27. Philippians 2:6-7.
28. John 17:9.
29. If you would like to further explore how Jesus shares the attributes of God, here are additional verses to check out: Matthew 8:5-13, 9:4, 11:27, 12:25, 14:15-21, 16:16-17, 21, 17:9-12, 21:17, 22-23, 18:20, 20:18-19, 28, 23:34, 37, 24:14, 25:34-46, 26:1-2, 20-25, 31-35, 28:18-20; Mark 2:6-8, 7:24-30, 8:31-32, 13:1-2, 14:17-21, 27-31; Luke 6:8, 7:1-10, 10:22, 13:34, 21:20-24, 32, 22:21-23, 31-34; John 1:1-3, 10, 14, 18, 47-49, 2:19, 4:46-54, 5:19, 6:70-71, 8:42, 56-59, 10:18, 36, 11:11-15, 12:39-41, 45, 13:3, 10-11, 21-29, 34, 36-38, 14:7-10, 15:12-13, 16:28, 30, 17:5, 20:28, 21:17; Acts 17:31; Romans 8:3; 1 Corinthians 1:24, 8:6, 10:4, 9; 2 Corinthians 2:4, 5:10; Galatians 4:4-6; Ephesians. 1:21, 4:10; Philippians 2:6, 9-11; Colossians 1:15-17, 2:3, 9-10; 1 Timothy 6:16; Hebrews 1:2-3, 10-12; 1 Peter 3:22; and Jude 5.
30. Wenham, Motyer, Carson, France, eds., *New Bible Commentary*, 129.
31. Matthew 1:23, quoting Isaiah 7:14.
32. Acts 3:6.
33. Acts 4:8b-12.
34. John 15:16.
35. Additional verses relating to the names of God ascribed to Jesus include: Matthew 3:3, 7:22, 10:22, 19:29, 22:2, 24:9, 25:1-13; Mark 1:3, 2:19, 9:38-39, 13:13; Luke 2:11, 3:4, 10:17, 21:12, 17; John 1:12, 14, 8:58, 15:21, 20:28, 31; Acts 1:24, 2:21, 38, 3:6, 16, 4:7, 17-18, 30, 5:28, 40-41, 7:59-60, 8:16, 9:15-16, 27-28, 10:43, 48, 15:26, 16:18, 19:5, 13-18, 20:28, 21:13, 26:9; Romans 1:4, 6:3, 9:5, 10:9-13, 15:6; 1 Corinthians 1:2, 13-15, 12:3, 15:24; 2 Corinthians 11:2; Galatians 1:4; Ephesians 1:21, 5:23, 25-27; Philippians 1:4, 2:9-11, 4:20; Colossians 3:7; 1 Thessalonians 1:3, 3:11, 13; 1 Timothy 2:13; Hebrews

CHAPTER 19: DIVINITY ON DISPLAY

      1:2-3, 8; 1 Peter 4:14; 2 Peter 1:1; 1 John 1:1, 3:23, 5:13; 3 John 7; Revelation 2:3, 13:3, 8, and 19:13.

35. John 1:3. See also 1 Corinthians 8:6 ("Jesus Christ, through whom all things came"), Colossians 1:16 ("in [Jesus] all things were created"), and Hebrews 1:2 ("the Son... through whom also [God] made the universe).
36. Colossians 1:16.
37. 1 Corinthians 8:6.
38. Matthew 8:23-27; Mark 4:35-41; Luke 8:22-25; see also Exodus 9:33; 14:21-22; Job 3:15-17, 37:15, 38:8; Psalm 33:7, 89:9, 107:29; Proverbs 30:4; Jeremiah 10:13; Jonah 1:15.
39. Matthew 14:22-33; Mark 6:45-50; John 6:16-21; see also Jeremiah 32:17; Psalm 135:6; Luke 18:27.
40. Matthew 14:13-21, 15:29-38; Mark 6:30-44, 8:1-9; Luke 9:10-17; John 6:1-13.
41. John 2:1-10.
42. John 11:38-44.
43. Bowman and Komoszewski, *Putting Jesus in His Place*, 199, with reference to Eric Eve, "Jewish Context of Jesus' Miracles" (*Journal for the Study of the New Testament* Supplement, No. 231).
44. Ibid.
45. John 14:6.
46. For additional verses supporting the case that Jesus proclaimed the power to forgive sins and grant eternal life, see Matthew 1:21, 7:13-14, 9:2-7, 16:25, 20:28; Mark 2:5-12, 8:35, 10:45, 16:16; Luke 5:20-24, 7:47-49, 19:9-10; John 3:15-17, 10:9-10, 12:47; Acts 2:21, 4:12, 5:31, 13:14, 16:31; Romans 1:17, 5:10, 19, 10:9-10, 13; 1 Corinthians 4:10, 15:1-4, 15:22; 2 Corinthians 5:19; Ephesians 2:8-9; 2 Timothy 1:9; Titus 2:13-14; Hebrews 5:9, 7:25, 9:28; 1 Peter 1:8-9, 3:21; and 1 John 5:12.
47. 2 Timothy 4:1.
48. John 5:22.
49. In addition to John 5:22 and 2 Timothy 4:1, a sample of New Testament verses that describe Jesus' role as the ultimate Judge include: Matthew 11:24, 12:41-42; John 3:18, 36, 5:24, 27, 8:16, 26, 9:39, 12:48; Acts 17:31; 1 Corinthians 4:4-5, 6:2, 11:32; 2 Timothy 4:8; Hebrews 10:30; James 4:12; 1 Peter 4:5-6; Jude 14-16; Revelation 6:10, 19:11, and 20:13.
50. Luke 22:69.
51. Mark 14:62.
52. Additional New Testament verses that provide evidence that the earliest Christians believed Jesus held a divine position of authority to rule over all creation include: Matthew 28:18; John 3:35, 13:3, 16:15; Acts 2:33-35, 10:36; Ephesians 1:20-22; Philippians 2:9-11, 3:20-21; 1 Corinthians

15:27-28; 1 Timothy 6:15; Hebrews 1:2, 2:8-9; Revelation 1:5, 3:14, and 17:14.

53 C. S. Lewis, *Mere Christianity* (San Francisco: HarperOne, 2009), 53.

54 Scott T. Allison and George R. Goethals, *Heroic Leadership: An Influence Taxonomy of 100 Exceptional Individuals* (New York: Routledge, 2013),185-186.

55 Kenneth S. Latourette, *A History of Christianity* (San Francisco: Harper San Francisco, 1953, 1975), 34.

56 Napoleon Bonaparte, "Napoleon's Argument for the Divinity of Christ and the Scriptures in a Conversation with General Bertrand at St. Helena," 7-8. Available online at https://archive.org/details/napoleonsargumen00napo/page/7.

57 Ibid.

58 Timothy Keller was summarizing a sermon by Jonathan Edwards, "On the Excellency of Jesus Christ." See Keller, *Making Sense of GOD: Finding God in the Modern World* (New York: Penguin Books, 2018), 232-233.

59 Timothy Keller, *The Reason for God* (New York: Penguin Group, 2008), 242.

The Bible is the only book which challenges unbelief by foretelling the future, staking it on the ultimate, certain, and complete fulfillment of its detailed predictions. It has been said that there were some 109 Old Testament predictions literally fulfilled at Christ's first coming.... If the law of Compound Probabilities is applied to all 109 predictions fulfilled at Christ's first coming, the chances that they could accidentally be fulfilled in the history of one person is one in billions.

—John Phillips, Bible scholar and author[1]

Other books claim divine inspiration, such as the Koran, the Book of Mormon, and parts of the [Hindu] Veda. But none of those books contains predictive prophecy. As a result, fulfilled prophecy is a strong indication of the unique, divine authority of the Bible.

—Norman Geisler and William Nix, biblical scholars[2]

20

Jesus' Coming Foretold

One Sabbath day, when Jesus was visiting his hometown of Nazareth, he participated in the synagogue services "as was his custom."³ As part of the service, the community leader handed out a scroll to be read aloud. On this day, Jesus received the scroll. Luke records that Jesus "stood up to read, and the scroll of the prophet Isaiah was handed to him." This is the section of Scripture that Jesus read on this day, the day he chose to launch his public ministry: "The Spirit of the Lord is on me, because he has anointed me to proclaim good news to the poor. He has sent me to proclaim freedom for the prisoners and recovery of sight for the blind, to set the oppressed free, to proclaim the year of the Lord's favor." But Jesus stopped in mid-sentence and "rolled up the scroll, gave it back to the attendant and sat down." With the "eyes of everyone in the synagogue" fixed on him, he then said, "Today this scripture is fulfilled in your hearing."⁴

Why did Jesus choose to read the scroll on this day? How was it fulfilled? Why did Jesus read all of the first verse of Isaiah 61 but then stop halfway through the second verse? (This is the likely reason that the people were staring at him when he handed the scroll back to the attendant and sat down; perhaps they were thinking it was strange that he had failed to finish.)

If we turn back one chapter—to the one just before this account in Luke's Gospel—we read that John the Baptist baptized Jesus in the Jordan River, at which point "the Holy Spirit descended upon him in bodily form like a dove."⁵ Luke follows this scene with Jesus' reading in the synagogue perhaps in anticipation of the question, "Why did the dove descend on Jesus?" or, as Jesus rephrased it, "Why is the Spirit of the Lord *on him*?"

CHAPTER 20: JESUS' COMING FORETOLD

Indeed, in the next three years of his public ministry, Jesus would give comforting news to the poor, free those who were bound by sin and death, open the eyes of both the physically and the spiritually blind, and proclaim God's love and favor.

But what about the last part of the verse, the part that Jesus stopped short of reading? The full second verse of Isaiah 61 states, "he has anointed me to proclaim the year of the Lord's favor *and the day of vengeance of our God*."[6] The Jewish people had expected their Messiah to accomplish *both* objectives upon his arrival: it would not only be a time to proclaim the good news that "God's favor" was being bestowed upon his people, but also a time when God would exercise divine vengeance, establish justice, and punish evildoers, especially the enemies of his people, the Israelites. By not reading the second half of the verse, Jesus may have been indicating that the second part would have to wait for future fulfillment. On his first visit to earth, his mission was to do the former. And, as Jesus explains elsewhere in the Gospels, he will return to execute judgment against evil at a future date.[7]

This is both an example of an Old Testament prophecy that Jesus fulfilled during his life, and also an example of an Old Testament prophecy that Jesus indicated he would fulfill at a later date, still future to us even today. We now turn to many other ways that Jesus' life, death, and resurrection had been foretold in the Old Testament. By fulfilling so many prophecies written hundreds of years before his birth, Jesus has given us one of the strongest lines of evidence that he really is who he claimed to be—the incarnate Son of God, the true Messiah whom the Israelites had been awaiting for centuries.

Even if one does not accept the Christian belief that the authors of the Bible wrote exactly what God directed—or "inspired"—them to write, there is no doubt that it is a remarkable book. Its collection of histories, poetry, and prophecies were penned by more than forty different authors and compiled into one volume over centuries, yet its imagery and themes form an amazing cohesion. As we look at some of the passages that point to the work of Jesus, we will discover a book like no other—and find that it is not such a great leap of faith after all to believe that the Bible is, as Christians say, "the word of God."

Prophecies Relating to Jesus' Lineage

A helpful term for understanding the Bible is "redemptive history." In other words, the purpose of the entire book is to show that humans need "redemption"—that is, each person must be "redeemed," or "saved from sin and death"[8]—and that the God who created humans has worked in history to do just that. A brief summary of the Bible is hardly adequate to show its depth and richness. But let's look at key moments in the Bible's story of redemptive history that prepare its readers to understand Jesus.

The history of humankind's salvation is told largely through a family tree. In Genesis, we read about Noah, who had three sons: Shem, Ham, and Japheth. Shem would become the father of the Jewish people (the "Shemites," or "Semites"), while Ham and Japheth would be the father of the Hamitic and Japhetic races. In the Bible, Noah speaks of his sons this way, obviously blessing Shem in greater measure:

> Praise be to the Lord, the God of Shem!
> May Canaan be the slave of Shem.
> May God extend Japheth's territory;
> may Japheth live in the tents of Shem,
> and may Canaan be the slave of Japheth.[9]

God fulfills Noah's blessing of Shem, for it was from Shem's line that his "chosen nation,"[10] Israel, would come. The Bible's redemptive history homes in on one man: Abraham. The twelfth chapter of Genesis contains a remarkable promise to Abraham: God said that *"all the people on earth* would be blessed through [him]."[11] God also promised that he would give a special homeland to Abraham's descendants.

Later in Genesis, God appeared to Abraham's son Isaac and repeated the promise:[12] "I will make your descendants as numerous as the stars in the sky and will give them all these lands, and through your offspring *all nations on earth* will be blessed."[13] And two chapters later, God reiterated the promise to Isaac's son, Jacob: "Your descendants will be like the dust of the earth, and you will spread out to the west and to the east, to the north and to the south. *All peoples on earth* will be blessed through you and your offspring."[14]

Jacob had twelve sons, the descendants of whom became the twelve tribes of Israel. The fourth son, Judah, was the next after Jacob to receive a promise from God regarding his descendants. When Jacob was about to die, he called his sons to him, saying, "Gather around so I can tell you what will happen to you in the days to come."[15] He made this statement regarding Judah:

> Judah, your brothers will praise you;
>> your hand will be on the neck of your enemies;
>> your father's sons will bow down to you.
> You are a lion's cub, Judah....
>> The *scepter* will not depart from Judah,
>> nor *the ruler's staff* from between his feet,
> until he to whom it belongs shall come
>> and the *obedience of the nations* shall be his.[16]

The scepter is an ornamental staff held by a ruler. A king or pharaoh would typically carry it during important ceremonies, and it came to symbolize sovereignty. And the Hebrew word for "ruler's staff" uses a root word that means "to cut" or "to inscribe," which is the verb used for the cutting of a decree or the inscription of a law. Thus, this prophecy states that someone from the tribe of Judah would, as one theologian put it, "wield the scepter with power and authority on the basis of a law or decree given to him."[17]

So, the blessing to the tribe of Judah indicates that the future ruling king would come from Judah's descendants. For this reason, Jews believed that the future Messiah would come from the line of Judah. This Messiah, or "Christ," from the Greek,[18] would usher in a period of abundance, peace, and joy.

In his blessing to Judah, Jacob also claimed that this future savior would have "the obedience of the nations." The surprise here is that "nations" is plural, not singular as it usually appears in references to the nation of Israel. Jacob was predicting that the ruler who would come from the line of Judah would rule over Israel as well as other nations beyond the borders of Israel.

The first Israelite leader to come from the tribe of Judah was King David, many centuries after Jacob's deathbed prophecy to Judah.[19] Once David became the king of Israel, a prophet named Nathan delivered this message from God to him:

> "The Lord declares to you that the Lord himself will establish a house for you: When your days are over and you rest with your ancestors, I will raise up your offspring to succeed you, *your own flesh and blood*, and I will establish his kingdom. He is the one who will build a house for my Name, and I will establish the throne of his kingdom forever.... Your house and your kingdom will endure forever before me; *your throne will be established forever*."[20]

It is obvious that God intends for David to die ("when your days are over and you rest with your ancestors"), and yet God repeated the word, "forever," several times with reference to David's dynasty. It sounds like God is referring to Solomon, David's son, who will "build a house for [God's] Name," since Solomon did build the first temple in the tenth century BC. But Solomon's rule lasted only 39 years. Furthermore, in 587 BC, the Davidic kingdom suffered defeat by the Babylonians,[21] and Zedekiah (the twenty-first king after David and the last descendant of David to rule as king) was blinded and taken into captivity. His kingdom became a Babylonian province ruled by Nebuchadnezzar, the king of Babylon. The Jewish people were left wondering, isn't there supposed to be a son of David who would rule with no end? Where is he?

Hundreds of years later, Luke reports that an angel spoke to a female descendant of David (engaged to a male descendant of David named Joseph):

> Do not be afraid, Mary; you have found favor with God. You will conceive and give birth to a son, and you are to call him Jesus. He will be great and will be called the Son of the Most High. The Lord God will give him *the throne of his father David*, and he will reign over Jacob's descendants *forever*; his kingdom *will never end*.[22]

It begins to make sense: Jesus is the one who will reign over Jacob's descendants forever; Jesus is the one whose kingdom will never end. That is why he emphasized, as we discussed in Chapter 18, that he is both "David's Lord" and "David's son." In other words, Jesus was saying,

"The scepter and the ruler's staff belong to me. Jacob was referring to *my* coming when he blessed his son Judah."

The author of the New Testament book of Hebrews explains how Jesus fulfilled the prophecy of Psalm 110 that describes the future Messiah sitting at the right hand of God while he waits for his enemies to be made his footstool:

> But when this priest [Jesus] had offered for all time one sacrifice for sins, he sat down at the right hand of God, and since that time *he waits for his enemies to be made his footstool*. For by one sacrifice he has made perfect forever those who are being made holy.[23]

The New Testament also refers to Jesus as the "Lion of the tribe of Judah," again alluding to the Messiah figure in Judah's blessing and to other Old Testament Messianic references.[24] Moreover, Jesus is the one through whom, by whom, and for whom God made his unbreakable promise to Abraham, Isaac, and Jacob to bless *all nations* throughout the entire world. How does Jesus do this? He offers eternal life to anyone in any nation who simply believes him.

Prophecies Relating to Jesus' Birth

Eight centuries before the birth of Christ, the prophet Isaiah rebuked a descendant of David named Ahaz, the thirteenth king after David (and at that time king of the nation of Judah, which had split with Israel).[25] King Ahaz was in a predicament. The powerful armies of the Assyrian nation had been overpowering the smaller kingdoms along the Mediterranean Sea and were closing in on Israel, Judah, and neighboring Damascus. Ahaz's faith was faltering. Either his throne would fall to Israel and Damascus, or the Assyrians would crush his kingdom. Either way, it was looking like the "throne of David" would come to an end, even though God had promised that it would last forever.

At this point, God sent Isaiah the prophet to reassure Ahaz that the dynasty would not fall and to give him a warning: "If you do not stand firm in your faith, you will not stand at all."[26] Ahaz was asked to believe this regarding the future line of David:

"Hear now, you house of David! Is it not enough to try the patience of humans? Will you try the patience of my God also? Therefore the Lord himself will give you a sign: *The virgin will conceive* and give birth to a son, and will call him *Immanuel*."[27]

Six centuries later, Matthew records the birth of Jesus, claiming, "All this took place to fulfill what the Lord had said through the prophet: 'The virgin will conceive and give birth to a son, and they will call him Immanuel' (which means 'God with us')."[28] Ahaz may have wondered how God intended to encourage him with a sign about a baby being born to a virgin, but God had intended this prophecy to encourage a much wider audience than just King Ahaz.

Two chapters after God's statement to Ahaz regarding the virgin, Isaiah prophesies even more details about this child:

> For to us a child is born,
>   to us a son is given,
>   and the government will be on his shoulders.
> And he will be called
>   Wonderful Counselor, Mighty God,
>   Everlasting Father, Prince of Peace.
> Of the greatness of his government and peace
>   there will be no end.
> He will reign on David's throne
>   and over his kingdom,
> establishing and upholding it
>   with justice and righteousness
>   from that time on and forever.[29]

These verses shed further light on what this baby born of a virgin would do: when he grew up, he would govern with greatness, peace, justice, and righteousness—forever. Here was the promised King who would reign eternally on David's throne.

The Gospel writers Matthew and Luke provide Jesus' genealogy from two perspectives, both of which demonstrate that he was indeed a descendant of Judah and David.[30] They also relate that he was the son of a virgin. As the perfect blend of human and God—mysteriously both

CHAPTER 20: JESUS' COMING FORETOLD

fully human and fully God—Jesus is the ultimate fulfillment of the name *Immanuel*, "God with us."

Another eighth century prophet, Micah, predicted this:

> "But you, *Bethlehem* Ephrathah,
>   though you are small among the clans of *Judah*,
> out of you will come for me
>   one who will be ruler over Israel,
> whose origins are from of old,
>   from ancient times."[31]

In addition to providing confirmation that the Messiah would come from the line of Judah, Micah names his birthplace. Bethlehem was the city where King David was born, but by New Testament times it had become a "has been" town. However, Matthew would have us believe that God chose *this humble place* for his entry into human history. It is interesting to contemplate the stark contrast between Jesus' birth and the type of grand entrance that a typical human ruler would make, if given the wherewithal to come into the world however he or she would choose.

Using a more literal translation of the Hebrew, Micah states that this "ruler over Israel" would "go forth" out of Bethlehem, and that his "going forths" are from long ago. Hebrew scholar Arnold Fruchtenbaum explains the tremendous emphasis that the text places on the eternality of this ruler:

> The Hebrew words for "from long ago, from the days of eternity" are the strongest Hebrew words ever used for eternity past. They are used of God the Father in Psalm 90:2. What is true of God the Father is also said to be true of this One who is to be born in Bethlehem.[32]

The verse in the Psalms that he mentions goes as follows, "Before the mountains were born or you brought forth the whole world, *from everlasting to everlasting* you are God." Thus, Micah's prophecy indicates that this everlasting God who existed before the world is equivalent to the "ruler over Israel" who was to come from Bethlehem.

Matthew refers to this prophecy in his account of Jesus' birth. The

Judean king, King Herod the Great, whom the Jews considered a usurper and vassal of the Roman occupiers, discovered that wise men (or magi) from the east were seeking a newborn "king of the Jews." Herod asked the chief Jewish priests and teachers of the law where the Messiah was to be born. They knew what the Scriptures had foretold and thus answered, "In Bethlehem in Judea," and they recited Micah's prophecy to Herod.[33]

The wise men eventually found the baby Jesus in Bethlehem, and "they bowed down and worshiped him" and "opened their treasures and presented him with gifts of gold, frankincense and myrrh."[34]

In Psalm 72, King David's son and successor King Solomon prays to the Lord to grant him righteousness and justice. He prays that through God's power the king (presumably himself) would "defend the afflicted among the people and save the children of the needy." He prays that God would enable this king to "crush the oppressor." So far, this is exactly what you'd imagine a good king would pray as he seeks God's guidance for his rule.

But in the next verse, Solomon prays: "May he endure as long as the sun, as long as the moon, through all generations.... In his days may the righteous flourish and prosperity abound till the moon is no more." This now sounds like an eternal king, and it is therefore possibly a reference to God himself, who, as the maker of heaven and earth, is the one true King. But the remainder of the psalm sounds eerily like the baby Jesus, the one whom the magi call "king of the Jews" and to whom they travel many miles so they can present him with precious gifts befitting of a king. We read:

> May he rule from sea to sea
>   and from the [Euphrates] River to the ends of the earth.
> May the desert tribes bow before him
>   and his enemies lick the dust.
> May the kings of Tarshish and of distant shores
>   bring tribute to him.
> May the kings of Sheba and Seba
>   present him gifts.
> May all kings bow down to him
>   and all nations serve him.
> For he will deliver the needy who cry out,
>   the afflicted who have no one to help.

CHAPTER 20: JESUS' COMING FORETOLD

> He will take pity on the weak and the needy
> > and save the needy from death.
> He will rescue them from oppression and violence,
> > for precious is their blood in his sight.
> Long may he live!
> > May gold from Sheba be given him.
> May people ever pray for him
> > and bless him all day long....
> May his name endure forever;
> > may it continue as long as the sun.
> Then all nations will be blessed through him,
> > and they will call him blessed.[35]

Though we could spend many pages examining the multiple ways that Jesus fulfills the cries of Solomon's heart for a king who hears the cries of the needy and crushes the oppressor, we will let the text speak for itself. We will just ask one question: Could the magi "from distant shores" who visit the baby Jesus be the first of many—from the ends of the earth—who will bow down before him?

From Isaiah, Micah, and the Psalms, therefore, we see that the Jewish people expected a promised Messiah who would be a descendant of Judah and David, born of a virgin in Bethlehem, and worshiped by people who hail from distant places, bow down to him, and present him with gold, honor, and other gifts.

Prophecies of Jesus' Triumphal Entry

To mark his entry into Jerusalem, Jesus insisted that his disciples bring him the colt of a donkey, "which no one has ever ridden."[36] Jesus chose to ride this colt into Jerusalem one week prior to his resurrection, a day now celebrated by Christians as Palm Sunday. The same crowd that later would be yelling, "Crucify him!" instead were crying out:

> "Hosanna! [Save!]"
> "Blessed is he who comes in the name of the Lord!"
> "Blessed is the coming kingdom of our father David!"
> "Hosanna in the highest heaven!"[37]

THE SHORTEST LEAP

The Jews were expecting a political Messiah who would deliver them from Roman control and rule over them forever. But Jesus entered Jerusalem riding the colt of a donkey. This unexpected, stunning fact should have clued in the bystanders that Jesus was not the typical king entering the city in victory. Though he was indeed entering Jerusalem in victory and ushering in the Kingdom of God, Jesus did not arrive on a warhorse or in a chariot. Instead he rode into town not just on a donkey, but on the colt of a donkey that had never been ridden. Jesus requested the colt for a reason—after all, he was always insisting that "the Scriptures must be fulfilled."[38] We can see what motivated him in this prophecy from Zechariah, who, writing in the early 500s BC, makes this prophecy regarding the way the future king would enter Jerusalem:

> Rejoice greatly, Daughter Zion [Israel]!
> Shout, Daughter Jerusalem!
> See, your king comes to you,
>   righteous and victorious,
>   lowly and riding on a donkey,
>   on a colt, the foal of a donkey.[39]

Knowing he was heading to the cross—where Christians believe he achieved the ultimate victory over sin and death—Jesus was indeed "righteous and victorious" as he entered Jerusalem on the foal of a donkey. Interestingly, in the ancient world, donkeys were primarily ridden by rulers in ceremonies that symbolized peace, such as the signing of a peace treaty. They were also associated with service, humility, and suffering, which was consistent with the mission that Jesus was entering Jerusalem to undertake. Moreover, a colt that had never been ridden was unlikely to cooperate with its rider, indicating that, in addition to proclaiming humility, service, and peace, Jesus was also displaying his power over the natural world.

But contrary to the expectations and desires of the Jewish people, it was not his plan—yet—to display power for the purpose of ousting the corrupt political system and establishing an eternal kingdom under his perfectly just rule. Accomplishing that objective, as we will discuss in Chapter 22, would come later. Let's now turn to the prophecies that describe this coming, powerful ruler in a totally unexpected way—a way that shows him enduring terrible suffering, self-sacrifice, and anguish.

CHAPTER 20: JESUS' COMING FORETOLD

QUESTIONS FOR COMPREHENSION AND DISCUSSION

1. How did Jesus fulfill the first verse of Isaiah 61? How did he fulfill the first part of the second verse of Isaiah 61? What is the likely reason Jesus stopped before reading the second part of verse 2 of Isaiah 61 in the synagogue before he started his ministry?
2. Why is the fulfillment of prophecy strong evidence that the Bible is God's Word and that Jesus is who he claimed to be?
3. What promise did God make to three generations (Abraham, Isaac, and Jacob) regarding their descendants?
4. What did Jacob's deathbed statement to his son Judah indicate would happen through Judah's descendants?
5. What did Nathan the prophet tell David that God said concerning one of his descendants?
6. How does the author of Hebrews explain that Jesus is the fulfillment of Psalm 110? By way of review, why did Jesus refer to this psalm, and how is it evidence that Jesus declared he was God?
7. What was the sign that God gave to Ahaz as the Assyrian army was closing in on him? For whom else did God intend this to be a sign?
8. What else did Isaiah foretell about this child who would be born?
9. What does Solomon pray for in Psalm 72 that concerns an event relating to Jesus' birth? What are other aspects of this psalm that seem to relate to Jesus?
10. What message was Jesus sending when he rode into Jerusalem on the foal of a donkey that had never been ridden? How did this differ from what his fellow Jews were expecting upon the arrival of the Messiah?

CHAPTER 20 ENDNOTES

[1] John Phillips, *Exploring the Scriptures* (Chicago: Moody, 1965, 1970), 124.
[2] Norman Geisler and William Nix, *An Introduction to the Bible* (Chicago: Moody, 1986), 196. They also footnote Gleason L. Archer, *A Survey of*

Old Testament Introduction, "Appendix 2: Anachronisms and Historical Inaccuracies in the Koran," 498-500; "Appendix 3: Anachronisms and Historical Inaccuracies in the Mormon Scriptures," 501-504.

3. Luke 4:16.
4. Luke 4:16-21.
5. Luke 3:22.
6. Isaiah 61:2b (the second part of Isaiah 61:2). All emphases in Bible passages are mine.
7. For Jesus' explanation of his second coming, a good place to start is Matthew 24. Jesus teaches that he will come again at a later date to "judge the living and the dead" (as it is phrased in 2 Timothy 4:1). The main point is that Jesus came two millennia ago to fulfill the first part of Isaiah 61:2—to proclaim the "good news" and "the year of the Lord's favor," but the day of judgment, which will happen when Jesus returns, is still future to us.
8. A few of the many verses that speak to the redemption that only Jesus can provide humans include Matthew 19:29, 26:28; Luke 1:68, 2:38, 21:28, 24:45-47; John 3:16, 36; Acts 2:21, 38, 10:43, 13:38, 26:18; Romans 3:24, 6:23, 8:23; 1 Corinthians 1:30; Galatians 3:13, 4:5; Ephesians 1:7, 14, 2:4-5; Colossians 1:14; Titus 2: 14; Hebrews 10:14; 1 Peter 1:18; 1 John 1:9.
9. Genesis 9:26-27.
10. See Deuteronomy 7:6-7 for the reason that Israel is called God's "chosen people."
11. Genesis 12:3.
12. The theological term for this promise is "covenant."
13. Genesis 26:4.
14. Genesis 28:14.
15. Genesis 49:1.
16. Genesis 49:8-9a, 10.
17. Walter C. Kaiser Jr., Peter H. Davids, F.F. Bruce, and Manfred T. Brauch, *Hard Sayings of the Bible* (Downers Grove, IL: InterVarsity Press, 1996), 134.
18. "Christ" (Χρίστος) is the Greek translation of "Messiah," which is used to describe Jesus in the New Testament.
19. Leaders prior to David had come from other tribes. Moses was from the tribe of Levi. Joshua, his successor, was from the tribe of Ephraim (one of Joseph's sons). The great warrior, judge, and prophet Gideon was from the tribe of Manasseh (another of Joseph's sons), and Samson, one of Israel's last judges before they established the monarchy, was from the tribe of Dan. Another great prophet, Samuel, also came from the tribe of Ephraim. And finally, Saul, the first king of Israel, came from the tribe of

CHAPTER 20: JESUS' COMING FORETOLD

Benjamin. Many years had passed, therefore, without any ruler from the line of Judah. But David, the king to follow Saul, was finally a potential candidate to be "the Messiah" (Every anointed king or high priest was called "*a* messiah," or an anointed one, so the Jews were looking forward to "*the* Messiah.")

20 2 Samuel 7:12-13,16.
21 This happened when the Babylonians destroyed the Jewish temple, and the kingdom of Judah came to an end. See the story in Jeremiah 52.
22 Luke 1:30-33.
23 Hebrews 10:12-14.
24 For references to the "Lion of Judah," see Genesis 49:8-10, Hosea 5:14, and Revelation 5:5. Note that in this era of redemptive history, Jesus also fulfills the prophecies relating to "Shiloh" in Genesis 49:10 and Ezekiel 21:27, and those relating to the "Branch of the Lord" and the "root of Jesse" in Isaiah 4:2, 11:1, 10, 53:2, Jeremiah 23:1-5, 33:15, Zechariah 3:8, 6:12, Romans 15:12, Revelation 5:5 22:16.
25 At the time, Ahaz was the young king of Judah. It is helpful to note that Saul and David had been the first two kings of the United Monarchy of Israel, which split into two nations around 930 BC during the reign of King David's grandson (and Solomon's son), Rehoboam. The ten tribes of northern Israel had rebelled against Rehoboam's rule, resulting in the division of the nation. Rehoboam remained the king of the southern kingdom of Judah (which consisted of the territory of the tribes of Judah and Benjamin), and a man named Jeroboam became the first king of the northern kingdom of Israel. Ahaz, who is the eleventh king of Judah after Rehoboam (thus thirteen generations removed from King David), took the throne when he was only 20, and he ruled for sixteen years in the second half of the seventh century BC (approximately 732-716 BC). Ahaz is described as an evil king who "did not do what was right in the eyes of the Lord" (2 Kings 16:2), and his son Hezekiah had to do a lot of cleaning up after his father when he succeeded him.
26 Isaiah 7:9b.
27 Isaiah 7:13-14.
28 Matthew 1:22-23.
29 Isaiah 9:6-7.
30 See Matthew 1 and Luke 3:21-38 for the two genealogies of Jesus.
31 Micah 5:2.
32 Arnold G. Fruchtenbaum, *Messianic Christology: A Study of Old Testament Prophecy Concerning the First Coming of the Messiah* (Tustin, CA: Ariel Ministries Press, 1998), 64.
33 Matthew 2:5-6.

34 Matthew 2:11.
35 Psalm 72.
36 Mark 11:2.
37 Mark 11:9-10.
38 Matthew 26:54; Mark 14:49; Luke 22:37, 24:44.
39 Zechariah 9:9.

Crucifixion was a Roman and a Grecian custom, but the Grecian and Roman empires were not in existence in David's time. Yet here is a prophecy written 1,000 years before Christ was born by a man who had never seen or heard of such a method of capital punishment as crucifixion. No other form of death could possibly correspond to the details David gives of the piercing of hands and feet, and the stripping of the tortured one to tell all the bones.

—Herbert Lockyer, Christian minister and author[1]

"*Fellow Israelites, I can tell you confidently that the patriarch David died and was buried, and his tomb is here to this day. But he was a prophet and knew that God had promised him on oath that he would place one of his descendants on his throne. Seeing what was to come, he spoke of the resurrection of the Messiah, that he was not abandoned to the realm of the dead, nor did his body see decay. God has raised this Jesus to life, and we are all witnesses of it.*"

—The apostle Peter to a crowd on Pentecost[2]

Crucifixion and Resurrection Foretold

It is understandable that the Jewish people were expecting the Messiah to come in kingly power and awesome might to establish peace on earth, to judge the world, and to avenge all evildoers. When instead Jesus was arrested and seemingly displayed little power to escape his predicament, they were even more confident that he could not possibly be their long-anticipated Messiah.

On many occasions, Jesus gave his disciples advance notice of his execution and resurrection. According to Luke, Jesus told his disciples three times that he would be delivered over to be killed. Here's the third time:

> Jesus took the Twelve aside and told them, "We are going up to Jerusalem, and *everything that is written by the prophets about the Son of Man will be fulfilled.* He will be delivered over to the Gentiles. They will mock him, insult him and spit on him; they will flog him and kill him. On the third day he will rise again."

Yet, the disciples "did not understand any of this… they did not know what he was talking about."[3] And at his arrest, Jesus had to command Peter to put away his sword and allow the soldiers to peaceably take him away, asking: "How then would the Scriptures be fulfilled that say it *must* happen this way?"[4]

So, it wasn't just the Jewish people in general who didn't expect a suffering Jesus to be their Messiah; even the disciples didn't grasp why Jesus had to die. But after his resurrection, Jesus aimed to clear up the confusion. He more fully explained what had happened to him and how his crucifixion and resurrection had fulfilled Scripture. Luke records that Jesus' first explanation was over dinner with two men he had met on the road to Emmaus.[5] Jesus asked them: "Did not the Messiah *have to suffer these things* and then enter his glory?"[6] Later, he filled in his disciples as he indulged in a piece of broiled fish.[7] Almost as if to say, "I told you so," Jesus said to them: "This is what I told you while I was still with you: *Everything must be fulfilled* that is written about me in the Law of Moses, the Prophets and the Psalms."[8]

The disciples and other Jews had rightfully been looking for a kingly, victorious Messiah. But they had not recognized that there are *other* prophecies in the Hebrew Scriptures that describe the Messiah as suffering for his people *in order to be* kingly and victorious. Seven hundred years before Jesus' birth, the prophet Isaiah wrote the most famous of these prophecies in a lengthy passage about "the suffering servant." Let's examine this section of Isaiah as evidence that Jesus' suffering and death were all part of God's plan of redemption. We'll then look at other prophecies relating to Jesus' crucifixion, including the poem that David wrote about someone who would suffer, yet emerge victorious. Finally, we'll take a quick look at a few ways that the Old Testament foresaw Jesus' resurrection.

PROPHECIES RELATING TO JESUS' SUFFERING

The section of Isaiah's prophetic book that most closely describes the suffering of the coming Messiah starts with the last three verses of the fifty-second chapter and continues through the entirety of the fifty-third. Isaiah starts to describe a "servant" who "will act wisely" and who will be "raised and lifted up and highly exalted."[9] Although a servant is generally considered lowly and inferior, this particular servant would be someone of high rank.

Because he gave his life to serve those whom he loved—even though they were unworthy of his love—you could say Jesus was the *ultimate* servant. He made this abundantly clear when he said that he "did not come to be served, but to serve, and to give his life as a ransom for

THE SHORTEST LEAP

many."[10] And yet, despite his self-proclaimed role as a servant, he was also highly regarded among men and acted with the utmost wisdom.

Describing the young Jesus, Luke states that "he grew and became strong; he was filled with wisdom, and the grace of God was on him.... And Jesus grew in wisdom and stature, and in favor with God and man."[11] And once Jesus began his ministry, Matthew notes that Jesus impressed those who met him: "When Jesus had finished saying these things, the crowds were amazed at his teaching, because he taught as one who had authority, and not as their teachers of the law."[12] Matthew also describes how those in Jesus' hometown, even though they didn't believe he was the Messiah, were impressed with his wisdom: "Coming to his hometown, he began teaching the people in their synagogue, and they were amazed. 'Where did this man get this wisdom and these miraculous powers?' they asked."[13]

According to Christian scholars, Isaiah's claim that the servant would be "raised and lifted up" is a prophecy of Jesus' being lifted up on the cross. One way to understand how the Jews at the time of Jesus understood the Book of Isaiah is by looking at the Greek translation of the Hebrew Scriptures, called the *Septuagint*. This translation uses the Greek verb *hupsóo* to describe what would happen to the servant. This Greek word could mean both "to be lifted up spatially" as well as "to be enhanced in honor, fame, position, power, or fortune."[14] Surprisingly, this Greek verb corresponds to a word in Jesus' native language of Aramaic (*zqf*, or אזדקיף) that actually means *both* "to be exalted" *and* "to be crucified."[15] You would never think these two meanings could be applied to the same word, and this seemingly contradictory double meaning only applies to the word in Jesus' native language of Aramaic. For this reason, one scholar even claims that the word "points to an origin probably in Jesus himself."[16] That is, Jesus himself coined the double meaning of the term, equating "to be exalted" with "crucifixion" for reasons that no one would understand except in hindsight.

Furthermore, Christian scholars claim that Isaiah's description of the servant being "highly exalted" is a reference to his ascension after his resurrection when "he left [his followers] and was taken up into heaven."[17] The Hebrew word that Isaiah originally used for "highly exalted" (*gabahh*, or גָּבַהּ) was translated *doxazó* in the *Septuagint*. The apostle John uses this verb 11 times in his Gospel to describe how Jesus would be "glorified."[18]

CHAPTER 21: CRUCIFIXION AND RESURRECTION FORETOLD

In one particular section of Paul's letter to the Philippians (which scholars believe quotes a hymn that began to circulate soon after Jesus' death), we hear an echo of Isaiah's words about a lowly servant who would be exalted. Paul exhorts believers to "have the same mindset as Christ Jesus," who was "in very nature God," but "did not consider equality with God something to be used to his own advantage," but instead "made himself nothing by taking the very nature of a *servant*, being made in human likeness." Jesus, Paul continues, "humbled himself by becoming obedient to death—even death on a cross!" In response to Jesus' servant-like obedience, "God *exalted* [*doxazó*] him to the highest place, and gave him the name that is above every name, that at the name of Jesus every knee should bow."[19]

Because this servant would be wise, lifted up, and highly exalted, the next verses from Isaiah 52 come as a surprising non-sequitur. Continuing his description of the servant, Isaiah prophesies that many would be "appalled at him" because "his appearance was so disfigured beyond that of any human being and his form marred beyond human likeness."[20]

Prior to being led out to be crucified, Jesus was flogged with thirty-nine lashes. According to Jewish law, the maximum number a criminal could receive was thirty-nine, one less than the forty lashes that would kill him.[21] Jesus received this maximum number of lashes (or "stripes"). To inflict these lashes, the Romans used a type of whip called a *flagrum*, which consisted of strips of leather that were attached to small fragments of bone and metal. Based on historians' understanding of Roman scourging, as Jesus was scourged, the flagrum tore away at his flesh and skin, and his shoulder blades, posterior ribs, and spinal vertebrae were thereby exposed (further fulfillment of the prophesy, which we will discuss shortly, that his bones would be "on display"[22]). After he was flogged, the Roman soldiers pierced his scalp with the crown of thorns and stripped, mocked, spit on, and struck him.[23]

All of this led up to Jesus' crucifixion. This particularly Roman method of execution is among the most excruciating ways that anyone can die. (In fact, the word, *excruciating*, comes from the Latin *excruciare*, meaning "out of the cross."[24]) Soldiers hammered iron spikes—seven inches long and almost a half inch in diameter—through the wrists, where they would hit the median nerve and send intense pain through the arms, shoulders, and neck. After the body was lifted vertically, they drove these same spikes through the feet. You can imagine (though you may not want to) that, once this bloody process was complete, Jesus' appearance was disfigured, marred beyond human likeness, and appalling to look upon, as Isaiah described the servant.

We next read in Isaiah 52 that, because the servant was "marred beyond human likeness," he would "sprinkle many nations."[25] After being flogged, Jesus was in a state of hypovolemia, having lost most of his blood. It sprinkled the path and the people who stood near him as he carried the horizontal crossbeam the distance of about two football fields.[26] The Hebrew verb translated "sprinkle" (*nazah*, or נָזָה) occurs twenty-four times in the Hebrew Scriptures.[27] Twenty-three times (all except this one in Isaiah), the term refers to the priestly duty of sprinkling the blood of a sacrifice or a special anointing oil in order to forgive sin or to consecrate or cleanse something considered unclean. For example, these are God's instructions for the consecration of the high priest's garments: "And take some blood from the altar and some of the anointing oil and sprinkle it on Aaron [the high priest] and his garments and on his sons and their garments. Then he and his sons and their garments will be consecrated."[28]

Another priestly duty that involved the sprinkling of blood was performed once a year on the Jews' most important holy day, Yom Kippur (about which we'll have more to say in Chapters 23 and 28). Before the high priest could enter the innermost room of the temple—the "Most Holy Place," where God symbolically dwelled in the Ark of the Covenant—he had to sprinkle blood on the thick curtain (called the "veil") that separated the outer "Holy Place" from the Most Holy Place. And upon entering the Most Holy Place, the high priest had to sprinkle blood on the cover of the Ark, called the "mercy seat" or "atonement cover," so that God would forgive the sins of the Israelites.[29] The main point is that the Hebrew word used for "sprinkle" in Isaiah 52:15, "he will sprinkle many nations," is the same word used in the instructions regarding forgiving, or atoning for, the people's sins on Yom Kippur. The correlation between the purpose of the Old Testament sprinkling and the purpose for which Jesus went to the cross—to forgive the sins of his people and thereby give them access to God for eternity—is unmistakable.

Let's continue with Isaiah's Suffering Servant prophecy, which next provides further background on the suffering servant: "He grew up before him like a tender shoot, and like a root out of dry ground. He had

CHAPTER 21: CRUCIFIXION AND RESURRECTION FORETOLD

no beauty or majesty to attract us to him, nothing in his appearance that we should desire him."[30] Scholars say that this verse most likely refers to Jesus' general appearance, rather than the "marred" appearance at his crucifixion. When he is depicted in art, Jesus generally appears handsome, drawn as most people would like to imagine him. But this verse indicates that he was most likely quite plain. Regarding his looks, Timothy Keller comments:

> One striking feature of the [Gospel] accounts is how they give us no description of Jesus' appearance. It is inconceivable that a modern journalistic account of any person would fail to tell us something of the kind of figure he cut or even what he wore. We live in an age intensely concerned with image and nearly obsessed with looks. But here all the emphasis is, we might say, not on the quality of his skin but on the content of his character. And that character was remarkable.[31]

Since the Gospel accounts never mention Jesus' appearance (except to note what he was wearing when the soldiers stripped him prior to his crucifixion), it seems likely that there was nothing remarkable, or kingly, to comment upon.

But what does Isaiah mean when he refers to this servant as "a tender shoot" and "a root from dry ground"? Here another passage from Isaiah helps. In his eleventh chapter, Isaiah refers to the future Messiah as a "shoot [that] will come up from the stump of Jesse [King David's father]" and states that "from his roots a Branch will bear fruit."[32] Elsewhere, Isaiah also writes this concerning the Messiah: "In that day the Branch of the Lord will be beautiful and glorious."[33] The prophet Jeremiah also writes about this Branch: "'The days are coming,' declares the Lord, 'when I will raise up for David a righteous Branch, a King who will reign wisely and do what is just and right in the land.'"[34]

Thus, with his reference to the "tender shoot" and "a root out of dry ground," Isaiah is telling us that the Suffering Servant—in stark contrast to his servant status and his plain-looking exterior—*is* the glorious king whom God promised would rule forever.

Moving on in Isaiah 53, the prophet continues to describe what this future ruler would endure: he would be "despised and rejected by mankind, a man of suffering, and familiar with pain." He was the type of man "from whom people hide their faces," he was "despised" (the word is used a second time to get the point across) and held "in low esteem."[35] Indeed, Jesus did not receive the public accolades of a long-awaited leader, nor did he seek them. Instead, many despised him and rejected his message (and still do).

Next, we read in Isaiah that the suffering servant "took up our pain and bore our suffering," even though "we considered him punished by God."[36] The irony in this verse is clear: the suffering servant was accomplishing something amazing on behalf of his people, and yet his people thought he was suffering and receiving punishment for something *he himself* had done wrong. The same irony comes across in all three of the synoptic gospels. Here's how Luke put it: "The people stood watching, and the rulers even sneered at him. They said, 'He saved others; let him save himself if he is God's Messiah, the Chosen One.'"[37] Though he easily could have saved himself, it was by *not saving himself* that he *did save* his people. Onlookers jeered at him as he suffered on the cross, believing him to be punished by God, when in fact he was bearing the penalty of sin on their behalf, as Isaiah had foreseen.

Isaiah drives this point home when he next states that the suffering servant was "pierced for our transgressions" and "crushed for our iniquities." Further, "the punishment that brought us peace was *on him*, and by *his wounds* we are healed."[38] These words accurately describe God's plan of redemption as revealed throughout the Bible. Jesus himself explained that he had come to "give His life as a ransom for many."[39] Note that Jesus claimed that he came to *give* his life; his life was not taken from him. He explained that he paid the "ransom" required to fulfill God's perfect justice *on behalf of* his followers, which was the only way they could have peace with God and live eternally in his presence. Because Jesus was pierced by the seven-inch nails, his followers would not be pierced by God's justice. And because Jesus received numerous wounds, his followers' broken relationship with their God could be healed.

Moving on, we come across a very common Old Testament metaphor for human beings: sheep. Emphasizing a common biblical theme, Isaiah states that all humans, "like sheep, have gone astray" and have "turned to [their] own way." Because of this, "the Lord has laid on [the suffering servant] the iniquity of us all."[40]

The Old Testament comparison of humans to sheep is fitting. Sheep

CHAPTER 21: CRUCIFIXION AND RESURRECTION FORETOLD

are easily led astray by their own desires, even to the point that they put their own survival at risk. Sheep notoriously will die without the care of a shepherd to protect them, feed them, give them medical care, and guide them. The Old Testament consistently portrays Israel's God-honoring rulers as good shepherds, while those who lead the people away from God are portrayed as evil shepherds. And repeatedly, God makes it clear through the prophets that *he himself* will shepherd his people because so many others have failed to do so properly.[41] He claims that he "will search for the lost [sheep] and bring back the strays," and he "will bind up the injured and strengthen the weak… [and] shepherd the flock with justice."[42]

Skipping from the Old to the New Testament, let's recall that Jesus called himself the "good shepherd." Not only did he protect and feed his sheep, he was willing to lay down his life for his sheep so that they could be with him forever. Here's how Jesus put it:

> "I am the good shepherd; I know my sheep and my sheep know me—just as the Father knows me and I know the Father—and *I lay down my life* for the sheep. I have other sheep that are not of this sheep pen. I must bring them also. They too will listen to my voice, and there shall be one flock and one shepherd.[43]

Jesus knew that his sheep had gone astray, and yet he loved them so much—he so badly wanted to restore them to his flock—that he was willing to lay down his own life for them. In so doing, the penalty for their iniquity was instead laid on him. In this way, the shepherd enabled his flock to spend eternity with him.

Isaiah then applies the sheep metaphor to the suffering servant himself, stating that "he was oppressed and afflicted, yet he did not open his mouth; he was led like a lamb to the slaughter, and as a sheep before its shearers is silent, so he did not open his mouth."[44] Fast forward to the New Testament: John the Baptist publicly called Jesus the "Lamb of God,"[45] a familiar symbol to the Jewish people, who sacrificed lambs on the Passover each year, another topic we will explore in more detail in Chapter 27. In keeping with Isaiah's prophecy, Jesus' behavior during his arrest and trial was notable: he remained calm, did not plead for his life, and stood in silent dignity when questioned—the way a sheep keeps quiet while it is sheared.

When the Roman governor of Judea, Pontius Pilate, interviewed Jesus to determine whether he deserved the death penalty, Jesus remained silent. When Pilate asked him, "Don't you hear the testimony they are bringing against you?" Jesus did not reply, "not even to a single charge—to the great amazement of the governor."[46] Moreover, when the Jewish leaders interrogated him and asked him to respond to the accusations against him, Jesus maintained his silence. The high priest asked him, "Are you not going to answer?" Matthew writes, "But Jesus remained silent."[47] Jesus did not open his mouth as he was being oppressed and afflicted. He had come for a purpose, and he had no need to defend himself from the false charges he faced. Jesus spoke only when charged under oath to answer the high priest.[48]

Isaiah then describes the suffering servant as "taken away" and "cut off from the land of the living," again stating that it was "for the transgression of my people" that "he was punished." Moreover, as they killed the servant, Isaiah rhetorically asks, "Yet who of his generation protested?"[49] The implied answer is, "No one." Standing before the Jewish and Roman authorities, accused of false crimes and sentenced to a penalty he did not deserve, Jesus was taken away to be flogged and then crucified. A crowd of people shouted, "Crucify him!" Pilate asked the crowd which prisoner to release (his custom during the festival of Passover): this Jesus or a dangerous criminal named Barabbas. The crowd chose freedom for Barabbas and death for Jesus. Even his most devoted disciple, Peter, denied three times that he knew him. Isaiah's prophecy is accurate: as Jesus was sent to his death, no one protested the injustice they were witnessing.

Isaiah's "suffering servant" prophesy continues. In the next verse, he claims that the servant was "assigned a grave with the wicked, and with the rich in his death, though he had done no violence, nor was any deceit in his mouth."[50] It was typical for those who were crucified to be buried with the other criminals or left on the cross to decompose as a grisly warning to would-be rebels. This was the type of grave that Jesus had been "assigned" due to the nature of his execution. However, a wealthy Jew named Joseph of Arimathea had other plans:

> Going to Pilate, he asked for Jesus' body, and Pilate ordered that it be given to him. Joseph took the body,

CHAPTER 21: CRUCIFIXION AND RESURRECTION FORETOLD

wrapped it in a clean linen cloth, and placed it in his own new tomb that he had cut out of the rock. He rolled a big stone in front of the entrance to the tomb and went away.[51]

Jesus fits the description provided by Isaiah: he never acted violently, and his teachings, though controversial, were delivered with integrity. Moreover, though he died a criminal's death, he was buried in a new tomb cut out of rock, a burial that only the wealthiest and most powerful could afford.

Peter quotes Isaiah 53 with these words of encouragement to those who trust in Jesus even as they are persecuted for their faith:

> But if you suffer for doing good and you endure it, this is commendable before God. To this you were called, because Christ suffered for you, leaving you an example, that you should follow in his steps.
>
> "He committed no sin, and no deceit was found in his mouth."
>
> When they hurled their insults at him, he did not retaliate; when he suffered, he made no threats. Instead, he entrusted himself to his Father, the one who judges justly. "He himself bore our sins" in his body on the cross, so that we might die to sins and live for righteousness; "by his wounds you have been healed."[52]

Jesus was crucified alongside two murderers, yet he was given a rich man's burial. Jesus was innocent of any violence or deception, yet he went to his death and was "cut off from the land of the living."

In the next verse, Isaiah explains that "it was the Lord's *will* to crush him and cause him to suffer," and "though the Lord makes [the servant's] life an offering for sin, he will see his offspring and prolong his days."[53] Christians believe that it was God's will, as Isaiah states, for Jesus to suffer and die as the offering for the sins of his people. Why would God's will require such a terrible thing, and why would Jesus so willingly comply? The author of Hebrews gives us an explanation: "For the joy set before him [Jesus] endured the cross, scorning its shame, and sat down at the right hand of the throne of God."⁵⁴ Christian theologians clarify that the "joy set before him"—the reason Jesus willingly went to the cross despite it being the most shameful and excruciating way to die—was to be with *his people*. That is, by his suffering to take the penalty for their sin, Jesus attained the joy of spending eternity with those who have faith in him.

Isaiah drives home the point even more: "After he has suffered, he will see the light of life and be satisfied; by his knowledge my righteous servant will *justify* many, and he will bear their iniquities."⁵⁵ Seven hundred years later, John writes, "[Jesus] is the atoning sacrifice for our sins, and not only for ours but also for the sins of the whole world."⁵⁶ The New Testament clearly teaches that Jesus went to the cross willingly to receive the punishment for "the iniquities" of those who trust in him. By the way, the Hebrew word used in this verse from Isaiah for "justify," (*tsadeq*, or צָדֵק), is used throughout the Old Testament to indicate "to be made righteous" or "to acquit."⁵⁷ Those who trust in Jesus are "acquitted," and no longer face judgment for their sins, not because of anything they have done, but because they have been given his perfect record through faith in him.

One other important note on this latest verse: here you can see that Isaiah also anticipated Jesus' resurrection: after the suffering servant was crushed, he would "see the light of life" again. Interestingly, before the discovery of the Dead Sea Scrolls, this part of Isaiah 53 was not in the Hebrew Scriptures (called the "Masoretic Text"). However, it *was* in the *Septuagint*, causing a bit of a debate regarding what the original text contained. But among the Dead Sea Scrolls was found the "Great Scroll of Isaiah" and two other fragments of Isaiah, and these turned out to be about 1,000 years older than the earliest manuscripts of the Masoretic Text, which date to the ninth century AD. These older manuscripts settled the debate, as they *do* contain the Hebrew words translated "light of life."

The last verse of this section of Isaiah describes the end result of the servant's suffering: God claims that he "will give [the servant] a portion among the great… because he poured out his life unto death" and because "he bore the sin of many, and made intercession for the transgressors."⁵⁸

Jesus clearly teaches that his purpose was to "lay down his life" for his sheep, to bear their sin for them, and to justify them in order to make them fit to live in God's presence for all eternity. Paul describes the transfer of his followers' sin to Jesus and the simultaneous transfer of Jesus' righteousness to his followers in this way: "God made him who had no sin to be sin for us, so that in him we might become the righteousness of God."[59] It was Isaiah's suffering servant—Jesus—who facilitated this great exchange.

Prophecies Relating to Jesus' Crucifixion

Though first-century Jews did not expect it—and no one would have thought to desire it—the Messiah came first to die.[60] All four Gospels clarify that this was Jesus' mission from the very start of his ministry. The launch of Jesus ministry was marked by the announcement that another prophecy of Isaiah was being fulfilled. John the Baptist, strangely clothed in camel's hair, had been asking the people to repent of their sins and be baptized in the Jordan River, for, he exclaimed, the "kingdom of heaven has come near."[61] A group of Jewish leaders came to the desert to find out who this man was and why he was baptizing people. John the Baptist immediately clarified, "I am not the Messiah." Then this exchange took place:

> "Then who are you?... Give us an answer to take back to those who sent us. What do you say about yourself?"
>
> John replied in the words of Isaiah the prophet, "I am the voice of one calling in the wilderness, 'Make straight the way for the Lord.'"[62]

John the Baptist was referencing this 700-year-old prophecy:

> A voice of one calling: "In the wilderness prepare the way for the Lord; make straight in the desert a highway for our God. Every valley shall be raised up, every mountain and hill made low; the rough ground shall become level, the rugged places a plain. And the glory of the Lord will be revealed, and all people will see it together."[63]

THE SHORTEST LEAP

When a king toured his kingdom, it was common for a straight road to be laid out for him so that he would have a comfortable route along which his people could gather to get a glimpse of him and greet him. The valleys would be filled in, the hills would be leveled, and the new highway would be level and straight as would befit the royal traveler. This prophecy spoke of not just any king, but God himself, coming to meet the people of his Kingdom.

So, first John the Baptist clarified that his mission was to prepare the way for the coming King. Then, when he saw Jesus, he declared: "Behold, the Lamb of God who takes away the sins of the world."[64] With these words, John publicly declared the astounding, unexpected purpose for which this king had come: to *be* the sacrificial lamb, which, for the Jews, had always symbolized the forgiveness of sins, freedom from slavery, and a restored relationship with their God. (Stay tuned for a more thorough explanation of the "Lamb of God" in Chapter 27.)

Let's take a look at a few other prophecies that, looking back from the vantage point of Jesus' life and death, predicted his death—the ultimate sacrifice for his people.

After the ancient Israelites had been kicked out of their land by rival nations, God used the prophet Zechariah to deliver a message of hope to them. He confirmed to the nation of Israel (which at the time of this prophecy was split into two kingdoms, Israel and Judah) that God would protect them from their enemies and restore them, such that "even the feeblest among them will be like [King] David." Zechariah continues:

> "And I will pour out on the house of David and the inhabitants of Jerusalem a spirit of grace and supplication. They will look on *me, the one they have pierced*, and they will mourn for him as one mourns for an only child, and grieve bitterly for him as one grieves for a firstborn son."[65]

Notice that God himself is speaking here, referring to himself as "the one they have pierced." For this reason, Christians claim that this is a prophecy concerning the way the Messiah would die. Jesus was pierced with stakes through his hands and his feet, and a Roman soldier also pierced him in the side with a spear. Not wanting any dead bodies hanging in public during their Sabbath,[66] the Jewish leaders asked the soldiers to break the legs of the men who had been crucified. This would

CHAPTER 21: CRUCIFIXION AND RESURRECTION FORETOLD

speed up their death, since they could no longer push themselves up with their legs and thus raise up their rib cage in order to breathe.

John sees this as the fulfillment of another prophecy, as he writes:

> But when they came to Jesus and found that he was already dead, they did not break his legs. Instead, one of the soldiers pierced Jesus' side with a spear, bringing a sudden flow of blood and water. The man who saw it has given testimony, and his testimony is true. He knows that he tells the truth, and he testifies so that you also may believe. These things happened so that the scripture would be fulfilled: "Not one of his bones will be broken," and, as another scripture says, "They will look on the one they have pierced."[67]

John is referring first to Psalm 34, where David writes: "The righteous person may have many troubles, but the Lord delivers him from them all; he protects all his bones, not one of them will be broken."[68] His second reference is to Zechariah 12, mentioned above.

Another clear prophecy of Jesus' death is found in Psalm 22, to which we alluded briefly earlier. This psalm, also by David, begins with the question, "My God, my God, why have you forsaken me?"[69] Matthew and Mark each record that Jesus cried out this same question from the cross just before he died. In Chapter 6, we noted that Jesus must have actually said this, for why would anyone concoct a statement that may unnecessarily confuse potential converts? Why does Jesus, whose followers believe is the omniscient God, sound confused about what's happening? And since he is calling out to his God, he doesn't seem to consider himself God. Moreover, if he is who he said he was—the Son of God—why is he claiming to have been forsaken by God? Scholars note that, before chapter and verse numbers, it was common to reference a psalm by reciting its first verse. Jesus wanted his audience to connect his death to Psalm 22, and as we examine additional details from this psalm, it becomes apparent why Jesus would want to point us there for an explanation of what was going on.

After the introductory question, the one that Jesus quoted, the next few verses of Psalm 22 state that the people of Israel have praised God and placed their trust in him because he had delivered them again and again. David, the author of this psalm, writes: "To you they cried out and were saved; in you they trusted and were not put to shame."[70] However, the tone in the next verses changes dramatically, and it gives us a hint as to how the people were saved:

> But I am a worm and not a man,
>   scorned by everyone, despised by the people.
> All who see me mock me;
>   they hurl insults, shaking their heads.
> "He trusts in the Lord," they say,
>   "let the Lord rescue him.
> Let him deliver him,
>   since he delights in him."[71]

What is going on? It makes sense when you read Luke's description of the crucifixion scene: "The people stood watching, and the rulers even sneered at him. They said, 'He saved others; let him save himself if he is God's Messiah, the Chosen One.'"[72]

Psalm 22 continues:

> I am poured out like water,
> and all my bones are out of joint.
>   My heart has turned to wax;
>   it has melted within me.
>   My mouth is dried up like a potsherd,
>   and my tongue sticks to the roof of my mouth;
>   you lay me in the dust of death.[73]

Jesus was experiencing the consequences of a loss of blood, an intense thirst, strain on his heart, and profound weakness. With his arms above his head and the full weight of his body pulling him down, his shoulder and elbow joints were dislocated, and it was a struggle for him to inhale. Because of the stress from blood loss, the difficulty in breathing, the depletion of oxygen in his brain, and the buildup of carbon dioxide and acid in his tissues, Jesus was in the initial stages of heart failure. Eventually, his heart gave out under this stress, the cause of his death. Psalm 22 is a poetic picture of terrible trauma.

The psalm goes on:

CHAPTER 21: CRUCIFIXION AND RESURRECTION FORETOLD

> Dogs surround me,
>   a pack of villains encircles me;
>   they pierce my hands and my feet.
> All my bones are on display;
>   people stare and gloat over me.
> They divide my clothes among them
>   and cast lots for my garment.[74]

Understandably, Jewish rabbis have interpreted the "me" of Psalm 22 as David himself, since they considered him the author of this psalm. And at the time in his life when he was next in line for the throne of Israel, David's enemies did indeed surround him.[75] Some claim that "pierced" is an incorrect translation of the Hebrew text, insisting that the more accurate translation is "like a lion." Thus, their translation is: "like a lion, they are at my hands and my feet," which does sound like something David would have written. Christians, they say, are misreading the original Hebrew word.

However, again, one of the Dead Sea scrolls sheds light on the debate.[76] Discovered in the 1950's, this text uses the form of the Hebrew word that is best translated "pierced." One scholar explains how one scroll, not examined until 1997, now reveals that "pierced," not "like a lion," is the best translation. He notes that the difference in meaning and the confusion is due to a very similar last letter in the Hebrew word (which is on the left, since Hebrew is read from right to left). After explaining that scholars did not believe this verse was in any of the Dead Sea scrolls, he then summarizes the big change in opinion in 1997 when they found a scroll that *did* contain it:

> This is where the discussion stood until about 1997. The Qumran Psalters do not contain this verse. However, a scroll from the same era found at nearby Nahal Hever known as 5/6HevPsalms reads, "They have pierced my hands and my feet"! Though the documents were found in 1951 or 52, this reading was not discovered until around 1997! Further, it did not appear in print until *The Dead Sea Scrolls Bible* was published in 1999. The implications are enormous. Here we have a Hebrew text over 1,000 years older than the oldest known copy of

the standard Hebrew Masoretic text, which supports the reading found in the Greek *Septuagint*, Syriac, and Vulgate. No longer can Hebrew scholars claim that the LXX [*Septuagint*], Syriac, and Vulgate are here faulty reflections of the original Hebrew. We see how easily such a change could occur in the Hebrew text when we compare the Hebrew word for pierced וראכ with the word יראכ for "like a lion." The only difference is the last character: ו vs. י.[77]

Thus, the earliest Hebrew version of Psalm 22:16 does indeed contain the word that is best translated as "pierced."

Several other points should be made with regards to verses 16 through 18 of Psalm 22. One of the worst aspects of dying by crucifixion was the shameful way that the victim's naked body would be displayed for all to see, with an enlarged rib cage due to the pressure from hanging by the wrists. Truly, Jesus' bones—especially his ribs—were on display as his enemies gloated and laughed in a circle around him.

There is also evidence from secular history that the Roman guards would strip search the criminal prior to leading him or her to the cross (probably to look for valuables in their clothing). They kept the clothing, if it were of value (and the seamless garments were especially valuable), and divided the pieces among themselves or cast lots for the more valuable items.[78] John explains this detail more fully than the other Gospel writers, incorporating a reference to Psalm 22:

> When the soldiers crucified Jesus, they took his clothes, dividing them into four shares, one for each of them, with the undergarment remaining. This garment was seamless, woven in one piece from top to bottom. "Let's not tear it," they said to one another. "Let's decide by lot who will get it." This happened that the scripture might be fulfilled that said, "They divided my clothes among them and cast lots for my garment." So this is what the soldiers did.[79]

Because crucifixion was the form of punishment that most effectively dissuaded others from committing the same crimes, it was crucial to make it as horrific as possible in the eyes of those passing by. The sight of the suffering criminal, hanging nude for all to see, in pain and struggling to lift his chest with his broken feet in order to take a breath—this sight would surely deter others from committing similar crimes. Also, as we mentioned earlier, the executioners generally left the dead body on the cross, where it would decay and be eaten by wild animals and birds of prey. The former curator of the Israel Antiquities Authority explains it this way:

> Giving the victim a proper burial following death on the cross, during the Roman period was rare and in most cases simply not permitted in order to continue the humiliation. Thus the victim was in many cases simply thrown on the garbage dump of the city or left on the cross as food for wild beasts and birds of prey.[80]

It is very likely, therefore, that wild dogs would gather around the crosses in eager anticipation of their next meal. Moreover, those who chose to watch crucifixions were not among the most sophisticated in the society, as you would imagine. Thus, the words, "Dogs surround me, a pack of villains encircles me," most likely applied to the scene of Jesus' death.

In his Gospel, John records Jesus' last words: "It is finished."[81] He had come to fulfill Psalm 22. And Christians believe that, in doing so, he completed the ultimate rescue mission, which would be validated when he rose from the grave on the third day.

Prophecies Relating to the Resurrection

In addition to Isaiah's reference to the suffering servant "seeing the light of life again," we will discuss several Old Testament prophecies that point to Jesus' future resurrection. For the first, we return to Psalm 22. As we've seen, the psalm provides a stark description that strikingly resembles Jesus dying on the cross. However, it ends valiantly. A few verses after describing the protagonist as "a worm and not a man," Psalm 22 changes its tone:

> For he has not despised or scorned
> > the suffering of the afflicted one;
> he has not hidden his face from him
> > *but has listened to his cry for help....*
> All the rich of the earth will feast and worship;
> > all who go down to the dust will kneel before him—
> > those who cannot keep themselves alive.
> Posterity will serve him;
> > future generations will be told about the Lord.
> They will proclaim his righteousness,
> > declaring to a people yet unborn:
> > He has done it![82]

The final verses of this psalm likely assured the Jewish people that one day, upon the arrival of their Messiah, they would be delivered from their enemies. Those who recognize this psalm as a prophecy pointing to Jesus see it as confirmation that God the Father accepted the payment that Jesus made through his suffering and death on the cross. In this way, Psalm 22 also hints at the resurrection. When Jesus rose on the third day, God answered his people's cries for help, and he declared Jesus worthy of all honor, praise, and worship. The triumphant sound of the cry in Psalm 22, "He has done it!" fittingly applies, and it echoes Jesus' cry from the cross soon before he died: "It is finished!"

Other Hebrew Scriptures provide additional hints regarding the future resurrection of Jesus, as well as the resurrection of those who trust in him. In another psalm David penned, he describes how God would not let "his faithful one" (also translated "his holy one") experience decay. David may well be referring to himself as God's faithful one. But one clue that he is referring to someone else is that he uses two distinct phrases connected by "nor," one for himself and another for "God's faithful one":

> Therefore my heart is glad and my tongue rejoices;
> > my body also will rest secure,
> because you will not abandon *me* to the realm of the dead,
> > *nor* will you let *your faithful one* see decay.[83]

David links this confidence in his own life after death to the assurance that the body of the greater "faithful one" will not rot in the

CHAPTER 21: CRUCIFIXION AND RESURRECTION FORETOLD

grave. As God's perfectly "faithful one," Jesus went to his death on the cross trusting the plan and knowing that he would rise again. Similarly, David—inspired by the Spirit to anticipate God's salvation—trusted that God would keep his body secure, which gave him clear cause for gladness and joy.[84]

Jesus himself pointed out that one Hebrew Scripture in particular foretold of his coming resurrection. When the Pharisees and teachers of the law asked "to see a sign from [him]," Jesus rebuked them (after all, he had already performed many "signs and wonders"!), saying:

> "A wicked and adulterous generation asks for a sign! But none will be given it except the sign of the prophet Jonah. For as Jonah was three days and three nights in the belly of a huge fish, so the Son of Man will be three days and three nights in the heart of the earth."[85]

Christian scholars universally claim that this "Sign of Jonah" was Jesus' resurrection, which happened on the third day after his crucifixion.[86]

Because Jesus did not fit the expectations of a powerful and kingly "Anointed One," it is understandable that his fellow Jews didn't recognize him as their Messiah. He had been born into poverty, starting life in a manger and as a refugee child. He was born into one of the most shameful scenarios of his culture: the apparent bastard child of a teenage mom and a man who felt sorry for her. He grew up in such a backwater town that Nathaniel exclaimed, "Nazareth! Can anything good come from there?"[87] From the time he began his ministry around age thirty, he had no home; Matthew quotes him saying: "Foxes have dens and birds have nests, but the Son of Man has no place to lay his head."[88] Though we read from his genealogy that he descended from King David, by the time of his birth there had not been a descendant of David on the throne of Israel for more than half a millennium. Such an unimpressive man couldn't possibly be the Messiah. But Isaiah's Suffering Servant and Psalm 22 paint a different portrait of Israel's Redeemer, a good shepherd who would lay down his life to rescue his sheep.

"The Message" Bible translation of Isaiah 53:1 fittingly describes just how misunderstood this beautiful Messianic prophecy has been. The translation goes like this: "Who believes what we've heard and seen?

Who would have thought GOD's saving power would look like *this*?"[89] In the next chapter, we'll examine the prophecies relating to the time Christians believe Jesus will return to earth a second time, when God's saving power will look completely different than how it looked when Jesus hung on a Roman cross.

QUESTIONS FOR COMPREHENSION AND DISCUSSION

1. Why did many of Jesus' fellow Jews not recognize him as the Messiah? What kind of Messiah were they expecting?
2. Explain the main ways that Isaiah's description of the "Suffering Servant" points to Jesus.
3. What is the significance of the suffering servant being "raised and lifted up" and "highly exalted"? What is another meaning of the Aramaic word for "exalted"? Why is this double meaning so applicable in Jesus' case?
4. Why does the Bible often compare humans to sheep? Why does God claim that he himself must be the shepherd for his people? How is Jesus a fulfillment of this prophecy?
5. Was Jesus killed, or did he give his life? Provide some evidence from the Bible that helps us know.
6. Why did Jesus willingly endure the cross? What was "the joy set before him"?
7. How is Psalm 22 a picture of death by crucifixion?
8. What was one important discovery made in 1997 when a scroll from a site near Qumran was rediscovered? How did this clarify the meaning of one of the words in Psalm 22?
9. Why do Christians believe Jesus' death and resurrection fulfilled the last cry of Psalm 22: "He has done it!"?
10. What does David write in one of his psalms that demonstrates his trust that God would not allow him to die? Who else did David trust God would not allow to "see decay"?

CHAPTER 21 ENDNOTES

1. Herbert Lockyer, *All the Messianic Prophecies of the Bible* (Grand Rapids, MI: Zondervan, 1973), 150.
2. Acts 2:29-32.
3. These quotes are from Luke 18:31-34. All emphases in Bible passages are mine. For other examples of when Jesus predicted his death, see Matthew 16:21-28, 17:22-23, 20:17-19; Mark 8:31-33, 9:30-32, 10:32-34; Luke 9:21-22, 43-45; and John 12:23, 31-33, 13:31-33.
4. Matthew 26:54.
5. See the story in Luke 24:13-35.
6. Luke 24:26.
7. See the story in Luke 24:36-49.
8. Luke 24:44.
9. Isaiah 52:13.
10. Matthew 20:28; Mark 10:45.
11. Luke 2:40, 52.
12. Matthew 7:28-29.
13. Matthew 13:54.
14. Walter Bauer and Frederick William Danker, *A Greek-English Lexicon of the New Testament and Other Early Christian Literature*, 3rd Edition (University of Chicago Press: 2001), 1046. Also available online at https://translate.enacademic.com/ὑψόω/el/en/.
15. "Passion Resurrection Predictions," *New Testament Studies*, 31, 1985, 217f. As referenced in Ibid.
16. Emilio G. Chavez, "The Hebrew and Aramaic Verbs for 'to lift up,'" available online at http://www.bible-explainer.com/ShortNotes/Hebrew and Aramaic Verbs for Lift Up.pdf.
17. Luke 24:51.
18. Bauer and Danker, *A Greek-English Lexicon of the New Testament and Other Early Christian Literature*, 258. John quotes Jesus using *doxazó* to describe himself as being glorified in John 8:54 (twice), 11:4, 12:16, 23, 28 (twice), 31 (twice). John also uses this verb another time when he claims "Jesus was not yet glorified" in 7:39.
19. See Philippians 2:5-11 for the full text.
20. Isaiah 52:14.
21. Jacob Neusner, *The Halakhah: An Encyclopedia of the Law of Judaism, Volume 3* (Brill, 2001), 224.
22. Psalm 22:17.
23. See Matthew 27:26-31 and Mark 15:16-20.

24. Julia Cresswell, *The Oxford Dictionary of Word Origins* (Oxford: Oxford University Press, 2010), 157.
25. Isaiah 52:15a.
26. Andre Moubarak, *One Friday in Jerusalem* (Jerusalem, Israel: Twin Tours & Travel Ltd., 2017), 13.
27. See the Englishman's Concordance at https://biblehub.com/hebrew/5137.htm.
28. Exodus 29:21.
29. See Leviticus 16.
30. Isaiah 53:2.
31. Timothy Keller, *Making Sense of God: Finding God in the Modern World* (New York: Penguin Group, 2016), 281.
32. Isaiah 11:1.
33. Isaiah 4:2.
34. Jeremiah 23:5.
35. Isaiah 53:3.
36. Isaiah 53:4.
37. Luke 23:35.
38. Isaiah 53:5.
39. Mark 10:45.
40. Isaiah 53:6.
41. For examples of God being the shepherd of his people, see Psalm 23, 28:9, 80:1; Isaiah 40:11; Jeremiah 31:10; Ezekiel 34, 37:24; and Zechariah 9:16.
42. Ezekiel 34:16.
43. John 10:14-16.
44. Isaiah 53:7.
45. John 1:29, 36.
46. Matthew 27:13-14.
47. Matthew 26:62-63a.
48. See Matthew 26:63b.
49. Isaiah 53:8.
50. Isaiah 53:9.
51. Matthew 27:57-59.
52. 1 Peter 2:24.
53. Isaiah 53:10.
54. Hebrews 12:1b-3.
55. Isaiah 53:11.
56. 1 John 2:2.
57. For an explanation of this Hebrew word and the verses that contain it, see the *Englishman's Concordance* at https://biblehub.com/hebrew/6663.htm.
58. Isaiah 53:12.

CHAPTER 21: CRUCIFIXION AND RESURRECTION FORETOLD

59 1 Corinthians 5:21.
60 John 1:29.
61 Matthew 3:2.
62 John 1:21-23.
63 Isaiah 40:3-5a.
64 John 1:29.
65 Zechariah 12:10.
66 See John 19:31.
67 John 19:34-37.
68 Psalm 34:19-20.
69 Psalm 22:1.
70 Psalm 22:5.
71 Psalm 22:6-8.
72 Luke 23:35.
73 Psalm 22:14-15.
74 Psalm 22:16-18.
75 See 1 Samuel 21-24.
76 These ancient scrolls were found in a cave in the region around Qumran, Egypt. They are the earliest copies of the Hebrew Scriptures, pre-dating the next oldest manuscripts by more than one thousand years.
77 Conrad R. Gren, "Piercing the Ambiguities of Psalm 22:16 and the Messiah's Mission," *Journal of the Evangelical Theological Society*, 48/2 (June 2005) 283–99, 287-288. He references Abegg, Flint, Ulrich, *Dead Sea Scrolls Bible* 519, and John R. Kohlenberger III, *The Interlinear NIV Hebrew-English Old Testament* (Grand Rapids, MI: Zondervan, 1987), 368.
78 William Barclay, *The Gospel of Matthew, Vol. 2* (Louisville, KY: Westminster John Knox Press, 2010), 428.
79 John 19:23-24.
80 Joseph Zias, "Crucifixion in Antiquity: The Evidence," http://www.mercaba.org/FICHAS/upsa/crucifixion.htm.
81 John 19:30. Commentators note that the word Jesus stated, "*Tetelestai*," can be translated either, "It is finished!" or "It is paid in full," which was an ancient accounting term to indicate that a debt had been paid and was no longer owed.
82 Psalm 22:24, 29-32.
83 Psalm 16:9-11.
84 Verses that demonstrate Jesus taught that he would rise again in three days include: Matthew 12:40, 26:61, 27:40, 63; Mark 8:31, 9:31, 10:34, 14:58, 15:29; and John 2:19-20.
85 Matthew 12:39-40.

86 Note that it was common in Jewish custom to use the phrases "three days and three nights" and "on the third day" interchangeably. This was because the Jews customarily considered any part of a day, regardless of the amount of time, to be a day. For example, in Esther 4:16, Esther instructs her people to not "eat or drink for three days, night nor day." Esther says she too will fast at the same time, after which she will go to the king (in order to plead that he save her people). Esther goes to the king "on the third day." This is another illustration that the Jewish expressions, "after three days and nights" and "on the third day," are equivalent to one another. See R. A. Jamieson, A. R. Fausset, and D. Brown, *A Commentary, Critical and Explanatory, on the Old and New Testaments* (Oak Harbor, WA: Logos Research Systems, 1997).

87 John 1:46.

88 Matthew 8:20.

89 Isaiah 53:1, Eugene H. Peterson, *The Message: The Bible in Contemporary Language*, originally published in 1993, emphasis mine.

The second coming of Christ will be so revolutionary that it will change every aspect of life on this planet. Christ will reign in righteousness. Disease will be arrested. Death will be modified. War will be abolished. Nature will be changed. Man will live as it was originally intended he should live.

—Billy Graham, Christian minister[1]

One great theme of Scripture is that God will judge a rebellious world en route *to establishing His righteous kingdom on earth. Accomplishing this will involve the defeat of God's enemies through the coming of the Messiah and His Kingdom reign from Jerusalem.*

—Michael J. Vlach, professor of theology[2]

22

The Victory to Come

Jesus' favorite name for himself, as we discussed in Chapter 18, was "the Son of Man," which comes from a reference the prophet Daniel makes to the future Messiah. Let's take another look at this prophecy for our purposes now. After Jerusalem fell to the Babylonians in 586 BC, Daniel was taken into captivity. While in Babylon, he wrote:

> In my vision at night I looked, and there before me was one like a *son of man,* coming with the clouds of heaven. He approached the Ancient of Days and was led into his presence. He was given authority, glory and sovereign power; *all nations and peoples of every language* worshiped him. His dominion is an everlasting dominion that will not pass away, and his kingdom is one that will never be destroyed."[3]

As we've seen, one of the reasons that the Jews did not believe Jesus was the Messiah was because he *had not* arrived in this manner. Though he didn't come with the clouds, he did have power, and when the people recognized it, their understandable inclination was to make him king. But Jesus refused to cooperate. John mentions one such incident:

> After the people saw the sign Jesus performed, they began to say, "Surely this is the Prophet who is to come into the world." Jesus, knowing that they intended to come and make him king by force, withdrew again to a mountain by himself.[4]

CHAPTER 22: THE VICTORY TO COME

Though Jesus surely had the power to overthrow the Roman occupiers and set up his Kingdom immediately, the mission of his first visit to earth was to live a sinless life and to be the Suffering Servant.

In this chapter, we'll take a look at the many prophecies throughout the Old Testament that gave the Jews reason to look for a king who would free them from their oppressors and establish a kingdom of perfect justice and righteousness. Rather than finding fulfillment in his first coming in the manger, Christians believe these prophecies will be fulfilled in the future when Jesus *returns* to judge the earth. Jesus himself declared to the high priest after his arrest that he would come again "on the clouds."[5] And when his disciples asked him for "the sign of your coming and of the end of the age," Jesus replied:

> "Then will appear the sign of the Son of Man in heaven. And then all the peoples of the earth will mourn when they see the Son of Man coming on the clouds of heaven, with power and great glory. And he will send his angels with a loud trumpet call, and they will gather his elect from the four winds, from one end of the heavens to the other."[6]

Jesus clearly applied Daniel's prophecy to himself, indicating that in the future he will return again in power to gather his followers. In Revelation, the apostle John describes a vision he had of Jesus' second coming in this way: "I looked, and there before me was a white cloud, and seated on the cloud was one like a son of man with a crown of gold on his head and a sharp sickle in his hand."[7] The sickle in his hand was for "harvesting the earth," a reference to the judgment of humans to determine if they were fit to live in God's presence. Let's take a closer look at why Christians believe many Old Testament prophecies concerning the Messiah will be fulfilled in this second coming of Jesus, when he would reign in power, gather his followers to him, and execute judgment on those who have not taken refuge in him through faith.

PROPHECIES OF JESUS' SECOND COMING

The Book of Isaiah, which contains many Messianic prophecies that we have already covered, also contains many references to the coming kingship that the Messiah would establish. Both Jews and Christians believe that these are references to a time that is still future to us. The difference between their stances, as we've noted, is that Jews believe that none of the prophecies concerning the Messiah have been fulfilled yet, while Christians believe that Jesus has already fulfilled them in part and will return as the future king to fulfill the rest. For our purposes, let's look at seven primary aspects of the coming Messiah, as foretold in the Old Testament, which both Jews and Christians believe have yet to be fulfilled.

The first aspect of the Messianic prophecies is that, when he comes, the Messiah will cause all nations, not just Israel, to come to him and look to him as their ruler.[8] For example, seven hundred years before Jesus' birth in the manger, Isaiah foresees that, "In the last days the mountain of the Lord's temple will be established as the highest of the mountains; it will be exalted above the hills, and *all nations* will stream to it."[9] The prophecy goes on to say that "many peoples" (that is, people from many different cultures) will say, "Come, let us go up to the mountain of the Lord, to the temple of the God of Jacob."[10] Moreover, the "word of the Lord" will go out from Jerusalem, and the Messiah "will judge *between the nations* and will settle disputes for *many peoples*."[11]

A second aspect of the Jewish expectations concerning the coming of the Messiah is the establishment of *shalom*, the Hebrew word for perfect peace and human flourishing. At this point, because the Messiah judges justly and settles all disputes, weapons and other instruments of war would no longer be needed. For example, Isaiah writes:

> He will judge between many peoples
>   and will settle disputes for strong nations far and wide.
> They will beat their swords into plowshares
>   and their spears into pruning hooks.
> Nation will not take up sword against nation,
>   nor will they train for war anymore.[12]

In such a peaceful world, plowshares and pruning hooks will replace swords and spears. The focus will be on enjoying food—and life in general, not on waging war.[13]

Before modern communications technology, at the end of a victorious battle, messengers would be sent back from the battlefield to deliver a

CHAPTER 22: THE VICTORY TO COME

message of peace to the people. They crossed mountains to the deliver the good news (or "gospel") that the people had been saved from their enemies, there was no more need to fear, and there would now be peace. The Jews—the citizens of "Zion"—were expectantly longing to hear the same type of message at the coming of their Messiah. Isaiah puts it this way:

> How beautiful on the mountains
>   are the feet of those who bring good news,
> who proclaim peace,
>   who bring good tidings,
>   who proclaim salvation,
> who say to Zion,
>   "Your God reigns!"[14]

Isaiah also describes the peace that will reign at the coming of the Messiah in this way:

> The wolf will live with the lamb,
>   the leopard will lie down with the goat,
> the calf and the lion and the yearling together;
>   and a little child will lead them.
> The cow will feed with the bear,
>   their young will lie down together,
>   and the lion will eat straw like the ox.
> The infant will play near the cobra's den,
>   and the young child will put its hand into the viper's nest.[15]

What a vivid poetic description of perfect shalom.[16]

Third, upon the arrival of the Messiah, the Jews expected that justice would prevail throughout the earth. And because he had come to establish this justice, the peoples of the earth would respect and admire him. This respect and admiration of God's power is often translated "fear of the Lord." The term describes a healthy fear of God flowing from respect, and those who fear the Lord thus eagerly seek to live according to his perfect will. A helpful analogy is the respect that soldiers have for an excellent commander, someone who may be tough, no-nonsense, and demanding, but who instills confidence in his or her soldiers because they trust that his or her decisions will benefit them, keep them safe, and lead them to victory.

After Isaiah says that "a shoot will come up from the stump of Jesse; from his roots a Branch will bear fruit,"[17] he states that "the Spirit of the Lord will rest on him—the Spirit of wisdom and of understanding, the Spirit of counsel and of might, the Spirit of the knowledge and fear of the Lord—and he will delight in the fear of the Lord."[18] Unlike typical rulers, this ruler "will not judge by what he sees with his eyes,"[19] nor will he make decisions based on "what he hears with his ears."[20] Instead, he will "judge the needy with justice."[21] This ruler will not depend on eyewitness evidence and hearsay, but will judge rightly because he knows all things, even the invisible and inaudible secrets of our hearts.[22]

Isaiah makes it very clear that the ruler from the line of David will establish justice: "In love a throne will be established; in faithfulness a man will sit on it—one from the house of David—one who in judging seeks justice and speeds the cause of righteousness."[23] Through Isaiah, God describes this future ruler as a servant whom God has chosen to bring justice to all nations:

> "Here is my servant, whom I uphold,
>   my chosen one in whom I delight;
> I will put my Spirit on him,
>   and he will bring justice to the nations.
> He will not shout or cry out,
>   or raise his voice in the streets.
> A bruised reed he will not break,
>   and a smoldering wick he will not snuff out.
> In faithfulness he will bring forth justice;
>   he will not falter or be discouraged
> till he establishes justice on earth."[24]

This is a picture of a ruler who is perfectly just and powerful, tenacious and unwavering. But it also describes a ruler who is perfectly gentle: not shouting, crying out, and raising his voice, nor breaking a tender blade of grass or snuffing out a candle that is still smoldering.[25] If one is honest, it is difficult not to think of Jesus when reading this description.

A fourth aspect of what the Jews believe will happen when their

Messiah comes is that he will usher in a time of feasting and abundance.²⁶ Here's one picture of this expectation:

> On this mountain the Lord Almighty will prepare
>   a feast of rich food for all peoples,
> a banquet of aged wine—
>   the best of meats and the finest of wines.²⁷

Since this feasting and abundance will arrive after a time of famine, difficulty, and suffering, it will be a time of incredible joy and celebration, as Isaiah describes:

> The Lord will surely comfort Zion
>   and will look with compassion on all her ruins;
> he will make her deserts like Eden,
>   her wastelands like the garden of the Lord.
> Joy and gladness will be found in her,
>   thanksgiving and the sound of singing.²⁸

It will be as if the people had been restored from a desert wilderness to the Garden of Eden. The prophet Ezekiel shares a similar message from God regarding the day he will restore Israel and "cleanse" his people from sin:

> "I will sprinkle clean water on you, and you will be clean; I will cleanse you from all your impurities and from all your idols. I will give you a new heart and put a new spirit in you; I will remove from you your heart of stone and give you a heart of flesh. And I will put my Spirit in you.... On the day I cleanse you from all your sins, I will resettle your towns, and the ruins will be rebuilt.... They will say, 'This land that was laid waste has become like the garden of Eden; the cities that were lying in ruins, desolate and destroyed, are now fortified and inhabited.'"²⁹ ³⁰

In some Messianic sections of Isaiah, all of these expectations are combined; that is, many nations will come together under the banner of the Messiah, he will establish peace, he will usher in a reign of justice and respect for God, and there will be feasts, abundance, joy, and comfort. For example, Isaiah records God as saying:

> "Listen to me, my people;
>   hear me, my nation:
> Instruction will go out from me;
>   my justice will become a light *to the nations*.
> My righteousness draws near speedily,
>   my salvation is on the way,
> and my arm will bring justice *to the nations*."[31]

As Isaiah continues to write, a fifth aspect of the Messiah's arrival surfaces, the fulfillment of the "everlasting throne of David." The Messiah will reign for all eternity, and in contrast, the present earth will deteriorate and come to an end. Speaking through Isaiah, God says:

> "Lift up your eyes to the heavens,
>   look at the earth beneath;
> the heavens will vanish like smoke,
>   the earth will wear out like a garment
>   and its inhabitants die like flies.
> But my salvation will last *forever*,
>   my righteousness will never fail."[32]

In this statement, God is claiming that the inhabitants of the earth will die like flies, but in other sections he emphasizes that the righteous (or, as the New Testament explains, those who have been made righteous through faith in Jesus) will live forever.

This leads into a sixth aspect of the Jews' expectations regarding the coming Messiah, their belief in the resurrection of all Jews upon the arrival of the Messiah. Soon after Isaiah writes that God will prepare a rich feast for all peoples, he states that God will also do the following:

> On this mountain he will destroy
>   the shroud that enfolds all peoples,
> the sheet that covers all nations;
>   he will swallow up death forever.

CHAPTER 22: THE VICTORY TO COME

> The Sovereign Lord will wipe away the tears
> from all faces;
> he will remove his people's disgrace
> from all the earth.[33]

Thus, the Messiah would destroy the "shroud" of death, which covers all people like a sheet, and he will "swallow up death forever."

Finally, for our purpose at least, the Jews expected that when the Messiah comes, the law would be "written on the hearts" of God's people. Until then, obedient Jews would memorize, recite, and teach their children God's law (the Torah). But when the Messiah comes, the law would be internalized in their hearts. Before the Messiah comes, Isaiah describes the people's treatment of God's law in this way:

> The Lord says:
> "These people come near to me with their mouth
> and honor me with their lips,
> but their hearts are far from me.
> Their worship of me
> is based on merely human rules they have been taught."[34]

But after the Messiah comes, the law will no longer be merely a list of rules to be followed outwardly through rote obedience lacking heartfelt devotion. God will put the law inside of his people, and they will obey it wholeheartedly and completely. God says it this way through the prophet Jeremiah: "'This is the covenant I will make with the people of Israel after that time,' declares the Lord. 'I will put my law in their minds and write it on their hearts. I will be their God, and they will be my people.'"[35]

These seven aspects of the arrival of the Messiah give us a better understanding of what the Jews were expecting in the Messiah, and why they believed Jesus was not the one whom God had promised through their prophets. When Jesus arrived, there was no immediate peace. People from all nations were not streaming to the temple in Jerusalem. The political structure remained corrupt, and the Romans were still demanding that the Jews pay taxes to Caesar. There was no increase in feasting. The Jews went on living the same dreary life—with beggars, lepers, widows, and the poor abounding as always. Moreover, the dead were still in their graves.

And the Torah remained a list of rules that they obligingly memorized and struggled to consistently obey. Jesus can't be the Messiah! Or could he be?

You can think of the prophecies in the Hebrew Scriptures as a view of a large mountain range from a distance. Peaks that seem to be at the same distance away are, in reality, separated by hundreds of miles. Similarly, the prophecies may seem to refer to the same Messianic arrival, but their fulfillment may come in stages that are separated by long spans of time. Christians believe the Messianic prophecies have already been fulfilled in part when Jesus came two millennia ago, but his second coming—when people from all nations will come to him, when he will judge the earth, establish peace, and set out great feasts, when he will write the law on his people's hearts—is still future to us.

The First Prophecies About Jesus

As we come to the end of our discussion of Old Testament prophecies that were fulfilled in Jesus, it is fitting for us to come full circle and return to the oldest biblical prophecies about the Messiah. We'll briefly discuss the very first prophecy about the Messiah in the Bible, as well as another of the earliest Messianic prophecies in the Bible, perhaps the earliest.

Though it's the first prophecy relating to Jesus that we come across as we read the Bible, it should make much more sense if we look at it last, now that we have covered other prophecies concerning Jesus' second coming when he will establish a Kingdom of perfect peace, justice, and flourishing. Following his resurrection, Jesus gave his disciples a comprehensive summary of how the entire Old Testament was about him: "Beginning with Moses and all the prophets, he explained to them what was written in all the Scriptures about himself."[36] Here Luke wrote "all the Scriptures" to mean the entirety of the Hebrew Scriptures, beginning with Genesis, the first book attributed to Moses. And it is at the very beginning in Genesis that we get the first glimpse of God's plan of salvation and how it would require a suffering savior.

We read that the first humans disobeyed God's command, bringing death and ruin upon their descendants, the entire human race. As a result of this "fall," God says the following words to the serpent who had tempted Adam and Eve:

CHAPTER 22: THE VICTORY TO COME

> "I will put enmity
> between you and the woman,
> and between your offspring and hers;
> he will crush your head,
> and you will strike his heel."[37]

Christian scholars largely agree that the offspring of the woman is Jesus, whose heel will be struck as he crushes the head of the serpent's offspring. Writing around 180 AD, the early Christian father Irenaeus expounds on this Genesis prophecy, describing how Jesus ultimately did trample on the serpent's head: "[Jesus] has therefore, in His work of recapitulation, summed up all things, both waging war against our enemy, and crushing him who had at the beginning led us away captives in Adam, and trampled upon his head."[38] Note that an injury to your heel will generally not kill you, but if your head is crushed, you don't live long. What does it all mean?

In the Gospels, we read of many clashes of power between Jesus and demons, clashes from which Jesus consistently emerged as the victor.[39] Jesus himself referred to his ultimate aim of crushing Satan's head once and for all in several places, such as with his reference to "binding the strong man" in order to "plunder" his house—a vivid image of rescuing people from the evil and darkness of this world.[40]

Jesus also referred to his victory over Satan ("the prince of the world") when he predicted his own death: "Now is the time for judgment on this world; now the prince of this world will be driven out. And I, when I am lifted up from the earth, will draw all people to myself."[41] In these verses, Jesus was referring to his future exaltation to the right hand of God, after he is crucified and rises again.[42] On the cross Jesus defeated the power of Satan and "drove him out," though Satan unfortunately remains active in the world until Jesus returns. But because of what the "offspring of the woman" accomplished on the cross, the "offspring of the serpent" no longer has deadly power over those who trust in Jesus. And when Jesus returns to judge the world, Satan will be crushed completely,[43] ushering in the Kingdom of God when peace, flourishing, justice, and love will prevail under Jesus' rule.

The epistles, too, refer to this first prophecy about Jesus in Genesis. In John's first letter, he writes, "The one who does what is sinful is of the devil, because the devil has been sinning from the beginning. The reason the Son of God appeared was to destroy the devil's work."[44]

Paul describes the final blow to Satan that is yet to come. At the time, Christians were being cruelly persecuted, and Paul wrote to them to encourage them. You can hear a clear echo of the Genesis prophecy in Paul's words: "The God of peace will soon crush Satan under your feet."[45] For those of us who eagerly await the day that Satan will be crushed, "soon" can't come soon enough.

The final prophecy about the future victory of the Messiah—at least for our discussion—comes from the oldest book of the Bible, the Book of Job. Many scholars believe Job is the oldest book of the Bible because Job contains no references to the Mosaic law, the priesthood, the prophets, or God's promises to Abraham, Isaac, and Jacob. Plus, the few similarities that Job does have with other parts of the Old Testament are most likely because those other parts were written later and were referencing Job, rather than vice versa.[46] Moreover, the only reference in the Bible to the name "Job" is in Ezekiel,[47] and Ezekiel was referring to the Job of the Book of Job. Meanwhile, the name "Job" only appears in extra-biblical sources that date between 2000 BC and 1400 BC, and not later.[48] Though there is still considerable debate, Job was most likely written around the time of Abraham, between 1900 and 1700 BC, about 400 years *before* the Book of Genesis was written. (But even though Genesis was probably written *later* than Job, it describes events that happened *before* the Book of Job was written.)

With that background on the age of the Book of Job, it is even more surprising to read Job's clear reference to the future Messiah. But before we get to it, let's first take a look at another statement by Job, one that is unexpectedly insightful given its early date. Job expresses a desire for a "mediator" to bridge the gap he feels exists between himself and the immortal God. He hopes for someone who will remove God's "rod of justice" that Job fears will fall on him. He explains it this way:

> [God] is not a mere mortal like me that I might answer him,
>   that we might confront each other in court.
> If only there were someone to mediate between us,
>   someone to bring us together,
> someone to remove God's rod from me,
>   so that his terror would frighten me no more.
> Then I would speak up without fear of him,
>   but as it now stands with me, I cannot.[49]

CHAPTER 22: THE VICTORY TO COME

Job expresses a common theme of not just the Old Testament but of many religions in general: the desire of a flawed, mortal human to approach a perfectly holy, immortal God without fear of punishment.

And yet, later we read Job's confident claim that he knows such a mediator exists and that one day he will come and enable him to approach the holy God. He calls this mediator his "Redeemer," and he succinctly states his trust that this mediator will physically stand on the earth in the future. Here is Job's famous assertion:

> I know that my redeemer lives,
>   and that in the end he will stand on the earth.
> And after my skin has been destroyed,
>   yet in my flesh I will see God;
> I myself will see him
>   with my own eyes—I, and not another.
>   How my heart yearns within me![50]

Not only did Job "know" that his redeemer was living—present tense—but he also knew that in the future, even after he died (his skin having been destroyed), he *himself* would take on flesh and see God. He even rephrased his claim, just in case we had misunderstood him, and emphasized who and how he would see God: "I *myself* will see him with *my own* eyes."

Fast forward to the New Testament, where Timothy explains that the mediator for whom Job longed has arrived: "For there is one God and one mediator between God and mankind, the man Christ Jesus."[51] The author of Hebrew further clarifies: "Christ is the mediator of a new covenant, that those who are called may receive the promised eternal inheritance—now that he has died as a ransom to set them free from the sins committed under the first covenant."[52]

In his Revelation, John describes the day that Job longed to see, when this mediator would return to earth. At that point, a "great multitude that no one could count, from every nation, tribe, people and language" will stand before the mediator's throne (whom he calls "the Lamb"). John then describes this great crowd of people, interspersing prophecies from Isaiah throughout:

> "Never again will they hunger;
>   never again will they thirst.

> The sun will not beat down on them,
>> nor any scorching heat.
> For the Lamb at the center of the throne
>> will be their shepherd;
>> 'he will lead them to springs of living water.'
>>> 'And God will wipe away every tear from their eyes.'"53

For those, like Job, who have suffered greatly in this world and have faith in this mediator, the day that John envisions will fulfill every longing of their heart, longings that no earthly prize could ever satisfy. Those who see Jesus as this future "redeemer," the one who will crush the serpent's offspring, understand how Job's heart was yearning within him. Four millennia ago, Job longed for a mediator, two millennia ago this mediator arrived, and sometime in the future this mediator will return to enable his followers to live in God's presence forever.

QUESTIONS FOR COMPREHENSION AND DISCUSSION

1. After he displayed his power, why did Jesus resist the people's efforts to make him king?
2. How does Daniel describe the coming of the Messiah, who is "like a son of man"? At what point in his life did Jesus say that he would one day come "on the clouds"?
3. Why is it somewhat surprising that the Jewish nation was expecting the Messiah to call people from *all* the nations of the earth?
4. What is *shalom*? What are some ways that the Old Testament describes the time when the Messiah will establish shalom?
5. What does it mean to "fear the Lord"? Why would people fear God upon the arrival of the Messiah?
6. What are some ways that the Old Testament describes God as destroying death?
7. When reading the Bible, what is the first prophecy about Jesus that we come across?

8. Who do Christian scholars believe are the "offspring of the woman" and the "offspring of the serpent"? What will happen to each?
9. What are ways that Jesus and the apostle Paul refer to this Genesis prophecy?
10. What is the oldest prophecy about Jesus in the Old Testament? What does Job long for that will make it possible for him to approach God? How does Jesus fulfill Job's yearning?

CHAPTER 22 ENDNOTES

1. Franklin Graham and Donna Lee Toney, *Billy Graham in Quotes* (Nashville, TN: Thomas Nelson, 2011), 123.
2. Michael J. Vlach, "Isaiah 24:21-23: The Victory and Rule of the Messianic King," in Michael Rydelnik and Edwin Blum, *The Moody Handbook of Messianic Prophecy: Studies and Expositions of the Messiah in the Old Testament* (Chicago, IL: Moody Publishers, 2019), 865.
3. Daniel 7:13-14. All emphases in Bible passages are mine.
4. John 6:14-15.
5. Matthew 26:64; Mark 14:62.
6. Matthew 24:30; see also Mark 13:26.
7. Revelation 14:14.
8. For a full commentary on these verses, see Rydelnik and Blum, *The Moody Handbook of Messianic Prophecy*, 785-802.
9. Isaiah 2:3-4. See Micah 4:1-5 for a similar prophecy.
10. Isaiah 4:3 and Micah 4:2.
11. Isaiah 2:2.
12. Micah 4:3. See also Isaiah 2:4.
13. Rydelnik and Blum, *The Moody Handbook of Messianic Prophecy*, 791.
14. Isaiah 52:7.
15. Isaiah 11:6-8.
16. John F. Walvoord, *Every Prophecy of the Bible* (Colorado Springs, CO: Chariot Victor Publishing, 1999), 98.
17. Isaiah 11:1.
18. Isaiah 11:2-3a.
19. Isaiah 11:3b.
20. Isaiah 11:3b.
21. Isaiah 11:4.
22. Mark Allen Powell, ed., *HarperCollins Bible Dictionary*, 3rd Edition (New York: HarperCollins, 2011), 104-105.

23. Isaiah 16:5.
24. Isaiah 42:1-4a.
25. Michael Rydelnik and Edwin Blum, *The Moody Handbook of Messianic Prophecy*, 934.
26. Ibid, 914.
27. Isaiah 25:6.
28. Isaiah 51:3.
29. Ezekiel 36:25-27a, 33b, 35.
30. For an explanation of how Ezekiel 36 has been partially fulfilled in the return of the Jewish people to the land of Israel, as well as how it points to future fulfillment in the second coming of Christ, see Kenneth L. Barker and John R. Kohlenberger III, *NIV Bible Commentary, Volume 1: The Old Testament* (Grand Rapids, MI: Zondervan, 1994), 1332-1333.
31. Isaiah 51:4-5a.
32. Isaiah 51:6.
33. Isaiah 25:7-8a.
34. Isaiah 29:13.
35. Jeremiah 31:33.
36. Luke 24:25.
37. Genesis 3:15.
38. Irenaeus of Lyons, *Irenaeus against Heresies*, 5.21.1, in A. Roberts, J. Donaldson and A. C. Coxe, eds., *The Apostolic Fathers with Justin Martyr and Irenaeus, Vol. 1* (Buffalo, NY: Christian Literature Company, 1887), 548.
39. See Matthew 4:24, 8:16, 28-33, 9:32-34, 12:22-28, 15:22, 17: 14, 18; Mark 1:32-34, 39, 3:22-27, 5:12-18, 6:13, 7:26-30, 16:9; Luke 4:33-36, 41, 8:2, 27-39, 9:37-43, 10:17, 11:14-26, and 13:32.
40. See Mark 3:20-35.
41. John 12:31-32.
42. See Luke 24:51.
43. In Revelation 20, John describes his vision of that day when Satan is ultimately defeated.
44. 1 John 3:8.
45. Romans 16:20.
46. Francis I. Anderson, *Job: An Introduction and Commentary*, Donald J. Wiseman, ed., *Tyndale Old Testament Commentaries*, Vol. 14 (Nottingham: InterVarsity Press, 1973), 66.
47. See Ezekiel 14:14, 20.
48. The sources that contain the name Job are: "a nineteenth-century BC Egyptian curse on a Palestinian clan chief; on an eighteenth-century Egyptian list of slaves, some of whom bear Semitic names; on eighteenth-century tablets from Alalakh and sixteenth-century tablets found at Mari;

CHAPTER 22: THE VICTORY TO COME

in the fourteenth-century Amarna letters; and in the thirteenth-century Ugaritic texts." Quoted in David R. Jackson, *Crying Out for Vindication: The Gospel According to Job* (Phillipsburg, NJ: P&R Publishing, 2007), 11. Jackson references David J. A. Clines, *Job 1-20, World Biblical Commentary* 17 (Dallas, TX: Word, 1989), 10-11.

49 Job 9:32-35.
50 Job:19-27.
51 1 Timothy 2:5.
52 Hebrews 9:15.
53 Revelation 7:16-17. John quotes prophecies from Isaiah 25:8 and 49:10.

You study the Scriptures diligently because you think that in them you have eternal life. These are the very Scriptures that testify about me, yet you refuse to come to me to have life.

—Jesus, to the Jewish leaders[1]

The New Testament overflows with echoes of imagery from Israel's history and Israel's Scriptures, showing how glimmers of grace in past events and practices were finally focused to crystal-clarity through the lens of Jesus, and then dawned in spreading luminescence in the people whom Christ redeemed.

—Dennis Johnson, theologian, professor, and author[2]

Old Testament Objects

The two men were dejected as they traveled the seven miles home to Emmaus from Jerusalem. The man they had hoped would "redeem Israel"—the Messiah, the Christ—had just been crucified. As they lamented this dreadful turn of events, a passerby struck up a conversation with them. To their surprise, he knew nothing of the events they had been discussing. After they explained what had unfolded over the previous few days, including the discovery of the empty tomb that same morning, the mysterious man said:

> "How foolish you are, and how slow to believe all that the prophets have spoken! Did not the Messiah have to suffer these things and then enter his glory?" And beginning with Moses and all the Prophets, he explained to them what was said in all the Scriptures concerning himself.... Then their eyes were opened and they recognized him, and he disappeared from their sight. They asked each other, "Were not our hearts burning within us while he talked with us on the road and opened the Scriptures to us?"[3]

This was Jesus himself, appearing in the flesh to Cleopas and his friend on the afternoon of the same day he had risen from the dead.[4] There is no indication that Jesus was bloodied or disfigured, and he apparently walked normally despite having had nails driven through his feet. It is understandable that they didn't recognize him.

Jesus uses the phrase, "Moses and all the Prophets," to refer to

CHAPTER 23: OLD TESTAMENT OBJECTS

what Christians call the Old Testament. They were composed of the *Torah* (the first five books of the Bible, also called the *Pentateuch*) and the "Prophets," which was further composed of the "former prophets" (Joshua, Judges, Samuel, and Kings) and the "later prophets" (Isaiah, Jeremiah, Ezekiel, and the Minor Prophets).[5]

Later this same day, Jesus mentioned a third section of Scripture that "must be fulfilled":

> He said to them, "This is what I told you while I was still with you: Everything must be fulfilled that is written about me in the Law of Moses, the Prophets and the Psalms." Then he opened their minds so they could understand the Scriptures. He told them, "This is what is written: The Messiah will suffer and rise from the dead on the third day, and repentance for the forgiveness of sins will be preached in his name to all nations, beginning at Jerusalem. You are witnesses of these things."[6]

Jesus uses "the Psalms" as a shorthand way of referring to the third section of the Hebrew Scriptures, also called the "Writings," which include Psalms, Proverbs, Job, Song of Songs, Ruth, Lamentations, Ecclesiastes, Esther, Daniel, Ezra, Nehemiah, and Chronicles.[7]

How interesting it would have been to be privy to the conversations Jesus had with his followers during the forty days he was with them after his resurrection![8] It would be ideal to have a word-for-word transcript of these post-resurrection "Bible studies" and to hear Jesus' own description of how the Old Testament points to him. But we do have the benefit of his words as they were recorded in the Gospels by eyewitnesses, as well as the perspective of the rest of the New Testament, which was written by those who were either eyewitnesses or interviewed eyewitnesses of Jesus' ministry and teaching.

The twenty-seven books that the early church carefully selected for inclusion in the New Testament canon provide many references to the Old Testament. In fact, the New Testament serves as a new lens through which we can study the Hebrew Scriptures, which Christians believe God provided to prepare people for what he would do through Jesus.

In his book *The Ancient Love Song: Finding Christ in the Old*

Testament, Charles Drew summarizes the way the Old Testament explains the New Testament:

> The Old Testament points to Jesus in many ways. The *Law* anticipates him by exposing our hearts and persuading us of our need for a savior. The *promises* anticipate him by kindling a longing at numerous levels that only Jesus can fulfill. The *Wisdom Literature* compels us to look to him for meaning and the ability to live wisely. Old Testament characters teach us to look beyond the seeable world to the Messiah's eternal kingdom, and they foreshadow his great work by the role they play in Israel's life. In Old Testament history, Christ visits his people in various ways, whetting our appetite for his incarnation [appearing in the flesh with a human body]. Old Testament psalmists and prophets often speak with the voice of Christ, anticipating his own anguish and exaltation. The Old Testament testifies to Jesus, in other words, with voices far richer and more numerous than a mere scattering of predictions (however many they may be).[9]

We do not have space to fully treat all of these "rich voices," but we will examine some of the many symbols and events that anticipate the coming of Jesus. Let's begin with a discussion of the primary *objects* in the Old Testament that provide an "advance echo" of Jesus hundreds— even thousands— of years before he was born in Bethlehem.

Symbols are an essential element of language. In fact, all languages are based on symbols, whether they are sounds we make or letters, characters, words, and punctuation on papyrus, parchment, paper, or screen. The earliest symbols that babies understand are sounds they hear, the pictures they see, even the stuffed toys they hold, all of which represent objects or concepts, either in real life or in our imaginations.

Even basic sign language or body language consists of symbols that babies will interpret as "pointers" to something else. When a baby points at something he wants, he intuitively knows that his finger is not the object of interest, but instead his finger is extended toward the object of interest, a cup of milk, for example. Similarly, a sign on the road

CHAPTER 23: OLD TESTAMENT OBJECTS

with, "Food →" is a symbol for a restaurant off the road to the right. We understand that the sign points to the restaurant; it is not the restaurant itself.

So it is in the Old Testament, where God unveils his plan for reconciling unholy humans to his perfectly holy self. Jesus did not suddenly show up expecting humans to understand his mission. God had prepared his people for the coming of his Son over hundreds of years through prophecies and symbols in the Hebrew scriptures.

The symbolic objects in the Old Testament did not themselves save people from death; instead, they point to the eventual means by which God would intervene in history to save people from death—his "rescue plan" for humanity. And just as a shadow of an object is not the object itself, but simply indicates that there is an object nearby that is producing the shadow, the Old Testament "shadows" were anticipating the arrival of the savior. Let's begin our tour of these "shadows" by examining some of the objects used to symbolize the coming savior. We'll then turn to the people, events, ceremonies, and holidays that point us to Jesus hundreds of years before he showed up as a baby in a manger.

NOAH'S ARK

Our tour begins with the well-known story of Noah's Ark (found in Genesis 6 through 9). Adam and Eve had multiplied in number as they were instructed, but their descendants have become so wicked that "every inclination of the human heart was only evil all the time."[10]

God spoke to a man named Noah, who is described as "blameless among the people of his time,"[11] warning him that he was planning to destroy humanity with a huge flood. Heeding this warning and following God's instructions, Noah built an ark to save his family, along with a male and female of every animal.

Noah's actions provide a beautiful example of the saving power of faith; in particular, his response to God's warning is an excellent example of what we'd call "faith in action." Even though, first, there was no evidence that a storm was approaching, and, second, he lived a good distance from the coast, Noah still believed God's warning of the coming flood. He also demonstrated his trust in God by obeying every detail of the instructions God gave him for the construction of the ark.

Although "Noah's Ark" has become, in the modern imagination, a children's story, Jesus considered it historical. He described the fate of unbelievers with a fearful warning:

> "As it was in the days of Noah, so it will be at the coming of the Son of Man. For in the days before the flood, people were eating and drinking, marrying and giving in marriage, up to the day Noah entered the ark; and they knew nothing about what would happen until the flood came and took them all away. That is how it will be at the coming of the Son of Man."[12]

What determined the difference between those who survived and those who were swept away? The ones who survived—who were "saved" from the storm—were the ones who trusted God and "entered the ark." Jesus compared this sudden storm in the days of Noah to the future "storm" when he returns to judge the world as the "Son of Man."

But at his second coming, the ark will not be a boat. It will be Jesus himself, and all who are "in Jesus" will be saved. Paul describes this safety from judgment in the letter he wrote to the church in Rome: "Therefore, there is now no condemnation for those who are *in Christ Jesus*."[13] Similarly, Paul writes to the Corinthians: "For as in Adam all die, so *in Christ* all will be made alive."[14]

There is actually evidence that this ancient flood did happen. One example of evidence is the plethora of flood myths in many ancient cultures.[15] But even if one does not accept the ark as literal, Noah's faith, which he demonstrated by boarding the ark and escaping judgment and destruction, points to the faith that Jesus requires his followers to have in order to survive the final judgment. The author of Hebrews commends Noah in this way: "By faith Noah, when warned about things not yet seen, in holy fear built an ark to save his family. By his faith he condemned the world and became heir of the righteousness that is in keeping with faith."[16]

The Stairway to Heaven

As we've mentioned, Noah had three sons, one of whom is named Shem. Shem's descendants became the Jewish nation (which is why they have

CHAPTER 23: OLD TESTAMENT OBJECTS

been called "Shemites," or "Semites"). As discussed in Chapter 20, God made a promise to one of Shem's descendants, Abraham, that he would "make him into a great nation" and through him "all peoples on earth will be blessed."[17] Abraham and his wife Sarah had a son in their old age, Isaac. Isaac married Rachel, and they had two sons, Jacob and Esau. Jacob fathered twelve sons, whose families became the twelve tribes of Israel.

Following a deceitful scheme in which Jacob had stolen his brother Esau's blessing from their father, Jacob fled to his uncle's house in Harran to escape a murderously vengeful Esau. On his first night *en route* to Harran, Jacob slept by the side of the road. It was there that "the Lord" appeared to him in a dream to reiterate the promise he had given Jacob's grandfather, Abraham. The story goes as follows: Jacob dreamed that he saw "a stairway resting on the earth, with its top reaching to heaven, and the angels of God were ascending and descending on it." At the top of the stairway, God said to Jacob:

> I am the Lord, the God of your father Abraham and the God of Isaac. I will give you and your descendants the land on which you are lying. Your descendants will be like the dust of the earth, and you will spread out to the west and to the east, to the north and to the south. All peoples on earth will be blessed through you and your offspring. I am with you and will watch over you wherever you go, and I will bring you back to this land. I will not leave you until I have done what I have promised you.

When Jacob awoke from his sleep, he thought, "Surely the Lord is in this place, and I was not aware of it." He was afraid and said, "How awesome is this place! This is none other than the house of God; this is the gate of heaven."[18]

This "gate of heaven" (sometimes called "Jacob's ladder" or "the stairway to heaven") is our second Old Testament object that symbolizes Jesus. Jesus himself directly referenced Jacob's dream in a conversation with a new disciple named Nathanael. After Jesus mentioned that he knew something about him (when he had been under a fig tree) that apparently no one other than God could have known, Nathanael declared, "Rabbi, you are the Son of God; you are the king of Israel." Jesus then replied:

> "You believe because I told you I saw you under the fig tree. You will see greater things than that." He then added, "Very truly I tell you, you will see 'heaven open, and the angels of God ascending and descending on the Son of Man.'"[19]

It sounds odd: Jesus was describing *himself* as the stairway of Jacob's dream. He will later refer to himself as "the way," meaning that he is the means by which we get to heaven.[20] It is notable that Jesus used the title "Son of Man" to describe himself just after Nathanael had called him "the Son of God." By connecting the two terms, Jesus may have been indicating that he does indeed connect "man" (i.e. people) to God.[21] Nathanael only got a glimmer of an understanding of what the New Testament writers will continue to unfold: that Jesus is, in fact, both fully human and fully God, and that he is the one who provides the means by which mere humans can approach a perfectly holy God.

Manna in the Wilderness

We now quickly forward through the stories of Jacob and his twelve sons, and the story of the youngest brother Joseph being sold into slavery by his brothers, rising to the top administrative position under the Egyptian pharaoh, and eventually forgiving his brothers when they come to Egypt during a famine to purchase grain. After the joyful reunion between Joseph and his father Jacob, the entire household moved to Egypt to escape the famine in Canaan.

Several generations passed, and the new pharaoh had forgotten the great things Jacob's son Joseph had done for Egypt. Instead, this new pharaoh enslaved the descendants of Jacob because they had become too plentiful and were a potential threat to his power. He even commanded that all Hebrew male babies be thrown into the Nile. One baby, however, was saved in a basket (or "ark," since the same Hebrew word is used for Noah's ark), which his mother had set to drift down the Nile, and he was rescued by Pharaoh's daughter and subsequently raised in Pharaoh's household. His name was Moses.

CHAPTER 23: OLD TESTAMENT OBJECTS

Moses grew up with all of the benefits of life in a palace and a royal education. But he eventually discovered that he was a Hebrew, not an Egyptian. From out of a burning bush, God called him to lead the Hebrew people out of slavery in Egypt and back to their "promised land." After ten plagues hit Egypt, Pharaoh finally agreed to release the Israelites. Moses led the freed Hebrew people across the dry seabed and through the desert towards the land that God had promised centuries earlier to Abraham, Isaac, and Jacob.

Though the people were no longer slaves, they began to grumble about life on the road, even if it was the road leading to the promised land, "flowing with milk and honey."[22] They complained to their leader Moses and his brother Aaron:

> "If only we had died by the Lord's hand in Egypt! There we sat around pots of meat and ate all the food we wanted, but you have brought us out into this desert to starve this entire assembly to death." Then the Lord said to Moses, "I will rain down bread from heaven for you."[23]

God's promise to rain down "bread from heaven" is fulfilled in the arrival of *manna*, which appeared on the ground six days a week as "thin flakes like frost." The Israelites called it manna because it sounded the same as the Hebrew words that are translated, "What is it?" Gathering it for food six days a week, they were able to survive for forty years in the desert.

Jesus interpreted the ultimate meaning of the event, startling his audience by describing himself as manna:

> Jesus said to them, "Very truly I tell you, it is not Moses who has given you the bread from heaven, but it is my Father who gives you the true bread from heaven. For the bread of God is the bread that comes down from heaven and gives life to the world."
>
> "Sir," they said, "always give us this bread."
>
> Then Jesus declared, "I am the bread of life. Whoever comes to me will never go hungry."[24]

Once again, Jesus clarified that an Old Testament object—in this case, the manna that God provided through Moses for his people—points to him. The manna came down from heaven to keep the Israelites from dying during their journey to the "promised land." Likewise, Jesus came down from heaven to save his people and enable them to complete their own journey to the "promised land" that God has reserved for them in heaven.

Symbolism of the Tabernacle and Temple

Though scholars have discussed many other objects in the Old Testament that symbolize Jesus, we will focus on the most vivid objects, ones that the nation of Israel preserved in their midst through the centuries leading up to Jesus, the furnishings of their place of worship: first, a portable tent called a tabernacle, and ultimately, the temple building that was erected by Solomon, the son of King David, in Jerusalem in the tenth century BC.

In the second book of the Old Testament, following the story of Moses' leading the people out of slavery in Egypt, God provided detailed instructions to the Israelites, still under Moses' leadership, for the construction of a symbolic "dwelling place" for him. The intent was to provide a physical structure where worship could be carried out, a place where the holy Creator could demonstrate his desire to have a relationship with humans. His instructions began with these words:

> "Then have them make a sanctuary for me, and I will dwell among them. Make this tabernacle and all its furnishings exactly like the pattern I will show you."[25]

Exodus is full of detailed instructions regarding how God wanted the tabernacle to be built, and the Israelites built it exactly "as the Lord had commanded Moses." In fact, the phrase, "as the Lord commanded Moses," occurs eighteen times in Exodus 39 and 40. The emphasis is clear: God specifies the way we are to worship him, and we are to follow his specifications, just as Noah followed his specifications when he built the ark. One scholar makes it clear: "The Tabernacle stood as a constant visible witness that salvation was God's way or no way."[26]

But why does God have his people build a place for him to dwell?

CHAPTER 23: OLD TESTAMENT OBJECTS

Doesn't the Bible say that God is present everywhere?[27] Does God really need a place to live? No, he does not. He was using the tabernacle as a visual aid to educate his people about himself and his future plans for them. Most importantly, the tabernacle was a visible sign to the people that God was *present with them*, and it was also a sign to them that God desired to *identify with them*.

So how does this worship tent symbolize Jesus? John opens his Gospel with these words: "The Word became flesh and made his dwelling among us."[28] The word John uses for "dwelling" is the same word that was used for God's "tabernacle" in the *Septuagint* (the Greek translation of the Hebrew Scriptures).[29] The tabernacle thus represented God taking on flesh to identify with humans and to dwell in their midst, as he would in Jesus.

Many centuries before Jesus, King David had expressed his desire to build a permanent, unmovable house for God, more permanent than the transportable tabernacle made of rods and curtains. In response, God tells David through the prophet Nathan:

> "You are not the one to build me a house to dwell in. I have not dwelt in a house from the day I brought Israel up out of Egypt to this day. I have moved from one tent site to another, from one dwelling place to another.... I declare to you that the Lord will build a house for you: When your days are over and you go to be with your ancestors, I will raise up your offspring to succeed you, one of your own sons, and I will establish his kingdom. He is the one who will build a house for me, and I will establish his throne forever. I will be his father, and he will be my son. I will never take my love away from him, as I took it away from your predecessor. I will set him over my house and my kingdom forever; his throne will be established forever."[30]

God was describing the dynasty ("house") that would lead to his Son. Jesus even called himself the temple, to the chagrin of his enemies: "Destroy this temple, and I will raise it again in three days."[31]

Let's take a closer look at how the tabernacle pointed forward to Jesus.

1. The Structure of the Tabernacle

The tabernacle was composed of three sections, the outer court, the Holy Place, and the Most Holy Place. Only members of the Israelite community could enter the outer court, and only priests could enter the Holy Place. The Most Holy Place, also called "The Holy of Holies," was located in the innermost section of the tabernacle.

As mentioned in Chapter 21, the only person who could enter the Most Holy Place was the high priest, who entered once a year on the Day of Atonement, or *Yom Kippur*. God was teaching the Israelites that his perfect holiness keeps them from having complete access to him. Moreover, there was one specific *way* that they were to approach him, as there was only one entrance into the tabernacle, one entrance into the Holy Place, and one entrance into the Most Holy Place.

The Book of Hebrews sheds light on the symbolism of the Most Holy Place, which the author calls the "inner room":

> But only the high priest entered the inner room, and that only once a year, and never without blood, which he offered for himself and for the sins the people had committed in ignorance. The Holy Spirit was showing by this that the way into the Most Holy Place had not yet been disclosed as long as the first tabernacle was still functioning. This is an *illustration* for the present time, indicating that the gifts and sacrifices being offered were not able to clear the conscience of the worshiper.[32]

That is, in the structure of the tabernacle, the people learned that the only true way into God's presence—from the world outside into the outer court, from the outer court to the Holy Place, and then from the Holy Place into the Most Holy Place—was to be provided later, but until that provision the tabernacle would be an "illustration" to symbolize the process. When Jesus became the "great high priest," the tabernacle was no longer necessary for worship, as he opened the way once and for all into God's presence for all who believe in him.

When the temple was built in Jerusalem about a millennium before Christ, a thick curtain separated the Holy Place from the Most Holy Place. It measured thirty feet by thirty feet and was about as thick as the

CHAPTER 23: OLD TESTAMENT OBJECTS

palm of a man's hand. The symbolism of the tabernacle providing a way for us to enter God's presence directly is clear from what happened upon Jesus' death. As soon as Jesus breathed his last breath we read that, "The curtain of the temple was torn in two from top to bottom."[33]

God was demonstrating in no uncertain terms that Jesus had achieved the mission for which he had been sent: by living the perfect life on behalf of his followers and by taking the penalty that his followers' sins deserved, Jesus provided full access into God's presence for everyone who trusts in him. But there's even more symbolism to drive this point home, just in case we still don't get the message.

2. THE FURNITURE OF THE TABERNACLE:

Even the furnishings inside the tabernacle and temple served as "object lessons" or "visual aids" to teach the people about the holiness of their God. The first item an Israelite would see upon entering the outer court of the tabernacle was the altar, which measured 7.5 by 7.5 feet and consisted of acacia wood and bronze grates. This was where priests would offer the animal sacrifices.

Our modern sensibilities find the idea of a blood sacrifice gruesome and archaic, but God made it very clear that blood was required to atone—or pay the penalty—for our sin. God spoke through Moses to emphasize the importance of the shedding of blood for the forgiveness of sins: "For the life of a creature is in the blood, and I have given it to you to make atonement for yourselves on the altar; it is the blood that makes atonement for one's life."[34]

"Atonement" is the English translation of a Hebrew word, *kaphar* (כפר), which was generally used to indicate "wiping away" or "covering over" of sin, as if to shield it from God's holy eyes. After atoning for the people's sins, God would see the people as if they were perfectly holy and had never sinned, which enabled them to live in his presence. An analogy, though imperfect, is to think of God's holiness as a consuming fire, such that in order to enable his people to live with him, they needed to be "fireproofed." Atonement would accomplish this fireproofing.

Our hearts are both warmed and broken when we hear stories in which people die in order to save the life of another. We therefore innately understand the significance of a blood sacrifice, the ultimate price anyone can pay for another person's life. Paul gets at the significance of this ultimate sacrifice when he explains that someone would possibly be willing to die "for a good person," implying that no one would usually consider dying for a bad person. However, Paul continues, "God shows his love for us in that while we were still sinners, Christ died for us."[35] The altar, therefore, pointed forward to the ultimate sacrifice of Jesus for his people.

Just beyond the altar before the entrance to the inner court (the Holy Place) was the bronze *laver*, or wash basin. The priests were to wash themselves after making sacrifices to atone for sin on the altar and before entering the Holy Place. The message is clear: sin makes us morally "dirty," and we must be cleansed in order to approach a perfectly holy God. In another outrageous statement, Jesus claimed that he is the means by which we become clean: "Already you are clean because of the word that I have spoken to you."[36] Paul also clarifies that Jesus' work on our behalf makes us clean:

> Husbands, love your wives, just as Christ loved the church and gave himself up for her to make her holy, *cleansing her by the washing with water* through the word, and to present her to himself as a radiant church, without stain or wrinkle or any other blemish, but holy and blameless.[37]

I should clarify that believers in Jesus are clean because God has transferred Jesus' perfect record to them and has forgiven their sins, but their actions on earth are still "dirty." However, those who truly trust in Jesus will demonstrate in their lives a gradual transition to "cleaner living" as they go through a process called *sanctification*.[38]

Once inside the Holy Place, the priests would see three items: the showbread, the lampstand, and the altar of incense. The showbread, or the "bread of faces" or "bread of the presentation" in Hebrew, was a table of pure gold on which the priests set out bread. The showbread was meant as a symbol of God's provision for the people.

As mentioned above when we discussed the manna in the desert, Jesus claimed, "I am the living bread that came down from heaven. Whoever eats this bread will live forever."[39] Moreover, Jesus also instructed his followers to observe what we call the Lord's Supper, or

CHAPTER 23: OLD TESTAMENT OBJECTS

communion, as a way to remember what he has done for them. At the "Last Supper," on the eve of Passover before Jesus' crucifixion, Luke records the following: "[Jesus] took bread, gave thanks and broke it, and gave it to them, saying, 'This is my body given for you; do this in remembrance of me.'"[40] Followers of Jesus eat the bread at communion to remember what Jesus did for them, when his body was broken on the cross, and it symbolizes the spiritual sustenance that Jesus provides.

The golden lampstand also stood just inside the Holy Place, across from the showbread. Composed of 75 pounds of solid gold, it had seven shafts ending with flower-shaped cups holding olive oil and a wick. Because the Jews considered the number seven symbolic of divine perfection, the priests kept the seven flames lit at all times, and these seven flames provided the only source of light within the Holy Place.

In the Bible, light is a ubiquitous symbol for goodness, illumination, and truth. As such, it is an especially common symbol for God, whether it was a flame in the holy place, a burning bush, a smoking firepot, or a pillar of fire. Jesus was thus making another outrageous claim to deity when he said, "I am the light of the world. Whoever follows me will never walk in darkness, but will have the light of life."[41] In the introduction to his gospel, John emphasizes that Jesus fulfills the light that had symbolized God throughout the Old Testament: "In [Jesus] was life, and that life was the light of all mankind."[42] Jesus is the fulfillment of the light from the seven flames that burned non-stop in the Holy Place.

The last item within the Holy Place was the altar of incense, located between the lampstand and the showbread next to the veil that separated the Holy Place from the Most Holy Place. Along with all of the other details for the tabernacle, God provided the recipe for the incense: "Take fragrant spices—gum resin, onycha and galbanum—and pure frankincense, all in equal amounts, and make a fragrant blend of incense, the work of a perfumer. It is to be salted and pure and sacred."[43]

The priests would take coals from the altar in the outer court and use them to light this fragrant blend of spices on the altar of incense in the morning and evening. The scent of the incense would waft into the Most Holy Place, symbolizing the prayers offered to God by the priests on behalf of the people. As an example of how incense symbolized prayer, King David writes: "I call to you, Lord, come quickly to me; hear me when I call to you. May my prayer be set before you like incense; may the lifting up of my hands be like the evening sacrifice."[44]

Prior to Jesus' coming, the priests interceded for the people—that is, they acted on behalf of the people to present their prayers to God. But the priests were no longer necessary after Jesus came. The author of Hebrews declares that Jesus is the ultimate priest, permanently replacing the priests who had come before:

> Now there have been many of those priests, since death prevented them from continuing in office; but because Jesus lives forever, he has a permanent priesthood. Therefore he is able to save completely those who come to God through him, because he always lives to intercede for them.[45]

Jesus provides intercession for us, just as he provides light, cleansing, and atonement. His life, death, and resurrection fulfilled what the furnishings in the tabernacle symbolized: he is the sacrifice that atones for our sin, he is the water that cleanses those who trust in him, he is the light of life to those who have faith in him, and he is the intercessor who enables his followers to boldly present their prayers to God.

The final piece of furniture in the tabernacle, the ark of the covenant, was placed in the Most Holy Place. The ark was the perfect representation of both God's residing with his people (his *immanence*) and also his being above and separate from his people (his *transcendence*). He wanted his people to know him, but they needed to understand that he was not to be treated casually.

The ark was inlaid with pure gold to symbolize the majesty and power of God. On the cover of the ark—the "atonement cover" or "mercy seat"—were two creatures called *cherubim* facing one another and spreading out their wings towards the center to cover the top of the ark. The cherubim are a type of angelic being, and in this case, they most likely resembled sphinxes (winged lions with human heads). The Bible describes God as being "enthroned between the cherubim."[46] Also, God spoke to Moses from between their wings.[47]

The contents of the ark were important items from Israel's history: the two stone tablets with the Ten Commandments, a jar of manna, and Moses' brother Aaron's staff.[48] When the high priest made atonement for the sins of the Israelites once a year on Yom Kippur, he would sprinkle (*nazah*, or נָזָה, as we discussed in Chapter 21) the blood of the sacrificed bull on the atonement cover. In this way, God would symbolically see the blood that covered the mercy seat *instead of* the broken law on the tablets beneath it.

Again, the author of Hebrews explains the rich symbolism of God's tabernacle, which pointed forward to the ultimate sanctuary that Jesus was to enter:

> For Christ did not enter a sanctuary made with human hands that was only a copy of the true one; he entered heaven itself, now to appear for us in God's presence. Nor did he enter heaven to offer himself again and again, the way the high priest enters the Most Holy Place every year with blood that is not his own. Otherwise Christ would have had to suffer many times since the creation of the world. But he has appeared once for all at the culmination of the ages to do away with sin by the sacrifice of himself. Just as people are destined to die once, and after that to face judgment, so Christ was sacrificed once to take away the sins of many; and he will appear a second time, not to bear sin, but to bring salvation to those who are waiting for him.[49]

The tabernacle—and all of the splendor and beauty of its furnishings—was a mere shadow of the means of salvation to which it pointed. The various components of the tabernacle were symbols foreshadowing God's ultimate plan of redemption that would enable his people to live in his presence eternally.

We now turn our attention to the people in the Old Testament who provided advance echoes of Jesus' arrival on earth. We'll see why many people claim that Jesus appears on every page of the Old Testament, whether in prophecies or in the form of object lessons, as we've seen already, or in the form of the fathers and leaders of the Israelites, as well as those who were considered "outsiders." We will also see in Chapters 27 and 28, God taught his people through the festivals and traditions that he established thousands of years ago and that are still practiced today.

THE SHORTEST LEAP

QUESTIONS FOR COMPREHENSION AND DISCUSSION

1. What did Jesus tell the two men on the road to Emmaus—and his disciples later the same day—about how the Old Testament relates to him? Which words did Jesus use to describe the Hebrew Scriptures?
2. Why is a study of the Old Testament helpful for understanding who Jesus is and what he came to earth to accomplish?
3. What is a symbol? What are some types of symbols that we use? Why are symbols useful?
4. How does Noah's ark point to Jesus? Why was Noah commended for his faith in Hebrews 11?
5. How does the stairway in Jacob's dream point to Jesus? What did Jesus say about himself that correlates with this symbol?
6. What is manna, and how does it point to Jesus? What did the manna do for the Israelites, and how is it like what Jesus does for his followers today?
7. Why was the tabernacle built? Why is it structured with three concentric sections? How does it point to Jesus as a whole?
8. What is the symbolism of the altar, the laver, the showbread, the lampstand, the altar of incense, and the curtain that separates the Holy Place from the Most Holy Place?
9. How do animal sacrifices teach us about God's ultimate plan for salvation? Why were sacrifices needed to please a God who is perfectly holy and just, but who also loves his people?
10. What is the significance of the ark of the covenant and the mercy seat? How were the people to enter into the presence of God, and how did Jesus change that?

CHAPTER 23 ENDNOTES

[1] John 5:39-40.
[2] Dennis Johnson, *Journeys with Jesus: Every Path in the Bible Leads Us to Christ* (Phillipsburg, NJ: P&R Publishing, 2018), 86.
[3] Luke 24:25-27, 31-32.

CHAPTER 23: OLD TESTAMENT OBJECTS

4   Because he is named, Cleopas was most likely the eyewitness who recounted this experience to Luke, as we covered in Chapter 9.
5   Johnson, *Journeys with Jesus*, 8-10.
6   Luke 24:45-48.
7   Johnson, *Journeys with Jesus*, 8-10.
8   Forty days lapsed between the resurrection of Jesus and his ascension, according to Acts 1:3.
9   Charles D. Drew, *The Ancient Love Song: Finding Christ in the Old Testament* (Phillipsburg, NJ: P&R Publishing, 2000), x.
10 Genesis 6:5.
11 Genesis 6:9.
12 Matthew 24:37-39, also in Luke 17:26-27.
13 Romans 8:1.
14 1 Corinthians 15:22.
15 A list of flood myths from cultures around the world is provided online at http://www.talkorigins.org/faqs/flood-myths.html.
16 Hebrews 11:7.
17 Genesis 12:2, 3.
18 Genesis 28:12-17.
19 John 1:50-58
20 See John 14:6.
21 See G.J. Wenham, J.A. Motyer, D.A. Carson, R.T. France, eds., *New Bible Commentary, 21st Century Edition* (Leister, England: Inter-Varsity Press, 2003), 1029.
22 "Land flowing with milk and honey" is the English translation of the Hebrew, שָׁבְדוּ בָלְחָ תְבָז, a term for the land that appears in Exodus 3:8, 17, 13:5, 33:3, Leviticus 20:24, Numbers 13:27, 14:8, 16:13-14, Deuteronomy 6:3, 11:9, 26:9, 15, 27:3, 31:20, Joshua 5:6, Jeremiah 11:5, 32:22, Ezekiel 20:6, 15.
23 Exodus 16:3-4.
24 John 6:32-35a.
25 Exodus 25:8-9.
26 Michael P.V. Barrett, *Beginning with Moses: A Guide to Finding Christ in the Old Testament* (Greenville, SC: Ambassador-Emerald International, 2001), 275.
27 For example, Jeremiah 23:23-24, 1 Kings 8:27, and Psalm 139:7-10.
28 John 1:14.
29 The Greek word used for "dwelled with" can also be translated "tabernacle with." Its form in John 1:14 is ἐσκήνωσεν, which comes from the lexical form, σκηνόω, translated "to have one's tent, dwell." This verb is used only five other times in the New Testament when it is used to indicate that God

will dwell with his people in the new heavens and new earth in Revelation 7:15, 12:12, 13:6, and 21:3.
30. 1 Chronicles 17:4b-5, 10b-14.
31. John 2:19.
32. Hebrews 9:7-9.
33. Mark 15:37-38.
34. Leviticus 17:11.
35. Romans 5:7-8.
36. John 15:3.
37. Ephesians 5:25-27.
38. James discusses the idea that good works are evidence of faith in James 2:14-26. Note that one is saved *by faith alone* and then proceeds to do good deeds; one is *not* saved by performing good deeds.
39. John 6:51.
40. Luke 22:19.
41. John 8:12.
42. John 1:4.
43. Exodus 30:34-36.
44. Psalm 141:1-2.
45. Hebrews 7:23-24.
46. See 1 Samuel 4:4; 2 Samuel 6:2; 2 Kings 19:15; 1 Chronicles 13:6; Psalm 80:1, 99:1; and Isaiah 37:16.
47. See Numbers 7:89.
48. From Hebrews 9:4. Aaron's staff, or rod, was composed of wood from an almond tree and had miraculously budded to indicate that God chose Aaron and his descendants (the tribe of Levi) as the priests who would serve in the tabernacle.
49. Hebrews 9:24-28.

The best evidence of the Bible's being the word of God is to be found between its covers. It proves itself.

—Charles Hodge, theologian[1]

What Satan put into the heads of our remote ancestors was the idea that they could 'be like gods'—could set up on their own as if they had created themselves—be their own masters—invent some sort of happiness for themselves outside God, apart from God. And out of that hopeless attempt has come nearly all that we call human history—money, poverty, ambition, war, prostitution, classes, empires, slavery—the long terrible story of man trying to find something other than God which will make him happy.... God cannot give us a happiness and peace apart from Himself, because it is not there. There is no such thing.

—C. S. Lewis, Christian apologist, novelist, and professor[2]

Old Testament Fathers

We have covered a few of the "object lessons" in the Hebrew Scriptures that become more fully understood in the New Testament. In addition to these objects, the accounts of people in the Old Testament, from the beginning of Genesis to the prophet Malachi at the end, anticipate the man who came as the Messiah.

In the next two chapters, we look at how God has explained his plan of redemption through the "insiders"—that is, through those who wielded power and influence in their society. In this chapter, we will discuss the first two generations of humans made in God's image and the early patriarchs, the forefathers of the Israelites. In the next chapter, we will discuss two other "insiders" who were great leaders of the Israelite nation.

ADAM AND EVE

Our first "insiders" are, appropriately, the very first humans "made in God's image." God created Adam and Eve to dwell with him peacefully in a paradisiacal garden lacking no good thing. Initially, they had no guilt and shame, no reason to "hide" from their Creator.

After creating the universe and animals, God declared that all that he had done was "good." But after he created Adam and Eve, God declared it to be "very good."[3] They were the crowning glory of his creation, and he sent them out to "be fruitful and increase in number" and to "fill the earth and subdue it."[4] They were truly "insiders" in God's creation, the "cherry on the top" of his world and the "apple of his eye."

CHAPTER 24: OLD TESTAMENT FATHERS

After these happy events of creation, we come to Genesis 3. At this point, Adam and Eve—as the first representatives of the human race created in God's image—made a terrible decision, since God had allowed his creatures to choose to obey him or disobey him, to follow him or reject him, to love him or despise him.

God gave Adam and Eve only one command—not to "eat of the tree of the knowledge of good and evil... or you will certainly die,"[5] but they chose to disobey. As a result of this choice, Adam and Eve certainly did die—not right away, but eventually, even though they had originally been created to live eternally. And because all humans are descendants of our first "representative," Adam, we too also sin (that is, we put ourselves first, God second), and we too also die.

It may sound unjust: "Why is everyone punished for what one man and one woman did?" The biblical teaching is that Adam was the representative of the human race, and as such the consequences of his decision were applied to all of his descendants. Moreover, Adam was as morally perfect as God could make him while still giving him the choice to obey or disobey. Any of his descendants, being morally *im*perfect, would make the exact same decision Adam did, but faster. We thus have no reason to cry "Unfair!"

Our modern sensibilities recoil at the word, *sin*. If you are like I was when I first began investigating the claims of Christianity, you are probably sensitive to this word as well. The reflexive human response to the word is almost always negative. Yet if we consider all of the evil there is in the world—the cause of every war, every crime, and every hurtful deed—we see that they originate in the selfish motives of human beings. Many sins seem fairly innocuous, but even the smallest sins, when combined, make the world a pretty terrible place. The Bible teaches that our sins are precisely what make us unhappy, unsatisfied, and unfulfilled. As a thought experiment to ponder the seriousness of sin, consider what the world would look like if every individual stopped acting selfishly and started to put others before themselves.

We have discussed extensive scientific, historical, and biblical evidence for the claim that Christianity requires the "shortest leap of faith." Could it be that our negative response to the word "sin" is not, after all, a rational response, but an emotional one? Obviously, no one likes the idea of human evil. But not liking something does not make it untrue.

The fourth-century African theologian, Augustine of Hippo ("St. Augustine"), used several Latin expressions to identify different states of the human heart. First, Adam and Eve were in a state that Augustine termed *"posse peccare, posse non peccare."* These terms describe how Adam and Eve originally had the choice to either sin or not sin. It was possible *(posse)* for them *to sin (peccare)*, but it was also possible *(posse)* for them to choose *not to sin (non peccare)*. Further, they were in a state of *posse mori, non posse mori*—it was possible for them to die, and it was also possible for them not to die, depending on their obedience.

But unlike Adam and Eve, God *cannot* sin. His state is therefore *"non posse peccare."* An omnipotent God can do anything—except sin. This is not some odd weakness, but simply a logical impossibility. It is impossible for God to violate his own perfectly holy nature, which is incapable of sinning. When we say, "God cannot sin," it is basically equivalent to saying, "God cannot *not* be God." God, therefore, can be described as *non posse peccare* and *non posse mori*—that is, it is *not possible* for God to sin, and it is *not possible* for God to die.

Once Adam and Eve chose to disobey God, they entered into a state of *"non posse non peccare"*—from then on, they couldn't *not* sin. This state of "not being able not to sin" has applied to all humans who have descended from Adam and Eve up to this day. We also are in a state of *non posse non mori*, which is evident from the fact that every human since Adam and Eve has died or eventually will die.[6]

Another biblical teaching is that *non posse non peccare* humans cannot be in the presence of a *non posse peccare* God, just as a piece of paper cannot be in the presence of a flame. But God wanted to bring his people back to himself—after all, he is perfectly loving as well as perfectly holy. The Bible's narrative stretches out from the "paradise lost" of Genesis, describing a God who wants to reconcile humans to himself. He directed the means, describing to Moses and the other Israelites how to construct the altar, conduct the sacrifices, and set up the wash basin, the showbread, the light, the incense, and the ark. These Old Testament symbols pointed forward to Jesus, who, as God in human flesh, was able to live a perfectly sinless life and thereby offer the perfect, once-for-all sacrifice.[7] Once you put your faith in Jesus, you lose a "non" and transfer from a state of *non posse non peccare* to a state of *posse non peccare*. If you depend on the power of the Holy Spirit that now indwells you as a believer, you become *capable* of *not* sinning, though you unfortunately still do sin (which to a true believer is quite frustrating).

When Adam and Eve chose to disobey God, God expelled them

from the Garden of Eden, and they lost their ability to live forever. They quickly became "outsiders," as they no longer could live in perfect communion with their creator. Because of Adam, the rest of humanity has suffered the same consequences: a life of selfishness, tears and pain, separated from their Creator, and inevitably cut short by death.

But then comes the good news. After Adam and Eve and their descendants were kicked out of the Garden of Eden, God implemented his "rescue plan," which he had devised even before creation.[8] God chose a people for himself (the descendants of Abraham), taught them about his holiness and his great love for them, and then came as Jesus to bring his people—this time from all people groups and all nations—back to himself.

By implementing this rescue plan, God provided a way for his people to once again live in his presence. But this time his people will enjoy a setting even better than the Garden of Eden, for they will live in "a new heaven and a new earth," and they will be in the states of *non posse peccare* and *non posse mori*. (Note the change from *posse non peccare* and *posse non mori* before death to *non posse peccare* and *non posse mori*—the placement of the "non" is crucial!) In heaven, people will no longer sin, they will no longer die, and they will live in perfect peace, or *shalom*, what the Old Testament prophets promised the Messiah would bring (as we discussed in the Chapter 22). Isaiah describes this time as follows: "Of the greatness of his government and peace there will be no end. He will reign on David's throne and over his kingdom, establishing and upholding it with justice and righteousness from that time on and forever."[9]

You may be asking, why didn't God just create humans in the *non posse peccare* state to begin with? A simple explanation is that he wanted to give humans the choice as to whether he is the Lord of their lives or they are the lords of their own lives. It is a complete mystery how God can be perfectly sovereign over all events in our lives, and yet at the same time allow us to choose him or reject him. But we can trust that through the "fall" of Adam and Eve and the "rescue" provided by Jesus Christ, God has orchestrated everything in such a way that neither his sovereignty nor our ability to choose are compromised. A finite mind like ours—bound by the four dimensions of space and time—cannot comprehend exactly how this all works out.

Adam teaches us about Jesus' purpose through contrast. Whereas Adam *disobeyed* God, Jesus *obeyed*, even to the point of death on a cross. Whereas through Adam all humans became *incapable of not sinning,* through Jesus, all who have faith in him become *capable of not sinning* in this life, and *not capable of ever sinning again* once they are in heaven. Whereas Adam's choice caused mankind to *have* to die, through faith in Jesus, God has provided mankind a way *not* to die. Whereas Adam was kicked out of the Garden of Eden, creating a chasm that separated him (and his descendants) from the Creator, Jesus has provided a way for his followers to cross the chasm and reunite with their Creator forever in the ultimate, perfected version of the Garden of Eden.

The apostle Paul provides the following more complete explanation of how Adam's failure points to our need for Jesus, comparing Jesus' work to a gift and Adam's work to a trespass:

> But the gift is not like the trespass. For if the many died by the trespass of the one man, how much more did God's grace and the gift that came by the grace of the one man, Jesus Christ, overflow to the many! Nor can the gift of God be compared with the result of one man's sin: The judgment followed one sin and brought condemnation, but the gift followed many trespasses and brought justification. For if, by the trespass of the one man, death reigned through that one man, how much more will those who receive God's abundant provision of grace and of the gift of righteousness reign in life through the one man, Jesus Christ!"[10]

Adam failed—we became outsiders and ultimately die. Jesus succeeded—those who trust in him become insiders and shall live forever.

ABEL

Following their expulsion from the Garden of Eden, Adam and Eve took the first steps in response to God's command to "multiply and fill the earth." Their first children were two sons, Abel, a farmer, and Cain, a keeper of livestock. Abel brought "some of the fruits of the soil as an offering to the Lord." Meanwhile, Cain also brought "an offering—fat portions from some of the firstborn of his flock."[11] Note that even as early as the second generation of God's people, there was an understanding that we owe our Creator an offering in return for all he has given us, and that we ought to offer a payment for our disobedience. Both sons complied, but for some reason, God looked "with favor" on Abel and his offering, but he did not look with favor on Cain and his.

Abel is the first "hero of the faith" mentioned in the eleventh chapter of the Book of Hebrews, what has been called the "Faith Hall of Fame." Hebrews states: "By faith Abel brought God a better offering than Cain did. By faith he was commended as righteous, when God spoke well of his offerings."[12] Jesus even called Abel "righteous" and considered him to be one of the Old Testament prophets.[13] From the text describing Cain and Abel's offerings in Genesis 4 alone, we are not entirely sure why Abel displayed faith through his offering, and why Cain did not. But from the commentary by the author of Hebrews, we do know that God could see Abel's faith, but Cain's faith was lacking.

God commended Abel as "righteous" on account of his unseen faith (perhaps expressed in his thoughts and attitude as he prepared and presented his offering to God), while Cain had not demonstrated the same "saving faith." It is a good reminder that God sees one's motivations and the "state of one's heart," and he looks past outward behavior to see one's true intentions. It behooves us to recognize that, unlike God, we humans cannot know for certain whether or not a person truly has faith in Jesus based on his or her outward behavior alone, though certainly outward behavior is a clue.[14]

We get further evidence that God focuses on our interior rather than our exterior when, centuries later, Samuel was about to choose the next king of Israel from among Jesse's eight sons. God made it clear to him that outward appearance was not the deciding factor for him with these words: "The Lord does not look at the things people look at. People look at the outward appearance, but the Lord looks at the heart."[15]

Similarly, this time in the New Testament, Jesus castigated the leaders in the Jewish sect known as the "Pharisees," who were obsessive in their nit-picky obedience to their own detailed interpretations of the law. He said to them: "You are like whitewashed tombs, which look beautiful on the outside but on the inside are full of the bones of the dead and everything unclean."[16] In the Sermon on the Mount, Jesus even made this startling and convicting comment:

> "Not everyone who says to me, 'Lord, Lord,' will enter the kingdom of heaven, but only the one who does the will of my Father who is in heaven. Many will say to me on that day, 'Lord, Lord, did we not prophesy in your name and in your name drive out demons and in your name perform many miracles?' Then I will tell them plainly, 'I never knew you. Away from me, you evildoers!'"[17]

Those who merely put on an outward show of obedience won't enter, but those who "do the will of my Father who is in heaven" will. Though it sounds like Jesus is telling them they should "do" something for him, we obtain a better understanding of what he means by "doing the will of his Father" in another question that he answers. When asked, "What must we do to do the works God requires?" Jesus answered, "The work of God is this: to *believe* in the one he has sent [i.e. Jesus]."[18]

All we have to do for Jesus to know us and to welcome us into his eternal kingdom in heaven is to "believe" in him. Just as Abel demonstrated faith in his Creator when presenting his offering, we demonstrate our faith in Jesus, also our Creator, when we present our lives as an offering, but only after we first believe. Our faith alone, not our outward obedience, is what makes our sacrifice acceptable to God.

The important take-away is that just one generation removed from Adam and Eve, we already see invisible faith—not just outward obedience—as crucial to whether or not God considers someone righteous. Cain even brought the best of his flock as an offering to God: the "fat portions of the firstborn." God saw the hearts of Abel and Cain, and he could determine whose faith was genuine and whose outward displays of obedience were just a veneer covering an ungrateful and faithless heart.[19]

ABRAM/ABRAHAM

Eight chapters after Cain and Abel, we come to the story of Abraham, the father of the Israelites. Of all God's people, Abraham was the ultimate insider—he was wealthy, honored, obedient, and the father of a great nation. God called Abraham to leave his comfortable and predictable life in Ur of the Chaldeans (the "New York City" of the ancient world), stopping part-way in Harran (the "Los Angeles" of the ancient world), to eventually settle in Canaan (what would become Israel, and what Abraham at first probably thought was the "ends of the earth").

Here is one version of the promise that God makes to Abraham:

> "I will make you into a great nation,
>   and I will bless you;
> I will make your name great,
>   and you will be a blessing.
> I will bless those who bless you,
>   and whoever curses you I will curse;
> and all peoples on earth
>   will be blessed through you."[20]

Many commentators note that the call of Abram from a familiar homeland to an unfamiliar "promised land" represents the steps a person takes after accepting the call to a life of faith in Jesus. Hebrews 11 confirms this analogy: "By faith Abraham, when called to go to a place he would later receive as his inheritance, obeyed and went, even though he did not know where he was going." Likewise, believers in Jesus are called by faith to trust that they will enter God's "eternal rest" in a beautiful, joyous, and perfectly peaceful place known as "heaven." We trust that God will fulfill his promise to take us to heaven eventually, and we endure the hardships of this world, knowing that we, like Abram, look "forward to the city with foundations, whose architect and builder is God."[21]

The amazing promise that God made to Abram is better translated as "an unbreakable, binding oath," since it comes from the Hebrew word *běrít*, (בְּרִית) most accurately translated as a "fetter" or "obligation" that "binds."[22] Theologians use the term *covenant* to emphasize that it is so much more than just a promise; it is a binding oath that can never be broken, forgotten, or weakened.

Three chapters later, God reiterated this covenant to make Abram's offspring as numerous as the stars and to give his descendants the land to which God had led him. Abram had been wondering how he could ever be the father of numerous offspring, since he and his wife Sarai had not had any children, and they were both beyond the usual child-bearing age. This time, in God's covenant "reminder," Abram had a mysterious, unexpected, and awe-inspiring experience.

Before describing the mysterious experience, it is helpful to provide background on a covenant-ratifying ritual that was used in the ancient Near East. When two parties made a solemn oath (for example, to enact a peace treaty), they would cut several animals in half, line the halves on either side of a pathway, and walk together along the path between the bloody animals. In so doing, the parties to the oath were essentially declaring to each other, "If I fail to keep my end of this bargain, may what happened to these animals happen to me."[23] It's basically a much more serious, ancient version of "cross my heart, and hope to die," and it definitely gets the point across regarding the solemnity of the contract.

In response to Abram's wondering how exactly God was going to fulfill his promise to make him the father of countless descendants, God asked Abram to get animals, cut them in half, and line them up along a pathway. At this point, Abram had probably figured out what was going to happen. He most likely expected God to force him, alone, to walk through the pieces. In doing so, Abram would promise to obey God and somehow earn the right to "numerous offspring" and the "promised land." But Abram was surprised in two ways. First, God appeared as a torch-like pot of fire and passed between the animal pieces. And second, God prevented Abram from accompanying him along the path. (God put Abram into a state in which he was aware of what was happening, but he was unable to move.)

Anyone in those days who was familiar with the custom of "walking through the pieces" would expect the two parties to walk through the pieces *together*. What's more, they never would expect God to walk through them *alone*. If anything, it would have been most appropriate for *Abram* to walk through the pieces alone, since God, in the position of power, could have easily demanded that Abram promise to be obedient or else face the consequences (by being killed as the animals had been). So, what does this strange ritual mean?

We'll get to the explanation shortly. First, let's examine a statement that Jesus made millennia later about Abraham. (God had changed his name from Abram to Abraham.) In the conversation when he claimed that "before Abraham was born, I am!" (discussed in Chapter 18), Jesus also shed light on Abraham's faith, claiming to the Jews that "Your father Abraham rejoiced at the thought of seeing my day; he saw it and was glad."[24]

CHAPTER 24: OLD TESTAMENT FATHERS

Both the description of Abraham's faith in Hebrews 11 above and this statement by Jesus make it clear that Abraham trusted God to fulfill his promises, and that Abraham looked forward to the day when God would do so. Jesus' statement that Abraham rejoiced indicates that the full extent of God's promises was fulfilled at his coming as the Son of God (what Jesus calls "my day"). Before Jesus came, God's promise had only been partially fulfilled by the Israelites arriving in the "promised land." Further fulfillment happened when Jesus came to earth, because he was the means by which Abraham's offspring would bless the entire world. God's promises will be fulfilled completely when Jesus comes again, and people from all nations, languages, and ethnicities will live eternally in his Kingdom. Jesus was essentially telling us, "This is it – this is what Abraham was trusting God to do: send a Savior through whom the entire world would be blessed, not for just a few years in this life, but for all eternity."

By appearing as a smoking firepot to walk alone through the pieces, God was making it abundantly clear to Abram that this promise was 100% certain. That is, God would definitely make Abram's descendants as numerous as the stars, he would definitely give him the "promised land," and he would definitely bless "all peoples on earth" through his descendants. God guaranteed it himself, and it depended not a single iota on Abram's actions. In fact, God would keep the promise *regardless* of Abram's future obedience or lack thereof. The only requirement for Abram to obtain the promises of God was *faith*. Abram had no way of knowing how God would fulfill his promises; he simply trusted that he would.

So, here's a question we can ask at this point: if you were in Abraham's position and saw this blazing torch levitating and traveling between the pieces, you'd believe too, wouldn't you? The amazing thing is that Abraham hadn't even seen the blazing pot of fire when he told God he believed him. Before God even asked Abram to gather the animals and cut them in half, we read:

> After this, the word of the Lord came to Abram in a vision: "Do not be afraid, Abram. I am your shield, your very great reward."
>
> But Abram said, "Sovereign Lord, what can you give me since I remain childless and the one who will inherit my estate is Eliezer of Damascus?" And Abram said, "You

> have given me no children; so a servant in my household will be my heir."
>
> Then the word of the Lord came to him: "This man will not be your heir, but a son who is your own flesh and blood will be your heir." He took him outside and said, "Look up at the sky and count the stars—if indeed you can count them." Then he said to him, "So shall your offspring be."
>
> Abram believed the Lord, and he credited it to him as righteousness.[25]

The final sentence is the key. God counted Abram as righteous because Abram *believed* his promises. That is, it wasn't Abram's works, but his faith, that made him fit for a relationship with God.[26] It was after this statement that God asked Abram to gather the animals in order to demonstrate that he would indeed do what he had promised, even if God himself somehow had to die to fulfill it. In fact, he did die to fulfill his promise—millennia later on a Roman cross.

Christians today have a better understanding of how God will fulfill his promise to bring us to the "promised land" (heaven). We know that God came in human form to live the perfect, sinless life *for us* and to die in order to pay the penalty for our sin *for us*. It is our faith in Jesus that makes us fit to live in God's presence, not any of our actions. Our active obedience—at least our paltry efforts to obey—come *after* we recognize what Jesus has done for us, when we seek to please him out of joy and gratitude, instead of out of guilt, fear, or obligation.

Before we leave Abraham, let's take a look at one other event in his life that helps us see his faith in action and better understand the salvation Jesus provides. Despite their old age, Abraham and his wife Sarai eventually had the son whom God had promised. Once this son, named Isaac, had grown up, we read about this horrendous command: "Take your son, your only son, whom you love—Isaac—and go to the region of Moriah. Sacrifice him there as a burnt offering on a mountain I will show you."[27] Skeptics often describe this event as God ordering "child sacrifice." But the purpose of this event, when properly understood, is magnificent; it points us to God's perfect love for his people. How so?

CHAPTER 24: OLD TESTAMENT FATHERS

As they ascended the mountain to make the sacrifice, Abraham kept his son in the dark about what the sacrifice would be. Thus, Isaac asked his father a perfectly logical question, "The fire and wood are here, but where is the lamb for the burnt offering?" Abraham was either afraid to tell his son the truth, or he trusted that God would somehow save Isaac from death, since God had demonstrated so clearly through the smoking firepot that Abraham would have many descendants through Isaac. Abraham therefore replied to Isaac, "God himself will provide the lamb for the burnt offering, my son."[28]

He may not have known exactly how, but Abraham had faith that God would save Isaac and provide another sacrifice to substitute for his precious boy. And this is exactly what God did. Here's how the story ends:

> But the angel of the Lord called out to him from heaven, "Abraham! Abraham!"
>
> "Here I am," he replied.
>
> "Do not lay a hand on the boy," he said. "Do not do anything to him. Now I know that you fear God, because you have not withheld from me your son, your only son."
>
> Abraham looked up and there in a thicket he saw a ram caught by its horns. He went over and took the ram and sacrificed it as a burnt offering instead of his son. So Abraham called that place *The Lord Will Provide*. And to this day it is said, "On the mountain of the Lord it will be provided."[29]

In this story, we learn several things about God: First, we can trust him absolutely, even when we don't understand what he is doing in our lives or why he's asking us to give up something that is very important to us. Secondly, God was pointing us to the ultimate demonstration of his love, the provision of his *own* Son, the perfect "Lamb of God," as the ultimate sacrifice on our behalf. And third, what God didn't require Abraham to do, sacrifice his only son, God *himself* did for us.

Since the idea of bloody sacrifices is completely distasteful to our modern-day sensitivities, it may make more sense if we use the language of accounting. Let's say you have worked your entire life as an attorney, eventually rising to become a judge. In those many years of hard work, you have managed to save a "nest egg" of ten million dollars. One day, you find out that your daughter has been found guilty of a crime and sentenced to life in prison. Not only that, but following the jury's verdict, *you* are the judge who must deliver the sentence. As the judge, you know that justice must be done, even though you also know that the sentence would mean that your daughter would live in prison, separate from you, for the rest of her life.

However, you know something else: there *is* a way for justice to be done and *at the same time* keep your daughter from spending her life in prison. The person she has wronged has agreed to drop all charges if you pay him ten million dollars. In so doing, you exchange your precious "nest egg" for your daughter. This exchange is the approximate equivalent of making the "perfect sacrifice" in the ancient Near East. The payment of your "nest egg" symbolizes the sacrifice, your daughter represents God's people, your daughter's prison sentence represents the debt we owe God for our rebellion against him (our sin), and the judge represents God the Father, who must execute justice perfectly, even when it concerns his precious children.

Of course, all analogies are imperfect, since the $10 million nest egg is meant to represent Jesus, and it doesn't even begin to compare to the value of his work on his followers' behalf. The main point is that the judge provided a way to execute perfect justice for his daughter's crime *and at the same time* to express his perfect love for and mercy to his daughter. In the same way, God the Father himself provided the payment for our sin—the penalty was paid by his Son on the cross—so that those who trust in him could live in his presence eternally.

What's more, the analogy fails to indicate that if we have faith in Jesus, our obedience or lack of obedience has *no impact* on our salvation (but once saved, we will want to obey Christ above all things). This is because God also provided his Son to live the *perfect, sinless life for us.* Forgiveness of our debt (like paying the "nest egg") gets us to the starting line, but Jesus' perfect life lived on our behalf takes us to the finish line, eternal life in God's presence.

CHAPTER 24: OLD TESTAMENT FATHERS

JACOB

After God provided a ram to substitute for him on the peak of Mount Moriah, Isaac grew up and married Rebekah. They had two sons, Jacob and Esau. One day, Jacob tricked his poor-sighted, elderly father Isaac into thinking that he was Esau. As a result, instead of giving his deathbed blessing to his eldest son Esau, Isaac gave it to Jacob. Esau was not happy. Jacob fled from his brother, whom he suspected would kill him. That night, Jacob had the "stairway to heaven" dream that we discussed in the last chapter.

After fleeing from Esau, Jacob eventually arrived in Harran, where he met his beautiful cousin Rachel. In order to have her hand in marriage, Jacob agreed to work seven years for his uncle Laban. He received a taste of his own deceitful medicine when Laban tricked him into marrying Rachel's less attractive sister Leah. Jacob ended up working for Laban another seven years in order to also marry Rachel. Eventually, Jacob had twelve sons, six by his wife Leah (Reuben, Simeon, Levi, Judah, Issachar, and Zebulun), two by his favorite wife Rachel (Joseph and Benjamin), two by Rachel's maidservant Bilhah (Dan and Naphtali), and two by Leah's maidservant Zilpah (Gad and Asher). In addition to sons, he had at least one daughter, Dinah, also by Leah. Altogether, the descendants of these twelve sons of Jacob would become the twelve tribes of Israel.

Note that God has never commanded or condoned polygamy, and the difficulties of this polygamous situation—and others in the Old Testament—wave like huge red flags warning us away from the practice! Yet despite the sinful dysfunction of this family, it was through them that God created the nation through which he would eventually bless the entire world, another sign that God was keeping his covenant with Abraham despite the behavior of his descendants.

When Jacob and his large family had settled in northwestern Mesopotamia (Paddan Aram), God asked Jacob to return with his entire household to Bethel, the same place where he had dreamed about the "stairway to heaven." God then reiterated to Jacob the same promise he had given to Abraham and Isaac:

> After Jacob returned from Paddan Aram, God appeared to him again and blessed him. God said to him, "Your

name is Jacob, but you will no longer be called Jacob; your name will be Israel." So he named him Israel.

And God said to him, "I am God Almighty; be fruitful and increase in number. A nation and a community of nations will come from you, and kings will be among your descendants. The land I gave to Abraham and Isaac I also give to you, and I will give this land to your descendants after you."[30]

In this way, God confirmed his covenant with Jacob, the same one he had made by "walking the pieces" as Abraham looked on, and the same one he had reconfirmed with Isaac. God would truly bring Jacob's descendants into the land he had promised to Abraham and Isaac, their offspring would truly be as numerous as the stars, and the whole world would truly be blessed through them. It was from the ancestral line of these imperfect men, Abraham, Isaac, and Jacob, that the Messiah would come to fulfill God's promise.

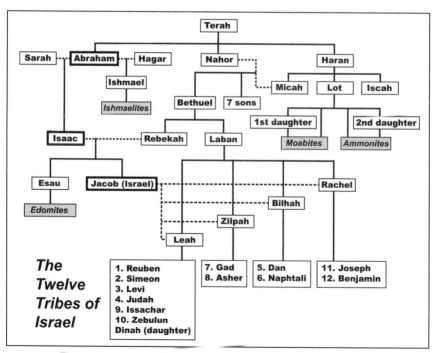

Figure 6: Family Tree from Terah to the Twelve Sons of Jacob

CHAPTER 24: OLD TESTAMENT FATHERS

JOSEPH

Jacob's eleventh son, Joseph, is another well-known biblical "insider," famous especially for his "coat of many colors." Because he was the first-born son of Jacob's favorite wife, Rachel, Joseph received special treatment from his father (including the gift of his famous coat), and his brothers resented him for it. Joseph initially came off as haughty and inconsiderate towards his brothers. With an amazing lack of social awareness, Joseph repeatedly shared with them that he had had dreams that they bowed down to him.

One day Jacob sent Joseph on an errand to report back on how his brothers were doing as they grazed their flocks. As soon as they saw Joseph in the distance, the brothers plotted to kill him. When Joseph arrived, they stripped him of his coat and threw him into an empty cistern in the ground. Judah then convinced the other brothers not to kill Joseph, but to "just" sell him into slavery to a passing caravan of Ishmaelite merchants on their way to Egypt. (The Ishmaelites were descendants of Ishmael, Abraham's son through his wife's Egyptian slave Hagar. The modern-day Arabs consider themselves descendants of the Ishmaelites.) To cover what they had actually done, the brothers tore and bloodied Joseph's coat so that their father thought he had been killed by a wild animal. (Again, Jacob became the object of his own former deception—a good lesson in itself.)

After many years in Egypt, as a slave for many of them and serving an unjust jail sentence for others, Joseph rose through God's assistance in interpreting Pharaoh's dreams to a high position as the "viceregent" in charge of all of Egypt, second in power only to Pharaoh. God then used Joseph to save the Egyptians from a terrible famine that had affected the entire region. Joseph went from favorite son to slave, and from slave to prisoner, and from prisoner to the second highest leader in Egypt. It's a wonderful riches to rags to riches story, which in itself parallels Jesus leaving heaven for earth and returning to heaven. But how else could it foreshadow Jesus and shed light on God's reason for sending his Son?

One commentary describes Joseph, whom Pharaoh had appointed as viceregent over all of Egypt, as a "better Adam," whom God had appointed as a sort of viceregent over the earth. Moreover, in his failings, Joseph points to an "even better Adam":

At many points in the story, Joseph appears to be represented as an "ideal" of what a truly wise and faithful man is like. He is a model of the ideal man, the ideal king. He accomplishes all that Adam failed to do. The story of Joseph is a reflection of what might have been had Adam remained obedient to God and trusted him for the "good." At the same time the picture of Joseph anticipates what might yet be, if only God's people would, like Joseph, live in complete obedience and trust in God. The picture of Joseph, then, looks back to Adam, but even more looks forward to one who was yet to come, the one from the house of Judah to whom the kingdom belongs.[31]

The story continues. Though they had no idea what became of Joseph after they had sold him into slavery many years earlier, his brothers traveled to Egypt from their home in Canaan to obtain grain during the famine. Ironically, it was their brother Joseph who had been instrumental in executing a plan to store extra grain to prepare for the future famine. After realizing that they had truly changed and were willing to sacrifice their lives for his younger brother, Benjamin, Joseph revealed his identity to his brothers and forgave them.

As an example of how a sovereign God can turn terrible circumstances around, Joseph tells his brothers: "You intended to harm me, but God intended it for good to accomplish what is now being done, the saving of many lives. So then, don't be afraid. I will provide for you and your children."[32] This is a beautiful picture of how God used what certainly was the most terrible event in history, the crucifixion of his Son, to "accomplish what is now being done, the saving of many lives." The cross, a terrible image of torture and death, takes on a whole new meaning for those who understand why Jesus went to it.

Joseph points to Jesus in many other ways, not the least of which is his obedience and trust in God throughout his difficult life. A brief list of similarities includes:

1. Both are their father's beloved son.[33]
2. Both were envied and hated without a cause.[34]
3. Both foretold that one day they would rule.[35]

4. Both were accused of being a dreamer or deluded.[36]
5. Both were sent by their father to seek the welfare of their brothers.[37]
6. Both willingly went to find their brothers.[38]
7. Both were rejected and condemned to die.[39]
8. Both were stripped of their clothing.[40]
9. Both were thrown into a pit, where they were abandoned.[41]
10. Both were sold for silver to be handed over to the Gentiles.[42]
11. Both became a servant.[43]
12. Both resisted temptations.[44]
13. Both were falsely accused.[45]
14. Both were exalted after and while going through humiliation.[46]
15. Both were unjustly placed among criminals.[47]
16. Both accurately predicted the future.[48]
17. All people were commanded to bow to both.[49]
18. Both provided food for all those in need.[50]
19. Both were not recognized by their brothers.[51]
20. Both allowed their brothers to suffer a "period of tribulation."[52] [53]

As great a man as he was, Joseph's behavior was far from perfect, and it was especially imperfect compared to that of Jesus, the man to whom he pointed. The clear message throughout the Old Testament is that even the best humans fall easy prey to pride and are unable to live a life that is perfectly pleasing to a holy God. We'll see the same pattern in other "biblical heroes" who point forward to Jesus, such as Moses and David, and it's to these insiders that we now turn.

Questions for Comprehension and Discussion

1. What were the main consequences of Adam and Eve's disobedience of God's one command not to eat the fruit of the tree of the knowledge of good and evil?
2. What can you say in response to the claim that it's "not fair" that all descendants of Adam and Eve have inherited the state of not being able *not* to sin (i.e. they are not able to live a perfectly sin-free life)?

3. Can you explain the concepts of (1) *posse peccare, posse non peccare*, (2) *non posse peccare*, (3) *posse non peccare*, and (4) *non posse non peccare*? What about the related concepts of *posse mori, posse non mori, non posse mori,* and *non posse non mori*? In which state were Adam and Eve? In which state is God? In which state are all humans who don't have faith in Jesus? And in which state are those who have faith in Jesus now, and then after they die?
4. What is one possible reason that God gave Adam and Eve *both* the ability not to sin *and* the ability to sin (admitting that we finite creatures are incapable of completely understanding God's thoughts and ways!)?
5. How does Adam foreshadow Jesus by means of contrast?
6. What do we learn about faith from Abel's offering to God? What does this say about one's outward behavior?
7. What was the promise God made to Abram, and how did God demonstrate that he was serious about it? What was strange about the way God made this promise? What is the meaning?
8. Why did God credit Abraham as "righteous"? What is the significance of this verse?
9. What did Abram not have to do that God would eventually do himself? Why did God do this?
10. What are some ways that Joseph foreshadowed Jesus?

CHAPTER 24 ENDNOTES

[1] Josiah Hotchkiss Gilbert, *Dictionary of Burning Words of Brilliant Writers* (1895), 35.
[2] C. S. Lewis, *Mere Christianity* (San Francisco: HarperOne, 2009), 50.
[3] Compare Genesis 1:4, 10, 12, 18, 21, and 25 with Genesis 1:31.
[4] Genesis 1:28.
[5] Genesis 2:17.
[6] See R.C. Sproul, "Radical Corruption," available online at https://www.ligonier.org/learn/articles/radical-corruption. Another useful explanation can be found at https://www.monergism.com/thethreshold/articles/onsite/augustinewill.html. Note that this topic is still debated in the Christian church, with some churches believing that it *is* possible for humans to not sin even without God's help. We will respond to this belief in Chapter

CHAPTER 24: OLD TESTAMENT FATHERS

31 when we look at the unique nature of Christian salvation, which takes human effort out of the picture.

7 There is debate as to whether Jesus was in the *posse peccare, posse non peccare* state or the *non posse peccare* state (he could have sinned but didn't, or he couldn't have sinned even if he tried). The main points the Bible teaches, in Hebrews 4:15 among other places, are that (1) Jesus was tempted in every way, just as we are, and yet (2) he never sinned. Both the *posse peccare, posse non peccare* and *non posse peccare* states are consistent with these biblical statements about Jesus.

8 God had worked out the "rescue plan" for his people before he created the world according to Ephesians 1:4, which states (along with the following verses to put it in context): "For [God] chose us in him before the creation of the world to be holy and blameless in his sight. In love he predestined us for adoption to sonship through Jesus Christ, in accordance with his pleasure and will— to the praise of his glorious grace, which he has freely given us in the One he loves. In him we have redemption through his blood, the forgiveness of sins, in accordance with the riches of God's grace that he lavished on us. With all wisdom and understanding, he made known to us the mystery of his will according to his good pleasure, which he purposed in Christ, to be put into effect when the times reach their fulfillment—to bring unity to all things in heaven and on earth under Christ."

9 Isaiah 9:7.

10 Romans 5:15-17.

11 See the story of Cain and Abel in Genesis 4.

12 Hebrews 11:4.

13 See Matthew 23:35 and Luke 11:50-51.

14 Good works generally result once a person comes to faith in Jesus and recognizes how much he has done for him or her. So, though we may be able to detect a lack of faith when good works are lacking, it is not our place to judge whether anyone has true faith in Jesus or not. Instead we are instructed to build up others, encouraging them to meditate on what Jesus has done for them and then to act out of joy and gratitude once they truly appreciate what he has done for them. See James 2:14-26, Ephesians 4:29, Colossians 3:1-3, John 14:15, and Romans 8.

15 1 Samuel 16:7.

16 Matthew 23: 27b.

17 Matthew 7:21-23.

18 John 6:28-29.

19 Walter C. Kaiser Jr., Peter H. Davids, F. F. Bruce, Manfred T. Brauch, *Hard Sayings of the Bible* (Downers Grove, IL: InterVarsity Press, 1996), 99-100.

20 Genesis 12:2-3.

21. Hebrews 11:10.
22. Walter A. Elwell, ed., *The Evangelical Dictionary of the Theology* (Grand Rapids: Baker Academic), 299.
23. Pat and David Alexander, *Zondervan Handbook to the Bible* (Oxford: Lion Publishing, 1999), 130-131.
24. John 8:56.
25. Genesis 15:1-6. All emphases in Bible passages are mine.
26. Kenneth L. Barker and John R. Kohlenberger III, *NIV Bible Commentary, Volume 1: The Old Testament* (Grand Rapids, MI: Zondervan, 1994), 24.
27. Genesis 22:2.
28. Genesis 22:7-8.
29. Genesis 22:11-14.
30. Genesis 35:9-12.
31. Kenneth L. Barker and John R. Kohlenberger III, *NIV Bible Commentary, Volume 1: The Old Testament* (Grand Rapids, MI: Zondervan, 1994), 50-51.
32. Genesis 50:20-21.
33. Genesis 37:3a and Matthew 3:17b.
34. Genesis 37:4 and Mark 15:10.
35. Genesis 37:7 and Matthew 26:64b.
36. Genesis 37:19 and Mark 3:21b.
37. Genesis 37:14a and Luke 20:13b.
38. Genesis 37:17b and John 1:11a.
39. Genesis 37:18b and Luke 19:14b, 23:21.
40. Genesis 37:23b and Matthew 27:28a.
41. Genesis 37:24a and Matthew 12:40b.
42. Genesis 37:28b and Matthew 26:15b.
43. Genesis 39:1-2 and Luke 22:27b, Philippians 2:7b.
44. Genesis 39:7-12 and Hebrews 4:15b, 7:26.
45. Genesis 39:17-18 and Matthew 26:60b, 61a.
46. Genesis 41:41, 45a and Philippians 2:9.
47. Genesis 39:20a and Luke 23:33.
48. Genesis 41:13a and John 13:19.
49. Genesis 41:43b and Philippians 2:10a.
50. Genesis 42:8 and John 6:35a
51. Genesis 42:8 and John 14:9, 2 Corinthians 3:14a.
52. Genesis 42:6-44:34 and Matthew 24:21a.
53. This is a partial list provided on the Jews for Jesus website: https://jewsforjesus.org/publications/newsletter/newsletter-sep-1985/a-comparison-between-joseph-and-jesus/.

It is fundamental to the Christian worldview in its truest form that what happened in Jesus of Nazareth was the very climax of the long story of Israel. Trying to understand Jesus without understanding what that story was, how it worked, and what it meant is like trying to understand why someone is hitting a ball with a stick without knowing what baseball, or indeed cricket, is all about.

—N. T. Wright, bishop and early Christian historian[1]

If you are willing to search, you will see glimpses of Jesus on every page in every book of the Old Testament—the Hebrew Scriptures. How could this be, apart from these Scriptures being inspired by God?

—Robert Beasley, theologian and author[2]

25

Old Testament Leaders

In the last chapter we limited our discussion to the father and mother of the human race and the fathers of the Israelite nation, all from the first book of the Bible. We now focus our discussion on two famed leaders of the Jewish nation, each of whom foreshadows Christ in multiple ways. Note that I chose two of Israel's "good" leaders, though Israel and Judah had many evil leaders throughout their history. But, as we'll see later, even the good guys did some pretty terrible things. Only Jesus, the Savior to whom they all point, is the perfect representative of his people, the perfect king, and the perfect source of ultimate flourishing and joy for this troubled world.

Let's take a look at Jesus through the examples of Moses and David.

MOSES

Moses is one of the most revered leaders of the Jewish people. As the "deliverer" of his people from slavery in Egypt, he provides a wonderful foreshadowing of Jesus, who delivered his people from their bondage to sin and death. Just as Moses led the Israelites across the Red Sea and out of slavery, Jesus leads his people out of their former life as "slaves to sin" and forward through their lives as his disciples on earth, "wandering through the wilderness" until they eventually reach the ultimate "promised land," the new heavens and the new earth.[3]

Though there are so many events in Moses' life that point to the coming of Jesus, I will highlight just three events for the purposes of this chapter. (We will also look at the first Passover in Chapter 27 when

CHAPTER 25: OLD TESTAMENT LEADERS

we study the feasts of the Israelites.) The first event occurred soon after Moses interceded with God for his grumbling people, and God provided the manna that satisfied their hunger, which we discussed in Chapter 23.

The people began to complain again. This time they were thirsty, and instead of relaxing and trusting that God would again come to their rescue, they screamed at Moses: "Why did you bring us up out of Egypt to make us and our children and livestock die of thirst?" I love Moses' heartfelt honesty in his ensuing cries to God: "What am I to do with these people? They are almost ready to stone me." Moses was a reluctant leader who had a love/hate relationship with his people.

This is the rest of the story:

> The Lord answered Moses, "Go out in front of the people. Take with you some of the elders of Israel and take in your hand the staff with which you struck the Nile, and go. I will stand there before you by the rock at Horeb. Strike the rock, and water will come out of it for the people to drink." So Moses did this in the sight of the elders of Israel. And he called the place *Massah* [meaning "testing"] and *Meribah* [meaning "quarreling"] because the Israelites quarreled and because they tested the Lord saying, "Is the Lord among us or not?"[4]

Fast forward sixteen hundred or so years to an event in John 4, where we read the story of the Samaritan woman at the well. When Jesus asked her to give him a drink of water, she replied, "You are a Jew and I am a Samaritan woman. How can you ask me for a drink?" In those days, Samaritans and Jews were not on friendly terms. The story continues:

> Jesus answered her, "If you knew the gift of God and who it is that asks you for a drink, you would have asked him and he would have given you living water."

> "Sir," the woman said, "you have nothing to draw with and the well is deep. Where can you get this living water? Are you greater than our father Jacob, who gave us the well and drank from it himself, as did also his sons and his livestock?"

Jesus answered, "Everyone who drinks this water will be thirsty again, but whoever drinks the water I give them will never thirst. Indeed, the water I give them will become in them a spring of water welling up to eternal life."[5]

Jesus made no secret of the fact that he is the ultimate provider of water, and not just water that temporarily satisfies one's thirst. He provides the water that sustains you eternally, so long as you "drink the water he gives" you (that is, receive the free gift of salvation through faith in him).

In this way, Moses' provision of water for the people foreshadows Jesus' provision of the "water welling up to eternal life" for his own people. Moreover, the staff with which Moses struck the rock is a symbol of God's judgment.[6] And many commentators note that by striking the rock to release the water, Moses was pointing forward to the crucifixion of Jesus, our "rock," whereby God "struck" his Son with the staff of judgment so that his death would pay the penalty for the sins of all who trust in him. The apostle Paul references this passage when he claims that the Israelites "drank the same spiritual drink; for they drank from the spiritual rock that accompanied them, and that rock was Christ."[7]

The second event of note is from Exodus 32, just as Moses returned from Mount Sinai, where God had given him the Ten Commandments. Upon entering the Israelite camp at the base of the mountain, he caught the Israelites singing, dancing, and worshiping the "golden calf." God had just demonstrated his enormous power to defeat their Egyptian captors, and yet Moses found them worshiping other false gods and giving them the credit for their rescue from slavery in Egypt. Instead of giving gratitude to Yahweh, the people worshiped the golden calf and said: "These are your gods, Israel, who brought you up out of Egypt."[8]

Before proceeding, let me point out that this statement is a perfect example of modern-day sin. Though we would never call it "idolatry" or "idol worship," we modern people do the same thing several millennia later by looking to anything other than God for our meaning in life. We look to our material possessions, our beauty or fitness, our children, our careers, our clothing, our cars, our fame, our Facebook likes, YouTube subscribers, and Instagram followers—you name it—instead of to the true source of all of these gifts. The true Giver is God, but we look instead to created things for our joy, worth, sense of purpose, identity, and meaning. One helpful definition of sin is to look to anything *besides* God for our ultimate source of meaning in life. It breaks God's heart, even if our "idols" are good things, like family and even ministry, if we give them priority rather than putting our personal relationship with him first. We'll have more to say on this in Chapter 32.

Back to the story: Upon seeing the Israelites worshiping an idol, Moses threw down the stone tablets containing the Ten Commandments, breaking them into pieces—a perfect symbol of what the Israelite people had just done to God's law. We pick up the story in Genesis 32:

> The next day Moses said to the people, "You have committed a great sin. But now I will go up to the Lord; perhaps I can make atonement for your sin."
>
> So Moses went back to the Lord and said, "Oh, what a great sin these people have committed! They have made themselves gods of gold. But now, please forgive their sin—but if not, then blot me out of the book you have written."
>
> The Lord replied to Moses, "Whoever has sinned against me I will blot out of my book. Now go, lead the people to the place I spoke of, and my angel will go before you. However, when the time comes for me to punish, I will punish them for their sin."[9]

What does it mean for God to "blot a name out of the book he has written"? King David gave us a clue in one of his poems, preserved for posterity in Psalm 69. He asked God for his enemies to be "blotted out of the book of life and not be listed with the righteous."[10] In the New Testament, Jesus instructed his disciples not to rejoice that the spirits submit to them, but to "rejoice that their names are written in heaven."[11] And the apostle Paul makes reference to this book of life when he states that the names of his co-workers who have "contended at [his] side in the cause of the gospel" are "in the book of life."[12]

Furthermore, the Book of Revelation mentions the "book of life" many times, clearly describing it as a book listing the names of those who are "righteous" and can thus enter heaven. The only reason anyone can be made righteous, based on Jesus' teachings and the rest of the New Testament, is to receive Jesus by faith as their representative, whereby they are "credited" with his righteous record. So how does this relate to Moses?

Looking at Moses' request now through the lens of the New Testament, we can see that Moses is asking to be a substitute for his people, so that he himself can take the penalty for their bad behavior, so that his name—not theirs—is blotted out of the book of life. There is a clear parallel here with what Jesus would do by offering himself as a substitute for his people. Instead of allowing Moses to do this for his people, God instead let the people off the hook for the moment, even offering his angel to go before them. But it is clear that punishment would come eventually.

Soon after this incident, Moses pleaded with God, imploring him to accompany them as they traveled through the desert on their way to the land he had given them. God responded: "I will do the very thing you have asked, because I am pleased with you and I know you by name." In return, Moses made this audacious request: "Now show me your glory." Amazingly, God agreed:

> And the Lord said, "I will cause all my goodness to pass in front of you, and I will proclaim my name, the Lord, in your presence. I will have mercy on whom I will have mercy, and I will have compassion on whom I will have compassion. But," he said, "you cannot see my face, for no one may see me and live."
>
> Then the Lord said, "There is a place near me where you may stand on a rock. When my glory passes by, I will put you in a cleft in the rock and cover you with my hand until I have passed by. Then I will remove my hand and you will see my back; but my face must not be seen."[13]

God wanted to show himself to Moses, but he did so in a way that made it quite apparent that it wasn't easy to reveal himself without risking Moses' life. Moreover, he had to put Moses in a cleft, or fissure,

CHAPTER 25: OLD TESTAMENT LEADERS

in a rock and cover Moses with his hand as he passed by. Plus, Moses could only see God's back. What is going on?! A famous hymn helps us understand. The hymn refers to Jesus as the "rock of ages" who was "cleft for" his followers. This portrait of Jesus as our "cleft in the rock" illuminates the role that Jesus plays in providing a way for us to "see" God.

John writes: "No one has ever seen God, but the one and only Son, who is himself God and is in closest relationship with the Father, has made him known."[14] The author of Hebrews concurs: "The Son is the radiance of God's glory and the exact representation of his being."[15] Jesus himself made this amazing claim, phrased as a question, right before they rolled back the stone that sealed his friend Lazarus' tomb. Lazarus had died four days earlier. Jesus said: "Did I not tell you that if you believe, you will *see* the glory of God?"[16] After opening the tomb, Lazarus walked out. Jesus provides us with a way to see God and his glory—without fear that we will die in the process.

Jesus, who left his throne in heaven and humbled himself, "made himself nothing by taking the very nature of a servant, being made in human likeness."[17] In doing so, he gives us the ability to see God. And through his perfect life lived for us, and through his death on the cross to pay sin's penalty for us, Jesus gave us his righteousness, making it possible for those who have faith in him to live in God's presence eternally. Moses received just a glimpse of God as he covered himself in the rock, but those who cover themselves by faith in Jesus will be able to see God for all eternity. This is how John explains it: "But we know that when Christ appears, we shall be like him, for we shall see him as he is."[18]

Let's look at one more incident (but by no means the last) in Moses' life that foreshadows Jesus. When a second generation of Israelites copied their parents and complained about their life in the desert, God sent venomous snakes among them. As if to remind the people that he sends both the good and the bad—and sometimes we need the bad to bring us back into a dependent relationship with him—the snakes brought the Israelites to their knees before Moses. They confessed that they had not trusted God, and they asked Moses to pray to God on their behalf, so that he would take away the snakes. So Moses prayed for the people, and in reply God revealed this strange plan for their "salvation":

> The Lord said to Moses, "Make a snake and put it up on a pole; anyone who is bitten can look at it and live."

> So Moses made a bronze snake and put it up on a pole. Then when anyone was bitten by a snake and looked at the bronze snake, they lived.[19]

Again, we ask, what in the world is going on? This is one of the many stories in the Old Testament that causes skeptics (and believers as well) to shake their head and dismiss the Old Testament as "bloody, archaic, and bizarre." But if you examine it through the lens of the New Testament, the seemingly weird pieces fall into sensical place. God's harsh response to the Israelites' lack of faith demonstrated his anger when they didn't recognize his provision and trust him for it. (After all, he had already freed them from slavery, parted the Red Sea to assist in their escape, and provided manna, quail, and water to sustain them in the wilderness.)

The snakes represent God's judgment on their sin (their lack of faith in him), and the means by which he healed the people demonstrates the power of Jesus' salvation. To be saved from the venom of the snake, all one had to do was glance up at the bronze serpent, which Moses lifted on a pole. (By the way, a serpent on a staff has become the most common symbol of medicine in the world, demonstrating the impact of this story.) So, to be saved from the serpent's poison, one simply had to look in faith at the serpent that was raised. Even someone who was too weak to do anything to "earn" this healing needed only to glance at the bronze serpent.

In John's Gospel, Jesus referred to this symbol when he was explaining the need to be "born again":

> "No one has ever gone into heaven except the one who came from heaven—the Son of Man. Just as Moses lifted up the snake in the wilderness, so the Son of Man must be lifted up, that everyone who believes may have eternal life in him."[20]

By being "lifted up" on the cross for us, Jesus provided the means whereby those who look to him in faith obtain healing and life, and not just temporary life only to die again, like Lazarus had received, but eternal life. Those who look to God "lifted up" (Jesus and his work on the cross) are thus saved from God's future judgment on sin. All we have to do is "look"—i.e. look in faith to Jesus for our salvation. Thus, salvation is not awarded on the basis of good works, though good works will flow out of gratitude and love in response to Jesus.

Before we wrap up our discussion of the bronze snake, one law that God had given his people through Moses applies in this circumstance: "And if a man has committed a crime punishable by death and he is put to death, and you hang him on a tree, his body shall not remain all night on the tree, but you shall bury him the same day, for a hanged man is cursed by God."[21] Paul, a former Pharisee and therefore familiar with the Mosaic law, makes this connection to Jesus: "Christ redeemed us from the curse of the law by becoming a curse for us, for it is written: 'Cursed is everyone who is hung on a pole.'"

The serpent, symbolizing sin, was *both* what was killing the Israelites *and* what would save the Israelites. Again, the apostle Paul helps us understand what Jesus was doing for his people: "God made him who knew no sin to be sin for us, so that in him we might become the righteousness of God."[22] On the cross, Jesus "became sin" for us—took our sin on himself—so that we could be saved from sin and obtain the righteousness that enables us to live in God's presence eternally. Moses saved his people by lifting up the snake on the pole so that those who looked at it in faith were saved. Jesus saved his people by being lifted up and becoming sin for them, such that anyone who looks to him in faith will be saved for all eternity.

DAVID

Alongside Moses, David is one of the most revered "insiders" in the Old Testament. We first meet David when God sent the prophet Samuel to Bethlehem with instructions to anoint the next king of Israel. Regarding whom to anoint, God simply told Samuel that he had selected "one of Jesse's sons" to be the next king of Israel.

Upon seeing Jesse's eldest son Eliab, Samuel felt confident that this son was the one God had selected. Eliab must have been tall, strong, and handsome—very "kingly." We referenced this incident in the discussion of Abel in Chapter 24. This is when God reminded Samuel that people look "at the outward appearance," but he "looks at the heart."[23] After seven sons were brought before him, Samuel received no confirmation from God that any were his choice for king, so he asked Jesse if he had any other sons.

Jesse never would have expected his youngest son to be chosen as the king; he hadn't even invited him to the meeting with Samuel. Upon hearing of the eighth son, who was out tending the family's sheep, Samuel asked for them to fetch him. In that society, the eldest son was the one who would inherit the blessing of the father. (Recall how Jacob had to deceive his father to obtain the blessing that should have gone to Esau.) In fact, the youngest son was the lowest in the rank, and therefore it must have been an extreme surprise to Jesse and the seven older brothers when Samuel asked for *David* to come in from the sheep.

When the young David walked in, God said to Samuel, "Rise and anoint him; this is the one."[24] Therefore, Samuel anointed David with oil in the presence of his father and older brothers. The *youngest* brother was God's choice for the successor to King Saul, the first king of Israel. Just as God looks at the heart and not at the exterior, God also does not choose as the world chooses. Instead of choosing the eldest, tallest, and strongest son, he chose the youngest son. In fact, this is a common theme throughout the Bible, indicating that God does not work as the world works. As Paul explains, "But God chose the foolish things of the world to shame the wise; God chose the weak things of the world to shame the strong."[25]

After his surprising anointing as the next king, the next incident in David's life is a famous one. It happened when Israel was just about to go to war with their worst enemy, the Philistines. David's three oldest brothers were among the Israelite soldiers camped on one hill overlooking the Valley of Elah to the south. On the other side of the valley, the Philistine army was assembled, ready for a fight.

Their largest warrior, "a champion named Goliath," shouted taunts across the valley at the Israelite soldiers: "Choose a man and have him come down to me. If he is able to fight and kill me, we will become your subjects; but if I overcome him and kill him, you will become our subjects and serve us."[26] King Saul and the Israelite soldiers were "dismayed and terrified" upon hearing Goliath's words, and "Whenever the Israelites saw the man, they all fled from him in great fear."[27]

In an echo of Jacob sending Joseph to check on his brothers centuries earlier, Jesse sent David out to bring food to his three brothers and check on them. Just as David arrived, the Israelites and Philistines were lining up to face each other in battle, shouting the war cry. David dropped his things with the keeper of supplies and ran to the battle lines to find out what was happening. Just then Goliath stepped forward from the Philistine line and shouted out his challenge for an Israelite to fight him on behalf of the whole army. Apparently fearless, David asked, "Who is this uncircumcised Philistine that he should defy the armies of the Lord?"[28]

In response, Eliab, the prideful older brother who doubted his younger brother was up to any good, accused David of abandoning his sheep alone in the field, of being wicked and conceited, and of coming just to watch the battle from the sidelines. He basically asked him, "What do you think you are doing here? Go away, you silly boy!" Moving on, David asked others what was going on with the huge Philistine warrior. Eventually, he asked the Israelite king, Saul, if he could fight Goliath himself. Despite Saul's advice not to do so, David insisted on facing Goliath, stating this clear expression of his faith, "The Lord who rescued me from the paw of the lion and the paw of the bear will rescue me from the hand of this Philistine."[29]

You are familiar with the end of the story. David defeated Goliath using a small stone and a sling shot. While his aim was impressive enough, what was even more impressive is what David told Goliath right before he slung the stone that killed him:

> "You come against me with sword and spear and javelin, but I come against you in the name of the Lord Almighty, the God of the armies of Israel, whom you have defied. This day the Lord will deliver you into my hands, and I'll strike you down and cut off your head. This very day I will give the carcasses of the Philistine army to the birds and the wild animals, and the whole world will know that there is a God in Israel. All those gathered here will know that it is not by sword or spear that the Lord saves; for the battle is the Lord's, and he will give all of you into our hands."[30]

David demonstrated amazing faith in the power of the Lord to save him and his people. He chose to risk his life as the representative of his people in combat against Goliath, the terrifying representative of their evil enemy, the Philistines. Whereas Adam failed in his role as the representative of the human race against our enemy, Satan, David proved to be a successful representative for the Israelites. David was clearly pointing to the "second Adam," Jesus, the representative for the human race who succeeded where Adam had failed. Just as David represented the Israelites and defeated the representative of the enemy, Goliath, Jesus defeated our ultimate enemy, Satan, and he continues to help his people—on a daily basis—as they fight the forces that Satan represents.

What's more, Jesus came as a baby in a stable in a poor backwater town in Israel, a Jewish boy apparently born out of wedlock to a poor girl and a carpenter. He came as a servant, not as a powerful conqueror, the way a king would normally arrive. And even his brothers thought he was crazy to make the claims he was making.[31] In the week leading up to his crucifixion, Jesus entered Jerusalem on a donkey instead of a warhorse, and he fought Satan without a sword, spear, or javelin. He is our perfect king and the only king that can bring perfect justice, peace, and flourishing for his people.

Before we leave David, there is an additional way that he foreshadowed Jesus that shouldn't go unmentioned. Before he was a king—and perhaps one of the main reasons God chose him to be king—David had worked as a shepherd caring for the family sheep, and he understood quite well how to care for them. As any shepherd can tell you, sheep are not the brightest of animals. They easily get into trouble, and when they fall over on their backs, they need help to get upright again. Sheep often want to escape from the flock, but they generally don't get very far before they became lost, injured, or cold, at best, or at worst, killed by more powerful and cunning predators. David even mentioned that he had to fight lions and bears that had threatened his sheep, which made him trust that God would also help him fight Goliath.[32]

David wrote one of his most beautiful and well-known poems to draw the parallel between his dependence on God and a sheep's dependence on the shepherd. You may recognize these opening lines:

> The Lord is my shepherd; I shall not want.
>   He makes me lie down in green pastures.
> He leads me beside still waters.
>   He restores my soul.
> He leads me in paths of righteousness

> for his name's sake.
> Even though I walk through the valley of the shadow of death,
> I will fear no evil,
> for you are with me;
> your rod and your staff,
> they comfort me.[33]

In *A Shepherd Looks at Psalm 23*, Phillip Keller, a shepherd himself, clarifies the deep nuances in this poem, illuminating it for modern-day urbanites who are not nearly as familiar with shepherding as people were in the days of David or Jesus. He notes that a shepherd would use a rod and staff for three main reasons: First, they were symbols respectively of the shepherd's authority over and concern for his sheep. Second, the shepherd used the rod to discipline the sheep when they went off course and put themselves in a dangerous situation, while he would use the staff to draw the sheep closer to each other and to himself. And third, the shepherd used the rod to fight off predators and the staff to guide the sheep in the right direction in order to keep them safe.

Because he had shepherding experience and because he was such a wonderful king, the Israelites lovingly referred to David as "the Shepherd King." About four hundred years later, when the Israelites had been defeated and were in Babylon, living in exile from their homeland, God spoke through the prophet Ezekiel to issue stern warnings to his people's leaders:

> "Woe to you shepherds of Israel who only take care of yourselves! Should not shepherds take care of the flock? You eat the curds, clothe yourselves with the wool and slaughter the choice animals, but you do not take care of the flock. You have not strengthened the weak or healed the sick or bound up the injured. You have not brought back the strays or searched for the lost. You have ruled them harshly and brutally. So they were scattered because there was no shepherd, and when they were scattered they became food for all the wild animals. My sheep wandered over all the mountains and on every high hill. They were scattered over the whole earth, and no one searched or looked for them."[34] [35]

THE SHORTEST LEAP

What is the solution that God proposed to protect his people from these "false shepherds"? He no longer trusted worldly shepherds. Instead God said he himself would come to be their shepherd:

> "For this is what the Sovereign Lord says: *I myself* will search for my sheep and look after them. As a shepherd looks after his scattered flock when he is with them, so will *I* look after my sheep. *I* will rescue them from all the places where they were scattered on a day of clouds and darkness. *I* will bring them out from the nations and gather them from the countries, and *I* will bring them into their own land. *I* will pasture them on the mountains of Israel, in the ravines and in all the settlements in the land. *I* will tend them in a good pasture, and the mountain heights of Israel will be their grazing land. There they will lie down in good grazing land, and there they will feed in a rich pasture on the mountains of Israel. *I myself* will tend my sheep and have them lie down, declares the Sovereign Lord. *I* will search for the lost and bring back the strays. *I* will bind up the injured and strengthen the weak, but the sleek and the strong *I* will destroy. *I* will shepherd the flock with justice."[36]

Though this prophecy has partially been fulfilled in the establishment of the State of Israel in 1948, when Jewish people scattered around the globe returned to what they claim is their rightful land, Christians believe the true fulfillment of this prophecy will take place when Jesus comes a second time to establish his Kingdom in the "new heavens and new earth." How do they defend this belief? In John's Gospel, Jesus made it clear that he was the ultimate "Good Shepherd" who has come to rescue his sheep:

> "I am the good shepherd. The good shepherd lays down his life for the sheep. The hired hand is not the shepherd and does not own the sheep. So when he sees the wolf coming, he abandons the sheep and runs away. Then the wolf attacks the flock and scatters it. The man runs

CHAPTER 25: OLD TESTAMENT LEADERS

away because he is a hired hand and cares nothing for the sheep.

"I am the good shepherd; I know my sheep and my sheep know me—just as the Father knows me and I know the Father—and I lay down my life for the sheep. I have other sheep that are not of this sheep pen. I must bring them also. They too will listen to my voice, and there shall be one flock and one shepherd."[37]

Just as the "Shepherd King" risked his life to save his people and defeat Goliath, Jesus came to lay down his life for his sheep. He is the fulfillment of the shepherd in Psalm 23, the one who provides green pasture and still waters to refresh his people's souls, and the one to whom they look as they pass through the valley of the shadow of death. His rod and his staff, they should comfort those who place their faith in him.

So, before closing this chapter, let's take a look at a few unfortunate events in the lives of our "insiders." We already know about Adam's failure, but we should point out that Abraham—the father of the Israelite nation, the amazing man who believed God and to whom God "credited it as righteousness," the man who trusted God so much that he even came close to sacrificing his own son—even Abraham was far from perfect.

Before Isaac was born, when Abraham and his wife Sarai traveled to Egypt, Abraham was afraid that the Egyptian men would kill him if they knew that Sarai, who must have been quite gorgeous, was his wife. He therefore hid the important fact that she was his wife from them, putting Sarai in a difficult situation when the Pharaoh heard of her beauty and called her to his palace. And many years later when they were still childless, Abraham doubted that his wife would ever be able to have a child, despite God's promise, thus deciding to sleep with Sarai's younger Egyptian slave, Hagar. The result was a son named Ishmael, from whom the modern-day Arabs descend. The family schism that resulted from Abraham's mistrust of God has had wide repercussions in world history even to this day.

In the last chapter, we discussed Jacob's deception of his brother Esau, as well as the dysfunctional treatment of his sons due to his favoritism of Joseph. Joseph, seemingly the epitome of a faithful follower of God, was foolish in his choice of words to share with his brothers, leading to resentment, jealousy, and a troubled relationship that fueled his brothers' terrible actions.

And even Moses, the steadfast leader that God chose to lead the Israelite people out of slavery in Egypt, had his very flawed moments. He killed an Egyptian in his younger years when he resided in Pharaoh's household, yet God still came to him in the burning bush years later and used him as one of the Israelites' greatest leaders.

Finally, David made many mistakes during his earthly rule, not the least of which was his adulterous relationship with Bathsheba, whom he watched from his balcony as she took a bath in the distance. Upon discovering that she was pregnant with his child, David first tried to deceive people into thinking that Bathsheba was carrying her husband's baby. When that didn't work, David attempted to get her husband, Uriah the Hittite, out of the way of their relationship, instructing his general to put Uriah in the most dangerous part of the battle, where he subsequently died.

The message is clear: while the Bible does contain a selection of amazing heroes who show us how to act courageously in faith, its main message is that even the best heroes are imperfect. It's not just the villains, like Goliath, who need a savior to set them free from evil, but the heroes of the faith, like David, also need a savior. And when a human king, like David, comes close to being what you may call a great leader, we are still left disappointed and hungering for someone who can truly bring lasting peace.

This yearning for a "perfectly just king" is something we all can understand, especially those of us who live in countries ravaged by corruption, racial and political divisions, injustice, and chaos. Fortunately, these "imperfect heroes" point to the perfect hero, the one who "will reign on David's throne," who will establish a kingdom that is founded on "justice and righteousness," and whose reign will bring peace not just for a generation or two, but for all time.

Upon hearing that a group of magi from the east were searching for the "King of the Jews," the current Jewish king, Herod the Great, asked the chief priests and teachers of the law where the Messiah was to be born. After hearing the prophecy from Micah 5 that the future king would come from Bethlehem, Herod ordered that all male babies two years old and younger be killed, just to make sure there would be no threats to his throne. Fortunately, Jesus' parents fled to Egypt in time to escape from Herod's soldiers and avoid the infamous "slaughter of the innocents."[38] Thus, the true King of the Jews escaped harm.

Several decades later, Jesus stood before the Roman governor of Palestine, Pilate, who asked the crowd: "What shall I do then, with the one you call the king of the Jews?"[39] The response from the crowd: "Crucify him!"[40] A few verses later, Mark continues the story:

> The soldiers led Jesus away into the palace (that is, the Praetorium) and called together the whole company of soldiers. They put a purple robe on him, then twisted together a crown of thorns and set it on him. And they began to call out to him, "Hail, king of the Jews!" Again and again they struck him on the head with a staff and spit on him. Falling on their knees, they paid homage to him. And when they had mocked him, they took off the purple robe and put his own clothes on him. Then they led him out to crucify him.[41]

While Jesus was hanging on the cross, the soldiers continued to mock him, saying, "If you are the king of the Jews, save yourself." And then, "There was a written notice above him, which read: THIS IS THE KING OF THE JEWS."[42] The mocking brings to mind Eliab's criticism of his youngest brother, David, just before he defeated Goliath. The irony of the mockery in Jesus' situation was that not only *was* he the king of the Jews, he was the Creator of the universe—in fact, he had created even the wood from which the Roman cross was made. Moreover, as mentioned in Chapter 21, it was precisely because he did *not* save himself that *he did save* all who trust him in him. If this isn't evidence that he is the one true King—both perfectly just and perfectly gracious—I'm not sure what else could convince you.

Questions for Comprehension and Discussion

1. How is Moses' leading his people across the Red Sea out of slavery in Egypt, through the wilderness, and to the promised land, a picture of the work that Jesus has done, does, and will do for his people?
2. How can one interpret the rod, the rock, and the water in the story of the Israelites at *Massah* and *Meribah*?
3. How does the worship of the Golden Calf reflect human behavior in our society today? What does Moses mean when he asks God to "blot his name out" of the "book of life"? How does this point to Jesus?
4. Why couldn't Moses "see" God? How did God allow Moses to see him? What is Jesus' role in enabling us to "see" God? How does he do this in more than one way?
5. What is the significance of the staff with the bronze serpent that Moses lifted up to heal people from the serpents that were killing them? How does the staff with the bronze serpent point to what Jesus did for his people?
6. Why was it odd for Samuel to choose the youngest of Jesse's sons to anoint as king? What does this tell us about God?
7. How does the young David's defeat of the frightening warrior, Goliath, point to Jesus? How were David and Goliath representatives of their people, just as Jesus and Adam are representative of theirs?
8. What aspects of his job as a shepherd translate to David's role as king? How does the shepherd symbolize the leaders God gave the Israelites? How is Jesus the ultimate "Good Shepherd"?
9. How are even the greatest heroes of the Bible imperfect? How does this give us a longing for a perfect king?
10. Why didn't Jesus save himself when he was on the cross? How is this a demonstration of both perfect justice and perfect mercy?

CHAPTER 25 ENDNOTES

1. N. T. Wright, *Simply Christian: Why Christianity Makes Sense* (New York: HarperCollins Publishers, 2006), 71.
2. Robert C. Beasley, *101 Portraits of Jesus in the Hebrew Scriptures* (Hendersonville, NC: LivingStone Books, 2008), xi.
3. Revelation 21:1-4.
4. Exodus 17:5-7.
5. John 4:10-14.
6. Edmund P. Clowney, *The Unfolding Mystery: Discovering Christ in the Old Testament* (Phillipsburg, NJ: P&R Publishing, 1988), 123-126.
7. 1 Corinthians 10:4.
8. Exodus 32:4b.
9. Genesis 32:30-34.
10. Psalm 69:28.
11. Luke 10:20.
12. Philippians 4:3.
13. Exodus 33:19-23.
14. John 6:46.
15. Hebrews 1:3.
16. John 11:40.
17. Philippians 2:7.
18. 1 John 3:2.
19. Numbers 21:8-9.
20. John 3:13-14.
21. Deuteronomy 21:22-23, ESV.
22. 2 Corinthians 5:21.
23. 1 Samuel 16:7.
24. 1 Samuel 16:12b.
25. 1 Corinthians 1:27.
26. 1 Samuel 17:9.
27. 1 Samuel 17:24.
28. 1 Samuel 17:26.
29. 1 Samuel 17:37.
30. 1 Samuel 17:45-47.
31. See John 7:5.
32. 1 Samuel 17:37.
33. Psalm 23:1-4, ESV.
34. Ezekiel 34:2b-6.

[35] Other Old Testament verses that refer to the people of Israel as sheep without a shepherd include: Numbers 27:17; 1 Kings 22:17; 2 Chronicles 18:16; Isaiah 13:14; Jeremiah 50:6; and Zechariah 10:2.
[36] Ezekiel 34:11-16. All emphases in Bible passages are mine.
[37] John 10:11-16.
[38] The story can be found in Matthew 2:16-18.
[39] Mark 15:12.
[40] Mark 15:13.
[41] Mark 15:16-20.
[42] Luke 23:47-48.

Nevertheless just as the chief teaching of the New Testament is really the proclamation of grace and peace through the forgiveness of sins in Christ, so the chief teaching of the Old Testament is really the teaching of laws, the showing up of sin, and the demanding of good. You should expect this in the Old Testament.

—Martin Luther, German monk and a seminal figure in the Protestant Reformation[1]

Scripture is like a river again, broad and deep, shallow enough here for the lamb to go wading, but deep enough there for the elephant to swim.

—Gregory the Great, sixth century pope[2]

26

Old Testament Outsiders

An overview of how the people of the Old Testament point to Jesus would be incomplete without the last two chapters and the discussion of the key forefathers and leaders of the Israelites. But many of my favorite stories from the Old Testament are those that are not as well-known, since their protagonists are the less powerful members of society, the ones excluded from positions of power and influence—the outsiders.

In the New Testament, Jesus loved the powerless and the excluded, and he often had harsh words for the religious or political insiders. He met regularly with "sinners and tax collectors," and insisted: "Let the little children come to me, and do not hinder them, for the kingdom of heaven belongs to such as these."[3] He was also remarkably interested in the plight of women, and many women were among his first followers. And even today, it is the outsiders who are more likely to "get" Jesus and the need to simply receive a free gift, compared to the insiders, who like to pridefully think that their own efforts are sufficient to be "good with God."

But even the Old Testament is replete with signs that the social, political, religious, and ethnic outsiders would be welcomed into heaven, despite their less than perfectly righteous lives. I'm sure many of the original hearers of these Old Testament stories couldn't quite understand how the blood of animals could bring moral outsiders into a reconciled relationship with a perfectly holy God. But on this side of the history relative to the cross, once we have understood the power of faith in Jesus, it makes much more sense: These outsiders could sense that their salvation was dependent on someone else, someone who would somehow give them salvation as an unearned, free gift. They thus had faith that God could save "even them."

CHAPTER 26: OLD TESTAMENT OUTSIDERS

The first group of outsiders we should discuss are the very people whose forefathers and leaders we just discussed as "insiders"—the Israelites. When God was giving his people the law through Moses, he told them that he had "set them apart from the nations." Moses made this beautiful statement in Deuteronomy:

> For you are a people holy to the Lord your God. The Lord your God has chosen you out of all the peoples on the face of the earth to be his people, his treasured possession.[4]

So far, it sounds like the Israelite people are somehow *better* than other nations. But wait.

Though he had set them apart from the other nations, God also made it clear to them that he *didn't* set them apart because of anything they had done. Moses wanted to be sure that the people understood this, so he immediately followed the last statement we read with this one:

> The Lord did not set his affection on you and choose you because you were more numerous than other peoples, for you were the fewest of all peoples. But it was *because the Lord loved you* and kept the oath he swore to your ancestors that he brought you out with a mighty hand and redeemed you from the land of slavery, from the power of Pharaoh king of Egypt.[5]

The reason that God chose the descendants of Abraham was simply because he loved them. It seems illogical, but God loved his people because, well, because he loved them. They were not more powerful than other nations, nor were they more numerous, nor were they "holier." God loved them because he had made an oath to their forefather Abraham to make them as numerous as the stars and to bless the whole world through them.

So, what does this mean? It simply means that the Israelites were not necessarily "insiders" because of anything they had done. They were loved by God and recipients of this love because God was keeping his own oath to a man he asked to leave Ur of the Chaldeans and travel to a land he promised to give him. All of Abraham's descendants were blessed by Abraham's faith in God, just as all of Adam's descendants were cursed by Adam's disobedience.

As we begin our discussion of "outsiders," it is crucial to emphasize this point—that God didn't choose his people based on their "performance" for him—because the reason many of the outsiders in this chapter are outsiders was simply because they were not among the "chosen race." But God is very clear that non-Israelites were *not* inferior because they were not descendants of Abraham. To illustrate this lack of favoritism, consider that the reason God saved the Hebrew firstborn children from being killed in Egypt on the first Passover was *not* because they were Jews, but because they had killed a spotless lamb and put the blood on their doorframe, trusting that this would save them (more on this in the next chapter). Anyone who did this, whether they were Egyptian, Hebrew, or any other race, would have been spared the death of the firstborn son within their home. And anyone who hadn't placed the blood of the lamb on their doorpost, even if they were Hebrew, would not escape judgment.

But, likewise, if we were to look at the examples of Israelites who were outsiders in a non-Jewish nation, such as Daniel, Shadrach, Meshach, and Abednego,[6] who were in exile in the Persian empire, we would have to refrain from thinking that they were superior in any way to their non-Israelite captors. The verse above, clarifying that God "did not set his affection" on the Jews for anything they had done, does not allow us to make those judgments about Israelites versus non-Israelites. It is clear from the behavior of other Israelites (including even their best leaders, Moses and David) that the reason they were insiders was not because of their perfect moral behavior. Let's begin with one of the earliest outsider stories, one that demonstrates that God can turn around even one of the most morally abhorrent circumstances.

Tamar

The account of Tamar is one of those Bible stories that makes the average person roll their eyes and think, "The Old Testament is so strange! How does this teach me to be a good person?!" But from these stories come interesting insights into God's plans for his people—the ones he set apart from the nations to be "holy"—and how he can transform our sin both for his glory and for the ultimate good of his people. Note that God doesn't want us to sin, but even if we do, he has the power to use it to produce an outcome that can bless us and/or others.

Before we get to the story, let us remind ourselves: God called Abraham and Sarai to leave their homeland and go to a "promised land." Their sons were Jacob and Esau, and Jacob (renamed Israel) had twelve sons, whose descendants became the twelve tribes of Israel. Jacob's fourth son, Judah, had a son Perez, who was the ancestor of Jesse.[7] Jesse had eight sons, the youngest of whom, David, was anointed as Israel's second king (and is still considered Israel's greatest king). And David's line eventually led to Jesus.[8]

Tamar first appears in the pages of the Bible when she married the eldest of Judah's three sons. When God put Tamar's husband, Er, to death because he was wicked, Tamar married the second son, Onan, as dictated by the ancient practice of "levirate marriage." By marrying the next oldest son (who hadn't yet been married), levirate marriage protected widows and, in the case when she had children, preserved the bloodline. Unfortunately, after Tamar married the second son, he too died (also because he was so wicked). This time, Judah was probably a bit worried about letting her marry his third son, Shelah, but since his third son was still too young to marry, Judah sent Tamar back to her father's home to wait for him to grow up.

Once the third son had become old enough to marry, Tamar realized she hadn't been sent for, as she had been promised. So, upon hearing that her father-in-law, Judah, was on a road trip to have his sheep sheared, Tamar dressed as a prostitute, covered her face with a veil, and placed herself along the path that her father-in-law would be taking. Amazingly, Judah fell for the trick and slept with her, but not before giving Tamar (still not knowing who she was) the promise that he would send a young goat as payment. He gave her his seal, cord, and staff (an ancient identity card) as a pledge that she could eventually exchange for the promised goat.

As it turns out, Judah had unknowingly fertilized two eggs within Tamar's womb. When he heard that his daughter-in-law had been prostituting herself and had become pregnant as a result, he ordered that she be burned to death. But as Tamar was brought out to be killed, she presented Judah's seal, cord, and staff to him, saying, "I am pregnant by the man who owns these.... See if you recognize whose seal and cord and staff these are."⁹ Probably a bit embarrassed, Judah claimed: "She is more righteous than I, since I wouldn't give her to my son, Shelah." Tamar's—and Judah's—twin sons were named Perez and Zerah. (Interestingly, Tamar's instructions to Judah to "examine" the seal, cord, and staff echo Judah's own instructions to his father Jacob to "examine" the bloodied robe of his son, Joseph,[10] demonstrating that deception perpetuates itself through the generations.)

Tamar used deception and sex with someone other than her husband (that is, adultery) to become a mother within the family she felt she rightfully belonged. One Jewish commentary puts it this way: "Tamar saw that her intended husband, Shelah, had grown up, and that Judah was deceiving her with false pretenses, and did not actually plan on marrying her to anyone. She took initiative, aspiring to free herself from being husbandless and to build a perpetuation for herself and for the household of Judah."[11] Tamar was being taken advantage of. She was a woman, which in those days was a position of very little power, and on top of that, she was a childless widow, which was the lowest status of all women. She had no hope, no future, and—almost—no power. Her only power was her beauty, which she used to "deceive the deceiver."

Were her actions morally upright? By no means. Were they justifiable? Probably not. But the main takeaway, regardless of your opinions as to the morality of Tamar's actions, is that she trusted that she had a future in the line of Judah. She may not have acted purely out of that motivation, but she acted in faith to seize hold of what she felt she deserved. And from her line, through Perez, both David and Jesus eventually would be born.

Rahab

Rahab provides another example of the "lowest of the low" in terms of power and influence. She was a woman, which was the first strike against her in the ancient world. Moreover, she was a Canaanite woman, not an Israelite. God "abhorred" the Canaanites' religious practices, which included the worship of many gods, the cults of the "high places," and even child sacrifice. And on top of this, she was a prostitute. It would be difficult to find anyone who was more of an outsider, as far as gender, politics, ethnicity, religion, and morality. But Rahab's profession did give

CHAPTER 26: OLD TESTAMENT OUTSIDERS

her one source of power: the information she gleaned from the men who visited her. Of special note, she learned about a tribe of people who were gathering across the Jordan River from her hometown of Jericho.

At the time when Rahab enters the Bible, in the Book of Joshua, the Israelite people have just completed their wandering in the wilderness of the Sinai Peninsula, forty long years after they had been freed from slavery in Egypt. The only remaining survivors from the time they left Egypt were Caleb and Joshua. In the first chapter of the Book of Joshua, Moses has just died, and Joshua has transitioned from his role as Moses' aide to his replacement as leader of the Israelites.

Forty years earlier, Joshua and Caleb had been two of the twelve spies Moses had sent out to investigate the land they were about to enter, and they were the only ones who had trusted God's promise to "give the land into their hands." The other ten spies had doubted that they could take the land, saying, "We can't attack those people; they are stronger than we are" and giving a bad report to their people about the land.[12] It was for this failure to trust him that God sent the Israelites into the desert for forty years, until all of the people whom he had rescued from slavery (except Caleb and Joshua) had died. The younger generation of Israelites were now at the border of the Promised Land, their hearts pounding with anticipation and excitement, as they were about to enter the land God had promised to Abraham more than four hundred and forty years earlier.

Like Moses had done, Joshua sent out spies ahead of them. Jericho was the first town across the Jordan River from their encampment in Shittim. The Bible doesn't record much between the time the spies were sent out and the time they entered the house of Rahab, simply this: "So they went and entered the house of a prostitute named Rahab and stayed there."[13] This seems a bit odd that we know nothing of the extent of their reconnaissance mission, except that they visited a prostitute's home. This isn't exactly a favorable accomplishment, and some people have tried to downplay her profession by translating the Hebrew word *zanah* as "hostess" or "tavernkeeper." But elsewhere in the Old Testament,[14] this word is clearly used to refer to prostitutes, and Rahab is called a prostitute twice in the New Testament.[15] There's no getting around it; the Hebrew spies were visiting a prostitute.

Somehow, the king of Jericho found out that Israelite spies had entered Rahab's home, and he sent a message to Rahab, ordering her to bring the spies out of her house. Not only did Rahab not do what her king asked her to do, but she hid the spies in her home and lied to the king, telling him they had already left (wisely sending the king's men in hot pursuit so they wouldn't search her home). Rahab provided this explanation for her actions:

> "I know that the Lord has given you this land and that a great fear of you has fallen on us, so that all who live in this country are melting in fear because of you. We have heard how the Lord dried up the water of the Red Sea for you when you came out of Egypt, and what you did to Sihon and Og, the two kings of the Amorites east of the Jordan, whom you completely destroyed. When we heard of it, our hearts melted in fear and everyone's courage failed because of you, for the Lord your God is God in heaven above and on the earth below."

Rahab clearly thought the Israelite God was stronger than her king. She had changed allegiances, and she was willing to protect the Israelite spies and lie to the king of Jericho, despite the risk. Replying excitedly, "Our lives for your life!" the spies came to an agreement with Rahab. They instructed her to hang a scarlet cord from her window as a sign to the invading Israelite army to save her and anyone else taking refuge within her home. As soon as she let the spies down from her window in the city wall (with instructions to hide in the hills for three days before crossing the Jordan), Rahab tied the scarlet cord in her window, as if she were afraid that she'd forget to do so by the time the Israelite army stormed the town.

We read a few chapters later that the Israelites did indeed save Rahab once the walls of Jericho fell and they invaded. Though the population of the city was completely wiped out, the Bible says this about Rahab:

> But Joshua spared Rahab the prostitute, with her family and all who belonged to her, because she hid the men Joshua had sent as spies to Jericho—and she lives among the Israelites to this day.[16]

Rahab went on to marry a man from the tribe of Judah by the name of Salmon (also spelled "Salma" or "Salmah" elsewhere). Salmon's father

CHAPTER 26: OLD TESTAMENT OUTSIDERS

was Nahshon, who was one of the twelve spies that Moses had originally sent into the promised land forty years before Rahab hid the second set of spies. In a strange twist, his father died in the wilderness due to his lack of trust in God's promises, while Salmon, who had been born in the wilderness, went on to marry the woman who protected the next group of spies because she *did* trust God's promises.

There are many symbols of salvation in the story of Rahab, which I will briefly summarize below:

1. Rahab was saved by faith in God, even though she wasn't an Israelite. This foreshadows the salvation of anyone who trusts in Jesus, both Jew and non-Jew alike. Her actions on behalf of the spies were outward signs that she had faith in their God, just as Christians' obedience to Jesus' teachings are outward signs of faith. That is, both Rahab and Christian believers are saved by faith, and as a result of that faith, they act in obedience to God. Jesus' brother James makes this point by using Rahab as an example:

    > Was not even Rahab the prostitute considered righteous for what she did when she gave lodging to the spies and sent them off in a different direction? As the body without the spirit is dead, so faith without deeds is dead.[17]

2. Rahab was saved in a particular way, by hanging the scarlet cord in the window. The cord acted as an outward sign of her faith in the Israelite God. When the Israelite soldiers saw the cord, they saved anyone in that house. This is very similar to the blood of the Passover lamb, which we will discuss in the next chapter, in that it was a sign that the members of the house trusted that God would not "strike down" their firstborn son. Understandably, many people today want to believe that there are many ways to God, but God has provided clear instructions in the Bible that there is one way to be saved, and that is by trusting in the blood of Jesus.[18] Even the color of the cord, scarlet, points to the color of blood, whether it is the blood of a

lamb at Passover or the blood of "Lamb of God, who takes away the sins of the world."[19]

3. As the first Gentile convert, Rahab is a picture of the future Christian church. Though the Jews were God's original chosen people, through whom he sent his Son as the ultimate sacrifice to end all sacrifices, the Gentiles—like Rahab—would be "grafted in" to the family tree.[20] Just as a man in the tribe of Judah marries Rahab, Jesus is the "Lion of Judah" who will marry "his bride"—those who have faith in him—to bring her into his family. Paul gives these beautiful instructions: "Husbands, love your wives, just as Christ loved the church and gave himself up for her."[21] Jesus even calls himself the "bridegroom,"[22] and John has a vision of "the Holy City, the new Jerusalem, coming down out of heaven from God, prepared as a bride beautifully dressed for her husband."[23]

Rahab presents a beautiful picture of the way God can change our lives. After trusting in God by faith, and then acting on that faith, her past was left in the past. She moved forward as a future grandmother of King David, and eventually of Jesus. As the apostle Paul writes in his letter to the church in Corinth: "Therefore, if anyone is in Christ, the new creation has come: The old has gone, the new is here!"[24]

RUTH

The next outsider, another woman, comes only a generation after Rahab. In fact, she is Rahab's daughter-in-law, Ruth. Ruth was a Moabitess, who became both a widow and the daughter-in-law of a widow within a short period of time. Just as Tamar was a childless widow, so Ruth was left without children or a husband to care for her. In those days, there were two women who were the most pitied of all women: widows and childless women, and to be both was the worst of all. You had neither a husband nor children to support you, and generally you were among the poorest of the poor, having to resort to begging on the street in order to feed yourself—unless, of course, you had a family who would support you if you returned home to them. But Ruth gave up even that comfort.

CHAPTER 26: OLD TESTAMENT OUTSIDERS

Ruth's (first) mother-in-law, Naomi, was an Israelite who had moved to Moab from Israel with her husband Elimelek, to escape a famine many years earlier. Their two sons, Mahlon and Kilion, had married Moabite women, Ruth and Orpah. Upon the death of Naomi's husband and two sons, Naomi insisted that her daughters-in-law return to their "mother's home" in order to find new husbands among their people. However, Ruth insisted on going with Naomi to Israel, eloquently demonstrating her faith in the God that Naomi worshiped:

> "Don't urge me to leave you or to turn back from you. Where you go I will go, and where you stay I will stay. Your people will be my people and your God my God. Where you die I will die, and there I will be buried. May the Lord deal with me, be it ever so severely, if even death separates you and me."[25]

Ruth left all that had been familiar to her to follow Naomi back to the land of Israel. She trusted that not even death would separate her from her beloved mother-in-law. Naomi finally gave up urging Ruth not to come with her. So Naomi and Ruth returned to Naomi's hometown of Bethlehem just as the barley harvest was beginning. Since Naomi was too old to gather grain, Ruth offered to go to the fields to "glean behind the harvesters." The law that God gave to his people through Moses shed light on what Ruth was planning:

> "When you reap the harvest of your land, do not reap to the very edges of your field or gather the gleanings of your harvest. Do not go over your vineyard a second time or pick up the grapes that have fallen. Leave them for the poor and the foreigner. I am the Lord your God."[26]

Ruth was not just poor, but she was also a foreigner. She had every right to follow the harvesters and pick up the leftovers. As it turned out, she was gleaning in the field that belonged to one of her deceased father-in-law's relatives, a man by the name of Boaz. You can read the rest of the story in the Book of Ruth. We will sum up our story with a spoiler (you have been warned!): Naomi encouraged Ruth to request Boaz to act as a "kinsman-redeemer" or "guardian-redeemer" (*goel* in Hebrew) for her. Boaz first went to another relative who was "next in line" to redeem Elimelech's daughter-in-law, and once he had double-checked that he wasn't interested, Boaz agreed to "redeem" Ruth by marrying her.

This was the exchange between Boaz and the elders and all the people at the gate, where he could make the redemption official:

> Then Boaz announced to the elders and all the people, "Today you are witnesses that I have bought from Naomi all the property of Elimelek, Kilion and Mahlon. I have also acquired Ruth the Moabite, Mahlon's widow, as my wife, in order to maintain the name of the dead with his property, so that his name will not disappear from among his family or from his hometown. Today you are witnesses!"
>
> Then the elders and all the people at the gate said, "We are witnesses. May the Lord make the woman who is coming into your home like Rachel and Leah, who together built up the family of Israel. May you have standing in Ephrathah and be famous in Bethlehem. Through the offspring the Lord gives you by this young woman, may your family be like that of Perez, whom Tamar bore to Judah."[27]

These four verses contain quite a few names that should be familiar to you. Boaz mentioned Naomi's husband and children, whose property he had purchased. As part of the deal, Boaz "acquired" Ruth as his wife (not a very romantic term for the deal, I agree). The people wished them well, praying that Ruth would build up the family of Israel as Rachel and Leah had done for Jacob, and as Tamar had done for Judah.

The main take-away from this beautiful story of grief turned to hope is that Boaz (the son of Rahab, by the way) provided a way for Ruth to be welcomed into the family of Israel, as well as a way to provide for her first mother-in-law and to have children. All of these things symbolized perfect flourishing in that culture. Ruth went from a widowed, childless foreigner to a married Israelite mother. And her child by Boaz, Obed, would become the father of Jesse and the grandfather of David. Ultimately, Ruth, along with Tamar and Rahab, would be

CHAPTER 26: OLD TESTAMENT OUTSIDERS

counted among the ancestors of Jesus, who was born in the same town, Bethlehem, to which Naomi and Ruth had returned in their grief.

The practice of "redeeming" the land and marrying a widow of a deceased relative is also a beautiful picture of the work of Jesus on behalf of believers. God cared so much about all of his people that he provided a way whereby a relative could pay to release someone from bondage, which may have happened if they owed a debt they couldn't pay themselves (a frequent cause of the form of slavery that was prevalent in the ancient Near East, unlike the race-based slavery that occurred from approximately 1300 to 1900 AD).

According to the Bible, all humans are in "bondage to sin" and cannot free themselves from the bondage (as we discussed in Chapter 21, they are in a state of *non posse non peccare*). They need a third party, a "redeemer," to pay a price, or ransom, to accomplish their freedom from bondage to sin. (Recall how Job's heart yearned for a redeemer, whom he trusted would stand upon earth!) Jesus tells us himself that he is that person who can free people from bondage; he can pay the ransom to release us: "For the son of man also came not to be served but to serve, and to give his life as a ransom for many."[28]

The author of Hebrews, who understood well the Israelite concept of the guardian-redeemer, clarifies:

> Since the children have flesh and blood, [Jesus] too shared in their humanity so that by his death he might break the power of him who holds the power of death—that is, the devil—and free those who all their lives were held in slavery by their fear of death.[29]

But instead of paying a ransom to the one who keeps us in bondage, sin or Satan, Jesus paid the ransom to his Father, because it is the Father whose holiness is offended by sin.[30] By paying the ransom, Jesus removed the barrier that separates humans from their Creator, ensuring that through faith, they transition from *non posse non peccare* to *posse non peccare* in this life, and eventually to the perfect peace of *non posse peccare* for all eternity.

Mephibosheth

Israel's first king, Saul, had four sons by his wife Ahinoam: Jonathan, Abinadab, Malchishua, and Ish-bosheth. Even though Jonathan was the son of Saul, the current king, he had befriended David, whom God had anointed the next king of Israel. Saul was jealous of David, whom he understandably felt was a threat to his rule, and he was thus seeking to kill David. But Jonathan protected David from his father. At one point, Jonathan asked David to "show [him] unfailing kindness like the Lord's kindness" and not to "ever cut off [David's] kindness from his family."[31] The account goes on to say that "Jonathan made a covenant with the house of David."[32]

Jonathan had a son named Mephibosheth, who was only five years old when his grandfather Saul, his father Jonathan, and two of his three uncles (Jonathan's brothers, Abinadab and Malchishua) all died in the Battle of Mount Gilboa. This young son of Jonathan is mentioned briefly in a parenthetical in the midst of the story about the murder of Saul's last surviving son Ish-Bosheth, who had been competing with David for his father's throne:

> (Jonathan son of Saul had a son who was lame in both feet. He was five years old when the news about Saul and Jonathan came from Jezreel. His nurse picked him up and fled, but as she hurried to leave, he fell and became disabled. His name was Mephibosheth.)[33]

So, this aside indicates that Jonathan had a son who became disabled at the age of five. Several years later, when he had become the king of Israel, David asked, "Is there anyone still left of the house of Saul to whom I can show kindness for Jonathan's sake?"[34] When he heard that one son, Mephibosheth, was still alive, David sent for him. The story continues:

> When Mephibosheth son of Jonathan, the son of Saul, came to David, he bowed down to pay him honor.
>
> David said, "Mephibosheth!"
>
> "At your service," he replied.

> "Don't be afraid," David said to him, "for I will surely show you kindness for the sake of your father Jonathan. I will restore to you all the land that belonged to your grandfather Saul, and you will always eat at my table."
>
> Mephibosheth bowed down and said, "What is your servant, that you should notice a dead dog like me?"
>
> Then the king summoned Ziba, Saul's steward, and said to him, "I have given your master's grandson everything that belonged to Saul and his family. You and your sons and your servants are to farm the land for him and bring in the crops, so that your master's grandson may be provided for. And Mephibosheth, grandson of your master, will always eat at my table."

The story ends with this sentence: "And Mephibosheth lived in Jerusalem, because he always ate at the king's table; he was lame in both feet."[35] Notice how the story ends with a restatement of Mephibosheth's handicap. Moreover, the book of 2 Samuel repeats the phrase "eat at the king's table" (or "eat at my table" when David says it) four times. What does this all mean, and how does it relate to Jesus?

Let's start with the covenant that Jonathan made with David, to show him "unfailing kindness like the Lord's kindness" and to "never cut off his kindness to his family." David was fulfilling his promise to his friend Jonathan by looking for his family in order to bless them. Other than this promise, there was absolutely no reason for David to reach out to Saul's grandson, since Saul had tried to kill David and had made David's life very difficult in the final years of his reign before he died. And it was also common practice in those days to kill all descendants of the former king to prevent them from becoming a rival for the throne.

But more than picturing God's fulfillment of his covenant to Abraham's family, the story of Mephibosheth points to grace, which is at the heart of the Gospel message that Jesus came to deliver. Childless women, widows, prostitutes—these were the women in the ancient world who represented the outsider, the hopeless, and the shameful. And in an age when either military prowess, religious piety, many wives and children, or large herds of livestock were the way a man proved his worth, Mephibosheth was the ultimate male outsider.

Though he was born the grandson of the king, at the age of five his grandfather and father, as well as two uncles, were killed in battle. Soon thereafter, his accident resulted in a severe disability that prevented him from walking. He was therefore unable to take part in most activities, not the least of which were military exercises and campaigns in which his brothers, cousins, and friends all participated. He also was probably not an attractive prospect to women, despite being in the royal line, though he apparently did marry, since he had one son, Mikah.[36] Mephibosheth is a picture of the biggest outsider in a family that had been pushed out of the palace and lost their power. For these reasons, he even called himself a "dead dog."

And yet, he ended up eating at the king's table and inheriting the wealth of his grandfather (which rightfully belonged to the new king, David). The ultimate outsider became an insider, eating with the king himself for the rest of his life. A devotional by the nineteenth century preacher, Charles Haddon Spurgeon, describes the analogy:

> Mephibosheth was no great ornament to a royal table, yet he had a continual place at David's board, because the king could see in his face the features of the beloved Jonathan. Like Mephibosheth, we may cry unto the King of Glory, "What is Thy servant, that Thou shouldst look upon such a dead dog as I am?" but still the Lord indulges us with most familiar intercourse with Himself, because He sees in our countenances the remembrance of His dearly-beloved Jesus. The Lord's people are dear for another's sake. Such is the love which the Father bears to His only begotten, that for His sake He raises His lowly brethren from poverty and banishment, to courtly companionship, noble rank, and royal provision.[37]

Jesus presented a picture of Mephibosheth at the king's table in his parable of the "great banquet." While he was dining at the house of a Pharisee, he advised the guests on whom to invite to a luncheon or dinner. Jesus said: "But when you give a banquet, invite the poor, the crippled, the lame, the blind, and you will be blessed."[38] One of the guests was inspired to state, "Blessed is the one who will eat at the feast in the

CHAPTER 26: OLD TESTAMENT OUTSIDERS

kingdom of God." In response, Jesus told the story of a man who was preparing a great feast for his friends and neighbors, and when the feast was ready to be served, the man sent his servant to gather all the people who had been invited. But all of the invitees were too busy to attend, and they all had an excuse for why they couldn't make it.

Angry with his closest friends, the man told his servant: "Go out quickly into the streets and alleys of the town and bring in the poor, the crippled, the blind, and the lame."[39] The servant did so, and there was still room for more at the table. So the man told the servant: "Go out to the roads and country lanes and compel them to come in, so that my house will be full. I tell you, not one of those who were invited will get a taste of my banquet."[40]

Though Jesus was teaching that his closest friends and brethren have rejected him, he was also making a wider claim that it's the "outsiders" who are more likely to respond to his invitation—to receive his free gift of eternal life—not those who are in positions of power and authority because they have followed all the rules and "pulled themselves up from their own bootstraps." Those who are more likely to recognize their *inability* to earn a place in heaven will be the ones who are more likely to seize the free ticket to the banquet.

The Jewish people had long anticipated the day when the Messiah would come, and the wedding feast had become a symbol of the joy and celebration that would take place when God came to rescue his people once and for all. As mentioned in Chapter 22, Isaiah makes this prophecy regarding that day:

> On this mountain the Lord Almighty will prepare
>   a feast of rich food for all peoples,
> a banquet of aged wine—
>   the best of meats and the finest of wines.
> On this mountain he will destroy
>   the shroud that enfolds all peoples,
> the sheet that covers all nations;
>   he will swallow up death forever.
> The Sovereign Lord will wipe away the tears
>   from all faces;
> he will remove his people's disgrace
>   from all the earth.[41]

In the Book of Revelation, the apostle John had a vision of the day when Jesus comes again and fully establishes the "Kingdom of God" in the new heavens and the new earth. After John heard a multitude shouting from heaven that "the wedding of the Lamb has come and his bride has made herself ready," an angel said to him, "Write this: Blessed are those who are invited to the wedding supper of the Lamb!"[42]

Like Mephibosheth, who could never have earned a place at the king's table on his own, those of us who receive the free ticket to God's banquet will dine with the King. We won't just be outsiders with a rare chance to eat with an insider. We will be, to use Jesus' words, "God's children"—the ultimate insiders, and for all eternity. Mephibosheth, who was lame in both feet, had a seat at the table of the king. Likewise, those who recognize their inability to stand in God's presence under their own effort but instead simply trust in Jesus and his "new covenant of grace," will have a seat at the table of the King of the universe forever.

NAAMAN

The last outsider we will discuss in this chapter—but by no means the last one we could discuss—is a man who had almost every reason to be considered an insider. Here is how he is introduced in 2 Kings:

> Now Naaman was commander of the army of the king of Aram. He was a great man in the sight of his master and highly regarded, because through him the Lord had given victory to Aram. He was a valiant soldier, *but he had* leprosy.[43]

In the original Hebrew text, the words "but he had" aren't there, and the flattering description of Naaman ends abruptly with the word "leprous," as if it were a big red stamp that covered the rest of his excellent qualifications. Here we have one of the most powerful and impressive men in all of Syria, the second in command to the Syrian king, who had won many victories in battle against the Assyrians—and even in raids against Israel—and yet he had a disease that would make people avoid him.

The Hebrew word, *tsara'ath*, is translated as "leprosy" 68 times in the Bible and refers to a range of skin conditions, perhaps not even

CHAPTER 26: OLD TESTAMENT OUTSIDERS

including Hansen's disease, the disease known as "leprosy" today. But the commonality of these various skin conditions was that close contact with a leper could result in the spread of the disease. The Jews had strict laws to prevent the spread of contagious skin diseases, even requiring lepers to cry out, "Unclean! Unclean!" as they walked through town in order to warn others to stay out of their way. Lepers were also required to dress in black and wear a hood that covered their face. Moreover, they were also excluded from their community and gathered together outside the city walls, where they often appeared begging on the side of the road.

Naaman is a portrait of the "almost perfect" insider with "just one problem" that made him an outsider, even in his own nation. Fortunately, an Israelite slave girl (probably one he had captured in his own raids on Israel) lived in his house and had heard that Naaman had tried everything to cure his disease. Thus, this Hebrew girl said to her mistress, Naaman's wife: "If only my master would see the prophet who is in Samaria! He would cure him of his leprosy."[44]

Naaman, desperate for any potential source of healing, decided it was worth a trip to Samaria (Israel) to inquire about healing. He took "ten talents of silver, six thousand shekels of gold and ten sets of clothing," along with a letter to the king of Israel from his boss, the king of Syria (Ben-Hadad). The letter stated, "With this letter I am sending my servant Naaman to you so that you may cure him of his leprosy."[45] As soon as the king of Israel (Jehoram) read the letter, he tore his robes, indicating his distress at being asked to do something that only God could do. (He probably feared that Ben-Hadad was using this occasion as a reason to wage war on Israel.)[46]

When he received the news that the king was distressed, Elisha the prophet sent for Naaman. Naaman's chariots headed over to Elisha's place, where Elisha didn't even open the door to greet him, as if to send the message that Elisha served a greater "boss" than Naaman's. Instead, he sent a messenger to Naaman with these instructions: "Go, wash yourself seven times in the Jordan, and your flesh will be restored and you will be cleansed."[47] Naaman was furious, declaring:

> "I thought that he would surely come out to me and stand and call on the name of the Lord his God, wave his hand over the spot and cure me of my leprosy. Are not Abana and Pharpar, the rivers of Damascus, better

than all the waters of Israel? Couldn't I wash in them and be cleansed?"⁴⁸

Naaman was whining because he was being treated in a manner that was not commensurate with his high position. Why had he traveled so far? Just to wash in a river? Why couldn't he have just stayed in his own country, where the rivers were even better? How dare this man not even greet him! Why did he simply send a messenger, and then give such lame instructions?

Fortunately, his aide convinced Naaman not to rush off, asking whether he'd have done "some great thing" if the prophet told him it would cure him. (Of course he would have—washing in the river just wasn't "impressive enough" for a man of Naaman's high rank.) So, probably dragging his feet and pouting all the way, Naaman took his aide's advice and figured he may as well try. He went down to the Jordan River and dipped himself in the water seven times (remember that seven is the biblical number for perfection), as Elisha had instructed him, "and his flesh was restored and became clean like that of a young boy."⁴⁹

Naaman was impressed, even to the point of exclaiming, "Now I know that there is no God in all the world except in Israel." He insisted on giving Elisha a gift in exchange for the healing, but Elisha refused and sent Naaman on his way. (In contrast, Elisha's servant Gehazi snuck away to follow Naaman and did ask him for a gift, a deceitful request that resulted in his own acquisition of leprosy.) Elisha granted Naaman his request to take two mule loads of Israeli soil back with him to Syria so that he could always place his knees on the soil of the true God of Israel when he was only pretending to bow down to the Aramean gods. Basically, he wanted to be a believer in Yahweh but to keep it secret.⁵⁰

So, what does it all mean? And how does this odd story about a Syrian general with bad skin point to Jesus? Let's start with the Israelite slave girl, who despite being stolen from her homeland, cared enough about her master that she recommended he go to see the prophet in Israel. Why would Naaman believe a slave girl from a foreign country? The answer is not in the text, but she must have lived a life that was an indication of her faith in the God of Israel. Naaman most likely trusted her recommendation because she reflected the kindness and confident poise of someone who trusted her God was taking care of her despite her terrible circumstances.

Note Naaman's typical *modus operandi*: he was a powerful man with a problem, so he loaded his chariots with expensive gifts, had the Syrian king write him a letter of recommendation, and headed out to discuss the matter with the king of Israel. He must not have heard the slave girl instruct him to go to the "prophet," not the king. Naaman may not have known how to find the prophet, but he immediately assumed the king would have the power to heal him. Instead he managed to threaten the Israelite king, who tore his clothing because he was so upset by Naaman's request.

Then Naaman's pride was bruised when Elisha didn't treat him the way he felt he deserved to be treated. He also found Elisha's instructions demeaning, and perhaps believed the prescription was too simple—Elisha must not be as powerful as people claimed he was. Washing in the river was all it would take to cure him of a disease no one else could cure? Anyone can wash in the river; Naaman was "good enough" to do something far more demanding. Naaman wanted to do "some great thing" to obtain his healing. After all, he felt he was quite capable of attaining this healing through his own efforts.

Many commentators have noted that leprosy is a symbol of sin throughout the Bible. It starts on the inside, but eventually manifests itself on the surface, like a scab or scale on your skin. It affects all people, regardless of social status. Even the powerful, wealthy, and famous can be afflicted by it. The more serious form of this group of skin diseases was incurable in the ancient world, just as there is no worldly cure for sin. The cleansing rituals for leprosy were analogous to the cleansing rituals that the priests practiced as a way to "become cleansed from sin" before a holy God. The less serious types of skin diseases lasted only a few years, so if someone was fortunate enough to have this type and waited long enough, he could have his skin inspected by a priest in order to be declared "clean." In an analogous manner, anyone who had sinned was required to offer sacrifices in order to be made "clean."

Because it kills the nerve endings in one's extremities, lepers would often injure themselves because they cannot detect pain. They wouldn't notice that they've put their foot in a fire, for example, until they smelled the burning flesh. Similarly, sin deadens our sensitivity to our need for God in order to experience true, deep-seated joy, and instead we look to things of this world that never satisfy for very long. It makes us callous and hard-hearted, causing us to refuse to humble ourselves and admit our need for outside help. Our sin causes spiritual blindness that makes us think we are "good enough" to go to heaven based on our own efforts.

Lepers were basically considered "dead men walking." Even though they were physically alive, their exclusion from society and their treatment by non-lepers made them feel dead (with regards to touching, the same rules applied to lepers as to corpses). Similarly, because of sin, humans are spiritually dead until they are "born again of the spirit," as Jesus explained in John 3. Moreover, just as this disease separates the leper from the rest of the community, sin separated humans from their perfectly holy Creator. The cleansing of a leper and his or her restoration to the community were symbols of forgiveness of sins, which restores the person to a right relationship with God.

Naaman was an insider who suffered from the same problem that makes all humans "outsiders" with respect to God. Even though he had everything—power, fame, success, money, good looks (his name meant "delightful, pleasant, beautiful")—he was unclean. He wanted to use his clout and his own strength to make himself clean, but the only way to receive cleaning was to do something simple, wash in the Jordan River.

Centuries later, we read the following story about another cleansing in the Jordan River:

> And so John the Baptist appeared in the wilderness, preaching a baptism of repentance for the forgiveness of sins. The whole Judean countryside and all the people of Jerusalem went out to him. Confessing their sins, they were baptized by him in the Jordan River.[51]

Though the action of baptism was not what actually cleansed a person from sin, it was a sign of the internal cleansing that takes place when someone trusts in Jesus for eternal life (salvation from sin and death). While God could have healed Naaman without having him dip himself in the Jordan seven times, this method of cleansing pointed forward to the only truly effective form of cleansing and the only way to restore humans to a reconciled relationship with their Creator: faith in Jesus. Something so simple, something any person can do—even a hardened criminal on his deathbed—is offensive to those of us who want to do it our own way or who think that we can earn it. But it really is that simple. So simple that our pride resists it.

Fortunately, Naaman had a slave girl and an aide to point him in the right direction, and the God of Israel gave even this rich, powerful, and prideful foreigner the free gift he offers us all, if we'd only take it and not

CHAPTER 26: OLD TESTAMENT OUTSIDERS

pass up the offer. Jesus himself insisted that John the Baptist baptize him in the Jordan River in order "to fulfill all righteousness."[52] Even though Jesus had never sinned, he wanted to live the perfect life on behalf of his followers, and this perfect life includes baptism. So even though those who have faith in Jesus receive forgiveness of sins, placing them at the "starting line" of a righteous life, they also are "imputed" Jesus' perfect life, which takes them to the "finish line" and makes them righteous enough to live in God's presence.

Two brothers, both of whom were among Jesus' original twelve disciples, asked Jesus if they could sit at his left and right in heaven. Jesus responded, "You don't know what you are asking. Can you drink the cup I drink or be baptized with the baptism I am baptized with?"[53] When they replied that they could, they demonstrated their misunderstanding of what it would require to do so. Jesus was referring to the "cup of wrath," which symbolized God's judgment on sin.[54]

Jesus drank this cup on the cross, when God the Father removed his presence from God the Son, and when Jesus received the penalty for the sin of all humans who trust in him. On the cross, Jesus suffered more than just having to hang from a cross of wood with spikes through his wrists and feet. The infinite pain of drinking God's cup of wrath fell like a hammer on Jesus. He drank the cup outside the city gates, and in so doing, he was able to rescue his followers from the bondage of sin, causing them to transition from outsiders estranged from God to the ultimate insiders who can sit at the king's table in heaven.

Peter makes this point in his letter to Christians who had been dispersed to various Roman provinces in Asia Minor in the first century:

> For Christ also suffered once for sins, the righteous for the unrighteous, to bring you to God. He was put to death in the body but made alive in the Spirit. After being made alive, he went and made proclamation to the imprisoned spirits—to those who were disobedient long ago when God waited patiently in the days of Noah while the ark was being built. In it only a few people, eight in all, were saved through water, and this water symbolizes baptism that now saves you also—not the removal of dirt from the body but the pledge of a clear conscience toward God. It saves you by the resurrection

of Jesus Christ, who has gone into heaven and is at God's right hand—with angels, authorities and powers in submission to him.[55]

Jesus went through the "baptism" of God's judgment (just as Noah did in his ark), so that we may be cleansed of sin, a cleansing symbolized by water baptism. The ultimate insider, Jesus, drank the cup of divine judgment for us, so that by faith in him, we outsiders can become insiders in the eternal Kingdom of God—not through our own insufficient work, but through faith alone in the sufficient work of Jesus.

Questions for Comprehension and Discussion

1. What had the Israelites done to qualify them to become God's chosen people, whom he set apart from other nations?
2. Why did Tamar believe she had a right to a child in the line of Judah? What had been done to her to cause her to feel wronged? How are Tamar's sinful actions evidence that she had faith that God wanted to use her? How did God use Tamar, despite her sin?
3. In what ways was Rahab an outsider? And how did she demonstrate faith in the God of Israel? What is the symbolism of the scarlet cord that Rahab hung in her window?
4. What are some ways that Rahab points to the future salvation of non-Jewish people?
5. How did Ruth display faith in the God of Israel, before she even set out on the journey back to Israel with her mother-in-law?
6. What is a "guardian-redeemer," and why would God set up this means of helping people who have fallen into debt and/or poverty? How does the guardian-redeemer point to Jesus?
7. How was Mephibosheth an outsider, especially with respect to King David? Why did David give Mephibosheth a seat at the king's table, and how is this analogous to sinful humans feasting with God for eternity?
8. How is Naaman an "insider with one problem that makes him an outsider"?

CHAPTER 26: OLD TESTAMENT OUTSIDERS

9. How is Naaman symbolic of all humans, and how is his cleansing in the Jordan River symbolic of what salvation by faith in Jesus accomplishes?
10. Why did Jesus have to be baptized? Why did he have to drink the cup of wrath? What is the significance of these two actions for a believer?

CHAPTER 26 ENDNOTES

1. Martin Luther, "Preface to the Old Testament," in *Luther's Works*, vol. 35, E. Theodore Bachmann, ed. (Philadelphia: Muhlenberg, 1960), 235-26.
2. Gregory the Great, *Commentary of the Blessed Book of Job*, available online at http://faculty.georgetown.edu/jod/texts/moralia1.html.
3. Matthew 19:14.
4. Deuteronomy 7:6.
5. Deuteronomy 7:7. All emphases in Bible passages are mine.
6. See the story of Shadrach, Meshach, and Abednego in Daniel 2:48-3:30.
7. See Ruth 4:18-22.
8. See Matthew 1.
9. Genesis 38:25.
10. Genesis 37:32.
11. Ephraim Chamiel, *To Know Torah: Volume 1, The Book of Genesis* (Jerusalem: Mendele Electronic Books, 2018), 198.
12. See the story in Numbers 13:26-33.
13. Joshua 2:1b.
14. Leviticus 21:7-14; Deuteronomy 23:18; Judges 11:1; and 1 Kings 3:16.
15. Hebrews 11:31; James 2:25.
16. Joshua 6:25.
17. James 2:24-25.
18. See John 14:6 and Acts 4:12.
19. John 1:29.
20. See Romans 11.
21. Ephesians 5:25.
22. John 3:29.
23. Revelation 21:2.
24. 2 Corinthians 5:17.
25. Ruth 1:16-17.
26. Leviticus 19:9-10.
27. Ruth 4:9-12.
28. Mark 10:45.

29. Hebrews 2:14-15.
30. Wayne Grudem, *Systematic Theology: An Introduction to Biblical Doctrine* (Grand Rapids, MI: Zondervan, 1994), 580.
31. 1 Samuel 20:14-15.
32. 1 Samuel 20:16.
33. 2 Samuel 4:4.
34. 2 Samuel 9:1.
35. 2 Samuel 9:13.
36. 2 Samuel 9:12.
37. Charles Haddon Spurgeon, *Morning and Evening,* May 27 morning devotion, available online at https://www.blueletterbible.org/devotionals/me/view.cfm?Date=0527&Time=am.
38. Luke 14:13.
39. 2 Samuel 14:12b.
40. Luke 14:16-24.
41. Isaiah 25: 6-8.
42. Revelation 19:9.
43. 2 Kings 5:1.
44. 1 Kings 5:3.
45. 1 Kings 5:6.
46. Kenneth L. Barker and John R. Kohlenberger III, *NIV Bible Commentary, Volume 1: The Old Testament* (Grand Rapids, MI: Zondervan, 1994), 543.
47. 1 Kings 5:10.
48. 1 Kings 5:11-12.
49. 2 Kings 5:14.
50. Barker and Kohlenberger, *NIV Bible Commentary,* 543.
51. Mark 1:4-5.
52. Matthew 3:15.
53. Mark 10:38.
54. See Job 21:20; Isaiah 51:17; Jeremiah 25:15; and Revelation 14:10, 16:19.
55. 1 Peter 3:18-22.

This is the significance of the Passover for the Israelite. But it has a message also for the conscience and the heart of all mankind.... God's protest against unrighteousness, whether individual or national. Wrong, it declares, may triumph for a time, but even though it be perpetrated by the strong on the weak, it will meet with its inevitable retribution at last.

—Morris Joseph, Jewish rabbi, teacher, and writer[1]

Therefore do not let anyone judge you by what you eat or drink, or with regard to a religious festival, a New Moon celebration or a Sabbath day. These are a shadow of the things that were to come; the reality, however, is found in Christ.

—Paul, in his letter to the Colossians[2]

27

Spring and Summer Feasts

We've seen in the last four chapters that God uses visual aids and stories to teach his people about him: how to know him, how to relate to him, and how to spend eternity with him. God uses the symbolism of objects, such as Noah's ark and the tabernacle, as well as characters in the stories recorded in the Hebrew Scriptures, ranging from Adam and Eve to the Syrian general, Naaman.

Through these symbols and stories, God teaches us that he originally made the world to be good, and he originally made the humans in that world to be "very good." But Adam and Eve chose to disobey God and "be their own gods" and were consequently kicked out of the Garden of Eden. Thereafter, "East of Eden," their descendants were devoted to their own wills, such that "everyone did what was right in his own eyes."[3] The result was—and still is—turmoil, conflict, hatred, racism, warfare, deception, murder—the list goes on.

But God intervened in history and set his affection on the descendants of a man named Abraham. They became God's people, "set apart to be holy, just as God himself is holy."[4] And God uses stories of people who are obedient—but also inevitably disobedient—to show us that no one can be as perfectly holy as he is, and if we want to live in his presence, we can't cleanse ourselves—we need a way to *be made* clean. He also uses stories of outsiders who become insiders to show us how we, as outsiders to heaven, can become the *ultimate* "insiders" and live in perfect peace in his presence for all eternity.

In the next two chapters, we'll discuss one more way God teaches us about his plan to rescue fallen humans from the consequences of their choice to live without him. In order to remind them about what he has done for them and point forward to what he will do for them in Jesus, God instructed his people to observe annual feasts, or festivals. The fulfillment of the Jewish festivals in Jesus is additional evidence that God is teaching his people—and the rest of the world through them—about his plan to restore them from "the fall," to rescue them from the evil of this world, and to give them everlasting life in the absence of sin, evil, pain, disease, and death.

THE HEBREW CALENDAR

Today we use the Gregorian calendar, named after Pope Gregory, who introduced it in 1582. This calendar is based on two astronomical events: the rotation of the earth on its axis, which takes one day, and the revolution of the earth around the sun, which takes 365¼ days. For this reason, the calendar has 365 days in a year for three years, and every fourth year is a "leap year" that has one extra day tacked on at the end of February.[5]

The Jewish calendar is based on these two astronomical events, plus one more: the revolution of the moon around the earth, which takes 29½ days. Dividing 365¼ days in a solar year by 29½ days in a lunar month results in 12.4 lunar months in a solar year. In other words, the moon goes around the earth 12.4 times in the time that the earth goes around the sun once.

So that the number of days in each month is a whole number, the twelve Hebrew months have either 29 days or 30 days. Each month starts at sunset on the day of the New Moon, or *Rosh Chodesh*. These months are:

1. Nisan   falls in March and April
2. Iyyar   falls in April and May
3. Sivan   falls in May and June
4. Tammuz   falls in June and July
5. Ab   falls in July and August
6. Elul   falls in August and September
7. Tishri   falls in September and October
8. Marchesvan   falls in October and November

9.	Kislev	falls in November and December
10.	Tebeth	falls in December and January
11.	Shebat	falls in January and February
12.	Adar	falls in February and March

To make up the difference between the length of these twelve months and the time it takes the earth to revolve around the sun, the calendar has two months of Adar ("Adar I" and "Adar II," or "Adar" and "Adar Beit") every two or three years.

In Leviticus 23, God instructed his people to observe seven "appointed feasts," or *Moadim*, on certain days of the Jewish calendar (but the days vary each year when converted to the Gregorian calendar). Every able-bodied Jew was required to travel to Jerusalem for three pilgrimage festivals, or *Regalim*. The three festival seasons and the seven appointed feasts are:[6]

A. Festival of Passover (March or April)
  1. Passover — Pesach — 14 Nisan
  2. Unleavened Bread — Hag NaMatzot — 15-21 Nisan
  3. Firstfruits — Reishit — 16 Nisan

B. Festival of Weeks (May or June)
  4. Weeks/Pentecost — Shavuot — 6 Sivan

C. Festival of Booths (September or October)
  5. Trumpets — Rosh Hashanah — 1 Tishri
  6. Day of Atonement — Yom Kippur — 10 Tishri
  7. Booths/Tabernacles — Sukkot — 15-22 Tishri

At the time of Jesus, the Jewish people were also celebrating two additional holidays that weren't instituted in the Book of Leviticus: the Feast of Dedication (*Hanukkah* or *Chanukah*) in November/December and Purim in February/March. We'll cover the spring and summer feasts in this chapter, and then talk about the autumn and winter feasts, along with Hanukkah and Purim, in Chapter 28.

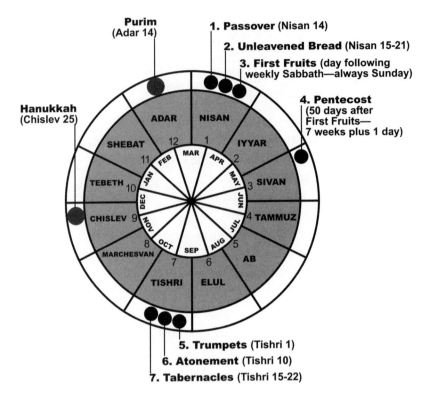

Figure 7: The Jewish Calendar Compared to Gregorian Calendar, with Jewish Feasts

THE PASSOVER (PESACH)

The Hebrew word, *Pesach*, means "to pass over." As we discussed in Chapter 25, God first spoke to Moses out of a burning bush and asked him to approach Pharaoh and request that he release the Israelites, who had been enslaved by the Egyptians for four hundred years. Pharaoh refused to let the Israelites go, even after God caused nine plagues to wreak havoc on Egypt.

After the ninth plague, Pharaoh continued to deny the Israelites freedom. So God gave these instructions to Moses and his brother Aaron: "This month is to be for you the first month, the first month of your year."[7] That was the new moon of the first month of Nisan. On the tenth day of this first month, the Israelites were to find one lamb for each household. But not just any lamb. It had to be a one-year-old male, completely devoid of any defect. Then, on the fourteenth day of the month, they were to slaughter the lamb at twilight. The instructions continue: "Then they are to take some of the blood and put it on the sides and tops of the doorframes of the houses where they eat the lambs."[8]

On the same evening on the fourteenth day of Nisan, when the moon was full, the family in the household would roast the lamb over a fire and eat the meat, along with "bitter herbs" and bread that contained no yeast. They were not to leave any of the leftovers to the next morning. God also gave his people instructions about how they were to eat the lamb: "[You must eat it] with your cloak tucked into your belt, your sandals on your feet and your staff in your hand," and they were to "eat it in haste; it is the Lord's Passover."[9] God described what he would do that night:

> "On that same night I will pass through Egypt and strike down every firstborn of both people and animals, and I will bring judgment on all the gods of Egypt. I am the Lord. The blood will be a sign for you on the houses where you are, and when I see the blood, I will pass over you. No destructive plague will touch you when I strike Egypt. This is a day you are to commemorate; for the generations to come you shall celebrate it as a festival to the Lord—a lasting ordinance."[10]

And, as he had warned his people, the Lord struck down the firstborn child of every family in Egypt, "from the firstborn of Pharaoh, who sat on the throne, to the firstborn of the prisoner, who was in the dungeon."[11] The households where the firstborn child survived—whether they were rich or poor, Egyptian or Israelite—had one thing in common: they had slaughtered a year-old male lamb, put the blood on their door frames, and eaten it. The Israelites ate in haste, with their cloaks tucked into their belts and their sandals at the ready, for they were rushing to flee Egypt and follow Moses out of slavery and toward the land God had promised them. This exit from Egypt is called the "Exodus," which is also the name of the biblical book that contains this story about the Israelites' rescue from slavery.

Nearly two millennia later, John the Baptist, who had been called to "prepare the way for the Lord," saw Jesus approach him for the first time and made these startling claims:

"Look, the Lamb of God, who takes away the sin of the world! This is the one I meant when I said, 'A man who comes after me has surpassed me because he was before me.' I myself did not know him, but the reason I came baptizing with water was that he might be revealed to Israel."[12]

Fast forward three years, and Jesus was celebrating Passover with his twelve disciples, one of whom would betray him that night. Jesus told them, "I have eagerly desired to eat this Passover with you before I suffer. For I tell you, I will not eat it again until it finds fulfillment in the kingdom of God."[13] Jesus was most likely making a reference to the Messianic banquet that Isaiah prophesied in Isaiah 25 and that he himself had mentioned in the parable of the Great Banquet, which we discussed in the last chapter.

The wine and the bread had always been a part of the Passover meal, and for the last two millennia, they have been integral parts of the Christian practice of the "Lord's Supper." Let's first discuss the bread. At the "Last Supper" before his crucifixion, Jesus gave his disciples the unleavened bread, saying, "This is my body given for you; do this in remembrance of me."[14] What is Jesus saying here?

Participants in the traditional Passover meal, called the Passover Seder, each break a piece of *matzah* or *matzo* (unleavened bread) in half, eat half, and then hide the other half in a cloth. In more recent times, they hide it throughout the room for the children to find. At the end of the meal, or when all of the pieces have been found for the children's game, the hidden halves are returned to the participants and eaten as a dessert.

The hidden half of matzah is called the *afikomen*, a Greek word that means "coming later" or "the coming one." Many Jews believe that it symbolizes the ultimate redemption from suffering, while others believe it is a reference to the Passover sacrifice that used to be made at the temple. Still others believe it signifies the importance of setting aside something for one's next meal, especially considering how often the Israelites have suffered from hunger. But many Jews who have become Christians believe that there is an unmistakable analogy between the afikomen and Jesus, described in the following way on the "Jews for Jesus" website:

We know that our Messiah's sinless body was "broken" in death, wrapped in a cloth and hidden as in burial, then brought back; resurrected by the power of God. It is truly a reward to those who find and partake in the life He offers. Yet the amazing parallels we see in the traditions of the afikomen remain hidden to those who reject Jesus' claims.[15]

Jesus clearly stated that the bread was a symbol of his body, which would be broken for those he came to save.

Now to the wine. At four points in the prescribed order of the Passover Seder program, four cups of wine are served. After they have eaten the supper, the participants drink from the third cup. At the Last Supper with his disciples, it was after they had eaten supper when Jesus raised the cup (that is, the third cup) and claimed: "This cup is the new covenant in *my* blood, which is poured out for you."[16] This third cup had always been referred to as the "Cup of Redemption." It symbolized the blood that had been shed when the lambs at the first Passover in Egypt were killed in order to "redeem" the lives of the eldest sons. If the blood of the lamb was on the doorpost, the eldest son was spared. At the Last Supper, Jesus was making it clear that he came to shed *his own* blood to redeem his people, and the third cup no longer pointed to the lambs killed for the first Supper. The Passover lamb had merely been a symbol to teach the people about God's ultimate plan of redemption. Just as a lamb was sacrificed annually during the time of the Old Covenant of works, Jesus shed his own blood on the cross in order to instigate a New Covenant of grace. Through his one-time sacrifice, Jesus provides eternal life to all who trust in him.

But what about the lamb served at the Last Supper? When you read the Gospel accounts of the Last Supper,[17] you'll notice that the traditional lamb was missing from the final Passover meal that Jesus shared with his disciples. Dr. Timothy Keller offers this explanation:

> Jesus' last meal with his disciples departed from the script in another way too. When Jesus stood up to bless the food, he held up the bread. All Passover meals had bread. He blessed the wine—all Passover meals had wine. But not one of the Gospels mentions a main course. There is

no mention of lamb at this Passover meal. Passover was not a vegetarian meal, of course. What kind of a Passover would be celebrated without lamb?

To most of us when we read about the Last Supper, we don't notice the missing main course. But Keller clarifies the stunning reason for its absence:

> There was no lamb *on* the table because the Lamb of God was *at* the table. *Jesus* was the main course.[18]

At the very first Passover meal, a lamb was slain and eaten, and the meal was immediately followed by freedom from physical slavery. Soon thereafter, the Israelites received the law on Mount Sinai, which ushered in the Old Covenant. But Jesus explained at his final Passover meal that he came to be the ultimate Lamb, and in so doing, he ushered in the New Covenant, through which believers in him would be released from slavery to sin and death. They would gain the ultimate freedom, but this time through faith alone, not through obedience to the law.

There is one final interesting tradition associated with the Jewish celebration of Passover. Because the majority of Jewish families in modern times don't even eat lamb at the Passover Seder, the only remaining aspect of the current Passover celebration that references the lamb is the *zeroa*, which can be either a roasted shank of lamb or a roasted chicken wing or neck. For Jews, the *zeroa* symbolizes the lamb that was slain as a sacrifice for sin. Many Jews serve the *zeroa*, but do not touch it or eat it during the meal because it was forbidden to make this sacrifice outside of the temple, and, since the temple had been destroyed in AD 70, they didn't want to give any impression that they had done so.

The same Hebrew word, *zeroa*, can be translated as "arm." Isaiah uses this word when he explains the coming "suffering servant" with these words: "Who has believed our message and to whom has the arm [*zeroa*] of the Lord been revealed?"[19] John refers to this verse in his Gospel:

> Even after Jesus had performed so many signs in their presence, they still would not believe in him. This was to fulfill the word of Isaiah the prophet: "Lord, who has believed our message and to whom has the arm of the Lord been revealed?"[20]

While Jews today believe the *zeroa* at the Seder meal represents the Passover sacrifice of a lamb, many Jews don't see its relevance to Jesus, whose death on their behalf is what the original symbol of the sacrificial lamb represented. God sent his Son as a way to reveal himself to and redeem his chosen people, yet many of them did not—and still do not—believe his message.

Jews claim that Passover is a celebration of freedom and a time to think about how others suffer, especially Jews who have suffered persecution for their faith throughout history. Christian Jews, also known as "Messianic Jews," would agree. Passover *is* a symbol of freedom, but it's not merely a symbol of freedom from the political systems and racial prejudices of this world. Passover represents the sacrifice that God made of *himself* in the person of the Son, so that all who trust in him will receive the free gift of complete forgiveness of their sins, and as a result, be freed from the worst oppressors of the human race—sin and death—for all eternity.

THE FEAST OF UNLEAVENED BREAD (HAG HAMATZOT) AND THE FEAST OF FIRSTFRUITS (REISHIT)

The Feast of Unleavened Bread starts on the day after Passover (a Sunday) and lasts for seven days through the next Saturday, which Jews call the *Sabbath* or *Shabat*. And the Feast of Firstfruits was celebrated on the first Sunday after Passover. After these two feasts the Spring pilgrimage festival concluded for the year.

These are God's instructions regarding the Feast of Unleavened Bread:

> On the fifteenth day of that month the Lord's Festival of Unleavened Bread begins; for seven days you must eat bread made without yeast. On the first day hold a sacred assembly and do no regular work. For seven days present a food offering to the Lord. And on the seventh day hold a sacred assembly and do no regular work.[21]

As a continuation of the Passover, this seven-day feast celebrated the Exodus of the Israelites from slavery in Egypt and the beginning of their history as a nation. It coincided with the end of the rainy season

CHAPTER 27: SPRING AND SUMMER FEASTS

and the beginning of the harvest season. The first crop to be harvested was barley (you will recall that Ruth returned with her mother-in-law in time for the barley harvest). On the second day of the seven-day Feast of Unleavened Bread, the people were to take the first ripe sheath of barley from that year's harvest—the "firstfruits"—and offer it to the Lord as a sign that they were dedicating the entire harvest to him. This required faith on the part of the Israelites, as this was the beginning of the season, and they were giving God the first part of the harvest, not knowing whether there would be much more to follow.

During the day of Passover and the seven days of the Feast of Unleavened Bread, the people were to eat no bread that contained leaven (yeast). They were even careful to only use utensils that had never touched leaven. The bread could not contain yeast because the Israelites had to leave Egypt in haste (hence their tucking their cloak into their belt during the meal and wearing sandals to be ready for departure). Leavened bread takes too long to rise before eating, and bread made without yeast lasts longer, making it more appropriate for a long trip. Some Jews also claim that the bread without leaven (*matzah* or *matzo*) also symbolizes the importance of humility—not getting "puffed up" with pride. In fact, in order to keep the matzo from puffing up from air bubbles, a special tool is used that pricks the matzo dough to pop the bubbles. This results in the lines of dotted holes that are typical of matzo.

In the New Testament, two verses clarify that leaven also represents sin, the cause of which in most every case is pride (putting oneself before others). Jesus issued this warning to his disciples: "Be on your guard against the yeast of the Pharisees, which is hypocrisy."[22] And Paul provides this admonishment to the church in Corinth: "Your boasting is not good. Don't you know that a little yeast leavens the whole batch of dough?"[23]

As we discussed in Chapter 18, Jesus called himself "the bread that comes down from heaven and gives life to the world," and more succinctly, he called himself "the bread of life." Not only is Jesus the fulfillment of the bread that fed the Israelites in the wilderness—the *manna*—but he is also the fulfillment of the unleavened bread of the Passover meal, since he was without sin, and therefore able to make atonement for all sinners. Even though Jesus never sinned, he was still tempted in the same ways that all humans are, as the author of the Book of Hebrews explains: "For we do not have a high priest who is unable to empathize with our weaknesses, but we have one [Jesus] who has been tempted in every way, just as we are—yet he did not sin."[24]

Many Messianic Jews (who believe Jesus is indeed the promised Messiah) see further symbolism in the stripes of pricked holes in the matzo served during this holy week. King David and the prophets Isaiah and Zechariah all wrote that the Messiah would be "pierced,"[25] as we discussed in Chapter 21. Isaiah added another detail concerning the Messiah: "By his stripes we are healed."[26] For those who appreciate what Jesus did for them, the stripes and piercings on the matzo bring to mind the stripes that he received with the Roman *flagrum* and the piercings he received during his crucifixion.

Thus, Jesus died on Passover as the one true "sacrificial lamb"; his body was broken, and his blood was poured out for his followers. Not only is he the perfect lamb without blemish, but he is also the bread of life that is free of yeast and was striped and pierced. The mixing of metaphors is intentional—God was making the meaning of his feasts as clear as possible in order to teach his people about the objective Jesus came to accomplish. And through his people's festivals, God would then teach the entire world about his plan for salvation.

The Offering of Firstfruits also points forward to the faith that believers in Jesus must have to obtain eternal life. Just as the Israelites trusted that God would provide the rest of the harvest when they gave the first of it away, those who trust in Jesus have faith that he will provide for them in this life, as well as in the life to come.

Firstfruits falls on the Sunday after the Passover, which is the same day that Jesus rose from the dead. The apostle Paul wrote to his fellow believers that if Jesus had not been raised from the dead, they were to be pitied the most of all people. He then delivered this exciting news: "But Christ has indeed been raised from the dead, the *firstfruits* of those who have fallen asleep (died)."[27] Because Jesus was raised on the day of the Offering of Firstfruits, his resurrection symbolizes the "firstfruits" of many resurrections to come—the resurrections of those who have faith in him.

THE FEAST OF WEEKS (SHAVUOT)

God instructed the Israelites to celebrate the Feast of Weeks seven weeks plus one day (50 days) after Passover. Also called the Feast of Harvest, the Latter Firstfruits, or Pentecost (which means "fifty" in Greek), the feast of *Shavuot* was established in order to present the first offering of new grain from the summer wheat harvest (as opposed to the barley harvest, which was offered at Firstfruits). It was a celebration in which the Israelites expressed their joy and thankfulness to the Lord for the blessings he had bestowed on them. The Jewish people also believe that God gave Moses the Ten Commandments during this time, which is why the feast is also called "Matan Torah," or "Giving of the Law."

Because they compare the Law with "milk and honey," the celebration of this holiday is accompanied by sweet dairy foods, such as cheesecake and cheese blintzes. People decorate their homes with greenery and flowers, symbolizing the harvest and the Torah, also known as a "tree of life." Many Jews read the Book of Ruth on this day, as well as study the Torah, sometimes all night.

In the New Testament, Jesus spent forty day after his resurrection visiting his disciples and teaching them about the kingdom of God and what they needed to know as they would bring the Gospel to all nations. Thus, it was forty-two days after his death on Passover that Jesus "was taken up before their eyes, and a cloud hid him from their sight."[28] Before he ascended, he had told his disciples: "You will receive power when the Holy Spirit comes on you; and you will be my witnesses in Jerusalem, and in all Judea and Samaria, and to the ends of the earth."[29]

Seven days later the disciples gathered to celebrate Shavuot, or Pentecost, in "the upper room," perhaps the same place where they had eaten the Last Supper with Jesus. During this gathering, the Holy Spirit descended on them, described by Luke in this way: "Suddenly a sound like the blowing of a violent wind came from heaven and filled the whole house where they were sitting."[30] Then "tongues of fire" appeared on the heads of the attendees in the upper room, and they began to speak in languages that non-Israelites were able to understand. A crowd of foreigners—"Parthians, Medes and Elamites; residents of Mesopotamia, Judea and Cappadocia, Pontus and Asia, Phrygia and Pamphylia, Egypt and the parts of Libya near Cyrene; visitors from Rome (both Jews and converts to Judaism); Cretans and Arabs"— gathered and were confused and surprised that these Galileans were speaking in words they could understand. Luke writes, "Utterly amazed, they asked: 'Aren't all these who are speaking Galileans? Then how is it that each of us hears them in our native language?'"[31] Something miraculous had happened to these Galilean men on the first Pentecost following Jesus' resurrection.

THE SHORTEST LEAP

For the Jews at least since the time of Jesus, Pentecost has been associated with the giving of the Law, but for the Christians it is associated with the giving of the Spirit. After reminding us that Luke, the author of Acts, had been a companion of the apostle Paul, one commentator explains it this way:

> By [Luke's] stress on Pentecost as the day when the miracle took place, he is also suggesting (1) that the Spirit's coming is in continuity with God's purposes in giving the law, and yet (2) that the Spirit's coming signals the essential difference between the Jewish faith and commitment to Jesus, for whereas the former is Torah-centered and Torah-directed, the latter is Christ-centered and Spirit-directed—all of which sounds very much like Paul.[32]

That is, for the Jews, Pentecost is a celebration of the giving of the Law, which teaches the people about God's holy standards of morality. But for those who follow Jesus, Pentecost is a celebration of the coming of the Spirit to empower them to deliver the message to the world—in all languages—that Jesus has *fulfilled the law* on their behalf. The Old Covenant had been replaced with the New. Once you trust in Jesus' work—his living a sinless life *for you* and dying to take the penalty of your sin *for you*—the Holy Spirit takes residence in your heart. At the moment of conversion, through the influence of the Holy Spirit, believers transition from the state of *non posse non peccare* (it is *not* possible *not* to sin) to the state of *posse non peccare* (it *is* possible *not* to sin), as we discussed in Chapter 24.

Paul sums it up in this way: "Therefore, there is now no condemnation for those who are in Christ Jesus, because through Christ Jesus the law of the Spirit who gives life has set you free from the law of sin and death."[33] By fulfilling the law perfectly, Jesus rescues those who place their faith in him because they recognize their utter inability to fulfill the law on their own. Because what Shavuot pointed to was fulfilled on the first Pentecost after Jesus' resurrection, any person who trusts in Jesus—regardless of their language, racial background, and culture—is freed from sin and given the free gift of eternal life in the presence of their Creator.

So far, we've covered just half of the Hebrew calendar. Let's move on to the fall and winter feasts and continue our discussion of the way the traditional Jewish festivals teach us about God's plan of redemption.

CHAPTER 27: SPRING AND SUMMER FEASTS

QUESTIONS FOR COMPREHENSION AND DISCUSSION

1. What is the difference between the Gregorian calendar that we use today and the Hebrew calendar? Describe the ways the two calendars record the passage of time, and the way they adjust the calendar to ensure that the seasons fall at the same time each year.
2. How many festival seasons are there, and how many feasts were appointed by God in Leviticus?
3. What did the Passover commemorate in the history of the Israelites?
4. What happened if a family did not kill a lamb and put the blood on the doorframe of their home? Did it matter if they were the Pharaoh's family or the family of a prisoner, or if they were Israelite or not?
5. What were the elements of the Passover meal, and how do they point to Jesus? What are the *afikomen* and the *zeroa*?
6. What is the significance that there was no lamb served at the Last Supper Jesus had with his disciples?
7. What two other feasts follow Passover and make up the rest of the spring pilgrimage festival?
8. What is the reason for eating only unleavened bread? What are some ways that the matzo represents the ultimate sacrifice for human sin?
9. What is one way that the Offering of Firstfruits points to Jesus and what he has done for his followers?
10. What is the significance of Pentecost to the Jew, and now to the Christian? What happened on the first Pentecost after Jesus' resurrection? How does the giving of the Law compare to the giving of the Spirit, and how does this describe the way the Old Covenant worked compared to the New Covenant?

CHAPTER 27 ENDNOTES

[1] Morris Joseph, *Judaism as Creed and Life* (Mishawaka, IN: Palala Press, 1919), 212.
[2] Colossians 2:16-17.

THE SHORTEST LEAP

3. Deuteronomy 12:8; Judges 17:6, 21:25; Job 32:1; Proverbs 12:15, 21:2.
4. See Leviticus 11:44-45, 19:2, 24, 20:7, 26, and 21:6. It is reiterated in the New Testament in Ephesians 1:4, Hebrews 12:14, and 1 Peter 1:13-16.
5. To further fine-tune the correlation of the years and seasons, there are no leap years in the years ending in "00" except if that year is divisible by 400. This is necessary because the amount of time it takes to go around the sun is slightly less than 365.25 days, so we skip the leap year once a century for three out of every four centuries. Confused now?
6. See Leviticus 23 for the instructions that God gave to Moses regarding these appointed feasts.
7. Exodus 12:1.
8. Exodus 12:7.
9. Exodus 12:11.
10. Exodus 12:12-14.
11. Exodus 12:29b.
12. John 1:29-31.
13. Luke 22:15-16.
14. Luke 22:19b.
15. David Brickner, "Mysterious Passover Symbols," April 1, 2010. Available online at https://jewsforjesus.org/publications/newsletter/newsletter-apr-2011/mysterious-passover-symbols/.
16. Luke 22:20.
17. See Matthew 26:17-29, Mark 14:12-25, and Luke 22:7-20.
18. Timothy Keller, *Jesus the King, Understanding the Life and Death of the Son of God* (New York: Penguin, 1988). Emphasis mine.
19. Isaiah 53:1.
20. John 12:38.
21. Leviticus 23:6-8.
22. Luke 12:1.
23. 1 Corinthians 5:6.
24. Hebrews 4:15.
25. Psalm 22:16, Isaiah 53:5, and Zechariah 12:10.
26. Isaiah 53:5.
27. 1 Corinthians 15:20.
28. Acts 1:9.
29. Acts 1:8.
30. Acts 2:2.
31. Acts 2:7-11.
32. Kenneth L. Barker and John R. Kohlenberger III, *NIV Bible Commentary, Volume 2: The New Testament* (Grand Rapids, MI: Zondervan, 1994), 387.
33. Romans 8:1-2.

The Midrash says that every blade of grass has an angel that whispers to it, 'Grow, grow!' So there is such an angel that tells us every Rosh Hashanah [Jewish New Year], 'Grow, grow!' You have the power to change and become the person God meant you to be. When we come to High Holy Day services, we need to be aware of our divine power to be a better person.... This is the meaning of Rosh Hashanah.

— Rabbi Dov Peretz and Dr. Arthur Green[1]

We should not be the same person the day after Yom Kippur that we were the day before Yom Kippur. We should be moving ahead, raising our lives to a higher level.

— Rabbi Marc D. Angel[2]

28

Fall and Winter Feasts

In the last chapter, we discussed the Spring and Summer festivals, Passover, the Feast of Unleavened Bread, and the Feast of Firstfruits, which cover one nine-day period (Sabbath through the Sunday after the next Sabbath). We also discussed the Feast of Weeks and Shavuot (or Pentecost), which starts fifty days after Passover. During these feasts, the Jewish people celebrated God's deliverance of their ancestors from slavery and the resulting blessings they receive from God every year, starting with the first of the barley harvest and ending with the first of the wheat harvest.

The fall festivals begin with the New Year, or *Rosh Hashana*, followed by the Day of Atonement, or *Yom Kippur*, ten days later, and then the Feast of Booths, or *Sukkot*, on the day after Yom Kippur. The Feast of Booths celebrates the blessings that God provided the Israelites between the Exodus and the time they crossed the Jordan River to enter the Promised Land. The other two feasts, in contrast, are much more solemn, focusing on the need to perform good works and to repent of one's sins. Let's take a closer look, focusing especially on the symbolism of each festival that finds its fulfillment in Jesus.

THE FEAST OF TRUMPETS (ROSH HASHANAH, THE JEWISH NEW YEAR)

The Feast of Trumpets, or *Rosh Hashanah*, is the first of the two "High Holy Days," the second of which is the Day of Atonement, or *Yom Kippur*, which comes nine days later. Rosh Hashanah takes place on the first day of the seventh month, Tishri (which falls in September and October), and kicks off a ten-day period of repentance and good deeds (also known as *Yamim Noraim*, the "Days of Awe"). Thus, the autumn pilgrimage festival starts on Rosh Hashanah and goes through Yom Kippur.

According to Jewish tradition, God writes the words, deeds, and thoughts of every person in the "Book of Life," and he opens this book on Rosh Hashanah to see how well each person has performed over the previous year. Thus, this holiday gives you an opportunity to reflect on your life, to repent of your sins, and to engage in good works to tip the scale—if necessary—to ensure that your good deeds outweigh your sins. If the good exceeds the bad, then your name will be inscribed for another year in the Book of Life. You therefore start off the New Year with a somewhat "clean slate" (though your sins are still present, just outweighed by your good deeds).

God specifically instructs the Israelites to have a "sacred assembly commemorated with trumpet blasts."[3] The *shofar*, or ram's horn, is the instrument that was used to sound the trumpet blasts 100 times during the synagogue service. The ram's horn was a frequent element of worship in the history of the Israelites, and when the people heard the priests "sound the ram's horn" they understood immediately that it was a time of celebration.

Psalm 81 associates the ram's horn with joy and worship of God:

> Sing for joy to God our strength;
> shout aloud to the God of Jacob!
> Begin the music, strike the timbrel,
> play the melodious harp and lyre.
> Sound the ram's horn at the New Moon,
> and *when the moon is full*, on the day of our festival.[4]

These verses refer to the autumn feasts: the new moon signified the start of the month, which in this month (Tishri) was the Feast of Trumpets. Yom Kippur took place on the tenth day of Tishri (that is, nine days after the Feast of Trumpets), and when the moon became full it was the start of the Feast of Tabernacles, which we will discuss next.

The first time we come across a ram's horn in the Torah is when we read about a ram that had been caught by its horns in a thicket at the summit of Mount Moriah. (By the way, the Torah, or Pentateuch, is the first five books of the Jewish Scriptures, or what Christians call the Old Testament.) Abraham was about to sacrifice his only son, Isaac, but God stopped him before he harmed his son. Abraham then sacrificed the trapped ram as a substitute for Isaac.

Another important event happened on Mount Moriah centuries later. It was on this same mountain that King Solomon built the temple to replace the temporary tabernacle as the symbolic dwelling place of God in the midst of his people. Recall that, after the Exodus, the Israelites wandered in the desert for forty years, packing up, transporting, and setting up the portable, tent-like tabernacle with every move they made. After entering the Promised Land, they finally settled into permanent cities, moved out of their tents, and had "peace on all sides."[5] At that point, Solomon built the temple to replace the tabernacle. The temple on Mount Moriah thus became the new location where the priests made sacrifices to atone for the people's sins.

The second time we come across a ram's horn in Scripture is on another mountain, Mount Sinai, when God explained the manner in which his people, whom he had *already* saved from slavery in Egypt, should approach him. God was going to descend on the mountain to give the law to Moses, and he gave these instructions for how the people should prepare:

> And the Lord said to Moses, "Go to the people and consecrate them today and tomorrow. Have them wash their clothes and be ready by the third day, because on that day the Lord will come down on Mount Sinai in the sight of all the people. Put limits for the people around the mountain and tell them, 'Be careful that you do not approach the mountain or touch the foot of it. Whoever touches the mountain is to be put to death. They are to be stoned or shot with arrows; not a hand is to be laid on them. No person or animal shall be permitted to live.' Only *when the ram's horn sounds a long blast* may they approach the mountain."[6]

Thus, about four hundred years after the ram's horns were caught in the thicket on Mount Moriah, the ram's horn was now a signal that the people could approach the mountain. Prior to the sound of the ram's

CHAPTER 28: FALL AND WINTER FEASTS

horn, they risked their lives to touch the foot of the mountain, but once the ram's horn had sounded, they could approach it, so long as they had "consecrated themselves." Again, we see a picture of God's holiness, like a furnace so hot that sinful humans cannot come near without being instantly incinerated.

The ram's horn was therefore a precious symbol to the Israelites of their ability to approach a perfectly holy God, who had given them instructions for how they could have a relationship with him. In Jesus, we find the fulfillment of the ram's horn. Jesus enables his people to not just approach God, but to *see* God and to *live with him for eternity*. The ram's horn announced to the people that God was now approachable, just as the tearing of the curtain that separated the Holy Place from the Most Holy Place symbolized the removal of the barrier between Jesus' followers and God.

Because Jesus has accomplished his goals of living the perfect life and taking the penalty of death for his followers, it is no longer necessary for his followers to calculate the balance between their good deeds and their sins. Once you trust in Jesus, your sins are forgiven and you are credited with Jesus' perfect life, as if you yourself had lived it. The "scale" is tipped "infinitely" towards good works and away from sins. In one of his poems, King David alluded to this type of transfer when he praised God, who "redeems your life from the pit and crowns you with love and compassion."[7] Through our faith in Jesus, God forgives our sins (he rescues us from a pit we could never escape on our own). And because of his love and compassion, he gives us Jesus' perfect record (he gives us a crown we could never earn on our own).

A few verses later, David writes, "For as high as the heavens are above the earth, so great is his love for those who fear him; and as far as the east is from the west, so far has he removed our transgressions from us."[8] Jesus' life, death, and resurrection demonstrate God's perfect love for his people, his willingness to pay the penalty of sin on their behalf, and therefore allow them to approach his "throne of grace with confidence."[9] Jesus is the fulfillment of Rosh Hashanah, since it is through his atoning sacrifice that he not only tilted his followers' scale towards good deeds and away from sins, but he got rid of the scale entirely (at least as far as salvation is concerned). And as a result, the names of those who place their faith in him are written in the "Lamb's Book of Life"[10] and can never be "blotted out."[11] Cleansed and forgiven, those who trust in Jesus for this salvation will live in God's presence for all eternity.

Many Jewish Christians believe that the *shofar* will sound for the last time to signal the Christian believer's ability to approach God for all eternity. Paul describes the sounding of the final shofar call in this way:

> For we believe that Jesus died and rose again, and so we believe that God will bring with Jesus those who have fallen asleep in him. According to the Lord's word, we tell you that we who are still alive, who are left until the coming of the Lord, will certainly not precede those who have fallen asleep [died]. For the Lord himself will come down from heaven, with a loud command, with the voice of the archangel and *with the trumpet call of God*, and the dead in Christ will rise first. After that, we who are still alive and are left will be caught up together with them in the clouds to meet the Lord in the air. And so we will be with the Lord forever.[12]

The *shofar* has always been and still is a beautiful and joyful sound. And one day its sound will be cause for the ultimate celebration and the reason for the greatest rejoicing! One last point: In addition to Rosh Hashanah, another time when the shofar would sound was at the coronation of a new king. At the time of Jesus' return, the final shofar blast will announce the arrival of the one true King, whose reign will never end.

DAY OF ATONEMENT (YOM KIPPUR)

For ten days after *Rosh Hashanah*, the Jewish people reflect on their sins, repent of them, and try to "make up" for them. Then they celebrate *Yom Kippur*, the Day of Atonement. This day is their most solemn holy day of the year. The word, *Kippur*, which translates to English as "atonement" or "covering," communicates that something must be done in order to reconcile impure humans to their perfectly pure Creator. There is a chasm between mankind and God, a chasm that can only be bridged by the payment of some sort of a penalty for sin and then by living a

CHAPTER 28: FALL AND WINTER FEASTS

perfectly holy life. No human being can cross the chasm—unless he or she can live a sinless life and offer the perfect payment for sin. And we're not talking about a life in which good deeds make up for sins—no sin must be committed at all. It's an impossible goal that no ordinary human could ever achieve.

As we discussed in Chapter 23, the high priest entered the Most Holy Place only once a year, and that was on the Day of Atonement. The entire sixteenth chapter of Leviticus describes the rituals that must take place on this one extremely important day, and the entire twenty-eighth chapter of Exodus describes the garments that the high priest must wear before entering the Most Holy Place. After making the requisite sacrifices and cleansing himself multiple times, the high priest could then take the blood of the sacrifice into the Most Holy Place and sprinkle it (*nazah*, or נָזָה, as we discussed in Chapter 21) on the atonement cover of the ark to pay for the sins of the people for the past year. According to Jewish tradition:

> A chain was tied to the feet of the High Priest, when he entered the Holy of Holies, so that if he dies there they will take him out, since it is forbidden to enter there.... Then [if he exits] there is joy among the higher and lower beings. If not, they were all in sorrow and all knew that their prayer was not accepted."[13]

Upon the high priest's exit from the Most Holy Place, the people felt relief that God had accepted the sacrifice made to cover their sins for the year.

When the Romans destroyed the Jewish temple in AD 70, the high priests could no longer enter the Most Holy Place to atone for the people's sins. Since then, therefore, there have been no sacrifices in the synagogues on Yom Kippur, and prayer, good works, and charitable donations have taken the place of the sacrificial rituals. Interestingly, there is one sacrificial tradition, the *kaparot*, that survives to this day among ultra-orthodox Jews in Israel. In this ceremony, the practitioners swing a chicken over their head, as a symbol of transferring their sins to it. The chickens are then slaughtered as payment for those sins.[14]

Back to the high priest on Yom Kippur. Even after he went through the extreme purification rituals, he was far from clean in relation to a holy God. God clearly communicated this in a vision that the prophet Zechariah had of the high priest, Joshua. When Zechariah saw him, Joshua had already gone through the extensive rituals to cleanse himself on Yom Kippur. But even then, Zechariah could see that Joshua's priestly vestments were still filthy, translated literally and more accurately as, *covered in excrement.* In the vision, Satan condemned Joshua, but the angel of the Lord took away his disgusting clothing and, in its place, provided clean vestments for him to wear. Here is an excerpt from Zechariah's account:

> Then he showed me Joshua the high priest standing before the angel of the Lord, and Satan standing at his right hand to accuse him. And the Lord said to Satan, "The Lord rebuke you, O Satan! The Lord who has chosen Jerusalem rebuke you! Is not this a brand plucked from the fire?" Now Joshua was standing before the angel, clothed with filthy garments. And the angel said to those who were standing before him, "Remove the filthy garments from him." And to him he said, *"Behold, I have taken your iniquity away from you, and I will clothe you with pure vestments."* And I said, "Let them put a clean turban on his head." So they put a clean turban on his head and clothed him with garments.... Hear now, O Joshua the high priest, you and your friends who sit before you, for they are men who are a sign: behold, I will bring my servant *the Branch.* For behold, on the stone that I have set before Joshua, on a single stone with seven eyes, I will engrave its inscription, declares the Lord of hosts, and *I will remove the iniquity of this land in a single day.*"[15]

This is a beautiful picture of how God cleanses the filth of human sin, which still tainted the most "holy" priest in the nation, even after he had gone through the cleansing rituals prescribed by God on Yom Kippur.

Zechariah claimed that the Lord would bring his servant, "the Branch," and would remove the iniquity of the land in one day. As we discussed in Chapters 21, Isaiah prophesied that "a shoot will come up from the stump of Jesse, from his roots a Branch will bear fruit."[16] Zechariah's reference to "the Branch," similarly, was an allusion to the Messiah, who would come to cleanse his people from the filth of sin. By living the perfect life and by dying to take the penalty for the sins of his followers, Jesus removed their iniquity and "clothed them in righteousness" in a single day. That single day was the Sunday when Jesus rose from the dead. At the resurrection of Jesus God accepted the "substitutionary atonement" that Jesus offered for his people.

Another component of the Day of Atonement festival in ancient times was the *Azazel*, literally translated from Hebrew as "the sender away," but now translated as "the scapegoat." These are the instructions regarding this tradition that were given to Aaron, who is generally regarded as Israel's first high priest:

> [The high priest] is to take the two goats and present them before the Lord at the entrance to the tent of meeting. He is to cast lots for the two goats—one lot for the Lord and the other for the scapegoat. Aaron shall bring the goat whose lot falls to the Lord and sacrifice it for a sin offering. But the goat chosen by lot as the scapegoat shall be presented alive before the Lord to be used for making atonement by sending it into the wilderness as a scapegoat.... When Aaron has finished making atonement for the Most Holy Place, the tent of meeting and the altar, he shall bring forward the live goat. He is to lay both hands on the head of the live goat and confess over it all the wickedness and rebellion of the Israelites—all their sins—and put them on the goat's head. He shall send the goat away into the wilderness in the care of someone appointed for the task. The goat will carry on itself all their sins to a remote place; and the man shall release it in the wilderness.[17]

Similar to the lamb that died for the Passover meal on the night the Israelites left Egypt, the scapegoat took "on its head" all of the sins of the Israelite people, such that they themselves would not receive the just penalty for them, which is exclusion from God's presence. The goat was sent into the wilderness as a symbol of what the Israelites deserved for their sin, separation from God.

On many occasions throughout the Old Testament, God makes this statement to his people: "I am the Lord, who brought you up out of Egypt to be your God; therefore be holy, because I am holy."[18] Note two things: first, God commanded his people to be holy *because* he had already rescued them from slavery in Egypt, *not so that* they could earn the rescue. And secondly, he wanted them to be holy—or free from sin—because he himself is holy. He was clarifying that in order for them to live in his presence, his holiness requires that they also be holy. When they aren't holy, God must somehow rid them of their sin in order to dwell in their midst. But because of the scapegoat, the people could continue to live in God's presence, since their sins had been removed from them (symbolically, at this point) and sent with the goat into the wilderness.

In the Book of Hebrews, the author gives a beautiful sermon to an audience of fellow Jews who understood the role of the high priest, especially on Yom Kippur. He encourages his listeners to "hold firmly to the faith" they profess in Jesus, since he is their "great high priest who has ascended into heaven."[19] After this claim that Jesus was their "great high priest," he goes on to explain Jesus' role as such:

> During the days of Jesus' life on earth, he offered up prayers and petitions with fervent cries and tears to the one who could save him from death, and he was heard because of his reverent submission. Son though he was, he learned obedience from what he suffered and, once made perfect, he became the source of *eternal salvation* for all who obey him and was designated by God to be high priest in the order of Melchizedek.[20]

Before proceeding, you'll want to know what is meant by "Melchizedek." In Genesis 14, we read about a mysterious king who blessed Abraham and to whom Abraham gave a tenth of the spoils from the battle he had just won (usually this tenth, or *tithe*, was reserved for God himself). The name Melchizedek translates to "the king of righteousness." The Bible states that Melchizedek was the king of "Salem," the Hebrew word for peace, שָׁלֵם, and thus translates as the "king of peace." In addition to a king, he was a "priest of God Most High." Christians believe Melchizedek symbolized Jesus, and many also believe he actually *was* Jesus, the ultimate prophet, priest, and king, the one to whom all of the other prophets, priests, and kings pointed.

On the Day of Atonement, Jews fasted and spent the day in prayer and petition to God, asked him to forgive their sins, offered sacrifices, and sent a scapegoat into the wilderness in order to rid themselves of the sin that separated them from God. Not only does Jesus fulfill the role of the high priest by offering these prayers and petitions for his people, Jesus fulfills Yom Kippur by also providing the final sacrifice to pay for sin—himself. By suffering and dying in our place, he takes the judgment we deserve. What's more, Jesus also fulfills the scapegoat, since he himself took the penalty for his followers' sins and was sent into the ultimate wilderness—hell itself—so that those who have faith in him won't have to go there (a place of complete separation from God's blessings). Jesus is the great high priest, the righteous king of peace, the perfect Lamb of God, *and* the scapegoat for his people.

Of the many times when God reminded his people to be holy, several times he clarified that it is he himself who makes them holy: "Keep my decrees and follow them. I am the Lord, *who makes you holy.*"[21] This is the Gospel message that Jesus delivers in the New Testament. We cannot ever make ourselves holy enough to live in God's presence—we can only *be made holy* by the free gift of salvation from our holy God.

At the end of the synagogue service on Yom Kippur, the shofar is sounded once again, signaling that the people can approach their God. It is because of the perfect life, the atoning death, and the resurrection of Jesus that the final shofar blast can be sounded, and at that time it will not be sounded for merely symbolic purposes.

THE FEAST OF TABERNACLES (SUKKOT)

The seventh feast that God instituted for his people in Leviticus 23 is *Sukkot,* which commemorated the forty years that the Israelites wandered in the wilderness after God had freed them from slavery in Egypt. It immediately follows the Day of Atonement, and it lasts for a full week from the 15th to the 22nd of Tishri (in September and/or October). The Feast of Tabernacles, also called the Feast of Booths, celebrates the fall harvest as well as God's provision for and protection of his people during the years that they wandered in the wilderness, when they lived in tents (also called booths).

THE SHORTEST LEAP

In ancient times there were two main ceremonies on the last day of Sukkot: First, people carried torches as they marched around the temple, and they lit the giant golden lampstands in the temple courtyard. This ceremony looked forward to the coming of the Messiah, who would, as the prophet Isaiah put it, be "a light for the Gentiles, that [God's] salvation may reach to the ends of the earth."[22] Second, a priest carried water from the Pool of Siloam to the temple, which also looked forward to the coming of the Messiah when, Isaiah also claimed, "the earth will be filled with the knowledge of the Lord as the waters cover the sea."[23]

To celebrate the Feast of Booths, each family constructs a *sukkah*, or booth. The booth is a temporary structure built of only wood or wood and canvas, with a roof of branches and leaves that had enough open space to provide a view of the stars. The family decorates their booth with leaves, fall flowers, fruits, and vegetables, and they eat at least one meal in the booth each day of the week-long festival. They also wave a *lulav* (made of bunches of leaves from certain trees) in all four directions, symbolizing God's presence everywhere.

As mentioned in Chapter 23 when we discussed the tabernacle, Jesus is the fulfillment of the tabernacle and the temple. He is the ultimate expression of "God with his people," and just as there was only one path to the Holy of Holies within the temple, Jesus is the only "way" to eternal life in God's presence. In his Gospel, John draws a parallel to the lights that were lit in the temple when he introduces Jesus: "In him was life, and that life was the light of all mankind."[24] He also records that Jesus said, "I am the light of the world. Whoever follows me will never walk in darkness, but will have the light of life."[25]

Moreover, John reports that it was during the Feast of Tabernacles that Jesus entered the temple courts and began to teach. It was on the last and greatest day of the Festival that Jesus made the following claim, possibly as the priest was bringing the water from the Pool of Siloam to the temple: "Let anyone who is thirsty come to me and drink. Whoever believes in me, as Scripture has said, rivers of living water will flow from within them."[26]

Recall that the prophet Isaiah said, "the Lord himself will give you a sign: the virgin will conceive and give birth to a son, and will call him Immanuel.[27] This word, *Immanuel*, means "God with us."[28] Just as God lived in the midst of his people while they wandered in the wilderness, Jesus came to earth as a human to literally live in the midst of his people.

Moreover, in this life, his Holy Spirit lives within those who place their trust in him,[29] and his followers will also live in his presence for all eternity. Jesus "tabernacled with"[30] humans two millennia ago, and he will do so for all eternity with those who have faith in him.

THE FEAST OF DEDICATION (HANUKKAH) AND PURIM

There are two other feasts that Jews celebrate today, though they were not instituted in the Pentateuch. We will discuss these briefly to round out our discussion of the Jewish festive holidays.

The Feast of Dedication, or *Hanukkah*, is celebrated from sunset on the 25th of Kislev through sunset on the 2nd of Tebeth (in November and/or December). It was instituted as a way to commemorate the victory of the Maccabean Jews over the Greeks and the rededication of the temple in 165 BC. Because Judea had been overtaken by the Seleucid Empire, the foreign king Antiochus Epiphanes ruled over the Jewish people. At the time, they were divided over the issue of assimilation: Some Jews were in favor of adopting Greek culture and becoming more Hellenized. But other Jews wanted to preserve their Jewish traditions and resist assimilation into the Hellenistic culture. The last straw came when the king of the Seleucids decided to replace the Jewish high priest with inappropriate people who had paid him bribes. A rebellion arose among the Jews who wanted to preserve their traditions, and they pitted themselves against the Jews who were in favor of assimilation. For this reason, the Jewish people have considered it more of a civil war than a rebellion.

The Maccabees were a group of brothers who fought against the Seleucid powers, or at least against the Jews who sided with the Seleucids. The two Books of the Maccabees (written in the time between the Old and New Testaments in the second century BC) record the story of this conflict. The outcome of the rebellion was a victory for the supporters of traditional Judaism, and it is this victory that Hanukkah commemorates. After cleansing the temple (because the Seleucids had defiled it), the oil in the lampstand miraculously lasted for eight days, though there had only been sufficient oil for one day of light. For this reason, the Feast of Dedication is also called the "Festival of Lights."

THE SHORTEST LEAP

When Jesus lived in Israel, the people had begun to celebrate the Feast of Dedication, which John references in the tenth chapter of his Gospel.[31] The earliest believers in Christ, many of whom were Jewish, understood the need to remain faithful in the face of persecution, which was the main message of the Feast of Dedication. Many of these Christians went to their deaths in order to remain faithful to Jesus Christ, just as the Maccabees had done to defend the traditions of their faith. And just as the Jews remained faithful to the one true God when the Seleucids defiled their temple and aimed to make them adopt the Greek culture, Christians who were being persecuted encouraged one another to remain faithful to their Lord and Savior, Jesus Christ. In fact, in his Sermon on the Mount, Jesus had praised those who would stand up to persecution:

> "Blessed are you when people insult you, persecute you and falsely say all kinds of evil against you because of me. Rejoice and be glad, because great is your reward in heaven, for in the same way they persecuted the prophets who were before you."[32]

Thus, just as the Jews celebrated the strength and loyalty of the Maccabees in the face of persecution on Hanukkah, Christians celebrate the same strength and loyalty to Jesus when faced with persecution. In his Gospel, John records that it was at the "Feast of Dedication" (Hanukkah) that Jesus made these claims: "My sheep listen to my voice; I know them, and they follow me. I give them eternal life, and they shall never perish; no one will snatch them out of my hand. I and the Father are one."[33] In response to these claims, the Jews picked up stones to kill Jesus, but Jesus was able to escape, for the time had not yet come for him to "lay his life down for his sheep."[34] The Maccabees went willingly to their deaths, trusting that God would bless them for their loyalty. And Christians have gone—and still go—willingly to their deaths, trusting that God will give them eternal life. What is the source of this confident trust? It is the evidence that their "Good Shepherd" went willingly to his own death so that his "sheep" would live again.

The Israelites also celebrate a feast known as Purim on the 14th day of the twelfth month, Adar, or Adar II in leap years (February or March). The feast of Purim was instituted as a way to commemorate the deliverance of the Jewish people while they were in exile in Persia in the fifth century BC.[35] The story is recorded in the book of Esther, which was named after the Jewish queen Esther. She foiled the plot of an evil man named Haman, who had tried to have Esther's husband, the Persian king Xerxes, execute all Jews in his kingdom. (The word "Purim" means "lots," since Haman had cast a lot to determine which day the Jews would be executed, and the lot fell on the twelfth month, Adar.)

Esther had become the Persian king's wife after winning a kingdom-wide beauty contest. In order to protect herself, Esther hid her identity as a Jew. But when her cousin Mordecai warned her of Haman's plot to wipe out the Jewish people in Persia, she risked her life and approached the king without being summoned (an act that could be punishable by death), disclosing to him that she was Jewish and asking him to save her people from Haman's plan. Anticipating that he would execute Mordecai, Haman had even built gallows for the occasion. But in a remarkable turn of events on account of Esther's bravery, the gallows were used to execute Haman instead.

Like Pesach, the Feast of Booths, Hanukkah, and the other festivals, Purim celebrates God's deliverance of his people from their enemies, as well as his provision and protection. Esther pointed forward to another member of a royal family who would not just risk his life for his people but would *give* his life to ensure that they would live. Jesus, the one true King, provided his own life as a payment so that his people would not just survive, but would live forever with him in his palace. The many rescues in the Bible, including the one in the Book of Esther celebrated on Purim, point to Jesus' final rescue of his people from sin and death.

THE SABBATH

The chapter would be incomplete without a discussion of a feast that the Jewish people were to observe once every seven days, the weekly *Shabbat*, or Sabbath. One possible reason that the number seven is considered a divine number is because God rested on the seventh day after six days of creation. Thus, "God blessed the seventh day and made it holy, because on it he rested from all the work of creating he had done."[36]

You'll note that seven is a common number in the feasts: The Feast of Unleavened Bread lasts for seven days. Pentecost happens seven weeks (seven sets of seven days), plus one day, after Passover. Another Jewish tradition was the Sabbath year, the *Shmita*, or שמיטה, which was every seventh year. In addition, the year after seven Sabbath years had passed was the *Jubilee*, or *Yobel*, יוֹבֵל, which happened every fifty years. (The English word "Jubilee" comes from the Hebrew word for the ram's horn, since the year began with the sounding of the ram's horn.) There were many laws concerning the Sabbath years and Jubilee years, for example, laws that required agricultural land to lay fallow, the forgiveness of debts, and the release of indentured servants to a life of freedom. (Interestingly, few people know that God instructed Noah to take with him *seven* pairs of every "clean" animal and every kind of bird. And then God told Noah that he would send rain on the earth seven days later.[37])

But back to the seventh day of the week. After the people had been freed from slavery in Egypt, God provided a form of bread to them in the wilderness, the manna we discussed in Chapter 23. God would send manna for six days of the week, but on the sixth day he sent twice as much, instructing the people to gather enough to feed their household on both the sixth day and the seventh day. That way, they wouldn't have to go out to gather the manna on the seventh day, when they were resting.

Though he had already taught his people about the seventh day through the way they had gathered manna for forty years, God emphasizes the importance of the seventh day as holy by instituting this command, "Remember the Sabbath day by keeping it holy," the fourth of the Ten Commandments. None of the other feasts even made it into the Ten Commandments! It is quite clear that the Sabbath was an extremely holy day, and even to this day, it is extremely important to Jews. Orthodox Jews don't operate any machinery or do any type of work on the Sabbath. Even operating an elevator is considered work, so there are special elevators that stop at every floor so that Jews can ride them on the Sabbath day without breaking any rules (like pushing buttons).[38] Though they are not all in the Bible, Jewish tradition recognizes 39 categories of activities, or *melakhoth*, which observant Jews avoid on the Sabbath. For orthodox Jews, it is only permissible to perform work on the Sabbath if it could save someone's life.

Jesus frequently debated the Jewish religious leaders concerning the Sabbath. Matthew, Mark, and Luke each tell one story about Jesus' disciples picking heads of grain from the wheat as they walked through a

CHAPTER 28: FALL AND WINTER FEASTS

field. Soon thereafter, Jesus healed a man with a withered hand. Both of these events took place on the Sabbath, and the Pharisees who witnessed them condemned these obvious infractions of the law. (The Pharisees were a sect of Judaism at the time of Jesus that was insistent on strict obedience to the law.)

The Gospel of Luke records another Sabbath healing: the story of Jesus restoring a woman who had been crippled for eighteen years. The Gospel of John includes two additional stories in which Jesus healed someone on the Sabbath: in John 3, Jesus healed a man who had been an invalid for 38 years, and in John 9, Jesus restored sight to a man born blind. Based on the last verse in John's Gospel,[39] we can assume that Jesus performed healings many other times on the Sabbath.

Jesus shed light on the reason he was able to heal on the Sabbath in several ways, but we'll look at three now. First, when confronted by the Pharisees about why he could heal on the Sabbath, Jesus asked, "If any of you has a sheep and it falls into a pit on the Sabbath, will you not take hold of it and lift it out? How much more valuable is a person than a sheep! Therefore it is lawful *to do good* on the Sabbath."[40] And secondly, Jesus made this statement to the Pharisees regarding his healing of the crippled woman: "You hypocrites! Doesn't each of you on the Sabbath untie your ox or donkey from the stall and lead it out to give it water? Then should not this woman, a daughter of Abraham, whom Satan has kept bound for eighteen long years, be *set free* on the Sabbath day from what bound her?"[41] And third, following the claim that his disciples had broken the law by removing heads of grain from the wheat, Jesus said, "The Sabbath was made *for man*, not man for the Sabbath."[42] In admittedly simplistic words, Jesus was clarifying that the Sabbath was made to help others, it was made to "free" his people, and it was made for man's benefit, not as a burden.

But the most enlightening statement concerning the Sabbath day that Jesus ever made is recorded in all three of the Synoptic Gospels. Jesus said, "The Son of Man is *Lord of the Sabbath*."[43] As mentioned in Chapter 18, Jesus' favorite title for himself was "the Son of Man." Thus, he was referring to himself in this statement. And by "Lord of the Sabbath," Jesus was indicating, not just that he was perfect in his obedience to the Sabbath law, which he was, but that he actually *created and instituted* the Sabbath. He was the one—in unity with the Father and the Holy Spirit—who communicated the fourth commandment to the Israelites through Moses. It was the people who had supplemented his commandment with the nitpicky rules. Why had they made so many rules for the Sabbath? Basically, by following the rules so well, they could then feel superior to others who did not follow them so well. In their self-righteousness, they looked down their noses at others, the very same people whom they should have taken the opportunity of the Sabbath day to help.

Jesus is "Lord of the Sabbath" in one other very crucial way. Because of his coming in human form, his living the perfect life free of sin, his dying on the cross as the "Lamb of God" and our scapegoat, and his resurrection on the feast of Firstfruits as a sign that God the Father had accepted his offering, Jesus *fulfilled* the Sabbath. He has put an end to the striving done to ensure one's good deeds outweigh one's sins. He has torn the curtain between humans and the Most Holy Place from top to bottom. And in so doing, the average, dirty, and completely unholy human—through faith in him—is cleansed and can confidently approach the throne of the perfectly holy God without being incinerated.

Knowing the burdens of trying to find worth and a sense of identity in life, Jesus urged and still urges us to find rest in him:

> Come to me, all you who are weary and burdened, and I will give you rest. Take my yoke upon you and learn from me, for I am gentle and humble in heart, and *you will find rest for your souls*. For my yoke is easy and my burden is light.[44]

Because of Jesus, the *shofar* will sound on the last day, and those who trust that he has done these things *for them* can receive it as a free gift and enjoy an *eternal* Sabbath rest. Moreover, those who trust in Jesus' work on their behalf can enter into a Sabbath rest for the remainder of their earthly lives, as they cease from the work to prove to themselves, to others, and to God that they are worthy. As the children of God, they have already been declared worthy to sit at the king's table, and they no longer have to work to demonstrate their worthiness. They can relax, knowing that God sees them as perfectly holy, even when they continue to fail, repent, fail, and repent. They can be humble and more readily own up to their sins. Instead of rationalizing their sin in order to minimize it or cover it up, they can admit to others how sinful they

CHAPTER 28: FALL AND WINTER FEASTS

are (though true believers seek to follow God's commandments, but for a different reason, as we will discuss in Chapter 32). But even when they fail, they can be confident that they are right with God because he has already forgiven their sin on account of Jesus' work on their behalf.

And most of all, Christians seek to be holy—not because they have to—but because they are driven by joy and gratitude to please the Lord of the Sabbath. They can be freed from the demands of living up to a law that they could never live up to, just as Jesus freed the crippled woman who had been physically bound by Satan. This is one of the reasons Jesus could say this to "the Jews who had believed him": "If you hold to my teaching, you are really my disciples. Then you will know the truth, and the truth will *set you free.*"[45]

With this chapter, we conclude the section of this book summarizing the symbols, people, and feasts of the Old Testament that point to Jesus. It is my hope that these symbols, types, shadows, and "advance echoes" of Jesus provide convincing evidence that Jesus is who he claimed to be: the fulfillment of "the Law of Moses, the Prophets, and the Psalms."[46]

QUESTIONS FOR COMPREHENSION AND DISCUSSION

1. Describe the significance of the three feasts of the autumn pilgrimage festival. How does the emphasis on good deeds versus sins compare to what Jesus has done for his followers?
2. When will the final shofar sound, according to many Jewish Christians?
3. What happened on Yom Kippur in ancient Israel?
4. How did the celebration of Yom Kippur change after the destruction of the temple in Jerusalem in 70 AD? How do modern Jews celebrate Yom Kippur?
5. How do the traditions of Yom Kippur (in ancient times and in modern times) point to Jesus?
6. What does the Feast of Booths commemorate? What were two ancient ceremonies during this feast, and how do they point to Jesus?
7. What are the stories of rescue in the feasts of Hanukkah and Purim? How does Jesus represent the ultimate rescue of God's people?

8. What is the significance of the weekly Sabbath? Why did Jesus heal on the Sabbath, and what did he teach about the Sabbath?
9. How is Jesus the fulfillment of the Sabbath rest?
10. How do the symbols, people, and feasts of the Old Testament provide evidence that Jesus really is the fulfillment of the Old Testament promises?

CHAPTER 28 ENDNOTES

1. Rabbi Dov Peretz and Dr. Arthur Green, *Rosh Hashanah Readings: Inspiration, Information and Contemplation* (Woodstock, VT: Jewish Lights Publishing, 2006), xv.
2. As quoted in Riddhima Kanetkar, "Yom Kippur: Significance of the Holiest Day in the Jewish Calendar," *International Business Times*, https://www.ibtimes.com/yom-kippur-significance-holiest-day-jewish-calendar-2595854.
3. Leviticus 23:23.
4. Psalm 81:1-3. All emphases in Bible passages are mine.
5. 1 Kings 4:24.
6. Exodus 19:13.
7. Psalm 103:4.
8. Psalm 103:11-12.
9. Hebrews 4:16.
10. Revelation 21:27.
11. Exodus 32:33.
12. 1 Thessalonians 4:14-17.
13. Zohar Vol. 16 Emor, Section 34. Yom Kippur, Par. 251.
14. *The Times of Israel*, "Chicken-swinging ritual endures despite animal welfare concerns," Available online at https://www.timesofisrael.com/chicken-swinging-ritual-endures-despite-animal-welfare-concerns/.
15. Zechariah 3:1-10.
16. Isaiah 11:1.
17. Leviticus 16:7-10, 20-22.
18. Leviticus 11:45.
19. Hebrews 4:14.
20. Hebrews 5:7-10.
21. Leviticus 20:8.
22. Isaiah 49:6.
23. Isaiah 11:9.
24. John 1:4.
25. John 8:12.

CHAPTER 28: FALL AND WINTER FEASTS

26. John 7:37-38.
27. Isaiah 7:14.
28. Matthew 1:23.
29. For verses about the indwelling of the Holy Spirit in believers, see Isaiah 63:11; Ezekiel 36:27; John 16:13; Acts 6:5; Romans 8:9, 11, 15; 1 Corinthians 3:16, 6:16, 19; Galatians 4:6, 5:18, 22; Ephesians 5:18; 2 Timothy 1:14.
30. As we mentioned in Chapter 23, in the introduction to his Gospel, John claims that Jesus ("the Word") "made his dwelling with us." These words can also be translated "tabernacled with us." (See John 1:14.)
31. John 10:22.
32. Matthew 5:11-12.
33. John 10:27-30.
34. See John 10:11.
35. See Esther 9:18-32.
36. Genesis 2:3.
37. See Genesis 7.
38. Elizabeth A. Harris, "For Jewish Sabbath, Elevators Do All the Work," *The New York Times*, March 5, 2012. Available online at https://www.nytimes.com/2012/03/06/nyregion/on-jewish-sabbath-elevators-that-do-all-the-work.html.
39. John 21:25: "Jesus did many other things as well. If every one of them were written down, I suppose that even the whole world would not have room for the books that would be written."
40. Matthew 12:11-12.
41. Luke 13:15-16.
42. Mark 2:27.
43. Matthew 12:8; Mark 2:28; Luke 6:5.
44. Matthew 11:28-30.
45. John 8:31-32.
46. Luke 24:44.

PART IV
The Explanatory Evidence

I believe in Christianity as I believe that the sun has risen: not only because I see it, but because by it I see everything else.

— C. S. Lewis, Christian apologist, novelist, and professor[1]

What can this incessant craving, and this impotence of attainment mean, unless there was once a happiness belonging to man, of which only the faintest traces remain, in that void which he attempts to fill with everything within his reach?

— Blaise Pascal, 17th century French mathematician, physicist, and religious philosopher[2]

29

Human Nature and Purpose

Jesus was born to a virgin who was "overshadowed by the power of the Most High." Jesus converted water into premium wine to ensure that a wedding celebration would continue. As Jesus was being baptized, the heavens opened up, the Holy Spirit alighted on him "like a dove," and a loud voice from heaven declared for all to hear: "This is my Son, whom I love; with him I am well pleased." Jesus brought sight to blind eyes, sound to deaf ears, steps to lame feet, and functionality to diseased tissue. He was able to feed thousands of people from one little boy's lunch. Even the wind and the waves followed his command. Molecules of water crowded together under his feet as he took a shortcut across the Sea of Galilee to meet up with his disciples in their boat. Glowing white as if his cells emanated photons, Jesus immediately acquired perfectly white clothing as he was "transfigured" before three stunned disciples.

About forty hours after his disfiguring death on a Roman cross, Jesus emerged from his tomb straight through his linen grave clothes, appearing "in the flesh" to his disciples and eating with them, but also walking through walls and appearing somewhat unrecognizable. After he spent forty days teaching his followers the meaning of his life, death, and resurrection, Jesus levitated in their midst and ascended into the clouds. The disciples stared up at the clouds, jaws dropping and necks craning, trying to see where Jesus had gone, when two men dressed in white appeared, saying: "Men of Galilee, why do you stand here looking into the sky? This same Jesus, who has been taken from you into heaven, will come back in the same way you have seen him go into heaven."

After presenting a brief summary of the supernatural elements of Jesus' earthly ministry, I have to admit that it's understandable that many people agree with this comment from Mark Twain: "Faith is believing something you know ain't true."[3] In fact, you might say Twain was wrong. If you believe something you know isn't true, that's not faith, it's stupidity.[4]

And I would actually agree: to believe something that you know isn't true really *is* stupidity. But Jesus doesn't demand this type of belief from his followers. Christians believe in something that they know *is* true, even though it sounds incredible. That makes all the difference.

I'd like to propose another definition of faith: "Faith is a trust or belief in a person, object, or truth claim that is based on scientific, historical, and experiential evidence, though it is not completely provable." For example, when I get on a plane, I have faith in the plane and the pilot, and I trust that they will safely take me to my destination. Is there a chance that the plane will crash? Indeed there is, and plane crashes unfortunately happen on occasion. But even so, the probability that my next plane flight will crash is still very small, about one in twenty million. Someone has done the math to make this statement: "Statistically speaking, a person would have to take a flight every day for 55,000 years before encountering a fatal accident. You are literally more likely to be killed by a falling coconut."[5] Even though I know there is a tiny chance my plane will crash, I can still have faith in the plane and choose to fly it. (I do not, however, have enough faith to walk under a coconut palm.)

Similarly, faith in the existence of God is not merely belief without any evidence. A belief in God *is* based on evidence. Some people require less evidence than others, and sometimes the evidence is in the form of an emotion or a sense that the world just "couldn't have happened by accident." Sometimes people find evidence for their faith in Jesus in the transformation they've experienced in their life since they came to believe in him. And often people find that the only evidence that they need for their faith in Jesus is the Bible, which "comes alive" to them as they read it. And, it is my hope and prayer that, following Chapters 18 through 28, you have a better appreciation for the reason so many people claim that the Bible is the only evidence they need. (And we didn't even discuss the many ways the Bible serves so effectively to guide and enrich our lives.)

These forms of faith that are based on "unscientific" evidence are not worthless, as if they indicate the person who possesses this type of faith is "stupid." One cannot judge the quality of someone else's evidence, since it is a personal experience that others cannot easily reproduce in the same exact manner. In fact, the Bible teaches that for anyone to have faith in Jesus, the Holy Spirit must first "open their eyes," so all of these forms of evidence are merely tools that the Holy Spirit uses to do so.[6]

Though a reliance solely on personal experience may be sufficient evidence for some people to have faith in Jesus, personal experience is insufficient proof for many others. And emotional experience, when it conflicts with the scientific and historical evidence, is very often misleading and inaccurate. In fact, I urge everyone to compare and contrast the rational evidence for Christianity with the evidence for any other supernatural worldview, including atheism. As we discussed in the Introduction, if our worldview is based on a rationale such as "it works for me" or "it just feels right" or "I don't want to be closed-minded like those Christians," then our faith may be overly based on emotion and not fully rooted in rational evidence. It is ironic that those who criticize Christians for "having a faith based on emotion and not on rational evidence" are precisely the ones whose faith regarding the supernatural is based on emotion and not on rational evidence. They reject Christianity for reasons such as, "I don't like that type of God," or "I think Christians are too narrow-minded," without noticing that these reasons are emotional rather than based on evidence.

This is the reason for my claim that the "leap of faith" leading to a wholehearted trust in Jesus as Lord is the "shortest leap," since Christianity rests on the most thorough examination of the rational evidence and is based therefore on the logical weight of the rational evidence. This is possible because Christianity is not only consistent with the latest, cutting edge scientific discoveries, but because it is also based on historical events and documentary evidence from eyewitness testimony. Moreover, Christianity rests on the amazing evidence from the fulfillment of prophecies and symbols that pointed to Jesus hundreds of years before he arrived on earth as a baby in a manger. You may still have to take a leap of faith to trust that Jesus is God in human form, your Savior, and the Lord of your life, but at least you do so rationally, and not by turning a blind eye to reality.

Since it's been a while, let's take a moment to review the ways that the latest scientific discoveries are consistent with the Christian worldview, which we discussed in chapters 1 through 4. Based on the evidence

CHAPTER 29: HUMAN NATURE AND PURPOSE

from astronomy, physics, biochemistry, molecular biology, paleontology, archaeology, and anthropology, we can confidently conclude the following:

1. The universe exploded into existence approximately 13.77 billion years ago.
2. In excess of one hundred conditions must be "just right" for the universe to exist and for life to be possible.
3. Even the simplest, single-celled organisms rely on biochemical systems and molecular machinery that are *irreducibly complex*, such that the chance they arose through blind chance alone—even given 13.77 billion years—is infinitesimally small.
4. DNA, the basic blueprint of all living organisms, is coded information, and as such, its *specified complexity* resembles computer programs and books, which have designers, engineers, and writers and don't just arise by blind chance.
5. The fossil record is characterized by *stasis* and *sudden appearance*, and it does not show convincing proof of a step-by-step, gradual transformation from less complex to more complex organisms, as evolution through blind chance would predict, especially with regards to the sudden appearance of complex organisms during the Cambrian period.
6. Around 150,000 years ago, human culture and the greatly enlarged *Homo sapiens sapiens* brain appeared suddenly in the fossil and anthropological records, not gradually over a million or more years as evolutionists would expect and blind chance would more than require.

These major findings—from all of the primary branches of scientific research—support the Bible's description of God. The Bible teaches that God created the world out of nothing, *ex nihilo*. He is therefore *omnipotent*. God is also *infinite* and *eternal*, and he himself, therefore, had no need to be created.

The Bible describes God as *omnipresent*. He is also *dimension-less*, existing outside the dimensions of time and space. Though he is present everywhere at all times throughout the universe, like water is present in a soaked sponge, God is also *distinct from* his creation, since he is not confined by the time-space dimensions of the universe he created.

Thus, God is like the water, while his creation is the sponge (an analogy that is far from perfect, of course). Thus, it is not accurate to state that the universe *is* God, or that nature *is* God, just as you would never say Leonardo da Vinci is "The Mona Lisa." In fact, the author of Hebrews compares Moses to a house and Jesus to its builder, which is another great analogy.[7]

As the creator of the universe, God is also *omniscient, logical,* and *wise,* having invented mathematics, logic, astronomy, physics, biology, ecology, and all other areas of knowledge, for that matter. Moreover, as the creator of the laws of physics, he alone would have the power to alter these laws to accomplish his will. Thus, miracles are within the power of an omnipotent creator.

Furthermore, the Bible teaches that God is *personal*—unlike both the *impersonal force* of many other worldviews, and unlike Allah, who is completely *transcendent* and whom Muslims would never dare to address as "Father." The God of the Bible is both *immanent* and *transcendent,* in that he is both near to us at all times and at the same time very far above us in terms of holiness (to an even greater extent than a human is above a worm!). The Bible teaches that God desires a relationship with the human beings he created. His words reveal a heart that yearns to reunite with us, and he even calls those who trust in him "his children" and refers to his people as "his bride."

The God of the Bible wants his people to come to know him—and though he certainly has the power to force us to know him, he gives humans the freedom to choose. Just as you would prefer someone to marry you of their own volition rather than because they are forced to, God gives his children the freedom to live independently from him, but he yearns for us to live in his presence from moment to moment. In fact, this is the relationship that would give us the most joy because it is the relationship for which God built us. Jesus describes this relationship as one in which we "remain in him":

> "As the Father has loved me, so have I loved you. Now remain in my love. If you keep my commands, you will remain in my love, just as I have kept my Father's commands and remain in his love. I have told you this so that my joy may be in you and that your joy may be complete."[8]

CHAPTER 29: HUMAN NATURE AND PURPOSE

God doesn't want his people to keep his commands in order to earn his love; he already loves us. We "remain in" his love if we keep his commands, which is the way our lives will be most joyful, blessed, and productive. We'll delve further into this unconditional love of God in Chapter 31 when we discuss grace-based salvation, which is unique among world religions.

Consistent with this personal God, discoveries of astrophysics have revealed that the earth is in the perfect position within the Milky Way galaxy, which is itself in the perfect position relative to other galaxies, in order to provide humans with a "front row seat" to study the universe. Moreover, the relative sizes of the moon and the sun and their relative distances from the earth are "just right," so that in a solar eclipse they overlap perfectly, as if God was presenting a beautifully wrapped gift to scientists who want to learn about stars and other aspects of our universe.

The very first book of the Bible describes humans as "made in God's image." This seemingly insignificant detail of our humanity opens up oceans' depths of theological implications. Humans are *not gods*, but we are made in the image of God, just as the image on a quarter is not really George Washington, but simply an image of the first president of the United States. As bearers of God's image, humans share God's *communicable* attributes, such as love, logic, creativity, spirituality, symbolic learning, goodness, an appreciation of beauty, and more.

Another implication of our being God's image bearers is that we have *inherent worth*, regardless of our gender, our race, our sexual orientation, our disabilities, our age, our wealth, our education, or our intelligence. Anthropology and archaeology continue to prove that modern *Homo sapiens sapiens* have a much larger brain than the next most recent hominids, and with this huge brain our species could handle symbolic communication, the creation of art, an appreciation of beauty, the development of rituals to prepare their dead for a supernatural afterlife, and the creation of complex tools to refine their ability to hunt, domesticate animals, grow crops, make clothing, migrate around the world, build housing, adapt to new environments, create music, trade with one another, and much more. These signs of culture seemed to have "popped out of nowhere" starting around 150,000 years ago, suggesting that our species originated as either a very, very fortuitous byproduct of random genetic mutations or the phenomenal product of a powerful and loving Creator.

Moreover, in Chapter 1, we discussed how the days of Genesis, when viewed in light of Einstein's law of relativity, fit quite consistently with the evidence for the big bang, the creation of the stars, sun, earth, and moon, the appearance of life on earth, the development of more complex life, and eventually the appearance of humans. Because the flow of time relative to an object depends on the speed of the object and the gravitational force acting on the object, a literal twenty-four-hour day could *also* be 8 billion years, depending on where the "timekeeper" is located within the expanding universe. In fact, the correspondence of the days of Genesis with what scientists now understand happened in the billions of years after the big bang is eerily accurate, especially for a document written thousands of years ago.

THE "CASTLE" OF EVIDENCE

The evidence that supports the claim that Jesus is God is much like a well-fortified and architecturally exquisite castle. The scientific evidence from chapters 1 through 4 forms the base of the castle, with supportive walls composed of thick, weighty, solid blocks of stone. The historical evidence in chapters 5 through 17 then forms the next few stories, with their ominous yet artistic ramparts and parapets. The biblical evidence from chapters 18 through 28 adds another few stories of strong and spectacular stone. At this point, our castle stands strong against attack, and the arrows of skeptics are easily deflected. In this chapter and the next four, we will lend further strength to our castle of evidence, just as flying buttresses did to medieval cathedrals, such that our refuge is not just strong in the face of attack, but breath-takingly beautiful.

Of course, a Christian's true strong castle, fortress, and high tower is the God who made us, sustains us, redeems us, and empowers us.[9] Those who trust in his strength will run to him at the first sign of an attack, and they will be warmed by his love and shielded by his powerful arm from all who would seek to harm them. But the metaphor I am using for our purposes now, this "castle of evidence," represents the strength of the "rational underpinnings" of Christianity. In order to destroy this castle, you must present evidence that refutes the many lines of

CHAPTER 29: HUMAN NATURE AND PURPOSE

scientific, historical, biblical, and explanatory evidence that support the castle. Just a few flying arrows won't do the trick. I encourage someone to write a "one-stop-shop" book that can convincingly refute all of the main lines of evidence presented in this book, which is itself a one-stop-shop rational defense of faith in Jesus. I sincerely doubt that anyone could do so.

So, let's get started with our final efforts to strengthen and beautify the rational evidence for faith in Jesus. First, we'll examine the two extremes of good and evil that characterize our world and the humans in our world (especially as opposed to other living creatures), in order to determine how well the biblical worldview explains it. We'll then examine the human desire for lasting purpose and significance, demonstrating that the biblical worldview accurately accounts for it. In the next chapter, we'll look at other aspects of human experience that are consistent with the biblical worldview: the existence of absolute standards of morality, an appreciation and pursuit of love and beauty, and the experiential evidence for a supernatural realm. In the last two chapters, we will look at the crowning glory of the evidence for the truth that Jesus is God: the "unique trajectory" of Christianity and the transformational power that this unique trajectory generates.

Let me present one last analogy to emphasize the value of evidence that experiential observations provide. When astronomers believed that the sun revolved around the earth, they found it difficult to accurately predict the motion of the stars. But when they understood that the earth was revolving around the sun, they experienced a "paradigm shift" with enormous explanatory and predictive power. Similarly, once we see the world through the biblical paradigm, we have a much better explanation for so much of our experiences, feelings, instincts, and motivations. As we piece together the jigsaw puzzle of human experience in light of the biblical worldview, the resulting picture comes into focus. All of the pieces fit. It all just makes sense. Let's begin.

WHAT AN AMAZING YET TERRIBLE WORLD

When Hamlet thought about human nature, he exclaimed, "What a piece of work is man!" He goes on to explain how wonderful man can be, but in the end, he feels that human beings are basically mere dust:

How noble in reason, how infinite in faculty, In form and moving how express and admirable, In action how like an Angel, In apprehension how like a god, The beauty of the world, The paragon of animals. And yet to me, what is this quintessence of dust?[10]

The Bible also teaches that God "made [humans] a little lower than the angels and crowned them with glory and honor,"[11] and yet it also teaches that all men have become "like one who is unclean," that "all our righteous acts are like filthy rags," and in the end "we all shrivel up like a leaf, and like the wind our sins sweep us away."[12]

King David ponders why God, who is so powerful and worthy, would want anything to do with mankind. Talking to God, David asks, "When I consider your heavens, the work of your fingers, the moon and the stars, which you have set in place, what is mankind that you are mindful of them, human beings that you care for them?"[13] The prophet Job even compares humans to maggots and worms—in contrast to the perfection of God: "If even the moon is not bright and the stars are not pure in his eyes, how much less a mortal, who is but a maggot—a human being, who is only a worm!"[14] Indeed, God even calls his beloved chosen people, the Israelites, "worms":

> "Do not be afraid, you worm Jacob,
>   little Israel, do not fear,
> for I myself will help you," declares the Lord,
>   your Redeemer, the Holy One of Israel."[15]

The Bible is clear that humans are *both* completely unworthy and completely worthy *at the same time*. So, how well does the Bible's description of humanity match up with the reality we see in the world around us and read in the news?

First, let's summarize the Bible's basic story regarding humanity: God created the world and called it "good," and God created humans *in his image* and called them "very good." But Adam and Eve made the choice to disobey God and set themselves up as their own gods. From then on, their descendants inherited this "original sin" nature. That is, all humans are born sinful because of Adam and Eve's failure. What's more, from Genesis 3, we learn that as a result of the fall, humans would experience difficulty in their toil on the earth, childbirth would become painful, there would be strained relations between husband and wife, and all humans would eventually die ("for dust you are and to dust you will return"[16]). And yet, God set his love on the humans he created, gave them a conscience to understand right from wrong, and provided a way to "rescue" them from the selfishness of their hearts.

Now, let's compare it to reality. I think we will all agree that our world is both incredibly beautiful and at the same time horrifyingly evil. The natural world is a museum without walls, where the most remarkable gems are on display in the form of waterfalls, roaring rapids, pristine blue waters, white sand beaches, plentiful and diverse life forms, and impressive natural wonders that are "bucket list worthy." And yet this same planet gives rise to deadly hurricanes, tornados, and tsunamis, forest fires, pestilences and pandemics, crop-destroying pests, and earthquakes.

Humans have tested our own physical limits by exploring the extreme limits of our world, whether it be at an altitude of 29,000 feet near the peak of Mount Everest, a depth of 36,000 feet at the bottom of the Mariana Trench, the farthest points from the equator, a short walk on the moon, a rover on the nearest planet, or a "free solo" climb of the 3,200 vertical rock face of El Capitan. Humans have also accomplished amazing feats, ranging from the world records set in the Olympics to the many discoveries of what had been mysteries about our universe, about the way our bodies function, and about the mechanisms ruling the smallest sub-atomic particles.

We can point to literary geniuses like Shakespeare, artistic masters like Michelangelo, insightful scientists like Einstein, masterful diplomats like Mandela, as well as the average person who inspires students as a teacher or professor, saves lives as a police officer, fire fighter, EMT, doctor, or nurse, works to improve society as a city planner, attorney, economist, or politician, maintains peace and protects citizens as a soldier, security guard, counselor, attorney, or arbitrator, creates new products to make life easier as an inventor, engineer, or entrepreneur, and so many others.

But just as humans continue to attain new heights of accomplishment, they have also scraped the bottom of the barrel in terms of atrocious acts. As we examine the human race over its history, we see a very wide spectrum from extreme good to extreme evil. Unlike other mammals, humans are capable of both far greater selflessness and far more sinister selfishness. Do other mammals sacrifice their lives for strangers? Do other mammals kill entire herds of their kindred species? By contrast, there are many humans who are willing to die for others, or at least live in poverty in order to help their fellow humans. And there are those who care not an iota for others, living only to deceive, steal, torture, and kill if it means they can acquire riches, power, or fame. Only twenty percent of the world earns more than $10 a day,[17] and yet these same people are also likely to complain that they don't earn enough, and they keep what they do earn for themselves. In fact, even in the countries that score the *highest* on the CAF World Giving Index (developed by the Charities Aid Foundation), half of their populations *do not* donate to charity, help a stranger, or volunteer their time.[18]

The point is that people perform amazing works of selflessness, and yet they are also responsible for wars, genocide, and mass murders. And the selflessness starts at birth. We may not like to call it sin, but yes, even the youngest, most "innocent" humans must be selfless to an extreme in order to survive, and they literally scream for their wants and insist on their way. It is only as we grow up that we learn to "share our toys," "not cut in line," "wait for our turn," and "say we're sorry." These selfless acts are not ingrained in human nature and must be learned, just like the ABC's. Those of us who live in a "decent," "civilized" society may sense that we are "inherently good." But, the truth is, if we are honest with ourselves, if we hadn't been born into this decent society, we wouldn't have been raised the way that makes us feel inherently good. In fact, most "decent" behaviors in modern, developed countries stem from Christian roots, though over the centuries the Judeo-Christian morality has been stripped of its reverence for a Creator. You'll find, in general, that countries that hadn't been influenced to a great extent by Judeo-Christian beliefs are not nearly as equal, prosperous, and supportive of equal rights for all races, religious beliefs, genders, and sexual orientations.[19]

The dichotomy of extreme good and extreme evil is found throughout the Bible. The result of Adam and Eve's "fall" was not a pretty picture. Within the first generation, the first son kills his brother over petty jealousy. The descendants of Adam and Eve were more interested in themselves than they were in the welfare of their neighbors, resulting in warfare, deception, racism, rape, torture, and all manner of evil. And yet, the descendants of

CHAPTER 29: HUMAN NATURE AND PURPOSE

Adam and Eve also sought to help their neighbors, to form alliances, and to establish systems of justice, lawful behavior, and orderliness. There are examples throughout the Bible of terrible evil alongside selfless love, just as we see these two extremes played out in the world today, which is filled with heroism, selfless love, and fights for justice, and yet at the same time replete with selfishness, hatred, and corruption.

The seventeenth-century scientist, mathematician, and philosopher, Blaise Pascal, argued for the truth of Christianity by proposing what is now termed the "anthropological argument." He summarizes the argument in this way:

> Greatness, wretchedness.... The more enlightened we are the more greatness and vileness we discover in man. Man's greatness and wretchedness are so evident that the true religion must necessarily teach us that there is in man some great principle of greatness and some great principle of wretchedness.... What sort of freak then is man! How novel, how monstrous, how chaotic, how paradoxical, how prodigious! Judge of all things, feeble earthworm, repository of truth, sink of doubt and error, the glory and refuse of the universe![20]

One literary masterpiece that brilliantly developed this theme of man's dual nature is the *Strange Case of Dr. Jekyll and Mr. Hyde*, by Robert Louis Stevenson. To deal with his inner struggle between good and evil, Dr. Jekyll develops a potion to mask his evil side. The potion works at first, but—to his utter devastation—his evil side periodically comes out in the form of Mr. Edward Hyde, who gains more and more power as the story proceeds.

Back to Pascal's anthropological argument. He claims that Christianity—of all philosophies—is the only one that can explain the dichotomy of human greatness and wretchedness, of human selflessness and selfishness. He writes, "For a religion to be true it must have known our nature; it must have known its greatness and smallness, and the reason for both." He then asks, "What other religion but Christianity has known this?"[21]

One explanation of the brilliance of Pascal's anthropological argument follows:

THE SHORTEST LEAP

> Pascal the empiricist starts with the data, notably the inexplicable phenomenon of mankind: unquestionably corrupt, subject to inconstancy, boredom, anxiety and selfishness, doing anything in the waking hours to divert the mind from human wretchedness, yet showing the vestiges of inherent greatness in the mind's realization of this condition. Mankind is also finite, suspended between twin infinities revealed by telescope and microscope, and aware of an inner emptiness which the finite world fails to satisfy. No philosophy makes sense of this. No moral system makes us better or happier. One hypothesis alone, creation in the divine image followed by the fall, explains our predicament and, through a redeemer and mediator with God, offers to restore our rightful state.[22]

There is thus a remarkable consistency between the Bible's description of human beings and the reality we see in the world. The explanatory power of Christianity—that man was made in the image of his divine creator and then chose to rebel against this creator—makes sense of the dichotomy of good and evil in our world.

Just as Dr. Jekyll does in the Robert Louis Stevenson novel, we can also experientially feel this "war" between good and evil waged on the forefronts of our conscience. This struggle is often symbolized by the angel and devil arguing as they sit on each of our shoulders. The apostle Paul explains this frustrating battle in terms we can all understand, if we are honest with ourselves. Paul writes, "So I find this law at work: Although I want to do good, evil is right there with me." He wants to do good—"in my inner being I delight in God's law"—but another side of him is waging war with this desire to do good. Exasperated, he exclaims, "What a wretched man I am! Who will rescue me from this body that is subject to death? Thanks be to God, who delivers me through Jesus Christ our Lord!"[23] Because Jesus came to defeat the sin nature—the devil on our shoulder—we can once and for all, and for all eternity, live in a way that is God-glorifying and that gives the angel on our other shoulder complete control. It will be as if Dr. Jekyll's potion works perfectly, and the evil Mr. Edward Hyde never appears.

CHAPTER 29: HUMAN NATURE AND PURPOSE

Before we move on, I must address those of you who are saying to yourselves, "But I like to live like Edward Hyde! It's more fun to be the rabble-rousing and rebellious partier!" Let me simply assure you that what awaits us in heaven will be the most amazing party, and yet it will have none of the frequent horrendously negative consequences, such as the hangover, the damage to property and one's health, the fights we didn't intend to get into, the inebriation that causes us to crash our car, and the other unenjoyable relational difficulties that inevitably happen. In heaven, there will be no need for drugs, alcohol, or other stimulants, since it will be pure bliss upon which it is impossible to improve.

Of course, we may still enjoy the taste of alcohol, and the Bible does say wine will flow in abundance. Just imagine all of the most wonderful things in your life without any of the terrible things. You will then get a much better understanding of why the true biblical concept of heaven is not only mischaracterized by our society as "boring and dull," but you will hopefully also recognize how much Satan deceives us into thinking that his ways are more fun, more exciting, and more fulfilling. It is a complete farce, and if you are honest with yourself, you will recognize it as such the more you *try to maintain* extended enjoyment in the sinful experiences. Over time, Satan's temptations bring less and less pleasure, and by the time we realize how unfulfilling they are, it is difficult to escape their grasp.

So, to summarize, the Christian biblical worldview has excellent explanatory power—more so than any other worldview—to make sense of the world we see around us, the history of human accomplishment and human depravity, and our own inner battle between good and evil.

A PURPOSE-DRIVEN LIFE

The Austrian psychoanalyst and atheist Sigmund Freud believed that science was superior to religion in at least the following way: "Religion is illusion, and it derives its strength from the fact that it falls in with our instinctual desires."[24] The German philosopher and economist Karl Marx would agree. He is known for this famous assertion that religion drugs the common people by comforting them with false hopes:

> The wretchedness of religion is at once an expression of and a protest against real wretchedness. Religion is the

sigh of the oppressed creature, the heart of a heartless world, and the soul of soulless conditions. It is the opium of the people.[25]

Both Freud and Marx are essentially saying that people look to religion to escape from the wretched difficulties of their lives, and in turning to religion, they find "real wretchedness." Freud and Marx agree that people turn to religion to fill a desire for meaning and hope that they know they can't find in their dreary lives. Thus, they'd say, people simply use religion as a "crutch" to assist them as they stumble along the difficult path of life.

Ironically, upon a thorough examination of the evidence in favor of the biblical worldview, it turns out that this gut level desire for meaning and significance is actually evidence that the Bible *is* true, and *not* that it is an illusion. There is a reason we want our lives to have purpose and a reason that we feel disappointed at being told that life is meaningless. These emotions aren't wishful thinking; they are instead evidence that supports the truth of the Bible. How so?

For one thing, these feelings are symptoms that we were made for a different world, one in which our deepest longings are fulfilled. C. S. Lewis describes it in this way:

> The Christian says, "Creatures are not born with desires unless satisfaction for those desires exists. A baby feels hunger: well, there is such a thing as food. A duckling wants to swim: well, there is such a thing as water. Men feel sexual desire: well, there is such a thing as sex. *If I find in myself a desire which no experience in this world can satisfy, the most probable explanation is that I was made for another world.* If none of my earthly pleasures satisfy it, that does not prove that the universe is a fraud. Probably earthly pleasures were never meant to satisfy it, but only to arouse it, to suggest the real thing. If that is so, I must take care, on the one hand, never to despise, or be unthankful for, these earthly blessings, and on the other, never to mistake them for the something else of which they are only a kind of copy, or echo, or mirage."[26]

CHAPTER 29: HUMAN NATURE AND PURPOSE

C. S. Lewis echoes St. Augustine, who 1,500 years earlier wrote these words to address God: "You move us to delight in praising You; for You have made us for Yourself, and our hearts are restless until they rest in You."[27]

Though we may disagree with C. S. Lewis and St. Augustine regarding our desire for God, we all can understand the desire for the world to have meaning and purpose. It just seems too terrible to admit that the entire universe "just happened," and we are merely a concatenation of molecules that shapes all we think, say, feel, and do. In an article he entitled "Where are the honest atheists?", one critic of atheism explains it as follows:

> If atheism is true, it is far from being good news. Learning that we're alone in the universe, that no one hears or answers our prayers, that humanity is entirely the product of random events, that we have no more intrinsic dignity than non-human and even non-animate clumps of matter, that we face certain annihilation in death, that our sufferings are ultimately pointless, that our lives and loves do not at all matter in a larger sense, that those who commit horrific evils and elude human punishment get away with their crimes scot free — all of this (and much more) is utterly tragic.[28]

There are plenty of atheists who insist that they can still lead meaningful lives and not believe in a transcendent Creator. (One recent book contains quotes and photographs from atheists to inspire other atheists that life still has meaning without God.[29]) But to do so, they must believe two contradictory truths simultaneously: (1) They are merely matter, and when they die they will be no more, and (2) Life has meaning. Of course, you can still have fun experiences, work to achieve justice, social progress, and environmental protection, and pursue fulfilling personal relationships as an atheist. But they are simply a means to pass the time until you die.

Your efforts may add a few more years to the duration of the planet, or the money you donate may help the next generations, or the product you invent may allow future generations to live longer and more comfortable lives, but one day our sun will die, and it will all come to an end. Former

Supreme Court justice Oliver Wendell Holmes Jr. once wrote a friend that there is "no reason for attributing to man a significance different in kind from that which belongs to a baboon or a grain of sand."[30] With regards to this quote, Timothy Keller notes, "No one with this set of beliefs can get peace and meaning for daily life unless he *stops* thinking about the implication of his beliefs."[31] Thus, atheists can indeed find meaning and significance in life, but only by *not* thinking out the implications of their worldview.

On the contrary, Christians will feel *more* peace and *more* purpose the *more* they meditate on the implications of their faith. Christians feel tremendous purpose the more they dwell on the biblical teachings that (1) God made them in his image, (2) he made them for a reason, and (3) he has given them specific skills to accomplish specific tasks in their lives. And, oh yes, this significance lasts beyond their earthly lives; they have a purpose that is *eternal*. This is one additional way that Christianity is *more* rational than atheism. Christians want to have purpose, and their worldview gives them rational evidence for them to have purpose. Atheists want to have purpose, but their worldview—if they rationally dwell on its implications—says their purpose is merely illusory and transient.

While you may not express the gut feeling that "life has meaning" in exactly those words, this desire for meaning and purpose comes out whenever we fight for a cause that we believe in. Whether we are seeking equal rights for humans of different races or sexual orientations, seeking justice for the poor and downtrodden, fighting for the rights of animals, or seeking to protect the beautiful world from damage inflicted by selfish humans, we are expressing our belief that the world has a purpose, and we are fighting for a cause that has meaning to us. But in a world without meaning, the only true purpose is to spread our genes and achieve "survival of the fittest."

The Christian worldview explains why we have a gut feeling that life has meaning and purpose. According to the Bible, God's creation of the world indicates at least three things about him: (1) He values physical matter, (2) he wants to establish a personal relationship with his people, and (3) he wants to involve his people in the work of establishing his Kingdom and defeating the powers of evil.

As we discussed earlier, Christianity is often misunderstood with respect to the first point (and many others, as we will discuss in Chapter

CHAPTER 29: HUMAN NATURE AND PURPOSE

31). Many people, including many Christians, believe that in heaven we will float around without bodies. And since bodiless spirits are difficult to imagine, we'll most likely look like winged angels levitating in the clouds strumming harps. But the Bible's description of heaven is completely different.

In the book *Heaven*, Randy Alcorn spends hundreds of pages discussing what the Bible says about heaven, and it may surprise you to hear that it never mentions that believers will become harp-playing angels in the clouds. Instead we will find "real people with real bodies enjoying close relationships with God and each other, eating, drinking, working, playing, traveling, worshiping, and discovering on a New Earth. Earth as God created it. Earth as he intended it to be."[32] Alcorn describes our desire for heaven in this way:

> We are homesick for Eden. We're nostalgic for what is implanted in our hearts. It's built into us, perhaps even at a genetic level. We long for what the first man and woman once enjoyed—a perfect and beautiful Earth with free and untainted relationships with God, each other, animals, and our environment. Every attempt at human progress has been an attempt to overcome what was lost in the Fall.[33]

We will be exactly as God originally created us to be, but we will no longer be able to perform the evil acts that have polluted this fallen world. Alcorn writes, "What God made us to desire, and therefore what we *do* desire if we admit it, is exactly what he promises to those who follow Jesus Christ: a resurrected life in a resurrected body, with the resurrected Christ on a resurrected Earth."[34]

In fact, God's plans for us, according to the Bible, are exactly what we naturally desire, not to float on clouds like angels, but to live in a world that is the best of our existing life without all of the bad stuff. Alcorn explains that, unlike what Freud and Marx claimed, "It's not that we want something, so we engage in wishful thinking that what we want exists. It's the opposite—the reason we want it is precisely because God has planned for it to exist."[35] Moreover, we "think of ourselves as fun-loving, and of God as a humorless killjoy. But we've got it backward. It's not God who's boring; it's us. Did we invent wit, humor, and laughter? No. God did."[36]

And another quote from *Heaven* drives home the point that all of our longings and desires in this life reveal the desire that God planted in our hearts for our true home with him:

> Nothing is more often misdiagnosed than our homesickness for Heaven. We think that what we want is sex, drugs, alcohol, a new job, a raise, a doctorate, a spouse, a large-screen television, a new car, a cabin in the woods, a condo in Hawaii. What we really want is the person we were made for, Jesus, and the place we were made for, Heaven. Nothing less can satisfy us.[37]

Not only will heaven fulfill all of the desires that the "shiny objects," "beautiful people," and "heights of fame and power" in this world never fully satisfy, we will have physical bodies that last forever. In response to the question, "What will our bodies be like?" Alcorn writes, "Our new bodies, I expect, will have a natural beauty that won't need cosmetics or touch-ups."[38] Moreover, not only will we have our physical senses in heaven, but they will be accentuated, and perhaps we will have more than just five. In addition, we won't have to worry about aging. Alcorn notes that the medieval theologian, Thomas Aquinas, argued that we will be the age that Jesus was when he was crucified, about thirty-three—*for all eternity.*

What an amazing hope this gives to us all, but especially to those who have experienced the pain and suffering caused by illnesses or disabilities in this life. Joni Eareckson Tada, who suffered an accident that left her a quadriplegic, delights in the hope of heaven:

> I still can hardly believe it. I, with shriveled, bent fingers, atrophied muscles, gnarled knees, and no feeling from the shoulders down, will one day have a new body, light, bright, and clothed in righteousness—powerful and dazzling.... No other religion, no other philosophy promises new bodies, hearts, and minds. Only in the Gospel of Christ do hurting people find such hope.[39]

So, besides the fact that God values the physical world and plans to restore the earth and his people to the way they were originally designed

CHAPTER 29: HUMAN NATURE AND PURPOSE

prior to the fall, we also know from the Bible that he desires a personal relationship with the humans he created, and it is for this reason that he came into the world. By providing a way for humans to spend eternity in his presence in heaven, Jesus rescues his followers from the pain and suffering of this evil world and gives them the hope that they will receive the home they have always yearned for. The difficulties we experience in this life will be completely redeemed when we arrive in heaven, such that our joy will be greater than if we had never experienced pain and suffering in the first place.

And third, the Bible teaches that God invites us to participate in the process whereby he redeems the world and establishes perfect justice on earth. We not only have hope of an eternal future in perfect bliss, but we also have purpose *in this life* as the God of the universe uses us to work alongside him in accomplishing his plans. He doesn't need our help, certainly, but he uses even human "jars of clay,"[40] created, formed, and refined in fire by the ultimate Potter,[41] in order to achieve his eternal purposes. An old saying, variously attributed to Thomas Watson, Martin Luther, and Ignatius Loyola, goes like this: "God uses crooked sticks to draw straight lines."

If the universe is a product of chance and human beings are simply "glorious evolutionary accidents," as evolutionist Stephen Jay Gould once stated,[42] how can we explain our search for a purpose beyond passing on our genes to the next generation? Sir John Templeton's question provides a good summary of the issue: "Would it not be strange if a universe without purpose accidentally created humans who are so obsessed with purpose?"[43]

Despite what many materialists and existentialists claim—humans search in vain for purpose in a universe where all things are a product of blind chance alone—the scientific evidence reveals that our universe may very well have been designed for a purpose. The weight of the evidence points to a Creator who brought the universe into being, who balanced the physical constants necessary for life on the edge of a fine razor blade, and who orchestrated the development of all living creatures, including the purpose-driven *Homo sapiens sapiens*.

The biblical plan is truly the opposite of meaningless, purposeless, and hopeless. And it is based on a mountain of evidence (refer to the previous 28 chapters of this book), not on wishful thinking. It may be a crutch, but in a world that is hopeless without it, the gospel is like no other crutch I can imagine.

THE SHORTEST LEAP

QUESTIONS FOR COMPREHENSION AND DISCUSSION

1. What is wrong with Mark Twain's claim that "faith is believing in something you know ain't true"? What is a better way to explain faith?
2. What are the six main lines of evidence in support of the biblical God from astronomy, physics, biochemistry, molecular biology, paleontology, and anthropology?
3. What are some ways we discussed in Chapters 4 that the scientific evidence is consistent with the way the Bible describes God, the creation of the universe, and the nature of human beings?
4. How is the evidence for Christianity similar to a castle? Can just a few "arrows" that are shot by skeptics destroy this castle?
5. What is the meaning of "explanatory power"? How does this concept relate to the model of the sun revolving around the earth versus the earth revolving around the sun?
6. What are some ways that the world is both wonderful and terrible? What are ways that humans are both extremes?
7. How does the Bible explain the "greatness" and "wretchedness" of humans?
8. How do atheists like Sigmund Freud and Karl Marx explain why humans look to religion to fulfill their desires? How does the Christian worldview explain these human desires?
9. What are three things that the Bible teaches regarding God's creation of the world and its implications for meaning, purpose, and hope in life?
10. What's wrong with the idea that we'll be bodiless spirits in heaven? How is this different from what the Bible teaches about heaven?

CHAPTER 29 ENDNOTES

1. C. S. Lewis, "They Asked for a Paper," in *Is Theology Poetry?* (London: Geoffrey Bless, 1962), 164-165.
2. Blaise Pascal, *Pensées*, para. 398, 425.
3. Mark Twain, Pudd'nhead Wilson's New Calendar, *Following the Equator*, 1897. Available online at http://twain.lib.virginia.edu/wilson/pwequat.html.

CHAPTER 29: HUMAN NATURE AND PURPOSE

4. Posted on Yahoo Answers by Abnormalbo, 2011. Accessible at https://answers.yahoo.com/question/index?qid=20110907230334AAqxvMZ.
5. Ben Bowman, "How Do People Survive Plane Crashes?" August 2, 2017, Curiosity Website, available https://curiosity.com/topics/how-do-people-survive-plane-crashes-o53cN3Xy/.
6. For verses that pertain to the how the Spirit opens one's eyes to the truth, see Numbers 22:31; 2 Kings 6:17; Isaiah 6:9-10, 29:18, 32:3, 35:5; Psalm 118:19, 146:8; Matthew 16:17; Luke 24:31, 45; John 9:39; Acts 26:18; 2 Corinthians 4:3-4; and Ephesians 1:18.
7. Hebrews 3:3.
8. John 15:9-11.
9. For Scripture that describes God as our "fortress," see Psalm 18:2, 28:8, 31:2-3, 46:7, 11, 48:3, 59:1, 9, 16-17, 62:2, 6, 71:3, 91:2, 94:22, 144:2; Proverbs 14:26; Isaiah 17:10; and Jeremiah 16:19.
10. William Shakespeare, *Hamlet*, Act IIk, Scene 2. Available online at http://shakespeare.mit.edu/hamlet/full.html.
11. Psalm 8:5.
12. Isaiah 64:6.
13. Psalm 8:3-4.
14. Job 25:5-6.
15. Isaiah 41:14b.
16. Genesis 3:19b.
17. Anup Shah, Poverty Facts and Stats, as of January 7, 2013. Available online at http://www.globalissues.org/article/26/poverty-facts-and-stats.
18. According to the CAF World Giving Index 2018 report, the "CAF World Giving Index score is calculated as a combined average of the proportion of people who reported one or more of the following in the month prior to interview: helping a stranger, donating money and volunteering time)." Available for download at www.cafonline.org.
19. For an overview of how Christianity led to freedom, equality, and technological and economic advancement, see Rodney Stark, *The Victory of Reason: How Christianity Led to Freedom, Capitalism, and Western Success* (New York: Random House, 2007). Also, for an overview of how Christianity treated minorities and women better than previous societies, see Rodney Stark, *The Rise of Christianity: How the Obscure, Marginal Jesus Movement Became the Dominant Religious Force in the Western World in a Few Centuries* (San Francisco: HarperSan Francisco, 1997).
20. Blaise Pascal, *Pensées*, available online at https://www.gutenberg.org/files/18269/18269-h/18269-h.htm.
21. Ibid.

22. D.G. Preston, *New Dictionary of Theology*, Sinclair B. Ferguson, David F. Wright, and J.I. Packer, eds. (Downers Grove, IL: InterVarsity Press, 1988), s.v. "Pascal, Blaise."
23. Romans 7:21-25a.
24. Sigmund Freud, *New Introductory Lectures on Psycho-Analysis* (New York: Carlton House, 1933), 239. Available online at https://archive.org/details/in.ernet.dli.2015.49982/page/n233.
25. Karl Marx, *Critique of Hegel's 'Philosophy of Right'* (Cambridge: Cambridge University Press, originally published in 1844), 131. Available online at https://books.google.com/books?id=uxg4AAAAIAAJ&pg=PA131.
26. C. S. Lewis, *Mere Christianity* (San Francisco: HarperOne, 2009), 137.
27. Augustine of Hippo, *Confessions*, written between 397 and 400 AD. Available online at https://www.gutenberg.org/files/3296/3296-h/3296-h.htm.
28. Damon Linker, "Where are the honest atheists?" *The Week*, March 8, 2013. Available online at https://theweek.com/articles/466865/where-are-honest-atheists.
29. Chris Johnson, *A Better Life: 100 Atheists Speak Out on Joy and Meaning in a World Without God* (Cosmic Teapot, 2014).
30. Richard Posner, ed., The Essential Holmes: Selections from the Letters, Speeches, Judicial Opinions, and Other Writings of Oliver Wendell Holmes, Jr. (Chicago: University of Chicago Press, 1997), 108.
31. Timothy Keller, *Making Sense of God: Finding God in the Modern World* (New York: Penguin Books, 2018), 87.
32. Randy Alcorn, *Heaven* (Carol Stream, IL: Tyndale House Publishers, 2004), inside front cover fold.
33. Ibid, 77.
34. Ibid, 7.
35. Ibid, 7-8.
36. Ibid, 411.
37. Ibid, 166.
38. Ibid, 289.
39. Joni Eareckson Tada, *Heaven: Your Real Home* (Grand Rapids, MI: Zondervan, 1995), 53.
40. 2 Corinthians 4:7.
41. See Isaiah 29:16, 64:8; Jeremiah 18:6.
42. Wim Kayzer, *A Glorious Accident* (New York: Freeman, 1997), 92.
43. John Templeton, *The Humble Approach: Scientists Discover God* (Philadelphia: Templeton Foundation, 1998), 19.

If this is ultimate reality, if this is what the God who made the universe is like, then this truth bristles and explodes with life-shaping, glorious implications for us. If this world was made by a triune God, relationships of love are what life is really all about.

— Timothy Keller, pastor and author[1]

Even those who have renounced Christianity and attack it, in their inmost being still follow the Christian ideal, for hitherto neither their subtlety nor the ardour of their hearts has been able to create a higher ideal of man and of virtue than the ideal given by Christ of old.

— Fyodor Dostoyevsky, *The Brothers Karamazov*[2]

Morality and Other Aspects of Real Life

In the last chapter, we discussed the spectrum of human goodness and evil, which ranges from the most selfless, even self-sacrificial, actions we can imagine to the most horrendously selfish and malicious deeds we can imagine. There is no need for examples, as any human with average experience and the ability to read or watch the news can see this wide range of human potential in either direction. Moreover, humans have an innate desire for purpose and meaning, regardless of whether they believe in God's existence.

Both of these phenomena of human experience are easily explained by the biblical Christian worldview, while the explanations offered by naturalistic evolution and "survival of the fittest" fall short. The Bible claims that a loving and all-powerful God created humans in his image, and even called them "very good," but he gave humans the choice to live separately from him—to be their own gods—and they consequentially lost their blissful state. That we are made in God's image explains human goodness, and our independent human choices that are opposed to God's purposes explain our frequent departure from goodness. Moreover, having lost "nirvana," humans have an innate desire to regain "paradise lost," though the things of this world never fully satisfy us for very long.

In this chapter, we turn our attention to four other aspects of human nature and life experience that the biblical worldview explains very well. First, it accounts for the feeling that some things are just wrong, regardless of what anybody else thinks—i.e., that there is such a thing as absolute morality. Secondly, we will examine how the biblical worldview accounts for the human "gut feeling" that love matters; it can't just be the result of chemicals in our brains. Third, we will explore the concept of beauty, and how an appreciation of beauty is more consistent with the biblical worldview than with materialism. And fourth, we will discuss the plausibility of the claim that billions of humans have made over the millennia: the claim that there is a supernatural realm beyond the physical world. Let's take a closer look at these human experiences—our sense of right and wrong, the feeling that love is important, the sense that beauty is real, and a belief in the supernatural—all four of which the biblical Christian worldview accounts for much better than any other philosophy.

IS THERE SUCH A THING AS RIGHT AND WRONG?

Another way that the Christian worldview has explanatory power is in its stance on morality. The question that has been asked in various ways for thousands of years is: Do "good and bad" exist, or are these concepts simply societal constructs based on "what's popular" in the culture, what feels good, or what some political scientist has determined will generate "the most good for the most people"? The Bible clearly teaches that right and wrong exist, and that there is absolute truth with regard to what is evil and what is good. But most people in today's society would beg to differ.

Let's say you have a friend who believes there are no moral absolutes. In other words, she believes everyone should determine what is right or wrong for himself or herself. No one has a right to insist something is wrong, and no one can insist that a particular way is right. This person might ask and claim, "How dare you impose your morals on me? I can decide what is right or wrong for myself!"

It is incredibly easy to point out the weakness of this argument. Here is one way to delve into her beliefs: "Some cultures believe it is fine to enslave minorities, since the majority can vote to do whatever it wants to do. What do you think?" Her response will most likely be something like, "Of course, that's wrong." At that point, her argument has crumbled, since to make the claim that "slavery is wrong" requires the existence of absolute morality. Individuals will thus want to choose for themselves where to draw the line between good and bad, and they then try to force this belief on others (usually unaware of what they are doing). They admit that there must be certain absolutes, but they disagree as to where actions pass from being OK to being "just wrong."

There have been centuries of philosophical debate on a rational method for determining morality. Thus, it may seem that we're getting closer to a scientific way to declare human equality and human rights intrinsically "good" and enslaving minorities and keeping women out of the jobs traditionally reserved for only men as intrinsically "bad." But even after many years of thinking by intelligent philosophers, we are no closer to developing a morality that is the "absolute best" for everyone without the existence of a supreme moral lawgiver. Here's how one book summarized the issue:

> Indeed, it is quite a bracing experience to go into a bookstore or browse online and see titles claiming to show "how science can determine human values," to uncover the "science of moral dilemmas," to disclose "the biological basis of morality" or "the science of right and wrong," to reveal "the universal moral instincts caused by evolution," to explain how a certain molecule is "the source of love and prosperity," to describe "how nature designed our universal sense of right and wrong," or to demonstrate "what neuroscience tells us about morality." These claims are all taken from the titles of recent books and articles, and these claims are pervasive.
>
> What pluck! These titles would seem to defy the age-old rule called "Hume's Law" that you can never derive an "ought" from an "is": that there is a decisive boundary separating prescription from description.[3]

In other words, you'd never know it by reading the claims of books on "non-theistic" morality available today, but even in this modern scientific age, there hasn't been any evidence proving that you can derive what someone "ought" to do based on what "is" about the physical universe. That is, science can provide "the *is*," but only philosophy can provide "the *ought*."

Science has not yet proven what is *absolutely* right and *absolutely* wrong in order for a society to flourish. There is no consensus, and there are only relative claims of right and wrong. Basically, there is no basis on which we can tell other cultures not to enslave minorities. We just feel it is wrong, but we can't declare it to be wrong without appealing to the "it just is" of absolute morality.

The Bible, however, teaches that there is a supreme lawgiver whose laws are perfectly just and perfectly fair. In fact, if every human followed his laws the world would be an amazing place to live. There would be no crime, no deception, no envy, no malice, no hatred, no poverty, no racism, no rape, no hunger, no murder—the list goes on. Unfortunately, in this fallen world, there would still be natural disasters, accidents that cause death, disabilities, and diseases, but humans would take care of one another much more, alleviating much of the negative fallout from these events. (However, in heaven, natural disaster, death, sickness, disability, and disease will no longer exist.)

But at this point, you are most likely not convinced that God is necessary for absolute morality to exist. You may be thinking that even without God's existence, we can still have human rights that aren't illusory, we can still make human equality a worthy goal on which everyone should agree, and we can still have the right to force other cultures not to enslave minorities. You may believe there is somehow a way to prove some things are "just right" and others are "just wrong" without appealing to a higher power.

There is not. Instead, there is only evidence that all morality is relative, that is, unless there is a higher power. Why is this? One of the best arguments to explain why absolute morality can only exist if God also exists is the "Sez Who?" argument presented by Yale professor Arthur Allen Laffer in his essay, "Unspeakable Ethics, Unnatural Law," published in the *Duke Law Journal* in 1979. The paper starts like this:

> I want to believe—and so do you—in a complete, transcendent, and immanent set of propositions about right and wrong, findable rules that authoritatively and unambiguously direct us how to live righteously. I also want to believe—and so do you—in no such thing, but rather that we are wholly free, not only to choose for ourselves what we ought to do, but to decide for ourselves, individually and as a species, what we ought to

be. What we want, Heaven help us, is simultaneously to be perfectly ruled and perfectly free, that is, at the same time to discover the right and the good and to create it.[4]

Laffer is essentially saying that even though we want to believe that perfect justice is achievable, at the same time we want to believe that we don't have to answer to anyone else's standards. We "want our cake and eat it too," creating a tension that is not easy to resolve (except, of course, in the Christian worldview, as we will see). Another quote that gets this same point across comes from sociologist James Davison Hunter:

> We want character but without unyielding conviction; we want strong morality but without the emotional burden of guilt or shame; we want virtue but without particular moral justifications that invariably offend; we want good without having to name evil; we want decency without the authority to insist upon it; we want more community without any limitations to personal freedom. In short, we want what we cannot possibly have on the terms that we want it.[5]

To understand the tension between our two contradictory sets of desires, Laffer sets out to demonstrate that "there cannot be any normative system ultimately based on anything but human will."[6] So, when someone states that you *ought* to do X or *ought not* to do Y, it is sufficient to simply respond, "Sez who?!"

For example, let's use the argument of enslaving minorities as part of a cultural practice. You say, "It is *not good* for a society to allow minorities to be enslaved, even if this has been done for centuries in this culture." This is a statement of a moral absolute: In all circumstances, even if it has been a cultural norm for a certain people group for centuries, it is not good to enslave minorities. We could then reply, "Sez who?" You would say something like, "Well, it's just not right. These minorities are powerless and innocent. They shouldn't be enslaved!" Again, we could reply, "Sez who?" You would say, "Says any decent person!" Again, "Sez who?" ("Who says decent people should say that?") The argument ultimately must go on until you admit that there must exist a universal law that dictates that we *ought not* to enslave minorities.

CHAPTER 30: MORALITY AND OTHER ASPECTS OF REAL LIFE

The Bible describes such universal laws as "God-given." The United States is founded upon the notion that "all humans are equal," which is one example of a God-given moral absolute. A supporter of slavery would have replied, "Sez who?" except that the ultimate person "who sez" that all humans are equal is God himself. And there's no higher authority to whom the "Sez who?" argument can refer.[7]

Laffer summarizes the dilemma we face when we try to make absolute truth claims without appealing to a supreme lawgiver:

> All I can say is this: it looks as if we are all we have. Given what we know about ourselves and each other, this is an extraordinarily unappetizing prospect; looking around the world, it appears that if all men are brothers, the ruling model is Cain and Abel. Neither reason, nor love, nor even terror, seems to have worked to make us "good," and worse than that, there is no reason why anything should. Only if ethics were something unspeakable by us, could law be unnatural, and therefore unchallengeable. As things now stand, everything is up for grabs.
>
> Nevertheless:
> Napalming babies is bad.
> Starving the poor is wicked.
> Buying and selling each other is depraved.
>
> Those who stood up to and died resisting Hitler, Stalin, Amin, and Pol Pot—and General Custer too—have earned salvation. Those who acquiesced deserve to be damned.
>
> There is in the world such a thing as evil.
> [All together now:] Sez who?
> God help us.[8]

In order to believe that moral absolutes exist, such as "napalming babies is bad," we must realize that we can't make our own set of morals just for ourselves. We can't in one moment believe that *one ought not* to do certain things (e.g. wear fur coats, drive gas-guzzling cars, forbid free speech, use capital punishment), and then in the next sentence insist that your morals are up to you to decide. Why can you make up your own morals that society should abide by, while the person with whom you disagree isn't allowed to "make up" *their* own? It is a logical contradiction.

Well, then, you say, we'll decide by a vote, and whoever wins the vote will establish the system of morality. In this case, what is to prevent the majority from voting to exterminate the minority? What's to prevent the claim that unproductive citizens, such as the mentally challenged, the physically disabled, or the elderly, should be eliminated (or at least not allowed to drain society's resources)? You then would argue, well, of course that would be wrong! We're then back to the question, "Who sez?"

The only worldviews that resolve the dilemma are those which acknowledge God as the divine law giver, and at the same time, recognize that humans can never perfectly keep his laws. The only worldview that I know of that truly resolves the dilemma is Christianity.

Here's why. God is perfectly holy. To live in his presence for eternity requires perfect holiness, which is impossible for humans. But God provided a way to live in his presence by sending his Son to live the perfectly holy life we could never live—for us—and to take the death penalty imposed in the Garden of Eden when Adam and Eve disobeyed—for us. Receiving the free gift of salvation by faith alone through Jesus Christ alone is the only way we can admit there is perfect justice, and yet not have to take the penalty for not adhering to perfect justice. This may not make sense to you, but please keep reading, as we will discuss it in more detail in Chapters 32 and 33.

Similarly, C. S. Lewis argued that "conscience reveals to us a moral law whose source cannot be found in the natural world, thus pointing to a supernatural Lawgiver."[9] Another theologian, John Henry Newman, also proposed that the existence of the conscience indicates that objective moral truths exist, such that people endeavor to act morally even when it goes against their best interests. Because these moral absolutes guiding our conscience exist, God must therefore exist as the one who has ultimate authority over morality.[10]

As one further explanation of this "Moral Argument" for God's existence, philosopher and theologian William Lane Craig makes these remarks:

CHAPTER 30: MORALITY AND OTHER ASPECTS OF REAL LIFE

> In a world without God, who's to say whose values are right and whose are wrong? There can be no objective right and wrong, only our culturally and personally relative, subjective judgments. Think of what that means! It means it's impossible to condemn war, oppression, or crime as evil. Nor can you praise generosity, self-sacrifice, and love as good. To kill someone or to love someone is morally equivalent. For in a universe without God, good and evil do not exist—there is only the bare, valueless fact of existence, and there is no one to say you are right and I am wrong.[11]

Christianity makes sense of our conscience, our feeling that certain things *really are* evil, and other things *really are* good. The existence of morality that transcends the opinions of humans and the power of the majority should comfort us because the Bible claims God will establish perfect justice on the earth when he rightly punishes everyone who has committed evil deeds. No wrong will go unpunished. But it should also send us running to Jesus for cover, as none of us has lived a life that is perfectly good, such that it is in line with God's perfectly holy standards.

One former atheist who is now a Christian wrote about her own realization that an absolute moral system only made sense within the framework of theism. While she was studying at Oxford, she considered herself an atheist and was eager to attend lectures by the atheist Peter Singer. But the lectures had an unexpected effect on her:

> I remember leaving Singer's lectures with a strange intellectual vertigo; I was committed to believing that universal human value was more than just a well-meaning conceit of liberalism. But I knew from my own research in the history of European empires and their encounters with indigenous cultures, that societies have always had different conceptions of human worth, or lack thereof. The premise of human equality is not a self-evident truth: it is profoundly historically contingent. I began to realise that the implications of my atheism were incompatible with almost every value I held dear.[12]

Another example of people acting on their conscience in the belief that absolute human rights must exist comes from an article in *Foreign Policy*, which summarizes the background for the quiet revolution that led to the collapse of the Soviet Union in the late 1980's. It quotes the Soviet leader at the time, Mikhail Gorbachev, who had written:

> The Soviet model was defeated not only on the economic and social levels; it was defeated on a cultural level. Our society, our people, the most educated, the most intellectual, rejected that model on the cultural level because it does not respect the man, oppresses him spiritually and politically.[13]

The Russian people sensed that the policies of their government were denying their freedom, and they gathered together to put an end to four generations of a one-party dictatorship. One Russian journalist made it clear that Russians sensed that their noblest of human qualities were being crushed:

> As Mikhail Antonov declared in a seminal 1987 essay, "So What Is Happening to Us?" in the magazine *Oktyabr*, the people had to be "saved" — not from external dangers but "most of all from themselves, from the consequences of those demoralizing processes that kill the noblest human qualities."[14]

The president of Kyrgyzstan, which had been a part of the USSR for decades, made this claim regarding the "inalienable rights" that an authoritarian government threatens: "The Almighty provided us with such a powerful sense of dignity that we cannot tolerate the denial of our inalienable rights and freedoms, no matter what real or supposed benefits are provided by 'stable' authoritarian regimes."[15]

So, how is it that a people can sense that an atheistic dictatorship is not "right"? What is to prevent this type of dictatorship from being implemented, if the leaders believe it is "for the common good"? Why do we cringe when we hear of the majority killing the minority, just because they are weak? Why do we want to help the homeless instead of vote for their removal from the streets in a way that threatens their human rights? Why do we want to save babies who are born with mental or physical abnormalities? All of these "gut feelings that it is just right" point to a Creator who made humans in his image, such that every human has dignity and inherent rights.

Only through faith in Jesus can we have our cake and eat it too. We can sincerely believe that all humans have dignity, and we can feel confident that this belief is compatible with our philosophical worldview. We can also trust that justice will be done, and at the same time trust that we will not be on the receiving end of it, even though we are not even close to living up to the standards of a perfectly holy God.

Why can we trust both of these? The first answer is because the Creator made us in his image, which gives all humans inherent dignity. Thus, he is responsible for giving us supreme laws and a conscience that feels certain things, like enslaving minorities, are definitely wrong, and other things, like freedom and love, are definitely right. And the second answer is because Jesus lived the perfect life *for us*, and he took on himself at the cross the judgment for our sins *for us*. This is how a perfectly just, perfectly loving God could accomplish *both* perfect justice *and* perfect love. The cross gives us our cake to admire in the refrigerator for all eternity, and yet we get to eat it, too.

The Existence of Love

Christianity explains love as no other religion or philosophy can. Atheists will claim that love is merely a feeling created by certain neurotransmitters in the synapses between our brain's neurons. This love has arisen, they explain, as a way to perpetuate our genes, ensuring that we mate, pass on our genes, and protect those with genes we share so they will pass them on to the next generation. Sex hormones, dopamine, epinephrine, and many other complex chemicals just happened to develop from less complex chemicals, and they then conferred survival benefits on the organisms who were fortunate enough to have them in the right quantities in the right places at the right times.

But there are problems with the atheist's explanation for love. Even noted atheist Richard Dawkins made this comment regarding the inability of science to explain love:

THE SHORTEST LEAP

> Just because science can't in practice explain things like the love that motivates a poet to write a sonnet, that doesn't mean that religion can. It's a simple and logical fallacy to say, "If science can't do something, therefore religion can".[16]

I agree with Dawkins in general. If science can't explain something, it does not automatically follow that religion should be able to explain it. However, in this case, religion *does* explain the existence of love better than the atheistic worldview. But the mere existence of love in the world does not prove that religion is true. In other words, I am not saying, "I see that love exists, therefore God must exist." What I am saying, however, is that a worldview in which a loving God exists has greater explanatory power for the existence of love than does a materialistic worldview in which all emotions are based on survival of the fittest.

But let's waste no further time. Let's take a look at just how religion—Christianity in particular—*can* explain love and *does* explain love much better than any other worldview. In the first book of the Bible, God states, "Let *us* make mankind in *our* image, in *our* likeness."[17] The original Hebrew documents contain these plural forms, which are in stark violation of the strict Jewish belief that there is only one God. For the many reasons we briefly and partially listed in Chapter 18, the earliest Christians developed the concept of a *triune* God, one God in three persons, termed the *Trinity*. One of the most convincing reasons to believe that the Trinity is true is that it isn't something humans would invent. It is truly a strange concept, and if humans were to invent a religion, it most likely wouldn't include the Trinity.[18]

Timothy Keller describes one of the most beautiful aspects of the concept of the Trinity:

> You see, different views of God have different implications. If there's no God—if we are here by blind chance, strictly as a result of natural selection—then what you and I call love is just a chemical condition of the brain.... On the other hand, if God exists but is unipersonal, there was a time when God was not love. Before God created the world, when there was only one divine person, there was no lover, because love can only

CHAPTER 30: MORALITY AND OTHER ASPECTS OF REAL LIFE

exist in a relationship. If a unipersonal God had created the world and its inhabitants, such a God would not in his essence be love. Power and greatness possibly, but not love. But if from all eternity, without end and without beginning, ultimate reality is a community of persons knowing and loving one another, then ultimate reality is about love relationships.[19]

Thus, because he has been in a three-way internal relationship for all eternity, God can actually *be* love. On the other hand, a unipersonal God, such as Allah or the Jewish conception of God, has great power, and he can use that power to create love. But only in Christianity do we find a God who *is love*.

John writes this clearly in his first letter: "Whoever does not love does not know God, because *God is love*.... And so we know and rely on the love God has for us. *God is love*. Whoever lives in love lives in God, and God in them."[20]

Keller goes on to explain the implications of the Trinity more fully:

> Why would a triune God create a world? If he were a unipersonal God, you might say, "Well, he created the world so he can have beings who give him worshipful love, and that would give him joy." But the triune God already had that—and he received love within himself in a far purer, more powerful form than we human beings can ever give him. So why would he create us? There's only one answer. He must have created us *not to get joy but to give it*.[21]

Only Christianity explains the origin of love, which has existed for all eternity in the mutually loving relationship between the Father, the Son, and the Holy Spirit. This the only way that God could have *been love* for all eternity. It is also the only way to explain that God *did not need* to create humans to have something to love. Instead of creating humans out of need, he created them out of the selflessness that flows from his nature: he wanted to *share his love* with them. In other words, (1) the triune God has always been giving and receiving love within himself, (2) he created humans to share in that love, and (3) it is this love that is the ultimate source of the joy that we all long for and frustratingly seek in mere worldly experiences.

The Christian understanding of love as originating in a triune God, who has been love for *all eternity*, also makes sense of our innate desire to see love last. Those of us who have had to watch our loved ones die understand this feeling. Though atheists can use non-theistic ways to explain the difficulty of watching our parents, siblings, friends, children, and other loved ones die (for example, we have evolved to want to preserve our gene pool, so death is not a good thing), the Christian worldview explains that humans were created to know love for all eternity. For this reason, it is such a painful shock to experience intense love cut short. Other mammals protect their family members and are indeed affected when loved ones die, but humans are far more impacted by the death of a loved one. The Christian worldview explains this much better than atheism.

The Reality of Beauty

One of the most fulfilling aspects of life on earth is beauty. Beauty is defined as a juxtaposition of qualities, like shape, form, color, sound, or texture, that pleases the senses. When something is beautiful, we desire to look at it, listen to it, smell it, touch it, and feel it as an end in itself, not as a means to another end. For example, you may go to work so that you can earn money to pay for a trip to Yosemite National Park. Your work is the means to an end, but the experience of beauty in Yosemite is the end in itself. As you stop at the first viewpoint to take in the splendor of Yosemite Valley, you do it for no other reason than to enjoy its beauty. You may hike for the physical benefits to your health, but the beauty of your surroundings is an end in and of itself. If you are like me, you'll try to preserve the beauty in photographs that always end up disappointing you compared to the real thing; though the images are still beautiful, they are merely a shadow of the true beauty.

Similarly, we may work to earn money to buy tickets to a play, symphony, or concert, or to travel to Paris to see the art in the Louvre and the architecture of Notre Dame. We may take a trip to the beach to watch the sunset, go snorkeling, or to collect seashells. We may make a special visit to the desert to enjoy the wildflower bloom, or to the forest

CHAPTER 30: MORALITY AND OTHER ASPECTS OF REAL LIFE

in the autumn to enjoy the colorful foliage. The scenery, birds, flowers, leaves, fish, and other natural objects are in themselves beautiful, and we don't need them to accomplish any other task. They are the ends to which we are attracted, and we often take any means possible to get to them.

In many ways, scientific discovery and inventiveness are also means to the end of viewing beauty, which can be found in understanding how a biochemical process works, building a robot that can accomplish a complex goal, getting an up-close view of new stars being born, understanding the intricate interrelationships of organisms within an ecosystem, or shedding light on how the brain stores memories. Many would not hesitate to speak of mathematics, physics, logic, and engineering as beautiful in and of themselves, though of course they are also quite powerful means of accomplishing other ends.

And those who love sports, martial arts, sewing, film-making, wood-working, music, art, fashion, gemology, knitting, wood-working, jewelry-making, videography, acting, cooking, baking, and other creative hobbies will see beauty in the moves of excellent players, practitioners, performers, and artists, as well as in the creative final products of those who are gifted with artistic, musical, and creative skill.

Often when we are struck by something of beauty, we have what we might call a "spiritual experience." Most people have this experience when they are surrounded by the beauty of nature, which is one of the reasons we easily identify with faiths that claim we are all "one with the universe." Indeed, we find much of the world's most beautiful architecture in places of worship or burial that have been built by practitioners of all world religions. These beautiful cathedrals, churches, mosques, temples, tombs, and shrines evoke in the visitor a sense of awe and reverence for the deity or deities that are worshiped in the building.

The art of medieval Europe sought to teach parishioners about God and the stories of the Bible, as well as give humans a sense of their insignificance compared to God through soaring arches, high ceilings, stained glass windows, and majestic and inspiring artistic details. In fact, it was in the beautiful churches of Italy that I first felt the presence of God, though I chalked it up to my imagination, which had somehow been inspired by beauty through "feel good" neurotransmitters.

Let's take a quick look at the beauty of the temple that God instructed his people to build, which demonstrates both his appreciation of beauty as well as a potentially significant theological point. God gives these instructions for the altar within the Inner Court of the tabernacle: "If you make an altar of stones for me, do not build it with dressed stones, for you will defile it if you use a tool on it."[22]

With regards to the remainder of the tabernacle, God still gives specific instructions, but he sets no limit on the use of tools. In fact, God's instructions for the details of the tabernacle insisted on the use of the most beautiful and expensive colors for the "finely twisted linen" of the curtains, pure gold and fine acacia wood for the lampstand, the showbread table, and the ark, and beautiful details of flowers, pomegranates, and cherubim on the lampstand, curtains, ark, and priestly garments. God even provided a precise recipe for the incense, which had to be "the work of a perfumer."[23]

And of special interest to those who find beauty in fashion, Exodus 28 and 39 provide absolutely stunning details for the crafting of the sacred, priestly garments, which God designed to give the priests "dignity and honor."[24] For example, these are the instructions for the breastpiece (or breastplate), which the high priest wore over his chest:

> They fashioned the breastpiece—the work of a skilled craftsman. They made it like the ephod: of gold, and of blue, purple and scarlet yarn, and of finely twisted linen. It was square—a span long and a span wide—and folded double. Then they mounted four rows of precious stones on it. The first row was carnelian, chrysolite and beryl; the second row was turquoise, lapis lazuli and emerald; the third row was jacinth, agate and amethyst; the fourth row was topaz, onyx and jasper. They were mounted in gold filigree settings. There were twelve stones, one for each of the names of the sons of Israel, each engraved like a seal with the name of one of the twelve tribes.[25]

It is quite apparent that God appreciates beauty, and he used beauty to teach his people how important they are to him. The twelve gems represented the twelve tribes of Israel, which served as symbols demonstrating that, just as the gems were close to the high priest's heart, the people were close to God's own heart. I have no doubt that the breastplate, if it still existed, would be one of the most visited artifacts in the world, right up there with the Crown Jewels, the Sistine Chapel, and the Taj Majal.

CHAPTER 30: MORALITY AND OTHER ASPECTS OF REAL LIFE

So, if the entire tabernacle was so beautiful and depended on the use of so many skilled craftsmen, weavers, and perfumers, why did God not allow anyone to use any tools, which were generally made of iron at that time, for the stones that comprised the altar? The Jewish *Mishna*, which is a collection of oral laws and commentary on the Torah, taught that the reason no iron tool could be used on the stones of the altar was because iron shortens a man's life, while the stones of the altar were intended to prolong a man's life.[26]

However, other commentators have provided an explanation that seems very reasonable, considering the rest of the Bible's teachings. They note that the altar represented the way that the sins of the people would be atoned. Therefore, God did not want the altar to in any way give humans the idea that their efforts played a role in this process. That is, just as the stones of the altar were created by God alone, the atonement for sins that the altar symbolized would be accomplished by God alone. Moreover, pagan altars were generally very ornate and beautiful, indicating that the humans who built them were working to earn the approval of the gods. In contrast, the Hebrew God wanted his people to know that his forgiveness of sins and their resulting salvation were offered freely to them, and their obedience was *a response to* this gift from God, not a way to earn God's love. We'll have more to say on "salvation by faith alone" in the next chapter.

But back to beauty: Beauty—and the spiritual feelings it inspires in us—are evidence for a divine Artist, who created not only all of the beauty in the world, but also gave us the ability to create beauty ourselves. This divine Artist also gives us an appreciation of beauty and therefore the desire to create it and to seek it out. And just as our photos are a mere shadow of the beauty of the scenery or objects they depict, earthly beauty is an imperfect substitute for the beauty of the Creator himself.

But according to materialists, our appreciation of beauty is simply an evolutionary adaptation. Our ancestors had an appreciation of beauty that somehow made it more likely for them to survive to childbearing age. They thus passed on this appreciation of beauty to the next generations. Our brains have been trained to admire a beautiful scene, to indulge in an amazingly delicious dessert, to relax as we inhale the sweet smell of lavender, or to enjoy a beautiful symphony. But the beauty in the scenery, dessert, lavender, and music is itself simply an illusion.

C. S. Lewis describes the way materialists view beauty in this way:

> You can't go on getting very serious pleasure from music if you know and remember that its air of significance is a pure illusion, that you like it only because your nervous system is irrationally conditioned to like it. You may still, in the lowest sense, have a "good time"; but just in so far as it becomes very good, just in so far as it ever threatens to push you on from cold sensuality into real warmth and enthusiasm and joy, so far you will be forced to feel the hopeless disharmony between your own emotions and the universe in which you really live.[27]

The beauty that we experience and that brings us such joy is consistent with the Christian worldview, but counterintuitive for those who believe the universe is a product of blind chance. We sense that beauty has real meaning, but in a materialistic world with no divine Artist, beauty is merely illusory and simply evolutionarily advantageous. When we see beauty, we sense that the beauty didn't "just happen." We sense that there is an Artist responsible for it. While this doesn't prove the existence of the biblical God, it is very consistent with the creative and personal God who is described in the Old and New Testaments.

THE SUPERNATURAL ALL AROUND US

The last way that we will discuss the explanatory power of Christianity is in the explanation of bizarre phenomena that can only be explained through an appeal to the supernatural. Of course, materialists refuse to appeal to the supernatural, claiming that there must be some scientific explanation for these phenomena that merely seem supernatural. But in asserting this, they are claiming that the experience of billions of people is merely an illusion caused by their brains playing tricks on them or by some other logical, scientifically provable event that has been misinterpreted. Could so many people have really been fooled into believing in the supernatural? Perhaps some of them, but *all* of them?!

Let's start with a scientific study that claims to have demonstrated the existence of a non-physical state separate from the body, something we would call "consciousness." A study by British researchers that was published in the journal *Resuscitation* found that consciousness

CHAPTER 30: MORALITY AND OTHER ASPECTS OF REAL LIFE

continues even after a person has been pronounced clinically dead and the brain has stopped functioning.[28] This research lends scientific support to the stories of the many people who claim to have undergone a near-death experience, or NDE, which is defined as "a lucid experience associated with perceived consciousness apart from the body occurring at the time of actual or threatened imminent death."[29]

In fact, a 1992 Gallup poll found that 13 million American adults (1 in 20 at the time) had experienced an NDE with at least some of the most common characteristics, such as the feeling of floating over and looking down on their own body following clinical death.[30] Since the poll found that approximately 774 people experience an NDE each day, approximately 8 million additional Americans have experienced an NDE since the 1992 poll.

A growing body of evidence, both scientific and experiential, leaves us to wonder: Perhaps we are more than just physical molecules; perhaps there is such a thing as a spiritual soul that is distinct from our bodies. Though materialists attribute these experiences to chemical reactions in the brain, people have provided uncanny evidence that they truly did experience an NDE. There are even examples of people who identified objects they had seen on the roof of the hospital during the NDE, and these objects were later confirmed to truly have been there.[31]

I will give another example of a supernatural experience that I myself experienced a little over twenty years ago. Before I became a Christian, a friend of mine opened up his home in California for a "sweat lodge ceremony." An American Indian chief flew down from Canada to perform a healing ceremony for a French woman who was dying of cancer. As a last resort, this woman, along with her husband and children, had flown in from France to at least try to obtain healing through alternative methods. At the time, I was an atheist.

We built a dome-shaped sweat lodge from flexible willow saplings and covered it with leather. Outside of it, we built a fire, where we heated several large stones. In the center of the sweat lodge we placed a bucket of water, and when we put the hot stones into it and closed the entrance, the steam was blinding and overpowering. We were in the sweat lodge for what felt like an eternity, while the American Indians chanted in their language. I was relieved to catch a breath of the cool California air when we stepped outside.

Earlier that day, we had covered the windows in a large room with black-out material, such that no light could enter, even in broad daylight.

That night, after we emerged from the sweat lodge, it was in that dark room that I had my "first" supernatural experience. With the lights on, several of the Indian chief's assistants rolled him in a blanket and tied him up with rope, using complex knots, such that it was doubtful he could ever untie himself, especially from within the blanket in which he had been rolled. The wrapped chief was laid in the middle of the room, and we were all gathered along the outer walls around him. The assistants set up what looked like coffee cans filled with sand in four corners of a small rectangle around their chief, and inside the coffee cans they put long poles of wood. Thus, the chief was surrounded on four corners by these four long poles that came up about five feet out of the sand-filled cans. A hand-made ball of leather laid lifeless on the floor. Then they turned off the lights.

What happened next changed my view on the existence of the supernatural, and largely because of this experience, within a few years I had investigated the various religions and eventually (and surprisingly, given my previous negative opinions of Christianity!) came to know Jesus as my Savior. The assistants sat on the far side of the room and beat rhythmically on drums as they chanted in their language. They explained that "the ball would come to us," at which point we should pray for the ill French woman. I had no idea what they meant until the leather ball lit up like a lantern and flew swiftly through the air, even between and around the poles, stopping on a dime in front of the first person's face. When the leather ball flew in front of their faces, the French family members prayed in French for their ill mother. When it stopped in front of my face, I prayed for her in English. And all the while the Indian chant and drum beats continued.

The experience lasted about fifteen minutes, with the leather ball flying around the room almost continuously (though there was a period of time when I thought it had finished, but it had merely taken a little break). I had set up that room. I knew there were no invisible strings or pulleys that could accomplish the strange flight of the glowing leather balloon, which lit up whenever it moved and hovered in front of our faces.

When the balloon finally settled on the floor and darkened again, we kept the lights off for a while, as if to be sure that it had finished its job of eliciting our prayers. Then the lights were turned on. The Indian chief was sitting calmly with his legs folded in front of him in the middle of the four sticks. The blanket was folded neatly by his side, and the rope

CHAPTER 30: MORALITY AND OTHER ASPECTS OF REAL LIFE

was coiled on top of the blanket. The poles around him were still vertical, though they could have easily been pushed over. I stared blankly at the scene for a long while, trying to figure out how it happened. I finally got up the nerve to go inspect the coffee cans, which were indeed filled with sand, and the leather ball, which was just that, an empty balloon-like casing of leather with nothing inside of it. By the way, the cancer unfortunately succeeded in its attack on the French woman's body. We were saddened to learn of her death a few weeks later.

I remember sharing the experience with a friend, a fellow atheist, who quickly rattled off possible explanations. I kept responding that his explanations were inadequate. There was no way, I insisted, to explain it without appealing to the supernatural. Thus began my journey into the spirit world. After reading several books on various religions (Buddhism particularly appealed to me), I found myself in a hotel in Rome, Italy with no reading material. There was a copy of the New Testament in the bedside table. Since it was printed in Italian, French, Spanish, German, and English, I figured I could easily switch between languages and thereby learn new vocabulary.

I ended up taking that New Testament with me on the rest of the trip, much to my traveling companion's embarrassment. I completed it one day while sunbathing on the beach in Nice, and of course I read it entirely in my first language of English! After finishing, I prayed to ask Jesus to be my Savior. It was July 4, 1998.

I share this story because most Christians have a similar one, though often not as crazy as mine is, I admit. Some Christians don't remember a day in particular when God "opened their eyes," either because they have been Christians all their life, or because it was such a gradual process. And many testimonies are much more amazing than mine, especially those you hear about Muslims in the Middle East claiming that Jesus appeared to them in a dream (which is one way that God is opening many people's eyes to his reality in countries where Christian missionaries are not allowed[32]).

But the common theme in Christian testimonies is that God reveals himself to those he chooses, especially if they are looking for him (and if they are looking for him, it's a sign he was first looking for them!).[33] The evidence in favor of the supernatural realm is extensive, though of course, we cannot observe it using the same techniques used to reveal truths in the physical world. But the human race is characterized by a desire to understand and know gods or God, and the belief in supernatural creatures, such as angels and demons, clearly is a part of the collective human consciousness. It makes sense of extreme evil, which can be attributed to the acts of the devil and demons, and it makes sense of extreme good, which Christians attribute to a perfectly loving and just God who made all humans in his image.

I find it also interesting that many religions have a sense that we "owe" God something as a payment for our inadequacies. There have thus been many systems of belief that prescribe a list of ways for humans to act or not to act in order to feel that they are "right" with God or the gods. Sacrificial systems, in addition to that of the ancient Jews, demonstrate that the human psyche feels the need to "pay" a price in order to please God or the gods. (By the way, the Bible is very clear that human sacrifice is abhorrent to God, and Jesus was in complete control when he offered himself as a sacrifice, which is completely unlike the human sacrifice of ancient religions.)[34]

The Greek and Roman myths about gods becoming humans may also reflect an aspect of the collective consciousness of humanity that we would like to see God and understand what he would be like as a fellow human (though the capricious gods of these myths are nothing like Jesus). Moreover, many of the most beautiful aspects of human nature come through religions, especially when it comes to living in the moment, meditating to clear our busy minds, sacrificing for others, seeking peace and refraining from violence, and so forth. That humans are inherently worshipers, whether it be of God, gods, nature, or their own "divine spark," doesn't prove that the supernatural realm exists, but it is strong evidence that it does.

I will close with my favorite Bible story about one time when God opened his people's eyes to the supernatural. The story begins when Israel was at war with the Kingdom of Aram, and the king of Aram told his officers where to set up camp. Though it was a private conversation, God revealed the location of the king of Aram's camp to the "man of God," Elisha, who then sent this intelligence to the king of Israel. This happened again and again—so often, in fact, that the king of Aram assumed that one of his officers was leaking information to the Israelites. But his officers insisted that they hadn't divulged the information to the king of Israel, explaining that, "Elisha, the prophet who is in Israel, tells the king of Israel the very words you speak in your bedroom."[35] In other words, Elisha somehow knew what the king of Aram was saying in secret. Therefore, the king of Aram ordered his men to send "horses and chariots and a strong force" to find and seize Elisha.

When this large force arrived at Elisha's place in Dothan, his servant saw the approaching army and exclaimed in panic, "Oh no, my lord! What shall we do?" The story continues:

> "Don't be afraid," the prophet answered. "Those who are with us are more than those who are with them."
>
> And Elisha prayed, "Open his eyes, Lord, so that he may see." Then the Lord opened the servant's eyes, and he looked and saw the hills full of horses and chariots of fire all around Elisha.[36]

Just as the horses and chariots of fire of God's heavenly army surrounded Elisha to protect him from the army of Aram, God's protection surrounds those who trust in him, and he rescues them from their primary foes, sin and death. Based on all of the evidence in chapters 1 through 28, as well as on the great explanatory power of the Christian faith discussed in this and the last chapters, we can be confident that the statement that Elisha made to his servant is also true for believers in Jesus: "Those who are with us are more than those who are with them."

Evidence for the spiritual world abounds, and so do the forces of evil that are behind the atrocious acts we read about in the news. Paul ends his letter to Christian believers in Ephesus with an urgent call for them to be prepared for the battle against the dark forces that are arrayed against those who trust in Jesus:

> Finally, be strong in the Lord and in his mighty power. Put on the full armor of God, so that you can take your stand against the devil's schemes. For our struggle is not against flesh and blood, but against the rulers, against the authorities, against the powers of this dark world and against the spiritual forces of evil in the heavenly realms. Therefore put on the full armor of God, so that when the day of evil comes, you may be able to stand your ground.[37]

The Bible teaches that the spiritual battle is real and that the spiritual battlefield is everywhere. It also teaches that God prepares his followers for the battle by giving them his "armor"[38] and, importantly, that he sends them out as "lambs in the midst of wolves."[39] Rather than use man-made weapons, they are to love their enemies and pray for those who persecute them. Though the battle is invisible, many Christians claim that it is quite tangible, especially so when they "fight" on the front lines to rescue people from the clutches of intense evil.

Having seen the way Christianity explains the existence of absolute morality, love, beauty, and the supernatural, we now move on to a discussion of the aspects of the Christian faith that set it apart from all other belief systems. These unique characteristics lend credibility to the claim the infinite, all-powerful Creator himself is the source of biblical Christianity.

QUESTIONS FOR COMPREHENSION AND DISCUSSION

1. How can you respond to someone who claims that morality is relative, and that every person must determine what is right or wrong for himself or herself?
2. Explain the "Sez who?" argument described by Arthur Laffer. Why can we reply, "Sez who?" to all moral claims?
3. Explain Hume's Law. That is, what does it mean that science can only explain what "is" and not what "ought to be"?
4. What is the problem with voting for moral laws through the political process? How does this demonstrate the existence of universal moral absolutes?
5. How can the Christian God have been love for all eternity? Can the same be true of a unipersonal God (as opposed to a triune God)?
6. What is one possible explanation that God did not want humans to use any tools when they built the altar? What is the theological message that God may have been delivering to his people?
7. How is the sense of beauty as an end in itself more consistent with a "divine Artist" than with a universe created through blind chance?

CHAPTER 30: MORALITY AND OTHER ASPECTS OF REAL LIFE

8. How is Christianity consistent with experiences of supernatural phenomena, such as NDEs, miracles, and so forth?
9. How does Christianity's understanding of the supernatural realm explain the extremes of good and evil in the world?
10. What did Elisha's servant see when God opened his eyes? How does this symbolize what God must do before anyone can receive Jesus as their Savior?

CHAPTER 30 ENDNOTES

1   Timothy Keller, *Jesus the King: Understanding the Life and Death of the Son of God* (New York: Penguin Random House, 2011), 9.
2   Fyodor Dostoyevsky, *The Brothers Karamazov* (New York: MacMillan, 1922), 178.
3   James Davison Hunger and Paul Nedelisky, *Science and the Good: The Tragic Quest for the Foundations of Morality* (New Haven and London: Yale University Press, 2018), Location 64. Referencing Sam Harris, *The Moral Landscape: How Science Can Determine Human Values* (New York: Free Press, 2010); Michael S. Gazzaniga, *The Ethical Brain: The Science of Our Moral Dilemmas* (New York: Harper-Perennial, 2006); E. O. Wilson, "The Biological Basis of Morality," *The Atlantic,* April 1998; Robert Johnson, *Rational Morality: A Science of Right and Wrong* (Great Britain: Dangerous Little Books, 2013); Paul Zak, *The Moral Molecule: The Source of Love and Prosperity* (New York: Dutton, 2012); Marc D. Hauser, *Moral Minds: How Nature Designed Our Universal Sense of Right and Wrong* (London: Abacus, 2006); Patricia Churchland, *Braintrust: What Neuroscience Tells Us about Morality* (Princeton, NJ: Princeton University Press, 2011); Laurence R. Tancredi, *Hardwired Behavior: What Neuroscience Reveals about Morality* (New York: Cambridge University Press, 2005).
4   Arthur Allen Laffer, "Unspeakable Ethics, Unnatural Law," *Duke Law Journal,* Vol. 1979, December, No. 6, 1229. Available online at https://digitalcommons.law.yale.edu/cgi/viewcontent.cgi?article=3810&context=fss_paper.
5   James Davison Hunter, *The Death of Character: Moral Education in an Age Without Good and Evil* (New York: Basic Books 2000), xv.
6   Ibid, 1229-1230.
7   Unfortunately, many Christians in America's history did not understand that slavery is abhorrent to God because he made all humans in his image, and all humans therefore have equal rights and dignity. Another note on this rightfully emotional topic, the "slaves" mentioned in the Bible were indentured servants, which was a position that helped people to get out of

debt. It was very different from the terrible practice of race-based slavery that was common in the United States in the sixteenth through mid-nineteenth centuries, which was, is, and always will be absolutely wrong because it violates the supreme moral code.

8   Hunter, *The Death of Character*, 1249.
9   Elsa Marty, *A Dictionary of Philosophy and Religion* (Continuum International Publishing Group, 2012), 154. Available online at https://books.google.com/books?id=78962vlrCDcC&pg=PA154.
10 See especially John Henry Newman, "A Letter Addressed to the Duke of Norfolk on Occasion of Mr. Gladstone's Recent Expostulation," published in *Newman and Gladstone: The Vatican Decrees*, (Notre Dame, 1962).
11 William Lane Craig, *On Guard: Defending Your Faith with Reason and Precision* (David C. Cook, 2010), Locations 529-533.
12 Sarah Irving-Stonebreaker, "How Oxford and Peter Singer Drove Me from Atheism to Jesus," *The Veritas Forum*, May 22, 2017. Available online at http://www.veritas.org/oxford-atheism-to-jesus/.
13 Quoted in Leon Aron, "Everything You Think You Know About the Collapse of the Soviet Union Is Wrong," *Foreign Policy*, June 20, 2011. Available online at https://foreignpolicy.com/2011/06/20/everything-you-think-you-know-about-the-collapse-of-the-soviet-union-is-wrong/.
14 Ibid.
15 Roza Otunbayeva, as quoted in Ibid.
16 Richard Dawkins, "Richard Dawkins at the Sydney Writers' Festival". "Science Show" with Robyn Williams, www.abc.net.au. September 8, 2007. Available online at https://www.abc.net.au/radionational/programs/scienceshow/richard-dawkins-at-the-sydney-writers-festival/3229706.
17 Genesis 1:26a.
18 If you'd like to read a sample of verses that support the concept of the Trinity in the New Testament, see 1 Corinthians 8:6, 2 Corinthians 1:21-22, 13:14, Ephesians 4:4-6, John 1:1, 3:16, 34-35, 5:19, 14:16, 26, 15:26, Hebrews 1:3, Isaiah 48:16, Luke 1:35, 3:22, Matthew 2:16-17, 3:16, 28:19, Mark 12:29, 1 Peter 1:2, Philippians 2:5-8, and 1 Timothy 2:5.
19 Timothy Keller, *Jesus the King: Understanding the Life and Death of the Son of God* (New York: Penguin Random House, 2011), 9.
20 1 John 4:8,16.
21 Keller, *Jesus the King*, 10.
22 Exodus 20:25.
23 Exodus 30:35.
24 Exodus 28:1.
25 Exodus 39:8-14.

26. Middot 3:4. Available online at https://www.sefaria.org/Mishnah_Middot.3.4.
27. C. S. Lewis, "On Living in an Atomic Age," in *Present Concerns* (San Diego, CA: Harcourt Books, 2002), 76. As quoted in Keller, *Making Sense of God*, 87-88.
28. S. Parnia, D.G. Waller, R. Yeates, and P. Renwick, "A Qualitative and Quantitative Study of the Incidence, Features and Aetiology of Near-Death Experience in Cardiac Arrest Survivors," *Resuscitation* (February 2001).
29. James Mauro, "Bright Lights, Big Mystery," *Psychology Today*, July 1992.
30. Ibid.
31. Kimberly Clark Sharp, *After the Light: What I Discovered on the Other Side of Life That Can Change Your World* (William Morrow & Company, 1995), 243.
32. J. Dudley Woodbury, Russell G. Shubin, and G. Marks, "Why Muslims Follow Jesus," *Christianity Today*, October 24, 2007. Available online at https://www.christianitytoday.com/ct/2007/october/42.80.html.
33. For a few verses describing how God calls or chooses his followers before they respond to him, see John 6:37, 44, 15:16; Matthew 22:14; Romans 8:28-29; Ephesians 1:4-5, 1:11, 2:10; 2 Thessalonians 2:13; 1 Peter 2:9.
34. See Leviticus 20:1-5.
35. 2 Kings 6:12.
36. 2 Kings 6:8-17.
37. Ephesians 6:10-13a.
38. See Ephesians 6:10-17.
39. Luke 10:3.

During a British conference on comparative religions, experts from around the world debated what, if any, belief was unique to the Christian faith.... [C. S.] Lewis responded, "Oh, that's easy. It's grace." After some discussion, the conferees had to agree. The notion of God's love coming to us free of charge, no strings attached, seems to go against every instinct of humanity.... Only Christianity dares to make God's love unconditional.

— Philip Yancey, Christian writer[1]

The doctrines of grace humble man without degrading him and exalt him without inflating him.

— Charles Hodge, former principal of Princeton Theological Seminary[2]

31

Unique Among Philosophies

Christianity is the only religion in which God was willing to suffer and die in order to rescue his people. No other religion proposes that God would do such a thing. Christianity is also unique in its claim that God has demonstrated his love to all people by entering human history in a tangible way. This is why we were able to spend thirteen chapters exploring how the central tenets of Christianity can be supported with historical evidence. Third, as we discussed in Chapter 30, Christianity is the only religion that explains how God can be love in and of himself. Because the Christian God has experienced mutual love within his triune nature for all eternity, he is like a powerhouse of love, just as the sun is a powerhouse of energy. The God of all other religions would have to first create an object of love before being able to extend love.

A fourth unique belief is that the biblical God claims that humans will one day live in renewed, physical bodies on a "New Earth." The Judeo-Christian God created the earth, and he proclaimed that it was "good," unlike many other religions and philosophies that disparage the physical world in favor of the spiritual. Jesus talked about an event in the future that he called *the palingenesia*, translated as "the renewal of all things."[3] It is crucial to note that Jesus used the definite article, "*the* renewal," as opposed to the indefinite article, "*a* renewal." This is a crucial distinction because the Greeks referred to each rebirth of the eternal universe as "renewals." Jesus was therefore communicating that there would be a *one-time* renewal, and that this renewed earth would subsequently last eternally and have no further need for renewal. This suggests that the law dictating that everything is wearing out over

CHAPTER 31: UNIQUE AMONG PHILOSOPHIES

time, known as the Second Law of Thermodynamics, will have been eradicated.

About seven centuries before Jesus' birth, the prophet Isaiah delivered these words from God to his people, whom he addresses as "Jerusalem," and whom Christians believe refers to everyone who has faith in Jesus, both Jews and non-Jews: "See, I will create new heavens and a new earth. The former things will not be remembered, nor will they come to mind." He goes on to explain how his plan will unfold: "And I... am about to come and gather the people of all nations and languages, and they will come and see my glory.... As the new heavens and the new earth that I make will endure before me,... so will your name and descendants endure."

And writing around the turn of the first century AD, the apostle John describes a vision God gave him of that day: "Then I saw 'a new heaven and a new earth.'" He also saw "the Holy City, the new Jerusalem, coming down out of heaven from God, prepared as a bride beautifully dressed for her husband." Then he heard "a loud voice from the throne," which said:

> "Look! God's dwelling place is now among the people, and he will dwell with them. They will be his people, and God himself will be with them and be their God. He will wipe every tear from their eyes. There will be no more death or mourning or crying or pain, for the old order of things has passed away.... I am making everything new!"[4]

No other religion claims that we will live forever in a new physical body on a new earth that has all of the good aspects of our current life, enhanced in ways "immeasurably more than all we ask or imagine,"[5] but without any of the terrible aspects of our current life. We won't just "become one with the universe" or exist as "bodiless spirits." Imagine your favorite activities on earth, and then imagine being able to do them for eternity. That's what God promises his people through the work of his Son.

A God who suffered for the people he loves, a God who himself entered human history, a God who in himself has been love for all eternity, and a God who values and seeks to restore the physical world—these are four amazing and unique aspects of Christianity.

But there is one other major unique aspect of the Christian faith that is the focus of this chapter: the Christian God *has already done everything necessary* for us to spend eternity with him. He offers a free ticket to heaven to all people, and his people are those who, by faith alone, "simply" receive it as a free gift. This is the unique aspect of the gospel, or the "good news," about what Jesus has accomplished, and it is the reason that the gospel has tremendous power to transform people from the inside out (our focus in the next chapter).

As C. S. Lewis claimed at the conference on comparative religions, it is this *grace*, or unearned merit, that sets Christianity apart from all other religions on earth. Let's find out what is so unique—and amazing—about grace.

THE UNIQUE TRAJECTORY OF THE GOSPEL

In all other religions, humans must perform various actions in order to climb up to God. Muslims seek to satisfy the five pillars of Islam. Buddhists seek to follow the Noble Eightfold Path to attain nirvana or enlightenment. Hindus perform the requirements of their societal class, or caste, in order to be reborn in a higher caste in their next life. And once he or she accumulates sufficient good karma over many lifetimes, the obedient Hindu will eventually reunite spiritually with the universal soul, or Brahman. As we discussed in the chapters concerning the Jewish feasts, Jews seek to obey God's detailed law, perform good deeds, and donate to charity in an effort to tip the balance and make their goodness outweigh their sinfulness. By studying the Torah, God's law, and living according to it the best that they can, Jews can improve the chances that God writes their name in his "Book of Life."

And if you ask atheists, agnostics, or the otherwise irreligious what makes them feel that their lives are worthwhile, you will get similar types of answers: succeeding in their career, lovingly raising a family, fighting for just causes, working to make the world a better place, donating to charity and volunteering, making a difference in others' lives. It all boils down to actions, or "works"—what humans do to prove to themselves and to others that they have significance, worth, an identity, a purpose, or a reason to feel proud. Even if you don't believe in God, as a human, you are working to achieve some semblance of meaning and purpose, to demonstrate that your life counts and won't have been lived in vain. This desire for significance is built into the human psyche, and our happiness depends upon how much significance we feel we have. If we don't feel significant, the result is generally depression, despair, and unfortunately, all too often, suicide.

As opposed to all of the religions of the world, including the ones not mentioned in the previous paragraphs, Christianity is based on the *reverse* of this typical, upward trajectory. Instead of humans working to climb their way *up* to God (or to achieve significance in other non-theistic ways), the Bible states that the Creator of the universe *came down* to humans. He came as a baby in a manger, humbling himself and becoming a servant who even washed his followers' dirty feet.[6] The Creator of the universe became a human being, which we've supported with historical and biblical evidence for the majority of this book so far. Moreover, he lived a perfectly holy life and suffered a terribly torturous death. Why? Because he knew that the humans whom he had created would never be able to live "the perfect life" his holiness demands. And because he loves his people and desires to spend eternity with them, he did not want them to take the penalty for their sins that his justice demands, which would separate them from the blessings of his presence for all eternity. It is crucial to note that Jesus taught extensively on this concept, called "hell," and he himself descended into hell while he was taking the penalty of sin on himself for those who trust in him.[7] So, the God of Christianity did for us what we could never do for ourselves.

But why did he have to do this? Why couldn't Jesus just forgive us and simply transfer his holiness over to us? Why did he have to come as a human, live perfectly, and then die a horrible death? If he is God, he surely could have done it an easier way, right? Unfortunately, just as God cannot sin (his state is *non posse peccare*, as we discussed in Chapter 24), he also cannot "just forgive" or "just transfer his holiness to us." It would violate his nature to do these things, as he is both perfectly loving and perfectly just. Because he is perfectly loving, he does not want to see us separated from him for eternity, which would be the case if he didn't rescue us. And because he is perfectly just, he can't just overlook our transgressions, forgive us, and give us his holy record. To satisfy his perfect justice, *someone* must take the penalty, so his solution was to send a substitute to do it for us—himself as the second person of the Trinity, Jesus Christ. Pastor Timothy Keller explains it in this way: "God could say, 'Let there be light!' but he couldn't just say, 'Let there be forgiveness!'"[8] Someone must pay the price for the sin of mankind. So, he paid it himself.

Keller gives us this example of how someone must always pay the price to forgive a debt. If your friend breaks your lamp, you can either ask him to pay to replace it, or you can forgive the debt and pay for a replacement yourself. Or, you could go without the lamp and have darkness where you would normally have had light. You forgive the debt either by paying money yourself for a new light or by enduring a lack of light.

It works the same way when you forgive someone who has wronged you. When you want to take revenge, you refrain. That requires effort. When you want to say terrible things about the person who hurt you, you refrain. That also is difficult. When you want to dwell on the incident, you refrain. Also tough. But by forgiving him or her, God uses it to grow you as a person, restore the relationship, and produce healing within you. Alternatively, you can pay the debt of forgiveness through revenge, saying terrible things, or dwelling on the incident, all of which have a negative impact on your character and emotional health, not to mention on the relationship with the person who hurt you.

Jesus chose the former, more difficult path. By taking the penalty for our sin on himself, he paid the price that we would have otherwise had to pay ourselves. In so doing, he restored the relationship between humans and their Creator, which Adam and Eve had originally broken. As a result, he also provides the power for those of us who emulate him to break the cycle of revenge when others hurt us. If we practice forgiveness, depending on the Holy Spirit for enablement, we can choose to "love our enemies" instead of strike back at them.

Many people also ask the question, "If God is perfectly good and also omnipotent, why does he allow suffering and evil in the first place? Isn't all of human sin his fault because he allowed it and lets it continue?" God allows evil and suffering because he allows humans to choose what they want to do, and human choices have caused the evil in the world. In *Mere Christianity*, C. S. Lewis explains it succinctly:

> The moment you have a self at all, there is a possibility of putting yourself first—wanting to be the centre—wanting to be God, in fact. That was the sin of Satan: and that was the sin he taught the human race.... What Satan

put into the heads of our remote ancestors was the idea that they could 'be like gods'—be their own masters—invent some sort of happiness for themselves outside God, apart from God. And out of that hopeless attempt has come nearly all that we call human history—money, poverty, ambition, war, prostitution, classes, empires, slavery—the long terrible story of man trying to find something other than God which will make him happy.[9]

So, when he let Adam and Eve have the option of disobeying him, God was willing to take the risk that evil would result (and of course, being omniscient, he knew it would!).

Though God didn't create evil and suffering, and only allowed it to exist because he wanted humans to be able to choose obedience or disobedience, there is a way that God actually uses evil and suffering for our good. Depending on our attitude to it, suffering will either make us miserable or it will strengthen us. Therefore, if we see suffering as a way to become stronger and grow as a person, it can play a useful role in our lives. Moreover, through suffering, we learn to empathize with others who have experienced the same difficulties. Please know that I in no way intend to minimize the heart ache and pain that suffering causes.

So, while God never causes evil or suffering, he can work his good purposes even through the evil and suffering that humans create. But even if you insist on pointing the finger at God and blaming him for evil, and even if you insist that he should be punished for this evil, your sentence has *already* been handed down. He *did* suffer for it. He *was* punished for it. God himself took the penalty for human evil on a Roman cross.

One story which exemplifies the power of sacrificial love comes from the book *To End All Wars* (formerly published as *Miracle on the River Kwai*). The author, Ernest Gordon, was a Scottish soldier who spent time working on the Burma Railway in a POW camp during World War II. He describes the horrendous conditions in the camp, where the prisoners were suffering from starvation and disease, and where fear, hatred, and selfishness ruled all relationships. At the end of one day of labor, the officer in charge insisted that a shovel was missing and threatened to kill all of the men unless the shovel was turned in. They all remained at attention, frozen with fear, wondering who could have stolen a shovel.

Then one man stepped forward to admit guilt, and the officer proceeded to mercilessly beat him to death. As the prisoners stared at his lifeless body on the ground, another soldier ran up, announcing that they had miscounted, and there was no missing shovel after all. The man had been innocent. He had stepped forward to save the lives of his fellow prisoners. The amazing result of this man's selfless action was the transformation of the atmosphere in the camp, as Gordon explains:

> Death was still with us, but we were slowly being freed from its destructive grip. We were seeing for ourselves the sharp contrast between forces that made for life and those that made for death. Selfishness, hatred, envy, jealousy, greed, self-intelligence, laziness, and pride were anti-life. Love, heroism, self-sacrifice, sympathy, mercy, integrity and creative faith, were the essence of life, turning mere existence into living in the truest sense. These were gifts of God to men. There was still hatred, but there was also love. There was death, but there was also life. God had not left us. He was with us, calling us to live the divine life in fellowship.[10]

This is the gospel trajectory. God himself paid our penalty for us, which then frees us up to "pay it forward." By satisfying—for us—the perfect holiness that his law demands, and by taking the penalty—for us—that his justice demands for our infractions, the Christian God provided a way for his people to live with him for all eternity. Our only requirement is to humbly receive the free gift.

WHY HUMAN NATURE INSTINCTIVELY DISLIKES GRACE

The natural instinct of human beings is to be self-sufficient, and this is more than ever the case in our modern, individualistic, freedom-focused, and meritocratic society. As a result, our natural inclination when we hear that God *had to come down* to pull us up to him, and that there is nothing else involved *on our part*, is to be turned off. After all, we are quite capable, thank you very much, of climbing up to God (or, in the case of those who don't believe in or think about God, to prove their worth on their own). It hurts our pride to hear that we aren't good enough to ever earn a place in heaven through our own will, determination, and effort.

When we are told how easy it is—just "have faith in Jesus" or simply "receive Jesus as your Savior"—we dismiss it. We act like Naaman, the Syrian general we discussed in Chapter 26, who didn't want to "just wash in the Jordan," which seemed too simple. He was a powerful, accomplished general—why should he do something any lowlife can do? And the rivers are better where he came from anyway! Why did he even bother to travel to Israel to solicit advice for his healing?[11]

Like Naaman, we reflexively recoil at the idea that getting into heaven is not up to us, and we especially hate being told that we could never do it on our own. At an early point in his ministry, Jesus mentioned Naaman's healing. Jesus had obviously insulted some people because we read that "all the people in the synagogue were furious when they heard" what he had just said. They even wanted to throw him off a cliff. Then Jesus told these law-abiding people: "And there were many in Israel with leprosy in the time of Elisha the prophet, yet not one of them was cleansed—only Naaman the Syrian."[12] Jesus was essentially claiming that a non-Jew had been healed, and the Jews' outward obedience to the law wouldn't have qualified them for the same healing. This is just one of many examples of how grace offends people of all backgrounds. It offended Naaman because he was a powerful military man who could do so much more to earn his healing, and it offended the Jews because they were God's chosen people, who followed God's law obediently.

What's more, we cry out, "Unfair!" when we hear that someone—even the worst criminal—can simply place their faith in Jesus right before they die and receive automatic access to heaven. And you mean to say that the sweet little old lady who bakes cookies for the firefighters isn't going to heaven just because she doesn't have faith in Jesus?! It all sounds so outrageously unjust and unjustifiable. Why would God make it so easy that just anyone can "play the Jesus card" and go to heaven, while the many who don't believe in Jesus aren't welcome there? Many people reject Christianity for this reason alone. And though it is a very difficult aspect of the faith, there are explanations, and to outright reject faith in Jesus merely because you are outraged is to potentially base your eternal destiny on an emotional reaction and not on reason. In the next chapter, when we talk about "the carrot and the stick" motivation of the human heart and how it inspires so many problems in our relationships, it will make more sense why God takes human effort out of the equation for our salvation. For now, it's helpful to note that if we trust that God is both omnipotent and perfectly loving—which the Bible teaches are both true—we can trust that his plan is perfect, though our finite minds cannot comprehend his infinite wisdom.

When we have these difficult questions, we can relax, knowing that God is in perfect control and he is perfectly wise, good, and just. Of course, we can still seek answers to our questions, but at some point, we must humbly admit we cannot understand the thinking of an infinite God, and it is irrational to disagree with his plan if we truly trust what the Bible says about him. As usual, C. S. Lewis explains this best:

> But there is a difficulty about disagreeing with God. He is the source from which all your reasoning power comes: you could not be right and He wrong any more than a stream can rise higher than its own source. When you are arguing against the very power that makes you able to argue at all: it is like cutting off the branch you are sitting on.[13]

But back to our knee-jerk dislike of "salvation by grace." One of the reasons people have an instinctual distaste for the idea of free, unearned grace is that we hate any form of grading that doesn't rely on our own effort. Those who are successful and accomplished are especially offended by grace, which is the main reason that poor people generally "get" the gospel of Christianity more easily than rich people, and outsiders, such as the prostitutes and tax collectors in Jesus' day, tend to "get" the gospel more than insiders who have positions of power in society. It is also why Christianity is spreading rapidly in places like Africa, while European churches are being converted into hostels and nightclubs, as a larger portion of the population no longer believes in the Christian God.

Another reason we hate the idea of free grace is that if God does all of the work, we lose our bargaining power with him. There is nothing he *can't* ask of us. If God has done everything, all we can do is obey him. In fact, the desire to obey God and please him is the most obvious sign of true faith. If we see how much God has done to ensure we spend eternity in paradise with him, we *will* desire to please him, and it becomes OK that we've lost our bargaining power. (This is also why deathbed conversions are rarely genuine. If someone waits until the last minute to put his faith in Jesus, it is most likely not true faith. Of course, it could be genuine—only God knows.)

Once God opens our eyes to what he has done for us through his Son, we will want to change our life to conform with his law. We will want to please him, but not because we have to. We will want to please him because we are grateful for what he has *already* done for us first.[14]

ETERNAL REST FOR OUR SOULS

Jesus has done everything for us. There are no other requirements, no pillars to obligingly perform, no righteous paths, no good karma to generate, no more lifetimes to live, no checklists of do's and don'ts. As hard as it is to believe, if you have faith in Jesus, there is nothing so terrible that you can do that could cause God to love you any less than he already loves you. And there is nothing so selfless that you can do that will cause God to love you anymore. God will always see you as if you had lived the perfect life he lived while he was on earth. Your salvation is eternally secure. What a relief!

As mentioned in Chapter 28, this is one of the reasons that Jesus calls himself the "Lord of the Sabbath." In him, we can find rest for our souls. We can relax into the understanding that "He has done it!", "It is finished," and "It is paid in full,"[15] as Jesus exclaimed just before he died. We can lean on the assurance that Jesus has removed our sins and given us his perfect record, and he will never say, "Oops, I didn't mean for you to get that gift—give it back!" This is why God tells us: "Be still, and know that I am God; I will be exalted among the nations, I will be exalted in the earth."[16] Everything will be all right. He has done it all. All of the evil in the world cannot thwart his, and his followers', ultimate victory. As the apostle Paul celebrated, "We are more than conquerors through him who loved us."[17]

Jesus understands our struggles to "live up" and "keep up" and "chin up." He experienced it himself. He was tempted in every way, just as we are. He wants us to relax and enjoy all of the good in the world he has made for us—the world he is planning to remake for us, without all of the iniquity of the current one. And he wants us to serve others and make sure they also know about his free gift.

CAN I LIVE ANY WAY I WANT?

Many people think, "Well, if you are saved no matter what, and if God loves you no matter what, it doesn't matter how you live! You can just go on living any way you please, right?" If you are a Christian and these are your thoughts, it is a sign that you haven't truly comprehended what Jesus has done for you. Once Christians realize the enormity of the gift they have received, once they are *captivated by grace,* they will desire to please Jesus and live in a manner that is worthy of his eternal gifts to them. Though only God knows whether anyone is truly a Christian, as Matthew writes, "You will know them... by their fruit."[18] That is, over time, true Christians will begin to bear the "fruit of the Spirit," which Paul states is "love, joy, peace, patience, kindness, goodness, faithfulness, gentleness, and self-control."[19] Note that Christians unfortunately won't display the fruit of the Spirit at all times throughout their lives. But they will seek to do so, and bearing fruit in greater abundance will be an ongoing process that will last their entire lives.

Jesus' brother James makes this point clear with these emphatic statements:

> You foolish person, do you want evidence that faith without deeds is useless? Was not our father Abraham considered righteous for what he did when he offered his son Isaac on the altar? You see that his faith and his actions were working together, and his faith was made complete by what he did.[20]

Here James is clarifying that it is through faith that we attain eternal life, but this faith—if it is genuine—will be accompanied by good deeds that are performed out of love, trust, and gratitude, rather than out of obligation or fear of punishment. Abraham had faith in God, who had promised to give him innumerable descendants through Isaac, and he demonstrated this faith through obedience, even when asked to surrender his most precious possession, his long-awaited son. He trusted that God was powerful enough to bring Isaac back to life, and his obedience was fueled by love, trust, and gratitude. James continues his explanation with a useful analogy: "As the body without the spirit is dead, so faith without deeds is dead."[21] A person who has true faith will seek to please God, even though he or she will not do so perfectly until that first day in heaven.

Jesus made it clear that the best way to demonstrate love for him is through obedience to his instructions. Just before he was arrested and condemned to die, Jesus told his disciples: "If you love me, keep my commands."[22] And a few verses later, Jesus repeated the same idea, to emphasize its importance: "Anyone who loves me will obey my teaching."[23] This is the trajectory of the gospel and our fitting response to it. First, God comes down to rescue his people. Second, his people (those who recognize what he has done for them) keep his commands out of gratitude to him and love for him. Sure, we believers mess up all of the time. But we are frustrated when we fail, we confess our sins, knowing that "he is faithful and just and will forgive our sins and purify us from all unrighteousness."[24] And we press on, determined to become more like Jesus, knowing we are eternally secure, and trusting that "he who began a good work in [us] will carry it on to completion until the day of Christ Jesus."[25]

In the following statement, Jesus emphasizes the importance of putting his words into practice after we believe that he is our "Lord":

> "Why do you call me, 'Lord, Lord,' and do not do what I say? As for everyone who comes to me and hears my words and puts them into practice, I will show you what they are like. They are like a man building a house, who dug down deep and laid the foundation on rock. When a flood came, the torrent struck that house but could not shake it, because it was well built. But the one who hears my words and does not put them into practice is like a man who built a house on the ground without a foundation. The moment the torrent struck that house, it collapsed and its destruction was complete."[26]

God saves us, and our appropriate response is to put his words into practice. In so doing, we build our house on a rock, and it won't be swept away during the torrents of this life.

You see this trajectory throughout the Bible: first God rescues, then his people respond in obedience out of love and gratitude. When the people forget what God has done for them, they turn to other gods or begrudgingly obey God out of obligation or guilt. There is no joy. But when they remember what God has done for them, the people's natural response is thankfulness, love, and joyful celebration.

In fact, one of the reasons God insisted that his people celebrate so many feasts was to ensure they would remember the many times he had rescued them and the many ways he had blessed them over the centuries. His people would often erect stone monuments to commemorate a time when God had rescued them. These "souvenirs" are sometimes referred to as "Ebenezers" from the Hebrew words, "Eben ha-Ezer," or "stone of the help." This is the name that the prophet Samuel gave to the stone he erected to commemorate the time when God helped the Israelites to defeat the Philistines at Mizpeh.[27] As our Creator, God knows how forgetful we can be, so he instituted these reminders to keep us focused on what is important, his rescues. All of the rescues in the Hebrew Scriptures point to the ultimate rescue—from sin and death—achieved through Jesus' sacrifice on our behalf.

Christianity maintains these opportunities to reflect on God's goodness through the repetitive celebrations of communion (also called Holy Communion or the Lord's Supper), as well as annual celebrations of Palm Sunday, Good Friday, Easter, and of course, Christmas. Interestingly, those who follow the tradition of the Eastern Orthodox church have twelve "Great Feasts," in addition to Easter, all of which are meant to remind the people of what God has done for them. The more we reflect on all that God has done for us, the more we can restore feelings of contentment, gratitude, and joy—even in the midst of the most difficult circumstances. Unfortunately, in the modern world, Santa Claus and the Easter Bunny have distracted us from what Jesus has done for us. And because we instinctively feel we have to earn God's approval, we also can easily turn these feasts into works we're obliged to perform (or church services we're obliged to attend) instead of treating them as reminders of God's gift of salvation and eternal life, which he gives us regardless of our works.

There is one final point to make regarding the unique trajectory of

CHAPTER 31: UNIQUE AMONG PHILOSOPHIES

the gospel: the purpose of the law. Most people are familiar with the Ten Commandments that God gave to his people in Exodus 20, though they probably couldn't recite them all. But most people are generally *not familiar with* the first two verses of Exodus 20, which immediately precede the first commandment. They go like this: "And God spoke all these words: 'I am the Lord your God, who brought you out of Egypt, out of the land of slavery.'"[28] *Before* he gives the law, God *first* reminds his people what he has *already* done for them, rescued them from slavery. They don't obey the law in order to earn this rescue, but they are to obey the law out of gratitude to God for *already* having rescued them.

God gave his people the law for at least three reasons, one of which was to show them the path to ultimate human flourishing in community with each other and with him. It's like an instruction manual that teaches us how we as human beings will perform optimally, how we can "build our house on the rock" so that it won't collapse in the torrent of life. The second reason God gave his people the law was to show the world what he is like, so that the Israelites—if they were obeying God's law—would be an example to other nations. And the third reason for the law was to show his people that they could never obey it perfectly. Their failure to keep the law (which was often!) would make his people aware of how unholy they were compared to a perfectly holy God. The law was meant to cause us to cry out for help: "We can't do it! Help us, Lord!" When Jesus came, this help arrived. We can now "take his yoke upon us and learn from him," and we can find in him the rest our souls need.

In the eighteenth century, the English revivalist and hymnist John Berridge composed this succinct rhyme to contrast the frustration of trying to fulfill the law, on the one hand, with the motivation and freedom that the gospel gives us, on the other:

> Run, John, run, the law commands,
> But gives us neither feet nor hands.
> Far better news the gospel brings:
> It bids us fly and gives us wings.[29]

Because our human hands and feet are incapable of obeying the law fully, God came down to us, and in so doing, he has given us wings to fly. Just as God rescued his people from Egypt, "carrying them on eagles' wings,"[30] he rescues his people today through grace. All a believer has to do is trust in the completed work of Jesus, which then empowers him or her to take flight. In the next chapter, we'll explore this great transformational and motivational power of the gospel.

I'd like to conduct a thought experiment to close this chapter. Let's begin with the assumption that the biblical God—the one who is consistent with the scientific evidence we discussed in the first part of the book—exists. If this all-powerful, perfectly wise, and infinitely holy Creator desired to share his love with the humans he created, how would he do so? I argue that the most unique aspect of Christianity—salvation by grace through faith alone—would be the most logical way for him to relate to humans. How so? If he is so perfectly holy, there is no way that humans—in their own effort—could reach the standard of holiness that he sets. And if is he so powerful, he has no need for humans to help him in any way. Further, if he is so wise, he recognizes that human effort, when successful, results in self-righteousness, and human effort, when unsuccessful, results in despair and self-deception. Neither result is attractive. Humans become either self-righteous and look down their nose at others who aren't as good, or they become angry and dejected, shifting the blame to others and deceiving themselves to keep from despair. My declaration, therefore, is that the type of God that the Bible describes (and the scientific evidence supports) would extend salvation in a way that was completely up to him, so that no human could boast.

Moreover, if this God is perfectly just, he could not overlook any evil. He would require that the penalty for any infraction be paid in full. And if this God is perfectly merciful and loving, he would be willing to take that penalty himself. Not only do we expect this type of salvation from the God of the Bible, but this type of salvation is also something that humans would never have invented themselves. Across the political and philosophical spectrum, all humans recoil at the idea that it's not up to us, that we can't "earn our way" into God's favor, that we are helpless unless God gives us a free gift and does everything that's required for us. Take your pick: (1) An all-powerful God who does everything for us to have a relationship with him, or (2) Humans competing with one another and arguing about who is most deserving of accolades. The former is beautiful and unique, more likely sourcing from a loving Creator, while the latter is what humans have

CHAPTER 31: UNIQUE AMONG PHILOSOPHIES

pursued for millennia and what has generated the mess that we see in the world today.

There are numerous other examples throughout the Old Testament of the "gospel trajectory": First God comes down to rescue his people, and second, the people respond in obedience that is motivated by love, joy, and gratitude. We covered many of these examples—though not all of them, by any means—in the previous chapters when we summarized the way the Old Testament foreshadows Jesus and the salvation that he offers us though our faith in him. Let's now turn to the way that the gospel trajectory fuels transformation in the lives of believers, empowering them in a way, I believe, no other religion or philosophy can.

QUESTIONS FOR COMPREHENSION AND DISCUSSION

1. What are a few unique aspects of Christianity with regard to suffering, historicity, love, and heaven?
2. How is the "renewal of all things" that Jesus talked about prophesied in the Old Testament? And how is it described in Revelation?
3. Describe the "trajectory" of all other human religions besides Christianity (when it is properly understood)? What are a few examples of this works-based, humans-up-to-God trajectory?
4. How do atheists or irreligious people follow the same trajectory, though it is not to a god or gods?
5. What is the trajectory of the gospel of Jesus Christ? Why is this trajectory necessary if there is any hope for sinful humans?
6. Why can't God just forgive sins? Why can't he just let us into heaven with him? That is, why did Jesus have to die?
7. Why is grace so contrary to the natural inclination of humans? Why do we tend to dislike the idea of grace?
8. How do believers respond to God's law, once we truly "get" what he has done for us?
9. If we say we have faith in Jesus, but we aren't showing any desire to obey and know Jesus more, what is this possibly indicating, according to Matthew and James?

10. What did God tell his people before he gave them the law? Why did he do this? How does this show the gospel trajectory? What are three reasons that God provided his law?

CHAPTER 31 ENDNOTES

1. Philip Yancey, *What's So Amazing About Grace?* (Grand Rapids, MI: Zondervan, 1997), 45.
2. Josiah Hotchkiss Gilbert, *Dictionary of Burning Words of Brilliant Writers* (1895), 334.
3. Matthew 19:28.
4. Revelation. 21:1-5a.
5. Ephesians 3:20.
6. See the story in John 13:1-17.
7. Theologians point out that, because God is omnipresent, those who do not receive his free gift of eternal salvation will not be fully separated from his presence. However, the Bible teaches that they will be separated from all of the good that emanates from him, which is everything good we experience in this life, whether we believe in him or not. For Jesus' own teachings on hell, see Matthew 5:22-30, 7:13-14, 19-20, 8:12, 10:28, 13:40-43, 49-50, 18:6-9, 22:11-14, 24:36-51, 23:33, 25:10-13, 29-30, 41-46; Mark 8:42-28, 9:45-47; Luke 6:49, 12:5, 13:22-30, 16:19-31, 17:26-35; John 15:6.
8. The source of much of the content in this chapter and the next two is many years of sermons by Timothy Keller at Redeemer Presbyterian Church in New York City and Theodore Hamilton at New Life Presbyterian Church in Escondido, California. These sermons are available online at https://gospelinlife.com and http://newlifepca.com.
9. C. S. Lewis, *Mere Christianity* (San Francisco: HarperOne, 2009), 49.
10. Ernest Gordon, *To End All Wars: A True Story about the Will to Survive and the Courage to Forgive* (Grand Rapids, MI: Zondervan, 2013), 105.
11. See the story in 2 Kings 5.
12. Luke 4:27-28.
13. C. S. Lewis, *Mere Christianity* (San Francisco: HarperOne, 2009), 48.
14. Read the apostle Paul's discussion of the question, "Shall we go on sinning that grace may increase?" in Romans 6. Those who truly recognize what Jesus has done for them are no longer "slaves to sin" but become "slaves to righteousness."
15. John 19:30.
16. Psalm 46:10.
17. Romans 8:37.
18. Matthew 7:16, 20.

CHAPTER 31: UNIQUE AMONG PHILOSOPHIES

19. Galatians 5:22-23, English Standard Version translation.
20. James 2:20-22.
21. James 2:26.
22. John 14:15.
23. John 14:23.
24. 1 John 1:9.
25. Philippians 1:6.
26. Luke 6:46-49.
27. 1 Samuel 7:12.
28. Exodus 20:1-2.
29. Charles H. Spurgeon, *The Salt-Cellars: Being a Collection of Proverbs, Together with Homely Notes Thereon* (London: Passmore and Alabaster, 1889), 200. From Jason Meyer, *The End of the Law: Mosaic Covenant in Pauline Theology* (B&H, 2010), 2 No. 3. Found online at https://www.thegospelcoalition.org/blogs/justin-taylor/run-john-run.
30. Exodus 19:4.

The gospel is this: We are more sinful and flawed in ourselves than we ever dared believe, yet at the very same time we are more loved and accepted in Jesus Christ than we ever dared hope.

— Timothy Keller, pastor and author[1]

Imagine yourself as a living house. God comes in to rebuild that house. At first, perhaps, you can understand what He is doing. He is getting the drains right and stopping the leaks in the roof and so on; you knew that those jobs needed doing and so you are not surprised. But presently He starts knocking the house about in a way that hurts abominably and does not seem to make any sense. What on earth is He up to? The explanation is that He is building quite a different house from the one you thought of — throwing out a new wing here, putting on an extra floor there, running up towers, making courtyards. You thought you were being made into a decent little cottage: but He is building a palace. He intends to come and live in it Himself.

— C. S. Lewis, Christian apologist, novelist, and professor[2]

Power to Truly Transform

So, other than our ability to "rest" in God's gift to us, what's the big deal about salvation by grace through faith in Jesus? First, let's compare how this trajectory—God coming to us—changes the motivations of the human heart. Then we'll examine how this fundamental difference in motivation transforms believers from the inside out.

THE DRIVE SHAFT OF THE HUMAN HEART

Just as there have been two main ways to get a horse to move forward, there are two main ways to motivate human beings: the "carrot" and the "stick." The carrot is some sort of incentive or reward we will *receive* if we achieve a goal. The "stick" is some sort of punishment that we will *avoid* if we achieve the goal.

There is one other analogy that is helpful in our discussion of human motivation: the drive shaft. In a car, the drive shaft—in the simplest of understandings—is what connects the power of the engine to the wheels. When the engine revs higher, the drive shaft delivers more force, or torque, to the axles, which causes the wheels to turn faster. Thus, the drive shaft connects the power of the engine to the wheels, which increases or decreases the speed of the car.

The Bible describes the human heart, *leb* or לֵב in Hebrew, as the engine that powers our motivation. The greatest desires of our heart will motivate us the most, just as our greatest fears will disincentivize us the most. The Bible understands the human heart as the "seat of the emotional and intellectual life" and the center of the "moral and spiritual as well as physical life."³ What modern psychologists ascribe to the "mind," the Bible ascribes to the heart, such that the heart alone is the seat of three functions: feeling, knowing, and willing. That is why Proverbs 4:23 instructs us to "above all else, guard your heart, for everything you do flows from it."

So back to the carrot and the stick. All religions, except biblical Christianity (when properly understood), operate on the basis of the carrot and the stick. Do good things and receive rewards; do bad things and receive punishment. What happens when a human being receives a reward for their good deeds, which could either be an actual reward or simply an internal feeling of accomplishment? He or she feels happy and proud. And what happens when a human being receives punishment, which could come in the form of rejection by one's peers, dissatisfaction with one's own performance, or just a feeling of guilt or failure? He or she feels demoralized, depressed, guilty, and perhaps even despair. (Note that this is true even in an atheistic or irreligious worldview.)

In this paradigm, the ultimate drive shaft of the human heart is to achieve the carrot and to avoid the stick. When we get the carrot, we experience happiness and pride. And if we fail to get the carrot, or if we get hit by the stick, the result is disappointment and despair. In short, if we succeed, we feel prideful, and if we fail, we feel despair. Moreover, as we go through the steps to climb up to heaven, paradise, nirvana, moksha, or whatever our own version of perfect happiness may be, we experience hope, but we also experience fear because our success may not last. One day we are doing well, and we are happy and proud. The next day we may make a mistake, and we are sad and disappointed at best, or filled with despair and despondent—even suicidal—at worst. We are hopeful of success but always afraid that one day we may fail. And we are never sure where we will end up at the point of our death. (Atheists and the irreligious also aren't certain what awaits them after death, but for a different reason.) We have no assurance unless we are always succeeding (or at least convincing ourselves that we are succeeding, or that our good deeds outweigh our bad deeds, or that it doesn't matter in the end if we're good).

Moreover, when we succeed, we are more likely to look down on others who are not as successful in the ways that we are. If we have worked hard to become wealthy, we are more likely to look down on (or not associate with) poor people. If we find worth because we are intelligent, we are more likely to criticize or disparage people who aren't as "rational" as we are. Similarly, if we have many educational degrees, we are more likely to look down on those who didn't work hard in school. If we are politically conservative, we are more likely to look down on the politically progressive, and vice versa. If we are beautiful or popular, we are generally more reluctant to be seen with those who are unattractive or socially clumsy. If we are good at sports, we are more likely to look down on those who are better at schoolwork, and vice versa. If we are church-goers or religious, we are more likely to look down on atheists or those of another faith. And if we are atheists, we are more likely to look down on those who have faith. You get the picture.

Since we are always seeking to establish our self-worth, identity, and significance, human beings are innately driven to focus on their own successes and on other people's comparative failures. This is the source of racism, misogyny, class conflict, political discord and gridlock, and many other relational problems in society. We also are much better at recognizing others' weaknesses and failures than we are at recognizing our own. Again, all of these tendencies are related to our drive to feel good about ourselves, and to maintain our sense of worth, whether religion is involved or not.

On the other hand, if we fail, our identity and self-worth are threatened, so we will unconsciously switch into one of several "coping" modes. One is "blame-shifting" mode, the earliest way that humans tried to cover up their failure. When her infraction was found out, Eve blamed the serpent, and Adam blamed Eve and therefore God, who had given him Eve.[4] If we aren't blame-shifting, we're in "minimizing" or "rationalizing" modes. It's not so bad, we tell ourselves. We had a good excuse to do what we did. Anyone in our place would have done the same. We compare ourselves to others and try to think of situations where other people behaved or failed worse. We actually enjoy seeing others fail, if we're honest with ourselves. It plays right into this attempt to minimize our own faults compared to those of others.

A woman who cheats on her husband may tell herself, "At least I'm a good mother, and after all, I deserve a little romance." A hit man in the Mafia may tell himself, "A man's got to earn a living somehow, and at least I treat my mother well." Hitler rationalized his actions in some way, too. As Keller has said in a sermon, "We don't know what Hitler told himself, but he told himself something." Keller also notes:

CHAPTER 32: POWER TO TRULY TRANSFORM

"Self-deception is not the worst thing we do, but it's the reason we can do the worst things."[5]

We humans are remarkably adept at self-deception, denial, and the ability to rationalize our faults. It's a survival instinct, a defense mechanism, and often a way to keep ourselves from despair. As a result, our worst sins are often the ones we are the best at hiding from ourselves, and they're especially insidious because we don't see them. Moreover, as we are exposed little by little to ways that are in opposition to God's law, we are like frogs in a pot of water that is slowly coming to a boil. Because our exposure is gradual, we don't realize how much trouble we are in until it is too late to jump out of the pot.

The reverse is also true: when we are successful, we are eager to claim all of the credit. We claim personal responsibility for our successes, and we don't recognize how much our childhood, our educational and career opportunities, our "being in the right place at the right time," and our God-given skills and intelligence are responsible. When we have excessive pride, we are less generous with our money ("it's mine—I earned it," is our attitude), and we are less likely to be sympathetic to others who aren't as successful. This is also a reason why we look down on others who aren't as moral or upright as we are, forgetting that much of the reason we are where we are is because of where we were born, our home life as a child, our opportunities, our friends and family, and so on.

Moreover, we often fail to give God the credit for so much of the good in our lives, since we think it's our own doing, forgetting that all good things come from him.[6] When we fail to give God credit, we are like children whose parents have done everything to ensure our future success, but when we grow up, we completely ignore the ones who made anything we've ever done even possible. When good things befall us, we are quick to claim credit, but when bad circumstances dog us, we more easily blame others, and often it is God we blame "for not answering our prayers." In fact, sometimes God doesn't answer our prayers because he knows what's better for us. He may allow us to go through trials in order to strengthen us, or because he wants to train us to depend on him instead of on the less reliable "idols" we usually seek for comfort, support, or significance.

To summarize, the drive shaft of our hearts is normally powered by pride and a fear of failure. As a result, we desperately seek to minimize or overlook our wrongs, to blame others, to exaggerate our accomplishments, or to compare ourselves to others whom we consider "lesser." When we succeed, we are likely to become prideful and self-righteous, and when we fail, we are likely to be envious, hateful, fearful, and despondent. Life becomes a roller coaster that is up one day and down the next, depending on our circumstances. What's more, with a whole world of people whose hearts operate by the carrot/stick drive shaft, we've all created a terrible place. Even good deeds are often inherently selfish, done so that we "look good to others," "build our college application or resume," or "feel good about ourselves," rather than out of true humility and selflessness. And bad deeds are everywhere. The carrot/stick drive shaft makes the world a mess.

If you doubt the relationship between the carrot and the stick mentality and the mess of the world, try this thought experiment. List as many types of evil in the world. I'll get the list started: lying, cheating, deception, robbery, bullying, vandalism, slander, murder, rape, fraud, racism, discrimination, corruption, falsehood, and so forth. Now try to think of the reasons that people would engage in this behavior. Usually they are motivated by selfishness, to gain something for themselves (pleasure, power, fame, or money), to make themselves feel better compared to others, or to avoid a negative consequence. Ironically, the same exact motivational drive that empowers people to do evil is what empowers people to earn religious rewards and avoid religious penalties. What we really need is for someone outside of us to provide a different drive shaft for our heart, one that doesn't depend on the carrot or the stick.

Instinctual Self-Justifiers

The Bible also explains that humans find significance and worth in their efforts to look good and to avoid looking bad. We want to "make ourselves right" in the eyes of others (and ultimately in the eyes of our Creator, for those of us who believe in God). If "justification" is the means by which Jesus makes us right with God, human beings are reflexively "self-justifiers." I also have heard this termed "self-savers"—we look only to ourselves for salvation. We put on an outward show of goodness, which doesn't match up with the state of our much dirtier hearts. We become very skilled at putting a pretty veneer over the dirt, so good that we ourselves don't even see what's inside us. That is why people take offense at being called "sinners." We tell ourselves, "Who, me? I'm a good person! I'm not a sinner! Those guys who steal and murder and sell drugs—those are the sinners, not me!"

Jesus was repulsed by this type of "exterior goodness," of which all humans are guilty. He calls the people who are good and obedient "on the outside," but who don't recognize the dirt on their insides, "whitewashed tombs."[7] They are clean, white, and slick on the exterior, but their interior is filled with rot. There is not a single one of us (except perhaps for sociopaths) who doesn't in some way try to put on an outward display of goodness to the general population, while hiding the inner hate, gossip, slander, envy, pride, deceit, refusal to forgive, ingratitude, and anger. It is human nature. King David writes about fallen human beings: "They are corrupt, their deeds are vile; there is no one who does good."[8] As we read in the prophecy of the suffering servant, "We all, like sheep, have gone astray, each of us has turned to our own way."[9] Isaiah also writes, "All of us have become like one who is unclean, and all our righteous acts are like filthy rags."[10] Feeling bad about yourself yet?! Hang in there. You must understand the bad news before you can appreciate the good news that is coming.

The biblical understanding of human nature is very nuanced, and actually quite accurate if you are honest. As we mentioned, the heart is the "engine" of the person, the source of all our motivations, drives, and actions. Thus, our external behavior will depend on what is driving our heart. In his Sermon on the Mount, Jesus clarified that our greatest desires are the "treasures" that motivate our hearts to action, kind of like the gas for a car engine. Jesus says:

> "Do not store up for yourselves treasures on earth, where moths and vermin destroy, and where thieves break in and steal. But store up for yourselves treasures in heaven, where moths and vermin do not destroy, and where thieves do not break in and steal. For where your treasure is, there your heart will be also."[11]

Our hearts follow our treasure. If we identify what our treasure is, we will understand what motivates us, inspires us, causes us to daydream, and dictates how we spend our time and money. A few of the most popular human treasures are wealth, beauty, fitness, popularity, comfort, love relationships, sex, friendships, family, success, career, children, possessions, fame, power, and the opinion of others. These treasures drive all of our actions. For the Pharisees in Jesus' time, their treasure was to look good in front of other people, which they tried to achieve through their obedience to the law. They even invented additional laws, so there would be more opportunities for themselves to succeed and for others to fail.

Seeing this "exterior obedience" of the Pharisees, Jesus explains how *not* to act when we pray:

> "And when you pray, do not be like the hypocrites, for they love to pray standing in the synagogues and on the street corners to be seen by others. Truly I tell you, they have received their reward in full. But when you pray, go into your room, close the door and pray to your Father, who is unseen. Then your Father, who sees what is done in secret, will reward you."[12]

Jesus emphasized that if our treasure is God, we will pray to him in secret where no one else can see us, but if our treasure is human opinion, we will pray out in the open where others will be impressed with how spiritual we are, which will be "our reward in full." (This is back in ancient times, of course—these days, someone praying in the street out loud would probably be considered mentally ill!) Many religious Christians behave in a way that is motivated by the desire to look good to others, rather than the desire to please God alone. Their outward actions, while appearing "good," are actually fueled by selfishness, just like the "whitewashed tombs" that Jesus criticized in his day. It is understandable that religious people often act this way, since the instinctual habit of the human heart is to "earn" our significance and to "save ourselves," since we so easily fall back on the carrot and the stick mentality. In the case of religion, the carrot is the pride we feel when we follow rules and demonstrate how holy we are to others. But Jesus warned us about this incorrect motivation.

The lessons here are, first, God sees our actions and our motivations when others don't, and secondly, our hearts are motivated by the treasure we are serving. For example, if we are serving the treasure of others'

CHAPTER 32: POWER TO TRULY TRANSFORM

positive opinion of us, we will act in a way to make our outward behavior align with the way we want others to view us. And if we are serving adventure or a wild nature, we will act in a way that is in line with this and will rebel against authority. However, if our treasure is God, we will act in a way that is pleasing to him—even when only he can see it, since we know that God sees past our external behavior right into our hearts. (This is a scary thought, which is another reason we are grateful that our salvation only depends on Jesus, not ourselves!)

Jesus used a helpful parable to emphasize how easy it is to focus on outward behavior rather than on inward humility and dependence on God's mercy:

> To some who were confident of their own righteousness and looked down on everyone else, Jesus told this parable: "Two men went up to the temple to pray, one a Pharisee and the other a tax collector. The Pharisee stood by himself and prayed: 'God, I thank you that I am not like other people—robbers, evildoers, adulterers—or even like this tax collector. I fast twice a week and give a tenth of all I get.'
>
> "But the tax collector stood at a distance. He would not even look up to heaven, but beat his breast and said, 'God, have mercy on me, a sinner.'
>
> "I tell you that this man, rather than the other, went home justified before God. For all those who exalt themselves will be humbled, and those who humble themselves will be exalted."[13]

Human beings are instinctively like the Pharisee, pridefully looking to our own accomplishments, whether we are religious or not. Even those who have low self-esteem are guilty of looking to themselves for significance (and yet they don't find it). In fact, true humility is not from thinking *less* of yourself, but thinking of yourself *less*. When you hang out with someone who is truly humble, you'll feel like they care only about you and how you are doing. Their focus is on others, and not on themselves. For someone who has false humility, they will most likely talk more about themselves and how they don't live up, and they will express minimal interest in you. Augustine of Hippo describes the natural human heart as *incurvatus in se*, or "curved inward on oneself," such that our inclination is to prop ourselves up relative to others. A truly humble person will always seek the opposite: to prop others up.[14]

But how does this relate to the carrot and the stick of human motivation? Here's how. Human beings are instinctively motivated to earn their treasure and to avoid losing their treasure. The carrot, therefore, is whatever we treasure. The stick is the removal of that treasure. In all religions, except for biblical Christianity, our heart is not changed. If we are religious people, our treasure is to earn God's approval (at least in the eyes of others). When we do the right things, check off the items on the "to do" list, and avoid the items on the "don't do" list, we feel proud. When we fail, we feel despondent and guilty. This is the drive shaft that is always operating in the human heart. All "religion" does is exacerbate the pride/despondency loop, as well as the ups and downs of the rollercoaster ride of life. It also wreaks havoc on human relationships, even to the extent of leading to violence, murder, and wars, since we look down on others who aren't as "good" as we are, or don't believe the right things, rather than loving all people regardless of how different they are from us. (Notice, however, that atheists do the same thing when they look down on the people who have a religious faith and insist that the world would be a better place if everyone believed as they do and religion just went away. That isn't the solution either!)

The reverse trajectory of the gospel completely *replaces* the drive shaft of the human heart by changing the way we are motivated. We have already received the reward, so our actions no longer matter for salvation. Instead of being driven by the reward of the "carrot" or the punishment of the "stick," the grace-empowered Christian is now motivated by gratitude and love. We have already received the carrot. We have already avoided the stick. We can celebrate with joy, act in gratitude, and obey out of love in response to the amazing gifts we have been given. The drive shaft of our heart—over time—can replace all of our previous "treasures" with the one and only treasure that is worthy of our lives: Jesus. We can still enjoy the other treasures that God gives us, but they have been replaced at the center of our heart by the most valuable treasure of all—one that will last for eternity and one that no one can ever take away from us.[15]

CHAPTER 32: POWER TO TRULY TRANSFORM

You may be thinking, "But, but... how is it even possible to replace our treasures with Jesus? You sincerely mean I will stop loving money, power, and fame and will love Jesus instead? I will stop loving my family and will love Jesus instead?" No, not instead, but more. He will be your primary treasure once what he has done for you has become more than just knowledge but has truly permeated your heart.

For example, read these statements that Jesus made to his followers with regards to money, family, and comfort and pleasures:

> Money: "No one can serve two masters. Either you will hate the one and love the other, or you will be devoted to the one and despise the other. You cannot serve both God and money."[16]

> Family: "Anyone who loves their father or mother more than me is not worthy of me; anyone who loves their son or daughter more than me is not worthy of me."[17]

> Comforts and pleasures: "Whoever does not take up their cross and follow me is not worthy of me."[18]

Jesus was using hyperbole to draw a sharp distinction between a focus on him versus a focus on money, family, and the pleasures of this world, thus making it crystal clear that our lives should be focused on him above all other things. He wasn't necessarily calling all of his followers to live a life of poverty, or to leave our family, or to deny ourselves all comforts. But he was insisting that we put him at the center of our lives and focus on him so much that the other things are not nearly as important to us as they used to be.

Yikes, you say, no one can do this! True, *no one can* do this. That is the point! Other than Jesus, the Son of God who became human, no human being is ever able to put God at the center of their life at all times, which would require that we are as perfect as God. If we try to reach God's holiness through our own actions, it is like jumping as high as we can in our own effort to touch the sun. But as we come to realize how far below his perfect holiness we are, we gain a deeper appreciation for what God has done for us, and we can confess our sin to him and to others, knowing that God will still love us because he has already forgiven every sin we have made and ever will make, and he has already given us Jesus' perfect record.

Over time, especially through prayer and hearing the gospel over and over, God changes the hearts of those of us who are believers, such that the things of this world lose their power over us, and pleasing Jesus becomes more important. It is at this point when we find true contentment and true joy, regardless of our circumstances. The author of Hebrews explains it beautifully:

> Therefore, since we are surrounded by such a great cloud of witnesses, let us throw off everything that hinders and the sin that so easily entangles. And let us run with perseverance the race marked out for us, fixing our eyes on Jesus, the pioneer and perfecter of faith. For the joy set before him he endured the cross, scorning its shame, and sat down at the right hand of the throne of God. Consider him who endured such opposition from sinners, so that you will not grow weary and lose heart.[19]

In order for the central treasure of our heart to become Jesus, we must "consider him who endured such opposition from sinners." As we meditate on what he has done for us—enduring opposition from the very people he came to help, "sinners"—it motivates us to put him at the center of our hearts and to seek to please him.

As we as believers focus on life from an eternal perspective, we also begin to value the things of this temporary world less and less, and it motivates us to "run with perseverance the race marked out for us," the relatively short Christian life on this earth, with its numerous difficulties. (The "great cloud of witnesses" is possibly those in heaven who are encouraging believers on earth, as though they are sitting in a huge, packed stadium cheering on the runners on the track below.) As we "fix our eyes on Jesus," it motivates us to appreciate what he has done for us more and more. The more we see ourselves as being "the joy set before him," the reason that he endured the cross, the more Jesus takes on "treasure status" in our hearts and the less likely that we will "grow weary and lose heart."

In humble recognition that we are not deserving, we believers will respond with gratitude, love, and joy. And if we don't feel this gratitude, love, and joy in our lives—and there will be many times when we

CHAPTER 32: POWER TO TRULY TRANSFORM

won't—we must "preach the gospel to ourselves," especially because grace goes against our instinctual works-motivated nature. On our own, we drift away from gratitude, love, and joy as the primary motivation for obedience, and we find ourselves back in the carrot and the stick paradigm—obeying out of obligation, fear of punishment, or guilt. We will also be more likely to look to our own accomplishments for "salvation," which causes us to look down on others who are different, rather than reaching out to them with the love of Jesus.

But if we continue to remind ourselves of how "the Lord has rescued us from the land of slavery" and set us apart as his chosen people, if we continue to remind ourselves of how much Jesus endured so that he could spend eternity with us, we will be drawn back into a life of love, joy, and gratitude, and away from the world of the carrot and the stick.

Allow me to encourage you to regularly attend a church that emphasizes grace as the motivation for good works. There are unfortunately quite a few "carrot and stick" churches that emphasize doing certain things and not doing other things as a way to earn God's approval. And unfortunately, there are many Christian churches that have removed the supernatural realm from their beliefs, and therefore deny all of the aspects of the faith that change the drive shaft of the heart. Be sure that the church you attend gives you regular reminders that Jesus has already accomplished your salvation *for you*, and as a result your fitting response is to obey his commands and to love and serve others. It is also essential that you have fellowship with other people who are "running the same race" as you are, if you really want God to change the drive shaft of your heart. Also crucial are regular prayer to confess sin and to ask for God's help, as well as regular study of the Bible in order to better understand what Jesus has done for us.[20]

All other religions, with their emphasis on effort and performance to earn one's way to heaven—or paradise, nirvana, enlightenment, or moksha—will never change the drive shaft of the human heart. If you succeed one day, you will feel prideful and look down on others who don't do as well as you. You can be confident, but not humble. And if you fail the next day, you feel disappointment, despair, guilt, or hopelessness (or you will rationalize or hide your failure from yourself). You will feel humbled, but not confident. In this carrot and stick paradigm, you will find yourself in slavery to obedience.

But the gospel of Jesus Christ sets you free from this endless cycle of obedience, pride, disobedience, and despair. Through faith in Jesus, you are already loved more than you could ever possibly imagine. Nothing you do would ever cause you to lose your adopted status as a child of God and your eternal place in his perfect, renewed earth. What an amazing source of confidence! But at the same time your "insides are so rotten" that it required the death of the Son of God to pay the penalty for them. You are, therefore, more evil than you could ever imagine. What an amazing source of humility! You are thus able to stand with both confidence and humility. You can always be humbly confident and confidently humble, as opposed to *either* confident (on your good days) *or* humble (on your bad days). Knowing that your eternal destiny in heaven is secure, you can be humble even when you succeed and confident even when you fail.

Moreover, when you fail you can readily admit your faults, and you are less likely to move into "blame-shifting," "minimizing," and "rationalizing" modes because you know that God has accepted you regardless of any wrong you have ever done. Christianity, understood rightly, is the only faith that offers humility *and* confidence, not just one or the other. And this humble confidence makes all the difference to relationships, with oneself, with each other, and with God. Let's take a closer look at how this works.

How the Gospel Transforms Our Relationships

The source of all power to improve and transform relationships is the love of God, which is poured out to all people, just as the energy of the sun warms all organisms on earth. But God has especially poured out his love to those who receive his free gift of eternal life through faith in Jesus. Those who trust in Jesus' work on their behalf no longer have to work to earn eternal life; they already have it. They are then released to serve God out of gratitude and love instead of out of obligation and fear, and this new drive shaft is truly powerful and transformative.

But just how do we receive the power that enables us to be humble, to endure suffering, and to live to serve others? Let's begin with an explanation from the apostle Paul:

CHAPTER 32: POWER TO TRULY TRANSFORM

Therefore, since we have been justified through faith, we have peace with God through our Lord Jesus Christ, through whom we have gained access by faith into this grace in which we now stand. And we boast in the hope of the glory of God. Not only so, but we also glory in our sufferings, because we know that suffering produces perseverance; perseverance, character; and character, hope. And hope does not put us to shame, because God's love has been poured out into our hearts through the Holy Spirit, who has been given to us. You see, at just the right time, when we were still powerless, Christ died for the ungodly. Very rarely will anyone die for a righteous person, though for a good person someone might possibly dare to die. *But God demonstrates his own love for us in this: While we were still sinners, Christ died for us.*[21]

Paul notes that first Christians have been "justified through faith," and second, as a result, they have peace with God. Simply put, because of what Jesus has done, those who trust in him are made to be "just as if" they had never sinned and "just as if" they themselves had lived Jesus' perfect life, thus giving them peace with God. *Therefore*, as a result of this justification through faith, believers "have gained access by faith into this grace in which [they] now stand." Simply put, Jesus' work allows believers to stand "in a state of grace." In this state of grace, they are empowered in several ways.

Before we move on to the transformational powers of the state of grace, let's explain why a state of grace is such a blessed and powerful place to be. In this state of grace, those of us who are believers are like prisoners who deserve the death penalty, but—instead of being sent to the electric chair—we have been released from prison. We are like the murderer Barabbas, who was released by Pontius Pilate. Soon thereafter, he probably shouted curses and looked on as Jesus, innocent of all wrongdoing, died on a cross that had been meant for him.[22] In addition, in a state of grace, we become "children of God."[23] Therefore, to make these analogies more accurate, the prisoners released from death row would become adopted children of Queen Elizabeth and would move into a wing of Buckingham Palace. And Barabbas would be welcomed as the adopted son of the King of Judea, entering his new home in the palace to get a hot shower, a delicious meal, new royal clothing, and a comfortable bedroom. This is a faint glimpse of what happens to someone the moment they choose to trust in Jesus, and it ought to stir the hearts of those who have faith in him, if they truly understand and believe it.

So, let's focus on the main outcomes of being in this state of grace, if those of us who are believers truly recognize it and remind ourselves that we are in it. The first consequence is that we don't have to depend on earthly sources of worth and significance because we have unshakable and eternal worth and significance as children of God. With both confidence and humility, we can admit fault when we have acted inappropriately, rather than finding excuses for our actions or blaming others. Like David, we can pray to God and ask him to "Search me, God, and know my heart; test me and know my anxious thoughts. See if there is any offensive way in me, and lead me in the way everlasting."[24] We can apologize more easily (though it's still not easy), and we can recognize and own up to the part we have played in a relationship that has grown sour. We also can take on a more "teachable spirit." Knowing that there is nothing we have done or can do that will make God love us any less, we are more likely to accept feedback from others, and we will be more likely to ask others for advice. Instead of lashing back when someone criticizes us, we can genuinely thank him or her for pointing out our error or offering feedback. We will find it is so much easier to take criticism when we aren't depending on others' opinions of us for our worth.[25]

Secondly, if those of us who are believers approach relationships from a "state of grace," we will refrain from judging others. Part of this comes from a newfound ability to first admit our own faults, which enables us to more readily admit, "Yeah, in his place, or with his background, I probably would have done the same." Jesus compared our own sins to logs, and those of the people we judge as mere specks, instructing us thus: "First take the log out of your own eye, and then you will see clearly to take the speck out of your brother's eye."[26] In a state of grace, those of us who are believers have the motivation to "find the logs in our eyes" because of the confident humility that the gospel gives us when we understand it fully.

A third main consequence of standing in a state of grace is that when those of us who are believers recognize how much God has forgiven us,

CHAPTER 32: POWER TO TRULY TRANSFORM

we are motivated to do the same for others. That is, because God has forgiven us and taken *our* debt on himself, we are empowered to forgive others and take *their* debts on *ourselves*. If we have faith in Jesus but hold grudges against others or withhold forgiveness to those who have wronged us, Jesus compares us to the "unmerciful servant" in a parable that Matthew records in his Gospel. Let's take a moment to discuss this parable, as it is very instructive with regards to forgiveness. A servant owes his master 10,000 gold talents. (One talent was the equivalent of twenty years' wages for a day laborer, so 10,000 talents amounted to 200,000 years of wages, approximately the equivalent of $6 billion today—obviously, an impossible sum for the servant to repay!) He begs his master to give him time to pay it back. Of course, the master knows the servant could never do this, so "the servant's master takes pity on him, cancels the debt and lets him go."[27] But on the servant's way out, he runs into a fellow servant who owes him 100 silver coins (about four months' wages, or $10,000, a comparatively tiny amount). And even though this other servant also begged for mercy and more time to repay the debt, the first servant has the fellow thrown into debtor's prison.

When the master finds out that the servant whom he had forgiven did not forgive his fellow servant a much smaller debt, he exclaims: "You wicked servant. I canceled all that debt of yours because you begged me to. Shouldn't you have had mercy on your fellow servant just as I had on you?"[28] In the same way, Jesus insists, those of us who are his followers must forgive our fellow humans, even when they harm us greatly, since God has already forgiven us the most enormous debt of all. Forgiveness is obligatory for all Christians, though not for salvation. But we should do so lovingly and willingly—though it's incredibly difficult—because we do it in response to what God has done for us. That is the gospel trajectory: God forgives us, so we forgive others.

When we readily and humbly admit our mistakes and ask for forgiveness, when we refrain from judging others, and when we forgive others who have wronged us, our relationships will thrive. This is one way we can follow Paul's recommendation: "If it is possible, as far as it depends on you, live at peace with everyone."[29] Forgiveness is difficult—after all, it required the death of the Son of God on a Roman cross to forgive us our sins. Paul then reminds us what God says in Deuteronomy 32: "Do not take revenge, my dear friends, but leave room for God's wrath, for it is written: 'It is mine to avenge; I will repay,' says the Lord."[30]

The cycle of violence and vengeance can stop, if we truly trust that God's perfect justice will one day be accomplished and all evil will be punished.

Returning to the verses from Romans 5 above, we see a fourth way that the gospel transforms those of us who are believers and thereby will improve our relationships: it gives us a hope that allows us to relax even in the midst of suffering. Paul emphasizes that those who have faith in Jesus can look forward to an eternal and glorious future in God's presence, and this hope empowers us to endure the sufferings of this life, which lasts a blink of the eye compared to eternity. In our suffering, we develop perseverance, which makes us people of character and depth, and our character contributes to the hope that we are looking forward to a day when our suffering will be redeemed. This character also improves our relationship with others, who are more likely to trust us, befriend us, share intimately with us, and pass the time with us.

Pastor Timothy Keller provides a helpful analogy for Christian hope in the midst of suffering. Imagine a situation in which you work for a year all alone doing mindless work in an uncomfortable chair in a boring, windowless room. In the first scenario, you will be paid $30,000 at the end of the year (or 300 silver coins, to use the ancient pay scale!). You grudgingly get through the day, the time creeps by, and you suffer through the year to get your $30,000. But imagine the same exact job, but this time you're told you will get $6 billion (or 10,000 talents!) at the end of the year. You whistle while you work, you smile all day, and you eagerly come to work each morning. Nothing has changed except what you are looking forward to receiving. Similarly, Christian hope is a certain expectation that this life is just a "waiting room" where we hang out in anticipation of the real adventure on the new earth. We can endure the sufferings of this life—though I don't intend to minimize or discount their difficulty—confident that God will eventually restore the world to the perfect state he had originally intended it to be.

A fifth way the "state of grace" transforms believers' relationships is by improving our ability to relate to "prickly" people—those whom we would otherwise avoid. Paul notes that God willingly sent his Son to die for us. At that time, we hadn't "proven our worthiness," not that anything we do would be sufficiently "worthy" for a perfectly holy God. We believers were completely undeserving of his dying for us. The most selfless humans may be willing to die for "a good person," but God was willing to die for us, *while we were still sinners*. As he was being crucified,

CHAPTER 32: POWER TO TRULY TRANSFORM

Jesus even said, "Father, forgive them, for they do not know what they are doing."[31] Yes, it is difficult for us mere mortals to extend this type of selfless love, but it should inspire us to try to emulate Jesus and to pray for God's help when we don't feel capable of helping or forgiving those who hurt us. Drawing on the infinite source of love we have in God, we can also spend time with those who are "draining," listening to and caring for them without requiring anything in return.

You can think of human relationships as financial exchanges. As you serve others, or practice patience with others, or resist the urge to insist on your way or lash out at others, you spend more and more of your "relational cash" on those people. The reverse is also true. When others serve you, are patient with you, or resist the urge to have their way or lash out at you, they are giving you more of their "cash." Left to ourselves in the carrot and the stick paradigm, we will spend this cash on others only when we expect them to give us some of their cash in return. But believers in Christ can tap into a never-ending source of relational cash, such that we can pour into others without receiving anything in return. We are "plugged into" a source of love that cannot be exhausted, and we don't have to look to others to fill our bank accounts anymore. We can freely give to others and trust that God will empower us to do so as we dwell on the amazing gifts that he has given us. Moreover, when someone wrongs us, we can "absorb" the wrong instead of reacting immediately to point it out. By drawing on the never-ending love of God that is "poured out into our hearts," we can overlook it. We don't have to "be right" and can respond in love instead of in anger. Of course, we don't have to be a doormat for others to walk all over. God still permits us to stand up for our rights and defend ourselves, but we should do so in love and with the goal of reconciliation.

A sixth way that the gospel transforms relationships—when we believers focus on it and thus stand in a "state of grace"—is by empowering us to catch ourselves before we put others down to make ourselves feel better, whether it would have been out loud or in our minds. We can remind ourselves that we are saved by grace, not by anything we do that makes us better than others. When we remember this, we are more willing to love others, regardless of our differences. God did not rescue us because we are more intelligent, rational, moral, or impressive in any way—he simply offers his "free ticket to heaven" to anyone who is willing to receive it. When we remind ourselves of this, we are more likely to lift others up rather than defaulting to criticism and attacks.

Seventh—and lastly, for our purposes—when we are in a "state of grace" through faith in Jesus, it changes our relationships by helping us identify the sinful desires that cause relational difficulties. As mentioned earlier, it is fine to have desires for good things like children, money, career, a love relationship, fun, comfort, and so forth. But even these good things become problems when they replace God at the center of our heart, which happens all the time. James describes the problem with these excessive desires of our heart:

> What causes fights and quarrels among you? Don't they come from your desires that battle within you? You desire but do not have, so you kill. You covet but you cannot get what you want, so you quarrel and fight. You do not have because you do not ask God. When you ask, you do not receive, because you ask with wrong motives, that you may spend what you get on your pleasures.[32]

When we fight with others, we do so because our desires or our worth have been threatened. We argue with our spouse when we don't get our way, or when he or she threatens our feelings of worth. We get angry with our children when they don't follow our wishes, or when they threaten our significance (especially if being a good parent is what we depend on for significance). We hate our colleagues when they interfere with our desire for career advancement or threaten the identity that we have built for ourselves with regards to our avocation.

Note that it is perfectly acceptable to experience emotions of sadness, anger, happiness, disappointment, embarrassment, fear, anxiety, and so forth. This is part of being human. But relationships are strained when these emotions are overblown. In the Bible, the Greek word used for "excessive desire" is *epithumia*. (The word, *thumia*, translates as "desire," while the prefix *epi* indicates that it is "above" or "over" the usual amount.) When we are excessively angry, excessively sad, excessively happy, excessively fearful, excessively anxious, excessively irritated, and so forth, it is a sign that our hearts are focused too much on a certain treasure, or we are depending too much on a worldly source of identity, significance, or worth.

CHAPTER 32: POWER TO TRULY TRANSFORM

The only way to replace that treasure at the center of our heart with Jesus—and to view ourselves as worthy based solely on what Jesus did for us—is to "fix our eyes" on him, to preach the gospel to ourselves, to spend time studying the Bible, to talk about our excessive desires in Christian community, and to pray for God to make himself real to us and remind us of what he has given us in Jesus.

The Bible calls these excessive desires and sources of significance and worth "idols," since they are objects of our worship that take the place of God. In ancient times, humans would worship idols made of stone or metal. In modern times, humans worship idols that take the form of cars, beauty, houses, boats, Hollywood stars, the royal family, sex, sports, fitness, career, children and family, comfort, control, freedom, and so on. These may all be good things, but as soon as they become "ultimate things" in our lives, we will find ourselves in trouble. The human heart is always worshiping something, and most of the time it is not God. Theologian John Calvin put it this way: "Man's nature, so to speak, is a perpetual factory of idols."[33]

The easiest way to spot your idols is to examine what makes you excessively angry, excessively sad, excessively happy, excessively fearful, excessively anxious, and so forth. You should be able to trace back these emotions to a root cause, and there you will find the idol that has been threatened. For example, if you find yourself excessively anxious when you speak in front of a group, your idol may be others' opinions. Or if you are excessively angry when one of your children gets a bad grade, your idol may be your children.

Other clues to your idols and where you get your sense of worth are what you spend most of your time doing, what you think about in your spare time, or where you spend most of your time and money. If your idol is your career, you are likely to be a workaholic. If your idol is love relationships, you are more likely to be extremely happy one day when he (or she) treats you well, and then extremely depressed the next day when he (or she) doesn't. If you spend a lot of your money on clothing, it is likely that your idol is beauty or popularity or other people's opinions of you. If you spend more of your time watching television or playing video games, your idol may be pleasure or entertainment. You get the picture.

Other than the fact that they make your life a roller coaster, depending on whether your idol is coming through for you or not, idols are also unable to support "the weight of your life." They will never be able to fully satisfy you, and the more you depend on them the more they will fail you. For example, if you make your significant other your idol or source of significance, you will expect too much of the relationship and put too many demands on it. So, if your love relationship is your idol, you are more likely to damage it. If you make your children the source of your worth, you will place excessive expectations on them, and you are more likely to turn them against you. If you make your career your idol, you will put too little emphasis on other relationships with family and friends, which is a common cause of divorce and loneliness. This is why Augustine of Hippo defined virtue as "rightly ordered love," with God at the top of the list of loves we should have in our life.[34] Once you learn to see your inordinate desires as your idols, you will have a much better understanding of what drives you and what you depend upon for your self-worth (other than Jesus). This is the first step in destroying these idols.

Another way to determine whether a desire is excessive or not is to ask yourself whether the object of your desire is the "ends" or the "means to an end." For example, if you value your career excessively, your career success is the "ends" to which all of your efforts are the "means." This could cause you to lie when you make a mistake, or to step on colleagues to climb the corporate ladder, or to take credit for the ideas of others in order to get ahead. But, if your career is simply a means to the end of honoring God by doing your best work and "shining" as a light for Christ, then you will be more likely to be honest, give others the credit, and help others rather than use them to get ahead.

Similarly, if your marriage is excessively important to you, you will place demands on your spouse that will push him or her away, but if your marriage is a means to the end of honoring God and demonstrating the love of Jesus to your spouse, then your marriage will be blessed, as you will be motivated to selflessly serve your spouse and not have to insist on being right when there are disagreements. You will not give just to receive back, and you will be more likely to seek compromises and to let go of your need to have your way.

In fact, God made humans to be in relationship with him, such that he would be the only "ends" in our life, and everything else would purely be a means to draw closer to him and honor him. When we have peace with God, joy, fulfillment, contentment, and love follow. But when we treat God as the "means" by which we can "earn" good gifts from him, we are putting those good gifts in the center, which for a life of joy, is where only God should be. When we make God the only "end" of our life and place everything else as a "means" to that end, our lives will be more content, and our relationships will be much healthier. After all, God is the only source of value, significance, worth, and meaning that cannot be taken away from us. All other idols will sooner or later disappoint us. Another C. S. Lewis quote drives this point home:

> Indeed, if we consider the unblushing promises of reward and the staggering nature of the rewards promised in the Gospels, it would seem that Our Lord finds our desires not too strong, but too weak. We are half-hearted creatures, fooling about with drink and sex and ambition when infinite joy is offered us, like an ignorant child who wants to go on making mud pies in a slum because he cannot imagine what is meant by the offer of a holiday at sea. We are far too easily pleased.[35]

These are just a few of the results of standing in "a state of grace," of living a life that is focused on the "inverse trajectory" of the gospel, and of constantly reminding ourselves how much we have been forgiven and how fortunate we are to have the right to be called children of God—for all eternity. The more we "fix our eyes on Jesus," the more we will find joy in the midst of sorrow, comfort in the midst of suffering, and peace in the midst of chaos.

Questions for Comprehension and Discussion

1. Explain how the carrot and the stick motivate humans.
2. How is the human heart like the drive shaft of a car? What powers the human heart?
3. Describe the Jewish understanding of the human heart. What role does the heart play in our lives?
4. What results when we get the carrot or when we avoid the stick? What results when we fail to get the carrot or when we get hit

by the stick? How does this lead to a roller coaster ride, as well as relational issues?

5. Why do we compare ourselves to others and look down on certain people?
6. When we fail, what are the various "modes" that we shift into, and why do we do it? When we're successful, why do we like to take the credit?
7. In the carrot and the stick world, explain what powers the human heart. How does the gospel change the drive shaft of the human heart?
8. How do we, over time, replace the treasures of our heart with God? How does this change our motivations?
9. What are a few ways that the gospel changes our relationships? How can it change our attitude about suffering and give us hope?
10. How can you identify the "treasures of your heart," that is, the idols that you worship? How do we go about replacing those idols with God?

CHAPTER 32 ENDNOTES

[1] Timothy Keller and Kathy Keller, *The Meaning of Marriage: Facing the Complexities of Commitment with the Wisdom of God* (New York: Penguin Group, 2011).
[2] C. S. Lewis, *Mere Christianity* (San Francisco: HarperOne, 2009), 205.
[3] Kaufmann Kohler, Tobias Schanfarber, Adolf Guttmacher, "Heart," *The 1905 Jewish Encyclopedia*, available online at http://www.jewishencyclopedia.com/articles/7436-heart.
[4] See Genesis 3:11-13.
[5] Timothy Keller, "Sin as Self-Deceit," January 28, 1996. Available online at https://gospelinlife.com/downloads/sin-as-self-deceit-6428/.
[6] James 1:17.
[7] Matthew 23:27.
[8] Psalm 14:1.
[9] Isaiah 53:6.
[10] Isaiah 64:6.
[11] Matthew 6:19-21.
[12] Matthew 6:5-6.
[13] Luke 18:9-14.
[14] See Ephesians 4:29.

CHAPTER 32: POWER TO TRULY TRANSFORM

15. This explanation for how Jesus replaces the treasures of our heart comes from the 18th century Scottish minister, Thomas Chalmers, "The Expulsive Power of a New Affection." Available online at https://www.monergism.com/threshold/sdg/Chalmers,%20Thomas%20-%20The%20Exlpulsive%20Power%20of%20a%20New%20Af.pdf.
16. Matthew 6:24.
17. Matthew 10:37.
18. Matthew 10:38.
19. Hebrews 12:1-3.
20. If you are looking for a good Bible study, I highly recommend Bible Study Fellowship International, which I have attended on and off since I became a Christian in 1998. Find out more at www.bsfinternational.org.
21. Romans 5:1-8.
22. See the story of the exchange of Barabbas for Jesus in Matthew 27:17-26; Mark 15:7-15; Luke 23:18-19; and John 18:39-40.
23. John 1:12 is the most concise description of how faith in Jesus gives believers the right to be called children of God. See also Romans 8:14, 16-17, 9:8; Galatians 3:26; Philippians 2:15; Hebrews 12:7; 1 John 3:1-2, 5:19; Revelation 21:7.
24. Psalm 139:23-24.
25. Proverbs 12:15 says that those who insist on being right are fools, while those who seek feedback are wise: "The way of a fool is right in his own eyes, but a wise man listens to advice."
26. Matthew 7:5.
27. Matthew 18:27.
28. Matthew 18:32-33.
29. Romans 12:18.
30. Romans 12:19.
31. Luke 23:34.
32. James 4:1-3.
33. John Calvin, *Institutes*, 1.11.8.
34. See Augustine of Hippo, *City of God* XV.23.
35. C. S. Lewis, *The Weight of Glory* (San Francisco: HarperOne, 2009), 26.

Christianity is a statement which, if false, is of no importance, and, if true, is of infinite importance. The one thing it cannot be is moderately important.

— C. S. Lewis, Christian apologist, novelist, and professor[1]

Contrary to the current secular understanding of "faith," true New Testament faith is not something that is made stronger by ignorance or by believing against the evidence. Rather, saving faith is consistent with knowledge and true understanding of facts.

— Wayne Grudem, Christian theologian[2]

Receiving the Free Gift

Just before he went to Jerusalem to die, Jesus asked his disciples, "Who do people say I am?" They answered, "Some say John the Baptist; others say Elijah; and still others, one of the prophets." Then Jesus asked: "But what about you? Who do you say I am?" When Peter replied, "You are the Messiah," Jesus stated, "Blessed are you, Simon son of Jonah, for this was not revealed to you by flesh and blood, but by my Father in heaven."[3]

The question Jesus posed to his followers is the same question he asks everyone today: "Who do you say that I am?" Do you say he was merely a teacher with helpful instructions for living a good life? Do you say he was merely another prophet who speaks on behalf of God? Do you say he was a fake who claimed to be the Messiah, but whose death proved that he wasn't? Do you prefer not to even answer the question, since you believe you have other more important things to worry about? (If you have read this book up to this point, you probably aren't in that category!) Or do you believe Jesus is the Messiah, both "David's Lord" and "David's Son," Son of God and Son of Man?

As scary as it sounds, your eternal destiny hangs on how you answer this question. And choosing not to answer the question is itself an answer. God has given you the choice as to how you answer the question, which is an enormous responsibility.[4] But God must also reveal the truth to you, as Jesus indicated above when he said the Father had revealed the answer to Peter. You must believe, but God must help you to believe.

Listen to Jesus emphasize the importance of what we believe about him: "Very truly I tell you, whoever hears my word and *believes* him who sent me has eternal life and will not be judged but has crossed over from death to life."[5] When Jesus was talking about giving eternal life, someone asked him the question, "What must we do to do the works God requires?" Jesus replied: "The work of God is this: to *believe* in the one he has sent."⁶ He went on to say, "For my Father's will is that everyone who looks to the Son and *believes* in him shall have eternal life, and I will raise them up at the last day."⁷ After he had raised his friend Lazarus from the dead, Jesus again claimed and asked: "The one who *believes* in me will live, even though they die; and whoever lives by *believing* in me will never die. Do you *believe* this?"⁸ This is just a fraction of the times that Jesus insisted that believing in him is linked to eternal life.

Jesus was clearly urging us to believe that he is the Son of God, and he is urging us today to make this belief the central part of our lives, from which everything else flows. And if Jesus' own statements weren't enough, John, who had been an eyewitness of Jesus' ministry, death, resurrection, and ascension, urges us to believe that what he has written about Jesus is true:

> The man who saw it has given testimony, and his testimony is true. He knows that he tells the truth, and he testifies so that you also may believe.... This is [i.e. I am] the disciple who testifies to these things and who wrote them down. We know that his [my] testimony is true. Jesus did many other things as well. If every one of them were written down, I suppose that even the whole world would not have room for the books that would be written.⁹

But why is it so difficult to believe, even after we have seen so much evidence?

THE GREAT BARRIERS TO BELIEF

Belief is a funny thing. To believe seems so easy, and yet we are constrained by our biases, our stereotypes, and our fears. We think rational evidence should be enough to sway our beliefs, but humans are capable of putting up walls, denying the evidence, and convincing themselves that there are still good reasons not to believe. The biggest hurdle for us to clear is our desire for autonomy. We don't want to answer to anyone, especially to an all-powerful God who can ask us to do anything. It is extremely scary.

Jesus described this refusal to believe as a game played by pouting children. After sending his disciples out on their first mission, Jesus spoke to a crowd that had gathered around him. He compared their generation to "children sitting in the marketplaces and calling out to others": "We played the pipe for you, and you did not dance; we sang a dirge, and you did not mourn."[10] Jesus then said that when John the Baptist came, he neither ate nor drank, and the people said he had a demon. And when he himself, the "Son of Man," came, he ate and drank, and they called him "a glutton and a drunkard, a friend of tax collectors and sinners."[11] What does Jesus mean?

In those days, the children would accompany their parents to the marketplaces, and while their parents were buying and selling, they would play "make believe" games with one another, just as children do today. The two most popular parties in ancient times were weddings and funerals, so it would probably be quite common for children to pretend to throw a wedding or a funeral. You can imagine one kid insisting, "Let's play wedding!" as he starts to pretend to play the pipe. And another would say, "Nah, that's boring." The first child would then suggest, "Well, then, let's play funeral!" and pretend to sing a dirge. And the second child would again say, "No, let's not. That's boring too." What the second child is basically saying is, "I don't want to play whatever *you* suggest. I only want to play what *I* suggest."[12]

Similarly, the people had criticized John the Baptist for being so ascetic, not eating anything but locusts and honey, and refraining from wine. But then they criticized Jesus for eating and drinking along with others, claiming he was "a glutton and a drunkard." The people who refused to believe John and Jesus were coming up with excuses not to believe them, and their excuses even contradicted each other, demonstrating their irrationality and the fact that emotion and pride were to blame for their unbelief. They were essentially saying, "We don't like what John the Baptist had to say, and we don't like what you have to say, Jesus. We want to keep the belief system to which we've grown accustomed, since it works best for us." They didn't *want* to believe, so they came up with excuses why they didn't *have* to believe.

The same is true today. Before I became a Christian, I had a million reasons why I wouldn't *ever* become a Christian. If someone managed

CHAPTER 33: RECEIVING THE FREE GIFT

to explain to me why one of my reasons wasn't sufficient to prevent me from believing, I would think of something else. If I were honest, I should have said that I simply didn't want to believe. Period. Moreover, I wanted to believe whatever allowed me to live my life the way I wanted to live my life. It was like God was a salad bar, and I could pick and choose the aspects of him that appealed most to me and leave the other ingredients that were unpalatable.

Here are a few of the issues I had with Christianity that were insurmountable, in my opinion: It's unfair that anyone who doesn't believe in Jesus goes to hell. Christians have done terrible things in the name of God in history. Christians are too sacchariny-sweet for me. I want to party, and Christians don't know how to have fun. Christians are so exclusive and narrow-minded. So, what happened to all of the people in history who didn't know about Jesus? Christians think the earth is only 5,000 years old—they're so unscientific. I don't need to believe in God to be a good person (in fact, I'm probably a better person than most Christians I know). Why would God send his son to die—isn't that child abuse? All religions are equally true; it doesn't matter what you believe as long as you don't hurt others. Christians are hypocrites—they're always judging others, and then they do the same exact things. I think Jesus is fine, but I don't like the angry, violent God of the Old Testament. And most of the shows I watched on television confirmed the stereotypes of Christians that I believed were true, keeping me stuck in unbelief.

The fact that I ever became a Christian is a testament to the power of God to change hearts! Once I became a believer and had read multiple books defending the rationality of the Christian faith, I began to see the gospel as an otherworldly, spectacular treasure of pure gold. What an amazing thing that Jesus accomplished *for me* a way that I could spend eternity with him, since he knew I could never accomplish it myself. What a treasure! But unfortunately, this treasure has been corrupted over the centuries, much like a treasure chest buried in the ocean for hundreds of years becomes covered with barnacles.

The beautiful treasure of the gospel was first distorted by early Christian leaders who, after Constantine made Christianity legal, were corrupted by power and wealth, forcing their parishioners to "earn" salvation through good works, obedience to their dictates, and even payments (the "indulgences" that set Martin Luther off). This went against everything Jesus taught about humility, renouncing earthly power and wealth, and salvation by faith alone. Barnacles began to grow on the treasure. The desire for Christians to take back the Promised Land from the Muslims during the crusades was a huge "public relations disaster" that caused many people to misunderstand Christianity and forget Jesus' original command to love one's enemies. More barnacles.

Another misunderstanding of Christianity results from outsiders seeing the joy of Christians and thinking that believers are either overly emotional and irrational, or just plain crazy. It doesn't help that "The end is near!" signs are generally held by Christians. The barnacles have obscured the treasure to such an extent that even those who call themselves Christians don't understand the implications that the gospel has for their life. They don't understand the trajectory of God coming down to rescue us, and they make it about their own good works. This is probably the biggest source of barnacles. Falling back on the instinctual drive shaft of the human heart, which is motivated by the carrot and the stick, they put so much emphasis on works that they become self-righteous, fake, judgmental, and prideful. There is also an emphasis on the stick, usually through "fire and brimstone" sermons and scare tactics. Ironically, by acting this way, they are also avoiding a meaningful, personal relationship with God. Let's discuss what this means.

Two Ways to Avoid God

There are two main ways that people avoid God, both of which involve our desire to rule our own lives and do things our own way. The first way people avoid God is symbolized by the "lost son" or "prodigal son" in the parable Jesus tells in Luke 15. The son asks the father for his inheritance (which he normally wouldn't receive until after the father's death) and goes off to live life on his own, away from the father. He enjoys what the father gives him, but he doesn't want anything to do with the father. He ends up penniless, "comes to his senses," and returns to his father with "his tail between his legs," prepared to work for him as a common laborer. This younger son represents the "irreligious" types, who want to enjoy the blessings of life but want to live their life without God's interference. But contrary to the son's expectations, the father sees him coming from a distance and runs to greet him. Then he throws a big party to celebrate his son's return.[13]

CHAPTER 33: RECEIVING THE FREE GIFT

Meanwhile, the older brother, who symbolizes the second way that people avoid God, is completely obedient and stays dutifully by his father's side while the younger brother is off partying and spending his inheritance. Upon the younger brother's return, the older brother is angry and refuses to go to the party celebrating his return. He tells his father:

> "All these years I've been slaving for you and never disobeyed your orders. Yet you never gave me even a young goat so I could celebrate with my friends. But when this son of yours who has squandered your property with prostitutes comes home, you kill the fattened calf for him!"[14]

The older brother reveals his true colors when he claims to have been "slaving" for his father. This is the legalistic, religious person, who obeys God in order to either earn the "carrot" or avoid the "stick." He has no joy in obeying the father, and he only does so to get some reward. He is prideful and looks down on the younger brother, and he is enraged when his brother returns and gets a party that he doesn't deserve.

In the modern world, the "younger brothers" are generally secular and focused on living the life that they make for themselves. They avoid God and don't even recognize that all good gifts come from him. The "elder brothers" are the religious types, who may go to church every Sunday, attend Bible studies, tick off all of the boxes on the "good Christian to do list," and avoid all of the actions on the "good Christian never do list." But they become upset when God does not bless them. They think they "deserve better" and that God "owes them" for all they do for him. They also obey begrudgingly, not joyfully and gratefully.

Jesus wants to have a relationship with his people that is neither like the father's relationship with the younger brother when he first sets out with his inheritance, nor like the father's relationship with the elder brother, who always grudgingly and "slavishly" obeyed. Jesus wants us *all* to come to him as the younger brother who recognizes the errors of his ways and returns with a repentant heart. Jesus wants those of us who are "younger brothers" to repent for running away from him and to recognize that God loves us despite our wanderings. And Jesus wants those of us who are "older brothers" to repent of the selfish reasons we perform good works—pride in our own efforts and our desire to put God in our debt. That is, he wants us elder brothers to humble ourselves and recognize that he has done everything for us already, so we can just rest in his completed work, obeying out of gratitude instead of obligation. He wants us both—younger and elder brothers alike—to come in and enjoy the party!

It is interesting to note that both brothers dislike the gospel—the trajectory of God coming down to rescue us—but for different reasons. The younger brother doesn't think he owes his father anything, and he is put off by the idea that he is a "sinner" who needs to repent. He likes the idea that God loves him; after all, God is love. On the other hand, the elder brother understands the concept of sin, and yet he spends so much effort trying not to sin that he believes he is without sin. He has become a master of self-deception. Moreover, he fails to recognize that he would never be able to live up to God's perfectly holy standards. He doesn't want to admit that only by God becoming a human and dying for his sins does he have any hope of going to heaven. He doesn't want to recognize that God owes him nothing, despite his "slaving away" to do good deeds.

Jesus wants the younger brothers to come to him in confidence, trusting that God loves them more than they could ever imagine, despite their past failures. And Jesus wants the older brothers to come to him in humility, recognizing that even their best works are "filthy rags" compared to God's holiness. He wants a personal relationship with both, without the younger son running away to do his own thing and without the older son slaving away to get on his good side.

You can have a personal relationship with God when the two sides of the gospel come together for you: (1) you recognize that you are so loved that nothing you can do will cause God to love you any less, and (2) you recognize that you are so sinful, despite all of your good works, that God had to take your punishment on himself to save you. God knows you completely, and yet he still loves you completely. You are fully known *and* fully loved. This is the personal relationship you have been seeking in all other relationships on earth that have never lived up and never will.

WHICH IS TRUE FREEDOM, FREEDOM IN CHRIST OR FREEDOM FROM CHRIST?

So, here's our main problem: we humans don't instinctively want to trust in God because, like Adam and Eve, we want to be our own gods.

CHAPTER 33: RECEIVING THE FREE GIFT

We either run away from God overtly, like the younger brother, or covertly, like the legalistic older brother. We want to have complete control over the steering wheel, brakes, and accelerator of our lives, and it's too frightening to give up that control. But to give up control is the beginning of freedom, as Jesus explains:

> "Very truly I tell you, everyone who sins is a slave to sin. Now a slave has no permanent place in the family, but a son belongs to it forever. So if the Son sets you free, you will be free indeed."[15]

We are like slaves trapped by the idols in our lives, idols we think will bring us long-lived satisfaction, but never will. Even the most successful people—both in terms of athletic ability, creative or musical skill, career success, wealth, movie star status, you name it—feel that there must be "something more." We think that we just have to earn that next degree, or achieve a certain rung on the corporate ladder, or meet "Mr. or Mrs. Right," or have a child, or buy the fancy car or the dream home, or raise the kids, or retire—the list goes on—and then we'll be content. But if we're honest with ourselves, the things of earth do not satisfy us the way we wish they did. We are a slave to our idols until we recognize that true satisfaction can only come from an eternal relationship with our Creator. That is what we were built for.

It is ironic that we think that giving our lives to God will take away our freedom, since it is only by placing our complete trust in God that we can truly be free. One writer explains freedom in Christ in this way:

> The False Self constructs all sorts of layers of ego and angst and striving and foolishness, while the True Self, deep at the center of a person, waits for the time when the False Self will die and allow the real life to begin.[16]

The "False Self" is the self that we have constructed in order to feel that we have purpose, significance, and worth in our own effort, whether it is the effort to be adventurous and free-wheeling (like the younger brother) or the effort to be legalistically obedient to our religion (like the elder brother). We put up a façade, especially with the people who don't know us very well, and we hide our "True Self." We may do this

THE SHORTEST LEAP

unconsciously, insisting that our true selves are exactly what we project to other people. But again, if we are honest with ourselves, we are not entirely the person we show to others. Most often, our true selves will come out with those who are closest to us, since we have learned to "let down our guard" around these people.

In Christ, we finally can put away all pretenses, though this is a long process and requires a lot of prayer, practice, and support. We can be our "True Self" because we know that God loves us this way. He wants to change us, of course, so that we become more like him, but in so doing, we actually become even more free. Let me explain using another analogy from Timothy Keller.

Freedom in Christ can be compared to a sailboat that has caught the wind and smoothly speeds through the water. A sailboat, if it is not operated properly, will not go in the direction that you want it to go. In fact, it is likely that it will capsize, run into a reef, crash into the rocks, or run aground. However, once you understand how to move the sails, operate the rudder, and determine the best angle of the boat relative to the direction of the wind, you will literally be "smooth sailing." Keller puts it this way:

> If you see a large sailboat out on the water moving swiftly, it is because the sailor is honoring the boat's design. If she tries to take it into water too shallow for it, the boat will be ruined. The sailor experiences the freedom of speed sailing only when she limits her boat to the proper depth of water and faces the wind in the proper angle.
>
> In the same way, human beings thrive in certain environments and break down in others. Unless you honor the givens and limits of your physical nature, you will never know the freedom of health. Unless you honor the givens and limits of human relationships, you will never know the freedom of love and social peace. If you actually lived any way you wanted—you would quickly die, and die alone.[17]

And further:

CHAPTER 33: RECEIVING THE FREE GIFT

> We were built to know, serve, and love God. If we try to live for anything else, it leads to slavery, but when we begin to live for God and follow his will, we find that we are actually becoming who we were meant to be, realizing our original design. We are a sailboat finally being put out into deep water. Someone may object that freedom should be doing what we really want to do. The Christian offer, however, includes this. It is not merely complying with the proper regulations of our creator; it also consists of a new, growing, inward passion to love and know our redeemer.[18]

Thus, the freedom of Christ permits us to be the person that God designed us to be, with our unique gifts, talents, and personality. We often think that God doesn't have our best interests in mind, that God is a demanding old codger shaking his finger at us and insisting that we stop doing anything that we enjoy. The "shiny objects" of this world often distract us from the truth and keep us busy trying to achieve what we think will make us happy. But in the end, the "treasures of the world" satisfy us only for a while before we need more, just as an addict must take more of a drug as he habituates to its effects.

THE OBJECT OF FAITH IS WHAT'S IMPORTANT, NOT THE STRENGTH OF THE FAITH

One of the most wonderful ways that Christians can experience freedom in Christ is to rest in him by faith alone. Faith alone. That means no works. Paul clarifies this succinctly in his letter to the Ephesians:

> For it is by grace you have been saved, through faith—and this is not from yourselves, it is the gift of God—not by works, so that no one can boast. For we are God's handiwork, created in Christ Jesus to do good works, which God prepared in advance for us to do.[19]

THE SHORTEST LEAP

As a former Pharisee, and one of the best, Paul was very familiar with the effects that religious works have on the heart. They puff it up, leading to boasting and looking down on others.

But through Jesus, God gives us a free gift that we don't deserve—that's *grace*. To receive this gift, we simply have faith that Jesus earned us a place in heaven with him for eternity. And then, to emphasize the difference, Paul goes on to state that we were created "to do good works." That is, we are saved by faith through nothing we do—i.e. "not by works." But once saved, we then "do good works" that God has created us to do. The first step—salvation—is by faith, and then—after being saved—true faith translates into good works.

So what is saving faith? There are three components: First, you must have a basic understanding of the facts of the gospel, that Jesus is the Son of God who had to live the perfect life on your behalf and die to take the penalty of sin on your behalf. Second, you must approve of, or agree with, these facts. That is, you should believe that the facts are true. And the third component is to trust with your heart that Jesus is your Savior. That is, Jesus saves you *from* sin and death, and he saves you *for* himself from the moment you believe and for all eternity in heaven. Theologian Wayne Grudem summarizes the second and third components of saving faith with these helpful details:

> Such agreement includes a conviction that the facts spoken of the gospel are true, especially the fact I am a sinner in need of salvation and Christ alone has paid the penalty for my sin and offers salvation to me. It also includes an awareness that I need to trust in Christ for salvation and that he is the only way to God, and the only means provided for my salvation. This approval of the facts of the gospel will also involve a desire to be saved by Christ. But all this still does not add up to true saving faith. That comes only when I make a decision of my will to depend on, or put my *trust* in, Christ as *my* Savior. This personal decision to place my trust in Christ is something done with my heart, the central faculty of my entire being that makes commitments for me as a whole person.[20]

CHAPTER 33: RECEIVING THE FREE GIFT

Over time, as you increase in your knowledge of the gospel, your faith will increase. You will also become more aware of your sin, since you will have a better understanding of the nature of sin (putting anything besides God at the center of your life). Moreover, you will also become more aware of sins that you used to deny, either because you refused to see them, you blamed others for their consequences, or you minimized or rationalized them. At these times, you are called to repent, that is, tell God that you are sorry for your sin and that you want to change. A great psalm to read for an example of repentance is Psalm 51, which David probably wrote after he had an adulterous affair with Bathsheba and murdered her husband.

So, yes, your faith will increase as you grow as a Christian. And you will learn to repent of sin more quickly and more frequently. But many Christians make their faith a work. They feel that "if they just had stronger faith," they'd deserve God's love, or they wouldn't keep failing, or God would bless them more. But even the simplest faith is sufficient for salvation. The important part is the *object* of the faith, Jesus. So long as your faith is in the right object, even the weakest faith is strong enough that nothing you can do will make God love you more or love you less.

Jesus had this exchange with a man whose son was possessed by "an impure spirit," which fortunately Mark records for those of us who think our faith is too weak:

> Jesus asked the boy's father, "How long has he been like this?"
>
> "From childhood," he answered. "It has often thrown him into fire or water to kill him. But if you can do anything, take pity on us and help us."
>
> "'If you can'?" said Jesus. "Everything is possible for one who believes."
>
> Immediately the boy's father exclaimed, "I do believe; help me overcome my unbelief!"[21]

Jesus went on to heal the boy. Not only does this story teach us that people can be possessed by spirits (a topic that is beyond the scope of this book!), but it also teaches us that it is not an irrational contradiction to say both, "I do believe," and "I need help overcoming my unbelief." So, during our times of doubt, we can go to God and ask him to restore our faith. We can also ask him to "restore to me the joy of your salvation,"[22] a common prayer of my own when I face discouragement and doubt.

When Jesus appeared to his disciples the Sunday afternoon after he was crucified, one disciple, Thomas, had not been there. The next week, this is what happened to the "doubting Thomas":

> A week later his disciples were in the house again, and Thomas was with them. Though the doors were locked, Jesus came and stood among them and said, "Peace be with you!" Then he said to Thomas, "Put your finger here; see my hands. Reach out your hand and put it into my side. Stop doubting and believe." Thomas said to him, "My Lord and my God!" Then Jesus told him, "Because you have seen me, you have believed; *blessed are those who have not seen and yet have believed.*"[23]

You, dear reader, are among those who did not have the privilege to see Jesus in the flesh. My prayer is that you will be among those who are blessed because they have not seen and yet have believed. Even though God is currently invisible, it is my hope that this book has clearly presented the many rational reasons that you can believe, despite not having seen.

THE DARTBOARD OF EVIDENCE

Before we close this final chapter, I want to summarize once again the evidence for the truth that Jesus is God and that he provides the only way into an eternal relationship with God. We began with the scientific evidence, which demonstrates that the belief in an all-powerful, all-knowing, personal God is more consistent with the evidence from astronomy, physics, molecular biology, biochemistry, paleontology, and anthropology than the belief that there is no God and the universe and all life on earth happened by accident. You can think of the scientific evidence as the outer ring on a dartboard.

CHAPTER 33: RECEIVING THE FREE GIFT

Figure 8: The Dartboard of Evidence

The next ring towards the center is the historical evidence for the truth of the accounts of Jesus' life, teachings, miracles, death, resurrection, and ascension. We demonstrated that the authors of the Gospels were eyewitnesses of Jesus, not only because they claim to be, but also because there are many signs within the Gospels that are consistent with eyewitness accounts and inconsistent with mythological, legendary, or concocted stories.

We also looked at the information that can be gleaned from secular outside sources—even anti-Christian sources—and found that these secular historical sources confirm many of the details about Jesus' life. Furthermore, we compared the Gospel stories to ancient myths that many skeptics have claimed Christianity is based upon. It became clear why scholars have dismissed these "Christ myth theories" as untenable. We also looked at the extensive archaeological evidence that confirms the historical nature of the biblical accounts, both in the Old Testament and the New Testament, giving us more reason to trust what the Bible says on matters of faith. The extensive documentary evidence from the thousands of extant manuscripts demonstrates that we can trust that we read essentially the same New Testament today that the original writers composed, and any differences are minor and don't affect the central tenets of Christianity.

We also compared traditional Christianity to the Gnostic documents, which, according to some liberal scholars, contain the true teachings of Jesus. Not only do these Gnostic documents contain a completely different philosophy than Christianity, one that is much more like ancient Greek philosophy, but they were also composed in the mid- to late second century. Therefore, their portrait of Jesus is less reliable than what we already know about Jesus' teachings from the Gospels of Matthew, Mark, Luke, and John, composed in the first century, or John's case, in the early second century at the latest. In addition, we saw that the opinions of liberal scholars, such as the Jesus Seminar, which assume that there is no supernatural realm, are clearly biased against traditional Christianity. Through their bogus assumptions, they end up finding the Jesus that they wanted to find when they set out to study him.

We also reviewed the evidence that supports the truth of Jesus' resurrection. We looked at the "five minimal facts" that the majority of historians agree upon, and then discussed how the various theories to explain these five facts are insufficient. The only way to adequately account for the five facts is to admit that the resurrection actually happened. Historians discount the resurrection because of a presupposition that the supernatural realm does not exist. But if an all-powerful God created the laws of physics, Jesus' resurrection is not just possible, it is also supported by the weight of the historical evidence.

The next ring of the dartboard represents the biblical evidence, which has become more trustworthy after reviewing the historical evidence that supports it. First, we looked at Jesus' own statements to demonstrate that he clearly referred to himself as God. We also looked at the teaching of the rest of the New Testament, which also clearly claims that Jesus is God. Next, we looked at the various prophecies concerning Jesus' life, his suffering and crucifixion, and his resurrection. We also noted that many of the Messianic prophecies refer to Jesus' second coming, and Jesus himself claimed that he would return to fulfill them. Finally, we spent six chapters exploring the symbols, people, and feasts of the Old Testament that God used to prepare us for what would happen after his arrival in a manger in Bethlehem.

The second to the last ring is the explanatory evidence, which doesn't prove Christianity is true, but give us further confidence that it is true because the Christian worldview explains so much of what we see and experience in the world. We see the extremes of good and evil in humans, and we feel a need for significance, meaning, and purpose in our lives. We also have a sense that some things are "just wrong," like murder and slavery, and others are "definitely good," like human rights and justice. We also have a sense that love and beauty are real, not just illusions created by a certain combination of chemicals in our brains that enabled us to pass on our genes more effectively. And finally, we talked about the experiential evidence for the supernatural realm, which billions of people across the planet and throughout history have experienced in one way or another.

The next ring of the dartboard is the transformational power that results from the unique downward trajectory of the gospel. Instead of our having to work our way up to him, God came down to us to live the perfect life that we can't live and to die to take the penalty for sin that we deserve. All other religions require certain works, but in Christianity, when it is properly understood, faith in Jesus is all that is required for salvation. Jesus has accomplished everything for his followers, and all we have to do is trust in his work on our behalf. Any other requirements would lead to self-righteousness and looking down on others. Good works should flow out of gratitude and joy, rather than out of obligation or fear of punishment.

This unique trajectory thus changes the drive shaft of the human heart, replacing the "carrot and stick" motivational drive with the drive to please the one who gives us so much. Over time, we will drift back to the carrot and the stick, but if we continue to remind ourselves that Jesus has done it all, we can rest in Jesus' completed work and gradually become the people he created us to be. And one day, we will transition to the life when evil, sin, disease, pain, and death will be no more, and we will enjoy life in the presence of our loving God forever. That is the center of the dartboard, and it is the most wonderful target for which we could ever aim. My prayer is that God will enable you to hit this "bullseye" of faith.

The Promises and the Prayer

I have collected thirty of my favorite promises that God gives his followers and reworded them a bit in order to summarize what happens when you "gain access by faith" in Jesus to a "state of grace." My prayer is that you will read this list and see that trusting in Jesus is not only the "shortest leap of faith" but is also the most rewarding. These are just a few of the promises that God makes to those who trust in him:

1. Even though you walk through the darkest valley, you don't have to fear evil, for God is with you.[24]
2. Surely goodness and lovingkindness will follow you all the days of your life, and you will dwell in the house of the Lord forever.[25]
3. Because you have been made righteous through faith in Jesus, when you cry out, the Lord hears you; he delivers you through all of your troubles.[26]
4. When you delight in the Lord, he will give you the desires of your heart in him.[27]
5. Remember the Lord's benefits: he forgives all your sins and heals all your diseases, he redeems your life from the pit and crowns you with love and compassion, he satisfies your desires with good things so that your youth is renewed like the eagle's.[28]
6. When you trust in the Lord with all your heart and lean not on your own understanding and when you submit all of your ways to him, he will make your paths straight.[29]
7. He gives strength to you when you are weary and increases your power when you are weak.[30]
8. When you hope in the Lord your strength is renewed. You will soar on wings like eagles; you will run and not grow weary, you will walk and not be faint.[31]
9. When you pass through the waters, God will be with you; and when you pass through the rivers, they will not sweep over you. When you walk through the fire, you will not be burned; the flames will not set you ablaze.[32]
10. Even if the mountains are shaken and the hills are removed, God's unfailing love for you will not be shaken nor will his covenant of peace be removed.

CHAPTER 33: RECEIVING THE FREE GIFT

11. God declares that he has plans to prosper you and not to harm you, plans to give you hope and a future.[33]
12. So do not worry about what to eat, drink, or wear, God knows what you need. But seek his kingdom and his righteousness first, and all these things will be given to you as well.[34]
13. If you know how to give good gifts to your children, how much more will your Father in heaven give good gifts to you when you ask him![35]
14. If you have left home or brothers or sisters or mother or father or children or fields for Jesus and the gospel, you will not fail to receive a hundred times as much in this present age: homes, brothers, sisters, mothers, children and fields—along with persecutions—and in the age to come eternal life.[36]
15. Ask and it will be given to you; seek and you will find; knock and the door will be opened to you.[37]
16. For God so loved the world that he gave his one and only Son, that when you believe in him you will not perish but will have eternal life.[38]
17. If you hear Jesus' word and believe the one who sent him, you have eternal life and will not be judged, but you have crossed over from death to life.[39]
18. God gives you eternal life, and you will never perish; no one will snatch you out of God's hand.[40]
19. Jesus will do whatever you ask in his name, so that the Father may be glorified in the Son. You may ask him for anything in Jesus' name, and he will do it.[41]
20. For the wages of sin is death, but the gift of God to you when you believe is eternal life in Christ Jesus your Lord.[42]
21. And you know that in all things God works for the good of you who love him and were called according to his purpose.[43]
22. Neither death nor life, neither angels nor demons, neither the present nor the future, nor any powers, neither height nor depth, nor anything else in all creation, will be able to separate you from the love of God that is in Christ Jesus your Lord.[44]
23. Your light and momentary troubles are achieving for you an eternal glory that far outweighs them all.[45]
24. You can be confident that God, who began a good work in you, will carry it on to completion until the day of Christ Jesus.[46]

25. You do not need to be anxious about anything, but in every situation, by prayer and petition, with thanksgiving, you simply present your requests to God. And the peace of God, which transcends all understanding, will guard your heart and your mind in Christ Jesus.[47]
26. If you lack wisdom, you should ask God, who gives generously to all without finding fault, and it will be given to you.[48]
27. The God of all grace, who called you to his eternal glory in Christ, after you have suffered a little while, will himself restore you and make you strong, firm and steadfast.[49]
28. If you confess your sins, he is faithful and just and will forgive you your sins and purify you from all unrighteousness.[50]
29. Jesus will never blot out your name from the book of life, but he will acknowledge your name before his Father and his angels.[51]
30. God's dwelling place is now among you, his people, and he will dwell with you. You will be his people, and God himself will be with you and be your God. He will wipe every tear from your eyes. There will be no more death or mourning or crying or pain, for the old order of things has passed away."[52]

For those who want to seize hold of these blessings and promises, the only requirement is to "declare with your mouth, 'Jesus is Lord,' and believe in your heart that God raised him from the dead."[53] But if you want to say it even more eloquently, we will close with a prayer that reflects David's prayer in Psalm 51.

I pray that you will recite this prayer to God with genuine honesty and excitement:

Dear God,

Please have mercy on me, a sinner who would rather follow my own will than yours. Your love never fails, and your compassion is so great, that I can trust you to cover over my transgressions and cleanse me from all sin.

I have not given you the credit you deserve for all of my blessings, and by putting other things in the place that

CHAPTER 33: RECEIVING THE FREE GIFT

only you should occupy in my life, I have not given you the honor and glory that you deserve.

I trust that Jesus lived the life that I could never live, and that Jesus took the penalty for my sins, which I could never pay myself. I also believe that he rose from the dead as confirmation that you accepted his perfect life and his perfect sacrifice on my behalf.

Therefore, I know that I am made holy and can live in your presence for eternity. May your Holy Spirit come to dwell inside my heart, changing its drive shaft so that I am motivated by love and gratitude instead of obligation or fear.

Please become the Lord of my life and change me so that my will aligns with your will. Help me to find gratitude and joy in the salvation you have given me, and guide me to follow your will for my life.

Help me to keep my eyes fixed on Jesus, to teach others about you, to praise you in all that I do, and to have a humble, contrite heart. Help me to always give you credit for everything good that I do, and empower me to love and serve others humbly, even if they are very different from me.

I look forward to enjoying a personal relationship with you, much like the one a child has with a perfectly caring and trustworthy father. And I look forward to the wonderful future that you promise me.

Amen.

Join the *Shortest Leap* community at www.shortestleap.com.

Questions for Comprehension and Discussion

1. Who do you say that Jesus is? Why is the answer to this question so important? What happens if you just ignore the question?
2. What did Jesus mean when he said the people were like children playing pretend in the marketplace? How does this describe people today who refuse to listen to the evidence for Christianity? What are some reasons people provide for not wanting to become a Christian?
3. How is Christianity like a pure gold treasure that has accumulated barnacles over the centuries? What are types of barnacles that have covered the treasure?
4. What are the two ways that people try to avoid God? What does it require for people who avoid God in each way to have a personal relationship with Jesus?
5. Why do both the younger brother and the elder brothers dislike the gospel? What are the differing reasons for their dislike of the gospel?
6. Do you identify more with the younger brother or the older brother? Why? How have you erred in thinking the Gospel was about you and your own behavior rather than faith in Jesus' work alone?
7. Though people think believing in the Christian God will cause them to lose their freedom, how does faith in Jesus actually lead to freedom? How is freedom through obedience to God like a sailboat that is gliding smoothly through the water?
8. How important is the strength of one's faith when it comes to receiving eternal life? How important is the object of faith in order to receive eternal life? What quote from the Bible illustrates the fact that one can "believe" but still have "unbelief"?
9. What are the three main components of saving faith in Jesus?
10. What are the rings in the "dartboard of evidence"? What is the bullseye? Have you "hit the bullseye" of faith?

CHAPTER 33 ENDNOTES

1. C. S. Lewis, *God in the Dock* (Grand Rapids, MI: Eerdmans Publishing Co., 2014), 102.
2. Wayne Grudem, *Systematic Theology: An Introduction to Biblical Doctrine* (Grand Rapids, MI: Zondervan, 1994), 712.
3. Matthew 16:17.
4. In Acts 17:30-31, Paul says: "The times of ignorance God overlooked, but now he commands all people everywhere to repent, because he has fixed a day on which he will judge the world in righteousness by a man whom he has appointed; and of this he has given assurance to all by raising him from the dead."
5. John 5:24.
6. John 6:29.
7. John 6:40.
8. John 11:25-26.
9. John 19:35, 21:24-25
10. Matthew 11:17.
11. Matthew 11:18-19.
12. This explanation comes from a sermon by Timothy Keller, "Rejecting the Real Jesus," June 16, 2016. Available at https://gospelinlife.com/downloads/rejecting-the-real-jesus-6459/.
13. For a complete explanation of the younger and elder brothers, and how both are avoiding a relationship with God, see Timothy Keller, *The Prodigal God: Recovering the Heart of the Christian Faith* (New York: Penguin Group, 2008).
14. Luke 15:29-30.
15. John 8:34.
16. Vinita Hampton Wright, *The Art of Spiritual Writing: How to Craft Prose That Engages and Inspires Your Readers* (Chicago: Loyola Press, 2013), 65-66.
17. Timothy Keller, *Making Sense of God: Finding God in the Modern World* (New York: Penguin Books, 2018), 130.
18. Ibid, 143.
19. Ephesians 2:8-10.
20. Grudem, *Systematic Theology*, 712.
21. Mark 9:21-24.
22. Psalm 51:12a.
23. John 20:26-29.
24. Psalm 23:4.
25. Psalm 23:6.

26. Psalm 34:17.
27. Psalm 37:4.
28. Psalm 103:2-5.
29. Proverbs 3:5-6.
30. Isaiah 40:29
31. Isaiah 40:31.
32. Isaiah 43:2.
33. Jeremiah 29:11.
34. Matthew 6:31-33.
35. Matthew 7:11.
36. Mark 10:29-30.
37. Luke 11:9-11.
38. John 3:16.
39. John 3:36.
40. John 10:28.
41. John 14:13-16.
42. Romans 6:23.
43. Romans 8:28.
44. Romans 8:38-39.
45. 2 Corinthians 4:17.
46. Philippians 1:6.
47. Philippians 4:6-7
48. James 1:5.
49. 1 Peter 5:10.
50. 1 John 1:9.
51. Revelation 3:5.
52. Revelation 21:3-4.
53. Romans 10:9.